About the Cover

Gaga rules!

In public relations terms, there is no brighter light on the planet than the former Stefani Joanne Angelina Germanotta, known to one and all as Lady Gaga. The New York City-born and bred singer, song writer, actress, record producer, clothes designer, social activist is a one-woman public relations conglomerate; earning upwards of $90 million a year. An online/ social media genius, Gaga bears influence on 47 million Facebook fans and 18 million Twitter followers, to say nothing of her Google+ followers, who numbered 21,000 four days after she signed up.

Oh sure, we could have chosen a preening politician or crafty corporate bigwig or hideous Hollywood starlet for our 12th Edition cover.

But in the wired world that is the second decade of the 21st century, as far as the practice of public relations is concerned – Gaga rules!

The Practice of
PUBLIC RELATIONS

Twelfth Edition

FRASER P. SEITEL
Foreword by David Rockefeller

Fraser P. Seitel

THE PRACTICE of PUBLIC RELATIONS

TWELFTH EDITION

Fraser P. Seitel

Managing Partner, Emerald Partners
Adjunct Professor, New York University

PEARSON

Boston   Columbus   Indianapolis   New York   San Francisco   Upper Saddle River
Amsterdam   Cape Town   Dubai   London   Madrid   Milan   Munich   Paris   Montréal   Toronto
Delhi   Mexico City   São Paulo   Sydney   Hong Kong   Seoul   Singapore   Taipei   Tokyo

Editor in Chief: Stephanie Wall
Director of Editorial Services: Ashley Santora
Editorial Project Manager: Kierra Bloom
Editorial Assistant: Jacob Garber
Director of Marketing: Maggie Moylan
Executive Marketing Manager: Anne Fahlgren
Senior Managing Editor: Judy Leale
Production Project Manager: Becca Groves
Operations Specialist: Nancy Maneri
Creative Director: Blair Brown
Senior Art Director: Janet Slowik
Interior Design: PreMediaGlobal
Cover Design: Wee Design Group

Cover Photo: Mandy Cheng/AFP/Getty Images/ Newscom
Senior Editorial Media Project Manager: Denise Vaughn
Production Media Project Manager: Lisa Rinaldi
Full-Service Project Management: PreMediaGlobal
Composition: PreMediaGlobal
Printer/Binder: Courier/Kendallville
Cover Printer: Lehigh-Phoenix Color/ Hagerstown
Text Font: 11/12 Apollo MT Standard

Credits and acknowledgments borrowed from other sources and reproduced, with permission, in this textbook appear on the appropriate page within text.

Many of the designations by manufacturers and sellers to distinguish their products are claimed as trademarks. Where those designations appear in this book, and the publisher was aware of a trademark claim, the designations have been printed in initial caps or all caps.

Library of Congress Cataloging-in-Publication Data

Seitel, Fraser P.
  The practice of public relations / Fraser P. Seitel, Managing Partner, Emerald Partners, Senior Counselor, Burson-Marsteller, Adjunct Professor, New York University, Visiting Professor, Florida International University.—Twelfth edition.
     pages cm
  ISBN-13: 978-0-13-308357-6
  ISBN-10: 0-13-308357-8
   1. Public relations—United States.   I. Title.
  HM1221.S45 2014
  659.2—dc23

                                                     2013005154

10 9 8 7 6 5 4 3 2 1

PEARSON

ISBN 10:   0-13-308357-8
ISBN 13: 978-0-13-308357-6

Dedicated to

Hunter Gittlin who, although but 5 years old, is nonetheless the boss of me.

Brief Contents

Contents

Foreword

David Rockefeller *(Photo courtesy of Virginia Sherwood)*

Opaque, confused, and inadequate communications by business and financial leaders characterized the 2008 financial crisis and the resulting dizzying descent into global economic recession. Unfortunately, their political brethren have not done much better in explaining what happened and what they are going to do about it. As a result, all institutions are under unprecedented stress and scrutiny.

As Fraser P. Seitel shows in the 12th edition of his text, good public relations will not solve these problems, but the dissemination of principled policies by seasoned professionals will allow the rest of us to understand the basic issues and lead to the formulation of more appropriate and effective policies.

Regaining and maintaining public confidence is essential as we move forward. But saying it and doing it are two different things. For students and even for professionals who have worked in the field for some time, *The Practice of Public Relations* is an excellent place to start. Seitel bridges the gap between theory and practice in a compelling and vivid way. His use of case studies, interviews, news photos, and other techniques, as well as his humorous and lucid text, brings the process brilliantly to life.

Leaders in the public, private, and not-for-profit sectors have learned from painful experience that they should rely on their public relations counselors for cogent advice on strategy and policy as well as communications. I learned to trust Mr. Seitel's instincts and abilities long ago when I was the chair and chief executive officer of The Chase Manhattan Bank. I continue to rely on his advice to this day.

For those who are working to restore and enhance the capacity of our institutions and their leaders to deal honestly and effectively with the public, this book will provide useful and essential guidance.

—*David Rockefeller*

David Rockefeller is one of the most influential figures in the history of U.S. business, finance, and philanthropy; he is considered by many to be "America's last great business statesman." Over four decades, Mr. Rockefeller served as an executive with The Chase Manhattan Bank, joining as assistant manager in the foreign department in 1946 and retiring in 1981, after 11 years as chair and CEO. Over his 90+ years, Mr. Rockefeller has met hundreds of world leaders and traveled around the globe many times. Since his retirement, Mr. Rockefeller has continued to stay active, with wide-ranging interests and involvement in the fields of international relations and civic affairs. He is the last remaining child of John D. Rockefeller Jr., who hired Ivy Lee in 1914 as the first modern-day public relations counselor.

Preface

First, thank you for buying my book. I appreciate it.

This book has been around for a good while, as have I.

Public relations continues to be a practice that is "contemporary" in every respect: new research findings, new communication methods, new social media communication techniques, and constantly changing case studies. Stated another way, a text like this one can't afford to rest on its laurels. It has to keep up to remain current.

In that context, your author is fortunate to continue to spend each day engaged in the practice of public relations, as a working consultant, with real clients, who demand real publicity and occasionally find themselves in real crises.

This helps keep the text fresh and up-to-date and practically grounded, so that events and innovations can be approached in proper public relations context. For example, social media, which has become so important in the field and has consequently moved up to Chapter 10 in this book, is approached here in a realistic, practical application sense as an important public relations "tool," but a tool nonetheless.

The point is that the approach of this book, unlike other basic texts, is intensely practical—long on reasoning and justification and applications that work and short on ethereal philosophy, dubious theory, or new wave communication panaceas. This 12th edition of *The Practice of Public Relations* will prepare you for public relations work in the second decade of the 21st century.

What's New in the 12th Edition of *The Practice of Public Relations*?

- **Eleven new, full cases featuring the most current and relevant topics in the industry, including:**
    - BP oil spill
    - Walmart bribery charges
    - Blackberry collapse
    - Hewlett Packard's CEO resignation
    - Amazon's pedophilia experience
    - McDonald's Twitter fiasco
    - Chrysler's F-bomb episode
    - Weinergate
    - Penn State's nightmare
    - Carnival Cruise Lines crash
    - Linsanity
- **Refortified emphasis on ethics with 18 brand-new ethics cases, including:**
    - Christian Dior and anti-Semitism
    - Burson-Marsteller and Facebook
    - Occupy Wall Street
    - Aflac and Gilbert Gottfried

- Mitt Romney and WAWA
- Goldman Sachs and its objecting employee
- Chick-fil-A and gay marriage
- Campbell's Soup and product labeling
- Kenneth Cole and the Arab Spring
- *Wall Street Journal* and Colorado theater tragedy
- Morning Joe
- Nancy Grace
- Pink slime

- **Six new "From the Top" interviews with today's top authorities in the worlds of management, media, and academia, including:**
  - Communication researcher Sandra Bauman
  - Agency CEOs Kathy Bloomgarden and Tadd Schwartz
  - Corporate public relations veterans Craig Rothenberg and Ned Raynolds
  - Military and government public relations expert Chuck Suits

- **New, expanded social media content in Chapter 10, "Public Relations and Social Media," encompassing the most up-to-date (at least as we write this) analysis of social media applications to public relations practice. In addition, comprehensive coverage of the role of social media in Public Relations is discussed throughout the text.**

- **Updated "Public Relations Library" features the most current public relations literature—primarily post-2004—as well as one new contemporary "Pick of the Literature" per chapter.**

- **Every chapter begins with a contemporary issue relating to the chapter content. Issues new to this edition include Taco Bell's "Thank you for suing us" PR campaign in Chapter 7, "The Law;" Rupert Murdoch's *News of the World* scandal in Chapter 9, "Media;" the Susan G. Komen Planned Parenthood controversy in Chapter 13, "Community Relations;" and Warner Brothers' response to the Aurora, Colorado, movie theater shooting in Chapter 17, "Crisis Management."**

Social media applications run throughout the chapters and, as noted, the chapter devoted to "Public Relations and Social Media" offers a comprehensive, updated discussion of social media vehicles and how they relate to public relations practice.

As important as social media has become to public relations work, the field still depends on technical skill, experience, and judgment, all grounded in solid relationships with colleagues, constituents, and media.

Above all, public relations responses and relationships must be based on the single concept of *doing the right thing*. Indeed, acting *ethically* lies at the heart of the solutions for the more than three dozen case studies that this edition presents.

With economic and political uncertainty around the world, the practice of public relations has never been a more potent force in society or a more valuable factor in an organization's reputation. In the second decade of the 21st century, public relations crises and opportunities are front-page news on a daily basis.

The field remains, at heart, a personal, relationship-oriented practice, demanding experienced judgment and finely honed interpersonal communications skills. And so, this 12th edition of *The Practice of Public Relations* places its emphasis on the principles, processes, and practices that lead to building positive relationships in a 24/7 communications environment.

This contemporary, real-life approach is intended to increase your enthusiasm for public relations study and practice.

Among the highlights of the 12th edition:

Comprehensive Social Media Content

As in so many other lines of work, mastering social media has become a key tool for public relations practitioners to engage in "direct conversations" with public relations publics. Public relations professionals must understand the communications opportunities and limitations of mobile and tablets, Facebook and Twitter and YouTube, blogs and podcasts and Pinterest, and all the rest.

No public relations textbook offers a more comprehensive discussion of social media than the 12th edition of *The Practice of Public Relations*.

Refortified Emphasis on Ethics

Proper public relations practice must be underpinned by a strong sense of ethics. The principle of *doing the right thing* is what should distinguish the practice of public relations.

This edition focuses on the ethical base that provides the theoretical foundation of effective communications and public relations.

The book's introductory chapters place significant attention on how an understanding of and facility with communications research, theory and public opinion can be applied to strategic public relations planning and creation of believable and persuasive messages.

Also included is a "PR Ethics Mini-Case" in each chapter. These cases bring to life the daily ethical dilemmas that confront professional public relations practitioners.

New Contemporary Cases

Public relations practice confronts an ever-changing landscape of problems and opportunities. It is imperative, therefore, that a textbook in the field keep current with the most contemporary examples of the good, the bad, and the ugly in public relations work.

This 12th edition does so by chronicling the most important contemporary public relations cases—from BP's Gulf of Mexico oil spill crisis to Penn State's catastrophic child abuse scandal to the transformation of an unknown Asian American basketball player into the international phenomenon of Linsanity.

Every case is designed to test your application of the theories discussed in solving real-world challenges.

Additional New Elements

The strength of this book continues to reside in its application of theory to real-life practice.

In addition to the new, contemporary cases and the expanded Social Media discussion, unique elements in the 12th edition include:

- **NEW! From the Top** interviews with distinguished communicators including agency CEOs and corporate and research leaders. These complement interviews with former Presidential Press Secretary and Obama Advisor Robert Gibbs; illustrious *USA Today* publisher Al Neuharth; legendary public relations counselors Harold Burson, Howard Rubenstein, and Richard Edelman; former Johnson and Johnson communications director Ray Jordan; and management guru, the late Peter Drucker; as well as an interview with the late Edward Bernays, one of the "fathers" of public relations

- **NEW! PR Ethics Mini-Cases**, which highlight the ethical challenges that public relations professionals face on a daily basis—from the public resignation of a Goldman Sachs executive to a campaign against gay marriage by the Chick-fil-A chicken restaurant to the questionable journalistic practices of prosecutor-turned-talk-show-host Nancy Grace.

- **NEW! Outside the Lines** features that expose off-line curiosities that make the practice of public relations such a fascinating art form.

- **NEW! Public Relations Library and Pick of the Literature** features, encompassing the most comprehensive, post-2004 bibliography in public relations literature.

- **NEW! Newscom photos**, taken straight from the news wire, add a real-life feel to this edition that isn't found in any other textbook.

All of these elements add to the excitement of this book. So, too, does the full-color format that underscores the liveliness, vitality, and relevance of the field.

Student Resources

Companion Website: This text's Companion Website at www.pearsonhighered .com/seitel offers free access to self-assessment quizzes and applicable links.

CourseSmart: CourseSmart eTextbooks were developed for students looking to save on required or recommended textbooks. Students simply select their eTextbook by title or author and purchase immediate access to the content for the duration of the course using any major credit card. With a CourseSmart eTextbook, students can search for specific keywords or page numbers, take notes online, print out reading assignments that incorporate lecture notes, and bookmark important passages for later review. For more information or to purchase a CourseSmart eTextbook, visit www .coursesmart.com.

Unique Perspective

Clearly, *The Practice of Public Relations*, 12th Edition, isn't your grandma's PR textbook.

This book is a lot different from other introductory texts in the field. Its premise is that public relations is a thoroughly engaging and constantly changing field. The extensive explanation of Social Media and its application to public relations practice is unique in public relations textbooks.

Although other texts may steer clear of the contemporary major cases, perplexing ethical mini-cases, thought leader interviews, "how to" counsel, and the public relations conundrums that force you to think, this book confronts them all.

It is, if you'll forgive the vernacular, an *in-your-face* textbook for an *in-your-face* profession.

Most important, *The Practice of Public Relations*, 12th Edition, is built around the technical knowledge of theory, history, process and practice, judgmental skills and personal relationships that underlie public relations practice and will be so essential in building the trust and respect of diverse communities in the second decade of the 21st century.

Happy reading, and thanks again for buying the book.

ACKNOWLEDGMENTS

The author and the publisher would like to thank the following reviewers for providing feedback for this revision.

Joseph Basso, Rowan University
Richard T. Cole, Michigan State University, East Lansing
Suzanne Fitzgerald, Rowan University
Dr. Andrew Lingwall, Clarion University
Jack Mandel, Nassau Community College
Michael Smilowitz, James Madison University

About the Author

Fraser P. Seitel is a veteran of four decades in the practice of public relations. (Although he claims still to be "extraordinarily young!") In 2000, *PR Week* magazine named Mr. Seitel one of the *100 Most Distinguished Public Relations Professionals of the 20th Century.*

In 1992, after serving for a decade as senior vice president and director of public affairs for The Chase Manhattan Bank, Mr. Seitel formed Emerald Partners, a management and communications consultancy, and also became senior counselor at the world's largest public affairs firm, Burson-Marsteller.

Mr. Seitel is a regular guest on television and radio. In addition to his appearances on a variety of programs on the Fox News Network, he has appeared on ABC's *Good Morning America*, CNBC's *Power Lunch*, CNN's *Larry King Live*, as well as on MSNBC, Fox Business Network, the Fox Radio Network, and National Public Radio.

Mr. Seitel has counseled hundreds of corporations, hospitals, nonprofits, associations, and individuals in the areas for which he had responsibility at Chase—media relations, speech writing, consumer relations, employee communications, financial communications, philanthropic activities, and strategic management consulting.

Mr. Seitel is an Internet columnist at odwyerpr.com and a frequent lecturer and seminar leader on communications topics. Over the course of his career, Mr. Seitel has taught thousands of public relations professionals and students.

After studying and examining many texts in public relations, he concluded that none of them "was exactly right." Therefore, in 1980, he wrote the first edition of *The Practice of Public Relations* "to give students a feel for how exciting this field really is." In four decades of use at hundreds of colleges and universities, Mr. Seitel's book has introduced generations of students to the excitement, challenge, and uniqueness of the practice of public relations.

Chapter **1**

Defining Public Relations

Chapter Objectives

1. To define the practice of public relations and underscore its importance as a valuable and powerful societal force in the 21st century.
2. To explore the various publics of public relations, as well as the field's most prominent functions.
3. To underscore the ethical nature of the field and to reject the notion that public relations practitioners are employed in the practice of "spin."
4. To examine the requisites—both technical and attitudinal—that constitute an effective public relations professional.

FIGURE 1-1 Public relations worrier.
On the first anniversary of his death, Osama bin Laden was remembered by anti-U.S. protestors in Pakistan.
(Photo: MUSA FARMAN/EPA/Newscom)

The year 2012 was a perplexing one for the practice of public relations.

On the one hand, after a century of high-level public relations activity, the field still struggled with defining itself, so much so that an effort by the Public Relations Society of America (PRSA) to reach a common definition was greeted, as *The New York Times* put it, with *"widespread interest, along with not a small amount of sniping, snide commentary and second-guessing."*[1] The PRSA received 927 suggested definitions from public relations professionals, academics, students, and the general public. Finally, in March, the winning definition was selected:

> *Public relations is a strategic communication process that builds mutually beneficial relationships between organizations and their publics.*

Not bad, although practitioners still grumbled and even the CEO of PRSA admitted, "Like beauty, the definition of 'public relations' is in the eye of the beholder."[2]

On the other hand, the power and value of public relations in the 21st century wasn't at issue; indeed, most accepted that the practice of public relations had become one of society's most potent forces.

The greatest testimony to that reality came from none other than the late, and not-so-great, former Al Qaeda terrorist-in-chief Osama bin Laden (Figure 1-1). According to letters unearthed from bin Laden's last-stand compound in Abbottabad,

Pakistan, a year after the terrorist was taken out by Navy SEALs, bin Laden spent his last months on the planet fretting about public relations. Among the bearded bomber's most pressing concerns were the following:

■ He contemplated ways to improve news media coverage, souring on MSNBC and favoring ABC News.

■ He worried about his place in history, writing "some in the media and among historians will construct a history for me, using whatever information they have, regardless of whether their information is accurate or not."

■ He was deeply concerned about Al Qaeda's image and contemplated a name change to give the group a more religious ring.

Finally, bin Laden argued that Al Qaeda attacks on Muslims in Muslim countries "would lead us to winning several battles while losing the war at the end," which, thankfully, he did.[3]

In the 21st century, few societal forces are more powerful than the practice of public relations, especially when combined with social media—the agglomeration of Facebook and Twitter messages, email, cell phone photos, blogs, wikis, Web casting, RSS feeds, and all the other emerging technologies of the World Wide Web.

Together, the combination of the two—social media and public relations—has revolutionized the way organizations and individuals communicate to their key constituent publics around the world.

Indeed, *revolution* was the watchword in the "Arab Spring" of 2011 when a wave of demonstrations, sparked by public relations messages on social media, brought down despotic rulers throughout the Arab world, from Tunisia to Egypt, from Libya to Yemen (Figure 1-2). Social media channels and public relations techniques combined to organize, communicate, and raise awareness to beat back state-sanctioned repression.

In the 21st century, even terrorists understood the impact of public relations messages and the reach of the World Wide Web to deliver them.

But what is *public relations*, anyway?

That is the question the PRSA tackled in 2012 and is still asked, even by many of the 200,000-plus people in the United States and the thousands of others overseas who practice public relations.

In a society overwhelmed by communications—from traditional and increasingly threatened newspapers and magazines, to 24/7 talk radio and broadcast and cable television, to nontraditional social media, instant messages, blogs, podcasts, wikis, and assorted other Internet exotica—the public is bombarded with nonstop messages of every variety. The challenge for a communicator is to cut through this clutter to deliver an argument that is persuasive, believable, and actionable.

The answer, more often than not today, lies in public relations. Stated another way, in the 21st century, the power, value, and influence of the practice of public relations have never been more profound.

FIGURE 1-2 Social media revolution.
Protestors gathered in Tahrir Square, focal point of Egypt's 2011 transfer of power. A year later, the country held its first democratic presidential election. *(Photo: ZUMA Press/Newscom)*

Prominence of Public Relations

In the initial decade of the 21st century, public relations as a field has grown immeasurably both in numbers and in respect. Today, the practice of public relations is clearly a growth industry.

- In the United States alone, public relations is a multibillion-dollar business practiced by 320,000 professionals, according to the U.S. Bureau of Labor Statistics. Furthermore, the Bureau says that "employment of public relations managers and specialists is expected to grow by 21% from 2010 to 2020, faster than the average for all occupations. New media outlets will create more work for public relations workers, increasing the number and kinds of avenues of communication between organizations and the public."[4]

- Around the world, the practice of public relations has grown enormously. The International Public Relations Association, now in its sixth decade, boasts a strong membership in more than 80 countries.

- Approximately 250 colleges and universities in the United States and many more overseas offer a public relations sequence or degree program. Many more offer public relations courses. Undergraduate enrollments in public relations programs at U.S. four-year colleges and universities are conservatively estimated to be well in excess of 20,000 majors. In the vast majority of college journalism programs, public relations sequences rank first or second in enrollment.[5]

■ The U.S. government has thousands of communications professionals—although none, as we will learn, are labeled *public relations specialists*—who keep the public informed about the activities of government agencies and officials. The Department of Defense alone has 7,000 professional communicators spread out among the Army, Navy, and Air Force.

■ The world's largest public relations firms are all owned by media conglomerates—among them Omnicom, The Interpublic Group, and WPP Group—which refuse to divulge public relations revenues. The field is dominated by smaller, privately held firms, many of them entrepreneurial operations. A typical public relations agency has annual revenue of less than $1 million with fewer than 10 employees. Nonetheless, the top 10 independent public relations agencies in the United States record annual revenues in excess of a billion dollars, with the top independent firm, Edelman Public Relations, with 4,120 employees, earning nearly $605 million in annual revenues.[6]

■ The field's primary trade associations have strong membership, with the Public Relations Society of America encompassing nearly 21,000 members and 10,000 college students in 100 chapters and the International Association of Business Communicators including 15,000 members in 80 countries.

In the 21st century, as all elements of society—companies, nonprofits, governments, religious institutions, sports teams and leagues, arts organizations, and all others—wrestle with constant shifts in economic conditions and competition, security concerns, and popular opinion, the public relations profession is expected to thrive because increasing numbers of organizations are interested in communicating their stories.

Indeed, public relations people have already attained positions of prominence in every aspect of society. Jay Carney, President Barack Obama's press secretary, is quoted daily from his televised White House press briefings. His predecessor, Robert Gibbs, is a close Obama advisor. Karen Hughes, a public relations advisor to George W. Bush for many years, moved from a Special Assistant to the President position in the White House to become Undersecretary of State for Public Diplomacy responsible primarily for changing attitudes internationally about the United States. Where once public relations was a profession populated by anonymous practitioners, today's public relations executives write books, appear on television, and are widely quoted. When United Parcel Service (UPS) appointed communications professional Christine Owens to its top internal body in 2005, CEO Mike Eskew said, "Communications is just too important not to be represented on the management committee of this company."[7]

Perhaps the most flattering aspect of the field's heightened stature is that competition from other fields has become more intense. Today the profession finds itself vulnerable to encroachment by people with non–public relations backgrounds, such as lawyers, marketers, and general managers of every type, all eager to gain the management access and persuasive clout of the public relations professional.

The field's strength stems from its roots: "A democratic society where people have freedom to debate and to make decisions—in the community, the marketplace, the home, the workplace, and the voting booth. Private and public organizations depend on good relations with groups and individuals whose opinions, decisions, and actions affect their vitality and survival."[8]

What Is Public Relations?

The PRSA's 2012 definition—"Public relations is a strategic communication process that builds mutually beneficial relationships between organizations and their publics"—is really pretty good.

Public relations is, indeed, a "strategic" process, which focuses on helping achieve an organization's goals. Its fundamental mandate is "communications," and its focus is "building relationships."

Another approach to a definition is, "Public relations is a planned process to influence public opinion, through sound character and proper performance, based on mutually satisfactory two-way communication."

At least that's what your author believes it is.

This definition adds the elements of "planning," so imperative in sound public relations practice, the aspect of "listening" through "two-way communications," as well as the elements of "character" or "ethics" and "performance." Public relations is most effective when it's based on ethical principles and proper action. Without these two essential requisites—character and performance—achieving sustained influence might be either transitory or impossible; in other words, you can fool some of the people some of the time but not all of the people all of the time; in other other words, "You can't pour perfume on a skunk!"

The fact is that there are many different definitions of public relations. American historian Robert Heilbroner once described the field as "a brotherhood of some 100,000, whose common bond is its profession and whose common woe is that no two of them can ever quite agree on what that profession is."[9]

In 1923, the late Edward Bernays described the function of his fledgling public relations counseling business as one of providing

> *Information given to the public, persuasion directed at the public to modify attitudes and actions, and efforts to integrate attitudes and actions of an institution with its publics and of publics with those of that institution.*[10]

And way back in 1975, when people didn't have a clue what "public relations" was, one of the most ambitious searches for a universal definition was commissioned by the Foundation for Public Relations Research and Education. Sixty-five public relations leaders participated in the study, which analyzed 472 different definitions and offered the following 88-word sentence:

> *Public relations is a distinctive management function which helps establish and maintain mutual lines of communications, understanding, acceptance, and cooperation between an organization and its publics; involves the management of problems or issues; helps management to keep informed on and responsive to public opinion; defines and emphasizes the responsibility of management to serve the public interest; helps management keep abreast of and effectively utilize change, serving as an early warning system to help anticipate trends; and uses research and sound and ethical communication techniques as its principal tools.*[11]

In adopting its 2012 definition, the Public Relations Society of America noted that its definition implied the functions of research, planning, communications dialogue, and evaluation, all essential in the practice of public relations.

No matter which formal definition one settles on to describe the practice, to be successful, public relations professionals must always engage in a planned and ethical process to influence the attitudes and actions of their target audiences.

Planned Process to Influence Public Opinion

What is the process through which public relations might influence public opinion? Communications professor John Marston suggested a four-step model based on specific functions: (1) research, (2) action, (3) communication, and (4) evaluation.[12] Whenever a public relations professional is faced with an assignment—whether promoting a client's product or defending a client's reputation—he or she should apply Marston's R-A-C-E approach:

1. **Research.** Research attitudes about the issue at hand.
2. **Action.** Identify action of the client in the public interest.
3. **Communication.** Communicate that action to gain understanding, acceptance, and support.
4. **Evaluation.** Evaluate the communication to see if opinion has been influenced.

The key to the process is the second step—action. You can't have effective communication or positive publicity without proper action. Stated another way, performance must precede publicity. Act first and communicate later. Indeed, some might say that public relations—PR—really should stand for *performance recognition*. In other words, positive action communicated straightforwardly will yield positive results.

This is the essence of the R-A-C-E process of public relations.

Public relations professor Sheila Clough Crifasi has proposed extending the R-A-C-E formula into the five-part R-O-S-I-E to encompass a more managerial approach to the field. R-O-S-I-E prescribes sandwiching the functions of objectives, strategies, and implementation between research and evaluation. Indeed, setting clear objectives, working from set strategies, and implementing a predetermined plan are keys to sound public relations practice.

Still others suggest a process called R-P-I-E for research, planning, implementation, and evaluation, which emphasizes the element of planning as a necessary step preceding the activation of a communications initiative.

All three approaches, R-A-C-E, R-O-S-I-E, and R-P-I-E, echo one of the most widely repeated definitions of public relations, developed by the late Denny Griswold, who founded a public relations newsletter.

> *Public relations is the management function which evaluates public attitudes, identifies the policies and procedures of an individual or an organization with the public interest, and plans and executes a program of action to earn public understanding and acceptance.*[13]

The key words in this definition are *management* and *action*. Public relations, if it is to serve the organization properly, must report to top management. Public relations must serve as an honest broker to management, unimpeded by any other group. For public relations to work, its advice to management must be unfiltered, uncensored, and unexpurgated. This is often easier said than done because many public relations departments report through marketing, advertising, or even legal departments.

Nor can public relations take place without appropriate action. As noted, no amount of communications—regardless of its persuasive content—can save an organization whose performance is substandard. In other words, if the action is flawed or the performance rotten, no amount of communicating or backtracking or post facto posturing will change the reality.

The process of public relations, then, as Professor Melvin Sharpe has put it, "harmonizes long-term relationships among individuals and organizations in society."[14] To "harmonize," Professor Sharpe applies five principles to the public relations process:

- Honest communication for credibility
- Openness and consistency of actions for confidence
- Fairness of actions for reciprocity and goodwill
- Continuous two-way communication to prevent alienation and to build relationships
- Environmental research and evaluation to determine the actions or adjustments needed for social harmony

And if that doesn't yet give you a feel for what precisely the practice of public relations is, then consider public relations Professor Janice Sherline Jenny's description as "the management of communications between an organization and all entities that have a direct or indirect relationship with the organization, i.e., its publics."

No matter what definition one may choose to explain the practice, few would argue that the goal of effective public relations is to harmonize internal and external relationships so that an organization can enjoy not only the goodwill of all of its publics but also stability and long life.

Public Relations as Management Interpreter

The late Leon Hess, who ran one of the nation's largest oil companies and the New York Jets football team, used to pride himself on *not* having a public relations department. Mr. Hess, a very private individual, abhorred the limelight for himself and for his company.

But times have changed.

Today, the CEO who thunders "I don't need public relations!" is a fool. He or she doesn't have a choice. Every organization *has* public relations whether it wants it or not. The trick is to establish *good* public relations. That's what this book is all about— professional public relations, the kind you must work at.

Public relations affects almost everyone who has contact with other human beings. All of us, in one way or another, practice public relations daily. For an organization, every phone call, every letter, every face-to-face encounter is a public relations event.

Public relations professionals, then, are really the organization's interpreters.

- On the one hand, they must interpret the philosophies, policies, programs, and practices of their management to the public.
- On the other hand, they must convey the attitudes of the public to their management.

Let's consider management first.

Before public relations professionals can gain attention, understanding, acceptance, and ultimately action from target publics, they have to know what management is thinking.

Good public relations can't be practiced in a vacuum. No matter what the size of the organization, a public relations department is only as good as its access to management. For example, it's useless for a senator's press secretary to explain the reasoning behind an important decision without first knowing what the senator had in mind.

So, too, an organization's public relations staff is impotent without firsthand knowledge of the reasons for management's decisions and the rationale for organizational policy.

The public relations department in any organization can counsel management. It can advise management. It can even exhort management to take action. But it is management who must call the shots on organizational policy.

It is the role of the public relations practitioner, once policy is established by management, to communicate these ideas accurately and candidly to the public. Anything less can lead to major problems.

Public Relations as Public Interpreter

Now let's consider the flip side of the coin—the public.

Interpreting the public to management means finding out what the public really thinks about the firm and letting management know. Regrettably, history is filled with examples of powerful institutions—and their public relations departments—failing to anticipate the true sentiments of the public.

- In the 1960s, General Motors (GM) paid little attention to an unknown consumer activist named Ralph Nader, who spread the message that GM's Corvair was "unsafe at any speed." When Nader's assault began to be believed, the automaker assigned professional detectives to trail him. In short order, GM was forced to acknowledge its act of paranoia, and the Corvair was eventually sacked at great expense to the company.

- In the 1970s, as both gasoline prices and oil company profits rose rapidly, the oil companies were besieged by an irate gas-consuming public. When, at the height of the criticism, Mobil Oil spent millions in excess cash to purchase the parent of the Montgomery Ward department store chain, the company was publicly battered for failing to cut its prices.

- In the 1980s, President Ronald Reagan rode to power on the strength of his ability to interpret what was on the minds of the electorate. But his successor in the early 1990s, George H. W. Bush, a lesser communicator than Reagan, failed to "read" the nation's economic concerns. After leading America to a victory over Iraq in the Gulf War, President Bush failed to heed the admonition "It's the economy, stupid," and lost the election to upstart Arkansas Governor Bill Clinton.

- As the 20th century ended, President Clinton forgot the candid communication skills that earned him the White House and lied to the American public about his affair with an intern. The subsequent scandal, ending in impeachment hearings before the U.S. Congress, tarnished Clinton's administration and ruined his legacy.

- In the first decade of the 21st century, Clinton's successor, George W. Bush, earned great credit for strong actions and communications following the September 11, 2001, attacks on the nation. The Bush administration's public relations then suffered when the ostensible reason for attacking Iraq—weapons of mass destruction—failed to materialize. Bush's failure to act promptly and communicate frankly in subsequent crises, such as Hurricane Katrina, hurt his personal credibility and irreparably tarnished his administration.

- Bush's successor, Barack Obama, was hailed for his messianic communications skills as he stormed into the White House with a message of "hope and change"

FIGURE 1-3   Dimon in the rough.
In the spring of 2012, JP Morgan Chase CEO Jamie Dimon, hailed as a leader with great communication skills, was put to the public relations test when his institution stubbed its toe on a $3 billion+ loss. (*Ouch!*) (*Photo: SAUL LOEB/AFP/Getty Images/Newscom*)

in 2008. By the end of his first term in 2012, with the economy flagging from an unprecedented financial meltdown and the Republicans chomping at the bit to replace him, Obama struggled to regain his "communication mojo" to earn reelection.

- Part of President Obama's problem was that his administration was met by a pervasive economic crisis, marked by CEOs from the nation's largest financial companies, among them Citigroup, AIG, Washington Mutual, Bear Stearns, Lehman Brothers, Countrywide Financial, Goldman Sachs, and Bank of America, exposed before the American public as inept—some would argue "law-breaking"—stewards of the public trust.

- The coup de grace occurred in the spring of 2012 when the nation's strongest financial institution, JP Morgan Chase, was rocked by a derivative trading loss in excess of $3 billion while trying to "protect" its investments. Outspoken CEO Jamie Dimon was forced to make a blunt, public apology for his bank's "stupid, self-inflicted mistakes" (Figure 1-3). And politicians piled on to use the bank's embarrassing public relations revelation to stiffen regulation.

In the first decade of the 21st century, then, the savviest individuals and institutions—be they government, corporate, or nonprofit—understood the importance of effectively interpreting their philosophies, policies, and practices to the public and, even more important, interpreting back to management how the public viewed them and their organization.

PR Ethics Mini-Case

Firing the Nazi in the House of Dior

In the spring of 2011, flamboyant John Galliano, creative director of the legendary Dior fashion house, was the hit of Paris.

For 15 years, Galliano had held forth as the universally praised arbiter of youth and vitality for the Dior line. His early collections, including one inspired by Paris' bums and spoofed in the movie *Zoolander*, were the talk of Paris. He was a master designer of all phases of fashion, from ready-to-wear collections to couture. And his outrageous getups—braids, pirate hats, astronaut suits, and other assorted wacky garb—stoked the anticipation of his presentations during Paris *Fashion Week* (Figure 1-4).

FIGURE 1-4   Walking the plank.
Gifted designer John Galliano was shown the door by Dior after anti-Semitic remarks challenged the firm's credibility. *(Photo: MAYA VIDON/EPA/Newscom)*

Galliano was credited with playing a major role in restoring the stuffy Dior brand back to relevance. The name Dior, itself, was credited with saving the French couture industry after World War II, when the Nazi occupation of Paris effectively shut down the haute couture industry. As the Germans threatened to move the entire industry to Berlin, a few Parisian designers continued to make dresses for Nazi officials' wives and French collaborators. One such designer was the young couturier Christian Dior, who worked for the house of Lucien Lelong. After the war in 1947, Dior opened his own house of fashion, and the industry in Paris, almost destroyed by war, was revived.

This history was brought into vivid display when, in late February 2011, Galliano was arrested after allegedly making anti-Semitic comments at a Paris bar. Hate speech is a crime in France. Dior suspended Galliano on the news of his arrest. Then, after the British tabloid *The Sun* published a damning video of Galliano at the bar saying "I love Hitler" and telling two women, "Your mothers, your forefathers, would all be f***ing gassed," Dior fired him.

Dior CEO Sidney Toledano was unforgiving in a statement issued to employees and the media. Toledano said, in part:

> What has happened over the last week has been a terrible and wrenching ordeal for us all. It has been deeply painful to see the Dior name associated with the disgraceful statements attributed to its designer, however brilliant he may be.
>
> Such statements are intolerable because of our collective duty to never forget the Holocaust and its victims, and because of the respect for human dignity that is owed to each person and to all peoples.
>
> So now, more than ever, we must publicly recommit ourselves to the values of the House of Dior.

Stated another way, no matter how talented or valuable their creative director, the credibility and reputation of the organization was eminently more important.*

Questions

1. What other options did Dior have beyond firing Galliano?

2. Do you agree with the categorical decision made by the House of Dior?

*For further information, see Raquel Laneri, "Why Dior Did the Right Thing Firing John Galliano," Forbes.com, www.forbes.com/sites /raquellaneri/2011/03/01/why-dior-did-the-right-thing-firing-john-galliano/, March 1, 2010.

The Publics of Public Relations

The term *public relations* is really a misnomer. *Publics* relations, or relations with the publics, would be more to the point. Practitioners must communicate with many different publics—not just the general public—each having its own special needs and requiring different types of communication. Often the lines that divide these publics are thin, and the potential overlap is significant. Therefore, priorities, according to organizational needs, must always be reconciled (Figure 1-5).

Technological change—particularly social media, mobile devices, blogs, satellite links for television, and the computer in general—has brought greater interdependence to people and organizations, and there is growing concern in organizations today about managing extensive webs of interrelationships. Indeed, managers have become interrelationship conscious.

Internally, managers must deal directly with various levels of subordinates as well as with cross-relationships that arise when subordinates interact with one another.

FIGURE 1-5   Key publics.
Twenty of the most important publics of a typical multinational corporation.

Externally, managers must deal with a system that includes nongovernmental organizations (NGOs), government regulatory agencies, labor unions, subcontractors, consumer groups, and many other independent—but often related—organizations. The public relations challenge in all of this is to manage effectively the communications between managers and the various publics, which often pull organizations in different directions. Stated another way, public relations professionals are mediators between client (management) and public (all those key constituent groups on whom an organization depends).

Definitions differ on precisely what constitutes a public. One time-honored definition states that a public arises when a group of people (1) faces a similar indeterminate situation, (2) recognizes what is indeterminate and problematic in that situation, and (3) organizes to do something about the problem.[15] In public relations, more specifically, a public is a group of people with a stake in an issue, organization, or idea.

Publics can also be classified into several overlapping categories:

- **Internal and external.** Internal publics are inside the organization: supervisors, clerks, managers, stockholders, and the board of directors. External publics are those not directly connected with the organization: the press, government, educators, customers, suppliers, and the community.

- **Primary, secondary, and marginal.** Primary publics can most help—or hinder—the organization's efforts. Secondary publics are less important, and marginal publics are the least important of all. For example, members of the Federal Reserve Board of Governors, who regulate banks, would be the primary public for a bank awaiting a regulatory ruling, whereas legislators and the general public would be secondary. On the other hand, to the investing public, interest rate pronouncements of the same Federal Reserve Board are of primary importance.

- **Traditional and future.** Employees and current customers are traditional publics; students and potential customers are future ones. No organization can afford to become complacent in dealing with its changing publics. Today, a firm's publics range from women to minorities to senior citizens to homosexuals. Each might be important to the future success of the organization.

- **Proponents, opponents, and the uncommitted.** An institution must deal differently with those who support it and those who oppose it. For supporters, communications that reinforce beliefs may be in order. But changing the opinions of skeptics calls for strong, persuasive communications. Often, particularly in politics, the uncommitted public is crucial. Many a campaign has been decided because the swing vote was won over by one of the candidates.

It's true that management must always speak with one voice, but its communication inflection, delivery, and emphasis should be sensitive to all constituent publics.

The Functions of Public Relations

There is a fundamental difference between the functions of public relations and the functions of marketing and advertising. Marketing and advertising promote a product or a service. Public relations promotes an entire organization.

The functions associated with public relations work are numerous. Among them are the following:

■ **Writing**—*the* fundamental public relations skill, with written vehicles from news releases to speeches and from brochures to advertisements falling within the field's purview.

■ **Media relations**—dealing with the press is another frontline public relations function.

■ **Social media interface**—creating what often is the organization's principle interface with the public: its Website, as well as creating links with social media options, such as Facebook, Twitter, YouTube, and the rest. Also important is monitoring the World Wide Web and responding, when appropriate, to organizational challenge.

■ **Planning**—of public relations programs, special events, media events, management functions, and the like.

■ **Counseling**—in dealing with management and its interactions with key publics.

■ **Researching**—of attitudes and opinions that influence behavior and beliefs.

■ **Publicity**—the marketing-related function, most commonly misunderstood as the "only" function of public relations, generating positive publicity for a client or employer.

■ **Marketing communications**—other marketing-related functions, such as promoting products, creating collateral marketing material, sales literature, meeting displays, and promotions.

■ **Community relations**—positively putting forth the organization's messages and image within the community.

■ **Consumer relations**—interfacing with consumers through written and verbal communications.

■ **Employee relations**—communicating with the all-important internal publics of the organization, those managers and employees who work for the firm.

■ **Government affairs**—dealing with legislators, regulators, and local, state, and federal officials—all of those who have governmental interface with the organization.

■ **Investor relations**—for public companies, communicating with stockholders and those who advise them.

■ **Special publics relations**—dealing with those publics uniquely critical to particular organizations, from African Americans to women to Asians to senior citizens.

■ **Public affairs and issues**—dealing with public policy and its impact on the organization, as well as identifying and addressing issues of consequence that affect the firm.

■ **Crisis communications**—dealing with key constituent publics when the organization is under siege for any number of urgent situations that threaten credibility.

This is but a partial list of what public relations practitioners do. In sum, the public relations practitioner is manager/orchestrator/producer/director/writer/arranger and all-around general communications counsel to management. It is for this reason, then, that the process works best when the public relations director reports directly to the CEO.

The Sin of "Spin"

So pervasive has the influence of public relations become in our society that some even fear it as a pernicious force; they worry about the power of public relations to exercise a kind of thought control over the American public.

Which brings us to *spin*.

In its most benign form, spin signifies the distinctive interpretation of an issue or action to sway public opinion, as in putting a positive slant on a negative story. In its most virulent form, spin means confusing an issue or distorting or obfuscating it or even lying.

The propensity in recent years for presumably respected public figures to lie in an attempt to deceive the public has led to the notion that "spinning the facts" is synonymous with public relations practice.

It isn't.

Spinning an answer to hide what really happened—that is, lying, confusing, distorting, obfuscating, whatever you call it—is antithetical to the proper practice of public relations. In public relations, if you lie once, you will never be trusted again—particularly by the media.

Nonetheless, public relations spin has come to mean the twisting of messages and statements of half-truths to create the appearance of performance, which may or may not be true.

This association with spin has hurt the field. *The New York Times* headlined a critical article on public relations practice, "Spinning Frenzy: P.R.'s Bad Press."[16] Other critics admonish the field as "a huge, powerful, hidden medium available only to wealthy individuals, big corporations, governments, and government agencies because of its high cost."[17]

In recent years, the most high-profile government public relations operatives have often fallen guilty to blatant spin techniques. The term *spin* was coined in the Clinton administration, when a bevy of eager communications counselors, such as James Carville, Paul Begala, and Lanny Davis, eagerly spun the tale that intern Monica Lewinsky was, in effect, delusional about an Oval Office affair with the president. (*She wasn't!*)[18] In the Bush administration, high-level advisors Karl Rove and Lewis Libby were implicated in a spinning campaign against former Ambassador Joseph Wilson, who questioned the motives of the war in Iraq. In 2005, Libby, Vice President Dick Cheney's top aide, was convicted for "obstruction of justice, false statement, and perjury" in the Wilson case.[19] In 2012, former senator and presidential candidate John Edwards was prosecuted for using political campaign funds to hide a mistress and their love child, while spinning a tale of "no mistress and somebody else's baby." Meanwhile, notorious media spinners from Donald Trump to Nancy Grace to Al Sharpton exaggerate indiscriminately and are rarely challenged.[20]

Faced with this era of spin and continued public uncertainty about the ethics of public relations, practitioners must always be sensitive to and considerate of how their actions and their words will influence the public.

Above all—in defiance of charges of spinning—public relations practitioners must consider their cardinal rule: *to never, ever lie.*

What Manner of Man or Woman?

What kind of individual does it take to become a competent public relations professional?

A 2004 study of agency, corporate, and nonprofit public relations leaders, sponsored by search firm Heyman Associates, reported seven areas in particular that characterize a successful public relations career:

1. Diversity of experience
2. Performance
3. Communications skills
4. Relationship building
5. Proactivity and passion
6. Teamliness
7. Intangibles, such as personality, likeability, and chemistry[21]

Beyond these success-building areas, in order to make it, a public relations professional ought to possess a set of specific technical skills as well as an appreciation of the proper attitudinal approach to the job. On the technical side, the following six skills are important:

1. **Knowledge of the field.** The underpinnings of public relations—what it is, what it does, and what it ought to stand for.
2. **Communications knowledge.** The media and the ways in which they work; communications research; and, most important, how to write.
3. **Technological knowledge.** Familiarity with computers and associated technologies, as well as with the World Wide Web, are imperative.
4. **Current events knowledge.** Knowledge of what's going on around you—daily factors that influence society: history, literature, language, politics, economics, and all the rest—from Kim Jong Un to Kim Kardashian; from Ben Stein to bin Laden; from Dr. Phil to Dr. Dre; from Three Penny Opera to 50 Cent; from Fat Joe to Lil' Kim to Pink. A public relations professional must be, in the truest sense, a Renaissance man or woman.
5. **Business knowledge.** How business works, a bottom-line orientation, and a knowledge of your company and industry.
6. **Management knowledge.** How senior managers make decisions, how public policy is shaped, and what pressures and responsibilities fall on managers.

In terms of the "attitude" that effective public relations practitioners must possess, the following six requisites are imperative:

1. **Pro communications.** A bias toward disclosing rather than withholding information. Public relations professionals should want to communicate with the public, not shy away from communicating. They should practice the belief that the public has a right to know.
2. **Advocacy.** Public relations people must *believe in* their employers. They must be advocates for their employers. They must stand up for what their employers represent. Although they should never ever lie (Never, ever!) or distort or hide facts, occasionally it may be in an organization's best interest to avoid comment on certain issues. If practitioners don't believe in the integrity and credibility of their employers, their most honorable course is to go to "Plan B"—find work elsewhere.

3. **Counseling orientation.** A compelling desire to advise senior managers. Top executives are used to dealing in tangibles, such as balance sheets, costs per thousand, and cash flows. Public relations practitioners deal in intangibles, such as public opinion, media influence, and communications messages. Practitioners must be willing to support their beliefs—often in opposition to lawyers or human resources executives. They must even be willing to disagree with management at times. Far from being compliant, public relations practitioners must have the gumption to say *no*.

4. **Ethics.** The counsel that public relations professionals deliver must always be ethical. The mantra of the public relations practitioner must be to *do the right thing*.

5. **Willingness to take risks.** Most of the people you work for in public relations have no idea what you do. Sad, but true. Consequently, it's easy to be overlooked as a public relations staff member. You therefore must be willing to stick your neck out . . . stand up for what you believe in . . . take risks. Public relations professionals must have the courage of their convictions and the personal confidence to proudly represent their curious, yet critical, role in any organization.

6. **Positive outlook.** Public relations work occasionally is frustrating work. Management doesn't always listen to your good counsel, preferring instead to follow attorneys and others into safer positions. No matter. A public relations professional, if he or she is to perform at optimum effectiveness, must be positive. You can't afford to be a "sad sack." You win some. You lose some. But in public relations, at least, the most important thing is to keep on swinging and smiling.

Last Word

Spin, cover-up, distortion, and subterfuge are the antitheses of good public relations.

Ethics, truth, credibility—these values are what good public relations is all about.

To be sure, public relations is not yet a profession like law, accounting, or medicine, in which all practitioners are trained, licensed, and supervised. Nothing prevents someone with little or no formal training from hanging out a shingle as a public relations specialist. Such frauds embarrass professionals in the field and, thankfully, are becoming harder to find.

Indeed, both the Public Relations Society of America (Appendix A) and the International Association of Business Communicators (Appendix B) have strong codes of ethics that serve as the basis of their membership philosophies.

Meanwhile, the importance of the practice of public relations in a less certain, more chaotic, over-communicated, and social media–dominated world cannot be denied.

Despite its lingering problems—in attaining leadership status, finding its proper role in society, disavowing spin, and earning enduring respect—the practice of public relations has never been more valuable or more prominent. In its first 100 years as a formal, integrated, strategic-thinking process, public relations has become part of the fabric of modern society.

Here's why.

As much as they need customers for their products, managers today also desperately need constituents for their beliefs and values. In the 21st century, the role of public relations is vital in helping guide management in framing its ideas and making its commitments. The counsel that management needs must come from advisors who understand public attitudes, moods, needs, and aspirations.

Contrary to what misinformed critics may charge, "More often than not, public relations strategies and tactics are the most effective and valuable arrows in the quiver of the disaffected and the powerless."[22] Civil rights leaders, labor leaders, public advocates, and grassroots movements of every stripe have been boosted by proven communications techniques to win attention and build support and goodwill.

Winning this elusive goodwill takes time and effort. Credibility can't be won overnight, nor can it be bought. If management policies aren't in the public's best interest, no amount of public relations effort can obscure that reality. Public relations is not effective as a temporary defensive measure to compensate for management misjudgment. If management errs seriously, the best—and only—public relations advice must be to get the truthful story out immediately. Indeed, working properly, the public relations department of an organization often serves as the firm's "conscience."

This is why the relationship between public relations and other parts of the organization—legal, human resources, and advertising and marketing, for example—is occasionally a strained one. The function of the public relations department is distinctive from that of any other internal area. Few others share the access to management that public relations enjoys. Few others share the potential for power that public relations may exercise.

No less an authority than Abraham Lincoln once said: "Public sentiment is everything . . . with public sentiment, nothing can fail. Without it, nothing can succeed. He who molds public sentiment goes deeper than he who executes statutes or pronounces decisions. He makes statutes or decisions possible or impossible to execute."[23]

Stated another way, no matter how you define it, the practice of public relations has become an essential element in the conduct of relationships for a vast variety of organizations in the 21st century.

Discussion Starters

1. How prominent is the practice of public relations around the world in the 21st century?
2. What is the PRSA's definition of public relations? How would you define the practice of public relations?
3. Why is the practice of public relations generally misunderstood by the public?
4. How would you describe the significance of the planning aspect in public relations?
5. Within the R-A-C-E process of public relations, what would you say is the most critical element?
6. In what ways does public relations differ from advertising or marketing?
7. If you were the public relations director of the local United Way, whom would you consider your most important "publics" to be?
8. What are seven functions of public relations practice?
9. How do professional public relations people regard the aspect of "spin" as part of what they do?
10. What are the technical and attitudinal requisites most important for public relations success?

Pick of the Literature

Rethinking Reputation: How PR Trumps Advertising and Marketing in the New Media World

Fraser P. Seitel and John Doorley. New York: Palgrave Macmillan, 2012

One outstanding educator and another guy critique how a social media–dominated society with declining journalistic societal standards impacts the quest for credibility.

The authors demonstrate how public relations can help build successful enterprises, even with a minimum of advertising support. The book focuses on real-life cases, including student designers of a successful footwear company who market themselves through networking, Facebook, and Twitter; Merck CEO Roy Vagelos, who developed a cure for river blindness and ensured the drug was made available where needed for free; and Exxon-Mobil, which resurrected its reputation through on-the-ground meetings with critics and a more accessible public relations posture.

The book also reviews the new 21st-century public relations realities, in which even "taking the low road" can lead to success, as in the cases of Donald Trump, Al Sharpton, Nancy Grace, and Dominic Strauss-Kahn. They forcefully argue, though, that "taking the high road," a la Paul Volcker and T. Boone Pickens, is eminently preferable. Worth buying, if for no other reason than one of the authors needs the money!

Case Study   BP's Loose Lips Sink Credibility Ship

For a company so assiduously devoted to polishing its reputation, the events of April 20, 2010, had to be particularly painful.

That morning, officials of the worldwide oil company BP, supervising drilling of the 18,000-foot Macondo Prospect well, 41 miles off the Louisiana coast, joined the 140 crew members on the company's prized oil rig, Deepwater Horizon, to celebrate the fabled rig's overall record for uninterrupted "safety."

How tragically ironic.

Ten hours later, gas, oil, and concrete from the Deepwater Horizon hurtled up the well bore onto the deck, unleashing a bone-rattling explosion and a massive fireball that killed 11 workers on the platform and submerged BP into the most disastrous public relations crisis in the history of the oil industry.

Bigger than the British Isle

BP was the world's third-largest energy company and the fourth-largest corporation in the world, employing 80,000 people and operating in 100 countries. Although BP, based in Great Britain, was the biggest company in the United Kingdom, it wanted the world to know it was a lot bigger than the British isle. So in 2001, the company formally dropped its legal name, British Petroleum, and became BP plc, to suggest its global clout and focus.

To corporate critics, environmentalists, and their ilk, BP was a particularly vulnerable target. In 1991, BP was cited as the most polluting company in the United States, based on Environmental Protection Agency toxic release data. In response, BP worked hard to distinguish itself from its generally hardnosed and standoffish oil industry brethren, as a responsible and concerned—and approachable—company.

- It broke with the industry in acknowledging the possible link between greenhouse gases and climate change.
- It invested heavily in sustainability and biofuels.
- It spent millions promoting its environmentally friendly views and programs in ads and public relations sponsorships around the world.

BP recognized that its reputation mattered, and it worked diligently to polish that reputation, while trolling the world for black gold.

This added to the company's shock and horror when on April 22, two days after the explosion, BP's Deepwater Horizon sunk to the bottom of the ocean floor. And the BP Corporation became embroiled in the most damaging corporate public relations catastrophe in history, costing the company billions of dollars and proving once again the ancient Chinese aphorism: "A reputation carefully honed over hundreds of years can be destroyed in a single moment."

Shockwaves from the Gulf to D.C. to London

The BP spill in the Gulf sent off public relations shockwaves all the way to the halls of Barack Obama's White House in Washington.

Dogged by an unpopular war in Afghanistan and economic problems at home, the last thing Barack Obama needed in April 2010 was a major oil spill in the Gulf of Mexico.

Initial administration response to the blowup in the Gulf was tepid. But as public anger rose, the Obama response morphed from one of "the Coast Guard is directing the response" to one of "the President is closely monitoring the situation" to one of "BP has the unique equipment to deal with the situation" to one of "my job is to get this fixed. BP will pay. If its CEO worked for me, he'd be fired."

Predictably with the American president breathing down its neck, at BP executive offices at St. James Square in London, all was chaos at the 100-year-old energy company.

The oil in the Gulf was leaking uncontrollably. The crisis was rapidly deteriorating into a full-blown media onslaught. And nobody at BP North American headquarters in sleepy Warrenville, Illinois, or at its international headquarters in London had the foggiest idea what to do.

The only thing BP knew for certain in those first days of oil spill Code Blue was: *We cannot become another* Exxon Valdez.

The *Exxon Valdez*, of course, was the mother of all public relations crisis catastrophes. In March 1989 in Prince William Sound, Alaska, an Exxon tanker (piloted by a captain who, as it turned out, was also reportedly "tanked") crashed into a reef and spilled 700,000 barrels of oil into the pristine Gulf of Valdez, soiling and killing everything in its wake.

Determined to prevent another *Valdez*, BP immediately took three actions:

- First, BP stepped up to take charge of handling the spill.

This wasn't necessarily a "given." There were other deep-pocketed players involved, from Transocean, which owned the rig, to Cameron International Corporation, which made the ill-fated blowout preventer, to Halliburton, which advised BP on plugging the well, to Anadarko Petroleum Corporation, which owned one-quarter of the BP well. When all of the others ducked for cover, BP stepped up to take the hit, alone.

- Second, also without prodding, BP stepped forward to pick up any "legitimate claims" associated with the Gulf spill.

One month into the spill, 65,000 compensation claims from assorted fishers, hotel and restaurant owners, and others had been filed, and BP had paid out $2 billion. The company also agreed, at the Obama administration's insistence, to set up a $20 billion claims fund—labeled a "shakedown" by one overzealous Republican congressman—to compensate those affected.

- Third, vowing to be public with its decisions, BP dispatched its young, dynamic chief executive, Anthony Bryan "Tony" Hayward, personally to take charge on the ground of the Gulf oil spill (Figure 1-6).

This final decision—assigning CEO Hayward to take charge of the crisis—proved a tragic miscalculation.

FIGURE 1-6   Tony on the spot.
BP dispatched its CEO, Anthony "Tony" Hayward, to Louisiana to deal with the worldwide oil spill media. *(Photo: Newscom)*

"I'd Rather be Sailing."

There is no question that CEO Hayward meant well.

But in a public relations crisis the magnitude of the burgeoning BP spill, with the eyes of the world on your every move and the ears of the world on your every word, the difference between "meaning well" and "performing admirably" is as wide as the vast ocean into which Hayward figuratively plunged upon opening his yap.

As the days wore on and Hayward continued to stumble rhetorically, the reputation that BP had built began to crumble. Its CEO's most egregious public relations errors included the following:

■ **He predicted a speedy conclusion to the crisis.**

One irrefutable rule of public relations crisis is *never, ever, predict.*

As much as the press and public want to know the likely outcome and timetable, in a crisis the worst thing one can do is predict what will happen.

Tony Hayward violated this principle almost immediately.

Early on, the BP CEO volunteered—to his and his company's ultimate detriment—that the environmental impact of the spill would be "very, very modest."

It made little difference that Hayward's full quote was a lot more measured, "It is impossible to say and we will mount, as part of the aftermath, a very detailed environmental assessment but everything we can see at the moment suggests that the overall environmental impact will be very, very modest."

Too late. The BP CEO's "modest impact" prediction snippet—played in an endless loop on cable TV—was enough to set a sinking early tone for Hayward and his company, right out of the box.

■ **He painted a perpetually upbeat picture.**

Just as you never predict in a public relations crisis, so, too, do you always attempt to *play down expectations.*

As BP's lead spokesperson, CEO Hayward, obviously "hoping for the best," once again violated this simple rule from the get-go.

One example: BP first estimated that perhaps 1,000 barrels a day would leak from the rig, making the problem seem manageable. When it quickly became obvious that the problem was eminently more significant, BP raised its estimates to 5,000 barrels a day.

A disbelieving Obama administration chartered its own panel of scientists to estimate the spill. By mid-June, the Obama panel estimated that, contrary to BP's Pollyannaish analysis, 35,000 to 60,000 barrels per day were leaking.

Had CEO Hayward downplayed expectations early on and warned that a greater amount of oil might leak, the company's credibility wouldn't have suffered so dearly in light of the constantly worsening reality.

■ **He whined.**

FIGURE 1-7   Tony off the rails.
CEO Hayward's recurring verbal faux pas inspired protestors and the public to downgrade BP's response to the spill.
(Photo: MICHAEL REYNOLDS/EPA/Newscom)

Another cardinal rule for any spokesperson is to *keep the focus on the individuals affected and not on yourself.*

Once again, CEO Hayward failed to heed simple public relations advice, committing yet another fatal faux pas for himself and his company.

After endless tracking of his every move, Hayward was growing testy with the press. On the morning of May 31, after another disappointing weekend of nonstop spillage, with the visibly downcast CEO once again cornered by the worldwide media, Hayward offered few answers beyond "how sorry we are for the massive destruction that cost lives, and there's no one who wants this thing over more than I do."

"I mean," concluded the CEO, "I'd like my life back."

Taken out of context—as it would be over and over again throughout the globe—Hayward's ad lib remark smacked of callous, condescending, self-centered whining, utterly devoid of any sensitivity to the 11 who died on the rig and the thousands in the Gulf whose lives had been ruined.

The CEO spokesperson was officially "toast." And Tony Hayward was relieved of his duties by BP, who would soon also relieve him of his CEO role (Figure 1-7).

■ **He went sailing.**

Eager, as he disastrously noted, to get "his life back," the day after being relieved of his public relations duties in the Gulf, Hayward decided to jet back overseas to watch his 52-foot yacht, *Bob,* compete in a swanky race off England's shore.

Predictably, as Hayward rooted on *Bob,* worldwide photographers and Internet bloggers recorded the fact that "when the going got tough, the CEO went sailing!"

BP tried to play down the Hayward yacht race. "He's spending a few hours with his family," said a BP spokesperson. "I'm sure that everyone would understand that. He will be back to deal with the response. It doesn't detract from that at all."

Well, actually it did. And BP felt the public's wrath.

The "end" for Tony Hayward came approximately three months after his company's oil well blew up in the Gulf of Mexico and one month after his yacht competed off the coast of England. On July 26, 2010, BP announced that BP Managing Director Bob Dudley would replace Hayward as BP CEO.

Hayward, it turned out, would remain with the company and reassigned to run a new BP unit—in Siberia!*

Questions

1. How would you assess BP's response to the Gulf of Mexico oil spill?

2. How could BP have prevented the damage done by its CEO spokesperson?

3. Had you been advising Hayward, what would you have suggested he say in response to the questions he was asked?

*For further information, see John M. Broder and Tom Zeller Jr., "Gulf Oil Spill Is Bad, But How Bad?" *The New York Times*, May 3, 2010; Justin Gillis, "Size of Oil Spill Underestimated, Scientists Say," *The New York Times*, May 13, 2010; Peter S. Goodman, "In Case of Emergency, What Not to Do," *The New York Times*, August 21, 2010; and Michael Sebastian, "BP Internal Pub Extols the Virtues of the Oil Disaster," ragan.com, June 23, 2010.

From the Top

An Interview with Harold Burson

Harold Burson is the world's most influential and gentlemanly public relations practitioner. He has spent more than a half century serving as counselor to and confidante of corporate CEOs, government leaders, and heads of public sector institutions. As founder and chairperson of Burson-Marsteller, he was the architect of the largest public relations agency in the world. Mr. Burson, widely cited as the standard bearer of public relations ethics, has received virtually every major honor awarded by the profession, including the Harold Burson Chair in Public Relations at Boston University's College of Communication, established in 2003.

How would you define public relations?

One of the shortest—and most precise—definitions of public relations I know is "doing good and getting credit for it." I like this definition because it makes clear that public relations embodies two principal elements. One is behavior, which includes policy and attitude; the other is communications—the dissemination of information. The first tends to be strategic, the second tactical—although strategy plays a major role in many, if not most, media relations programs.

How has the business of public relations changed over time?

Public relations has, over time, become more relevant as a management function for all manner of institutions—public and private sector, profit and not-for-profit. CEOs increasingly recognize the need to communicate to achieve their organizational objectives. Similarly, they have come to recognize public relations as a necessary component in the decision-making process. This has enhanced the role of public relations both internally and for independent consultants.

How do ethics apply to the public relations function?

In a single word, pervasively. Ethical behavior is at the root of what we do as public relations professionals. We approach our calling with a commitment to serve the public interest, knowing full well that the public interest lacks a universal definition and knowing that one person's view of the public interest differs markedly from that of another. We must therefore be consistent in our personal definition of the public interest and be prepared to speak up for those actions we take.

At the same time, we must recognize our roles as advocates for our clients or employers. It is our job to reconcile client and employer objectives with the public interest. And we must remember that while clients and employers are entitled to have access to professional public relations counsel, you and I individually are in no way obligated to provide such counsel when we feel that doing so would compromise us in any way.

What are the qualities that make up the ideal public relations man or woman?

It is difficult to establish a set of specifications for all the kinds of people wearing the public relations mantle. Generally, I feel five primary characteristics apply to just about every successful public relations person I know.

■ They're smart—bright, intelligent people; quick studies. They ask the right questions. They have that unique ability to establish credibility almost on sight.

- They know how to get along with people. They work well with their bosses, their peers, their subordinates. They work well with their clients and with third parties like the press and suppliers.

- They are emotionally stable—even (especially) under pressure. They use the pronoun "we" more than "I."

- They are motivated, and part of that motivation involves an ability to develop creative solutions. No one needs to tell them what to do next; instinctively, they know.

- They don't fear starting with a blank sheet of paper. To them, the blank sheet of paper equates with challenge and opportunity. They can write; they can articulate their thoughts in a persuasive manner.

What is the future of public relations?

More so than ever before, those responsible for large institutions whose existence depends on public acceptance and support recognize the need for sound public relations input. At all levels of society, public opinion has been brought to bear in the conduct of affairs both in the public and private sectors. Numerous CEOs of major corporations have been deposed following initiatives undertaken by the media, by public interest groups, by institutional stockholders—all representing failures that stemmed from a lack of sensitivity to public opinion. Accordingly, my view is that public relations is playing and will continue to play a more pivotal role in the decision-making process than ever before. The sources of public relations counsel may well become less structured and more diverse, simply because of the growing pervasive understanding that public tolerance has become so important in the achievement of any goals that have a recognizable impact on society.

Public Relations Library

Broom Glen M. *Cutlip and Center's Effective Public Relations.* 10th ed. Upper Saddle River, NJ: Prentice Hall, 2008. The granddaddy of comprehensive textbooks in the field.

Dillenschneider, Robert L. *The AMA Handbook of Public Relations.* New York: American Management Association, 2010. A legendary practitioner offers his prescription for communicating in the 21st century.

Dinan, William, and David Miller. *A Century of Spin: How Public Relations Became the Cutting Edge of Corporate Power.* Ann Arbor, MI: Pluto Press, 2008. A review of corporate public relations with a decidedly Scottish twist.

Doorley, John, and Helio Fred Garcia. *Reputation Management: The Key to Successful Public Relations and Corporate Communication.* New York: Routledge, 2010. The two smartest professors in the field discuss what really counts in terms of public relations effectiveness.

Ewen, Stuart. *PR! A Social History of Spin.* New York: Basic Books, 1996. A not-nice-at-all analysis of the growth of public relations in society, written by a sociologist who doesn't seem to have much regard for the burgeoning profession.

Gehrt, Jennifer, and Colleen Moffitt. *Strategic Public Relations: 10 Principles to Harness the Power of PR.* Xlibris Corporation, 2009. Two veteran public relations counselors use lessons from others to respond to the new 21st-century communication landscape.

Guth, David W., and Charles Marsh. *Public Relations: A Values-Driven Approach,* 5th ed. Upper Saddle River, NJ: Pearson Education, 2012. Two distinguished professors offer a look at today's public relations, including such unique theoretical aspects as contingency theory of accommodation, reflective paradigm, and heuristic versus theoretical approaches.

Hall, Phil. *The New PR: An Insider's Guide to Changing the Face of Public Relations.* North Potomac, MD: Larstan Publishing, 2007. Written by a former editor of the newsletter *PR News,* the book presents a valid portrait of the state of the public relations business in the first decade of the 21st century.

Heath, Robert L. *The Sage Handbook of Public Relations.* Thousand Oaks, CA: Sage Publications, 2010. A comprehensive overview of the field, including sections on investor relations, sports public relations, and the role of public relations in promoting healthy communities.

Heath, Robert L., and W. Timothy Coombs. *Today's Public Relations: An Introduction.* Thousand Oaks, CA: Sage Publications, 2006. Two eminent professors suggest that relationship building is "more than just a buzzword" and, rather, constitutes the essence of public relations.

Lattimore, Dan (Ed.). *Public Relations: The Practice and the Profession* (Kindle Edition). New York: McGraw-Hill College, 2011. Worthwhile contributions from a variety of scholars and professionals in the field.

Newsom, Doug, Judy Vanslyke Turk, and Dean Kruckeberg. *This Is PR: The Realities of Public Relations.* 9th ed. Belmont, CA: Wadsworth Publishing Company, 2007. Well regarded text authored by top-line academic practitioners.

Pohl, Gayle M. *No Mulligans Allowed: Strategically Plotting Your Public Relations Course.* Dubuque, IA: Kendall Hunt Publishers, 2005. A fresh, creative, and useful perspective on charting a public relations career, authored by one of the nation's foremost public relations educators.

Rampton, Sheldon, and John Stauber. *Trust Us, We're Experts: How Industry Manipulates Science and Gambles with Your Future.* New York: J.P. Tarcher/Putnam, 2002. A super-cynical look at what public relations people do for a living, authored by two of the industry's most ardent—yet lovable—critics.

Ries, Al, and Laura Ries. *The Fall of Advertising and the Rise of PR.* New York: Harperbusiness, 2004. An old ad hand and his daughter blow the lid off the advertising profession.

Slater, Robert. *No Such Thing as Over-Exposure: Inside the Life and Celebrity of Donald Trump.* Upper Saddle River, NJ: Financial Times/Prentice Hall, 2005. The story, if you can bear it, of Donald Trump, in which the promotion-craving megalomaniac sat for 100 hours of private conversations. (Not for the faint of heart!)

Solis, Brian, and Deidre Breakenridge. *Putting the Public Back in Public Relations*. Upper Saddle River, NJ: Pearson Education, 2009. Two experts on public relations for the Social Media Age present new concepts to engage old and new publics.

Wilcox, Dennis, and Glen T. Cameron. *Public Relations: Strategies and Tactics*. 10th ed. Boston: Allyn & Bacon, 2010. Fine, long-standing text; good introduction.

Yaverbaum, Eric. *Public Relations Kit for Dummies 2nd Edition*. Foster City, CA: IDG Books Worldwide, 2006. A tongue-in-cheek, but useful, primer.

Chapter 2

The History and Growth of Public Relations

Chapter Objectives

1. To track the development of the practice of public relations from ancient times to the present.

2. To underscore the contribution to the field of two pioneers, in particular, Ivy Lee and Edward Bernays, whose philosophies and policies set the tone for modern-day public relations.

3. To chart the growth of public relations and its emergence as a major societal force in the 21st century.

4. To examine the field's most famous critical case, the murders of individuals who consumed Tylenol and the choices Johnson & Johnson made in handling the crisis.

FIGURE 2-1 **On the hot seat.**
In the fall of 2012, Johnson & Johnson's pristine public relations reputation was on the line when a raft of recalls caused Congress to seek answers from CEO William Weldon and Consumer Group head Colleen Goggins, both of whom eventually left J&J. *(Photo: ZUMA Press/ Newscom)*

The practice of public relations came of age three decades ago when the Johnson & Johnson (J&J) Company of New Brunswick, New Jersey, confronted the most diabolical crisis in the field's young history—the sabotaging of company products resulting in the murder of company customers. The respectful and public way that J&J handled "The Tylenol Murders" is the subject of the case at the end of this chapter and a large reason why the field enjoys such prominence today. Johnson & Johnson's "Credo" of corporate values it considers sacrosanct is a model for companies around the world.

But public relations is a continually evolving social science. And none other than the legendary Johnson & Johnson company learned that in the fall of 2010, when J&J was once again thrust into the nation's headlines for problems with its products. In a rapid succession of announcements, J&J was forced to recall a series of products, from its children's liquid Tylenol to tens of thousands of artificial hips to millions of contact lenses, all produced by J&J units.

The spate of highly publicized product problems cast a pall over the commodity that Johnson & Johnson had fought so valiantly to uphold in the face of the Tylenol murders 30 years earlier— its integrity.[1] Ultimately, the problems cost the company millions of dollars in profits, triggered a congressional inquiry, forced the senior executive in charge of its consumer businesses to leave, and hastened the ultimate departure of J&J's CEO William Weldon (Figure 2-1).

Such is the fragility of a public relations reputation.

Unlike accounting, economics, medicine, and law, the modern practice of public relations is still a young field, a little more than 100 years old.

Modern-day public relations is clearly a 20th-century phenomenon. The impetus for its growth might, in fact, be traced back to one man.

John D. Rockefeller Jr. (Figure 2-2) was widely attacked in 1914 when the coal company he owned in Ludlow, Colorado, was the scene of a bloody massacre staged by Colorado militiamen and company guards against evicted miners and their families. When a dozen women and small children were killed at the Ludlow massacre, Rockefeller called in journalist Ivy Ledbetter Lee to help him deal with the crisis.

Lee, whom we discuss later in this chapter, would go on to become "the father of public relations." His employer, John D. Rockefeller Jr., whose legendary father had always adhered to a strict policy of silence, would bear responsibility for the birth of a profession built on open communications.

The relative youthfulness of the practice of public relations means that the field is still evolving. It is also getting *stronger* and gaining more *respect* every day. The professionals entering the practice today are by and large superior in intellect, training, and even experience to their counterparts of decades ago (when nobody studied "public relations").

The strength of the practice of public relations today is based on the enduring commitment of the public to participate in a free and open democratic society. Several society trends have influenced the evolution of public relations theory and practice:

1. **Growth of big institutions.** The days of small government, local media, mom-and-pop grocery stores, tiny community colleges, and small local banks have

FIGURE 2-2
Pondering a crisis.
John D. Rockefeller, Jr.
(center) needed public
relations help in 1914,
when the Colorado
coal company he
owned was the scene
of a massacre of
women and children.
*(Photo: Rockefeller
Archive Center)*

largely disappeared. In their place have emerged massive political organizations, worldwide media and social networks, Walmarts, Home Depots, statewide community college systems, and nationwide banking networks. The public relations profession has evolved to interpret these large institutions to the publics they serve.

2. **Heightened public awareness and media sophistication.** First came the invention of the printing press. Then came mass communications: print media, radio, and television. Later it was the development of cable, satellite, videotape, videodisks, video typewriters, portable cameras, word processors, fax machines, and cell phones. Then came the Internet, blogs, podcasts, wikis, and, most prominently, social media that have helped fragment audiences. Fifty years ago, McGill University Professor Marshall McLuhan predicted the world would become a "global village," where people everywhere could witness events—no matter where they occurred—in real time. In the 21st century, McLuhan's prophecy has become a reality.

3. **Increasing incidence of societal change, conflict, and confrontation.** Minority rights, women's rights, senior citizens' rights, gay rights, animal rights, consumerism, environmental awareness, downsizings, layoffs, and resultant unhappiness with large institutions all have become part of day-to-day society. With the growth of the Web, activists have become increasingly more daring, visible, and effective. Today, anyone who owns a computer can be a publisher, a broadcaster, a motivator of others.

4. **Globalization and the growing power of global media, public opinion, and democratic capitalism.** While institutions have grown in size and clout in the 21st century, at the same time the world has gotten increasingly smaller and more interrelated. Today, news of a cyclone that ravages Myanmar or an earthquake that imperils China is broadcast within moments to every corner of the globe. The outbreak of democracy and capitalism in China, Latin America, Eastern Europe, the former Soviet Union, South Africa, and even, in recent years, in Middle East nations from Afghanistan and Iraq to Libya and Egypt has heightened the power of public opinion in the world. The process has been energized by media that span the globe, especially social media that instantaneously connect like-minded individuals. In China alone, there are 75 million blogs, often carrying—at great risk—criticisms of the government. Public opinion is a powerful force not only in democracies such as the United States but also for oppressed peoples around the world. Accordingly, the practice of public relations as a facilitator for understanding has increased in prominence.

5. **Dominance of the Internet and growth of social media.** Nearly 245 million of the world's people today use the Internet.[2] The extraordinary growth of the Internet and the World Wide Web has made hundreds of millions of people around the world not only "instant consumers" of communication but also, with the advent of social media, "instant generators" of communication as well. The profound change this continues to bring to society—and the importance it places on communications—is monumental.

Ancient Beginnings

Although modern public relations is a 20th-century phenomenon, its roots are ancient. Leaders in virtually every great society throughout history understood the importance of influencing public opinion through persuasion. For example, archeologists have found bulletins in Iraq dating from as early as 1800 B.C. that told farmers of the latest techniques of harvesting, sowing, and irrigating.[3] The more food the farmers grew, the better the citizenry ate and the wealthier the country became—a good example of planned persuasion to reach a specific public for a particular purpose—in other words, public relations.

The ancient Greeks also put a high premium on communication skills. The best speakers, in fact, were generally elected to leadership positions. Occasionally, aspiring Greek politicians enlisted the aid of sophists (individuals renowned for both their reasoning and their rhetoric) to help fight verbal battles. Sophists gathered in the amphitheaters of the day to extol the virtues of particular political candidates. Thus, the sophists set the stage for today's lobbyists, who attempt to influence legislation through effective communications techniques. From the time of the sophists, the practice of public relations has been a battleground for questions of ethics. Should a sophist or a lobbyist—or a public relations professional, for that matter—"sell" his or her talents to the highest bidder, regardless of personal beliefs, values, and ideologies? When modern-day public relations professionals agree to represent repressive governments, such as Iran or Zimbabwe or North Korea, or to defend the questionable actions of troubled celebrities, from Charlie Sheen and Floyd Mayweather to Mel Gibson and R. Kelly, these ethical questions remain a focus of modern public relations.

The Romans, particularly Julius Caesar, were also masters of persuasive techniques. When faced with an upcoming battle, Caesar would rally public support through published pamphlets and staged events. Similarly, during World War I, a special U.S. public information committee, the Creel Committee, was formed to channel the patriotic sentiments of Americans in support of the U.S. role in the war. Stealing a page from Caesar, the committee's massive verbal and written communications effort was successful in marshaling national pride behind the war effort. According to a young member of the Creel Committee, Edward L. Bernays (later considered by many to be another "father of public relations"), "This was the first time in U.S. history that information was used as a weapon of war."[4]

Even the Catholic Church had a hand in the creation of public relations. In the 1600s, under the leadership of Pope Gregory XV, the church established a College of Propaganda to "help propagate the faith." In those days, the term *propaganda* did not have a negative connotation; the church simply wanted to inform the public about the advantages of Catholicism. Today, the pope and other religious leaders maintain communications staffs to assist in relations with the public. Indeed, the chief communications official in the Vatican maintains the rank of Archbishop of the Church. It was largely his role to deal with perhaps the most horrific scandal ever to face the Catholic Church—the priest pedophile issue of 2002. In the aftermath of that scandal, the Vatican has launched a clear public relations effort to enact procedures and punishments dealing with such abuse.[5]

Early American Experience

The American public relations experience dates back to the founding of the republic. Influencing public opinion, managing communications, and persuading individuals at the highest levels were at the core of the American Revolution. The colonists tried to persuade King George III that they should be accorded the same rights as English men and women. "Taxation without representation is tyranny" became their public relations slogan to galvanize fellow countrymen and countrywomen.

When King George refused to accede to the colonists' demands, they combined the weaponry of sword and pen. Samuel Adams, for one, organized Committees of Correspondence as a kind of revolutionary Facebook to disseminate anti-British information throughout the colonies. He also staged events to build up revolutionary fervor, such as the Boston Tea Party, in which colonists, masquerading as American Indians, boarded British ships in Boston Harbor and pitched chests of imported tea overboard—as impressive a media event as has ever been recorded sans television.

Thomas Paine, another early practitioner of public relations, wrote periodic pamphlets and essays that urged the colonists to band together. In one essay contained in his *Crisis* papers, Paine wrote poetically: "These are the times that try men's souls. The summer soldier and the sunshine patriot will, in this crisis, shrink from the service of their country." The people listened, were persuaded, and took action—testifying to the power of early American communicators.

Later American Experience

The creation of the most important document in America's history, the Constitution, also owed much to public relations. Federalists, who supported the Constitution, fought tooth and nail with anti-Federalists, who opposed it. Their battle was waged in newspaper articles, pamphlets, and other organs of persuasion in an attempt to influence public opinion. To advocate ratification of the Constitution, political leaders such as Alexander Hamilton, James Madison, and John Jay banded together, under the pseudonym Publius, to write letters to leading newspapers. Today those letters are bound in a document called *The Federalist Papers* and are still used in the interpretation of the Constitution.

After its ratification, the constitutional debate continued, particularly over the document's apparent failure to protect individual liberties against government encroachment. Hailed as the father of the Constitution, Madison framed the Bill of Rights in 1791, which ultimately became the first 10 amendments to the Constitution. Fittingly, the first of those amendments safeguarded, among other things, the practice of public relations:

> *Congress shall make no law respecting an establishment of religion, or prohibiting the free exercise thereof; or abridging the freedom of speech, or of the press, or the rights of the people peaceably to assemble, and to petition the government for a redress of grievances.*

In other words, people were given the right to speak up for what they believed in and the freedom to try to influence the opinions of others. Thus was the practice of public relations ratified.[6]

Into the 1800s

The practice of public relations continued to percolate in the 19th century. Among the more prominent, yet negative, antecedents of modern public relations that took hold in the 1800s was press agentry. Two of the better-known—some would say notorious—practitioners of this art were Amos Kendall and Phineas T. Barnum.

In 1829, President Andrew Jackson selected Kendall, a Kentucky writer and editor, to serve in his administration. Within weeks, Kendall became a member of Old Hickory's "kitchen cabinet" and eventually became one of Jackson's most influential assistants.

Kendall performed just about every White House public relations task. He wrote speeches, state papers, and messages, and he turned out press releases. He even conducted basic opinion polls and is considered one of the earliest users of the "news leak." Although Kendall is generally credited with being the first authentic presidential press secretary, his functions and role went far beyond that position.

Among Kendall's most successful ventures in Jackson's behalf was the development of the administration's own newspaper, the *Globe*. Although it was not uncommon for the governing administration to publish its own national house organ, Kendall's deft editorial touch refined the process to increase its effectiveness. Kendall would pen a Jackson news release, distribute it for publication to a local newspaper, and then reprint the press clipping in the *Globe* to underscore Jackson's nationwide popularity. Indeed, that popularity continued unabated throughout Jackson's years in office, with much of the credit going to the president's public relations advisor.*

Most public relations professionals would rather not talk about P. T. Barnum as an industry pioneer. Barnum, some say, was a huckster whose motto might well have been "The public be fooled." Barnum's defenders suggest that although the impresario may have had his faults, he nonetheless was respected in his time as a user of written and verbal public relations techniques to further his museum and circus.

Like him or not, Barnum was a master publicist. In the 1800s, as owner of a major circus, Barnum generated article after article for his traveling show. He purposely gave his star performers short names—for instance, Tom Thumb, the midget, and Jenny Lind, the singer—so that they could easily fit into the headlines of narrow newspaper columns. Barnum also staged bizarre events, such as the legal marriage of the fat lady to the thin man, to drum up free newspaper exposure. And although today's practitioners scoff at Barnum's methods, in this day of Paris Hilton, Lindsay Lohan, Donald Trump, and Al Sharpton, not to mention the Kardashians, there are still many press agents practicing the ringmaster's techniques. Indeed, when today's public relations professionals bemoan the specter of shysters and hucksters that still overhangs their field, they inevitably place the blame squarely on the fertile mind and silver tongue of P. T. Barnum.

Emergence of the Robber Barons

The American Industrial Revolution ushered in many things at the turn of the century, not the least of which was the growth of public relations. The 20th century began with small mills and shops, which served as the hub of the frontier economy, eventually giving way to massive factories. Country hamlets, which had been the centers of commerce and trade, were replaced by sprawling cities. Limited transportation and communications facilities became nationwide railroad lines and communications wires. Big business took over, and the businessman was king.

The men who ran America's industries seemed more concerned with making a profit than with improving the lot of their fellow citizens. Railroad owners led by William Vanderbilt, bankers led by J. P. Morgan, oil magnates led by John D.

---

*Kendall was decidedly not cut from the same cloth as today's neat, trim, buttoned-down press secretaries. On the contrary, Jackson's man was described as "a puny, sickly looking man with a weak voice, a wheezing cough, narrow and stooping shoulders, a sallow complexion, silvery hair in his prime, slovenly dress, and a seedy appearance." (Fred F. Endres, "Public Relations in the Jackson White House," *Public Relations Review* 2, no. 3 [Fall 1976]: 5–12.)

Outside the Lines

P. T. Barnum Redux

Kourtney, Kim, Khloé, and Kris and the Never-Ending Quest for Publicity

Self-respecting public relations professionals despise the legacy of P. T. Barnum, who created publicity through questionable methods. They lament, as noted in Chapter 1, that public relations communication should always reflect "performance" and "truth."

Ah, were it so.

Alas, Barnum's bogus methods are just as effective with 21st-century media as they were with 19th-century media.

Doubt it?

Then consider the Kardashians, those walking/talking/publicity-generating masters of media, who have parlayed their peculiar personal predicaments into reality-TV fame, public relations renown, and oodles of nonstop cash. P. T. Barnum never met publicity he didn't like, and neither have the Kardashians.

The Kardashian girls—Kourtney, Kim, Khloé, mother Kris Jenner (former wife of Los Angeles attorney Robert Kardashian and remarried to U.S. Olympic gold medalist Bruce Jenner), and younger sisters Kendall and Kylie—are celebutantes, famous for, well, being "famous."

The Kardashian girls parlayed their fame into a reality-TV series, *Keeping Up with the Kardashians*, which spawned the reality show *Khloé and Lamar* about Khloé and professional basketball-playing husband Lamar Odom. The Kardashians also cashed in on clothing lines, perfume franchises, a retail store in Las Vegas, and Kim's 72-day wedding to professional basketball player Kris Humphries.

While cynics doubted the staying power of the Kardashians, the media continued to report their every movement. Somewhere, P. T. Barnum is smiling (Figure 2-3).

FIGURE 2-3   Kardashian khaos.
That was the moniker of both the new Las Vegas shop that Kourtney, Kim, Khloé, and Kris opened in late 2011 and also the hysteria that perpetually surrounded the Kardashians, who treasured publicity above all else. *(Photo: Raoul Gatchalian/starmaxinc.com/Newscom)*

Rockefeller, and steel impresarios led by Henry Clay Frick ruled the fortunes of thousands of others. Typical of the reputation acquired by this group of industrialists was the famous—and perhaps apocryphal—response of Vanderbilt when questioned about the public's reaction to his closing of the New York Central Railroad: "The public be damned!"

Little wonder that Americans cursed Vanderbilt and his ilk as "robber barons" who cared little for the rest of society. Although most who depended on these industrialists for their livelihood felt powerless to rebel, the seeds of discontent were being sown liberally throughout society.

Enter the Muckrakers

When the axe fell on the robber barons, it came in the form of criticism from a feisty group of journalists dubbed *muckrakers*. The "muck" that these reporters and editors "raked" was dredged from the supposedly scandalous operations of America's business enterprises. Upton Sinclair's novel *The Jungle* attacked the deplorable conditions of the meatpacking industry. Ida Tarbell's *History of the Standard Oil Company* stripped away the public façade of the nation's leading petroleum firm. Her accusations against Standard Oil Chair Rockefeller, many of which were unproven, nonetheless stirred up public attention.

Magazines such as *McClure's* struck out systematically at one industry after another. The captains of industry, used to getting their own way and having to answer to no one, were wrenched from their peaceful passivity and rolled out on the public carpet to answer for their sins. Journalistic shock stories soon led to a wave of sentiment for legislative reform.

As journalists and the public became more anxious, the government got more involved. Congress began passing laws telling business leaders what they could and couldn't do. Trust-busting became the order of the day. Conflicts between employers and employees began to break out, and newly organized labor unions came to the fore. The Socialist and Communist movements began to take off. Ironically, it was "a period when free enterprise reached a peak in American history, and yet at that very climax, the tide of public opinion was swelling up against business freedom, primarily because of the breakdown in communications between the businessman and the public."[7]

For a time, these men of inordinate wealth and power found themselves limited in their ability to defend themselves and their activities against the tidal wave of public condemnation. They simply did not know how to get through to the public. To tell their side of the story, the business barons first tried using the lure of advertising to silence journalistic critics; they tried to buy off critics by paying for ads in their papers. It didn't work. Next, they paid publicity people, or press agents, to present their companies' positions. Often these hired guns painted over the real problems of their client companies. The public saw through this approach.

Clearly, another method had to be discovered to get the public to at least consider the business point of view. Business leaders were discovering that a corporation might have capital, labor, and natural resources, yet be doomed to fail if it couldn't influence public opinion. The best way to influence public opinion, as it turned out, was through honesty and candor. This simple truth—the truth that lies at the heart of modern-day, effective public relations practice—was the key to the accomplishments of American history's first great public relations counselor.

Ivy Lee: The Real Father of Modern Public Relations

Ivy Ledbetter Lee was a former Wall Street reporter, the son of a Methodist minister, who plunged into publicity work in 1903 (Figure 2-4). Lee believed neither in Barnum's public-be-fooled approach nor Vanderbilt's public-be-damned philosophy. For Lee, the key to business acceptance and understanding was that the public be informed.

Lee disdained the press agents of the time, who used any influence or trick to get a story on their clients printed, regardless of the truth or merits. By contrast, Lee firmly believed that the only way business could answer its critics convincingly was to present

FIGURE 2-4   Father of public relations.
Ivy Lee. *(Photo: Courtesy of Seely G. Mudd Manuscript Library, Princeton University Library, Ivy Lee Papers, Public Policy Papers, Department of Rare Books and Special Collections)*

its side honestly, accurately, and forcefully. Instead of merely appeasing the public, Lee thought a company should strive to earn public confidence and goodwill.

In 1914, John D. Rockefeller Jr., son of one of the nation's most maligned and misunderstood men, hired Lee to assist with the fallout from the Ludlow massacre, which was affecting his Colorado Fuel and Iron Company. Lee's advice to Rockefeller was simple:

> *Tell the truth, because sooner or later the public will find it out anyway. And if the public doesn't like what you are doing, change your policies and bring them into line with what the people want.*[8]

Despite the tragedy of Ludlow, Lee encouraged Rockefeller to create a joint labor–management board to mediate all workers' grievances on wages, hours, and working conditions. It was a great success. The mine workers—and the public—began to see John D. Rockefeller Jr. in a different light. Most important, he began to see them in a new light as well. As Rockefeller's youngest son, David, recalled nearly a century later, "My father was changed profoundly by his meetings with the workers. It was a lesson that stayed with him throughout the rest of his life and one of the most important things that ever happened to our family."[9]

In working for the Rockefellers, Lee tried to "humanize" them, to feature them in real-life situations such as playing golf, attending church, and celebrating birthdays. Simply, Lee's goal was to present the Rockefellers in terms that every individual could understand and appreciate.

Ironically, even Ivy Lee could not escape the glare of public criticism. In the late 1920s, Lee was asked to serve as advisor to the parent company of the German Dye Trust, which, as it turned out, was an agent for the policies of Adolf Hitler. For his involvement with the Dye Trust, Lee was branded a traitor and dubbed "Poison Ivy" by members of Congress investigating un-American activities. Ironically, the smears against him in the press rivaled the most vicious ones against any of the robber barons.[10]

Ivy Lee's critics cite his unfortunate involvement with the Dye Trust and even his association as spokesperson for John D. Rockefeller Jr. as proof that his contributions weren't particularly profound. They argue that Lee "was not someone who was particularly effective at getting business to change its behavior."[11]

Ivy Lee's proponents, on the other hand (and your author is one of them), argue that Lee was among the first to counsel his clients that "positive public relations starts with action, with performance" and that positive publicity must follow positive performance.[12] This is why Ivy Lee is recognized as the individual who began to distinguish "publicity" and "press agentry" from "public relations" based on honesty and candor. For his seminal contributions to the field, Ivy Lee deserves recognition as the *real* father of public relations.

The Growth of Modern Public Relations

Ivy Lee helped to open the gates for modern public relations. After he helped establish the idea that high-powered companies and individuals have a responsibility to inform their publics, the practice began to grow in every sector of American society.

Government

During World War I, President Woodrow Wilson established the Creel Committee under the leadership of journalist George Creel. Creel's group, composed of the nation's leading journalists, scholars, and public relations leaders, mounted an impressive effort to mobilize public opinion in support of the war effort and to stimulate the sale of war bonds through Liberty Loan publicity drives. Not only did the war effort get a boost, but so did the field of public relations. The nation was mightily impressed with the potential power of publicity as a weapon to encourage national sentiment and support.

During World War II, the public relations field received an even bigger boost. The Office of War Information (OWI) was established to convey the message of the United States at home and abroad. Under the directorship of Elmer Davis, a veteran journalist, the OWI laid the foundations for the U.S. Information Agency as America's voice around the world.

World War II also saw a flurry of activity to sell war bonds, boost the morale of those at home, spur production in the nation's factories and offices, and, in general, support America's war effort as intensively as possible. By virtually every measure, this full-court public relations offensive was an unquestioned success.

The proliferation of public relations officers in World War II led to a growth in the number of practitioners during the peace that followed. One reason companies saw the need to have public relations professionals to "speak up" for them was the more combative attitude of President Harry Truman toward many of the country's largest institutions. For example, Truman's seizure of the steel mills touched off a massive public relations campaign, the likes of which had rarely been seen outside the government.

Later in the century, the communications problems of President Richard Nixon, surrounding the "cover-up" of the Watergate political scandal, brought new criticism of public relations. It didn't matter that Nixon was surrounded by alumni of the advertising industry, rather than public relations professionals. The damage to the field's reputation was done. But the administration of the "great communicator" Ronald Reagan reaffirmed the value of public relations. And later, the communications skills of President Bill Clinton—before a nasty scandal in the Oval Office submerged him in scandal—added to the importance of the practice in government. In the 21st century, the masterful communications ability of President Barack Obama reinforced the power of communication in the White House, especially early in his first term.

Counseling

The nation's first public relations firm, the Publicity Bureau, was founded in Boston in 1900 and specialized in general press agentry. The first Washington, D.C., agency was begun in 1902 by William Wolff Smith, a former correspondent for the *New York Sun* and the *Cincinnati Enquirer*. Two years later, Ivy Lee joined with a partner to begin his own counseling firm.

The most significant counselor this side of Ivy Lee was Edward L. Bernays, who began as a publicist in 1913 and was instrumental in the war bonds effort. He was the nephew of Sigmund Freud and author of the landmark book *Crystallizing Public Opinion* (see interview at the end of this chapter).

Bernays was a giant in the public relations field for nearly the entire century. In addition to contributing as much to the field as any other professional in its history, Bernays was a true public relations scholar. He taught the first course in public relations in 1923 and was also responsible for "recruiting" the field's first distinguished female practitioner, his wife Doris E. Fleischman.

Fleischman, former editor of the *New York Tribune*, was a skilled writer, and her husband was a skilled strategist and promoter. Together they built Edward L. Bernays, Counsel on Public Relations into a top agency. In many ways, Fleischman was the "mother" of public relations, paving the way for a field that is today dominated by talented women (Figure 2-5).

FIGURE 2-5
Dynamic duo.
Edward L. Bernays and his wife, Doris Fleischman, formed the 20th century's greatest public relations tandem.
(Photo: Courtesy of the Museum of Public Relations, www. prmuseum.com)

Bernays's seminal writings in the field underscored the importance of strategic communications advice for clients. For example, Bernays wrote:

At first we called our activity "publicity direction." We intended to give advice to clients on how to direct their actions to get public visibility for them. But within a year we changed the service and its name to "counsel on public relations." We recognized that all actions of a client that impinged on the public needed counsel. Public visibility of a client for one action might be vitiated by another action not in the public interest.[13]

Due to his background, Bernays was fascinated by a wide range of psychological theories and practices beginning to emerge in society. One of his major contributions to the practice of public relations was transforming the practice from a purely journalistic-based approach to one underpinned by psychology, sociology, and social-psychology to reach individuals in terms of their unconscious desires, fears, and needs.[14]

After Bernays's pioneering counseling efforts, a number of public relations firms, most headquartered in New York, began to take root, most notably among them Hill & Knowlton, Carl Byoir & Associates, Newsom & Company, and Burson-Marsteller. One of the earliest African American counselors was D. Parke Gibson, who authored two books on African American consumerism and advised companies on multicultural relations.

For many years, Hill & Knowlton and Burson-Marsteller jockeyed for leadership in the counseling industry. One early counselor, Harold Burson (see From the Top in Chapter 1), emphasized marketing-oriented public relations "to help clients sell their goods and services, maintain a favorable market for their stock, and foster harmonious relations with employees." In 2000, Burson was named the most influential PR person of the 20th century.[15]

In the 1990s, the counseling business saw the emergence of international super-agencies, many of which were merged into advertising agencies. Indeed, both Hill & Knowlton and Burson-Marsteller were eventually merged under one corporation, WPP, which also included the J. Walter Thompson and Young & Rubicam advertising agencies. Another mega-communications firm, Omnicom Group, owned seven major public relations firms, including Fleishman-Hillard, Porter Novelli, and Ketchum. With the growth of such large agencies, occasional lapses in ethical standards confronted the profession (see PR Ethics Mini-Case in this chapter). Despite these communications conglomerates, most public relations agencies still operate as independent entities. And local agencies, staffed by one or several practitioners, dominate the industry.

In the 21st century, then, the public relations counseling business boasts a diverse mix of huge national agencies, medium-sized regional firms, and one-person local operations. Public relations agencies may be general in nature or specialists in everything from consumer products to entertainment to health care to social media and technology.

Corporations

After World War II, as the 20th century rolled on, the perceptual problems of corporations and their leaders diminished. Opinion polls ranked business as high in public esteem. People were back at work, and business was back in style.

Smart companies—General Electric, General Motors (GM), and American Telephone & Telegraph (AT&T), for example—worked hard to preserve their good names through both words and actions. Arthur W. Page became AT&T's first public relations vice president in 1927. Page was a legendary public relations figure—memorialized in today's Arthur Page Society of leading corporate and agency public relations executives—helping to maintain AT&T's reputation as a prudent and proper corporate citizen.

PR Ethics Mini-Case

Burson Fumbles Facebook Flap

As noted, there is no more respected individual in the practice of public relations than Harold Burson. The agency he founded, Burson-Marsteller, has a long and proud tradition of ethical practice. (Your author, himself, is a proud alumnus of the firm.)

But in the spring of 2011, Burson-Marsteller was caught red-handed in an embarrassing scheme to make a client's competitor look bad. The fact that the client was Facebook and the competitor was Google—two of the most powerful names in the social media world—only added to Burson's dilemma (Figure 2-6).

It all started when two Burson staff members—both former journalists—approached daily newspapers and Internet bloggers about authoring articles critical of a feature on Google's Gmail service called "Social Circle." The social media feature, said the Burson representatives, was guilty of trampling the privacy of millions of users and violating federal fair trade rules.

When the bloggers pressed Burson to reveal its client, Burson refused. One blogger was so enraged with the Burson whispering campaign that he posted Burson's entire pitch online. The blogger reported that Burson offered to ghost write an op-ed column, let the blogger sign his name to it, and then help get it published in the *Washington Post*, *Politico*, *The Hill*, *Roll Call*, and *The Huffington Post*.

This led to a chain reaction in the media. *USA Today* ran a Money section front-page story, "PR Firm's Google Attack Fails," exposing the two former journalists, one former CNBC news anchor Jim Goldman and the other, former *National Journal* political columnist John Mercurio, as the surreptitious leakers.

Meanwhile, Google began fielding media calls about the little-known service and issued its own statement: "We have seen this email reportedly sent by a representative of the PR firm Burson-Marsteller. We're not going to comment further. Our focus is on delighting people with great products."

Facebook quickly came out to separate itself from its public relations agency. Said a Facebook spokesperson, "No 'smear' campaign was authorized or intended," adding that it hired Burson to "focus attention on this issue, using publicly available information that could be independently verified by any media organization or analyst."

A chastened Burson said Facebook asked to be anonymous but acknowledged that the misguided effort was "not at all standard operating procedure and is against our policies."

The public relations industry was quick to denounce the clumsy "fake news" efforts of Burson and the two reporters-turned–public relations professionals. Said the chair of the Public Relations Society of America, "This reflects poorly upon the global public relations profession. Burson took the road of misleading and not disclosing who they were representing. In the essence of the public relation code of ethics 101, that's a no-no."*

No-no.

Questions

1. How should Burson have handled its Facebook assignment?

2. Should a public relations client always be identified?

FIGURE 2-6 Thumbs down.
Facebook was caught with egg on its face(book) as a result of the sneaky campaign of its public relations agency to plant incriminating stories about its competitor, Google. *(Photo: PORNCHAI KITTIWONGSAKUL/AFP/ Getty Images/Newscom)*

*For further information, see Bryon Acohido and Jon Swartz, "PR Firm's Google Attack Fails," *USA Today*, May 10, 2011, pp. B-1, 2; and Greg Hazley, "Burson Becomes Target in Facebook Flap," *O'Dwyer's*, June 2011, p. 10.

Page also was one of the few public relations executives to serve on prestigious corporate boards of directors, including Chase Manhattan Bank, Kennecott Copper, Prudential Insurance, and Westinghouse Electric.[16]

Page's five principles of successful corporate public relations are as relevant now as they were in the 1930s:

1. To make sure management thoughtfully analyzes its overall relation to the public
2. To create a system for informing all employees about the firm's general policies and practices
3. To create a system giving contact employees (those having direct dealings with the public) the knowledge needed to be reasonable and polite to the public
4. To create a system drawing employee and public questions and criticism back up through the organization to management
5. To ensure frankness in telling the public about the company's actions[17]

Another early corporate public relations luminary was Paul Garrett. A former news reporter, he became the first director of public relations for mighty GM in 1931, working directly for GM's legendary CEO Alfred Sloan. Garrett once reportedly explained that the essence of his job was to convince the public that the powerful auto company deserved trust, that is, "to make a billion-dollar company seem small." Ironically, as good as Garrett was, according to the late maestro of management Peter Drucker (see From the Top in Chapter 5), he nevertheless reflected the universal public relations complaint, still common today, of "never feeling like an insider" within his organization. Drucker, who counseled CEO Sloan, said that because Garrett was a "communications professional" and not a "car man," GM executives often treated him with wariness.[18]

One would think that companies today all recognize the importance of proper public relations in the conduct of their business. Most do. But, as the corporate financial scandals of the first decade of the 21st century—that torpedoed entrenched firms such as Lehman Brothers, Bear Stearns, Countrywide, and Washington Mutual and laid low the respected names of Goldman Sachs, Morgan Stanley, Merrill Lynch, Bank of America, and Citigroup—show, CEOs don't know everything. The point is that in a day dominated by social media and cable TV, smart corporate leaders more than ever need to seek out the counsel of trained public relations professionals in dealing with their key constituent publics.

Public Relations Comes of Age

As noted, public relations came of age largely as a result of the confluence of five general factors in our society:

Growth of Large Institutions

Ironically, the public relations profession received perhaps its most important thrust when business confidence suffered its most severe setback. The economic and social upheaval caused by the Great Depression of the 1930s provided the impetus for corporations to seek public support by telling their stories. Public relations departments sprang up in scores of major companies, among them Bendix, Borden, Eastman Kodak, Eli Lilly, Ford, GM, Standard Oil, and U.S. Steel. The role that public relations played in regaining post-Depression public trust in big business helped project the field into the relatively strong position it has enjoyed since World War II.

Today, businesses of every size recognize that aggressively communicating corporate products and positions can help win public receptivity and support and ward off government intrusion. The best companies in the 21st century are those that have learned, as Ivy Lee preached, that proper action results in the best public relations.

Heightened Public Awareness and Media Sophistication

In the 1970s and 1980s, companies were obligated to consider minority rights, consumer rights, environmental implications, and myriad other social issues. Business began to contribute to charities. Managers began to consider community relations a first-line responsibility. The general policy of corporations confronting their adversaries was abandoned. In its place, most large companies adopted a policy of conciliation and compromise.

This new policy of corporate social responsibility (CSR) continued into the 1990s. Corporations came to realize that their reputations are a valuable asset to be protected, conserved, defended, nurtured, and enhanced at all times. In truth, institutions in the 1990s had little choice but to get along with their publics. The general prosperity of the 1990s, fueled by enormous stock market gains, helped convey goodwill between organizations and their publics.

By 2012, 98% of American homes had television, more than 50% of Americans subscribed to basic cable, and 273 million North Americans used the Internet.[19] Where once three television networks—ABC, CBS, and NBC—dominated America's communication nexus, now a plethora of channels and cable networks, talk radio stations, as well as millions of blogs and social media outlets cater to every persuasion, enabling media consumers to choose what they want to view.

As a result of all this communication, publics have become much more fragmented, specialized, and sophisticated.

Societal Change, Conflict, and Confrontation

Disenchantment with big institutions peaked in the 1960s, coincident with an unpopular Vietnam War.

The social and political upheavals of the 1960s dramatically affected many areas, including the practice of public relations. The Vietnam War fractured society. Movements were formed by various interest groups. An obscure consumer advocate named Ralph Nader began to look pointedly at the inadequacies of the automobile industry. Women, long denied equal rights in the workplace and elsewhere, began to mobilize into activist groups such as the National Organization for Women (NOW). Environmentalists, worried about threats to the land and water by business expansion, began to support groups such as the Sierra Club. Minorities, particularly African Americans and Hispanics, began to petition and protest for their rights. Homosexuals, AIDS activists, senior citizens, birth control advocates, and social activists of every kind began to challenge the legitimacy of large institutions. Not since the days of the robber barons had large institutions so desperately needed professional communications help.

By the 21st century, such movements had morphed into established, well-organized, and powerful interest groups. Nongovernmental organizations (NGOs), united by the Internet, proliferated around the globe. By the presidential election of 2008, public disapproval of the Iraq War, concerns about energy supplies and prices, climate change

FIGURE 2-7   Meet the new bosses.
Hillary Clinton and Barack Obama not only shared a bench in 2008, they represented the evolving leadership of minorities throughout society, as Obama was elected president and Clinton was named his first Secretary of State. *(Photo: White House photo by Pete Souza)*

and global warming, and a host of other issues, as well as renewed disenchantment with those in charge of government and business, generated a new round of activism. Women rallied around the candidacy of Senator Hillary Clinton. The enthusiasm, among young people, generated by Senator Barack Obama and his call for "hope and change" was illustrative of the mood. When Senator Obama was elected the nation's first African American president and Senator Clinton was named his secretary of state in 2009, it was clear that traditional times in America had, indeed, "changed" (Figure 2-7).

Globalization and Growth of Global Media, Public Opinion, and Capitalism

In the 21st century, democracy and capitalism, as someone once said, have "broken out everywhere."

In recent years, significant events to spur democracy—all conveyed in real time by pervasive global media—have been breathtaking.

■ In 2005, after the defeat of Saddam Hussein signaled the potential for a democratic Iraq, an astounding 10 million citizens—70% of eligible voters—went to the polls to elect new leaders.

■ In 2008, Kosovo declared its independence from Serbia in a stunning signal of freedom. Also, democratic revolutions in Georgia and Ukraine challenged Russian dominance.

■ In 2011, the political uprising that swept through the Middle East represented the most significant challenge to authoritarian rule since the collapse of Soviet communism. Champions of democracy demanded that tyrants cede power as the "Arab Awakening" extended into totalitarian nations such as Syria well into the winter of 2013.

While the world remains a troubled place, the growth of democracy remains an inexorable force that can't be denied. Even in nations that aren't democracies, like China, the spirit of capitalism, of individuals free to earn a living based on their own industriousness and entrepreneurship, pervades. Moreover, with the world near-completely "wired," the power of communication and public relations to bring down tyrants and build up democracy is profound.

Dominance of the Internet and Growth of Social Media

In the 21st century, true two-way communication has arrived largely as a result of the growth of online access. Social media, cable, satellite, mobile, instant messaging, pagers, bar code scanners, voice mail systems, videodisk technologies, and a multitude of other developments revolutionized the information transmission and receiving process. The emergence of the Internet and the World Wide Web radically intensified the spread of communications even further.

The Internet began during the cold war in 1969 as a U.S. Department of Defense system (and not, as Nobel Prize winner but failed U.S. presidential candidate Al Gore may have intimated, as his invention!). In 2000, 22% of Americans had bought a product online. The rate grew to 49% in 2007. Revenues from Internet purchases grew from $7.4 billion in the third quarter of 2000 to an estimated $34.7 billion in the third quarter of 2007. And today, with close to 70% of online adults connected to social media platforms, sales via social commerce alone are expected to reach $30 billion.[20]

The impact of the Internet on public relations practice has been phenomenal. Email dominates internal communications. Journalists, like many other Americans, regard the Internet as their primary choice of most organizational communications. In the 21st century, knowledge of and facility with the Internet—from Facebook to Twitter, from Instagram to Pinterest to mobile apps of every variety—has become a front-burner necessity for public relations practitioners.

Public Relations Education

As the practice of public relations has developed, so too has the growth of public relations education. In 1951, 12 schools offered major programs in public relations. Today, well in excess of 200 journalism or communication programs offer concentrated study in public relations, with nearly 300 others offering at least one course dealing with the profession.

The last major study of public relations education was done more than a decade ago by the Commission on Public Relations Education, chartered by the Public Relations Society of America. This commission recommended a public relations curriculum imparting knowledge in such nontraditional but pivotal areas as relationship building, societal trends, and multicultural and global issues.[21]

While public relations education isn't generally incorporated into most business schools, it should be. As noted, the practice has become an integral part in the daily workings and ongoing relationships of most organizations—from companies to churches, from governments to schools. Therefore, business students should be exposed to the discipline's underpinnings and practical aspects before they enter the corporate world.

Likewise, in journalism, with more than 70% of U.S. daily newspaper copy—and 80% of UK newspaper copy—estimated to emanate from public relations–generated releases, journalists, too, should know what public relations is all about before they graduate.[22]

Last Word

From humble beginnings 100 years ago, the practice of public relations today is big business around the world.

- The U.S. Bureau of Labor Statistics reports that close to 320,000 individuals practice public relations across the country.[23]

- The Public Relations Society of America, organized in 1947, boasts a growing membership of 21,000 in 100 chapters nationwide.

- The Public Relations Student Society of America, formed in 1968 to facilitate communications between students interested in the field and public relations professionals, has more than 10,000 student members at close to 300 college chapters in the United States and one in Argentina.

- The International Association of Business Communicators boasts 15,000 members in more than 80 countries.

- More than 5,000 U.S. companies, 2,100 trade associations, 189 foreign embassies, and 350 federal government departments, bureaus, agencies, and commissions have public relations departments.[24]

- More than 3,000 public relations agencies exist in the United States, with more than 700 public relations firms residing in 80 foreign countries.[25]

- Top communications executives at major companies and agencies draw six-figure salaries, and more than a few make in excess of a million dollars a year.

The scope of modern public relations practice is vast. Media relations, government relations, Web relations, employee communications, public relations counseling and research, local community relations, audiovisual communications, contributions, interactive public relations, and numerous other diverse activities fall under the public relations umbrella. This may be one reason public relations is variously labeled *external affairs, corporate communications, public affairs, corporate relations,* and a variety of other confusing euphemisms.

Just as the name of the field generates confusion, so too does its purpose. Specifically, public relations professionals lament that the practice is still often accused of being a haven for snake oil salespeople peddling cosmetics, subterfuge, and spin. What many fail to understand is that proper public relations—the kind that builds credibility—must begin and end with one important commodity: *truth.*

Indeed, there is no more important characteristic for public relations people to emulate than the candor that comes from high ethical character. The field's finest ethical moment, in fact, occurred when the Johnson & Johnson Company, in the wake of unspeakable tragedy brought about by its lead product Tylenol, didn't hesitate to choose the ethical course. As the case study at the conclusion of this chapter suggests, the handling of the Tylenol tragedy was public relations' most shining hour. (And as the J&J example at this chapter's commencement indicates, positive public relations must be refortified all the time.)

Despite the stereotypes that still overhang the field, with hundreds of thousands of men and women in its practice in the United States and thousands more overseas, public relations has become solidly entrenched as an important, influential, and professional component of 21st-century society.

Discussion Starters

1. What societal factors have influenced the spread of public relations?
2. Why do public relations professionals think of P. T. Barnum as a mixed blessing?
3. What is the significance to the practice of public relations of American revolutionary hero Samuel Adams?
4. What did the robber barons and muckrakers have to do with the development of public relations?
5. Why are Ivy Lee and Edward Bernays considered two of the fathers of public relations?
6. What impact did the Creel Committee and the Office of War Information have on the development of public relations?
7. What was the significance of Arthur Page to the development of corporate public relations?
8. Where should the practice of public relations be situated in a university?
9. What are some of the yardsticks that indicated that public relations had "arrived" in the latter part of the 20th century?
10. What are some of the issues that confront public relations in the 21st century?

Pick of the Literature

A Century of Spin: How Public Relations Became the Cutting Edge of Corporate Power (paperback)

David Miller and William Dinan, London, England: Pluto Press, 2008

Two British sociology professors present a not-so-flattering view of how public relations developed and became the powerful societal force it is today.

The authors' bias is that public relations was hatched by covertly political types, interested in "spinning" propaganda to forward their purposes. It traces these roots to modern-day British politicians, right up to British Prime Minister David Cameron.

The book begins by calling public relations one of the world's most powerful forces, conceived by corporations to impose business interests on public policy. The notion of "public relations ethics" is an oxymoron, according to these professors.

Worth reviewing, at least to see how the naysayers think.

Case Study   The Tylenol Murders

Arguably, the two most important cases in the history of the practice of public relations occurred within four years of each other to the same product and company.

For close to 100 years, Johnson & Johnson Company of New Brunswick, New Jersey, was the epitome of a well-managed, highly profitable, and tight-lipped consumer products manufacturer.

Round I

That image changed on the morning of September 30, 1982, when Johnson & Johnson faced as devastating a public relations problem as had confronted any company in history.

That morning, Johnson & Johnson's management learned that its premier product, extra-strength Tylenol, had been used as a murder weapon to kill three people. In the days that followed, another three people died from swallowing Tylenol capsules loaded with cyanide. Although all the cyanide deaths occurred in Chicago, reports from other parts of the country also implicated extra-strength Tylenol capsules in illnesses of various sorts. These latter reports were later proved to be unfounded, but Johnson & Johnson and its Tylenol-producing subsidiary, McNeil Consumer Products Company, found themselves at the center of a public relations trauma the likes of which few companies had ever experienced.

Tylenol had been an astoundingly profitable product for Johnson & Johnson. At the time of the Tylenol murders, the product held 35% of the $1 billion analgesic market. Throughout the years, Johnson & Johnson had not been—and hadn't needed to be—a particularly high-profile company. Its chairperson, James E. Burke, with the company for almost 30 years, had never appeared on television and had rarely participated in print interviews.

Caught by Surprise

Johnson & Johnson's management was caught totally by surprise when the news hit. The company recognized that it needed the media to get out as much information to the public as quickly as possible to prevent a panic. Therefore, almost immediately, Johnson & Johnson made a key decision: to open its doors to the media.

On the second day of the crisis, Johnson & Johnson discovered that an earlier statement that no cyanide was used on its premises was wrong. The company didn't hesitate. Its public relations department quickly announced that the earlier information had been false. Even though the reversal embarrassed the company briefly, Johnson & Johnson's openness was hailed and made up for any damage to its credibility.

Early on in the crisis, the company was largely convinced that the poisonings had not occurred at any of its plants. Nonetheless, Johnson & Johnson recalled an entire lot of 93,000 bottles of extra-strength Tylenol associated with the reported Chicago murders. In the process, it telegrammed warnings to doctors, hospitals, and distributors and suspended all Tylenol advertising.

But what about all those millions of dollars worth of Tylenol capsules on the nation's shelves?

The company was convinced such a massive recall wasn't warranted by the facts. It was convinced that the tampering had taken place during the product's Chicago distribution and not in the manufacturing process. Further, the FBI was worried that a precipitous recall would encourage copycat poisoning attempts. Nonetheless, five days later, when a copycat strychnine poisoning occurred in California, Johnson & Johnson did recall all extra-strength Tylenol capsules—31 million bottles—at a cost of more than $100 million.

Although the company believed it had done nothing wrong, Johnson & Johnson acted to assuage public concerns. It also posted a $100,000 reward for the killer or killers. Through advertisements promising to exchange capsules for tablets, through thousands of letters to the trade, and through statements to the media, the company hoped to put the incident into proper perspective.

Loyal Users but . . .

At the same time, Johnson & Johnson commissioned a nationwide opinion survey to assess the consumer implications of the Tylenol poisonings. The good news was that 87% of Tylenol users surveyed said they realized that the maker of Tylenol was "not responsible" for the deaths. The bad news was that 61% still said they were "not likely to buy" extra-strength Tylenol capsules in the future. In other words, even though most consumers knew the deaths weren't Tylenol's fault, they still feared using the product.

But Chairperson Burke and Johnson & Johnson weren't about to knuckle under to the deranged saboteur or saboteurs who had poisoned their product. Despite predictions of the imminent demise of extra-strength Tylenol, Johnson & Johnson decided to relaunch the product in a new triple-safety-sealed, tamper-resistant package

FIGURE 2-8 New packaging.
The triple-safety-sealed, tamper-resistant package for Tylenol capsules had (1) glued flaps on the outer box, (2) a tight plastic neck seal, and (3) a strong inner foil seal over the mouth of the bottle. A bright yellow label on the bottle was imprinted with a red warning: "Do not use if safety seals are broken." As it turned out, all these precautions didn't work. *(Photo: Courtesy of Johnson & Johnson)*

(Figure 2-8). Many on Wall Street and in the marketing community were stunned by Johnson & Johnson's bold decision.

So confident was Johnson & Johnson's management that it launched an all-out media blitz to make sure that people understood its commitment. Chairperson Burke appeared on television shows and in newspaper interviews.

Welcoming *60 Minutes*

The company even invited the investigative news program *60 Minutes*—the scourge of corporate America—to film its executive strategy sessions to prepare for the new launch. When the program was aired, reporter Mike Wallace concluded that although Wall Street had been ready at first to write off the company, it was now "hedging its bets because of Johnson & Johnson's stunning campaign of facts, money, the media, and truth."

Finally, on November 11, 1982, less than two months after the murders, Johnson & Johnson's management held an elaborate video news conference in New York City, beamed to additional locations around the country, to introduce the new extra-strength Tylenol package.

In the months that followed Burke's news conference, it became clear that Tylenol would not become a scapegoat. In fact, by the beginning of 1983, despite its critics, Tylenol had recaptured an astounding 95% of its prior market share. Morale at the company, according to its chairperson, was "higher than in years." It had acted true to the "Credo," which spelled out the company's beliefs (Figure 2-9). The euphoria lasted until February 1986 when, unbelievably, tragedy struck again.

FIGURE 2-9
The Johnson & Johnson credo.
(Photo: Courtesy of Johnson & Johnson)

OUR CREDO

We believe our first responsibility is to the doctors, nurses and patients,
to mothers and fathers and all others who use our products and services.
In meeting their needs everything we do must be of high quality.
We must constantly strive to reduce our costs
in order to maintain reasonable prices.
Customers' orders must be serviced promptly and accurately.
Our suppliers and distributors must have an opportunity
to make a fair profit.

We are responsible to our employees,
the men and women who work with us throughout the world.
Everyone must be considered as an individual.
We must respect their dignity and recognize their merit.
They must have a sense of security in their jobs.
Compensation must be fair and adequate,
and working conditions clean, orderly and safe.
We must be mindful of ways to help our employees fulfill
their family responsibilities.
Employees must feel free to make suggestions and complaints.
There must be equal opportunity for employment, development
and advancement for those qualified.
We must provide competent management,
and their actions must be just and ethical.

We are responsible to the communities in which we live and work
and to the world community as well.
We must be good citizens — support good works and charities
and bear our fair share of taxes.
We must encourage civic improvements and better health and education.
We must maintain in good order
the property we are privileged to use,
protecting the environment and natural resources.

Our final responsibility is to our stockholders.
Business must make a sound profit.
We must experiment with new ideas.
Research must be carried on, innovative programs developed
and mistakes paid for.
New equipment must be purchased, new facilities provided
and new products launched.
Reserves must be created to provide for adverse times.
When we operate according to these principles,
the stockholders should realize a fair return.

Johnson & Johnson

Round II

Late in the evening of February 10, 1986, news reports began to circulate that a woman had died in Yonkers, New York, after taking poisoned capsules of extra-strength Tylenol.

Unbelievably, the nightmare for Johnson & Johnson was about to begin again.

And once again, the company sprang into action. Chairperson Burke addressed reporters at a news conference a day after the incident. A phone survey found that the public didn't blame the company. However, with the discovery of other poisoned Tylenol capsules two days later, the nightmare intensified. The company

recorded 15,000 toll-free calls at its Tylenol hotline. Once again, production of Tylenol capsules was halted. "I'm heartsick," Burke told the press. "We didn't believe it could happen again, and nobody else did either."

This time, the firm decided once and for all to cease production of its over-the-counter medications in capsule form. It offered to replace all unused Tylenol capsules with new Tylenol caplets, a solid form of medication that was less tamper-prone (Figure 2-10). The withdrawal of its capsules cost Johnson & Johnson more than $150 million after taxes.

Once again, in the face of tragedy, the company and its CEO received high marks. As President Reagan said at a White House

A special message from the makers of TYLENOL® products.

If you have TYLENOL capsules, we'll replace them with TYLENOL caplets.

And we'll do it at our expense.

As you know, there has been a tragic event. A small number of Extra-Strength TYLENOL® Capsules in one isolated area in New York have been criminally tampered with.

This was an outrageous act which damages all of us.

Both federal and local authorities have established that it was only capsules that were tampered with.

In order to prevent any further capsule tampering, we have removed all our capsules from your retailers' shelves. This includes Regular and Extra-Strength TYLENOL capsules, CO-TYLENOL® capsules, Maximum-Strength TYLENOL® Sinus Medication capsules, Extra-Strength SINE-AID® capsules, and DIMENSYN® Menstrual Relief capsules.

And Johnson & Johnson's McNeil Consumer Products Company has decided to cease the manufacture, sale, and distribution of **all** capsule forms of over-the-counter medicines.

If you're a regular capsule user, you may be wondering what to use instead. That's why we'd like you to try TYLENOL caplets.

The caplet is a solid form of TYLENOL pain reliever, which research has proven is the form most preferred by consumers. Unlike tablets, it is specially shaped and coated for easy, comfortable swallowing.

And the caplet delivers a full extra-strength dose quickly and effectively.

So, if you have any TYLENOL Capsules in your home, do one of the following:

1. Return the bottles with the unused portion to us, together with your name and address on the form below. And we'll replace your TYLENOL capsules with TYLENOL Caplets (or tablets, if you prefer). We'll also refund your postage. Or...

2. If you prefer, you can receive a cash refund for the unused capsules by sending the bottle to us along with a letter requesting the refund.

We are taking this step because, for the past 25 years, over 100 million Americans have made TYLENOL products a trusted part of their health care.

We're continuing to do everything we can to keep your trust.

Send to:
TYLENOL® Capsule Exchange
P.O. Box 2000
Maple Plain, MN 55348
Please send my coupon for free replacement caplets or tablets to:
Please print
Name _____
Address _____
City _____
State _____ Zip _____
Offer expires May 1, 1986

(Courtesy of Johnson & Johnson)

reception two weeks after the crisis hit, "Jim Burke of Johnson & Johnson, you have our deepest appreciation for living up to the highest ideals of corporate responsibility and grace under pressure."

Today, 30 years after the first customers were murdered after ingesting Tylenol capsules, the Tylenol case study stands as a model in how to conduct positive public relations—honestly, openly, transparently—even in the face of unspeakable tragedy.

Questions

1. What might have been the consequences if Johnson & Johnson had decided to "tough out" the first reports of Tylenol-related deaths and not recall the product?

2. What other public relations options did Johnson & Johnson have in responding to the first round of Tylenol murders?

3. Do you think the company made a wise decision by reintroducing extra-strength Tylenol?

4. In light of the response of other companies not to move precipitously when faced with a crisis, do you think Johnson & Johnson should have acted so quickly to remove the Tylenol product when the second round of Tylenol murders occurred in 1986?

5. What specific lessons can be derived from the way in which Johnson & Johnson handled the public relations aspects of these tragedies?

6. What was the media environment when the Tylenol crises occurred? How might the results have differed if the crises occurred today?

7. See what information Johnson & Johnson offers for its customers on the Tylenol website (www.tylenol.com). Follow the links to the Care Cards, House Calls, and FAQ sections. How do these sections demonstrate Johnson & Johnson's concern for customers? How do you think Johnson & Johnson would use this website to communicate with the public if new health scares surfaced?

For further information on the first round of Tylenol murders, see Jerry Knight, "Tylenol's Maker Shows How to Respond to Crisis," *Washington Post* (October 11, 1982): 1; Thomas Moore, "The Fight to Save Tylenol," *Fortune* (November 29, 1982): 48; Michael Waldholz, "Tylenol Regains Most of No. 1 Market Share, Amazing Doomsayers," *The Wall Street Journal* (December 24, 1982): 1, 19; and *60 Minutes,* CBS-TV (December 19, 1982).

For further information on the second round of Tylenol murders, see Irvin Molotsky, "Tylenol Maker Hopeful on Solving Poisoning Case," *The New York Times* (February 20, 1986); Steven Prokesch, "A Leader in a Crisis," *The New York Times* (February 19, 1986): B4; Michael Waldholz, "For Tylenol's Manufacturer, the Dilemma Is to Be Aggressive—But Not Appear Pushy," *The Wall Street Journal* (February 20, 1986): 27; and "Tylenol II: How a Company Responds to a Calamity," *U.S. News & World Report* (February 24, 1986): 49.

For an overall view of Johnson & Johnson and Tylenol, see Lawrence G. Foster, *Robert Wood Johnson: The Gentleman Rebel.* State College, PA: Lillian Press, 1999.

From the Top

An Interview with Ray Jordan

Ray Jordan is Senior Vice President of Corporate Affairs at Amgen. For nine years, he was Corporate Vice President, Public Affairs and Corporate Communication for Johnson & Johnson, responsible for public relations and corporate communication for the broadly based, diversified global health care company. He oversaw the public affairs responsibilities and activities of the company's more than 250 operating companies in 57 countries around the world. This interview is based on his tenure at J&J, which ended in 2012.

What was your primary mission as Johnson & Johnson's chief communications officer?

Our function had a clear vision and strategy, broad enough to be relevant and applicable to all our businesses, and my principal role was to drive that throughout the organization. Our mission involved three primary components: (1) maintaining and enhancing the reputation of the company and our businesses, (2) ensuring our core values, and (3) improving the environment for growth.

How did you manage the worldwide J&J communications network across international borders?

We managed more than 200 people around the world, including those who reported up through various solid and dotted lines. We didn't have communications people in all of our countries. Our corporate team was about 20 professionals. We operated through a council of senior communications officers, responsible for each of our four primary groups: (1) consumer, (2) pharmaceuticals, (3) surgical care, and (4) comprehensive care.

How did you influence perceptions in different geographies?

At Johnson & Johnson, our *Credo* was the galvanizing element across all geographies and businesses. That was at the core of driving reputation externally and our behavior inside the company.

Has the Tylenol case influenced the way J&J conducts itself around the world?

Yes. It's a powerful story and representation of how J&J thinks as a company. Those stories, like Tylenol, and the people who have lived and carry them are powerful influencers in the J&J culture.

How important is it for communications officers to interact constructively with corporate lawyers?

To be effective in my job, this is essential. Our lawyers are "facilitators," not "roadblocks." One obligation we have as communicators is to help ensure that our company's actions are consistent with who we are. That means we need to reflect on how other constituencies might react to a particular corporate action—before we take it. Lawyers are always engaged around potential actions. So a good relationship with lawyers means they will bring us into an assessment of whether an impending action may have consequences for other stakeholders. We were fortunate that at the corporate level of Johnson & Johnson, the communications group was always invited into discussions of this sort. And I lobbied our communications staff around the world to build strong working relationships with their senior lawyer—and also their senior finance officer. It's curious that many communications people tend to wither in terms of dealing with legal or finance groups. But they are both critically important for a communicator to get to know and work with.

How do you measure your success in your job?

Measurement in our business has always been a conundrum. My CEO gave me good guidance early on. He suggested focusing on a five-year mission at any given time. You need that much time to make meaningful "change" in terms of realizing a particular mission. So we managed our group in terms of "priorities" over the next five years. We assessed progress against these larger objectives clearly embraced by management. We met each fourth quarter with our senior executives to review what, if anything, we needed to change in our framework, what environmental factors will weighed on our priorities, and what commitments we planned to make for the year ahead. We used these updates to strike the theme for all subsequent communications—annual report, internal town hall meetings, analyst meetings, etc. In this way, our communications messages were consistent across geographies and businesses. And we could track progress in conveying these messages.

What qualities do you value most in a communications professional?

I look for three things:

1. *Business acumen is vital.* You must be able to relate to business leaders on the basis of what the business is and how to think about it.

2. *Excellent writing or editing capacity.* This is still vitally important in what we do.

3. *Tenacity to help the business operate in "the right way" is third.* You've got to possess a passion for this.

Public Relations Library

Bernays, Edward L. *Crystallizing Public Opinion.* New York: Liveright, 1961. The original 1923 version was the first significant book in the field. It deserves to be read for its historical value as well as for the amazingly progressive ideas that its author forwarded about the modern practice for which he was so responsible.

Bernays, Edward L. *Public Relations.* Norman: University of Oklahoma Press, 1963. This book offers an informative history of public relations, from Ancient Sumeria through the 1940s, and includes Bernays's view of what public relations ought to stand for.

Bernays, Edward L. *The Later Years: Public Relations Insights, 1956–1986.* Rhinebeck, NY: H & M, 1987. Essentially, this is a series of columns that Edward Bernays authored for the late *Public Relations Quarterly.*

Boorstin, Daniel J. *The Image: A Guide to Pseudo Events in America.* New York: Harper & Row, 1964. A not-very-flattering account of America's emphasis on image over reality, written 40 years ago by one of the nation's most eminent 20th-century thinkers.

Burson, Harold. "A Decent Respect to the Opinion of Mankind." Speech delivered at the Raymond Simon Institute for Public Relations (Burson-Marsteller, 866 Third Avenue, New York, NY 10022), March 5, 1987. This speech highlights public relations activities that have influenced the United States from colonial times to the present day.

Burson, Harold. *E Pluribus Unum: The Making of Burson-Marsteller.* New York: Burson-Marsteller, 2004. This 166-page memoir traces the life of one of the patriarchs of public relations, Harold Burson, from newspaperman in Memphis through war correspondent to founding his legendary public relations firm.

Chomsky, Noam. *Necessary Illusions: Thought Control in Democratic Societies.* Boston: South End Press, 1989. A contrary view to Bernays's concept of public relations, this book, written by a well-known social critic, expresses all "that is wrong" about the media and attempts to persuade the public.

Cutlip, Scott M. *Public Relations History from the 17th to the 20th Century.* Hillsdale, NJ: Lawrence Erlbaum Associates, 1995. A one-of-a-kind historical reference.

Cutlip, Scott M. *The Unseen Power—Public Relations, A History.* Hillsdale, NJ: Lawrence Erlbaum Associates, 1994. This 800-page book is perhaps the definitive history of public relations in the 20th century. And it's not always "positive," either.

Marchand, Roland. *Creating the Corporate Soul: The Rise of Public Relations and Corporate Imagery in American Big Business.* Berkeley and Los Angeles: University of California Press, 2001. An important part of public relations, the work in Corporate America.

Nevins, Allan. "The Constitution Makers and the Public, 1785–1790." An address before the Conference of the Public Relations Society of America, November 13, 1962. Reprinted as "At the Beginning . . . A Series of Lecture-Essays." Gainesville, FL: The Institute for Public Relations Research and Education, 1997.

Olasky, Marvin N. "Roots of Modern Public Relations: The Bernays Doctrine." *Public Relations Quarterly,* Winter 1984. Olasky wages a spirited defense of Bernays as a more pragmatic and effective public relations representative than Ivy Lee.

Slater, Robert. *No Such Thing as Over-Exposure: Inside the Life and Celebrity of Donald Trump.* Upper Saddle River, NJ: Prentice Hall, 2005. If you've ever wondered about the phrase "a legend in his own mind," read this book and find out what it means.

Tedlow, Richard S. *Keeping the Corporate Image: Public Relations and Business, 1900–1950.* Greenwich, CT: JAI Press, 1979. An analytical and comprehensive history of corporate public relations in the first half of the 20th century.

Tye, Larry. *The Father of Spin: Edward L. Bernays and the Birth of Public Relations.* New York: Henry Holt, 1998. The author's background as a *Boston Globe* journalist, not a public relations practitioner or professor, both limits the depth of this biography and offers the refreshing viewpoint of an "outsider."

Chapter **3**

Communication

Chapter Objectives

1. To discuss the goals and theories of modern communication as they relate to the practice of public relations.

2. To explore the importance and proper use of words and semantics to deliver ideas and persuade others toward one's point of view.

3. To discuss the various elements that effect communication, including the media, the bias of receivers, and the individuals or entities delivering messages.

4. To examine the necessity of feedback in evaluating communication and formulating continued communication.

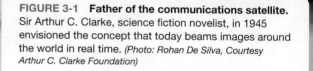

FIGURE 3-1 Father of the communications satellite. Sir Arthur C. Clarke, science fiction novelist, in 1945 envisioned the concept that today beams images around the world in real time. *(Photo: Rohan De Silva, Courtesy Arthur C. Clarke Foundation)*

Social media so dominates communications practice today that the most venerable of communication staples, the Encyclopedia Britannica, has been uprooted by an upstart online reference source called Wikipedia.

In today's online world, Wikipedia is the first source that most people—683 million visitors annually—consult. Its name is a blend of the words *wiki*, a technology for creating collaborative Websites, and *encyclopedia*. Launched in 2001 by Jimmy Wales and Larry Sanger, it is the largest, fastest-growing, and most popular general reference work on the Internet.[1]

And sometimes, that's not such a good thing. All too often, Wikipedia's "collaborators" are biased, either for or against the subject about which they are "objectively" writing. For example, in the spring of 2007, Wikipedia's founders were shocked when one of the service's most influential contributors and administrators, a chap who billed himself as "Essjay," was found not to be the tenured professor in Catholic law he had claimed but rather a 24-year-old community college dropout. That revelation—along with the knowledge that every day, scores of anonymous, self-styled "correctors" of questionable knowledge are anonymously editing Wikipedia copy—made people wonder about the accuracy of all those millions of articles in 250 languages on Wikipedia.[2] The lesson: Believe Wikipedia at your peril.

Such were the problems with communication in the age of social media.

In the 21st century, nearly the whole world is truly "wired." The power of communication, through the oral and written word and the images that flash around the world to millions of people in real time, is more awesome than any individual, group, or even nation.

What happens at a market in Baghdad is witnessed in a matter of seconds in Berlin and Bangkok and Boise. The world has truly become a "global village."

And perhaps no individual is more responsible for this global phenomenon than a British science fiction novelist who died in 2008 (Figure 3-1). Sir Arthur Clarke wrote a short article in 1945 that talked about combining the technologies of rocketry, wireless communications, and radar to envision an extraterrestrial system that relied on orbiting space stations to relay radio signals around the world.

Today, more than a half century later, Sir Arthur's vision has morphed into the global system of two dozen geo-synchronous satellites that orbit 22,300 miles above the earth, transmitting words and images around the world at the speed of light.[3] Thanks to the "Clarke Orbit" and the uplink technology that continues to be developed, events from coronations to courtroom trials to courageous efforts in the face of overwhelming tragedy are now broadcast globally at 186,000 miles per second (Figure 3-2).

As a consequence, *communication* has never been a more potent tool, and *communications* must be handled with great care.

FIGURE 3-2   **The world is watching.**
In the summer of 2012, as Syrian dictator Bashar al-Assad slaughtered his people and thumbed his nose at the world, opposition forces in the country used the Internet to keep the world abreast of the carnage. This placard reads, "Thank you for killing us." *(Photo: JAMAL NASRALLAH/EPA/Newscom)*

Which brings us back to public relations.

First and foremost, the public relations practitioner is a professional communicator. More than anyone else in an organization, the practitioner must know how to communicate.

Fundamentally, communication is a process of exchanging information, imparting ideas, and making oneself understood by others. It also includes understanding others in return. Indeed, *understanding* is critical to the communications process. If one person sends a message to another, who disregards or misunderstands it, then communication hasn't taken place. But if the idea received is the one intended, then communication has occurred. Thus, a boss who sends subordinates dozens of emails isn't necessarily communicating with them. If the idea received is not the one intended, then the sender has done little more than convert personal thoughts to words—and there they lie.

Although all of us are endowed with some capacity for communicating, the public relations practitioner must be better at it than most. Before public relations practitioners can earn the respect of management and become trusted advisors, they must demonstrate a mastery of many communications skills—writing, speaking, listening, promoting, and counseling. Just as the comptroller is expected to be an adept accountant, and the legal counsel is expected to be an accomplished lawyer, the public relations professional must be the best communicator in the organization. Period.

Goals of Communication

When communication is planned, as it should be in public relations, every communication must have a goal, an objective, and a purpose. If not, why communicate in the first place?

What are typical communications goals?

1. **To inform.** Often the communications goal of an organization is to inform or educate a particular public. For example, before holidays, the Automobile Association of America (AAA) will release information providing advice on safe driving habits for long trips. In so doing, AAA is performing a valuable information service to the public.

2. **To persuade.** A regular goal of public relations communicators is to persuade people to take certain actions. Such persuasion needn't be overly aggressive; it can be subtle. For example, a mutual fund annual report that talks about the fund's long history of financial strength and security may provide a subtle persuasive appeal for potential investors.

3. **To motivate.** Motivation of employees to "pull for the team" is a regular organizational communications goal. For example, the hospital CEO who outlines to her managers the institution's overriding objectives in the year ahead is communicating to motivate these key employees to action.

4. **To build mutual understanding.** Often communicators have as their goal the mere attainment of understanding of a group in opposition. For example, a community group that meets with a local plant manager to express its concern

about potential pollution of the neighborhood is seeking understanding of the group's rationale and concern.

The point is that whether written release, annual report, speech, or meeting, all are valid public relations communications vehicles designed to achieve communications goals with key constituent publics. Again, the best way to achieve one's goals is through an integrated and strategically planned approach.

Traditional Theories of Communication

Books have been written on the subject of communications theory. This book is *not* one of them. Consequently, we won't attempt to provide an all-encompassing discussion on how people ensure that their messages get through to others. But in its most basic sense, communication commences with a source, who sends a message through a medium to reach a receiver, who, we hope, responds in the manner we intended.

Many theories exist—from the traditional to the contemporary—about the most effective ways for a source to send a message through a medium to elicit a positive response. Here are but a few.

- One early theory of communication, the *two-step flow theory*, stated that an organization would beam a message first to the mass media, which would then deliver that message to the great mass of readers, listeners, and viewers for their response. This theory may have given the mass media too much credit. Indeed, when media is less "mass" than it is "targeted"—through social media, Websites, blogs, cable TV, talk radio, etc.—people today are influenced by a great many factors, of which the mass media may be one but is not necessarily the dominant one.

- Another theory, the *concentric-circle theory*, developed by pollster Elmo Roper, assumed that ideas evolve gradually to the public at large, moving in concentric circles from great thinkers to great disciples to great disseminators to lesser disseminators to the politically active to the politically inert. This theory suggests that people pick up and accept ideas from leaders, whose impact on public opinion may be greater than that of the mass media. The overall study of how communication is used for direction and control is called *cybernetics*.

- The communications theories of the late Pat Jackson have earned considerable respect in the public relations field. Jackson's public relations communications models, too, emphasized "systematic investigation—setting clear strategic goals and identifying key stakeholders."[4] One communications approach to stimulate behavioral change encompassed a five-step process:

  1. **Building awareness.** Build awareness through all the standard communications mechanisms that we discuss in this book, from publicity to advertising to public speaking to word of mouth.
  2. **Developing a latent readiness.** This is the stage at which people begin to form an opinion based on such factors as knowledge, emotion, intuition, memory, and relationships.
  3. **Triggering event.** A triggering event is something—either natural or planned—that makes you want to change your behavior. Slimming down in time for beach season is an example of a natural triggering event. Staged functions, rallies, campaigns, and appearances are examples of planned triggering events.

4. **Intermediate behavior.** This is what Jackson called the "investigative" period, when an individual is determining how best to apply a desired behavior. In this stage, information about process and substance is sought.
5. **Behavioral change.** The final step is the adoption of new behavior.

■ Another traditional public relations theory of communications is the basic *S-E-M-D-R communications process*. This model suggests that the communication process begins with the source (S), who issues a message (M) to a receiver (R), who then decides what action to take, if any, relative to the communication. Two additional steps, an encoding stage (E), in which the source's original message is translated and conveyed to the receiver, and a decoding stage (D), in which the receiver interprets the encoded message and takes action, complete the model. It is in these latter two stages, encoding and decoding, that the public relations function most comes into play.

■ Dissonance theory, formulated in the 1950s, suggests that people seek out messages that agree with or are "consonant" to their own attitudes; they avoid messages that disagree or are "dissonant" to their own attitudes. So the fact that liberals watch MSNBC and conservatives watch Fox News is an example of such "cognitive dissonance."[5]

■ There are even those who focus on the growing import of the "silent" theories of communication. The most well known of these, Elisabeth Noelle-Neumann's *spiral of silence*, suggests that communications that work well depend on the silence and nonparticipation of a huge majority. This so-called silent majority fears becoming isolated from and therefore ostracized by most of their colleagues. Thus, they invariably choose to "vote with the majority."[6]

All of these theories and many others have great bearing on how public relations professionals perform their key role as organizational communicators.

Contemporary Theories of Communication

Many other communications theories abound today as Internet communication changes the ways and speed at which many of us receive our messages. Professor Everett Rogers talks about the unprecedented "diffusion" of the Internet as a communications vehicle that spans cultures and geographies. Others point to the new reality of "convergence" of video, data and voice, mobile and fixed, traditional and new age communications mechanisms with which public relations professionals must be familiar.

The complexity of communications in contemporary society—particularly in terms of understanding one's audience—has led scholars to author additional "audience centric" theories of how best to communicate.

■ *Constructivism* suggests that knowledge is *constructed*, not transmitted. Constructivism, therefore, is concerned with the cognitive process that precedes the actual communication within a given situation rather than with the communication itself.

This theory suggests that in communicating, it is important to have some knowledge of the receiver and his or her beliefs, predilections, and background. Simply dispensing information and expecting receivers to believe in or act on it, according to this theory, is a fool's errand. The task of the communicator, rather, is to understand and identify how receivers think about the issues in question and then work to challenge these preconceived notions and, hopefully, convert audience members into altering their views.[7]

■　*Coordinated management of meaning* is a theory of communications based on social interaction. Basically, this theory posits that when we communicate—primarily through conversation—we construct our own social realities of what is going on and what kind of action is appropriate. We each have our own "stories" of life experience, which we share with others in conversation. When we interact, say the creators of this theory, we attempt to "coordinate" our own beliefs, morals, and ideas of "good" and "bad" with those of others so that a mutual outcome might occur.

　　　The point, again, is that communication, rather than being the simple "transmission" of ideas, is a complex, interconnected series of events, with each participant affected by the other.[8]

■　Other widely discussed theoretical models of public relations communications are the *Grunig-Hunt public relations models*, formulated by Professors James E. Grunig and Todd Hunt. Grunig and Hunt proposed four models that define public relations communications.

1. **Press agentry/publicity.** This early form of communication, say the authors, is essentially one-way communication that beams messages from a source to a receiver with the express intention of winning favorable media attention.

2. **Public information.** This is another early form of one-way communication designed not necessarily to persuade but rather to inform. Both this and the press agentry model have been linked to the common notion of "public relations as propaganda."

3. **Two-way asymmetric.** This is a more sophisticated two-way communication approach that allows an organization to put out its information and to receive feedback from its publics about that information. Under this model, an organization wouldn't necessarily change decisions as a result of feedback but rather would alter its responses to more effectively persuade publics to accept its position.

4. **Two-way symmetric.** This preferred way of communicating advocates free and equal information flow between an organization and its publics, based on mutual understanding. This approach is more "balanced"—*symmetrical*—with the public relations communicator serving as a mediator between the organization and the publics.[9]

These are but a few of the prominent theories of communications—all revolving around "feedback"—of which public relations practitioners must be aware. In Chapter 4, we review relevant theories in forming public opinion.

The Word

Communication begins with words. Words are among our most personal and potent weapons. Words can soothe us, bother us, or infuriate us. They can bring us together or drive us apart. They can even cause us to kill or be killed. Words mean different things to different people, depending on their backgrounds, occupations, education, and geographic locations. As anyone who has ever walked into a Starbucks and ordered a "small" caramel mocha macchiato only to be handed a "tall" caramel mocha macchiato knows, what one word means to you might be dramatically different from what that same word means to someone else. For example, when President Obama's surrogates, in the heat of the 2012 Republican presidential nomination process, labeled eventual presidential opponent Mitt Romney as "elitist," his wealthy rival lashed back in anger, the implication being that he couldn't relate to blue-collar voters. The study of what words really mean is called *semantics,* and the science of semantics is a peculiar one indeed.

Words are perpetually changing in our language. Every day, especially with the Internet, words are added to the lexicon. In 2012, when Marc Zuckerberg's Facebook stock floundered in its initial public offering, those who bought the stock were said to have been *Facebooked* or, worse, *Zucked.* Indeed, *Zuck* became an instant, new four-letter word.[10] What a word denotes according to the dictionary may be thoroughly dissimilar to what it connotes in its more emotional or visceral sense. Even the simplest words—*liberal, conservative, profits, consumer activists*—can spark semantic skyrockets. For example, in 2007, McDonald's launched a petition to get the Oxford English Dictionary to alter its definition of *McJob* as "an unstimulating low-paid job with few prospects."[11]

Particularly sensitive today is so-called discriminatory language—words that connote offensive meanings—in areas such as gender, race, ethnicity, and physical impairment. Words such as *firemen, manpower, housewife, cripple, midget,* and *Negro* may be considered offensive. While "political correctness" can go too far, it is nonetheless incumbent on public relations communicators to carefully assess words before using them.

Many times, without knowledge of the territory, the semantics of words may make no sense. Take the word *fat.* In U.S. culture and vernacular, a person who is fat is generally not associated with the apex of attractiveness. A person who is thin, on the other hand, may indeed be considered highly attractive. But along came 50 Cent and Kanye West and Jay-Z and hip-hop, and pretty soon *phat*—albeit with a new spelling—became the baddest of the bad, the coolest of the cool, the height of fetching pulchritudinousness (if you smell what I'm cookin').

Words have a significant influence on the message conveyed to the ultimate receiver. Thus the responsibility of a public relations professional, entrusted with *encoding* a client's message, is significant. Public relations encoders must understand, for example, that in today's technologically changing world, words and phrases change meaning and drop out of favor with blinding speed (see Outside the Lines in this chapter). During the past century, the English language has added an average of 900 new words every year.[12]

For an intended message to get through, then, a public relations "interpreter" must accurately understand and effectively translate the true meaning—with all its semantic complications—to the receiver.

The Message

The real importance of words, in a public relations sense, is using them to build the messages that move publics to action. Framing "key messages" lies at the top of every public relations to-do list.

Messages may be transmitted in myriad communications media: social media, speeches, newspapers, radio, television, news releases, press conferences, broadcast reports, and face-to-face meetings. Communications theorists differ on what exactly constitutes the message, but here are three of the more popular explanations.

1. **The content is the message.** According to this theory, which is far and away the most popular, the content of a communication—what it says—constitutes its message. According to this view, the real importance of a communication—the message—lies in the meaning of an article or in the intent of a speech. Neither the medium through which the message is being communicated nor the individual doing the communicating is as important as the content. This is why

Outside the Lines
Profizzle of Lexicizzle

The 21st-century lexicon of current words and phrases is ever-changing. What's *in* today is *out* tomorrow.

Doubt it?

Then translate the following phrases that your parents considered colloquial.

- *I'll be a monkey's uncle*
- *This is a fine kettle of fish*
- *Knee high to a grasshopper*
- *Going like 60*
- *Iron Curtain*
- *Domino theory*

Or explain what they meant by the following items.

- *Boob tube*
- *L.D.*
- *Segregation*
- *Mailman*
- *Stewardess*

Or reconcile what you mean with what they mean by the following terms.

- *Gay*
- *Menu*
- *Virus*
- *Crack, smack, snow,* and *blow*

Words change so quickly these days that we even have new instant languages being created before our eyes. Among them, the *gangsta* lexicon of one, Snoop Dogg (Figure 3-3), affectionately known as *izzle speak*, is designed primarily to confuse anyone who isn't an urban Black rapper. To wit:

- *Valentizzle*
- *Tonizzle*
- *Televizzle*
- *President Barack Obizzle*
- *Mitt Romnizzle*

All of which means that for public relations professionals in the 21st century, properly interpreting messages to key publics has become a complicated proposition.

Fo shizzle.

FIGURE 3-3 Profizzle of Lexicizzle.
Rapper Snoop Dogg. *(Photo: Snapper Media/Splash News/Newscom)*

professional public relations people insist on accurate and truthful content in the messages they prepare.

2. **The medium is the message.** Other communications theorists argue that the content of a communication may be less important than the medium in which the message is carried. This theory was originally proffered by the late Canadian communications professor Marshall McLuhan. This theory is relevant in today's hyper-media society, where the reputation and integrity of a particular media source may vary wildly. For example, a story carried on an Internet blog would generally carry considerably less weight than one reported in *The New York Times*. That is not to say that for some receivers, a particular blog's

credibility might surpass that of the *Times*. Personal bias, as we will discuss, is always brought to bear in assessing the power and believability of communications messages. In other words, to some cognitively dissonant citizens, conservative Fox News is the "fair-and-balanced last word" in credibility; to others, it's the liberal MSNBC.

3. **The man—or, to avoid political incorrectness, the person—is the message.** Still other theorists argue that it is neither the content nor the medium that is the message, but rather the speaker. For example, Führer Adolf Hitler was a master of persuasion. His minister of propaganda, Josef Goebbels, used to say, "Any man who thinks he can persuade, can persuade." Hitler practiced this self-fulfilling communications prophecy to the hilt. Feeding on the perceived desires of the German people, Hitler was concerned much less with the content of his remarks than with their delivery. His maniacal rantings and frantic gestures seized public sentiment and sent friendly crowds into frenzy. In every way, Hitler himself was the primary message of his communications.

Today, in a similar vein, we often refer to a leader's charisma. Frequently, the charismatic appeal of a political leader may be more important than what that individual says. Such was the historic appeal of Fidel Castro in Cuba or Muammar Gaddafi in Libya, for example. Political orators in particular, such as former Presidents Bill Clinton and Ronald Reagan, could move an audience by the very inflection of their words. The smooth and confident speaking style of Barack Obama was a major plus in his winning the presidency in 2008. Experienced speakers, from Rachel Maddow on the left to Rush Limbaugh on the right, to retired military leaders such as Colin Powell and Stanley McChrystal, to sports coaches such as John Gruden and Mike Krzyzewski, can also rally listeners with their personal charismatic demeanor.

The point is that a speaker's words, face, body, eyes, attitude, timing, wit, presence—all form a composite that, as a whole, influences the listener. In such cases, the source of the communication becomes every bit as important as the message itself.

Receiver's Bias

Communicating a message is futile unless it helps achieve the desired goal of the communicator. As the bulk of the communications theories cited in this chapter suggest, the element of feedback is critical. This is why Web 2.0 technology—social media, interactive wikis, blogs, and the like—is important and pervasive. Key to feedback is understanding the precognitions and predilections that receivers bring to a particular message.

Stated another way, how a receiver decodes a message depends greatly on that person's perception. How an individual comprehends a message is a key to effective communications. Everyone is biased; no two people perceive a message identically. Personal biases are nurtured by many factors, including stereotypes, symbols, semantics, peer group pressures, and—especially in today's culture—the media.

Stereotypes

Everyone lives in a world of stereotypical figures. Gen Xers, policy wonks, feminists, bankers, blue-collar workers, bluebloods, PR types, and thousands of other characterizations cause people to think of specific images. Public figures, for example, are typecast regularly. The dumb blond, the bigoted right-winger, the bleeding-heart liberal,

FIGURE 3-4 Seeing stars.
Some of Hollywood's finest, courtesy of Madame Tousssaud's Wax Museum, pose below the iconic Hollywood sign. Located on Mount Lee in Griffith Park, the Hollywood sign is the most famous sign in the world. Originally built in 1923 for $21,000 as an advertising gimmick to promote home sales, the 45-foot-high, 450-foot-long, 480,000-pound sign was restored in 1978—Tinseltown's most enduring and instantly identifiable symbol. *(Photo: Jim Sulley/newscast/Newscom)*

the computer geek, and the snake oil used car salesperson are the kinds of stereotypes perpetuated by our society.

Like it or not, most of us are victims of such stereotypes. For example, research indicates that a lecture delivered by a person wearing glasses will be perceived as significantly more believable than the same lecture delivered before the same audience by the same lecturer without glasses. The stereotyped impression of people with glasses is that they are more trustworthy and more believable. (Or at least that's the way it was before Lasik surgery!)

Also, like it or not, such stereotypes influence communication.

Symbols

The clenched-fist salute, the swastika, and the thumbs-up sign all leave distinct impressions on most people. Marshaled properly, symbols can be used as effective persuasive elements (Figure 3-4). The Statue of Liberty, the Red Cross, the Star of David, and many other symbols have been used traditionally for positive persuasion. On the other hand, the symbols chosen by the terrorists of September 11, 2001—the World Trade Center, the Pentagon, and most likely the U.S. Capitol and the White House—were clearly chosen because of their symbolic value as American icons.

Semantics

Public relations professionals make their living largely by knowing how to use words effectively to communicate desired meanings. Occasionally, this is tricky because the same words may hold contrasting meanings for different people. Today's contentious debate about abortion is a case in point, with the debate buttressed by confusing semantic terms—*pro-life* to signify those against abortion and *pro-choice* to signify those in favor of allowing abortions. By the same token, Republican semanticist Frank Luntz warns his party to talk about the *death tax*, rather than the "estate tax," and *economic freedom*, rather than "capitalism."[13]

Controversy also surrounds the semantics associated with certain forms of rap and hip-hop music. To critics, some artists preach a philosophy of violence and hate and prejudice against women. But misogynist gangsta rappers, from the self-promoting Kanye West to the downright filthy Lil John, claim that they are merely "telling it like it is" or "reporting what we see in the streets." When reporters and record company executives give credence, that is, "street cred," to such misguided rhetoric, they become just as responsible as the artists for the often-unfortunate outcomes that result—for example, the child pornography charges against and subsequent 2008 trial of singer R. Kelly.

Because language and the meanings of words change constantly, semantics must be handled with extreme care. Good communicators always consider the consequences of the words they plan to use before using them.

PR Ethics Mini-Case
The Name That Slimed an Industry

The microbiologist at the U.S. Department of Agriculture had a couple of choice names for the lean, finely textured beef filler, used in hamburgers to kill bacteria: *pink paste* or *pink goo*.

But wait, said USDA meat inspector Gerald Zirnstein when he pondered the product in 2002, "it's pink. It's pasty. And it's slimy looking. So I called it pink slime" (Figure 3-5).

Perfect.

Or at least it was for a decade.

Then, in 2012—a decade after pink slime had been used regularly, and safely, in ground beef products—a food blogger posted an online petition asking the USDA to stop using the filler in school lunches, using the controversial name as her battering ram.

Within nanoseconds, the net furor had fueled newspaper headlines decrying "pink slime," and opportunistic celebrity chefs, such as Jamie Oliver, quickly denounced the product. Under pressure, McDonald's and other fast-food companies discontinued their use of it. And major supermarket chains, including Kroger and Stop & Shop, vowed to stop selling beef with the low-cost filler, heated and treated with ammonium to kill bacteria.

It was only a matter of time before the company that led production of the beef filler for 10 years, Beef Products, Inc. of South Dakota, closed down the products and three of its four plants, costing 650 jobs.

The company insisted that the product, which remained perfectly safe according to the USDA, was victim to "unfounded attacks and media-perpetuated myths."

And also a very catchy, yet unfortunate, name.*

FIGURE 3-5 **What's in a name?**
Plenty, especially if the name is "pink slime." *(Photo: Creativ Studio Heinemann/Westend61/Newscom)*

Questions

1. How "fair" was the debate over "pink slime," and what does it say about the use of semantics in popular controversy?

2. If you were Beef Products, what public relations approach would you have adopted?

*For further information, see Candice Choi, "The Making of the Term 'Pink Slime,'" salon.com, May 21, 2012.

Peer Groups

In one famous study, students were asked to point out, in progression, the shortest of the following three lines.

A _____

B _____

C _____

Although line B is obviously the shortest, each student in the class except one was told in advance to answer that line C was the shortest. The object of the test was to see whether the one student would agree with his peers. Results generally indicated that, to a statistically significant degree, all students, including the uncoached one, chose C.

Such an experiment is an example of how peer pressure prevails in terms of influencing personal bias. Public relations professionals, intent on framing persuasive communications messages, must understand the importance of peer group influences on attitudes and actions.

Media

The power of the media—particularly as an agenda setter—is substantial. Agenda-setting is the creation of public awareness by the media—the ability to tell us what issues are important. As early as 1922, the legendary newspaper columnist Walter Lippman was concerned that the media had the power to present biased images to the public. Indeed, two basic assumptions underlie most research on agenda-setting: (1) the press and the media do not reflect reality; they filter and shape it; (2) media concentration on a few issues and subjects leads the public to perceive those issues as more important than other issues.[14]

Today, with social media and the Internet so pervasive, cable news and talk radio so popular, and newspaper readership down, some argue that traditional media have lost some clout as agenda-setters. Perhaps. But it is still the case that most national agendas are set by the most powerful national media, such as *The New York Times*, *The Washington Post*, and *USA Today*. For example, in the presidential campaign of 2012, both the Obama and Romney camps responded daily to front-page *Times* and *Post* pieces—on everything from politically motivated national security leaks to the impact of lobbyist money on the campaigns to where the candidates chose to spend their pre-election summer vacations—that dominated the news cycles.

By the same token, in interesting the media to pursue client-oriented stories, public relations professionals also have a direct role in setting the agenda for others. The point is that people base perceptions on what they read or hear, often without bothering to dig further to elicit the facts. This is a two-edged sword: Although appearances are sometimes revealing, they are also often deceiving.

Feedback

A communicator must get feedback from a receiver to know what messages are or are not getting through and how to structure future communications.

You really aren't communicating unless someone is at the other end to hear and understand what you're saying and then react to it. This situation is analogous to the old mystery of the falling tree in the forest: Does it make a noise when it hits the ground if there's no one there to hear it? Regardless of the answer, effective communication doesn't take place if a message doesn't reach the intended receivers and exert the desired effect on those receivers.

Even if a communication is understood clearly, there is no guarantee that the motivated action will be the desired one. In fact, a message may trigger several different effects.

1. **It may change attitudes.** This result, however, is difficult to achieve and rarely happens.
2. **It may crystallize attitudes.** This outcome is much more common. Often a message will influence receivers to take actions they might already have been thinking about taking but needed an extra push to accomplish.
3. **It may create a wedge of doubt.** Communication can sometimes force receivers to modify their points of view. A persuasive message on cable TV can cause viewers to question their original thinking on an issue.
4. **It may do nothing.** At times, the best laid communication plans result in no action at all.

Whether the objectives of a communication have been met can often be assessed by such things as the amount of sales, number of followers, viewers, or votes obtained. If individuals take no action after receiving a communication, feedback must still be sought. In certain cases, although receivers have taken no discernible action, they may have understood and even passed on the message to other individuals.

Last Word

Knowledge of how and when and to whom to communicate is the primary skill of the public relations practitioner. Above all else, public relations professionals are professional communicators. That means they must not only be knowledgeable about the various Web-based techniques and tactics available to communicators in the 21st century but also understand the theoretical underpinnings of what constitutes a credible message and how to deliver it.

The early years of the 21st century indicate that effective communication has never been more important. With the emergence of worldwide terrorism; the Arab Spring; the deepening cultural chasm between West and East, rich and poor, and haves and have-nots; along with economic challenges from the soaring cost of energy to the threat of global recession, to the emergence of China and India as economic super powers—the need for honest, straightforward, and credible communication is critical.

There is no trick to effective communication. In addition to mastery of techniques, it is knowledge, experience, hard work, and common sense that are the basic guiding principles. Naturally, communication must follow action; organizations must back up what they say with what they do. Omnipresent advertising, a winning Website and social media presence, slick brochures, engaging speeches, intelligent articles, and good press may help capture the public's attention, but in the final analysis the only way to obtain continued public support is through proper performance.

Discussion Starters

1. Why is it important that public relations professionals understand communication?
2. What are some principal goals of communication, and what are some contemporary examples?
3. Why do words such as *liberal*, *conservative*, *profits*, and *consumer activist* spark semantic sky-rockets?
4. What is the role of a public relations professional in the S-E-M-D-R communications process?

5. What is the difference between the symmetric and asymmetric models of communication?
6. What is meant by constructivism and coordinated management of meaning?
7. What is meant by the media as *agenda setter*?
8. Why is feedback critical to the communications process?

9. What common mistakes do people make when they communicate?
10. What are some contemporary examples of the changing meanings of words over time?

Pick of the Literature

The Power of Communication

Helio Fred Garcia, Upper Saddle River, NJ: Pearson Education, 2012

One of the brightest lights in the communication profession, Professor Garcia draws on first-hand experience to detail how communication is as powerful as any factor in the 21st century.

The book draws heavily on current examples to link leadership and communication. From Bill Gates to John McCain, David Letterman to Steve Jobs to the CEOs of Hewlett-Packard and Netflix, Garcia applies sensible lessons to contemporary cases.

Through his experience as a teacher and practitioner and especially as counselor to leaders in the military, Garcia offers a valuable text for any public relations practitioner. As the author puts it, "Words matter. Words shape world views." And as one contributor adds, "If you can't communicate, you can't lead."

Case Study   Walmart's Bribery Shutdown

For the Sunday *New York Times*, the story was unprecedented.

On April 22, 2012, the world's most respected daily newspaper published a lead story on its front page that extended to three additional full pages inside the paper. The story concerned a multiyear investigation by the *Times* into bribery allegations at the largest foreign subsidiary at the largest retailer in the world.

Walmart de Mexico, the story said, was responsible for orchestrating a campaign of bribery to win market dominance. In its rush to build stores, "the company had paid bribes to obtain permits in virtually every corner of the country," according to the *Times*.

The dispatching of bribes to government officials was not only unethical, it was illegal—a violation of Mexican laws and Foreign Corrupt Practices Act, a federal law that makes it a crime for American corporations and their subsidiaries to bribe foreign officials.

And that was only part of it.

Further, the *Times* alleged, Walmart was fully aware of the bribery accusations against it; but rather than proceeding with a full-scale investigation to reach conclusions, it chose to shut down its internal investigation.

Internal Tug of War

By most accounts, Walmart, the world's largest retailer, was also among the world's most beleaguered companies.

Walmart Stores, Inc., founded by the legendary Sam Walton in bucolic Bentonville, Arkansas, is the world's largest private employer, serving an astounding 138 million customers per week in 8,500 stores in 15 countries under 55 different names. It makes $419 billion in annual sales—or about $35 billion a month—and controls about 20% of the retail grocery and consumables business in the United States.

Walmart is also the world's largest private employer, with 2.1 million worldwide employees, or, as the company puts it, "associates." In Mexico, Walmart employs 209,000 people, making it the country's largest private employer.

Over the years, Walmart has been a lightning rod for controversy. It has been charged with everything from being anti-union to anti-female to anti-community. Through it all, Walmart has adopted a commitment to the highest moral and ethical standards. It has worked to improve its public relations, becoming a more open and transparent company.

So when a former executive in the company's Mexican subsidiary notified Walmart management of the alleged bribery scandal in 2005, it set off, according to the *Times*, "a prolonged struggle at the highest levels of Walmart" between those eager to uphold the public standards the company had embraced and others intent on downplaying any allegations that might interrupt Walmart's relentless pursuit of growth.

Indeed, although Walmart's investigation of the alleged Mexico bribery allegations extended to the highest reaches of the company, the company failed to report the existence of its internal investigation to the U.S. Justice Department until December of 2011—seven years after the first reports of problems—and right after it learned that *The New York Times* was snooping around in Mexico.

El Lobo Guarding the Hen House

In its exhaustive four-page story, the *Times* suggested that its investigation, which included reviewing thousands of government documents and extensive interviews including 15 hours with the former Walmart executive who originally blew the whistle, showed "credible evidence that bribery played a persistent and significant role in Walmart's rapid growth in Mexico."

According to its accusers, Walmart's strategy was to build stores so fast in Mexico that its competitors would have little time to react. To accomplish this rapid expansion, according to the *Times*, required bribes, bribes, and more bribes to change zoning maps, reduce environmental objections, and otherwise expedite ordinarily lengthy permit processes. To deliver bribes to officials at every level of the Mexican bureaucracy, the company hired "gestores," a fixture in Mexican society, who are paid as "fixers" to do everything from lobby officials to stand in line for individuals at motor vehicle offices to grease the skids for building permits.

The *Times* reported that of all people, Walmart's attorneys led the charge to get management to focus on the bribery allegations and stop those responsible. The lawyers' entreaties, according to the *Times*, were met with delay and skepticism by senior management. While outside lawyers recommended a major top-to-bottom analysis of what was going on, Walmart's top management rejected this suggestion in favor of a more limited analysis.

Walmart's ethics policy, meanwhile, clearly stated, "Never cover up or ignore an ethics problem." Nonetheless, at a meeting in early 2006, reported by the *Times*, in the office of Walmart CEO H. Lee Scott Jr., it was decided to adopt a new, "modified protocol" for internal investigations. And in the case of the continuing Mexican investigation, it was decided to transfer control of the bribery inquiry to the office of a top executive in Mexico, a man who was one of the earliest targets of the bribery allegations.

Incredibly, just a few months after the assignment, the Mexican executive concluded in his final report to management that "no evidence" of bribes was found in Walmart de Mexico. The report further recommended against any "criminal pursuit" of any Walmart executive and with that, the case was closed—until the *Times* reopened it several years later.

Righteous, if Reluctant, Indignation

Walmart's reaction to the *Times*'s expose was one of righteous indignation.

As a spokesperson told the *Times*, "If these allegations are true, it is not a reflection of who we are or what we stand for. We are deeply concerned by these allegations and are working aggressively to determine what happened."

Specifically, Walmart said it was taking steps in Mexico to strengthen compliance with the Foreign Corrupt Practices Act. One "step" Walmart would not take was to allow the *Times* to speak with Mr. Scott or other executives involved in the scandal.

The immediate reaction to the *Times*'s story was most felt in the stock market, where Walmart shares on the Monday following the weekend revelation sunk like a stone, accounting for about one-fifth of the losses in the Dow Jones industrial average. Predictably, politicians from Washington to Mexico City called for outside investigations into Walmart's conduct. In Mexico, President Felipe Calderon said he was "indignant" about the company's behavior.

Perhaps most damaging to the company, Walmart building permits from Boston to New York City to Los Angeles were reportedly undergoing increased scrutiny, in the aftermath of the bribery allegations. Over the years, Walmart had worked assiduously to polish its image as it intensified efforts to move from its rural routes into big—and historically hostile—cities. The cries by local merchants that "Walmart will put us out of business" seemed to gain credibility in the wake of the bribery charges.

One venue where fireworks were expected but never materialized was the Walmart Annual Meeting, held a month after the *Times*'s story in Fayetteville, Arkansas. With Chairperson Rob Walton presiding over the 50th anniversary of the company his father founded and with a star-studded cast of marquee entertainers—Justin Timberlake, Taylor Swift, Lionel Richie, Celine Dion, Aerosmith, and Cheap Trick—the 14,000 employees and shareholders in attendance were positively buoyant (Figure 3-6). One reason that shareholders seemed oblivious to the bribery problems was that by the annual meeting, the company's stock had recovered, reaching a 12-year high.

Lest shareholders were concerned about the problems the *Times*'s story had raised, Walmart CEO Michael T. Duke assured them, "Let me be clear: Walmart is committed to compliance and integrity everywhere we operate."*

Questions

1. Had you been public relations advisor to CEO Scott at the time of the bribery allegations, what would you have counseled him to do?

2. How would you characterize Walmart's internal and external response to the bribery charges?

3. How significantly do you think the bribery allegations impacted the company's reputation?

4. What should Walmart's public relations posture be going forward, relative to the bribery charges?

*For further information, see David Barston, "Vast Mexico Bribery Case Hushed Up by WalMart After Top Level Struggle," *The New York Times*, April 22, 2012, pp.1, 8–10; Stephanie Clifford, "Wal-Mart Stock Falls Nearly 5%," *The New York Times*, April 23, 2012; Stephanie Clifford, "The Annual Shareholders' Meeting for Wal-Mart, Like Its Stock, Is Buoyant," *The New York Times*, June 1, 2012; and Stephanie Clifford and Steven Greenhouse, "WalMart's U.S. Expansion Plans Complicated by Bribery Scandal," *The New York Times*, April 28, 2012.

FIGURE 3-6   A big tent.
Chairperson Rob Walton, eldest son of the founder, welcomes 14,000 Walmart shareholders to the company's 2012 annual meeting extravaganza to celebrate its 50th anniversary. *(Photo: Richie Miller/Cal Sport Media/Newscom)*

From the Top

An Interview with Edward L. Bernays

Edward L. Bernays, who died in 1995 at the age of 103, was a public relations patriarch. A nephew of Sigmund Freud, Bernays pioneered the application of the social sciences to public relations. In partnership with his late wife, he advised presidents of the United States, industrial leaders, and legendary figures from Enrico Caruso to Eleanor Roosevelt. This interview was conducted with the legendary counselor in his 98th year.

When you taught the first public relations class, did you ever envision the field growing to its present stature?
I gave the first course in public relations after *Crystallizing Public Opinion* was published in 1923. I decided that one way to give the term "counsel on public relations" status was to lecture at a university on the principles, practices, and ethics of the new vocation. New York University was willing to accept my offer to do so. But I never envisioned at that time that the vocation would spread throughout the United States and then throughout the free world.

What were the objectives of that first public relations course?
The objectives were to give status to the new vocation. Many people still believed the term "counsel on public relations" was a euphemism for publicity man, press agent, flack. Even H. L. Mencken, in his book on the *American language*, ranked it as such. But in his *Supplement to the American Language*, published some years later, he changed his viewpoint and used my definition of the term.

What are the most significant factors that have led to the rise in public relations practice?
The most significant factor is the rise in people power and its recognition by leaders. Theodore Roosevelt helped bring this about with his Square Deal. Woodrow Wilson helped with his New Freedom, and so did Franklin Delano Roosevelt with his New Deal. And this tradition was continued as time went on.

Do you have any gripes with the way public relations is practiced today?
I certainly do. The meanings of words in the United States have the stability of soap bubbles. Unless words are defined as to their meaning by law, as in the case of professions—for instance, law, medicine, architecture—they are in the public domain. Anyone can use them. Today, any plumber or car salesman or unethical character can call himself or herself a public relations practitioner. Many who call themselves public relations practitioners have no education, training, or knowledge of what the field is. And the public equally has little understanding of the meaning of the two words. Until licensing and registration are introduced, this will continue to be the situation.

What pleases you most about current public relations practice?
What pleases me most is that there are, indeed, practitioners who regard their activity as a profession, an art applied to a science, in which the public interest, and not pecuniary motivation, is the primary consideration; and also that outstanding leaders in society are grasping the meaning and significance of the activity.

How would you compare the caliber of today's public relations practitioner with that of the practitioner of the past?
The practitioner today has more education in his subject. But, unfortunately, education for public relations varies with the institution where it is being conducted. This is due to the lack of a standard definition. Public relations activity is applied social science to the social attitudes or actions of employers or clients.

Where do you think public relations will be 20 years from now?
It is difficult to appraise where public relations will be 20 years from now. I don't like the tendency of advertising agencies gobbling up large public relations organizations. That is like surgical instrument manufacturers gobbling up surgical medical colleges or law book publishers gobbling up law colleges. However, if licensing and registration take place, then the vocation is assured a long lifetime, as long as democracy's.

Public Relations Library

Argenti, Paul A. *Corporate Communication*. Burr Ridge, IL: Irwin Professional Publishing, 2005. A fine introduction to corporate public relations practice.

Brown, Paul B., and Alison Davis. *Your Attention, Please: How to Appeal to Today's Distracted, Disinterested, Disengaged, Disenchanted, and Busy Audiences*. Avon, MA: Adams Media, 2006. Excellent treatise on how to deal with the information overload with which all of us are afflicted. The trick to getting through, according to the authors: Be fast and write punchy.

COMM.PR.biz, commpro_daily_headlines@commpro.biz, 362 Atlantic Avenue, Brooklyn, NY 11217. Guest columnists discuss the pertinent public relations news of the day. And it's free!

Cone, Steve. *PowerLines: Words that Sell Brands, Grip Fans, and Sometimes Change History*. New York: Bloomberg Press, 2008. A fascinating synopsis of the memorable words and phrases indelibly etched in the public cranium, from "Bond, James Bond" to "Virginia Is for Lovers" to "Live Free or Die."

Demers, David. *Mass Communication and Media Research*. Spokane, WA: Marquette Books, 2005. Up-to-date dictionary of communication and media history and terms.

Diggs-Brown, Barbara, *The PR Style Guide: Formats for Public Relations Practice* (3rd ed.). Boston, MA: Wadsworth, 2013. A compendium of public relations vehicles, from annual reports to audio news releases, brochures to direct mail campaigns, media tours to new media.

D'Vario, Marisa. *Building Buzz: How to Reach and Impress Your Target Audience*. Franklin Lakes, NJ: Career Press, 2006. This is a combination pop psychology/communication primer on how to get you and your company and its products noticed.

Green, Andy. *Effective Communication Skills for Public Relations*. London, England: Kogan Page Ltd., 2005. A British perspective on how to transform personal communication by managing the way you think, act, create messages, and network.

Hackman, Michael Z., and Craig E. Johnson. *Leadership: A Communication Perspective* (5th ed.). Long Grove, IL: Waveland Press, Inc., 2009. Examples, case studies, and explanation on the intersection between leadership and effective communication.

McPhail, Thomas L. *Global Communications: Theories, Stakeholders, and Trends* (2nd ed.). Malden, MA: Blackwell Publishing, 2006. Contemporary view of global communications innovations and challenges.

Pacelli, Lonnie. *The Truth about Getting Your Point Across . . . and Nothing But the Truth*. Upper Saddle River, NJ: Prentice Hall, 2006. This book is a terrific primer on how to get your message across convincingly whether writing or speaking, texting or tweeting.

PR Daily News Feed, webmgr@ragan.com, *Ragan.com*, Lawrence Ragan Communications, 111 East Wacker Drive, Chicago, IL 60601. Pointed online commentary on current communications issues. And it's also free!

Shepherd, G. J., J. St. John, and T. Striphas (Eds.). *Communications as . . . Perspectives on Theory*. Thousand Oaks, CA: Sage Publications, 2006. Communications, the authors say, is a "process of relating," and this book explains how relationships are built.

Chapter 4

Public Opinion

Chapter Objectives

1. To discuss the phenomenon of public opinion, contemporary examples of it, the areas that impact it, and how it is formed.

2. To explore the issue of attitudes, how they are influenced, motivated, and changed.

3. To discuss the area of persuasion, its various theories, and how individuals are persuaded.

4. To examine reputation, particularly corporate image, and how companies might enhance their reputation.

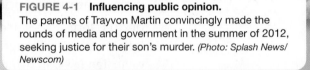

FIGURE 4-1   Influencing public opinion.
The parents of Trayvon Martin convincingly made the rounds of media and government in the summer of 2012, seeking justice for their son's murder. *(Photo: Splash News/ Newscom)*

Public opinion is an elusive and fragile commodity. It can take an organization or individual many years to build the credibility and nurture the trust that goes into winning favorable public opinion. But it can take only a matter of minutes to destroy all that has been developed.

That's why in the summer of 2012, some of America's largest companies, from Coca-Cola and Pepsi to Walmart and Johnson & Johnson, found themselves on defense when they were unwittingly dragged into a highly charged shooting incident that mushroomed into a national conflagration of race, guns, and justice.

The February 2012 shooting death of Trayvon Martin, a black 17-year-old staying at an Orlando-area gated community, was a minor story for weeks until it exploded onto the national stage in March. That's when the boy's parents and civil right leaders went public that

young Martin was shot dead by a neighborhood watch captain, George Zimmerman, who had invoked Florida's "Stand Your Ground" law, which allowed deadly force in self-defense. The boy was "armed," according to the police report, with a can of iced tea and a bag of Skittles. And the public relations campaign waged by the boy's parents began to gain traction across the land[1] (Figure 4-1).

By June, the "Stand Your Ground" law was undergoing intense scrutiny, with detractors claiming it encouraged vigilantism. And that's where the big companies came in. They all supported a group called the American Legislative Exchange Council (ALEC), which billed itself as supporting "free-market solutions that create jobs and improve the economy," a mission that few could debate. But ALEC also supported "Stand Your Ground Laws" and voter ID laws that groups such as the Congressional Black Caucus labeled as "suppressing minority participation." When a New York–based civil rights group went after ALEC's big corporate sponsors, most big companies, bailed immediately and severed their memberships.[2]

Regardless of ALEC's primary purpose and track record or whether the law was or wasn't used properly in the Zimmerman case, none of the big companies involved wanted to stick around in defiance of public opinion.

Suffering a loss in public opinion isn't a trivial matter. Individuals and companies in the public eye can't afford to tarnish their reputations. Often, this translates into a loss of prestige and business. And that's why most public relations agencies bill themselves as experts in the field of "reputation management."

Society is littered with the reputational carcasses of once respected organizations and individuals who tested the goodwill of the public once too often. For example:

- In 2008, the nation witnessed a parade of several of its richest financial leaders, from Citigroup CEO Chuck Prince to Merrill Lynch CEO Stanley O'Neal to Bear Stearns CEO Alan Schwartz to Lehman Brothers CEO Richard Fuld, being pilloried by media and Congress for squandering shareholder trust and resources in the disastrous subprime mortgage lending fiasco.

- In 2011, former presidential candidate and senator John Edwards was indicted by a North Carolina grand jury on six felony charges for violating federal campaign laws, in using donations to hide the fact that he had a mistress and had fathered an illegitimate son. In 2012, Edwards was found not guilty on one count, and the judge in Edwards's case declared a mistrial on the other charges. The government announced it wouldn't pursue Edwards further. It made no difference. His reputation, once so bright, was ruined.[3]

- In 2012, the vaunted U.S. Secret Service was rocked by scandal when it was reported in April that 11 agents, including supervisors, had engaged prostitutes prior to President Obama's trip to Colombia. Most of those involved left the agency or were demoted.[4] That same month, it was reported that employees of the General Services Administration, responsible for monitoring the federal budget, had spent $820,000 of taxpayer money to fly 300 bureaucrats to Las Vegas for a "congratulatory conference" at a lavish spa and casino.[5]

The point is that these individuals and the organizations they represented, like many others in all areas of society, suffered serious setbacks in terms of their standing with the public as a result of their actions.

The related point is, as we put it in Chapter 1, *You can't pour perfume on a skunk*.

The best public relations campaign in the world can't build trust when reality is destroying it. If your product doesn't work, if your service stinks, if you are a liar, then no amount of "public relations" will change that. You must change the "action" before credibility or trust can be built.

Such are the vulnerabilities of public opinion in a culture driven by media, fueled by the Internet, and dominated by celebrity. Public opinion in the 21st century is a combustible and changing commodity.

As a general rule, it's difficult to move people toward a strong opinion on anything. It's even harder to move them away from an opinion once they reach it. Nonetheless, the heart of public relations work lies in attempting to affect the public opinion process.

Public relations professionals therefore must understand what public opinion is, how it is formed, how it evolves from people's attitudes, and how it is influenced by communication. This chapter discusses attitude formation and change and public opinion creation and persuasion.

What Is Public Opinion?

Public opinion, like public relations, is not easily explained. Newspaper columnist Joseph Kraft called public opinion "the unknown god to which moderns burn incense." Edward Bernays called it "a term describing an ill-defined, mercurial, and changeable group of individual judgments."[6]

Princeton Professor Harwood Childs, after coming up with no fewer than 40 different yet viable definitions, concluded with a definition by Herman C. Boyle: "Public opinion is not the name of something, but the classification of a number of something."[7]

Splitting public opinion into its two components, *public* and *opinion*, is perhaps the best way to understand the concept. Simply defined, *public* signifies a group of people who share a common interest in a specific subject—stockholders, for example, or employees or community residents. Each group is concerned with a common issue: the price of the stock, the wages of the company, or the building of a new plant.

An *opinion* is the expression of an attitude on a particular topic. When attitudes become strong enough, they surface in the form of opinions. When opinions become strong enough, they lead to verbal or behavioral actions.

Attitudes
   └──▶ *Opinions*
           └──▶ *Actions*

A forest products company executive and an environmentalist from the Sierra Club might differ dramatically in their attitudes toward the relative importance of global warming and continued industrial production. Their respective opinions on a piece of environmental legislation might also differ radically. In turn, how their organizations respond to that legislation—by picketing, petitioning, or lobbying—might also differ.

Public opinion, then, is the aggregate of many individual opinions on a particular issue that affects a group of people. Stated another way, public opinion represents a consensus. That consensus, deriving as it does from many individual opinions, begins with people's attitudes toward the issue in question. Trying to influence an individual's attitude—how he or she thinks on a given topic—is a primary focus of the practice of public relations.

What Are Attitudes?

If an opinion is an expression of an attitude on a particular topic, what then is an *attitude*?

Unfortunately, that also is not an easy question to answer. It was once generally assumed that attitudes are predispositions to think in a certain way about a certain topic. But research indicates that attitudes may more likely be evaluations people make about specific problems or issues. These conclusions are not necessarily connected to any broad attitude.[8] For example, an individual might favor a company's response to one issue but disagree vehemently with its response to another. Thus, that individual's attitude may differ from issue to issue.

Attitudes are based on a number of characteristics.

1. **Personal**—the physical and emotional ingredients of an individual, including size, age, and social status.

2. **Cultural**—the environment and lifestyle of a particular country or geographic area. The cultures of the United States and off again/on again ally Pakistan, for example, differ greatly; on a less global scale, cultural differences between rural and urban America are vast.

3. **Educational**—the level and quality of a person's education. To appeal to the increased number of college graduates in the United States today, public communication has become more sophisticated.

4. **Familial**—people's roots. Children acquire their parents' tastes, biases, political partisanships, and a host of other characteristics.

5. **Religious**—a system of beliefs about God or a higher power. Religion is making a comeback. After a period of people turning away from religion, in the 21st century, even after several evangelical scandals, religious fervor has reemerged.

6. **Social class**—position within society. As people's social status changes, so do their attitudes. For example, college students, unconcerned with making a living, may dramatically change their attitudes about such concepts as big government, big business, wealth, prosperity, and politics after entering the job market.

7. **Race**—ethnic origin, which today increasingly helps shape people's attitudes. Minorities in our society, as a group, continue to improve their standard of living and their relative position. African Americans head major corporations, hold cabinet positions, sit on the Supreme Court, and, in 2008, become president. Latinos and Asian Americans have become coveted interest groups. And women, in many sectors—among them, college students and public relations professionals—are no longer considered a minority.

Research indicates that attitudes and behaviors are situational—influenced by specific issues in specific situations. Nonetheless, when others with similar attitudes reach similar opinions, a consensus, or public opinion, is born.

How Are Attitudes Influenced?

Strictly speaking, attitudes are positive, negative, or nonexistent. A person is for something, against it, or neutral. Studies show that for any one issue, most people don't care much one way or the other. A small percentage expresses strong support, and another small percentage expresses strong opposition. The vast majority is smack in the so-called muddled middle—passive, neutral, indifferent. Many years ago, former U.S. Vice President Spiro T. Agnew called this group "the silent majority."

It's hard to change the mind of a person who is staunchly opposed to a particular issue or individual. Likewise, it's easy to reinforce the support of a person who is wholeheartedly in favor of an issue or individual.

Social scientist Leon Festinger discussed this concept when he talked about the *theory of cognitive dissonance.* He believed that individuals tend to avoid information

FIGURE 4-2   **Save the seals.**
The Humane Society's campaign to stop Canada's commercial seal hunt used graphic mailings, Web video, and photos to influence public opinion. *(Photo: Courtesy of the Humane Society of the United States)*

that is dissonant or opposed to their own points of view and tend to seek out information that is consonant with, or in support of, their own attitudes.[9]

Similarly, *social judgment theory* suggests that people may have a range of opinions on a certain subject, anchored by a clear attitude.[10] Again, while it is seldom possible to change this anchor position, communicators can work within this range, called a person's "latitude of acceptance," to modify a person's opinion.

For example, while most people might not discriminate against eating Canadian seafood products, they might object to the clubbing of baby seals. Therefore, in trying to pressure Canada to stop the seal hunt, the Humane Society of the United States attempts to link the hunt with Canada's seafood industry. In so doing, it attempts to sway the undecided to take action and also to influence others within an acceptable range (Figure 4-2).

Understanding the potential for influencing the silent majority is extremely important for the public relations practitioner, whose objective is to win support through clear, thoughtful, and persuasive communication. Moving a person from a latent state of attitude formation to a more aware state and finally to an active one becomes a matter of motivation.

Motivating Attitude Change

People are motivated by different factors, and no two people respond in exactly the same way to the same set of circumstances. Each of us is motivated by different drives and needs.

The most famous delineator of what motivates people was Abraham Maslow. Maslow's *hierarchy of needs theory* helps define the origins of motivation, which in turn helps explain attitude change. Maslow postulated a five-level hierarchy:

1. The lowest order is physiological needs: a person's biological demands—food and water, sleep, health, bodily needs, exercise and rest, and sex.

2. The second level is safety needs: security, protection, comfort and peace, and orderly surroundings.

3. The third level is love needs: acceptance, belonging, love and affection, and membership in a group.

4. The fourth level is esteem: recognition and prestige, confidence and leadership opportunities, competence and strength, intelligence and success.

5. The highest order is self-actualization, or simply becoming what one is capable of becoming; self-actualization involves self-fulfillment and achieving a goal for the purposes of challenge and accomplishment.[11]

According to Maslow, the needs of all five levels compose the fundamental motivating factors for any individual or public.

Another popular approach to motivating attitude change is the *elaboration likelihood model*, which posits that there are essentially two ways that people are persuaded:

1. When we are interested and focused enough on a message to take a direct "central route" to decision making, and

2. When we are not particularly engaged on a message and need to take a more "peripheral" route.

Translating this theory into action means that the best way to motivate interested people is with arguments that are strong, logical, and personally relevant. On the other hand, the way to motivate people who are less interested might be through putting them in a better mood—with a joke, for example, or demonstrating, through speech or clothes or mannerism, that you are very much "like" them. Such techniques, according to this theory, might help encourage listeners to accept your arguments.[12]

Power of Persuasion

Perhaps the most essential element in influencing public opinion is the principle of persuasion. Persuading is the goal of the vast majority of public relations programs.

Persuasion theory has myriad explanations and interpretations. Basically, persuasion means getting another person to do something through advice, reasoning, or just plain arm-twisting. Books have been written on the enormous power of advertising and public relations as persuasive tools.

According to classic persuasion theory, people may be of two minds in order to be persuaded to believe in a particular position or take a specific action.

■ First is the "systematic" mode, referring to a person who has carefully considered an argument—actively, creatively, and alertly.

■ Second is the "heuristic" mode, referring to a person who is skimming the surface and not really focusing on the intricacies of a particular position to catch flaws, inconsistencies, or errors.[13]

That is not to say that all systematic thinkers or all heuristic thinkers think alike. They don't. Things are more complicated than that. Let's say your little brother wants a pair of basketball shoes and your dad accompanies him to the store to buy them. Both are systematic thinkers. But they have different questions.

Your dad asks:

1. How much do they cost?
2. How long will they last?
3. Is the store nearby so I can get back to watch the ball game?
4. Will they take a personal check?

Your brother asks:

1. Does LeBron James endorse them?
2. Do all my homeboys wear them?
3. Will Wanda Sue go out with me if I buy them?

The point is that all of us are persuaded by different things, which makes the challenge of public relations persuading much more a complex art form than a science. No matter how one characterizes persuasion, the goal of most communications programs is, in fact, to influence a receiver to take a desired action.

What kinds of "evidence" will persuade?

1. **Facts.** Facts are indisputable. Although it is true, as they say, that "liars figure and figures lie," empirical data are a persuasive device in hammering home a point of view.

2. **Emotions.** Maslow was right. People do respond to emotional appeals—love, peace, family, patriotism. Arguably, the most riveting moment in George W. Bush's presidency came in the Oval Office on September 13, 2001, two days after the most horrific event in U.S. history, when a reporter asked about Bush's personal concerns.

   The President: *Well, I don't think about myself right now. I think about the families, the children. I am a loving guy, and I am also someone, however, who has got a job to do—and I intend to do it. And this is a terrible moment. But this country will not relent until we have saved ourselves and others from the terrible tragedy that came upon America.*[14]

   In less than 50 words, a visibly shaken Bush had made an emotional connection with the American public that proved elusive through much of his presidency.

3. **Personalizing.** People respond to personal experience.

   - When poet Maya Angelou talks about poverty, people listen and respect a woman who emerged from the dirt-poor environs of the South in a day of segregation.
   - When *America's Most Wanted* TV host John Walsh crusades against criminals who prey on children, people understand that his son was abducted and killed by a crazed individual.
   - When former baseball pitcher Jim Abbott talks about dealing with adversity, people marvel at a star athlete born with only one arm.

   Again, few can refute knowledge gained from personal experience.

4. **Appealing to "you."**   The one word that people never tire of hearing is *you*. *What is in this for me?* is the question that everyone asks. One secret to persuading, therefore, is to constantly think in terms of what will appeal most to the audience.

As simple as these four precepts are, they are often difficult for some to grasp. Emotion, for example, is a particular challenge for business leaders, who presume, incorrectly, that showing it is a sign of weakness. This, of course, is wrong. The power to persuade—to influence public opinion—is the measure not only of a charismatic but also of an effective leader.[15]

Influencing Public Opinion

Public opinion is a lot easier to measure than it is to influence. However, a thoughtful public relations program can crystallize attitudes, reinforce beliefs, and occasionally change public opinion. First, the opinions to be changed or modified must be identified and understood. Second, target publics must be clear. Third, the public relations professional must have in sharp focus the "laws" that govern public opinion—as amorphous as they may be.

In that context, the "Laws of Public Opinion," developed many years ago by social psychologist Hadley Cantril, remain pertinent. The events following the September 11 attacks on America are a case in point.[16]

1. **Opinion is highly sensitive to important events.** Events of unusual magnitude are likely to swing public opinion temporarily from one extreme to another. Opinion doesn't become stabilized until the implications of events are seen in some perspective. For example, after the terrorist attacks, President Bush's popularity rose to unprecedented heights.

2. **Opinion is generally determined more by events than by words—unless those words are themselves interpreted as an event.** In a speech to a joint session of Congress nine days after the terrorist attacks, the president vowed to "lift the dark threat of violence from our people and our future. We will rally the world to this cause by our efforts, by our courage. We will not tire, we will not falter, and we will not fail." Bush's words became a rallying cry for the nation and, temporarily at least, transformed his presidency.[17]

3. **At critical times, people become more sensitive to the adequacy of their leadership. If they have confidence in it, they are willing to assign more than usual responsibility to it; if they lack confidence in it, they are less tolerant than usual.** Relatively few voices rose in protest when the Bush administration, in the cause of fighting terrorism, imposed sweeping changes in privacy rights regarding such traditional areas as library use and securing court orders before wiretapping suspected American evildoers.

4. **Once self-interest is involved, opinions are slow to change.** Even after the United States invaded Iraq to oust Saddam Hussein in March 2003, American support continued for the war effort. That support began to wane when the 2,000th American soldier was killed in October 2005.[18]

5. **People have more opinions and are able to form opinions more easily on goals than on methods to reach those goals.** For example, few questioned the need for a new U.S. Department of Homeland Security to protect the land within our borders from terrorism.

6. **By and large, if people in a democracy are provided with educational opportunities and ready access to information, public opinion reveals a hardheaded common sense.** In the weeks and months following the attacks of September 11, as Americans became more enlightened about the implications and threats of terrorism within the United States, the administration's strategy

of continuous communication helped solidify public opinion.[19] But again, as progress in the Middle East waxed and waned and American troops were made to serve extended tours in long, drawn-out conflicts, by 2011—after 4,500 American deaths and 30,000 Americans wounded—public opinion clearly agreed when President Obama formally declared the end of the Iraq war.[20]

PR Ethics Mini-Case

Occupy: Si, Changing Public Opinion: Not Exactly

Ironically, the movement to protest the inequities of America's financial system in September 2011 originated in Canada. "Occupy Wall Street," which took over Zuccotti Park in Lower Manhattan, was inspired by the Canadian activist group Adbusters.

The Occupy protest movement was designed to expose social and economic inequality in the United States and elsewhere by exposing greed, corruption, and the undue influence of corporations on everyday life. While the movement attracted copious press coverage and did engrain its slogan, "the other 99 percent," in the public psyche, from a public relations perspective, Occupy Wall Street's results were mixed.

One criticism of Occupy was that it flailed out in too many directions, issuing news releases at breakneck speed to attract publicity to stay relevant in the public's mind (Figure 4-3). The shifting focus of Occupy targets, its detractors argued, tended to dissipate the important messages about inequality that the movement had committed to confront.

Critics also argued that the protestors showed little respect for local residents and merchants, whose daily lives and businesses they interrupted; engaged in criminal activities in their encampment; and practiced questionable hygiene (Figure 4-4).

In terms of changing public opinion, Occupy Wall Street was plagued by having unclear and constantly evolving goals, no unified message, no one leader or spokesperson to crystallize objectives, and appearing to be more concerned with publicity than with evoking positive change. Indeed, it was difficult to follow the movement's targets—one day the banks, the next hedge funds, the next educational institutions.

When the movement began to fizzle in the winter of 2011, the New York Occupy and its derivatives around the

FOR IMMEDIATE RELEASE December 3, 2011
Contact: press@occupywallst.org (press queries)
For this event: Diego Ibanez (OWS Hunger Striker),
801 636 4108, DiegoJorgelbanez@gmail.com
Laura Gottesdiener (OWS Hunger Strike, Co-ordinator),
617 519 5659, LauraGottesdiener@gmail.com

OWS Hunger Strike For Open Spaces

New York City—On Saturday, December 3, in Liberty Plaza, we—THE OWS HUNGER STRIKERS—will begin a hunger strike. We are striking to demand outdoor space for a new occupation. We will hold our strike, for its duration, outside at Duarte Square on Sixth Avenue and Canal Street in Manhattan as part of a continued effort seeking sanctuary on Trinity Wall Street's unused and vacant lot of land. Should we be arrested, we will continue the strike in jail. We are calling on Occupiers across the nation to join us.

This is a call for escalation in response to the escalated levels of government-enacted violence and repression The Occupy Movement has endured over the last few weeks. In cities across the nation, Mayors chose to stifle freedom of speech and the right to assemble by evicting peaceful occupations using illegal and unconstitutional force. Here in NYC, in the middle of the night on November 14, billionaire Mayor Bloomberg used the NYPD to illicitly evict our community from Liberty Square.

We recognize the long history of hunger strikes as a radical action that has liberated countries, communities and individuals from repression, slavery and injustice. From colonial India to modern Turkey; from the Northern Ireland H-Block cells to Palestinian prisons; from 1970s Cuba to present-day California, hunger strikes have amplified the voices of the oppressed.

Occupy Wall Street is a people-powered direct action movement that began on September 17, 2011 in Liberty Square in Manhattan's Financial District. OWS is part of a growing international movement fighting against neoliberal economic practices, the crimes of Wall Street, government controlled by monied interests, and the resulting income inequality, unemployment, environmental destruction, and oppression of people at the front lines of the economic crisis. For more, visit www.occupywallst.org

FIGURE 4-3   Non-stop news releases.
Critics charged Occupy Wall Street with disseminating too many news releases about too many issues.
(Courtesy of Occupy Wall Street)

FIGURE 4-4 Rag tag warriors.
In the winter of 2011, Occupy Wall Street protestors tried to move public opinion toward uniting behind the cause of the "99 percent." *(Photo: SAUL LOEB/AFP/Getty Images/Newscom)*

nation had spurred as much attention as they had outrage. While the *New York Times* editorialized, "The Occupy Wall Street protesters had achieved a great deal," the *Wall Street Journal* took another view, concluding, "OWS botched an opportunity to capture public opinion and achieve something."*

Questions

1. How successful do you believe Occupy Wall Street was?

2. Had you been running the movement's public relations initiative, how would you have improved its approach?

*For further information, see Fraser P. Seitel, "Organizing for Impact," odwyerpr.com, October 31, 2011; James Taranto, "Follow Those Kids!" *Wall Street Journal*, November 18, 2011.

Polishing the Corporate Image

Most organizations today and the people who manage them are extremely sensitive to the way they are perceived by their critical publics. The days of "The public be damned!" are long behind us.

Today, organizations—particularly large ones—have little choice but to go public. CEOs are regular guests on CNBC, Fox Business, and Bloomberg financial television programs. The accounting and corporate scandals of the early years of the 21st century that embroiled such now-former companies as Enron, Worldcom, and Arthur Andersen threatened the confidence of the American capitalistic system. The credit crisis and financial meltdown at the end of the decade, which triggered the demise of companies such as Bear Stearns, Countrywide, Washington Mutual, and Lehman Brothers, was yet another reminder that smart companies and their leaders simply couldn't "hide" any longer from public scrutiny.

■ In 2008, with the price of oil skyrocketing, ExxonMobil faced criticism from shareholders, including heirs of Standard Oil Company founder John D. Rockefeller.[21] Exxon responded with a far-reaching program addressing the controversial area of climate change.

■ In 2009, when the existence of the American auto industry was threatened by recession, rising fuel prices, and unpopular vehicles, the traditionally silent executives of General Motors (GM), Chrysler, and Ford became much more vocal in pleading their case before government and the public. After some well-publicized missteps in Washington, the industry rebounded enough to avoid disaster.

■ In 2010 and 2011, Wall Street was rocked by a continuous stream of Ponzi schemes, insider trading scams, and other assorted disasters that threw formerly respected multi-millionaire investors, such as Bernie Madoff, Allen Sanford, and Raj Rajaratnam, in the slammer and threatened a similar fate to former McKinsey & Company head Rajat Gupta and former New Jersey Senator and Governor Jon Corzine. All, to their detriment, demurred from public view.

■ In 2012, having learned that such "silence isn't golden," JP Morgan Chase CEO Jamie Dimon didn't shrink from public view when his company reported an embarrassing $2 billion trading loss. Dimon confronted the issue with two congressional appearances, took the heat, and came out relatively unscathed.

The point is that most organizations and individuals in the spotlight today understand, first, that credibility is a fragile commodity, and second, to maintain and improve public support they must operate with the "implicit trust" of the public. That means that for a corporation in the 21st century, winning favorable public opinion isn't an option—it's a necessity, essential for continued long-term success.

Outside the Lines
Winning Reputation . . .

How do you measure reputation?

Each year for the past 13, survey firm Harris Interactive has polled consumers on what companies they feel have the highest reputation.

Harris asks 17,555 respondents to rank organizations on six primary measures of reputation: (1) emotional appeal, (2) financial performance, (3) products and services, (4) vision and leadership, (5) workplace environment, and (6) social responsibility. Other characteristics, such as ethics and sincerity of corporate communications, were also probed.

The 2012 Harris data underscore the ephemeral quality of corporate reputation. Only half of the companies ranked among the Top 10 in 2008 repeated in 2012. Tech companies dominated the most recent list, with Apple and Google first and second, Amazon fourth, and Microsoft ninth. Meanwhile, recalls drove traditional reputation bellwether Johnson & Johnson from second to seventh. And not one financial or oil company made the list.

Here are the top 10 companies for 2012 and 2008.

Top 10—2012

1. Apple
2. Google
3. The Coca-Cola Company
4. amazon.com
5. Kraft Foods Inc.
6. The Walt Disney Company
7. Johnson & Johnson
8. Whole Foods Market
9. Microsoft
10. UPS

Top 10—2008

1. Google
2. Johnson & Johnson
3. Intel Corporation
4. General Mills
5. Kraft Foods Inc.
6. Berkshire Hathaway Inc.
7. 3M Company
8. The Coca-Cola Company
9. Honda Motor Co.
10. Microsoft

For further information, see "The 2012 Harris Poll Annual RQ Public Summary Report," Harris Interactive, 2011.

Outside the Lines

. . . Losing Reputation

And then there was the poor Adidas running shoe company.

Sick of playing second fiddle to its arch competitor, Nike, Adidas decided in the summer of 2012 to "go bold."

So it hired edgy designer Jeremy Scott to design a shoe "so hot you lock your kicks to your ankles." Literally. Scott's design of the company's gray, purple, and black JS Roundhouse Mids included bright orange shackles—just like the kind they wear in prison and also, in a bygone century, as slaves (Figure 4-5).

The condemnation of Adidas on Facebook and in the media for its creative, "slavery chic" shoe was swift and unforgiving. One user called the new design "offensive and inappropriate, not to mention ugly." Another asked, "How would a Jewish person feel if Nike decided to have a shoe with a swastika on it?" And a Syracuse University professor added, "Shackles . . . the stuff that our ancestors wore for 400 years while experiencing the most horrific atrocities imaginable." Within nanoseconds, race-watcher Jesse Jackson was condemning Adidas for rekindling the fires of slavery, and the Adidas Facebook page lit up with equally stupefied responders.

Adidas, perhaps understandably, was reeling from the immediate and intense criticism. A spokesperson meekly defended the designer's past work and added, "Any suggestion that this is linked to slavery is untruthful."

And obviously, the Adidas public relations person was right, but in a viral world, where instant perception becomes

FIGURE 4-5 **Slavery chic?**
Adidas quickly dropped the shackles from its new training shoe—because it evoked images like this—when the controversy went viral in the summer of 2012. *(Photo: Bernd Wuestneck/dpa/picture-alliance/Newscom)*

unfortunate reality, the reputation of Adidas had taken a direct and gut-wrenching hit. The day after the shackle shoe controversy went viral, Adidas, correctly, dropped the shackles from its new shoe.*

*For further information, see Meagan Clark, "Adidas: Shoes with Shackles Are Unrelated to Slavery," *Daily Caller*, June 18, 2012; Michael Hiestand, "Adidas Isn't Talking about Sneakers That Were a Gaffe," *USA Today*, June 19, 2012; and Jesse Solomon, "Adidas Cancels 'Shackle' Shoes after Outcry," CNN.US, June 19, 2012.

Managing Reputation

For an organization or an individual concerned about public opinion, what it comes down to is managing reputation. Reputation is gained by what one *does,* not by what one *says.* Reputation is present throughout our lives. It's how we choose business partners, which dentist or mechanic to visit, the stores we frequent, the neighborhood we live in, and the friends we keep. In recent years, *reputation management* has become a buzzword in public relations and in the broader society. At the start of the century, the term was little known. Today, a Google search on "reputation management" produces nearly 55 million results.

Many public relations firms have introduced reputation management divisions, and some have even billed themselves as being in the business of "relationship management."

Generally defined, relationship management aligns communications with an organization's character and action. It creates recognition, credibility, and trust among key constituents. It stays sensitive to its conduct in public with customers and in private with employees. It understands its responsibilities to the broader society and is empathetic to society's needs.

While reputation itself may be difficult to measure, its value to an organization or an individual is indisputable.[22] And it's also indisputable that "managing" reputation is a front-line responsibility of public relations.

Last Word

Influencing public opinion remains at the heart of professional public relations work. Public opinion is a powerful force that can impact the earnings of corporations through such actions as product boycotts, union threats, strikes, and the misdeeds of key executives; influence government legislation through campaign support, product recalls, and letters and emails from constituents; and even unify a nation through calls to action by strong and committed leaders.

To influence public opinion, public relations professionals must anticipate trends in our society. At the start of the 21st century, one self-styled prognosticator, John Naisbitt, predicted the new directions that would influence American lives in the near future. Among them were the following:

- Inflation and interest rates will be held in check.
- There will be a shift from welfare to workfare.

- There will be a shift from public housing to home ownership.
- CEOs in a global economy will become more important and better known than political figures.[23]

With the second decade of the new century underway, a number of Nesbitt's "megatrends" appear to be coming to pass. Public relations professionals need to take note of these and other trends in gauging how public opinion will impact their organizations. They also should consider what the late public relations counselor Philip Lesly once pointed out: "The real problems faced by business today are in the outside world of intangibles and public attitudes."[24]

To keep ahead of these intangibles, public attitudes, and kernels of future public opinion, managements will turn increasingly for guidance to professional public relations practitioners.

Discussion Starters

1. What is the relationship between public relations and public opinion?
2. What are attitudes, and on what characteristics are they based?
3. How are attitudes influenced?
4. What is Maslow's hierarchy of needs?
5. What is the theory of cognitive dissonance?
6. How difficult is it to change a person's behavior?
7. What are several key public opinion laws, according to Cantril?
8. What kinds of evidence persuade people?
9. What are the elements involved in managing reputation?
10. In assessing the list of best and worst companies in terms of reputation, what specific characteristics influence these rankings?

Pick of the Literature

The New York Times, nytimes.com, and *The Wall Street Journal*, wsj.com

Public relations can be practiced only by understanding public opinion, and two of the most prominent daily forums in which to study it are *The New York Times* and *The Wall Street Journal.*

Despite the 21st-century problems of newspapers, these two most venerable news organizations reveal the diverse views of pundits, politicians, and plain people. The *Times* is arguably the primary source of printed news in the world. The *Journal,* likewise, is the primary printed source of the world's business and investment news—an area of increasingly dominant importance.

Both papers, through their opinion pages and in-depth stories, express the attitudes of leaders in politics, business, science, education, journalism, and the arts, on topics ranging from abortion rights to genetic engineering to race relations. Occasionally, the *Times* and the *Journal* supplement their usual coverage with public opinion polls to gauge attitudes and beliefs on particularly hot issues.

It may, indeed, be the Internet age, but if you really want to know what's going on in the world and be a lot more knowledgeable than most of those with whom you work, read *The New York Times* and *The Wall Street Journal* every day. You can even do it online. Sure, the news is often infuriating, but it's also a joy to know more about what's going on than virtually anyone else.

The *Times* and the *Journal* are clearly the most important reference works any public relations professional can read (even including this book!).

Case Study | The Rise and Fall and Rise of Queen Martha

In the winter of 2001, few Americans could dispute that Martha Stewart was "Queen of the Kitchen." Few Americans enjoyed more robust acclaim in terms of public opinion.

The tough-willed, hot-tempered, blunt-speaking perfectionist had morphed from a modest upbringing to become the undisputed, multimillionaire-closing-in-on-billionaire, domestic doyenne—the homemaker's homemaker, arbiter of all things tasteful in the home, *numero uno* in all matters of domesticity.

Her parents, Martha and Edward Kostyra, were Polish Americans, her mother a school teacher and her father a pharmaceutical salesman, who raised their five children in Nutley, New Jersey. Her mother taught young Martha cooking and baking and sewing, and her father taught her how to garden. That was just the start the serious-minded model student needed. After a brief fling in the stock brokerage business and a failed marriage, Stewart began to build an empire that would become the stuff of legends.

- She coauthored a book called *Entertaining,* which became an instant bestseller.
- She followed that with lucrative publishing ventures, producing videotapes, dinner-music CDs, television specials, and dozens of books on matters of domesticity— from hors d'oeuvres to pies, from weddings to Christmas, from gardening to restoring old houses.
- She appeared regularly on NBC's *Today Show,* becoming a household name.

- She became a board member of the New York Stock Exchange.
- She delivered lectures for $10,000 a pop and charged eager attendees $900 a head to attend seminars at her farm.
- She signed an advertising/consulting contract with department chain Kmart for $5 million.
- She presided over a long-running syndicated television show, *Martha Stewart Living.*
- She parlayed the program into the creation of multimillion-dollar company Martha Stewart Living Omnimedia (MSO), with branches in publishing, merchandising, and Internet/direct commerce, selling products in eight discrete categories.

Without exaggeration, Stewart was Queen of the Kitchen, until one day when it all came tumbling down.

Selling in the Nick of Time

In December 2001, Stewart sold nearly 4,000 shares of biotech company ImClone Systems stock under mysterious circumstances. The company was run by Stewart's pal Samuel Waksal, who had presided over a rapid stock price ascension, due principally to the company's promising cancer-fighting drug, Erbitux, which had been submitted for approval to the Food and Drug Administration (FDA).

With everything looking good for the company, it was surprising on December 27 that Stewart decided suddenly to unload all her shares at a $60 price. The next day, the case got even more curious: On December 28, the FDA rejected ImClone's application for Erbitux. The stock cratered. But Stewart, having presciently decided to sell the day before, avoided a $51,000 loss.

Serendipity perhaps?

The government didn't think so.

Charges of Insider Trading

Stewart may have been smart, but according to the U.S. attorney for the Southern District of New York, she was not smart enough to know about the FDA's timing in rejecting Erbitux. Rather, argued the government, Stewart had learned about the FDA's intention from her stockbroker. The stockbroker had received an urgent call from Waksal, then relayed the information to Stewart, who immediately decided to sell.

If true, Stewart had acted on classic insider information, a federal crime, which gives privileged investors an unfair advantage over all other shareholders. Indeed, prosecutors argued that this was precisely what had happened and that Stewart and her stockbroker were both guilty of illegally acting on insider information. Accordingly, in June 2003, the U.S. Attorney formally indicted both of them.

Stewart's attorneys argued that this was not the case at all. Stewart, they said, had always had a "plan" to sell her stock when it reached the $60 level.

After Waksal was sentenced to seven years in prison and family members he had tipped off were fined, attention turned to Stewart. The question was: Would she come forward and acknowledge "mistakes," or would she hold firm and deny any impropriety?

Silence of the Diva

The answer, painfully revealed over the next excruciating two years, was that Stewart became the "silent diva." She said little to elaborate on the case, preferring instead to allow her attorneys to speak for her. In one celebrated appearance on the *CBS Morning Show,* Stewart defiantly cut cabbage while an exasperated host tried to get her to react to the charges against her.

Soon thereafter, Stewart's guest appearances on television became fewer and fewer. She stopped lecturing. Her ubiquitous Kmart ads ceased to appear. She resigned as chair and CEO of MSO. Indeed, the woman who had seemed to be everywhere was now virtually out of sight.

In her place, a battery of lawyers negotiated with the Feds and argued with the judge to have her charges reduced. U.S. District Judge Miriam Cedarbaum, taking a page from the domestic doyenne herself, adamantly refused to throw out the charges.

Those who expected the typically feisty Stewart to come out fighting were sadly disappointed. In June 2003, Stewart unveiled a personal Website on which she proclaimed her innocence and insisted she would fight to clear her name. But beyond those Website notations, she remained tight-lipped. Meanwhile, in the vacuum of Stewart's silence, the Internet, cable television, and the public press were flooded with "experts" surmising on just what poor Martha Stewart had done to herself.

FIGURE 4-6 Fall of a diva.
Grim-faced Martha Stewart is flanked by lawyers and court security after she was sentenced to five months in prison in July 2004. *(Photo: Justin LANE/EPA/Newscom)*

An Excruciating Trial

Stewart's trial began January 27, 2004, two full years after the alleged insider trading violation.

The trial was excruciating for Martha. For two months, she was forced to endure a phalanx of cameras greeting her in the morning for her arrival at the lower Manhattan courthouse and waiting for her each evening when the day's session was over (Figure 4-6). She said nothing, again relying on attorneys to explain to the media exactly what went on that day in court. As her lawyers spoke each night, a stone-faced Stewart would stare straight ahead. Meanwhile, the share price of her company's stock plummeted, and her reputation wasn't far behind.

On March 5, 2004, with the world waiting breathlessly for the verdict, Stewart was found guilty on all four counts of obstructing justice and lying to federal investigators. Her broker was also found guilty, and both faced prison time.

About an hour after the verdict was read, Stewart—radiant as ever with a fur around her neck, a black overcoat, and a tasteful, brown leather bag at her side—strode poker-faced down the stairs of the courthouse, accompanied by her lawyers. She did not respond to questions shouted at her by reporters. Instead, the following statement was posted on her Website:

Dear Friends,
I am obviously distressed by the jury's verdict but I take comfort in knowing that I have done nothing wrong and that I have the enduring support of my family and friends.

Her lawyers vowed to appeal.

Four months later, after losing her job, her company, close to $500,000 in stock market wealth, and her reputation, Martha

Stewart lost her freedom. She was sentenced to five months in prison and two years' probation.

Still, Stewart was defiant, telling a television interviewer that "many, many good people have gone to prison" and comparing herself to Nelson Mandela, South Africa's persecuted anti-apartheid hero. And outside the courthouse, after her sentencing, an unrepentant Stewart vowed, "I'll be back."

Winter at Camp Cupcake

Stewart's attorneys, taking the lead from their defiant client, appealed her conviction and vowed to spare her hard time. But suddenly, in mid-September 2004, Stewart had a change of heart.

Shocking her supporters, the domestic doyenne announced that she would not wait for the verdict on her appeal and rather wished to begin serving her five-month prison sentence early "to put this nightmare behind me, both personally and professionally."

And so on October 8, 2004, Stewart, 63 and a multimillionaire, slipped into the women's federal prison in Alderson, West Virginia, to join petty thieves and embezzlers and drug offenders, all performing day labor at rates between 12 and 40 cents an hour.

And wonder of wonder, Stewart was an ideal prisoner. Reports from "Camp Cupcake," as it was labeled, were glowing in their praise of Stewart.

- She praised her guards, the warden, and fellow prisoners.

- She wrote passionately about the unfairness of federal sentencing guidelines, which shackled many of those whom she met behind the walls.

- She even participated in prison events—failing to win the "prison bakeoff."

On Thursday, March 3, 2005, when Stewart was sprung from the slammer to return to her 153-acre Westchester Estate, she was met with cameras, microphones, and a hero's welcome.

Comeback Kid

It was a new Martha Stewart who emerged from prison. She was more relaxed, more open, and more available to questioners. She also was very much back in business.

- She signed deals to begin two new television shows—one a daytime lifestyles show, the other a spinoff of Donald Trump's *The Apprentice.*

- She signed a $30 million deal for a Sirius satellite radio program.

- She signed a lucrative book deal to produce a Martha memoir, discussing her time in prison.

By the winter of 2005, Stewart was back with a vengeance. She still hadn't acknowledged—even after her conviction and subsequent jail time—that she had done anything "wrong." But there would be ample opportunity for an admission, as Martha momentum—"Martha Mo"—began to build and the "queen" set out to retake her throne.

On January 6, 2006, the United States Court of Appeals for the Second Circuit rejected the arguments of Stewart's lawyers and upheld her conviction.

With time, Martha Stewart was back on television and prominent once again. But the layoff in prison had clearly taken its toll. While Martha was gone, a number of other homemaking heroines—led by the younger Rachel Ray—and celebrity chefs had moved eagerly to supplant her.

And while it was clear that Martha Stewart would never again want for money, fame, or power, it was also safe to assume that in terms of public opinion, she would never get back to where she had been prior to taking her fatal fall.

Questions

1. How would you characterize Martha Stewart's initial public relations response to the charges against her?

2. What key public relations principle did Martha Stewart violate?

3. Had you been advising her, what public relations strategy and tactics would you have recommended? How "vocal" should she have been?

4. How important, from a public relations perspective, was her decision to go to jail early?

5. What public relations strategy should Stewart adopt now?

6. Should she acknowledge that she made mistakes?

For further information, see Michael Barbaro, "Court Rejects Appeal by Martha Stewart," *The New York Times* (January 7, 2006): C3; Krysten Crawford, "Martha: I Cheated No One," *CNN Money* (July 20, 2004); Krysten Crawford, "Martha, Out and About" (March 4, 2005); Gene Healy, "Lessons of Martha Stewart Case," *Cato Institute* (July 16, 2004); "Martha Stewart Wants to Enter Prison Early," *CBC News* (September 16, 2004); Brooke A. Masters, "Stewart Begins Prison Term," *Washington Post* (October 9, 2004): EO1; Fraser P. Seitel, "Martha's Final PR Hurdle," www.odwyerpr.com (March 6, 2005); Fraser P. Seitel, "Martha Finally Gets PR Religion" (August 26, 2005); "Stewart Convicted on All Charges," *CNN Money* (March 5, 2004); "Timeline of Martha Stewart Scandal," *Associated Press,* Copyright 2005.

From the Top

An Interview with Ned Raynolds

Ned Raynolds is a veteran corporate communications executive and strategic advisor experienced in all phases of external and internal communications, corporate and agency public relations. Mr. Raynolds's broad industry experience includes travel and transportation, banking and finance, pharmaceuticals, and electric and gas utilities. He has managed corporate communications for American Airlines for the East Coast and has served in executive capacities at Hill + Knowlton Strategies, GPU, Inc., Valley National Bank, and the American Stock Exchange.

How important is "reputation" for a company today?
It is everything. A company's reputation—shaped largely by news media coverage—influences the actions of everyone who determines its success or failure. In these days of lightening communications, news spreads like wildfire and a company's fine reputation can fall within hours. When it does, demand for its products can dry up, regulators and legislators can saddle it with draconian measures, and even the board of directors can turn against management. Rebuilding a lost reputation typically takes years of exemplary performance—effectively communicated.

How can a communications department help build reputation?
The time-honored definition of public relations, "good performance, publicly appreciated," is truer than ever today. The public spotlight is too bright to paper over poor or deceptive behavior. A communications department helps build a corporation's reputation when it (a) draws public attention to the company's good works, gaining credit where due, (b) persuades management to face up publicly to shortcomings, being accountable and setting forth a corrective plan, and (c) advises management about how the plans it is considering are likely to affect public opinion.

How should a communications group accommodate social media?
Social media has taken its place as an essential element in the corporate communicator's media mix. It can present a valuable opportunity when used to enlist support for a company's products or services, events, or pro-bono activities. Or, it can make for rough going when people use social outlets to jump on real or perceived failings. Negative social media posts can quickly mushroom into full-blown crises. Communications departments, especially those of consumer companies, should strongly consider 24/7 social media monitoring to nip incipient problems in the bud.

How important is the CEO in building positive public opinion for a company?
All important. Since the media and the public think of organizations in human terms, the CEO becomes the target for their praise or scorn. Absent negative issues, a CEO can build a positive reputation for his/her company through an effective program of executive communications. In a crisis, the CEO must stand up for the company. He/she must be available, informative, and open with the media and take responsibility, insofar as appropriate, for what has gone wrong.

How important is it for the communications department to report to the CEO?
It is desirable for the communications department to report to the CEO, because public perceptions affect companies at the highest level. However, it can also be a successful arrangement for the communications department to report to another officer who understands and supports the communications mission and has the ear of the CEO. Communicators should also be part of any meetings with the CEO involving reputational or public perception issues.

Why use a public relations agency?
A public relations agency's greatest value is that it presents an experienced outside view. While company staffers often tend to look at the corporation from the inside out, agency advisors are more likely to view it through the eyes of the company's constituents and the news media. Agencies also tend to offer broad, deep experience with specific industries and a variety of specialized skills that most companies cannot afford to support internally.

What are the skills that public relations people in the 21st century must possess?
They should be clear, concise communicators—both with the written and spoken word. They should understand how the news media works and be able to think like journalists. They should be able to react quickly to unexpected developments. They should understand enough about business to recommend communications activities that will advance the goals of their employer or client. And they should be creative in coming up with ideas that will capture the attention of the media and the public, to the company's benefit.

Public Relations Library

Alsop, Ron J. *The 18 Immutable Laws of Corporate Reputation: Creating, Protecting, and Repairing Your Most Valuable Asset.* New York: Free Press, 2004. A *Wall Street Journal* veteran's step-by-step guide to winning a positive reputation and communicating it.

Asher, Herbert. *Polling and the Public* (7th ed.). Washington, DC: CQ Press, 2007. A comprehensive examination of research methods and public opinion surveys.

Berinksky, Adam J. (Ed.) *New Directions in Public Opinion.* New York: Routledge, 2012. A contemporary discussion of what influences public opinion in such controversial topics as same-sex marriage, politics, and trust in public opinion polls.

Bloomgarden, Kathy. *Trust: The Secret Weapon of Effective Business Leaders.* New York: St. Martins Press, 2007. Ruder Finn's co-CEO traces a road map for corporations to build support among their most important publics.

Claggett, William J.M., and Byron E. Shafer. *The American Public Mind.* New York: Cambridge University Press, 2010. Worthwhile historical background on the major events that underpin the United States, including the Depression, New Deal, and civil rights.

Friedman, Barry. *The Will of the People.* New York: Farrar, Strauss, and Giroux, 2009. A study of how public opinion has influenced Supreme Court interpretation of the Constitution.

Kotler, Philip, and Nancy Lee. *Corporate Social Responsibility: Doing the Most Good for Your Company and Your Cause.* Hoboken, NJ: John Wiley & Sons, 2005. Two well-known marketing professors provide their perspective on CSR.

Manheim, Jarol B. *Biz-War and the Out-of-Power Elites: The Progressive-Left Attack on the Corporation.* Mahwah, NJ: Lawrence Erlbaum Associates, 2004. What certain critics in society would like public opinion to resemble.

McCombs, Max, Lance Holbert, Spiro Kiousis, and Wayne Wanta. *The News and Public Opinion.* Cambridge, UK: Polity Press, 2011. A British view on how what's reported influences public opinion.

Murray, Allan. *Revolt in the Boardroom.* New York: HarperCollins, 2007. A *Wall Street Journal* editor traces reasons why the "reputations" of corporations are prone to suffering in a post-Enron world.

Oxley, Zoe M. *Public Opinion: Democratic Ideals, Democratic Practice* (Paperback). Washington, DC: CQ Press, 2008. A scholarly discussion of public opinion research and its relation to social psychology.

Shapiro, Cynthia. *Corporate Confidential: 50 Secrets Your Company Doesn't Want You to Know—and What to Do About Them.* New York: St. Martin's Press, 2005. A human resources executive opens the curtain on the real truth about such issues as free corporate speech, age discrimination, and being too smart in a corporation.

Sobel, Richard, Peter Furia, and Bethany Barratt. *Public Opinion and International Intervention.* Dulles, VA: Potomac Press, 2012. Fascinating exposition on the different views of the Iraq war in 12 countries.

Chapter 5

Management

Chapter Objectives

1. To discuss public relations as a "management" function that serves the organization best when it reports to the CEO.
2. To explore in detail the elements that constitute a public relations plan.
3. To discuss public relations objectives, campaigns, and budgets.
4. To compare and contrast the internal public relations department and the external public relations agency.

FIGURE 5-1   Wotta headache!
For years until his retirement in 2013, U.S. Rep. Barney Frank, ranking member of the House Financial Services Committee, greeted noncommunicative bankers and CEOs with disdain and occasional derision.
(Photo: MATTHEW HEALEY/UPI/Newscom)

CEOs have seen better days.

According to Booz & Co., which annually monitors such things, at the 250 top companies by market capitalization, CEO turnover averaged 14% over 12 years through 2012. One researcher observed, "As the rate of CEO turnover returns to historical levels, we are seeing executives face more intense pressure to perform."[1]

One area in which CEOs were obliged to "perform" was the realm of communication. After the corporate scandals of the early 2000s, the Madoff Ponzi scheme of 2009 and the other insider trading calamities that followed, coupled with the U.S. financial meltdown of 2010 and European stresses of 2012, it became more important than ever for management to express itself convincingly to shareholders, regulators, and the general public.

Often the results were disastrous.

■ Research in Motion (RIM), creator of the immortal BlackBerry handheld device, squandered its reputation and franchise with years of failed promises and botched communication. For example, when RIM in the winter of 2012 finally acquiesced to shareholders and dumped its two founders as co-CEOs, it appointed a relatively unknown operations type to head the company. His first decision: to make huge payouts to the two failed co-CEOs and "continue their legacy." The stock plummeted.[2]

■ In April 2012, another underperforming company, beauty firm Avon Products, named Johnson & Johnson executive Sherilyn McCoy to be its new CEO. The timing was auspicious, as Avon received a $10 billion buyout bid from the world's largest fragrance maker, Cody, backed by investor Warren Buffett. If Avon accepted, its stock would have been valued around $22 a share. Cody set a time limit for Avon to respond to its bid, and Avon's new CEO responded by—doing nothing! Not only did CEO McCoy not accept the Cody bid, she didn't even communicate with the courtesy of a response. Avon's stock immediately sunk 30% on its new silent CEO's non-reply.[3]

■ A much different tack—thankfully!—was taken by our old friend JP Morgan Chase CEO Jamie Dimon when he was called to testify in the summer of 2012 for his bank's $2 billion + trading loss. Not only did Dimon gladly appear before the vultures in both the U.S. Senate and House, he was articulate, straightforward, and kept his cool, despite brow-beating by notorious business critics such as retiring Congressman Barney Frank, who wondered if CEO Dimon would allow his own compensation to be "clawed back" as a result of the loss (Figure 5-1).[4]

It has been said that the only difference between the public relations director and the CEO is that the latter gets paid more.

In many ways, that's quite true. The CEO, after all, is the firm's top manager, responsible for, in addition to setting strategy and framing policy, serving as the organization's chief spokesperson, corporate booster, and reputation defender—not at all unlike the responsibilities assigned to the public relations professional.

To be effective—and respected—in his or her job, the public relations professional in the 21st century must understand management. That means that public relations people must master knowledge of such management functions as planning, budgeting, objective setting, and how top management thinks and operates. That's what this chapter discusses.

It also deals with the differences between working as a staff public relations practitioner inside a corporation, nonprofit, or other organization, where the job is to support management in achieving its objectives, and working as a professional in a public relations agency, where the job is to contribute to the revenue generation of the company. Finally, it provides some feel of what to expect in terms of income in public relations.

Management Process of Public Relations

Like other management processes, professional public relations work emanates from clear strategies and bottom-line objectives that flow into specific tactics, each with its own budget, timetable, and allocation of resources. Stated another way, public relations today is much more a planned, persuasive social managerial science than a knee-jerk, damage-control reaction to sudden flare-ups.

Don't get me wrong. As we will learn later, the public relations professionals who have the most organizational clout and get paid the most are those who demonstrate the ability to perform in a crisis. Thinking "on your feet" is a coveted ability in the practice of public relations. But so, too, is the ability to think strategically and plan methodically to help change attitudes, crystallize opinions, and accomplish the organization's overall goals.

Managers insist on *results,* so the best public relations programs can be measured in terms of achieving results in building the key relationships on which the organization depends. The relevance of public relations people in the eyes of top management depends largely on the contribution they make to the management process of the organization.

With nearly a century under its belt, the practice of public relations has developed its own theoretical framework as a management system. According to communications professors James Grunig and Todd Hunt, public relations managers perform what organizational theorists call a *boundary* role: They function at the edge of an organization as a liaison between the organization and its external and internal publics. In other words, public relations managers have one foot inside the organization and one outside. Often this unique position is not only lonely but also precarious.

As boundary managers, public relations people support their colleagues by helping them communicate across organizational lines both within and outside the organization. In this way, public relations professionals also become systems managers, knowledgeable about and able to deal with the complex relationships inherent in the organization.[5]

Top managers are forced to think strategically about reaching their goals. So, too, should public relations professionals think in terms of the strategic process element of their own roles.

It is this procedural mindset—directed at communicating key messages to realize desired objectives to priority publics—that makes the public relations professional a key advisors to top management.

Reporting to Top Management

The public relations function, by definition, must report to top management.

If public relations, as noted in Chapter 1, is truly to be the "interpreter" for management philosophy, policy, and programs, then the public relations director should report to the CEO.

In many organizations, this reporting relationship is not the case. Public relations is often subordinated to advertising, marketing, legal, or human resources. Whereas marketing and advertising promote the product, public relations promotes the entire organization. Therefore, if the public relations chief reports to the director of marketing or advertising, the job mistakenly becomes one of promoting specific products rather than one of promoting the entire organization.

For the public relations function to be valuable to management, it must remain independent, credible, and objective. This mandates that public relations professionals have not only communication competence but also an intimate knowledge of the organization's business. Without the latter, according to research, public relations professionals are much less effective as top-management advisors.[6]

Public relations should be the *corporate conscience*. An organization's public relations professionals should enjoy enough autonomy to deal openly and honestly with management. If an idea doesn't make sense, if a product is flawed, if the general institutional wisdom is wrong, it is the duty of the public relations professional to challenge the consensus. As Warren Buffet, the legendary CEO of Berkshire Hathaway, put it, "We can afford to lose money—even a lot of money. But we cannot afford to lose reputation—even a shred of reputation."[7]

This is not to say that advertising, marketing, and all other disciplines shouldn't enjoy a close partnership with public relations. Clearly, they must. All disciplines must work to maintain their own independence while building long-term, mutually beneficial relationships for the good of the organization. However, public relations should never shirk its overriding responsibility to enhance the organization's credibility by ensuring that corporate actions are in the public interest.

PR Ethics Mini-Case

A Publicity Tie Too Far

Traditionally, one way to attract publicity is to tie one's product to a current news story.

But sometimes, the "tie-in" goes over the line.

That's what the management of international public relations firm Fleishman-Hillard discovered in the summer of 2012, when one of its clients issued a news release that tied its product to the recent arrest of Canada's "body parts killer," a male porn star accused of killing and dismembering a former lover (Figure 5-2).

The company, Backcheck, which conducts background checks, issued the release, which suggested that the landlord who leased apartments to the alleged killer could have used the company's product to reveal "red flags."

Canadian media felt the release stretched the bonds of ethical disclosure, and so, too, did Backcheck's public relations firm, Fleishman-Hillard. The president of Fleishman-Hillard Canada issued this immediate apology:

FIGURE 5-2   Smoking kills.
And so, too, apparently, did Luka Rocco Magnotta, the accused "body parts killer," whose 2012 arrest was used as fodder for an ill-conceived tie-in news release. *(Photo: AFP /Getty Images/Newscom)*

APOLOGY FROM FLEISHMAN-HILLARD CANADA

Today, our firm experienced first-hand, the type of public criticism and threat to our reputation that we are often called upon to counsel our clients through. Good public relations starts with transparency, honesty and a willingness to address a problem head-on. Our firm made an inappropriate decision—leveraging recent headlines in an attempt to gain coverage for a client. Using such tragic events in this context was a clear mistake in judgment on the part of our firm.

The reaction from the media and general public aligns with our own feelings of regret and we apologize to anyone who was offended.

We feel it is important to address this error in judgment, and are counseling ourselves as we would counsel any client in a similar situation.

This is an isolated incident. We do great work for our clients in Canada and around the globe each and every day. Shocking headlines and the need to break through the content clutter should never come at the sacrifice of common sense and good taste.

John Blyth, President and Senior Partner, Canada

Fleishman's client, however, still wasn't convinced the release was that bad. Said Backcheck CEO Dave Dinesen, "I apologize if anyone thought it was in poor taste, but if I was renting out my basement, I'd want to know who I was renting it to."*

Questions

1. What was offensive about the Backcheck news release?

2. What do you think of Fleishman's handling of the crisis and its apology?

*For further information, see Michael Sebastian, "Company, PR Firm Apologize for 'Tackiest Press Release in Human History,'" ragan. com, June 5, 2012; and Dylan Stapleford, "Luke Magnotta, Canada's Alleged 'Body Parts Killer,' Arrested in Berlin," Yahoo!News, June 4, 2012.

To perform that function effectively, it needs to report directly to top management, and ultimately to the CEO.

Conceptualizing the Public Relations Plan

Strategic planning for public relations is an essential part of management. Planning is critical not only to know where a particular campaign is headed but also to win the support of top management. Indeed, one of the most frequent complaints about public relations is that it is too much a "seat-of-the-pants" activity, impossible to plan and difficult to measure. Management's perspective is, "How do we know the public relations group will deliver and fully leverage the resources they're asking for?" They must see a plan.[8] With proper planning, public relations professionals can indeed defend and account for their actions.

Before organizing for public relations work, practitioners must consider objectives and strategies, planning and budgets, and research and evaluation. The broad environment in which the organization operates must dictate the overall business objectives. These, in turn, dictate specific public relations objectives and strategies. Once these have been defined, the task of organizing for a public relations program should flow naturally.

Environment
 └──➤ *Business objectives*
   └──➤ *Public relations objectives and strategies*
      └──➤ *Public relations programs*

Setting objectives, formulating strategies, and planning are essential if the public relations function is to be considered equal in stature to other management processes. Traditionally, the public relations management process involves four steps:

1. **Defining the problem or opportunity.** This requires researching current attitudes and opinions about the issue, product, candidate, or company in question and determining the essence of the problem.

2. **Programming.** This is the formal planning stage, which addresses key constituent publics, strategies, tactics, and goals.

3. **Action.** This is the communications phase, when the program is implemented.

4. **Evaluation.** The final step in the process is the assessment of what worked, what didn't, and how to improve in the future.

Each of these four process steps is important. Most essential is starting with a firm base of research and a solid foundation of planning.

Creating the Public Relations Plan

The public relations plan must be spelled out in writing. Its organization must answer management's concerns and questions about the campaign being recommended. Here's one way it might be organized and what it should answer.

1. **Executive summary**—an overview of the plan.

2. **Communication process**—how it works, for understanding and training purposes.

3. **Background**—mission statement, vision, values, events that led to the need for the plan.

4. **Situation analysis**—major issues and related facts the plan will deal with.

5. **Message statement**—the plan's major ideas and emerging themes, all of which look to the expected outcome.

6. **Audiences**—strategic constituencies related to the issues, listed in order of importance, with whom you wish to develop and maintain relationships.

7. **Key audience messages**—one- or two-sentence messages that you want to be understood by each key audience.

8. **Implementation**—issues, audiences, messages, media, timing, cost, expected outcomes, and method of evaluation—all neatly spelled out.

9. **Budget**—the plan's overall budget presented in the organization's accepted style.

10. **Monitoring and evaluation**—how the plan's results will be measured and evaluated against a previously set benchmark or desired outcome.[9]

The beauty of creating a plan is that it clearly specifies tactics against which objectives can be measured and evaluated. In devising the public relations plan along these lines, an organization is assured that its public relations programs will reinforce and complement its overall business goals.

Activating the Public Relations Campaign

Any public relations campaign puts all of the aspects of public relations planning—objectives, strategies, research, budgeting, tactics, and evaluation—into one cohesive framework. The plan specifies a series of *what's* to be done and *how* to get them done—whatever is necessary to reach the objectives.

Every aspect of the public relations plan should be designed to be meaningful and valuable to the organization. The four-part skeleton of a typical public relations campaign plan resembles the following:

1. **Backgrounding the problem.** This is the so-called situation analysis, background, or case statement that specifies the major aims of the campaign. It can be a general statement that refers to audiences, known research, the organization's positions, history, and the obstacles faced in reaching the desired goal.

2. **Preparing the proposal.** The second stage of the campaign plan sketches broad approaches to solve the problem at hand. The elements of the public relations proposal may vary, depending on the subject matter, but generally include the following:
   - Situational analysis—description of the challenge as it currently exists, including background on how the situation reached its present state.
   - Scope of assignment—description of the nature of the assignment: What the public relations program will attempt to do.
   - Target audiences—specific targets identified and divided into manageable groups.
   - Research methods—specific research approach to be used.
   - Key messages—specific selected appeals: What do we want to tell our audiences? How do we want them to feel about us? What do we want them to do?
   - Communications vehicles—tactical communications devices to be used.
   - Project team—key players who will participate in the program.
   - Timing and fees—a timetable with proposed costs identified.

3. **Implementing the plan.** The third stage of a campaign plan details operating tactics. It may also contain a time chart specifying when each action will take place. Specific activities are defined, people are assigned to them, and deadlines are established. This stage forms the guts of the campaign plan.

4. **Evaluating the campaign.** To find out whether the plan worked, evaluation methods should be spelled out here.
   - Did we implement the activities we proposed?
   - Did we receive appropriate public recognition for our efforts?

■ Did attitudes change—among the community, customers, management—as a result of our programs?

The inclusion of a mechanism for evaluation is imperative in terms of verifying results based on shifts in public opinion or actions taken to benefit an organization and its goals.[10]

Finally, although planning the public relations campaign is important, planning must never become an end in itself. The fact is that no matter how important planning may be, public relations is still assessed principally in terms of its action, performance, and practice.

Setting Public Relations Objectives

An organization's goals must define what its public relations goals will be, and the only good goals are ones that can be measured. Public relations objectives and the strategies that flow from them must achieve results. As the baseball pitcher Johnny Sain used to say, "Nobody wants to hear about the labor pains, but everyone wants to see the baby."

So, too, must public relations people think strategically. Strategies are the most crucial decisions of a public relations campaign. They answer the general question, *How will we manage our resources to achieve our goals?* The specific answers then become the public relations tactics used to implement the strategies. Ideally, strategies and tactics should profit from pretesting.

As for objectives, good ones stand up to the following questions:

■ Do they clearly describe the end result expected?

■ Are they understandable to everyone in the organization?

■ Do they list a firm completion date?

■ Are they realistic, attainable, and measurable?

■ Are they consistent with management's objectives?

Increasingly, public relations professionals are managing by objectives (MBO) and by results (MBR) to help quantify the value of public relations in an organization. The two questions most frequently asked by general managers of public relations practitioners are, *How can we measure public relations results?* and *How do we know whether the public relations program is making progress?* MBO can provide public relations professionals with a powerful source of feedback. MBO and MBR tie public relations results to management's predetermined objectives in terms of audiences, messages, and media. Even though procedures for implementing MBO programs differ, most programs share four points:

1. Specification of the organization's goals, with objective measures of the organization's performance

2. Conferences between the superior and the subordinate to agree on achievable goals

3. Agreement between the superior and the subordinate on objectives consistent with the organization's goals

4. Periodic reviews by the superior and the subordinate to assess progress toward achieving the goals

Again, the key is to tie public relations goals to the goals of the organization and then to manage progress toward achieving those goals. The goals themselves should be clearly defined and specific, practical and attainable, and measurable.

Outside the Lines

Cooking Gilbert's Goose

Sometimes the best-laid public relations plans are foiled by management's overwhelming desire to stay out of trouble. And when it's your well-paid, very public spokesperson who gets you in trouble, well . . . fuggedaboutit.

Such was the lesson learned by one Gilbert Gottfried, hyperactive comedian and erstwhile spokesperson for the Aflac insurance company. In the spring of 2011, Gilbert was riding high as the unmistakable—and slightly grating—voice of the revered Aflac duck (Figure 5-3). The omnipresent Aflac commercials, utilizing the duck and Mr. Gottfried's voice for 10 years, were well known throughout the world, particularly in Japan where Aflac was the country's number-one insurer.

But in March 2011, a vicious earthquake followed by a tsunami struck Japan, leaving the country devastated. For some suicidal reason, the tsunami caused the 56-year-old Mr. Gottfried to tweet to his many followers the following pearls:

- "I just split up with my girlfriend, but like the Japanese say, 'There'll be another one floating by any minute now.'"
- "What does every Japanese person have in their apartment? Flood lights!"
- "Japan called me. They said: 'Maybe those jokes are a hit in the U.S., but over here, they're all sinking.'"

So, too (sink, that is!), did Mr. Gottfried's spokesperson career. Aflac wasn't amused with the Twitter postings, so the company's CEO immediately flew to Japan, and the firm donated $1.2 million to the International Red Cross aid fund for Japan.

And, oh yes, Aflac also fired Mr. Gottfried.*

*For further information, see "Gilbert Gottfried Fired by Japanese Firm Aflac for Making Tsunami Jokes," Daily Mail Online, March 15, 2011.

FIGURE 5-3   Before the quackup.
Aflac spokesperson Gilbert Gottfried and friend, in happier times. *(Photo: Everett Collection/Newscom)*

Budgeting for Public Relations

Like any other business activity, public relations programs must be based on sound budgeting. After identifying objectives and strategies, the public relations professional must detail the particular tactics that will help achieve those objectives. No organization can spend indiscriminately. Without a realistic budget, no organization can succeed. Likewise, public relations activities must be disciplined by budgetary realities.

In public relations agencies responsible for producing revenue, *functional budgeting* is the rule; that is, dollars for staff, resources, activities, and so on are linked to specific revenue-generating activities. Employees are required to turn in time sheets detailing hours worked on behalf of specific clients. In organizations where public relations is a "staff" activity and not responsible for revenue generation, *administrative budgeting* is the rule; that is, budget dollars are assigned generally against the department's allocation for staff and expenses.

The key to budgeting may lie in performing two steps: (1) estimating the extent of the resources—both personnel and purchases—needed to accomplish each activity, and (2) estimating the cost and availability of those resources. With this information in hand, the development of a budget and monthly cash flow for a public relations program becomes easier. Such data also provide the milestones necessary to audit program costs on a routine basis and to make adjustments well in advance of budget crises.

Most public relations programs operate on limited budgets. In a growing number of instances, "pay-for-performance" public relations has emerged. The premise of this arrangement is that the buyer pays only for what he or she gets, meaning that fees are based on the depth of coverage and the circulation or audience rating of the venue in which coverage appears. If no coverage is achieved, no fee is paid. Most public relations agencies, however, make "no guarantees" that their efforts will be successful and therefore frown on pay-for-performance contracts.[11]

Most public relations agencies treat client costs in a manner similar to that used by legal, accounting, and management consulting firms: The client pays for services rendered, either on a monthly or yearly retainer basis or on minimum charges based on staff time. Time records are kept by every employee—from chairperson to mail clerk—on a daily basis to be sure that agency clients know exactly what they are paying for. Hourly charges for public relations agency employees can range from low double figures per hour to upwards of $500 an hour and even as high as $1,000 an hour for a handful of agency superstars.

Because agency relationships are based on trust, it is important that clients understand the derivation of costs. In recent years, debate has raged over markups on expenses paid on behalf of clients by public relations firms. Out-of-pocket expenses—for meals, hotels, transportation, and the like—are generally charged back to clients at cost. But when an agency pays in advance for larger expense items—printing, photography, graphics, design—it is standard industry practice to mark up such expenses by a factor approximating 17.65%. This figure, which the vast majority of agencies use, was borrowed from the advertising profession and represents the multiplicative inverse of the standard 15% commission that ad agencies collect on advertising placement.

The guiding rule in agency budgeting is to ensure that the client is aware of how charges are being applied so that nasty surprises might be avoided when bills are received.

Implementing Public Relations Programs

The duties and responsibilities of public relations practitioners are as diverse as the publics with whom different institutions deal. Specific public relations tasks are as varied as the organizations served. Here is a partial list of public relations duties:

- **Media relations:** Coordinating relationships with the online, print, and electronic media, which includes arranging and monitoring press interviews, writing news releases and related press materials, organizing press conferences, and answering media inquiries and requests.

- **Social media marketing:** The digital revolution has introduced a whole new component to public relations skills sets. The Web, where everyone is a publisher and conversations are the rule, has transformed the publication of information into a legitimate two-way street. Marketing via social networking sites, from Facebook to Twitter, from Pinterest to Tumblr to all the rest has become a frontline responsibility of public relations professionals.

- **Internal communications:** Informing employees and principals through a variety of means, including intranet, newsletters, television, and meetings. Traditionally, this role has emphasized news-oriented communications rather than benefits-oriented ones, which are usually the province of personnel departments.

- **Government relations and public affairs:** Coordinating activities with legislators on local, state, and federal levels. This includes legislative research activities, lobbying, and public policy formation.

- **Community relations:** Orchestrating interaction with the community, perhaps including open houses, tours, and employee volunteer efforts designed to reflect the supportive nature of the organization to the community.

- **Investor relations:** Managing relations with the investment community, including the firm's present and potential stockholders. This task emphasizes personal contact with securities analysts, institutional investors, and private investors.

- **Consumer relations:** Supporting activities with customers and potential customers, with activities ranging from hard-sell product promotion activities to "soft" consumer advisory services.

- **Public relations research:** Conducting opinion research, which involves assisting in the public policy formation process through the coordination and interpretation of attitudinal studies of key publics.

- **Public relations writing:** Coordinating the institution's printed voice with its publics through reprints of speeches, annual reports, quarterly statements, and product and company brochures.

- **Special interest publics relations:** Coordinating relationships with outside specialty groups, such as nongovernmental organizations, suppliers, educators, students, nonprofit organizations, and competitors.

- **Institutional advertising:** Managing the institutional—or non-product—advertising image as well as being called on increasingly to assist in the management of more traditional product advertising.

- **Graphics:** Coordinating the graphic and photographic services of the organization. To do this task well requires knowledge of desktop publishing, typography, layout, and art.

- **Website management:** Coordinating the organization's online "face," including Website design and ongoing counsel, updating, and even management of the site.

- **Philanthropy:** Managing the gift-giving apparatus, which ordinarily consists of screening and evaluating philanthropic proposals and allocating the organization's available resources.

- **Special events:** Coordinating special events, including travel for company management, corporate celebrations and exhibits, dinners, groundbreakings, and grand openings.

- **Management counseling:** Advising managers on alternative options and recommended choices in light of public responsibilities.

■ **Crisis management:** Taking charge when crisis strikes is another first-line responsibility of public relations professionals, who are looked to provide guidance to management in confronting the media and the often perilous situation.

Again, this is but a partial list of the tasks ordinarily assigned to public relations professionals.

Public relations managers frequently use the visualization tools of Gantt and PERT charts to control and administer these project tasks. The Gantt chart, developed by Charles Gantt in 1917, focuses on the sequence of tasks necessary for completion of the project at hand. Each task on a Gantt chart is represented as a single horizontal bar. The PERT chart shows the relationship between each activity. These relationships create pathways through the process. The "critical path" is a series of tasks that must be completed in a certain time period for the project to be completed on schedule (see Figure 5-4).

The Public Relations Department

Public relations professionals generally work in one of two organizational structures: (1) as a staff professional in a public relations department of a corporation, university, hospital, sports franchise, political campaign, religious institution, and so on, whose task is to support the primary business of the organization; or (2) as a line professional in a public relations agency, whose primary task is to help the organization earn revenue.

Consider the public relations department. Once an organization has analyzed its environment, established its objectives, set up measurement standards, and thought about appropriate plans, programs, and budgets, it is ready to organize a public relations department. Departments range from one-person operations to far-flung networks of hundreds of people, such as at the U.S. Department of Defense, Johnson & Johnson, or ExxonMobil, with staff around the world, responsible for relations with the press, investors, civic groups, employees, and many different governments.

Today, appropriately, about half of all corporate communications departments report to the chairperson, president, and/or CEO. This is an improvement from the past and indicative of the higher stature that the function enjoys. About one-sixth of public relations departments report to advertising or marketing, and another one-sixth report to a vice president of administration.[12] Clearly, reporting to the CEO is eminently preferable to reporting to a legal, financial, or administrative executive, who may tend to "filter" top-management messages.

In government, public relations professionals (although, as we will see later in this book, they're not called *public relations*) typically report directly to department heads. In universities, the public relations function is frequently coupled with fundraising and development activities. In hospitals, public relations is typically tied to the marketing function.

In terms of structure, corporate public relations departments today are faced with stakeholders who are more "empowered" than ever. It's not just the media who publish about the company—it's everybody on the Internet—activists, employees, consumers, bloggers of every stripe and attitude. For the first time in history, corporate communicators no longer control the conversation.[13] This group of diverse influencers means that companies must organize communications departments to reflect a new diverse

Prototype Gantt Chart
Packaged Goods Product
Target Start of Ship at Start of Year, Retail Availability in March, Marketing Support in April

Category	Activity	Jan	Feb	Mar	Apr	May	Jun	Jul	Aug
Product	Exploratory Research	XXX							
	Concept Development		XXX						
	Quantitative Research				XXX				
	Product Development			XXX	XXX	XXX	XXX	XXX	
Package	Structural Package Dev			XXX	XXX	XXX	XXX	XXX	
	Graphics Development			XXX	XXX	XXX	XXX	XXX	
Financial	Pricing & Profit	XXX							
	Volume Projections	XXX							
	Budget Development					XXX			
Marketing Plan	Sales Promotion				XXX	XXX	XXX	XXX	
	Advertising				XXX	XXX	XXX	XXX	
	Publicity							XXX	
	Produce Ads/Collateral Material						XXX		
Purchasing	Long Lead Supplies				XXX	XXX	XXX	XXX	
	Shorter Lead Supplies						XXX	XXX	
Begin Production	Inventory Build								XXX
	Ship To Field Warehouses								XXX
Sales Meetings	Present To Sales Force								XXX
	Present To Trade								XXX
Start Shipping	Begin Delivery To Trade								

FIGURE 5-4 Critical path chart.
Daniel Jay Morrison & Associates (www.djmconsult.com) created this prototypical chart to trace the critical path of a product coming to market. *(Courtesy of Daniel Jay Morrison & Associates, Inc.)*

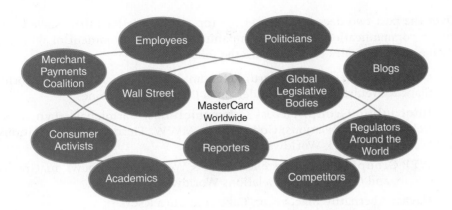

FIGURE 5-5
Organizing for public relations.
These diverse publics are some of those who make up the evolving ecosphere of influencers of MasterCard Worldwide.
(Courtesy MasterCard Worldwide)

group of influencers (see Figure 5-5). This new reality suggests that corporate communications departments must focus more on "engaging" their constituent publics in two-way dialogue, to keep informed about their views and to keep them informed as to the company's motives and actions.

The Public Relations Agency

Now consider the public relations agency. The biggest difference between an external agency and an internal department is perspective. The former is outside looking in; the latter is inside looking out (sometimes literally for itself!). Here's what is meant by "perspective." Sometimes the use of an agency is necessary to escape the tunnel-vision syndrome that afflicts some firms, in which a detached viewpoint is desperately needed. An agency, unfettered by internal corporate politics, might be better trusted to present management with an objective reading of the concerns of its publics.

An agency has the added advantage of not being taken for granted by a firm's management. Unfortunately, management sometimes has a greater regard for an outside specialist than for an inside one. This attitude frequently defies logic but is nonetheless often true. Generally, if management is paying (sometimes quite handsomely) for outside counsel, it tends to listen carefully to the advice.

Agencies generally organize according to industry groupings, with specialization in industry functions—media relations, government relations, social media, investor relations, etc. Larger agencies are divided into such areas as health care, sports, fashion, technology, finance, and so on. Account teams are assigned specific clients. Team members bill clients on an hourly basis, with most firms intending to retain two-thirds of each individual's hourly billing rate as income. In other words, if an account executive bills at a rate of $300 per hour—and many senior counselors do—the firm expects to retain $200 of that rate toward its profit. As to billing rates, one survey indicated that agency CEOs average an hourly rate of $322, with the hourly rate of an account executive averaging $140.[14]

In recent years, as clients have begun to manage resources more rigorously, agencies have gotten much more systematic in measuring success and in keeping customers from migrating to a competitor. Indeed, the most difficult part of agency work is not *attracting* clients but *retaining* them.

Public relations agencies today, as noted, are huge businesses. And public relations, itself, is a multibillion-dollar industry. In 2010, the global public relations industry recorded fee income of $8.8 billion, employing about 60,000 people, according to the Holmes Report.[15]

Over the past two decades, most of the top public relations firms have been subsumed by communications holding companies, the most prominent of which, along with some of the agencies they own, are the following:

- ■ **Omnicom:** Fleishman-Hillard, Ketchum, Porter-Novelli, Brodeur Worldwide, Clark & Weinstock, Gavin Anderson & Company, and Cone
- ■ **Interpublic Group:** Access Communications; Carmichael, Lynch, Spong; DeVries Public Relations; Golin-Harris; MWW; Tierney Public Relations; and Weber-Shandwick Worldwide
- ■ **WPP Group:** Burson-Marsteller, Cohn & Wolfe, Hill & Knowlton, Grey Global Group, and Ogilvy Public Relations Worldwide
- ■ **Havas:** Abernathy MacGregor, Cake, and Euro RSCG
- ■ **Publicis:** Manning, Selvage & Lee, Publicis Dialog, Rowland Worldwide, and, in 2008, Kekst and Company
- ■ **Chime Communications PLC:** Bell Pottinger, Stuart Higgins, Good Relations, Corporate Citizenship, and others

Public relations purists bemoan the incursion of these mammoth companies because many are dominated by advertising agencies. Defenders point to the potential synergy between the two disciplines. One casualty of the takeover of the world's leading public relations firms by these holding companies is that the largest agencies no longer make public their annual revenues and earnings. Nonetheless, a compilation of the net fees of the largest independent public relations firms still shows robust annual revenues (Table 5-1), with the largest, Edelman, earning in excess of $600 million annually. What is indisputable is the tremendous growth of the profession.

Reputation Management

Many public relations agencies in recent years, particularly those purchased by the large advertising agency conglomerates, have declared special emphasis on what they suggest is the more "strategic" *reputation management*. Venerable Hill & Knowlton even went so far as to rebrand itself in 2011 as *Hill & Knowlton Strategies* to more accurately capture the research essence of its reputation management efforts.[16]

What is reputation management? Public relations purists argue that this is precisely what they have been doing all along—helping to "manage strategically" an organization's "reputation," that is, its brand, position, goodwill, or image.

Essentially, an organization's reputation is composed of two elements: (1) the more "rational" products and performance, and (2) more "emotional" behavioral factors, such as customer service, CEO performance, personal experience with the company, and the like. Stated another way, reputation is gained by what one *does*, not by what one *says*.[17]

Reputations matter because a company with a good reputation can charge premium prices, have greater access to new markets and products, have greater access to capital, profit from greater word-of-mouth endorsement, and possess an unduplicated identity. Such distinctive organizations as Tiffany, Google, Dreamworks, and the New York Yankees are all examples of entities with unique and positive reputations that translate into hard-nosed advantages. One quantitative study of reputation concluded that more than one-quarter of a company's stock market value was attributable to intangibles such as its reputation.[18]

TABLE 5-1   O'Dwyer's Rankings: Worldwide Fees of Top Independent PR Firms with Major U.S. Operations—May 2012

Beyond the largest public relations firms, most owned by advertising-oriented multinational holding companies, are thousands of independent public relations firms—many entrepreneurial in nature. Others, like the family-owned Edelman Company—begun by father Dan and now run by son Richard (see From the Top in Chapter 10)—are huge organizations.

Many of these independent shops are thriving. In 2011, many of the top 25 independent public relations firms enjoyed double-digit gains in fee income, testifying to the strength of the public relations counseling business.

	Firm	2011 Net Fees	Empl.	% Fee Change from 2010
1.	Edelman, New York	$604,740,732	4,120	+15.9
2.	APCO Worldwide, Wash., DC	120,701,000	603	+6.4
3.	Waggener Edstrom Worldwide, Bellevue, WA	115,832,000	878	+3.5
4.	Ruder Finn, New York	81,281,000	644	flat
5.	Text 100 Global PR, San Francisco	50,425,771	500	+10.0
6.	W2O Group, San Francisco	47,577,000	231	+29.0
7.	MWW Group, East Rutherford, NJ	38,626,000	202	+11.0
8.	ICR, Norwalk, CT	32,030,483	92	+21.0
9.	Qorvis Communications, Wash., DC	29,500,000	102	flat
10.	DKC, New York	26,800,000	150	+12.1
11.	Finn Partners, New York	23,618,000	196	new
12.	Regan Communications Group, Boston	20,824,340	65	+7.0
13.	Cooney/Waters Group, New York	20,433,000	70	+45.0
14.	Allison+Partners, San Francisco	19,400,000	120	+25.0
15.	Taylor, New York	19,100,000	90	flat
16.	Coyne PR, Parsippany, NJ	18,010,000	107	+13.6
17.	Padilla Speer Beardsley, Minneapolis	17,834,808	106	+4.0
18.	Atomic, San Francisco	15,008,254	92	+35.0
19.	Gibbs & Soell, New York	14,705,882	95	−8.0
20.	Zeno Group, New York	13,926,036	77	+11.7
21.	French | West | Vaughan, Raleigh	13,325,710	72	−2.0
22.	CJP Communications, New York	12,574,399	52	+24.4
23.	Levick Strategic Communications, Wash., DC	12,459,523	51	+38.1
24.	5W Public Relations, New York	12,455,065	72	+9.0
25.	RF | Binder Partners, New York	12,450,000	75	+1.5

Courtesy of Jack O'Dwyer Company, www.odwyerpr.com

Reputation management, then, is *the ability to link reputation to business goals to increase support and advocacy and increase organizational success through profits, contributions, attendance, and so on.*

What do reputation managers do? The behaviors they attempt to influence include (1) persuading consumers to recommend and buy their products, (2) persuading investors to invest in their organization, (3) persuading competent job seekers to enlist as employees, (4) persuading other strong organizations to joint venture with them, and (5) persuading people to support the organization when it is attacked.

As the extraordinarily successful commissioner of the National Basketball Association, David Stern, puts it, "I am the protector of the brand and its integrity. That's a job that every CEO has, and I consider it my job to be out there to be protective and to respond so that I can be the spokesperson."[19]

Assisting the CEO in "managing" the reputation of the organization is the public relations professional. Indeed, for the public relations person, reputation management reflects the function's fundamental mandate to promote, maintain, defend, enhance, and sustain the organization's credibility, as the economists put it, "in perpetuity"; in other words, forever.

Where Are the Jobs?

Like other support functions, public relations suffered when the high-tech stock market bubble burst at the beginning of the 21st century. In recent years, however, even with recession clouds hovering over much of the world, the field has shown newfound resilience.

Indeed, the long-term future of the practice of public relations promises to be steady and strong.

- In terms of areas of specialization, social media outreach has become an integral part of a public relations specialist's responsibilities. Social media is a mechanism through which Generation X and Y communicate, and has, therefore, introduced new public relations opportunities for them in particular.

- In terms of other functional areas of specialization, the function of managing a company's reputation ranks high on the public relations job scale. So, too, do the areas of investor relations and crisis management. The increase in demand for specialists in these three high-level areas probably explains why the number of public relations people earning between $100,000 and $249,000 has grown markedly in recent years.[20]

  Worldwide corporations, faced with increased scrutiny from the media, government, and the general public to act ethically and behave responsibly, have recognized the need for talented, top communications managers. Once the media never gave public relations news much notice, but in 2012, *The New York Times* considered it "major news" when image-suffering Goldman Sachs hired a new public relations director.[21] And the practice has grown exponentially beyond the United States.

- Public relations agencies, wiser and more experienced after the boom-bust phenomenon of the early years of the 21st century, will continue to expand.

- In the nonprofit realm, public relations positions in hospitals, in particular, are likely to grow as managed care becomes the reality and health care organizations become more competitive in attracting patients and winning community approval. Other nonprofits—charities, schools, museums, associations—all faced with fewer resources and more competition for community funding—will also require increased public relations help to attract development and membership funds.

- Finally, one other public relations skill that will be in increased demand, certainly for the remainder of this decade, is employee communications. Employees in the 21st century, empowered by the Internet and burned by layoffs, pension fund losses and restructurings, and failures of management to be credible, must be convinced that their organizations deserve their allegiance. This will be a job largely for public relations practitioners—to win back employee trust.[22]

And if you still aren't convinced that public relations jobs will blossom in the years ahead, consider this. Pope Benedict XVI, in the summer of 2012, hired Vatican Fox News correspondent Greg Burke to assist the church in its sometimes-wanting public relations policy around the globe.[23] So even the Pope needs public relations!

What Does It Pay?

Without question, the communications function has increased in importance and clout in the new century. Top communications professionals in many large corporations today draw compensation packages well into six figures, with a select few earning more than $1 million annually. According to the U.S. Bureau of Labor Statistics, the media annual wage for public relations specialists was $52,090 in 2010, with a range of $30,560 to $92,500. The highest paid public relations specialists, according to the Bureau, worked in Victoria, Texas; San Jose, California; and Washington, DC.[24]

According to the Public Relations Society of America (PRSA), average salaries for public relations professionals by job title in 2012 ranged thusly:

Executive vice president	$160,600
Senior vice president	$138,300
Vice president	$112,700
Account supervisor	$75,600
Senior account executive	$60,600
Account executive	$37,400

The survey, quoted by the PRSA, found that salaries were higher in New York, Los Angeles, Atlanta, and Chicago and lower in Boston, Dallas, Houston, Washington, and San Francisco.[25] Another survey indicated that public relations agency vice president/group directors earned between $112,000 and $185,000 annually and that corporate public relations vice presidents earned between $113,500 and $182,000 annually.[26] Another PRWeek study described the "typical PR vice president" as a "female, married with kids, who works more than 50 hours per week and earns $137,800 per year."[27]

A 2012 Korn/Ferry study of 148 "chief communications officers (CCO)" polled the senior-most communication executives at Fortune 500 companies. This survey revealed a wide disparity among companies in terms of pay packages for communication officers. Two-thirds of those polled earned $175,000 and $349,000 a year. A handful had salaries in excess of $700,000 a year. And most were entitled to bonuses and equity compensation, with such annual bonuses averaging between $150,000 and $200,000.

The Korn/Ferry study was instructive in that nearly half these high-earning respondents reported to the company CEO and possessed an advanced degree, more than half were in the 46- to 55-year-old category, and most supervised a staff of less than 50 people. The survey concluded that "the CCO function is becoming broader and more vital to companies, especially as they are challenged to manage all of their stakeholder relations and their reputations."[28]

Women and Minorities

Two decades ago, the practice of public relations was overwhelmingly a bastion of white males. Today, it is women who predominate in public relations work. And minorities—African Americans, Asians, and Hispanics—while still small in total numbers in the field, have nonetheless increased their participation in public relations.

Fifty years ago, 27% of public relations practitioners were female; today that figure has grown to nearly 85%. Of the PRSA's 21,000 members, 73% are women.[29]

The issue of increased feminization of public relations—the establishment of a so-called velvet ghetto—is a particularly thorny one for the practice. One area of constant consternation is the traditional discrepancy between men's and women's salaries and upper-management positions—the glass ceiling for women in public relations.

The PRSA's "2010 Work, Life & Gender Survey" indicated that the average annual income for men in public relations was about $120,000; the figure for women was about $72,000. The study's conclusion: While the numbers of women entering public relations is growing, the salary gap between men and women is widening.[30] Many scholars have examined this troubling phenomenon and come up with theories. One researcher noted the fact that many in top management consider women as "natural born communicators," possessing "general feminine values such as cooperation, respect, interconnection, justice, equity, honesty, sensitivity, intuition, fairness, morality, commitment, etc." Such a belief "is a dangerous myth and represents highly questionable gender stereotypes."[31] Another researcher bluntly concluded that the 14% differential in pay between men and women in public relations could only be attributable to one thing: "gender discrimination."[32]

Predictably, 90% of chief communications officers at Fortune 500 companies are white men, while 2% are African American or black, 2% are Hispanic, and 6% are either Asian/Pacific Islander, multiracial, Native American/Alaska Native, or declined to state.[33]

One brighter ray in this gender picture is that recent experience may suggest that times are changing, albeit more slowly than some would prefer. University public relations programs across the country report a preponderance of female students, outnumbering males by as much as 80%. Moreover, the number of women executives in public relations has also increased in recent years. While the number of male public relations executives still exceeds the number of female public relations executives, the existence of a glass ceiling may be a phenomenon in decline.[34]

The fact remains, however, that the practice of public relations still has a ways to go in providing women and minorities opportunity for growth, development, and higher pay.

Last Word

In the 21st century, the practice of public relations is firmly accepted as part of the management process of any well-run organization. Indeed, the function of a CCO—chief communication officer—is a growing one throughout industry.

Public relations objectives and goals, strategies, and tactics must flow directly from the organization's overall goals. Public relations strategies must reflect organizational strategies, and tactics must be designed to realize the organization's business objectives. Stated another way, public relations programs are worth little if they fail to further management's and the organization's goals.

As media communications have proliferated and an organization's reputation has become more essential, the practice of public relations enjoys a significant management role and challenge in this new century. Coming out of the corporate and accounting scandals of the early 2000s and the loss of confidence in business and CEOs in the latter part of the first decade of the century, management must depend on the able assistance of proper public relations practice to help reestablish trust in society's major institutions.

That may be one reason why CNN Money listed public relations specialists as one of the fastest-growing professional jobs between now and 2014, predicted to increase by more than 22% annually.[35] Or, in the words of one public relations recruiter, "There has never been a better time to be in the business. And that will continue for the next 10 to 20 years."[36]

Discussion Starters

1. What is the management process of public relations?
2. Why is it imperative that public relations report to top management?
3. What are the elements that make up a public relations plan?
4. What questions must be answered in establishing valid public relations objectives?
5. What elements go into framing a public relations budget?
6. What were the "ethical implications" that confronted Fleischman-Hillard with its Canadian client?
7. What are the fundamental differences between working in a corporation and working in an agency as a public relations professional?
8. What are several of the primary tactical tasks assigned to the public relations function?
9. What may be the primary areas of opportunity for public relations professionals in the years ahead?
10. Why has the field of public relations been accused of being a "velvet ghetto"?

Pick of the Literature

Reputation Management: The Key to Successful PR and Corporate Communication

John Doorley and Helio Fred Garcia, New York: Taylor and Francis Group, 2006

Two eminent public relations professors (full disclosure: I work with 'em, but they're still "eminent!") prescribe a best-case formula for achieving positive recognition for any organization.

Both authors bring a wealth of corporate and consulting experience to this seminal work that transcends any other in the area of "reputation management." For one thing, the authors contend that reputation management can be measured, and they present methods to help quantify the elusive, but essential, commodity.

The authors dissect the various elements of managing one's reputation, from community relations to crisis. In terms of the latter, they detail, as definitively as anyone ever has, how an organization can respond effectively in the midst of crisis, by assessing specific measures that trigger strategic action. And they also offer five guest chapters, written by experienced practitioners, who have helped build reputations at leading corporations. Clearly, Doorley and Garcia have written the number-one text on "reputation management" in the practice of public relations.

Case Study   Crushing the CrackBerry

It hardly seemed possible.

By the summer of 2012, the company that created the legendary BlackBerry—the "crackberry," the use of which caused loyal users to become addicted—seemed on a collision course with oblivion. All signs pointed to Research in Motion—RIM, the company that at the start of the new century invented the handheld device that spread like wildfire—either being eviscerated for its parts or sold at fire sale prices.

As RIM announced yet another quarter of disappointing earnings in July 2012, its reputational fall from grace was stunning in its slope and severity.

RIM's decline was also testimony to the importance of effective public relations in the growth and development of a company and its products.

From Dominance to Devastation

RIM was founded in Waterloo, Ontario, Canada by Greek Canadian Mike Lazaridis, a computer genius who at the age of 12 won a prize for reading every science book in his local library. Together with his RIM co-chief executive Jim Balsille, Lazaridis introduced the revolutionary BlackBerry wireless mobile device in 1999, and the results were electric.

Celebrities from Lady Gaga and Brad Pitt to Nicki Minaj and Kim Kardashian were pictured with their BlackBerry devices by their side. The rise of "CrackBerry Nation" seemed unstoppable. Until, that is, the Apple iPhone entered the fray.

Competition from the iPhone and later Verizon's Droid Razr and many other upstarts caused RIM to lose its business focus and its public relations edge. By 2011, bad news for RIM turned *very* bad—and kept on coming.

- **Collapse of the U.S. market.** In 2011, BlackBerry's share of the U.S. smartphone market dropped to 10% from 49% in 2009.

- **Unfinished PlayBook Tablet.** In April, RIM released the BlackBerry PlayBook to compete against Apple's iPad. The half-finished PlayBook was greeted with underwhelming reviews. Why, people wondered, would the company introduce something that wasn't complete? RIM was forced to cut the tablet's price to $200 from $500, costing the company a $485 million write-down.

- **BlackBerry blackout.** In October, RIM's network suffered a well-publicized failure, causing service interruptions for customers around the world. RIM's restoration from the "BlackBerry blackout" took a full week, making it the longest service delay for the device in its 12-year history.

- **Sovereign conflicts.** As RIM worked to expand globally, it tangled with security regulations around the world. India threatened to ban BlackBerry service if RIM didn't comply with government rules. The country demanded access to communications sent over RIM's corporate services, and the two sides continued to debate.

- **Disappointing earnings.** In September, RIM announced that its quarterly income fell by nearly 60% from the year earlier. Its gross profit margins dropped, cash evaporated, and inventories more than doubled because of unwanted PlayBook tablets. In a conference call with analysts, the company's co-chief executives seemed oblivious to the bad news. Balsillie told analysts that one new model was "a thing of beauty to behold," sentiments founder Lazaridis echoed. Analysts weren't convinced. Said one conference call participant, "We question the company's long-term viability."

- **Phone delays.** In December, RIM announced it would have to delay the introduction of smartphones running the vaunted, new BlackBerry 10 operating system. The BlackBerry 10, viewed by many as the company's "last hope," wouldn't be ready until late in 2012.

By year-end 2011, BlackBerry had vacated its place as the smartphone of choice for serious professionals.

"Funny" Public Relations

At the start of 2012, with RIM's stock price in free fall, the company decided—finally!—to work on its public relations to try to right the ship.

In January, RIM named a new CEO to replace Lazaridis and Balsillie. The new man, Thorsten Heins, was a little known operations manager recruited from Siemens four years earlier (Figure 5-6). Rather than encourage a new start for the company, Heins spent his press conference introduction reiterating that the strategy his

FIGURE 5-6   Bizarro world.
New Research in Motion CEO Thorstein Heins looks lonely as he chairs a BlackBerry World event in Orlando in May 2012. *(Photo: DAVID MANNING/REUTERS/Newscom)*

predecessors had begun "was sound and destined for success." In fact, said CEO Heins, he had asked both former co-CEOs to remain with the company in advisory capacities.

Immediately after the new CEO's introductory news conference, shares of RIM stock fell 8.5%.

RIM followed its new CEO launch with another launch in February—a quartet of masked and caped superhero characters to serve as marketing symbols for the company's new and improved tag line, "Be bold."

The caped crusaders—Gogo Girl (the Achiever), Max Stone (the Adventurer), Justin Steele (the Advocate), and Trudy Foreal (the Authentic)—appeared in cartoon form on the company's BlackBerry blog. The company invited blog reader feedback.

Big mistake.

Among the responses:

- "Did you really just waste all of your innovation points on marketing Blackberrys to tweens with Pixar inspired cartoon characters?"

- "Disgusted. Target audience has always been business people. Are you quitting on them and targeting kids?"

- "Are you kidding me? A product line that the entire world knows is completely archaic and uncool and you think cartoon superheroes will help save you?"

To combat the vituperative viral vivisection, CEO Heins said the superheroes would be making only a one-time appearance on the blog.

A month later, RIM was back with another cockamamie idea. It hired two young comedians as part of a youth-oriented campaign called "The New 2012 Challenge Council Project." The job of the two comics, according to a company online posting, was to "shut down BlackBerry trash talk once and for all."

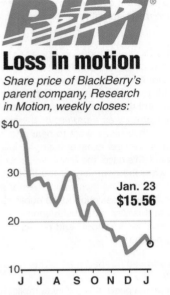

Loss in motion

Share price of BlackBerry's parent company, Research in Motion, weekly closes:

Jan. 23
$15.56

J J A S O N D J

FIGURE 5-7   Going down.
The precipitous decline of the stock of a once-promising company was a bitter pill for gullible RIM stockholders (one of whom wrote this furshlugginer book!). *(Photo: Staff/MCT/Newscom)*

In June, with RIM's stock down a breathtaking 80% in one year, hovering on the verge of single digits (Figure 5-7), the doomed device maker disclosed one additional piece of news that spoke volumes for where the once-proud company found itself.

The company said in a securities filing that it had awarded its two former co-chief executives $12 million in exit payments earlier in the year.

Just when all seemed lost, in 2013, RIM officially changed its corporate name to "BlackBerry" and introduced its long-awaited Z10 hand held device—to surprisingly good reviews. Let's hope.*

Questions

1. How would you describe RIM's business response to increased mobile device competition?

2. How would you describe its public relations reaction?

3. What's your reaction to its attempts at comedic public relations responses to competitive pressures?

4. What would be your overall public relations strategy if you were RIM's public relations director?

*For further information, see Brian X. Chen, "RIMS's Year of Misery," *The New York Times*, December 16, 2011; Ian Austen, "RIM Suffers as Profit Falls 58.7%," *The New York Times*, September 15, 2011; Ian Austen, "BlackBerry Owners Aren't Big Fans of Cartoons," *The New York Times*, February 1, 2012; Ian Austen, "RIM Tries Being Funny," *The New York Times*, March 8, 2012; Ian Austen, "Research in Motion Reveals Multimillion-Dollar Pay for Former Chief Executives," *The New York Times*, June 14, 2012; Ian Austen and Kevin J. O'Brien, "Markets Are Not Convinced by a New Leader at RIM," *The New York Times*, January 23, 2011; and Daniel Tencer, "BlackBerry Outage: Can RIM's Reputation Survive This PR Disaster," *Huffington Post*, December 13, 2011.

From the Top
An Interview with Peter Drucker

Peter Drucker, who died in 2005 at the age of 95, was called the "greatest thinker management theory has produced" by the *London Economist.* His work influenced Winston Churchill, Bill Gates, Jack Welch, and the Japanese business establishment. His more than three dozen books, written over 66 years and translated into 30 languages, also delivered his philosophy to newly promoted managers just out of the office cubicle. Dr. Drucker counseled presidents, bishops, baseball managers, CEOs, and symphony conductors on the finer points of management success. In his 88th year, Dr. Drucker sat with the author for this interview.

What would you say have been your greatest contributions to business and society?
One, I made management visible. People say I've discovered management—that's nonsense. I made it into a discipline.

Second, I was also the first one who said that people are a resource and not just a cost, and they have to be placed where they can make a contribution. The only ones who took me up on it were the Japanese for a long time.

The third one is knowledge—that knowledge work would be preeminent.

Four, I was the first to say that the purpose of business is to create the customer and to innovate. That I think is a major contribution. That took a long time to sink in—that management is not this mad dog of internal rules and regulations, that it's a discipline that can be learned and taught and practiced.

I think those four. The rest are secondary.

What is your view of today's public relations practice?
There is no public relations. There's publicity, promotion, advertising; but "relations" by definition is a two-way street. And the more important job and the more difficult is not to bring business and the executives to the outside but to bring the outside to these terribly insulated people. And this will be far more important in the next 20 years, when the outside is going to change beyond all recognition. I'm not only talking business CEOs but also university presidents and even bishops—several of my charity patients are bishops—all need to know what's going on outside.

Can you elaborate?
With an example. Have you ever heard of Paul Garrett?

Paul Garrett came out of journalism. He wanted to build a proper public relations department, to bring to General Motors what the outside was like. He would have been very effective. But GM didn't let him. Alfred Sloan (GM's CEO) brought Garrett

in 1930 to keep GM out of *Fortune. Fortune* was founded as a muckraking magazine with investigative journalism.

Why didn't Sloan, supposedly one of the greatest managers of all time, want to listen to Garrett?
Neither Sloan nor anybody else in top management of General Motors wanted to hear what Garrett would have told them. And this was still the case much later.

Paul Garrett was a professional who would have told them things they didn't want to hear and wouldn't believe. Killing the messenger is never the right policy.

And in GM's case, the employee relations people totally failed to warn the company of the horrible sit-down strike they would suffer. And then when investor relations became important, it wasn't assigned to the public relations people.

And to this day, most institutions still look upon public relations as their "trumpet" and not as their "hearing aid." It's got to be both.

What do you see as the future of the practice of public relations?
I think there is a need. It is a very complicated and complex function. The media are no longer homogenous and are much more critical. But there is a need for an intermediary to tell the truth to management. Public relations people today don't do that because they're scared, because the people they work for don't like to hear what they don't want to hear.

Let's face it. There's an old saying, "If I have you for a friend, I don't need an enemy."

Public Relations Library

Austin, Erica Weintraub, and Bruce E. Pinkleton. *Strategic Public Relations Management* (2nd ed.). Mahwah, NJ: Lawrence Erlbaum Associates, 2006. Solid emphasis on public relations planning and research theory and technique.

Aylward, Scott, and Patty Moore. *Confessions from the Corner Office.* New York: John Wiley & Sons, 2007. Two communications executives, who rose through the ranks, credit their mastery of "the art of survival and behavior."

Bloom, Robert H., and Dave Conti. *The Inside Advantage: The Strategy that Unlocks the Hidden Growth in Your Business.* New York: McGraw-Hill, 2007. Words of wisdom from an experienced business CEO, who suggests that every company has "hidden strengths," which it must find, unleash, and communicate.

Croft, A. C. *Managing a PR Firm for Growth and Profit.* New York: Haworth Press, 2006. A public relations agency executive offers advice on attracting, winning, and keeping clients.

Dilenschneider, Robert. *A Time for Heroes.* Bell Gardens, CA: Phoenix Press, 2005. A public relations veteran interviews business leaders and others on who they consider to be "heroes" and why.

Gregory, Anne. *Planning and Managing Public Relations Campaigns* (3rd ed.). London, England: Kogan, 2010. Detailed discussion on how research, planning, and theory contribute to solving public relations problems.

Ihlen, Oyvind, Betteke Van Ruler, and Magnus Fredrikkson (Eds.). *Public Relations and Social Theory.* New York: Routledge, 2009. Confronting public relations as a social phenomenon with a decidedly global perspective.

Lukaszewski, James E. *Why Should the Boss Listen to You? The 7 Disciplines of the Trusted Strategic Advisor.* New York: Jossey Bass/Wiley, 2008. An experienced management counselor offers advice on landing a seat at the management table, based on trustworthiness, thinking strategically, and developing a management perspective.

Rivkin, Steve, and Fraser P. Seitel. *Ideawise: How to Transform Today's Ideas into Tomorrow's Innovations.* New York: John Wiley & Sons, 2002. Two communications veterans (one of whom is exceedingly good looking) provide common sense rules on sparking creativity and "finding the muse."

Smith, Ronald D. *Strategic Planning for Public Relations.* New York: Routledge, 2009. Worthwhile explanation of the importance of reasoned and logical planning in solving public relations problems, with a wide array of contemporary cases included.

Swann, Patricia. *Cases in Public Relations Management.* New York: Routledge, 2010. Good discussion of contemporary cases in media relations, ethical public relations, and other areas.

Theaker, Alison. *The Public Relations Handbook* (4th ed.). New York: Routledge, 2012. Soup-to-nuts glossary of public relations practice, with elements of management.

Toth, Elizabeth (Ed.). *The Future of Excellence in Public Relations and Communication Management.* Mahwah, NJ: Lawrence Erlbaum, 2007. A research-oriented, scholarly discussion, with contributions from leading academics in the field.

Chapter **6**

Ethics

Chapter Objectives

1. To discuss the one aspect that should differentiate public relations from the law and other business pursuits—ethics.
2. To explore ethics—or the lack thereof—in today's business, government, media, and public relations cultures.
3. To discuss the concept of corporate social responsibility.
4. To underscore the bedrock importance of public relations professionals "doing the right thing."

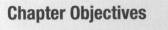

FIGURE 6-1 From parking lot to slammer.
Fleishman-Hillard's convicted public relations chief in more carefree times. *(Photo: ZUMA Press/Newscom)*

*L*OS ANGELES, CA Jan. 7, 2011—*A former executive for an international public relations firm must begin serving his prison sentence after an appeals court refused to overturn his conviction for defrauding Los Angeles taxpayers.*

An attorney for 61-year-old Douglas Dowie tells the Los Angeles Times *Friday that the former head of the Los Angeles office of Fleishman-Hillard Inc. will begin serving the 3 1/2-year term in federal prison next month.*

Dowie was convicted in 2006 of conspiracy and wire fraud for padding consulting bills to the city Department of Water and Power and other clients for more than $500,000 from 2000 to 2003.

The firm paid the city $6 million in 2004 to settle a related lawsuit.

Dowie's former aide, John Stodder Jr., was sentenced to one year and three months in prison. His appeal is pending.[1]

Poor Douglas Dowie, public relations man turned jailbird (Figure 6-1).

Dowie, former power broker as head of the Fleishman-Hillard public relations office in Los Angeles during the mayoral administration of Jim Hahn, used his friendship with the mayor to overcharge the city's Department of Water and Power about $50,000 a month for three years, according to those who testified against him.[2] Dowie and two Fleishman-Hillard subordinates were fined and sent to prison.

The fate of the three was just one indication that more and more society expected public relations professionals to conduct themselves ethically in pursuit of their increasingly high-powered assignments.

- In 2010, the U.S. Federal Trade Commission settled a complaint against public relations firm Reverb Communications for using employees to pose as ordinary customers to post glowing reviews of client video games on Apple's iTunes store.[3]

- In 2011, former Bill Clinton White House apologist Lanny Davis grudgingly resigned from serving as public relations representative for murderous Ivory Coast leader Laurent Gbagbo. Davis, who wrote a book about the importance of "transparency" in public relations, was the subject of withering criticism for serving as a hired gun for a Gbagbo regime that reportedly committed legendary human rights abuses.[4]

- In 2012, Walmart cut its ties with Mercury Public Relations after a junior staff member at the L.A. public relations firm showed up at an anti-Walmart union news conference, posing as a reporter. The union discovered the ruse and alerted the media.[5]

The practice of public relations is all about earning *credibility*. Credibility, in turn, begins with telling the truth. Public relations, then, must be based on "doing the right thing"—in other words, acting ethically.

In the 21st century, with scandals popping up periodically in every sector of society—from politics to religion, from business to sports—the subject of ethics is a pervasive one.

What precisely are *ethics*?

A sociologist posed that question to business people and got these answers:

- "Ethics has to do with what my feelings tell me is right or wrong."
- "Ethics has to do with my religious beliefs."
- "Being ethical is doing what the law requires."
- "Ethics consists of the standards of behavior our society accepts."
- "I don't know what the word means."

Classical ethics means different things to different people. Ethics theories range from utilitarianism (i.e., the greatest good for the greatest number) to deontology (i.e., do what is right, though the world should perish).

While the meaning of ethics may be hard to pin down, there's no secret to what constitutes unethical behavior. Unfortunately, it's all around us. Consider the following:

- In **government**, ethical lapses know no party affiliation. Washington seems perpetually rocked by ethical scandals. In 2010, longtime New York congressman Charley Rangel was convicted of a variety of ethical offenses, all stemming from his misuse of power.[6] (The disgraced Rangel, whose career would have been doomed in any other profession, came back to win primary reelection in 2012. But hey, that's politics!) In 2011, Rangel's New York colleague Anthony Weiner resigned from the House after it was revealed he had sent provocative tweets to female followers (see Case Study in Chapter 12).[7] In the summer of 2012, President Obama's Justice Department was called to task for its questionable Operation Fast and Furious, which allowed thousands of guns to be bought by arms traffickers in the hopes of exposing Mexican drug cartels. On the Republican side, when former George W. Bush Presidential Press Secretary Scott McClellan wrote a tell-all memoir in 2008, critics decried his ethical impropriety (see PR Ethics Mini-Case in this chapter).

- In **business**, insider trading scandals, where Wall Street fat cats bilked unsuspecting investors out of millions, have dominated the news in recent years. Hedge fund titans Bernie Madoff, Allen Stanford, Raj Rajaratnam, and disgraced former McKinsey & Co. CEO Rajat Gupta all faced hard time after their unethical behavior was displayed before the world.

- In **sports**, several of history's most legendary baseball players, from slugging Mark McGwire to fire-balling Roger Clemens to slammin' Sammy Sosa to all-everything Alex "A-Rod" Rodriguez, were all tarnished in the wake of the sport's 21st-century steroids scandal. Even revered cyclist Lance Armstrong couldn't escape the reality that doping gave him an unfair advantage.[8]

- In **education**, the president of Penn State University was drummed out in 2011 in the wake of the pedophilia scandal that also cost football coach Joe Paterno his job—and, some argued, his life. President Graham Spanier, whom all agreed did a superlative job in building Penn State's reputation, nonetheless was found wanting in covering up the awful Jerry Sandusky scandal (see Case Study in Chapter 13).[9]

- Similar charges of sexual abuse embroiled the venerable **Catholic Church** in ethical scandals from the beginning of the decade under Pope John Paul II and later under his successor, Pope Benedict XVI.

- In the realm of **nonprofit organizations,** supposed to aid those less fortunate, ethical improprieties also weren't uncommon. For example, in 2012, CNN revealed that a charity designed to serve veterans with disabilities had instead squandered millions of dollars on marketing costs that benefited Disabled Veterans National Foundation's organizers.[10]

- As noted, not even the practice of **public relations** could escape serious ethical lapses, as the Fleishman-Hillard, Walmart, Lanny Davis, and other ethical scandals revealed.

Again, public relations professionals are expected to *do the right thing*. The cardinal rule of public relations is to *never lie*.

Nonetheless, in one startling survey at the turn of the century of 1,700 public relations executives, it was revealed that 25% of those interviewed admitted they had "lied on the job," 39% said they had exaggerated the truth, and another 44% said they had felt "uncertain" about the ethics of what they did.[11]

While the industry never repeated that survey (Wonder why?), the Public Relations Society of America (PRSA) did invest $100,000 in revamping its code of ethics. The code (see Appendix A), underscored by six fundamental values that the PRSA believes vital to the integrity of the profession (see Figure 6-2), demonstrates the significance of ethics to the practice of public relations.

FIGURE 6-2 **PRSA's six values.**
The values of advocacy, honesty, expertise, independence, loyalty, and fairness form the basis of the PRSA ethical code.
(Copyright Public Relations Society of America. Reprinted by permission)

PRSA Member Code of Ethics 2000

PRSA Member Statement of Professional Values

This statement presents the core values of PRSA members and, more broadly, of the public relations profession. These values provide the foundation for the Member Code of Ethics and set the industry standard for the professional practice of public relations. These values are the fundamental beliefs that guide our behaviors and decision-making process. We believe our professional values are vital to the integrity of the profession as a whole.

ADVOCACY

We serve the public interest by acting as responsible advocates for those we represent. We provide a voice in the marketplace of ideas, facts, and viewpoints to aid informed public debate.

HONESTY

We adhere to the highest standards of accuracy and truth in advancing the interests of those we represent and in communicating with the public.

EXPERTISE

We acquire and responsibly use specialized knowledge and experience. We advance the profession through continued professional development, research, and education. We build mutual understanding, credibility, and relationships among a wide array of institutions and audiences.

INDEPENDENCE

We provide objective counsel to those we represent. We are accountable for our actions.

LOYALTY

We are faithful to those we represent, while honoring our obligation to serve the public interest.

FAIRNESS

We deal fairly with clients, employers, competitors, peers, vendors, the media, and the general public. We respect all opinions and support the right of free expression.

The Public Relations Society of America, 33 Irving Place, New York, NY 10003-2376

Doing the Right Thing

What exactly are ethics? The answer isn't an easy one.

The Josephson Institute, which studies ethics, defines ethics as *standards of conduct that indicate how one should behave based on moral duties and virtues.*

In general, ethics are the values that guide a person, organization, or society—concepts such as right and wrong, fairness and unfairness, honesty and dishonesty. An individual's conduct is measured not only against his or her conscience but also against some norm of acceptability that society or an organization has determined.

Roughly translated, an individual's or organization's ethics comes down to the standards that are followed in relationships with others—the real integrity of the individual or organization. Obviously, a person's ethical construct and approach depend on numerous factors—cultural, religious, and educational, among others. Complicating the issue is that what might seem right to one person might not matter to someone else. No issue is solely black or white but is rather a shade of gray—particularly in making public relations decisions.

That is not to say that classical ethical distinctions don't exist. They do. Philosophers throughout the ages have debated the essence of ethics.

- *Utilitarianism* suggests considering the "greater good" rather than what may be best for the individual.

- To Aristotle, the *golden mean of moral virtue* could be found between two extreme points of view.

- Kant's *categorical imperative* recommended acting "on that maxim which you will to become a universal law."

- Mill's *principle of utility* recommended "seeking the greatest happiness for the greatest number."

- The traditional *Judeo-Christian ethic* prescribes "loving your neighbor as yourself." Indeed, this golden rule makes good sense as well in the practice of public relations.

Because the practice of public relations is misunderstood by so many—even including some of those for whom public relations people work—public relations people, in particular, must be ethical. They can't assume that ethics are strictly personal choices without relevance or related methodology for resolving moral quandaries. Public relations people must adhere to a high standard of professional ethics, with truth as the key determinant of their conduct.

Indeed, ethics must be the great differentiator between public relations practice and other functions. Public relations people must always tell the truth. That doesn't mean they divulge "everything" about those for whom they work. But it does mean that they should never, ever lie. All one has in public relations is his or her reputation. When you lie, you lose it. So a high sense of ethical conduct must distinguish those who practice public relations.

Professional ethics, often called *applied ethics,* suggests a commonly accepted sense of professional conduct that is translated into formal codes of ethics.

The essence of the codes of conduct of both the PRSA and the International Association of Business Communicators is that honesty and fairness lie at the heart of public relations practice. Indeed, if the ultimate goal of the public relations professional is to enhance public trust of an organization, then only the highest ethical conduct is acceptable.

Inherent in these standards of the profession is the understanding that ethics have changed and continue to change as society changes. Over time, views have changed on such issues as discrimination, the treatment of women and minorities, pollution of the environment, concern for human rights, acceptable standards of language and dress, and so on. Again, honesty and fairness are two critical components that will continue to determine the ethical behavior of public relations professionals.

Boiled down to its essence, the ethical heart of the practice of public relations lies, again, in posing only one simple question to management: *Are we doing the right thing?* In posing that critical question, the public relations officer becomes the "conscience" of the organization.

Often the public relations professional will be the only member of management with the nerve to pose such a question. Sometimes this means saying no to what the boss wants to do. Public relations professionals must be driven by one purpose—to preserve, defend, sustain, and enhance the health and vitality of the organization. Simply translated, the bottom line for public relations professionals must always be to counsel and to do what is in the best long-term interests of the organization.

Ethics in Business

For many people today, regrettably, the term *business ethics* is an oxymoron. Its mere mention stimulates images of disgraced CEOs being led away in handcuffs after bilking their shareholders and employees out of millions of dollars. In one period alone, the 2012 "summer of shame," a dizzying array of corporate executives was charged with ethical violations.

- The summer began with Irving H. Picard, the trustee overseeing the liquidation of Bernard Madoff's investment advisory firm, receiving permission to "claw back" profits from those Madoff rewarded in his Ponzi scheme that bilked investors out of some $7.3 billion—the most costly swindle in investing history.

- The Madoff number was just slightly more than high-flying Texas financier R. Allan Stanford was convicted of swindling out of investors over a two-decade scam involving 30,000 investors in 113 countries.

- In June, the conviction of Rajat Gupta was perhaps the most shocking scandal of all. Gupta, former McKinsey CEO and a member of the board of premier investment banker Goldman Sachs, was an eminently respected business leader. But he also turned out to be a common criminal, feeding insider information to convicted hedge fund felon Raj Rajaratnam (Figure 6-3).

Gupta's conviction culminated a wave of insider trading cases that yielded 66 indictments and 60 convictions over two-and-a-half years. These followed business scandals earlier in the decade that exposed subprime lenders as crooks, banks and other financial institutions as less-than-responsible stewards of public wealth, and CEOs as suspect in terms of ethics and credibility. With venerable companies such as Bear Stearns and Lehman Brothers going out of business and others, such as AIG and General Motors (GM), tottering, the early part of the 21st century was not a stellar period for business credibility.

No wonder confidence in business has deteriorated. One 2011 survey by the Ethics Resource Center found that although employees seemed more ethical in their own jobs, more employees had negative views of the ethics of their supervisors. Confidence in senior leadership fell to 62% in 2011, matching the historic low of 2,000 and down six points from just two years earlier. One-third of U.S. employees said their own managers "didn't exercise ethical behavior."[12]

FIGURE 6-3
Escort service.
Raj Rajaratnam, one of Wall Street's most powerful hedge fund managers, is escorted by the FBI in 2009 after being arrested for earning millions from illegally obtained stock tips. *(Photo: BRENDAN MCDERMID/REUTERS/ Newscom)*

Indeed, many believed "crooked CEO" was redundant. One book, written by former management consultants, described CEOs thusly:

> *Among the more than 14,000 publicly registered companies in the U.S. and the even larger number of privately held companies there is a class of people who will lie to the public, the regulators, their employees and anyone else in order to increase personal wealth and power.*[13]

To stem the feeling that chief executives and their companies weren't acting ethically, a number of firms increased their efforts to make their activities more transparent to the public. Companies from Coca-Cola to Amazon.com to General Electric announced plans to make accounting procedures more understandable. One CEO, Henry Paulson of investment banking giant Goldman Sachs, called on his fellow CEOs, in a memorable speech, to reform before regulation forced them to do so: "In my lifetime, American business has never been under such scrutiny. To be blunt, much of it is deserved."[14] Paulson's call for business ethics helped secure his selection as Secretary of the Treasury under President George W. Bush; where later he presided over the meltdown and thankful recovery of the U.S. financial system.

Corporate Codes of Conduct

By the second decade of the 21st century, most organizations devoted an increasing amount of time and attention to corporate ethics.

The vast majority of companies conducted periodic risk assessments, with more than half doing so annually. Three-quarters of all companies conducted training in such areas as sexual/workplace harassment, conflicts of interest, and protecting confidential information. Many firms devoted upwards of $500,000 a year, exclusive of personnel costs, for ethics and compliance programs.[15]

Most organizations also adopted formal codes of conduct to guide their activities. A code of conduct is a formal statement of the values and business practices of a corporation. A code may be a short mission statement, or it may be a sophisticated document that requires compliance with articulated standards and that has a complicated enforcement mechanism. Whatever its length and complexity, the corporate code of conduct dictates the behavioral expectations that an organization holds for its employees and agents.

Formal codes of conduct can help accomplish a number of public relations purposes.

- **To increase public confidence.** Scandals, credit crises, oil shocks, etc., have all shaken investor confidence and have led to a decline of public trust and confidence in business. Many firms have responded with written codes of ethics.

- **To stem the tide of regulation.** As public confidence has declined, government regulation of business has increased. Some estimated the cost to society of compliance with regulations at $100 billion per year. Corporate codes of conduct, it was hoped, would help serve as a self-regulation mechanism.

- **To improve internal operations.** As companies became larger and more decentralized, management needed consistent standards of conduct to ensure that employees were meeting the business objectives of the company in a legal and ethical manner.

- **To respond to transgressions.** Frequently, when a company itself is caught in the web of unethical behavior, it responds with its own code of ethics.

Ralph Waldo Emerson once wrote, "An organization is the lengthened shadow of a man." Today, many corporate executives realize that just as an individual has certain responsibilities as a citizen, so, too, does a corporate citizen have responsibilities to the society in which it is privileged to operate.

As business becomes globalized, companies are being encouraged by interest groups, governments, educational institutions, industry associations, and others to adopt codes of conduct. Accordingly, formal ethical codes, addressing such topics as executive compensation, accounting procedures, confidentiality of corporate information, misappropriation of corporate assets, bribes and kickbacks, and political contributions, have become a corporate fact of life for every company executive, up to and including the members of the board of directors.

Corporate Social Responsibility

Closely related to the ethical conduct of an organization is its corporate social responsibility (CSR). Simply stated, CSR is about how companies manage the business processes to produce an overall positive impact on society. This implies that any social institution, from the smallest family unit to the largest corporation, is responsible for the behavior of its members and may be held accountable for their misdeeds.

In the late 1960s, when this idea was just emerging, initial responses were of the knee-jerk variety. A firm that was threatened by increasing legal or activist pressures and harassment would ordinarily change its policies in a hurry. Today, however, organizations and their social responsibility programs are much more sophisticated. Social responsibility is treated just like any other management discipline: Analyze the issues, evaluate performance, set priorities, allocate resources to those priorities, and implement programs that deal with issues within the constraints of the organization's resources. Many companies have created special committees to set the agenda and target the objectives.

Social responsibility touches practically every level of organizational activity, from marketing to hiring, from training to work standards. A partial list of social responsibility categories might include the following:

- **Product lines**—dangerous products, product performance and standards, packaging, and environmental impact
- **Marketing practices**—sales practices, consumer complaint policies, advertising content, and fair pricing
- **Corporate philanthropy**—contribution performance, encouragement of employee participation in social projects, and community development activities
- **Environmental activities**—pollution control and climate change projects, adherence to federal standards, and evaluation procedures for new packages and products
- **External relations**—support of minority enterprises, investment practices, and government relations
- **Employment diversity in retaining and promoting minorities and women**—current hiring policies, advancement policies, specialized career counseling, and opportunities for special minorities such as the physically handicapped
- **Employee safety and health**—work environment policies, accident safeguards, and food and medical facilities

More often than not, organizations have incorporated social responsibility into the mainstream of their practices. Most firms recognize that social responsibility, far from being an add-on program, must be a corporate way of life. They recognize that in a skeptical world, business must be responsible to act ethically and improve the quality of life of their workforce, their families, and the broader society.

Outside the Lines
Test Your Workplace Ethics

So you want to enter the workplace? The question of ethics looms larger today than at any previous time, especially with the advent of technology and the potential abuses it brings.

To test how you might measure up as an ethical worker, answer the following questions. And don't cheat!

Questions

1. Is it wrong to use company email for personal reasons?
2. Is it wrong to use office equipment to help your family and friends with homework?
3. Is it wrong to play computer games on office equipment during the workday?
4. Is it wrong to use office equipment to do Internet shopping?
5. Is it unethical to visit pornographic Websites using office equipment?
6. What's the value at which a gift from a supplier or client becomes troubling?
7. Is a $50 gift to a boss unacceptable?
8. Is it okay to take a pair of $200 football tickets as a gift from a supplier?
9. Is it okay to take a $120 pair of theater tickets?

10. Is it okay to take a $100 holiday fruit basket?

11. Is it okay to take a $25 gift certificate?

12. Is it okay to accept a $75 prize won at a raffle at a supplier's conference?

Answers

From a cross-section of workers at nationwide companies, the answers to these questions were compiled by the Ethics Officer Association, Belmont, Massachusetts, and the Ethical Leadership Group, Wilmette, Illinois.

1. 34% said personal email on company computers is wrong.

2. 37% said using office equipment for homework is wrong.

3. 49% said playing computer games at work is wrong.

4. 44% said Internet shopping at work is wrong.

5. 87% said it is unethical to visit pornographic sites at work.

6. 33% said $25 is the amount at which a gift from a supplier or client becomes troubling. Another 33% said $50. Another 33% said $100.

7. 35% said a $50 gift to the boss is unacceptable.

8. 70% said it is unacceptable to take $200 football tickets.

9. 70% said it is unacceptable to take $120 theater tickets.

10. 35% said it is unacceptable to take a $100 fruit basket.

11. 45% said it is unacceptable to take a $25 gift certificate.

12. 40% said it is unacceptable to take the $75 raffle prize.

Ethics in Government

Politics has never enjoyed an unblemished reputation when it comes to ethics. In the first two decades of the 21st century—with the U.S. political system polarized between harsh right and hard left—politicians seemed to be losing more ground in terms of trustworthiness and ethical values.

Both the legislative and executive branches of the federal government took a beating in the public eye. Congress, according to Gallup polling, "reduced its public approval rating in the winter of 2013 to 14%. That means that the other 86%" of the nation had real trouble with the ethics and ability of Congress. But at least the rating was better than the 10% congressional approval rating recorded at the beginning of 2012.[16] The president generally fared better than Congress, but presidential approval still had trouble consistently piercing the 50% approval barrier.

The advent of 24-hour cable news and the 24/7 Internet blogosphere cast a perpetual 21st-century spotlight on the activities of the president and his allies. No administration could escape the harsh glare of prying eyes noting ethical failures. President Bill Clinton suffered the ultimate ethical ignominy: being impeached by the House of Representatives for his inexplicable and shocking behavior with a young intern in the White House. Both President George Bush and Vice President Dick Cheney were criticized harshly for everything from the disposition of and reasons for war in Iraq to their past corporate energy affiliations. President Obama, as he ran for reelection in 2012, also was attacked by critics for everything from politicizing his declaration of a path to citizenship for children of illegal immigrants to his Justice Department's "Fast and Furious" decision to provide guns to Mexican arms traffickers.

The "sleaze factor" in government continued to poison politics.

■ In 2008, New York's crusading Democrat Governor Elliott Spitzer was forced from office when he was found to have been a client of a high-priced prostitution ring. Later that year, Congressman Rangel faced a series of ethics violations and failure to comply with tax laws.

■ In 2009, Republican Mark Sanford refused to resign as South Carolina governor after his extramarital affair was exposed. He ultimately lost his family and his job.

■ In 2011, Democrat Congressman Anthony Weiner was drummed out of the House for sexting young women pictures of his . . . well, never mind. Later that year, Republican presidential primary candidate Herman Cain was upended by allegations of sexual misconduct.

■ In 2012, former Democrat senator and presidential candidate John Edwards was exonerated from charges of using campaign funds to hide a mistress and love-child, although the damage to his career was done.

Whew!

After all the white-collar crime and political scandals that have marked the first two decades of the 21st century, the public is less willing to tolerate such ethical violations from their elected officials. It is likely that ethics in government will become an even more important issue as voters insist on representatives who are honest, trustworthy, and ethical.

PR Ethics Mini-Case
The Sad Memoir of Scott McClellan

By 2006, when he was "relieved" of his duties as President George W. Bush's press secretary, Scott McClellan was a dazed and bitter man.

Arguably one of the weakest presidential press secretaries in history, McClellan was labeled "the human piñata" because of the way he was battered at White House press conferences.

Forced to deal with several embarrassing White House problems, not the least of which was the accusation against Vice President Dick Cheney and his deputy, Lewis Libby, in leaking the name of a CIA operative, McClellan was forced to endure constant battering at the hands of an empowered White House press corps. If nothing else, he served the Bush Administration as a "good soldier" (Figure 6-4).

FIGURE 6-4   Et tu Brute?
President George Bush welcomes incoming Press Secretary Scott McClellan to the White House as successor Ari Fleischer looks on. *(Photo: Shawn Thew/EPA/Newscom)*

In the spring of 2006, McClellan was mercifully replaced by Fox News broadcaster Tony Snow, who quickly brought order and credibility back to the press secretary job with a confident, open approach.

A year later, inexplicably, Scott McClellan turned on the hand that had fed him for his entire career as a government employee. Indeed, George W. Bush had loyally taken McClellan with him from the State House in Texas to the White House in Washington for the better part of two decades.

But when McClellan left the White House, he let his former patron have it with both barrels blazing.

In his memoir, segments of which were leaked less than a year after his White House departure, McClellan ripped into Bush, claiming his former mentor, among other things:

- Relied on "propaganda" to sell the Iraq war,
- Veered "terribly off course" in war policy,
- Refused to be "open and forthright on Iraq," and
- Took a "permanent campaign approach" to governing.

The McClellan memoir sent shockwaves through Washington and was an instant bestseller. Democratic opponents of President Bush hailed it as a "smoking gun," revealing all the improprieties of the Bush White House.

But others wondered about the "ethics" of a former press secretary choosing to attack the only former client he ever had, a man whom the press secretary had publicly praised just months before the tell-all book.

Moreover, if the essence of public relations counsel is to advise an employer on "how to act," some wondered why McClellan hadn't offered the advice to the president when he served next to him, rather than criticizing him, for money, well after the fact.*

Questions

1. How would you assess Scott McClellan's ethical responsibility to be loyal to his boss versus his ethical responsibility to reveal what happened at the White House?

2. What are the public relations ethical considerations revealed by the McClellan case?

*For further information, see Mike Allen, "McClellan Rips Bush, White House," Politico.com (May 27, 2008); Elisabeth Bumiller, "In Ex-Spokesman's Book, Harsh Words for Bush," *The New York Times* (May 28, 2008); and Fraser P. Seitel, "The Sad Memoir of Scott McClellan," odwyerpr.com (November 26, 2007).

Ethics in Journalism

The Society of Professional Journalists is quite explicit on the subject of ethics (Figure 6-5).

Journalists at all times will show respect for the dignity, privacy, rights, and well-being of people encountered in the course of gathering and presenting the news.

1. The news media should not communicate unofficial charges affecting reputation or moral character without giving the accused a chance to reply.

2. The news media must guard against invading a person's right to privacy.

3. The media should not pander to morbid curiosity about details of vice and crime.

And so on.

Unfortunately, what is in the code often doesn't reflect what appears in print or on the air. More often than not, journalistic judgments run smack into ethical principles—especially in a day when every citizen is a publisher on the Internet.

- Plagiarism scandals at three of the nation's leading newspapers—*The New York Times, Washington Post,* and *Boston Globe*—resulted in the firings of high-profile journalists. The *Times* fell victim to the new century's most embarrassing instance of suspect journalistic ethics. In 2003, the "Great Gray Lady" was stunned when one of its promising young reporters, Jayson Blair, was discovered to have fabricated numerous dispatches for the paper over an extended period. The *Times* found out about Blair's fraud only when a reporter from another paper tipped it off. Blair was immediately fired, and the *Times* took a major reputation hit.

- In 2005, the *Times* was shocked again after one of its star reporters, Judith Miller, served 85 days in prison for refusing to reveal confidential administration sources related to stories involving the leak of the name of a CIA operative

FIGURE 6-5
Journalists' code.
The Society of Professional Journalists has elaborated in some detail on the ethical guidelines that should govern all journalists. *(Photo: Copyright © 1996–2007. Reprinted by permission of the Society of Professional Journalists, www.spj.org)*

THE SOCIETY OF PROFESSIONAL JOURNALISTS, SIGMA DELTA CHI

Code of Ethics

THE SOCIETY of Professional Journalists, Sigma Delta Chi believes the duty of journalists is to serve the truth.

WE BELIEVE the agencies of mass communication are carriers of public discussion and information, acting on their Constitutional mandate and freedom to learn and report the facts.

WE BELIEVE in public enlightenment as the forerunner of justice, and in our Constitutional role to seek the truth as part of the public's right to know the truth.

WE BELIEVE those responsibilities carry obligations that require journalists to perform with intelligence, objectivity, accuracy and fairness.

To these ends, we declare acceptance of the standards of practice here set forth:

RESPONSIBILITY:
The public's right to know of events of public importance and interest is the overriding mission of the mass media. The purpose of distributing news and enlightened opinion is to serve the general welfare. Journalists who use their professional status as representatives of the public for selfish or other unworthy motives violate a high trust.

FREEDOM OF THE PRESS:
Freedom of the press is to be guarded as an inalienable right of people in a free society. It carries with it the freedom and the responsibility to discuss, question and challenge actions and utterances of our government and of our public and private institutions. Journalists uphold the right to speak unpopular opinions and the privilege to agree with the majority.

ETHICS:
Journalists must be free of obligation to any interest other than the public's right to know the truth.
1. Gifts, favors, free travel, special treatment or privileges can compromise the integrity of journalists and their employers. Nothing of value should be accepted.
2. Secondary employment, political involvement, holding public office and service in community organizations should be avoided if it compromises the integrity of journalists and their employers. Journalists and their employers should conduct their personal lives in a manner which protects them from conflict of interest, real or apparent. Their responsibilities to the public are paramount. That is the nature of their profession.

3. So-called news communications from private sources should not be published or broadcast without substantiation of their claims to news value.
4. Journalists will seek news that serves the public interest, despite the obstacles. They will make constant efforts to assure that the public's business is conducted in public and that public records are open to public inspection.
5. Journalists acknowledge the newsman's ethic of protecting confidential sources of information.

ACCURACY AND OBJECTIVITY:
Good faith with the public is the foundation of all worthy journalism.
1. Truth is our ultimate goal.
2. Objectivity in reporting the news is another goal, which serves as the mark of an experienced professional. It is a standard of performance toward which we strive. We honor those who achieve it.
3. There is no excuse for inaccuracies or lack of thoroughness.
4. Newspaper headlines should be fully warranted by the contents of the articles they accompany. Photographs and telecasts should give an accurate picture of an event and not highlight a minor incident out of context.
5. Sound practice makes clear distinction between news reports and expressions of opinion. News reports should be free of opinion or bias and represent all sides of an issue.
6. Partisanship in editorial comment which knowingly departs from the truth violates the spirit of American journalism.
7. Journalists recognize their responsibility for offering informed analysis, comment and editorial opinion on public events and issues. They accept the obligation to present such material by individuals whose competence, experience and judgment qualify them for it.
8. Special articles or presentations devoted to advocacy or the writer's own conclusions and interpretations should be labeled as such.

FAIR PLAY:
Journalists at all times will show respect for the dignity, privacy, rights and well-being of people encountered in the course of gathering and presenting the news.
1. The news media should not communicate unofficial charges affecting reputation or moral character without giving the accused a chance to reply.
2. The news media must guard against invading a person's right to privacy.
3. The media should not pander to morbid curiosity about details of vice and crime.
4. It is the duty of news media to make prompt and complete correction of their errors.
5. Journalists should be accountable to the public for their reports and the public should be encouraged to voice its grievances against the media. Open dialogue with our readers, viewers and listeners should be fostered.

PLEDGE:
Journalists should actively censure and try to prevent violations of these standards, and they should encourage their observance by all newspeople. Adherence to this code of ethics is intended to preserve the bond of mutual trust and respect between American journalists and the American people.

married to a Bush administration critic. On her release, the *Times* criticized her for being too cozy with the White House. Miller hastily resigned after 28 years at the *Times* and was hired by Fox News.

■ In 2009, the *Times* was faced with a different kind of ethical dilemma, when Editor Bill Keller decided to keep quiet the kidnapping by the Taliban in Afghanistan of investigative reporter David Rohde. When Rohde escaped to freedom seven months later, the *Times* was criticized by some for suppressing the news. In 2010, Keller made the decision to publish a cache of a quarter million confidential diplomatic cables, purloined by WikiLeaks, an organization dedicated to revealing secret documents. Some questioned the ethics of putting diplomats and the nations they worked for at risk.[17]

■ In the new millennium, with 152 blogs on the Internet, 25 billion tweets sent each year, and two billion YouTube videos watched each day, as well as the exponential increase in TV news, cable stations, and programming on the Internet, the pressure has increased on news outlets to get stories at any cost.[18] Network television news organizations—once the bastion of heralded journalists from Edward R. Murrow and Walter Cronkite to Chet Huntley and David Brinkley—resorted to paying news sources to appear on their airwaves. In 2011, after ABC was embarrassed when it was revealed the network paid accused baby killer Casey Anthony $200,000 for photos, the network became the first to adopt a policy that it would no longer "pay for play."[19]

■ And then, of course, there were the screamers. Cable television news, in particular, was rocked by the phenomenon in the 21st century of "nonstop screaming," where adversaries on either side spent most of their air time declaring a "my way or the highway" point of view. Partisanship was the order of the day. Such popular programs as Fox News Channel's *The O'Reilly Factor with Bill O'Reilly*, MSNBC's *Hardball with Chris Matthews*, and *CNN Headline News' with Nancy Grace*, all distinguished by their voluble hosts, added plenty of heat but little light to the national dialogue. Indeed, by 2012, CNN, the one cable network that tried to remain neutral, had lost miserably in the only thing that mattered to TV executives: ratings.[20] And many times, it was non-journalist late-night comedians who landed the top name guests—or "gets" as they say in the news biz (Figure 6-6).

A Gallup poll in 2012 revealed that Americans rated journalists at 26% in terms of "Honesty/Ethics," just ahead of bankers and lawyers. Nurses ranked first at 84%.[21] Such was the demoralized state of journalistic ethics in the last half of the first decade of the 21st century.

FIGURE 6-6 **The new "journalists."**
Late-night comics, such as Jay Leno, out-muscled journalists in the 21st century to interview the really big "gets." *(Photo: White House Photo by Pete Souza)*

Ethics in Public Relations

Ethics is—or at least, should be—the great differentiator between public relations and other professions. In light of numerous misconceptions about the practice of public relations, it is imperative that practitioners emulate the highest standards of personal and professional ethics (Figure 6-7). Within an organization, public relations practitioners must be the standard bearers of corporate ethical initiatives. By the same token, public relations consultants must always counsel their clients in an ethical direction—toward accuracy and candor and away from lying and hiding the truth.

The public relations department should be the seat of corporate ethics. At least four ethical theories are relevant to the practice of public relations.

- The *attorney/adversary model*, developed by Jay Barney and Ralph Black, compares the legal profession to that of public relations in that (1) both are advocates in an adversarial climate and (2) both assume counterbalancing messages will be provided by adversaries. In this model, Barney and Black suggest practitioners have no obligation to consider the public interest or any other outside view beyond that of their client.

Council of PR Firms Code of Ethics

Members of the Council commit to standards of practice that assure clients, the public and media, employees, and business partners and vendors the highest level of professionalism and ethical conduct in every relationship with a Council member. This commitment is a requirement for application and continued membership in the Council.

Member firms will serve their **clients** by applying their fullest capability to achieve each client's business objectives, and charging a fair price for that service. Members and their employees will be honest and accurate when recording time charges and seeking reimbursement of expenses, and member firms will not solicit or accept kickbacks or under-the-table payments in connection with business development efforts. Members will avoid representing any conflicting client interests without the expressed approval of those concerned. Council firms and their employees will respect client confidences and the privacy of client employees, and will refrain from directly soliciting client employees with whom they are engaged in ongoing projects.

In communicating with the **public** and **media**, member firms will maintain total accuracy and truthfulness. To preserve both the reality and perception of professional integrity, information that is found to be misleading or erroneous will be promptly corrected and the sources of communications and sponsors of activities will not be concealed.

Council members will respect the personal rights of their **employees** and former employees. They will provide employees the necessary tools to serve their clients and opportunities to develop their professional skills. They will safeguard the privacy and handle with respect the professional reputation of current and former employees. Members will adopt policies that assure equal opportunity for all job candidates without regard to race, color, religion, national origin, sex, sexual orientation, age, veteran status, disability or any other basis prohibited by applicable federal, state or local law.

Commercial relationships with business **partners** and **vendors** will be handled in a businesslike manner, and credit will be given for ideas and services provided by others.

FIGURE 6-7   Doing the right thing.
The Council of Public Relations Firms board of directors revised its Code of Ethics in 2009 to exhort members to commit to the highest level of ethics. *(Courtesy Council of Public Relations Firms)*

- The *two-way communication model*, developed by Jim Grunig, is based on collaboration, working jointly with different people, and allowing for both listening and give-and-take. In this model, Grunig suggests that the practitioner balances his or her role as a client advocate with one as social conscience for the larger public.

- The *enlightened self-interest model*, developed by Sherry Baker, is based on the principle that businesses do well by doing good. In this model, Baker suggests that companies gain a competitive edge and are more respected in the marketplace if they behave ethically.

- The *responsible advocacy model*, developed by Kathy Fitzpatrick and Candace Gauthier, is based on the ideal of professional responsibility. It postulates that practitioners' first loyalty is to their clients, but they also have a responsibility to voice the opinions of organizational stakeholders. In this model, Fitzpatrick and Gauthier suggest that the practitioner's greatest need for ethical guidance is in the reconciliation of being both a professional advocate and a social conscience.

The PRSA has been a leader in the effort to foster a strong sense of professionalism among its membership, particularly in its new code of ethics. Its six core values underpin the desired behavior of any public relations professional.

- **Advocacy.**   The PRSA Code (see Appendix A) endorses the Fitzpatrick and Gauthier model in stating: "We serve the public interest by acting as responsible advocates for those we represent." For example, public relations professionals must never reveal confidential or private client information, even if a journalist demands it. The only way such information might be revealed is after a thorough discussion with the client.

- **Honesty.**   For example, a client asking a public relations representative to "embellish" the performance the company expects to achieve should be told diplomatically, but firmly, no. Public relations people don't lie.

- **Expertise.**   For example, a client in need of guidance as to whether to accept a sensitive interview invitation for a cable TV talk show must be carefully guided through the pros and cons by a skilled public relations practitioner.

- **Independence.**   For example, when everyone in the room—lawyer, human resources, treasurer, and president—agree with the CEO's rock-headed scheme to disguise bad news, it is the public relations professional's duty to strike an independent tone.

- **Loyalty.**   For example, if a competing client offers a practitioner more money to abandon his or her original employer, the public relations professional should understand that his or her loyalties must remain constant.

- **Fairness.**   For example, when a rude and obnoxious journalist demands information, a practitioner's responsibility is to treat even the most obnoxious reporter with fairness.

What these tenets indicate is that proper public relations practice is just the opposite of what many accuse public relations people of being—deceivers, obfuscators, con artists, spinners, or even liars. Rather, public relations people and practice ought to be "transparent."[22]

Sadly, the practice hasn't always lived up to these ethical principles. As a consequence, the field, even more sadly, regularly ranks toward the bottom on credibility surveys.[23] Changing this view to one of a more ethical and honest practice is a great challenge for public relations leaders in the 21st century.

Outside the Lines
Defending a Dictator

Public relations ethics are sometimes slippery.

So it was in 2011, with the United States in recession and the world ablaze in the "Arab Spring," with Middle East dictators clinging to power.

To help in the task, the despots reached out to American public relations units to help cleanse their name back in the good, old U.S. of A. A slew of American public relations firms were hired by the world's most repressive governments. Brown Lloyd James, Bell Pottinger, Potomac Square Group, Qorvis Communications, and former Bill Clinton aide Lanny Davis were just a few of the public relations names—most headquartered in Washington—called in to assist the image of ruthless tyrants, in exchange for significant fees.

One organization, Monitor Group of Cambridge, Massachusetts, made up of Harvard academics and former diplomats, was asked to promote the beneficent deeds of Libyan dictator Colonel Moammar Gadaffi (Figure 6-8). This, the group did gladly to the tune of $3 million from the besieged dictator. A portion of that money was passed on by Monitor to leading academics and policymakers in the United States, in the form of honorariums, consultancy fees, and travel expenses. The former officials and Harvard professors accepted the blood money gladly and attempted to present the scary Gadaffi in a positive light.

Alas for Monitor and its hired guns, the Libyan leader met an untimely demise at the hands—literally—of his less-than-admiring countrymen in October 2011. Monitor subsequently admitted its error in representing the brutal Libyan strongman but apparently didn't give back any money.*

FIGURE 6-8   Col. Goofball.
Why would any self-respecting public relations firm represent this man? 'Cuz he was *rich* (until his loyal subjects caught up with him in 2011)! *(Photo: Donatella Giagnori/ZUMA Press/Newscom)*

*For further information, see Rosanna Fiske, "Destroying America's Reputation by Rebuilding Libya's," The Hill's Congress Blog, August 15, 2011; and "U.S. Firm Monitor Group Admits Mistakes Over $3 Million Gadaffi Deal," *The Guardian*, March 3, 2011.

Last Word

The scandals in government and business in the first two decades of the 21st century have placed a premium in every sector of society on acting ethically. More than half of the 3,000 workers who took part in a National Business Ethics Survey said they witnessed at least one type of ethical misconduct on their job.[24] That's disgraceful. As the CEO of Eaton Corporation, the manufacturing giant, put it, "There is no truer window into a corporation's soul than its approach to ethics."[25]

The same can be said for the practice of public relations.

The success of public relations in the 21st century will depend largely on how the field responds to the issue of ethical conduct. Public relations professionals must have credibility in order to practice. They must be respected by the various publics with which they interact. This is as true overseas as it is in the United States. To be credible and to achieve respect, public relations professionals must be ethical. It is that simple.

Stated another way, for public relations practice in general and individual public relations professionals in particular, credibility in the next few years will depend on how scrupulously they observe and apply the principles and practice of ethics in everything they do.

Discussion Starters

1. How would you define ethics?
2. How would you describe the state of ethics in business, government, and journalism?
3. How important is the ethical component of the practice of public relations?
4. Why have corporations adopted corporate codes of conduct?
5. What is corporate social responsibility?
6. What were the ethical implications of Scott McClellan's memoirs?
7. What are the pros and cons of the attorney/adversary public relations model compared to the enlightened self-interest model?
8. Is the public more tolerant or less tolerant of ethical violators today? Why?
9. What is the significance of the six ethical values that underscore the Public Relations Society of America Code of Ethics?
10. What are the ethical responsibilities of a public relations professional?

Pick of the Literature

Ethics in Public Relations 2nd ed.

Patricia J. Parsons, Philadelphia, PA: Kogan Page Ltd., 2008

Excellent overview of the various aspects of ethics in the practice of public relations, authored by a distinguished professor at Mount St. Vincent University in Halifax, Nova Scotia, Canada.

The bias of this book is that most public relations professionals conduct themselves with honesty and integrity, and that "spin" is the enemy (She's right!).

She writes that "recognizing, facing, and dealing with ethical dilemmas in everyday practice are the three most important aspects of ethics." (Again, she's right!) The book proposes an ethical framework for practitioners, beginning with history and definitions and evolving into moral relativism and situational ethics. In the process, she examines such germane aspects as ethics in media relations, whistleblowing, ethics and client relations, ethics in decision-making, and a host of other issues.

This is truly an exhaustive summary of an imperative topic in the practice of public relations.

Case Study | Doing the Right Thing by Making a "Hurd" Decision

For decades, the Hewlett-Packard Company—or HP, as it was known—was one of Silicon Valley's most respected technology companies. Its founders, Stanford classmates David Packard and William Hewlett, created their partnership in 1939 and built a worldwide computer colossus.

Both Hewlett and Packard, after they retired, became well known as philanthropists, each of them the epitome of high ethics and propriety.

The hugely successful company they developed was built on a platform of innovative competence complemented by an understated public profile and high moral fiber. All that began to change when in 1999, HP stunned the macho, high-tech world by recruiting an actual *woman* to be its CEO. Carly Fiorina, high-profile executive vice president of AT&T, was the surprise selection to take the Hewlett-Packard reins, becoming one of the most powerful women in business. Fiorina's tenure was marked by a contentious merger with rival computer maker Compaq, dissension in the ranks, and a most un-HP-like parade of personal CEO publicity. *Carly mania* reigned in the media. Publicity about HP's woman chief seemed to be all over the place. In 2005, having had enough fireworks, the Hewlett-Packard board ushered CEO Fiorina out the door.

Fair-Haired Boy

As Fiorina's replacement, Hewlett-Packard chose Mark Hurd, a no-nonsense, 25-year computer industry veteran. Unlike his predecessor, Hurd proved himself a solid, low-key leader, well respected by Wall Street and the media, if not always by the people who worked for him. (He laid off 10% of the HP workforce shortly after being named CEO.) Hurd generally managed the company skillfully, regaining much of the credibility it had sacrificed in the Fiorina era.

Hurd's one slip was in 2006 when HP was embroiled in an embarrassing crisis that resulted from its board chair hiring spies to snoop on fellow HP board members, staff members, and journalists who covered the company. Upshot of the scandal was national publicity exposing the HP practices and the California Attorney General charging the HP board chair, Patricia Dunn, with four felonies for her role in the HP investigation into the unauthorized disclosure of company information.

Throughout the crisis, CEO Hurd adopted a low profile. Ultimately, when the smoke cleared, he announced that the board chair had resigned, and he apologized profusely for HP's violation of the privacy of directors and company employees. Not only did Hurd escape the board crisis relatively unscathed, he was named to add to his CEO title as the new HP chair.

"A Close Personal Relationship"

For five years, Hurd navigated Hewlett-Packard through steadily better years; the company appeared to be back on its profitable/ethical track. That's why it was such a bolt from the blue on Friday, August 6, 2010, when it was announced that CEO Hurd had decided to resign.

According to HP's board, which made the announcement after the market closed, CEO Hurd resigned, technically, for "fudging on his expenses." Less technically, but more importantly, Hurd was found to be having a two-year "close personal relationship" with a female contractor. Part of Hurd's "relationship" with the contractor included dinners, often on business trips, for which the CEO charged the company but failed to report that he dined with his friend, the contractor.

And so, because of these "expense irregularities," the HP board fired the CEO. Not incidentally, the "contractor" in question happened to be a blonde bombshell, former aspiring B movie actress-turned-seminar leader, featured in such cinematic properties as *Intimate Obsession, Blood Dolls,* and the immortal *Body of Influence 2.*

Biting the Bullet

In making its announcement about its well-regarded CEO, HP went to great lengths to acknowledge that after an extensive investigation, it found that he committed no violations of law but rather violated the *Hewlett-Packard Code of Conduct.* So the board had "no recourse" but to ask for and receive Hurd's resignation.

Hurd, himself, was candid in admitting that he had not always represented the corporation in the manner in which he should have (Figure 6-9). He said, "I realized there were instances in which I did not live up to the standards and principles of trust, respect and integrity that I have espoused at HP and which have guided me throughout my career. . . . I believe it would be difficult for me to continue as an effective leader at HP and I believe this is the only decision the board and I could make at this time."

The HP board, also to its credit, acknowledged that getting rid of such a well-respected leader was a difficult decision. Said its lead independent director, "The board deliberated extensively on this matter. It recognizes the considerable value that Mark has contributed to HP over the past five years in establishing us as a leader in the industry. . . . This departure was not related in any way to the company's operational performance or financial condition, both of which remain strong. The board recognizes that this change in leadership is unexpected news for everyone associated with HP."

HP's critics were livid at the decision.

FIGURE 6-9   Curtains for the CEO.
Hewlett-Packard CEO Mark Hurd grimly stepped down in 2010, after an ethics scandal forced him to resign. (*Photo: MANDEL NGAN/AFP/Getty Images/Newscom*)

■ Larry Ellison, billionaire cofounder of software giant Oracle and a tennis buddy of Hurd's, declared, "The HP Board just made the worst personnel decision since the idiots on the Apple Board fired Steve Jobs many years ago," adding that the HP board capitulated to "cowardly corporate political correctness."

■ Corporate governance watchdog Nell Minow took the board to task for failing "to make it clear enough to (Hurd) what their expectations were or this would not have happened." After all, Minnow argued, the board is responsible for "making sure the CEO knows he will be held accountable."

■ Finally, industry analysts in the financial community and the press joined in to pile on HP for getting rid of such a market-friendly CEO. The tech analyst at Sanford Bernstein & Co. said it was "difficult to view Hurd's departure as anything but negative for HP." Likewise, argued *e-Week*, a leading IT management journal, "The goal of any major tech company is to maximize shareholder value. The only way to do that is to reduce expenses, increase revenues, and *ultimately see profits soar.* When a CEO who has done as good a job as Hurd leaves, shareholders tend to get worried. And when that happens, they usually start selling off shares for fear of the next CEO ruining things."

Which is, of course, what happened immediately after Hurd's departure from HP: its shares tumbled. But in short time, investors realized—even if industry analysts didn't—that a successful company that actually *stands for something* is a good investment in the long run. Accordingly, HP shares soon regained the value they had lost.

Taking the Ethical Road

Hewlett-Packard's critics had a point. The company's board did have at least two other options, both employed time and again by organizations facing similar crises.

■ **One**, it could have looked the other way, quietly slapped the CEO on the wrists, and hoped nothing would be made public.

■ **Two**, HP could have announced Hurd's resignation to "pursue personal business opportunities" and offered no further explanation.

Hewlett-Packard chose neither of these two easier courses. The action it took reinforced that the company's *Code of Conduct* wasn't just a piece of paper that meant nothing; by contrast, it represented a mandatory pact to which every employee, regardless of rank, was a subject. In taking strong action against the highest ranking individual in the company, HP's board remained true to the ethical framework established by its founders and demonstrated the three-step template to which all companies should subscribe in similar management crisis.

While reasonable observers might disagree with aspects of the HP decision and response, they can't quibble that the Hewlett-Packard board displayed admirable courage in taking a clearly unpopular action in order to safeguard the principles upon which the company was built. The board took the high road and distinguished itself.

As to Mark Hurd, he landed on his feet, hired by none other than Larry Ellison as co-president and board member of Oracle Corporation. Oracle, as it turned out, also had a Corporate Code of Conduct which, among other things, stated the following:

Our reputation and our success depend upon the personal commitment that each of us makes to uphold our values and practice ethical behavior in all of our business dealings. All of us, regardless of employment level, position, or geographic location, are expected to make this commitment daily, both individually and collectively, to uphold the standards of business conduct outlined in this Code.

Which, as it turned out, was exactly what Hewlett-Packard's Board did in firing Mark Hurd.*

Questions

1. What other options did Hewlett-Packard have in dealing with Mark Hurd?

2. Do you think the board did the right thing?

3. Had HP decided to slap its CEO on the wrists for his infraction, what might have been the outcome for the company?

*For further information, see Ashlee Vance, "H.P. Ousts Chief for Hiding Payments to Friend," *The Wall Street Journal*, August 6, 2010.

From the Top

An Interview with Howard J. Rubenstein

Howard J. Rubenstein, president of Rubenstein Associates since founding the firm in 1954, is one of the world's most well-known and respected public relations counselors, advising some of the world's most influential corporations, organizations, and opinion leaders. In addition to managing the day-to-day activities of his firm, Rubenstein is involved in numerous civic and philanthropic organizations. A Phi Beta Kappa graduate of the University of Pennsylvania, he finished first in his class in the night school division of St. John's University School of Law, which subsequently awarded him an honorary Doctor of Law degree. As an attorney, he served as assistant counsel to the House of Representatives Judiciary Committee.

How would you define the practice of public relations?
Public relations is the art of conveying an idea or message to a wide variety of publics utilizing multiple forms of communications. It can be broadly applied and used to advance the interests of businesses, governments, and society in general. It can achieve objectives as narrow as promoting a product or as broad as creating a movement. The communications themselves can be targeted to the general public or to very select groups of individuals, conveyed via media or person to person. The tools employed encompass a wide array, from press releases, news conferences, special events, speaking engagements, webinars, blogs, and grassroots organizations down to a single conversation with one influential person.

How important is communications for organizations in today's society?
Communications in its many forms creates and projects messages with the power to affect great change and achieve tremendous success, while a breakdown in communications can lead to dismal failure. Clearly, communications is critical for organizations as they seek public acceptance, support, and understanding of their activities. Communication today is a major focus for presidents, prime ministers, and legislators, as well as religious leaders, as they try to shape the directions of entire societies and world events.

What are the key attributes that distinguish the best public relations professionals?

Ethics, intelligence, and willingness to put in the time and hard work are core characteristics. Good PR professionals should have the ability to write well and speak effectively. The final attribute is creativity and imagination, combined with an understanding of reality and practicality. Professionals in the field should be able to stretch the envelope as far as technique and methodology go, without forgetting what they are trying to achieve.

What is the key to interesting a journalist in a client's story?

There are many keys to piquing media interest. First, however, you must know the media outlet and understand what a news story is and what a reporter wants to see as the components of a story. You must target and reach out selectively, rather than just send out releases. Then, once you know where to go, find the human-interest angle, keep the pitch succinct, and offer what the reporter needs to cover the story. Forget the term *spinmeister*. Offer a story that is accurate, do it in an honorable and forthright way, and help the reporter do his or her job well. Above all, don't waste reporters' time with something that isn't right for the publication or the beat the reporter covers. And don't be nasty if your idea is rejected. You'll likely want to approach that reporter again some day. Instead take that rejection as a sign that you need to refine the pitch or find a better fit for it.

What inspired you, personally, to go into public relations?

I was inspired to enter public relations by my father, who was a crime reporter with the *New York Herald Tribune*. From his perspective as a journalist, he believed that PR had the untapped potential to be a great career. Not only did he get me my first account, he explained to me the importance of ethics, honesty, and integrity in dealing with the press, conducting business, and communicating with the public. He taught me the importance of good writing, finding the news value in a story, and working hard to achieve coverage in the media. He was very supportive when I began my company with that single account at my new office, which was also known as *my mother's kitchen table!* He encouraged me and always believed that public relations had a bright future. I remember him saying that public relations as a field was malleable, like clay, and could be formed to fit any idea that I had. As a result, I started out believing that if I was honest, thoughtful, and hard working, I could be successful, earn a living, and establish a good reputation in what was then a barely recognized field. That's what happened, so I guess my father was right.

What are the greatest challenges facing the practice of public relations?

In every aspect of society, leaders seek public relations counsel. Because media scrutiny is so intense today, it takes a professional to understand and advise society's leaders as to how best to respond and engage. As a result, PR people today are professionals with as much credibility and weight as lawyers, accountants, bankers, architects, or engineers. We alone offer the ability to design communications programs, judge their potential, and execute them to achieve results. That guarantees for PR professionals tremendous opportunity and a seat at the table at the highest levels.

Yet for all that progress in the evolution of the profession, there are still too many people, especially in the general public, who hold public relations in low esteem. PR professionals are still viewed in many quarters as snake-oil salesmen, ready to stoop to conquer or employ deceptive tactics. The great challenge today is changing that perception and winning for the profession the respect that it deserves. The way to meet that challenge as an industry is through superb professional performance and continued adherence to the highest ethical and business standards.

Public Relations Library

Black, Jay, and Chris Roberts. *Doing Ethics in Media*. New York: Routledge, 2011. A discussion of the ethics that people in communication—journalism, public relations, advertising, marketing—ought to emulate.

Fitzpatrick, Kathy, and Carolyn Bronstein (Eds.). *Ethics in Public Relations: Responsible Advocacy*. Thousand Oaks, CA: Sage Publications, Inc., 2006. A book all about "responsible advocacy," representing clients and organizations.

Hartley, Robert F. *Business Ethics: Mistakes and Successes*. New York: John Wiley & Sons, 2005. This book discusses all the notorious ethical cases of our time, from Ford's Explorer and Firestone tires to WorldCom's accounting fraud to "Chainsaw" Al Dunlap's duplicity at Sunbeam.

McClellan, Scott. *What Happened*. New York: Public Affairs, 2008. The prodigal son of the George W. Bush White House gives his side of the events that led him to turn on his former employer with this tell-all memoir.

O'Leary, Rosemary. *The Ethics of Dissent*. Washington, DC: CQ Press, 2006. A lively treatise, focusing on ethical issues, problems, and downright abominations in government.

Seymann, Marilyn, and Michael Rosenbaum. *The Governance Game: Restoring Boardroom Excellence and Credibility in Corporate America*. Mahwah, NJ: Aspatore, 2003. This book explores one of corporate America's most prominent ethical vulnerabilities, the board of directors. The authors suggest what corporate boards can do to improve their performance in terms of management of the board and the ethical behavior of directors. They stress that corporate boards must go beyond making sure their companies are simply complying with existing laws and regulations.

Stauber, John, and Sheldon Rampton. *Trust Us, We're Experts*. New York: Penguin Putnam, 2001. The anti–public relations authors of *Toxic Sludge Is Good for You* are at it again. This time they explain—from their unique perspective—how "corporations and public relations firms have seized upon remarkable new ways of exploiting your trust to get you to buy what they have to sell." Strap yourself in.

Trevino, Linda K., and Katherine A. Nelson. *Managing Business Ethics: Straight Talk About How to Do It Right*, 3rd ed. New York: John Wiley & Sons, 2004. Discusses not only what business ethics are but also why business should care.

Chapter 7

The Law

Chapter Objectives

1. To discuss the relationship between public relations professionals and lawyers and the importance to public relations practitioners of understanding the law.

2. To explore, in particular, the First Amendment, from which free speech emerges.

3. To discuss the various areas of the law relevant to public relations professionals, including defamation, disclosure, insider trading, copyright and Internet law.

4. To underscore the new importance in the 21st century of litigation public relations.

FIGURE 7-1 Where's the beef?
Taco Bell used TV stars like Heidi Montag and Spencer Pratt to promote its good works and gave no ground when sued in 2011. *(Photo: Tonya Wise/London Ent/Splash/Newscom)*

In the winter of 2011, Taco Bell was hot, and we're not just talking about the enchiladas!

In January, a disgruntled customer sued the restaurant chain on the grounds that its taco mixture contained more fiber than meat. As this is the day when no nuisance lawsuit goes unreported, news of the suit spread widely on the Internet. Soon, that intrepid reporter Stephen Colbert parodied the claim on his Comedy Central *The Colbert Report*.

But Taco Bell, a chain known for its out-of-the-box thinking and public relations sophistication (Figure 7-1), struck back in a most unusual way: It publicized the lawsuit on Facebook and YouTube and with a full page ad, headlined, "Thank You for Suing Us." The video and the ad

proclaimed that Taco Bell's taco mixture contained 88% beef—not the 35% the suit claimed—with ingredients such as water, oats, spices, and cocoa powder added to provide flavor, texture, and moisture. The company's counterintuitive viral and public rebuttal effectively squelched publicity about the negative legal action.[1]

In recent years, as public relations has gained stature, the practice has become more aggressive in communicating during legal cases—although generally not as "aggressively" as Taco Bell—and with and through lawyers.

Indeed, there has always been a natural tension between public relations practitioners and lawyers. Ideally, public relations counselors and lawyers should work together to achieve a client's

FIGURE 7-2 Where are my lawyers?!? Among the most innovative and persuasive—and public relations conscious—nonprofit organizations is People for the Ethical Treatment of Animals, which has featured celebrities such as Charlize Theron and Pink to get across messages that gave their adversaries and the attorneys of their adversaries fits. *(Courtesy of PETA)*

desired outcomes. And this is often the case. But there is also a fundamental difference in legal versus public relations advice.

- Lawyers correctly advise clients on what they *must* do, within the letter of legal requirements, to defend themselves in a court of law.
- Public relations advisors counsel clients on not what they *must* do but what they *should* do to defend themselves in a different court—the court of public opinion.

There is a vast difference between the two.

In recent years, however, lawyers have moved increasingly to pursue the publicity turf traditionally manned by public relations professionals. Some lawyers have become ubiquitous—on radio and television and in the middle of press conferences—in using public relations techniques to further their clients' and their own ends.

In many ways, it makes sense that lawyers and public relations people should work in concert. Public relations and the law both begin with the First Amendment to the Constitution that guarantees freedom of speech in our society.

But in the 21st century, ensuring freedom of speech is not as easy as it sounds. One question is, *Where does one's freedom start and another's end* (Figure 7-2)? Another question is, *How much freedom of speech is appropriate—or advisable—in any given situation?* And yet another question is, *How does the freedom of the Internet impact on communications rights and responsibilities?*

Such are the dilemmas in the relationship between public relations principles and the law.

Public Relations and the Law: An Uneasy Alliance

While public relations professionals and lawyers have worked more closely in recent years, the legal and public relations professions have historically shared an uneasy alliance. Public relations practitioners must always understand the legal implications of any issue with which they become involved, and a firm's legal position must always be the first consideration.

From a legal point of view, normally the less an organization says prior to its day in court, the better. That way, the opposition can't gain any new ammunition that will become part of the public record. A lawyer, the saying goes, tells you to say two things: *"Say nothing, and say it slowly!"*

From a public relations standpoint, though, it may make sense to go public early on, especially if the organization's integrity or credibility is being called into public question. In the summer of 2003, for example, when NBA star Kobe Bryant was accused of raping a woman at a Colorado hotel, on the advice of his lawyers and public relations counsel Bryant immediately held a press conference, with his wife at his side, to acknowledge he had erred but denied the charges. A year later, the sexual assault charge was dismissed, and by 2009, Kobe Bryant, his credibility restored, had led his Los Angeles Lakers to the NBA championship. By contrast, as we've seen, Martha Stewart listened to her lawyers' exhortation to remain silent when charged with lying to federal prosecutors, and she wound up in Camp Cupcake (see Case Study in Chapter 4).

The point is that legal advice and public relations advice may indeed be different. In an organization, a smart manager will carefully weigh both legal and public relations counsel before making a decision.

It also should be noted that law and ethics are interrelated. The Public Relations Society of America's Code of Professional Standards (see Appendix A) notes that many activities that are unethical are also illegal. However, there are instances in which something is perfectly legal but unethical and other instances in which things might be illegal but otherwise ethical. Thus, when a public relations professional reflects on what course to take in a particular situation, he or she must analyze not only the legal ramifications but also the ethical considerations.[2]

This chapter examines the relationship between the law and public relations and the more prominent role the law plays in public relations practice and vice versa. The discussion introduces the legal concerns of public relations professionals today: First Amendment considerations, insider trading, disclosure law, ethics law, privacy law, copyright law, and the laws concerning censorship of the Internet—issues that have become primary concerns for public relations practitioners in the 21st century.

Public Relations and the First Amendment

Any discussion of law and public relations should start with the First Amendment, which states: "Congress shall make no law . . . abridging the freedom of speech or the press." The First Amendment is the cornerstone of free speech in our society: This is what distinguishes democratic nations from many others.

Recent years have seen a blizzard of problems and challenges regarding the First Amendment.

- In 2005, *The New York Times* reporter Judith Miller was jailed for failing to disclose her sources in the outing of CIA agent Valerie Plame, wife of a former ambassador and enemy of the Bush administration. Miller pleaded that under the First Amendment, she had a right to protect her sources. But the court disagreed.[3]

- In 2006, when an obscure Danish newspaper published cartoons depicting the prophet Muhammad in a tasteless way, Muslims protested around the world, resulting in destruction, injuries, and deaths. While the Western world considered the cartoons—as offensive as they were—examples of "freedom of expression," much of the Muslim world was outraged. Two years later, a Danish anti-Koran film triggered a renewal of Muslim outrage.

- In 2008, a former *USA Today* reporter faced fines and imprisonment, in a suit by former Army scientist Steven Hatfill, when she was ordered to reveal her sources about the anthrax attacks on America, which killed five people in 2001. Hatfill had been labeled a "person of interest" in the attacks but was never charged. Ultimately, the government wound up paying him $4.6 million for accusing him undeservedly. And the threats against the reporter were dropped.[4]

- In 2010, WikiLeaks, an international online organization that billed itself as a "publisher of private, secret and classified media from anonymous news sources, leaks and whistleblowers," shocked the diplomatic world by collaborating with international newspapers to publish secret U.S. State Department diplomatic cables. WikiLeaks' strange founder, an Australian computer programmer/hacker named Julian Assange, defiantly defended the "public's right to know" (Figure 7-3).[5]

As these cases suggest, interpreting the First Amendment, especially in the Internet age, is no simple matter. One person's definition of obscenity or divulging state secrets may be someone else's definition of art or freedom of expression. Because the First Amendment lies at the heart of the communications business, defending it is a frontline responsibility of the public relations profession.

FIGURE 7-3 **Hacker or hero?**
WikiLeaks founder Julian Assange, citing his First Amendment rights, disclosed online secrets angering diplomats and generals. In 2013, he continued to fight charges against extradition from the UK to Sweden on sexual assault charges. *(Photo: FACUNDO ARRIZABALAGA/EPA/Newscom)*

Public Relations and Defamation Law

The laws that govern a person's privacy have significant implications for journalists and other communicators, such as public relations professionals, particularly laws that touch on libel and slander—commonly known as defamation laws—by the media.

Defamation is the umbrella term used to describe libel—a printed falsehood—and slander—an oral falsehood. For defamation to be proved, a plaintiff must convince the court that certain requirements have been met, including the following:

1. The falsehood was communicated through print, broadcast, or other electronic means.

2. The person who is the subject of the falsehood was identified or easily identifiable.

3. The identified person has suffered injury—in the form of monetary losses, reputational loss, or mental suffering.[6]

Generally, the privacy of an ordinary citizen is protected under the law. A citizen in the limelight, however, has a more difficult problem, especially in proving defamation of character through libel or slander.

To prove such a charge, a public figure must show that the media acted with actual malice in their reporting. *Actual malice* in a public figure slander case means that statements have been published with the knowledge that they were false or with reckless disregard for whether the statements were false. In a landmark case in 1964, *The New York Times* v. *Sullivan,* the Supreme Court nullified a libel award of $500,000 to an Alabama police official, holding that no damages could be awarded "in actions brought by public officials against critics of their official conduct" unless there was proof of actual malice. And proving actual malice is a difficult task.

Several historic libel cases have helped pave the case law precedent.

- In 1992, *The Wall Street Journal* and its award-winning reporter Bryan Burrough were served with a $50 million libel suit by Harry L. Freeman, a former communications executive of American Express. The suit stemmed from the way Freeman was characterized in Burrough's book, *Vendetta: American Express and the Smearing of Edmund Safra.*[7]

- In an earlier celebrated case, Israeli General Ariel Sharon brought a $50 million libel suit against *Time* magazine. The jury criticized *Time* for negligent journalism in reporting Sharon's role in a massacre in a Palestinian refugee camp. However, the jury couldn't conclude *Time* acted with "malice" and didn't render a libel verdict. Sharon got nothing.

- In 1996, Atlanta security guard Richard A. Jewell sued both *NBC News* and the *Atlanta Journal-Constitution* for reporting that he was the lead suspect in the Atlanta Olympic bombing, which led to two deaths. The reports caused a media feeding frenzy, which disrupted Jewell's life and tarnished his name. A decade later, Jewell was cleared of any involvement in the bombing and reached a settlement with his media accusers, averting a libel lawsuit.

The 21st-century proliferation of blogs, tweets, Facebook posts, and cable and radio talk shows, where hosts and guests say what they want regardless of factual accuracy or impact on a person's life, has resulted in the definition of "defamation" becoming more complex and more global.

FIGURE 7-4   Very nice.
Actor Sacha Baron Cohen, aka Borat, won a defamation suit against him in 2008 after a random businessman-turned-extra claimed he suffered "public ridicule, degradation, and humiliation" for his unwitting and involuntary role in Cohen's film. *(Photo: GOLD/MILLER PRODUCTIONS/Album/Newscom)*

- In the United States, celebrities sue and are sued all the time on grounds of defamation. In 2008, when he was accused by his former trainer of taking steroids, baseball pitcher Roger Clemens sued for defamation. In 2012, Clemens was hauled into U.S. federal court and was exonerated. When a businessman sued for defamation against actor Sacha Baron Cohen for chasing him down Fifth Avenue in a movie in which Cohen's alter ego, "Borat," pretended to be a documentary producer, a judge tossed out the case on the grounds that the movie, "while vulgar," was an attempt at ironic commentary (Figure 7-4).[8]

- In 2009, journalists were shocked when a federal appeals court in Boston ruled that even though the content of an email was true, the writer of that email could still be guilty of "libel." The case involved a Staples, Inc., employee who padded his expense account and was fired. When Staples announced the firing and its cause to 1,500 employees, the company was sued, and the court found that even though the email's content was true, Staples had shown "actual malice" in sending it. The ruling challenged the long-held belief that "truth is a defense against libel."[9]

- In 2011, punk rocker and actress Courtney Love agreed to pay $430,000 to a fashion designer who claimed that the Hole lead singer had defamed her by posting multiple remarks on Twitter that the designer was a "drug-pushing prostitute with a history of assault and battery."[10] Ouch!

Public relations practitioners must be aware of situations involving libel and slander. Many public relations professionals create, write, and edit internal print and online newsletters. In this context, they must be careful not to defame fellow employees or others in what they write. The same caution should be the rule for public relations professionals who make statements to the media on behalf of their organizations. Care must be the watchword in such public speech.

Public Relations and Insider Trading

Every public relations professional should know the laws that govern his or her organization and industry.

With 100 million Americans participating in the securities markets, either directly or through private pension plans, nowhere in public relations practice is an understanding of the law more important than in the area of securities law.

Every public company has an obligation to deal frankly, comprehensively, and immediately with any information that is considered *material*. A material announcement is one that might cause an investor to buy, hold, or sell a stock. The Securities and Exchange Commission (SEC)—through a series of court cases, consent decrees, complaints, and comments over the years—has painted a general portrait of disclosure requirements for practitioners, with which all practitioners in public companies should be familiar. The SEC's mandate stems from the Securities Act of 1933 and the Securities Exchange Act of 1934, which attempted to protect the public from abuses in the issuance and sale of securities.

The SEC's overriding concern is that all investors have an opportunity to learn about material information as promptly as possible. Basically, a company is expected to release news that may affect its stock market price as quickly as possible. Through its general antifraud statute, Rule 10b-5 of the Securities and Exchange Act, the SEC strictly prohibits the dissemination of false or misleading information to investors. It also prohibits insider trading of securities on the basis of material information not disclosed to the public.

In the first years of the 21st century, one celebrated insider trading case involved ImClone Systems' CEO Sam Waksal, who, along with family members, unloaded ImClone stock after he learned that the Food and Drug Administration was about to reject a key ImClone drug. The stock was subsequently crushed, as was CEO Waksal, his family, his stockbroker, and his good friend Martha Stewart (see Case Study in Chapter 4)—all embroiled in an insider trading scandal.[11]

In 2011, billionaire hedge fund manager Raj Rajaratnam was sentenced to 11 years in jail and fined more than $150 million for using insider tips to buy stocks. One of those from whom he allegedly received tips was Rajat Gupta, a former McKinsey and Company CEO, Goldman Sachs director and White House state dinner guest, who was convicted of insider trading charges in 2012.

Nor did journalists escape the accusation of insider trading convictions. In the late 1990s, a columnist at *The Wall Street Journal* was convicted of illegally using his newspaper column to give favorable opinions about companies in which a couple of his stockbroker friends had already invested heavily. He went to jail. In the early 2000s, wild-eyed stock picker James Cramer was accused by a former colleague of "pumping up stocks by feeding rumors" to friendly broadcasters at CNBC.[12] Cramer denied the allegations, and when no charges were brought, Cramer became a popular program host at CNBC.

As to public relations counselors, they, too, must be careful to act only on public information when trading securities. In 2008, for example, the public relations firm Brunswick suspended its Dow Chemical account executive when her husband traded on confidential news that Dow was considering an acquisition.[13] Dow Chemical promptly dropped its relationship with Brunswick.

Outside the Lines

Criminal Attorneys—Literally

"Let he who is without sin, throw the first stone." Thus sayeth the Bible. And, of course, it is not nice to disparage those who have fallen on hard times.

But, on the other hand, when a public relations person observes a pompous, sanctimonious, and self-righteous fat-cat lawyer finally getting his comeuppance, well. . . .

Such was the case in 2008, when a number of the world's most high-profile and public relations–savvy trial lawyers, aka plaintiff's attorneys—all known for going after large companies in front-page class action suits, many of which reaped gargantuan settlements (mostly for themselves!)—were sentenced to prison for misdeeds.

- Richard Scruggs, wealthy and flamboyant Mississippi attorney, received the maximum sentence of five years in prison for attempted bribery in suits against insurance companies, after Hurricane Katrina.

- Melvyn Weiss, 72-year-old "dean" of the trial lawyers, got 30 months in the slammer and was ordered to pay $10 million for using kickbacks to gain advantage in class actions.

- And William Lerach, Mr. Weiss's partner and perhaps America's highest profile plaintiff's attorney, drew two years in federal prison for his role in helping pay $11 million in kickbacks to people who became plaintiffs in lawsuits targeting, among others, AT&T, Lucent, WorldCom, Microsoft, Prudential Insurance, and Enron (Figure 7-5).

The sentencing of counselor Lerach, one of the more controversial and press-conscious of the breed, evoked particular glee from corporate executives. Said one unsympathetic CEO, "He's getting what he deserves. I once likened Lerach to a low-life form, somewhat below pond scum. Thank goodness, he's met my highest expectations."*

Whatever happened to following the good book?

*For further information, see Andrew Ross Sorkin, "Lerach Is Sentenced to 2 Years in Prison," *The New York Times* (February 11, 2008).

FIGURE 7-5 I object!
When high-powered plaintiff's attorney William Lerach was found guilty of providing kickbacks to witnesses, he was sentenced to hard time. *(Photo: Steve Ueckert/Rapport Press/Newscom)*

Public relations people are privy to all manner of confidential information. When they violate that confidentiality, they risk not only losing clients but also violating the law.

Public Relations and Disclosure Law

Besides cracking down on insider trading, the SEC has challenged corporations and public relations firms on the accuracy of information they disseminate for clients. Today, in an environment of mergers, takeovers, consolidations, and the incessant rumors that circulate around them, knowledge of disclosure law, a sensitivity to disclosure requirements, and a bias toward disclosing rather than withholding material information are important attributes of public relations officials.

In the new millennium, with securities trading extending beyond the traditional 9:30 a.m.–4 p.m. stock market trading day and with instantaneous online trading a reality for millions of investors, the responsibilities on public relations people for full and fair and immediate disclosure have intensified. The SEC, in turn, has increased its focus on private meetings between companies and analysts, which are closed to the media and therefore to individual investors who rely on the media for financial information.

To combat such selective disclosure, the SEC in 2000 adopted Regulation FD, or "fair disclosure." Basically, Regulation FD requires companies to widely disseminate any material announcement.

In the past, companies would share such material news with securities analysts or large investors, who then might act on it before the public found out. Under Regulation FD, even if a material announcement slips out to an analyst, the company is obligated to issue a news release within 24 hours "to provide broad, non-exclusionary disclosure information to the public."[14]

In 2002, Regulation FD was bolstered by the passage of the Sarbanes-Oxley Act, sponsored by U.S. Senator Paul Sarbanes and U.S. Representative Michael Oxley. Sarbanes-Oxley came as a result of the large corporate financial scandals involving Enron, WorldCom, Global Crossing, and Arthur Andersen. Among other requirements, Sarbanes-Oxley mandated all publicly traded companies to increase financial disclosure and submit an annual report of the effectiveness of their internal accounting controls to the SEC, with criminal and civil penalties for noncompliance.[15]

Although many corporations, analysts, and investors complained that the combination of Regulation FD and Sarbanes-Oxley would have a costly, "chilling impact" on companies that previously were willing to communicate, Congress and the regulators were unwilling to yield.

As the 21st century continued, with the world in recession, allegations against stock swindlers came fast and furious. The two most notorious, Bernard Madoff in New York and Robert Allen Stanford in Texas, who duped investors out of billions of dollars, underscored the vital need to strengthen disclosure law. And regulating financial markets was high on President Barack Obama's agenda when he took office in 2009 and remained when he campaigned for reelection in 2012.

Never since the Great Depression of the 1930s had the need been more apparent to ensure that all investors were provided full, fair, and immediate disclosure of "material" facts regarding their investments.

Public Relations and Ethics Law

The laws on ethical misconduct in society have gotten quite a workout over the last two decades.

- In a celebrated case, translated into the 1999 movie *The Insider,* the late public relations counselor John Scanlon faced a grand jury subpoena stemming from his efforts to discredit Jeffrey Wigand, an internal critic of Scanlon's cigarette client Brown & Williamson.[16]

- In the political public relations arena, the activities of lobbyists, in particular, have been closely watched by Congress since the imposition of the Federal

PR Ethics Mini-Case
Fall from Grace

One other unnecessary phenomenon of the 21st century is the proliferation of lawyers on cable television. (Public relations people on cable, on the other hand, is fine.) Lawyers have become all too willing to dish out opinions to any cable interviewer who asks—whether or not they have any expertise in the specific or general subject matter at issue.

The princess of them all is Nancy Grace (Figure 7-6).

Grace, a former Georgia prosecutor once described by an appeals court as playing "fast and loose" with the facts, has used that very "attribute" to become a 21st-century TV star.

Grace first came to media attention by using the murder of her college fiancé as a rallying cry to seek truth and justice. It was later revealed that Grace's "recollections" of the facts of that case were a bit off. Among them, her fiancé was killed by a coworker, not a random stranger as Grace repeated; the coworker had no criminal record and admitted the crime,

FIGURE 7-6   Dancing with the devil.
Legal diva Nancy Grace struts her stuff on *Dancing with the Stars* in 2011. *(Photo: Steve Ueckert/Rapport Press/Newscom)*

contrary to how Grace characterized him; and he filed no appeals after conviction, again contrary to Grace's story.

Grace, a staple on CNN's rabid *HLN* (*Headline News*) has made mincemeat of America's time-honored "guilty till proven innocent" standard. Grace's one-woman judge and jury routine has, among other travesties of justice:

- Claimed unequivocally that a drifter suspected in the Utah kidnapping of a teenager in 2002 "was guilty." The drifter died in custody and later was posthumously exonerated, when two other individuals confessed to the crime.

- Accused members of the 2006 Duke lacrosse team of "gang raping" a stripper. The more it became clear that the young men were innocent, the more she used her bully TV pulpit to persecute them.

- Badgered unmercifully the mother of a missing two-year-old. The day the interview was scheduled to air, the woman killed herself. Relatives blamed her death on Grace's over-the-top interview and sued. Grace settled with the woman's estate.

- Railed against the exoneration of Casey Anthony in 2011 in the death of her young daughter, Caylee. Said Grace of the court's verdict, "It's tough . . . when you think about all those days that Tot Mom went about partying as if Caylee had never existed. . . . The devil is dancing tonight."

- Wondered loudly in 2012 whether singer Whitney Houston's death in a Hollywood bathtub might be the result of foul play, despite the Los Angeles Police Department's repeated denials.

Not only were Nancy Grace and her employers unrepentant for the verbal damage she had wrought, she—and they and the ratings—reveled and prospered in the notoriety. Grace was even drafted to appear on *Law and Order* and chosen in 2011 to compete on *Dancing with the Stars,* where she embarrassingly exposed a telltale nipple in a particularly vigorous quickstep. Grace, typically, was unfazed.*

Questions

1. Have you any objection to Nancy Grace's opinions in the ongoing legal cases cited here?

2. What were the public relations implications for Grace's network, *HLN,* with respect to its outspoken lawyer?

*For further information, see David Carr, "TV Justice Thrives on Fear," *The New York Times,* May 22, 2011; and Stephen Hudak, "Josh Duckett Calls Settlement of Nancy Grace Lawsuit 'A Blessing,'" *Orlando Sentinel,* November 9, 2010.

Regulation of Lobbying Act of 1946. The late White House Deputy Chief of Staff Michael K. Deaver, a well-known public relations professional, was found guilty of perjury over his lobbying activities, fined $100,000, and sentenced to community service. In 2005, political public relations professional Michael Scanlon, an associate of crooked lobbyist Jack Abramoff, also was sentenced to hard time as a result of conspiracy to bribe public officials.

■ In 2012, Governor Nikki R. Haley of South Carolina was cleared of charges that she violated ethics rules when she was a state representative and lobbied on behalf of two businesses she worked for.

In recent years, campaign finance reform to limit—if not eradicate—the acceptance by legislators of favors and money from wealthy interest groups intensified until 2010. In that year, the Supreme Court's decision in the *Citizens United* v. *FEC* case held that the First Amendment prohibited the government from restricting independent political expenditures by corporations and unions, thus stemming the tide for campaign finance reform in the 2012 election. Consequently, the emergence of so-called Super PACs, political action committees that could accept unlimited contributions from individuals, unions, and corporations for the purpose of making independent expenditures, proliferated.[17]

Public Relations and Copyright Law

One body of law that is particularly relevant to public relations professionals is copyright law and the protections it offers writers. Copyright law provides basic, automatic protection for writers, whether a manuscript is registered with the Copyright Office or even published. Under the Copyright Act of 1976, an "original work of authorship" has copyright protection from the moment the work is in "fixed" form. The word *fixed* means that the work is sufficiently permanent to permit it to be perceived, reproduced, or otherwise communicated.[18]

Copyright law gives the owner of the copyright the exclusive right to reproduce and authorize others to reproduce the work, prepare derivative works based on the copyrighted material, and perform and/or display the work publicly. That's why the late Michael Jackson had to pay $47.5 million for the rights to the Beatles' compositions to the duly sworn representatives and heirs of John, Paul, George, and Ringo.

Copyright law is different from trademark law, which refers to a word, symbol, or slogan, used alone or in combination, that identifies a product or its sponsor—for example, the Nike swoosh.

What courts have stated again and again is that for the purposes of criticism, news reporting, teaching, scholarship, or research, use of copyrighted material is not an infringement but rather constitutes *fair use*. Although precise definitions of fair use—like everything else in the law—is subject to interpretation, such factors as "the effect on the future market" of the copyrighted work in question or the "volume of quotation used" or even whether the "heart" of the material was ripped off are often considered.[19]

That's why the Associated Press (AP), one of the nation's largest news organizations, announced in 2008 that it had had it with bloggers copying its works and would impose strict guidelines on the blogosphere as to how much quoting and copying of AP stories would be tolerated. The AP dictum was aimed squarely at the vague doctrine of *fair use*.[20]

Over time, the Supreme Court has strengthened the copyright status of freelance artists and writers—many of whom are independent public relations practitioners—ruling that such professionals retain the right to copyright what they create "as long as they were not in a conventional employment relationship with the organization that commissioned their work." As a result of this ruling, public relations professionals must carefully document the authorization that has been secured for using freelance material. In other words, when engaging a freelance professional, public relations people must know the law.

Public Relations and Internet Law

The Internet has introduced a new dimension to the law affecting free speech. The premise in American law is that "not all speech is created equal."[21] Rather, there is a hierarchy of speech, under Supreme Court precedents dating back many decades, that calibrates the degree of First Amendment protection with, among other tests, the particular medium of expression. For example, speech that would be perfectly acceptable if uttered in a public park could constitutionally be banned when broadcast from a sound truck.

Dealing with the Internet has introduced new ramifications to this legal principal. Indeed, cyberlaw has brought into question many of the most revered communications law principles.

Censorship

In 1996, Congress passed the Communications Decency Act (CDA) as an amendment to a far-reaching telecommunications bill. The CDA introduced criminal penalties, including fines of as much as $250,000 and prison terms up to two years, for making "indecent" speech available to "a person under 18 years of age." A Philadelphia court a few months later struck down the law, contending that such censorship would chill all discourse on the Internet.[22]

Then, in the summer of 1997, the Supreme Court, in a sweeping endorsement of free speech, declared the CDA unconstitutional. The decision, unanimous in most respects, marked the highest court's first effort to extend the principles of the First Amendment into cyberspace and to confront the nature and the law of this new, powerful medium. In summarizing the Court's finding, Justice John Paul Stevens said the Court considered the "goal of protecting children from indecent material as legitimate and important" but concluded that "the wholly unprecedented breadth of the law threatened to suppress far too much speech among adults and even between parents and children."[23]

In 1998, Congress passed the Children's Online Privacy Protection Act (COPPA), which details what a Website operator must include in a privacy policy, when and how to seek verifiable consent from a parent or guardian, and what responsibilities an operator has to protect children's privacy and safety online including restrictions on the marketing to those under 13. While children under 13 can legally give out personal information with their parents' permission, many Websites altogether disallow underage children from using their services due to the amount of COPPA paperwork involved. The Federal Trade Commission enforces COPPA.

In the 21st century, the most raging Internet censorship battles have been waged overseas, with nations such as China, Iran, Turkey, and others notorious for their Internet filters. In 2010, Google closed its search service in China because of the country's harsh restrictions.[24]

Intellectual Property

Few cyberlaw cases have drawn more headlines than the 2001 case against Napster, the popular application that allowed users to exchange music files. Because Napster ran the file-swapping through a central server, it was an easy target for legislation.

In the end—for Napster—the protest, led by those heavy-metal defenders of the First Amendment, Metallica, and backed by the large music companies, convinced the Court that the company was infringing on copyright protections of intellectual property. Two years later, the recording industry waged all-out war on those who downloaded intellectual property without paying.

On a broader level, intellectual piracy of everything from video games to music to software has become rampant, with estimates that 90% of virtually every form of intellectual property in China is pirated.[25] In 2012, a pitched battle was waged in Congress on the piracy of intellectual property. On one side stood the Hollywood producers of records, books, and movies who fretted that the fruits of their labors were being stolen. On the other side stood Internet firms such as Google, Twitter, Facebook, and Reddit, which saw the Stop Online Piracy Act (SOPA) momentum as a threat to creativity. In the end, the might of the upstart Internet crowd proved too strong, and SOPA was defeated.[26]

The SOPA conflict was a harbinger of battles to come, with media companies on one side and Internet providers on the other. While a number of nations, including the United States, Japan, Canada, South Korea, and Australia, signed the Anti-Counterfeiting Trade Agreement, in July 2012, European legislators rejected the international treaty to crack down on digital piracy. While the United States vowed to put the treaty into effect, even without European Union involvement, the debate into international piracy of intellectual property was destined to continue.[27]

Cybersquatting

Another complex issue is that of cybersquatting—grabbing domain names in bad faith, expressly for the purpose of tormenting or "shaking down" a rightful registrant. It costs an infiltrator about $35 to register a variation of a domain name.

Companies from Wendy's to General Motors to Walmart, politicians, celebrities, and athletes have all been beset by cybersquatters. Kmart Corporation successfully mounted a legal challenge to fight a rogue Website, Kmartsucks.com. Ultimately, the site was forced to change its name to Themartsucks.com. The basketball player Chris Bosh won a landmark ruling in 2010 that reclaimed his online identity and that of 800 other athletes and celebrities.[28]

Current trademark law prohibits a company from registering a name that exactly duplicates a registered trademark, but cybersquatters frequently register names that differ only slightly. They know that Web surfers will type in a variation of a company's name when searching for its site. They then either attempt to sell the names or use the sites to disrupt the company's commerce.[29]

E-Fraud

Fraud is fraud, no matter where it is domiciled. And on the World Wide Web, where anyone who wants to can choose anonymity, strip in a logo, and pretend to be someone he or she is not, fraud runs rampant. (Just check your inbox for "inheritance gift" emails from Nigeria!)

The problem is that e-crooks are not only difficult to stop but also difficult to define, at least in legal terms. Often it depends on companies policing the Internet themselves, frequently to go after former employees.

For example:

- Varian Medical Systems of Palo Alto won a $775,000 verdict against two former employees who posted 14,000 messages on 100 message boards accusing the firm of being homophobic and of discriminating against pregnant women.

- A California court ruled against a fired Intel employee who sent emails to about 35,000 staffers, criticizing the company.

- St. Paul–based insurer Travelers accused one former vice president of trying to sabotage the company with anonymous blog postings, charging, among other things, that one executive was little more than a "glorified secretary" and another "would stab his own mother in the back to make money." Travelers took the case all the way to federal court.[30]

And then there's "click fraud," which threatens to disrupt the largest search engines. Search engines rank listings by the number of clicks they receive: the more clicks, the higher the ranking. Click fraud occurs when a concerted effort is initiated to register multiple clicks to drive specific listings higher in a search-ranking algorithm. Such fraudulent activity affects marketers, who advertise on a site and pay rates based on usage.[31]

Social Media

The advent of social networking has introduced yet another legal dimension to the Internet. This is a particularly thorny issue in terms of employee relations.

In 2010, the National Labor Relations Board accused a company of illegally firing an employee after she criticized her supervisor on her Facebook page. The Board argued that "whether it takes place on Facebook or at the water cooler, it was employees talking jointly about working conditions, in this case about their supervisor, and they have a right to do that."[32]

Or do they?

With organizations now sensitive to the potential use of social media to discuss employment matters, lawyers recommend that employers "review their Internet and social media policies to determine whether they are susceptible to an allegation that the policy would reasonably tend to chill employees in the exercise of their rights to discuss wages, working conditions and unionization."[33]

Increasingly, universities and potential employers are seeking access to social media to monitor activities. The University of North Carolina at Chapel Hill, for example, adopted a student athlete policy that appointed a coach to be responsible "for having access to and regularly monitoring the content of team members' social networking sites and postings."[34]

These are but a few of the burgeoning legal issues that surround the World Wide Web.

Litigation Public Relations

In court cases, plaintiffs and defendants are often scrupulously warned by judges not to influence the ultimate verdict outside the courtroom.

Forget it.

In the 21st century, with the Internet, CNN, MSNBC, Fox News Channel, CNBC, Headline News, and talk radio incessantly jabbering about possible trials, upcoming trials, and current trials, there is little guarantee that any jury can be objective about any high-profile legal case.

That's why litigation public relations has become so important.

Litigation public relations can best be defined as managing the media process during the course of any legal dispute so as to affect the outcome or its impact on the client's overall reputation.

Although court proceedings have certain rules and protocols, dealing in the public arena with a matter of litigation has no such strictures. The Sixth Amendment to the Constitution guarantees accused persons "a speedy and public trial, by an impartial jury," but television commentary by knowledgeable—and in many cases, unknowledgeable—"experts" can help influence a potential jury for or against a defendant (Figure 7-7).

As a consequence, communication has become central to the management of modern litigation.[35] Smart lawyers understand that with the Internet and cable TV, in particular, being so pervasive, they have little choice but to engage in litigation public relations to provide their clients with every advantage.

For example, in 2008, when three Duke lacrosse players were prosecuted for allegedly raping a stripper, supporters set up a Website to communicate views on the case, which ultimately fell apart. When several parents of the lacrosse players filed a countersuit against the university, they set up a blog to provide information to the public. In 2011, when International Monetary Fund President Dominique Strauss-Kahn was charged with rape by a New York City chambermaid, his surrogates engaged in a blistering publicity attack of the woman's history and character. The case was dropped.

FIGURE 7-7
Litigation public relations.
The Institute for Justice (IJ) epitomized the best of litigation public relations when it publicized the story of Doreen Flynn, a mom with three young daughters, each of whom would need a bone marrow transplant to survive. IJ challenged the prohibition on compensating bone-marrow donors in the National Organ Transplant Act and won the case in 2012.
(Courtesy of Institute for Justice, photo by Don Wilson)

According to one counselor who works exclusively with litigation, there are seven keys to litigation visibility.

1. **Learn the process.** All involved should be aware of the roadmap for the case and the milestones ahead, which may lend themselves to publicity.

2. **Develop a message strategy.** Think about what should be said at each stage of a trial to keep the press and public focused on the key messages of the client.

3. **Settle fast.** Settlement is probably the most potent litigation visibility management tool. The faster the settlement, the less litigation visibility there is likely to be. This is often a positive development.

4. **Anticipate high-profile variables.** Often in public cases everybody gets into the act—judges, commentators, jury selection experts, psychologists, and so on. Always anticipate all that could be said, conjectured, and argued about the case. Always try to be prepared for every inevitability.

5. **Keep the focus positive.** Ultimately, it's a positive, productive attitude that leads to effective negotiations with the other side. So the less combative you can be—especially near settlement—the better.

6. **Try settling again.** Again, this ought to be the primary litigation visibility strategy—to end the agony and get it out of the papers.

7. **Fight nicely.** Wars are messy, expensive, and prone to producing casualties. It is much better to be positive. This will give both sides a greater chance of eventually settling.[36]

Last Word

As our society becomes more contentious, fractious, and litigious, public relations must become more concerned with the law. On the one hand, because management must rely so heavily on legal advice and legal judgments, it is imperative that public relations people understand the laws that govern their organizations and industries. Public relations people must understand that their views may differ from those of an attorney. As a defense lawyer once described his role, "You should do what a client wants, period. That's what you're paid for." By contrast, public relations people are paid to advise their clients what is "the right thing to do." And they should never shrink from that obligation.

On the other hand, public relations advisors must depend on "buy-in" from others in management. Lawyers are among the most influential of these associates. Therefore, knowing the law and forming an alliance with legal counselors must be a frontline objective for public relations professionals.

Beyond the working relationship between public relations people and lawyers, the practice of public relations has, itself, wrestled with legal questions in recent years. The government has gone after firms that "deceptively advertised" online, through such tactics as posting fictitious online reviews of products or restaurants or similarly endorsing clients' wares through blogs and Twitter.[37] Increasingly, public relations practice is based on legal contracts: between agencies and clients, employers and employees, purchasers and vendors. All contracts—both written and oral—must be binding and enforceable.

In recent years, controversy in the field has erupted over noncompete clauses, in which former employees are prohibited, within certain time parameters, from working for a competitor or pitching a former account. Time and again the courts have ruled in favor of public relations agencies and against former clients in noncompete cases.

Likewise, legal challenges have been made relative to the markup of expenses that public relations agencies charge clients. Standard practice in the industry is to mark up by 15 to 20% of legitimate printing and advertising bills submitted to clients.

Add to these the blurring of the lines between public relations advice on the one hand and legal advice on the other, and it becomes clear that the connection between public relations and the law will intensify dramatically in the 21st century.

Discussion Starters

1. What is the difference between a public relations professional's responsibility and a lawyer's responsibility?
2. What have been recent challenges to the First Amendment?
3. How can someone prove that he or she has been libeled or slandered?
4. What is meant by the term *insider trading*?
5. What is the SEC's overriding concern when considering disclosure?
6. How have Regulation FD and Sarbanes-Oxley changed the disclosure environment?
7. Whom does copyright law protect?
8. What are some of the dominant issues in laws affecting the Internet?
9. What are several general principles with respect to litigation public relations?
10. What general advice should a public relations professional consider in working with lawyers?

Pick of the Literature

Advertising and Public Relations Law, 2nd Edition

Roy L. Moore, Carmen Maye and Erik L. Collins. New York: Routledge, 2011

This book offers an exhaustive examination of the First Amendment as it relates to the advertising and public relations businesses.

It traces the history of the First Amendment and tracks the interpretation of the amendment through the decades. The real merit of this volume is in its discussion of New Media implications on free speech law in terms of both individuals and corporations. Libel, defamation, privacy, and related public relations–oriented statutes are discussed in depth.

Copyright, patents and trademarks, Federal Trade Commission regulations, and others are explained. An excellent legal primer for public relations professionals.

Case Study   Amazon Shuts Free Speech Door on Pedophile Book

There is no thornier issue for Internet providers than "free speech." For Google, Facebook, Twitter, and the rest, conundrums involving free speech are omnipresent.

- Is all speech "free"?
- If not, where does free speech end?
- What "sanctions" should be placed on groups such as WikiLeaks that publish secret documents?
- And what about limits on pornography?

In the winter of 2010, one of the Internet's champions of "free speech," Amazon.com, confronted such an issue, which quickly went viral and immersed the company in a messy public contretemps.

Standing Its Ground

In November, when pressed by journalists, Amazon didn't flinch in defending its sale of a $4.79 self-published electronic book offering a guide to pedophilia. The author, Philip Greaves of

Pueblo, Colorado, was a former nurse's aide who described himself as a "rogue scholar with respect to the topics of religion, sexuality and politics." Greaves also self-published four other books, including *Our Gardens of Flesh* and *The Grand Book of the Godless.*

Amazon offered Greaves's *The Pedophile's Guide to Love and Pleasure*, which described itself as a guide for so-called pedosexuals, because, said the company, pulling it would amount to censorship. Over the years, Amazon's CEO and founder Jeff Bezos had been one of those Internet stalwarts who argued against censoring Internet properties, on the grounds that the Internet was a safe haven for freedom of personal choice.

Although CEO Bezos was off the radar screen when publicity for the pedophile book emerged, an Amazon representative defended the company's decision to sell the book. Said he:

> Amazon believes it is censorship not to sell certain books simply because we or others believe their message is objectionable. Amazon does not support or promote hatred or criminal acts, however, we do support the right of every individual to make their own purchasing decisions.

Several Amazon reviewers were repulsed by the company's logic and decision.

> As a mother of a child who has been molested, shame on Amazon for allowing such garbage to be sold on its site. The author of this book is a predator and should never have been allowed to write or promote this trash that is called a book of information. How many children will be assaulted because of this. Amazon take it off your site.

A few Amazon reviewers, however, hailed the company's gutsy decision.

> This is the single best book ever written . . . if for no other reason than the horde of frothy-mouthed crusaders shouting for its utter annihilation. The subject matter is all but irrelevant, as I'm sure the very same people decrying someone willing to write outside of their moral comfort zone would be completely aghast at someone saying the same thing about a devout Christian book.

In terms of the law, sexual activity with a minor is a federal crime and luring children across state lines for the purposes of either prostitution or sexual activity is also a violation of federal law. However, publishing a book that talks about pedophilia isn't a crime.

Losing Its Ground

Perhaps heartened by the online publisher's defense, author Greaves, in the wake of the national publicity, offered his own defense of his work.

> This is my attempt to make pedophile situations safer for those juveniles that find themselves involved in them, by establishing certain rules for these adults to follow. I hope to achieve this by appealing to the better nature of pedosexuals with hope that their doing so will result in less hatred and perhaps lighter sentences should they ever be caught.

And that's when Amazon reversed course.

Although the company made no formal announcement, the very next day after Amazon's defense and Greaves's explanation, the book became inaccessible on Amazon's site. In addition, Amazon removed author Greaves's other titles as well.

While Amazon steadfastly refused to elaborate on its next-day decision, other than saying the company "reserves the right to determine the appropriateness" of items sold on its site, author Greaves was unrepentant. Said he, "I wrote the book to establish guidelines so that people would behave in a manner that is non-injurious to each other."

Police in Greaves's hometown, however, weren't convinced. Said one, "When free speech fuels the motive for people on how to approach kids, how to find kids, how to touch kids and sexually abuse them, that's just wrong."

A month after the Amazon controversy came to light, author Greaves was arrested in Polk County, Florida, for violating the state's obscenity law that prohibits the "distribution of obscene material depicting minors engaged in conduct harmful to minors."

Legal experts questioned whether Greaves's right to free speech would come into play. If prosecutors could charge Greaves for shipping his book, they asked, what would prevent booksellers from facing prosecution for selling Vladimir Nabokov's *Lolita*, a novel about a pedophile?

In April, Greaves pleaded "no contest" and got two years probation. Said the non-plussed author, "True pedophiles love children and would never hurt them" (Figure 7-8).*

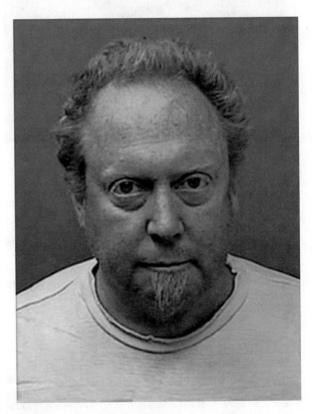

FIGURE 7-8 The author at (ar)rest.
Philip Greaves. *(Photo: PacificCoastNews/Newscom)*

Questions

1. Do you agree with Amazon's first or second decision?

2. Where should Amazon draw the line on distributing books that contain questionable content?

3. What do you think of Amazon's public relations posture in this case?

*For further information, see Lauren Frayer, "Amazon Yanks Pedophilia E-Book Amid Boycott Talk," AOL.COM, November 11, 2010; Mark Hachman, "Amazon Refuses to Pull Pro-Pedophilia E-Book," PCMAG.COM, November 10, 2010; "Pedophilia Book Removed from Amazon, But Others Remain," *The Wall Street Journal*, November 11, 2010; and Alan Pendergast, "Philip Greaves: Amazon Removes Other Titles by Pedophile's Guide to Love and Pleasure Author," Dever Westword Blog, November 12, 2010.

From the Top

An Interview with Robert Shapiro

Robert Shapiro (right) and a former client. *(Photo: Michael NELSON Agence France Presse/Newscom)*

Celebrity attorney Robert Shapiro, cofounder of LegalZoom, has represented many of Hollywood's most famous and notorious defendants, from his tenure as a member of football great and accused murderer O. J. Simpson's "dream team" to his defense of legendary record producer and convicted murderer Phil Spector. After his successful defense of O. J. Simpson, Shapiro offered the following insights into how a modern-day lawyer views public relations.

How do you view a lawyer's public relations responsibilities?

When we are retained for those high-profile cases, we are instantly thrust into the role of a public relations person—a role for which the majority of us have no education, experience, or training. The lawyer's role as spokesperson may be [as] equally important to the outcome of a case as the skills of an advocate in the courtroom.

How important is the media to a trial?

The importance and power of the media cannot be overemphasized. The first impression the public gets is usually the one that is most important. The wire services depend on immediate updates. Therefore, all calls should be returned as quickly as possible.

"No comment" is the least appropriate and least productive response. Coming at the end of a lengthy story, it adds absolutely nothing and leaves the public with a negative impression.

How important are relationships with the media in a trial setting?

Initial relationships with legitimate members of the press are very important. Many times a lawyer will feel it is an intrusion to be constantly beset by seemingly meaningless questions that take up a tremendous amount of time. But the initial headlines of the arrest often make the sacred presumption of innocence a myth. In reality, we have the presumption of guilt. This is why dealing with the media is so important.

How carefully should lawyers construct answers to reporters' questions?

Just as you would do in trial, anticipate the questions a reporter will pose. Think out your answers carefully. . . . Use great care in choosing your words. Keep your statements simple and concise. Pick and choose the questions you want to answer. You do not have to be concerned with whether the answer precisely addresses the question, since only the answer will be aired.

What about dealing with the tabloids?

My experience is that cooperating with tabloid reporters only gives them a legitimate source of information which can be misquoted or taken out of context and does little good for your client. My personal approach is not to cooperate with tabloid reporters.

What about dealing with television?
The television media, either consciously or unconsciously, create an atmosphere of chaos. Immediately upon arriving at the courthouse, you are surrounded by television crews. We have all seen people coming to court and trying to rush through the press with their heads down or covering them with newspapers or coats. Nothing looks worse. I always instruct my clients upon arrival at the courthouse to get out in a normal manner, to walk next to me in a slow and deliberate way, to have a look of confidence and acknowledge with a nod those who are familiar and supportive.*

*Excerpted from Robert Shapiro, "Secrets of a Celebrity Lawyer," *Columbia Journalism Review* (September/October 1994): 25–29. Copyright © 1994 Columbia Journalism Review. Reprinted by permission.

Public Relations Library

Bybee, Keith. *Bench Press: The Collision of Courts, Politics and the Media.* Stanford, CA: Stanford University Press, 2007.

Coffey, Kendall. *Spinning the Law.* Amherst, NY: Prometheus Books, 2010. A famous attorney takes a spin at spinning, offering a media primer for barristers.

Collins, Matthew. *The Law of Defamation and the Internet.* New York: Oxford University Press, 2005. Useful overview of evolving Internet law.

Goldsmith, Jack, and Tim Wu. *Who Controls the Internet? Illusions of a Borderless World.* New York: Oxford University Press, 2008. Two legal scholars examine the reality of the laws that attempt to govern the Internet.

Levick, Richard, and Larry Smith. *Stop the Presses: The Crisis and Litigation PR Desk Reference* (2nd ed.). Ann Arbor, MI: Watershed Press, 2008. Two agency veterans focus on litigation public relations in crisis situations. Good book.

Mitchell, Paul. *The Making of the Modern Law of Defamation.* Oxford, England: Hart Publishing, 2005. Libel, slander, and hate speech share center stage in this useful compendium.

Moore, Roy L., and Michael D. Murray. *Media, Law and Ethics* (3rd ed.) New York: Taylor and Francis Group 2008. An updated compendium of the laws that govern the media.

Parkinson, Michael G., and L. Marie Parkinson. *Public Relations Law.* New York: Routledge, 2008. Candid appraisal of the legal rights and responsibilities of public relations professionals.

Sinclair, Adriana. *International Relations Theory and International Law.* Cambridge, UK: Cambridge University Press, 2010. Good discussion of the legal boundaries of operating in international markets.

Zittrain, Jonathan. *The Future of the Internet and How to Stop It.* Harrisonburg, VA: R.R. Donnelly, 2008. Especially pertinent is the chapter on "cybersecurity."

Chapter 8

Research

Chapter Objectives

1. To discuss the importance of research as the essential first step in every public relations assignment.

2. To explore research principles, types, and methods.

3. To discuss the various research tools and evaluative techniques available to public relations professionals.

4. To underscore the importance of Web monitoring and tools available for Internet research.

An early look at 2012

President Barack Obama faces a challenging electoral map for the 2012 presidential election, as analyzed by the Cook Political Report; 270 electoral votes are needed to win:

Obama		Tossup	Republican	
■ Solid	■ Leaning	■ Tossup	■ Solid	■ Leaning/likely
186	35	98	159	60

Number of electoral votes to win: 270

Source: Cook Political Report
Graphic: Raoul Ranoa, Los Angeles Times

© 2011 MCT

FIGURE 8-1   Purple nation?

Not so much, especially if you get behind the numbers that indicate that most U.S. voters, whether they claim to be "independent" or not, still side with one of the two major political parties. *(Photo: Ranoa/MCT/Newscom)*

By the presidential election of 2012, most Americans had had it with political parties. With radical blue-state liberals dominating the Democrats and radical red-state conservatives dominating the Republicans, the great muddled middle seemed to be dominant.

And that's pretty much why public relations pollster Mark Penn concluded in *Time* magazine that the American voter was changing. Wrote Penn, "Polls reveal that some 40 percent of U.S. voters now classify themselves as independents, a record number. America is becoming a purple nation, where the biggest party is no party at all"[1] (Figure 8-1).

Sounds correct. But is it?

"It's overblown," said marketing guru Steve Rivkin. "In fact according to Gallup, the number of independents has stayed about the same since the mid-1990s. Penn is referring to non-aligned party identification. If you ask independents which party they lean toward, the number of true independents goes down to about 10 percent." Indeed, according to Gallup, when "independent party leanings" are included, Democrats and Republicans come out to be about 45% each.[2]

In other words, while Penn's numbers may have been correct, his interpretation of those numbers—that the 2012 election would reveal a sea change in American voters—was far from historical reality. Sure enough, it didn't.

Such are the peculiarities of research, where the old adage, "Figures lie, and liars figure," must still be considered in evaluating empirical data.

Despite its interpretative issues, research is the natural starting point for any public relations assignment—from plotting a political campaign to promoting a product to designing a program to confronting a crisis. The first step in solving any public relations challenge is to conduct research.

At the same time, it should be recognized that research, particularly in an art form as intuitive as public relations, is no panacea. Research is but a foundation upon which a sensible programmatic initiative must be based. Research must always be complemented by analysis and judgment.

Nonetheless, in public relations it is obligatory to begin with research.

Why?

Frankly, the answer stems from the fact that few managers understand what public relations is and how it works. Managers—particularly those guided by quantitative, empirical measurement—want "proof" that what we advise is based on logic and clear thinking.

In other words, most clients are less interested in what their public relations advisors *think* than in what they *know*. The only real way to know your advice is on the right track is by ensuring that it is grounded in hard data whenever possible. So before recommending a course of action, public relations professionals must analyze audiences, assess alternatives, and generally do their homework.

In other words, do research.

Essential First Step

Every public relations program or solution should begin with research. Most don't, which is a shame.

The various approaches to public relations problem solving, discussed in Chapter 1, all start with research.

Instinct, intuition, and gut feelings all remain important in the conduct of public relations work, but management today demands more—measurement, analysis, and evaluation at every stage of the public relations process. In an era of scarce resources, management wants facts and statistics from public relations professionals to show that their efforts contribute not only to overall organizational effectiveness but also to the bottom line. For example:

- **Outputs**—Did we get the coverage we wanted?
- **Outtakes**—Did our target audience see and/or believe our messages?
- **Outcomes**—Did audience behavior or relationships change, and did sales increase?[3]

Questions such as these must be answered through research.

In a day when organizational resources are precious and companies don't want to spend money unless it enhances results, public relations programs must contribute to meeting business objectives.[4] That means that research must be applied to help segment market targets, analyze audience preferences and dislikes, and determine which messages might be most effective with various audiences. Research then becomes essential in helping realize management's goals.

Research should be applied in public relations work both at the initial stage, prior to planning a campaign, and at the final stage to evaluate a program's effectiveness. Early research helps to determine the current situation, prevalent attitudes, and difficulties that the program faces. Later research examines the program's success, along with what else still needs to be done. Research at both points in the process is critical.

What Is Research?

Research is the systematic collection and interpretation of information to increase understanding. Most people associate public relations with conveying information; although that association is accurate, research must be the obligatory first step in any project. A firm must acquire enough accurate, relevant data about its publics, products, and programs to answer these questions:

- How can we identify and define our constituent groups?
- How does this knowledge relate to the design of our messages?
- How does it relate to the design of our programs?
- How does it relate to the media we use to convey our messages?
- How does it relate to the schedule we adopt in using our media?
- How does it relate to the ultimate implementation tactics of our program?

It is difficult to delve into the minds of others, whose backgrounds and points of view may be quite different from our own, with the purpose of understanding why they think as they do. Research skills are partly intuitive, partly an outgrowth of individual temperament, and partly a function of acquired knowledge. There is nothing mystifying about them. Although we tend to think of research in terms of impersonal test scores, interviews, or questionnaires, these methods are only a small part of the process. The real challenge lies in using research—knowing when to do what, with whom, and for what purpose.

Principles of Public Relations Research

For years, public relations professionals have debated the standards of measuring public relations' effectiveness. The Institute for Public Relations Research and Education offered several guiding principles in setting standards for public relations research.

- Establish clear program objectives and desired outcomes tied directly to business goals.
- Differentiate between measuring public relations "outputs," generally short term and surface (e.g., amount of press coverage received or exposure of a particular message), and measuring public relations "outcomes," usually more far-reaching and carrying greater impact (e.g., changing awareness, attitudes, and even behavior).
- Measure media content as a first step in the public relations evaluation process. Such a measure is limited in that it can't discern whether a target audience actually saw a message or responded to it.
- Understand that no one technique can be expected to evaluate public relations effectiveness. Rather, this requires a combination of techniques, from media analysis to cyberspace analysis, from focus groups to polls and surveys.
- Be wary of attempts to compare public relations effectiveness with advertising effectiveness. One particularly important consideration is that while advertising placement and messages can be controlled, their equivalent on the public relations side cannot be.
- The most trustworthy measurement of public relations effectiveness is that which stems from an organization with clearly identified key messages, target

Outside the Lines

Figures and Faces—Lie

If you don't believe the old maxim that "figures lie and liars figure," consider the following: In often repeated research, randomly selected participants are shown the two faces in Figure 8-2 and asked, "Which woman is lovelier?" Invariably, the answer is split 50–50.

However, when each woman is named; one "Jennifer" and the other "Gertrude," respondents overwhelmingly—more than 80%—vote for Jennifer as the more beautiful woman.

Why? "Jennifer" is more hip, more happening, more, uh, "phat." (Sorry, all you Gertrudes out there!)

The point is that people can't help but introduce their own biases, including even in presumably "objective" research experiments. This factor always should be taken into account in evaluating public relations research.

FIGURE 8-2 Jennifer/Gertrude. *(Courtesy of Fraser P. Seitel)*

audiences, and desired channels of communication. The converse of this is that the more confused an organization is about its targets, the less reliable its public relations measurement will be.

Public relations evaluation cannot be accomplished in isolation. It must be linked to overall business goals, strategies, and tactics.

Types of Public Relations Research

In general, research is conducted to do three things: (1) describe a process, situation, or phenomenon; (2) explain why something is happening, what its causes are, and what effect it will have; and (3) predict what probably will happen if we do or don't take action. Primary, or original, research in public relations is either theoretical or applied. Applied research solves practical problems; theoretical research aids understanding of a public relations process.

Most public relations analysis, however, takes the more informal form called secondary research. This relies on existing material—books, articles, Internet databases, and the like—to form the research backing for public relations recommendations and programs.

Applied Research

In public relations work, applied research can be either strategic or evaluative. Both applications are designed to answer specific practical questions.

- **Strategic research** is used primarily in program development to determine program objectives, develop message strategies, or establish benchmarks. It often examines the tools and techniques of public relations. For example, a firm that wants to know how employees rate its candor in internal publications would first conduct strategic research to find out where it stands.

■ **Evaluative research**, sometimes called summative research, is conducted primarily to determine whether a public relations program has accomplished its goals and objectives. For example, if changes are made in the internal communications program to increase candor, evaluative research can determine whether the goals have been met. A variant of evaluation can be applied during a program to monitor progress and indicate where modifications might make sense.

Theoretical Research

Theoretical research is more abstract and conceptual than applied research. It helps build theories in public relations work about why people communicate, how public opinion is formed, and how a public is created.

Knowledge of theoretical research is important as a framework for persuasion and as a base for understanding why people do what they do.

Some knowledge of theoretical research in public relations and mass communications is essential for enabling practitioners to understand the limitations of communication as a persuasive tool. Attitude and behavior change has been the traditional goal in public relations programs, yet theoretical research indicates that such a goal may be difficult or impossible to achieve through persuasive efforts. According to such research, other factors are always getting in the way.

Researchers have found that communication is most persuasive when it comes from multiple sources of high credibility. Credibility itself is a multidimensional concept that includes trustworthiness, expertise, and power. Others have found that a message generally is more effective when it is simple, because it is easier to understand, localize, and make personally relevant. According to still other research, the persuasiveness of a message can be increased when it arouses or is accompanied by a high level of personal involvement in the issue at hand.

The point here is that knowledge of theoretical research can help practitioners not only understand the basis of applied research findings but also temper management's expectations of attitude and behavioral change resulting from public relations programs.

Secondary Research

Secondary research is research on the cheap. Basically, secondary research allows you to examine or read about and learn from someone else's primary research, such as in a library.

Also called "desk research," secondary research uses data that have been collected for other purposes than your own. Database monitoring is particularly important for public relations researchers. Such online resources as Claritas, which supplies marketing analysis and demographic tools; SurveyMonkey.com, which provides the resources to create tailored online surveys (Figure 8-3); and the omnipresent Google search engine are popular outlets to aid public relations researchers.

Because public relations budgets are limited, it always makes sense first to consider secondary sources in launching a research effort.

Methods of Public Relations Research

Observation is the foundation of modern social science. Scientists, social psychologists, and anthropologists make observations, develop theories, and, hopefully, increase understanding of human behavior. Public relations research, too, is founded on

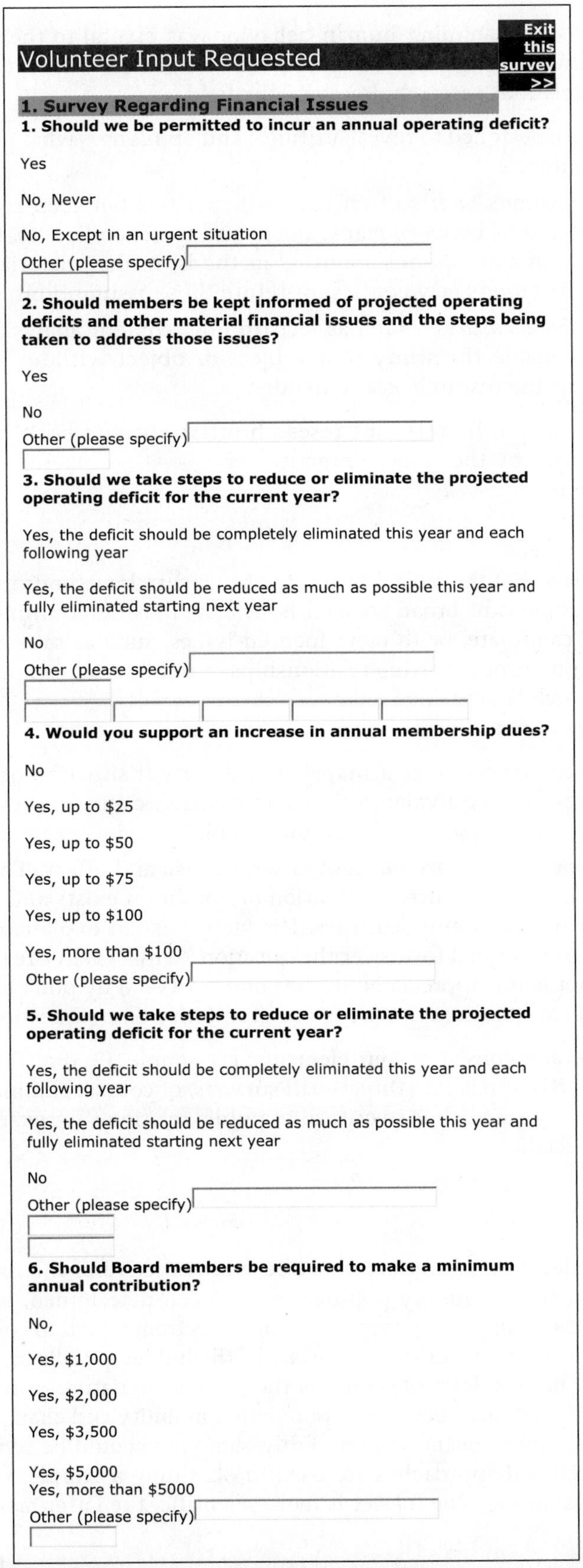

Volunteer Input Requested

Exit
this
survey
>>

1. Survey Regarding Financial Issues

1. Should we be permitted to incur an annual operating deficit?

Yes

No, Never

No, Except in an urgent situation

Other (please specify)

2. Should members be kept informed of projected operating deficits and other material financial issues and the steps being taken to address those issues?

Yes

No

Other (please specify)

3. Should we take steps to reduce or eliminate the projected operating deficit for the current year?

Yes, the deficit should be completely eliminated this year and each following year

Yes, the deficit should be reduced as much as possible this year and fully eliminated starting next year

No

Other (please specify)

4. Would you support an increase in annual membership dues?

No

Yes, up to $25

Yes, up to $50

Yes, up to $75

Yes, up to $100

Yes, more than $100

Other (please specify)

5. Should we take steps to reduce or eliminate the projected operating deficit for the current year?

Yes, the deficit should be completely eliminated this year and each following year

Yes, the deficit should be reduced as much as possible this year and fully eliminated starting next year

No

Other (please specify)

6. Should Board members be required to make a minimum annual contribution?

No,

Yes, $1,000

Yes, $2,000

Yes, $3,500

Yes, $5,000
Yes, more than $5000

Other (please specify)

FIGURE 8-3 **Survey monkey.** Services, such as SurveyMonkey.com, allow you to design your own online survey, such as the hypothetical one shown here.

observation. Indeed, examining human behavior was pivotal to the early public relations work of Edward Bernays, a disciple of his uncle, Sigmund Freud. Three primary forms of public relations research dominate the field.

- *Surveys* are designed to reveal attitudes and opinions—what people think about certain subjects.
- *Communications audits* often reveal disparities between real and perceived communications between management and target audiences. Management may make certain assumptions about its methods, media, materials, and messages, whereas its targets may confirm or refute those assumptions.
- *Unobtrusive measures*—such as fact-finding, content analysis, and readability studies—enable the study of a subject or object without involving the researcher or the research as an intruder.

Each method of public relations research offers specific benefits and should be understood and used by the modern practitioner.

Surveys

Survey research is one of the most frequently used research methods in public relations. Surveys can be applied to broad societal issues, such as determining public opinion about a political candidate, or to more focused issues, such as satisfaction of hospital patients or hotel guests or reporting relationships of public relations people (Figure 8-4). Most survey research is now done online.

Surveys come in two types.

1. *Descriptive surveys* offer a snapshot of a current situation or condition. They are the research equivalent of a balance sheet, capturing reality at a specific point in time. A typical public opinion poll is a prime example.

2. *Explanatory surveys* are concerned with cause and effect. Their purpose is to help explain why a current situation or condition exists and to offer explanations for opinions and attitudes. Frequently, such explanatory or analytical surveys are designed to answer the question "why?" Why are our philanthropic dollars not being appreciated in the community? Why don't employees believe management's messages? Why is our credibility being questioned?

Surveys generally consist of four elements: (1) sample, (2) questionnaire, (3) interview, and (4) analysis of results. (Direct-mail surveys, of course, eliminate the interview step.) Because survey research is so critical in public relations, we examine each survey element in some detail.

The Sample

The sample, or selected target group, must be representative of the total public whose views are sought. Once a survey population has been determined, a researcher must select the appropriate sample or group of respondents from which to collect information. Sampling is tricky. A researcher must be aware of the hidden pitfalls in choosing a representative sample, not the least of which is the perishable nature of most data. Survey findings are rapidly outdated because of population mobility and changes in the political and socioeconomic environment. Consequently, sampling should be completed quickly.

Two cross-sectional approaches are used in obtaining a sample: random sampling and nonrandom sampling. The former is more scientific, the latter more informal.

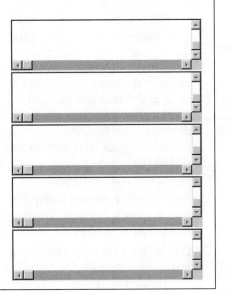

PR News/IABC Joint Survey: Getting a Taste of the C-Suite

Please take a few minutes to fill out the following survey by April 25th. Coverage of the study's results will appear in the May 4th issue of PR News as well as the May 2005 edition of IABC's CW Bulletin. We're hopeful that the results will enable senior PR pros to devise strategies that will help them reach the corporate summit—and stay there.

1. I report directly to the CEO — Please Choose ▼

2. I am a member of the top management team — Please Choose ▼

3. I regularly attend meetings of the top management team (whether or not I am a member) — Please Choose ▼

4. How many employees are there in your corporate affairs/PR department? — Please Choose ▼

5. What country are you in? — Please Select ▼

	Strongly Agree	Agree	Neither Agree nor Disagree	Disagree	Strongly Disagree
6. My CEO:					
a . . . understands the importance of communication, not just when there is an issue or crisis	○	○	○	○	○
b. . . . sees PR as an investment in the future not just a cost	○	○	○	○	○
c. . . . asks my opinion about PR implications of future directions of the business	○	○	○	○	○
d. . . . usually accepts my recommendations	○	○	○	○	○
e. . . . would say I understand the business	○	○	○	○	○
7. My CEO values corporate affairs / PR advice at least as much as that from:					
a. . . . Advertising	○	○	○	○	○
b. . . . Sales	○	○	○	○	○
c. . . . Marketing	○	○	○	○	○
d. . . . Legal	○	○	○	○	○
e. . . . Human Resources	○	○	○	○	○
8. My CEO makes an effort (e.g. willingly puts in time) to maintain good relations with the following stakeholders:					
a. . . . employees	○	○	○	○	○
b. . . . stockholders	○	○	○	○	○
c. . . . analysts	○	○	○	○	○
d. . . . customers/clients	○	○	○	○	○
e. . . . business or alliance partners	○	○	○	○	○
f. . . . media	○	○	○	○	○

9.
a. What do you mostly discuss at your meetings with the CEO? (e.g. high-level strategy, business reputation, communication tactics, your career path, media relations, CEO presentations, analyst relationships, publications?)

b. Has the CEO redefined your role or mandate at any stage (e.g. upgraded it, expanded it, downgraded it, etc.)? Please explain what and why.

10.
a. To what extent does your CEO expect PR results to be measured? Does he/she take PR less seriously because measurement is not easy to do? To what extent is your CEO skeptical of anything without numbers attached?

b. What demands does the CEO have of the PR function that are not currently being met?

c. What three things would you like to see improved in regard to the CEO and PR/coms function or your relationship with him/her?

FIGURE 8-4 Reaching the corporate summit survey.
This survey, cosponsored by *PR News* and the International Association of Business Communicators, polled reporting relationships among public relations professionals. *(Reprinted with permission from the International Association of Business Communicators)*

Random Sampling In random sampling, two properties are essential—equality and independence. *Equality* means that no element has any greater or lesser chance of being selected. *Independence* means that selecting any one element in no way influences the selection of any other element. Random sampling is based on a mathematical criterion that allows generalizations from the sample to be made to the total population. There are four types of random or probability samples.

1. **Simple random sampling** gives all members of the population an equal chance of being selected. First, all members of the population are identified, and then as many subjects as are needed are randomly selected—usually with the help of a computer. Election polling uses a random approach; although millions of Americans vote, only a few thousand are ever polled on their election preferences. The Nielsen national television sample, for example, consists of only 10,000 homes, encompassing 25,000 people, despite the fact there are 112 million TV households in the United States.[5] Despite the relatively small sample size, TV networks live and die on the basis of Nielsen data.

   How large should a random sample be? The answer depends on a number of factors, one of which is the size of the population. In addition, the more similar the population elements are in regard to the characteristics being studied, the smaller the sample required. In most random samples, the following population-to-sample ratios apply, with a 5% margin of error:

Population	Sample
1,000	278
2,000	322
3,000	341
5,000	355
10,000	370
50,000	381
100,000	383
500,000	383
Infinity	384

   Random sampling owes its accuracy to the laws of probability, which are best explained by the example of a barrel filled with 10,000 marbles—5,000 green ones and 5,000 red ones. If a blindfolded person selects a certain number of marbles from the barrel—say, 400—the laws of probability suggest that the most frequently drawn combination will be 200 red and 200 green. These laws further suggest that with certain margins of error, a very few marbles can represent the whole barrel, which can correspond to any size—for example, that of a city, state, or nation.

2. **Systematic random sampling** is closely related to simple random sampling, but it uses a random starting point in the sample list. From then on, the researcher selects every nth person in the list.

3. **Stratified random sampling** is a procedure used to survey different segments or strata of the population. For example, if an organization wants to determine the relationship between years of service and attitudes toward the company, it may stratify the sample to ensure that the breakdown of respondents accurately reflects the makeup of the population.

4. **Cluster sampling** involves first breaking the population down into small heterogeneous subsets, or clusters, and then selecting the potential sample from

the individual clusters or groups. A cluster may often be defined as a geographic area, such as an election district.

Nonrandom Sampling   Nonrandom samples come in three types: convenience, quota, and volunteer.

1. **Convenience samples,** also known as accidental, chunk, or opportunity samples, are relatively unstructured, rather unsystematic, and designed to elicit ideas and points of view. Journalists use convenience samples when they conduct person-on-the-street interviews. The most common type of convenience sample in public relations research is the focus group.

2. **Quota samples** permit a researcher to choose subjects on the basis of certain characteristics. For example, the attitudes of a certain number of women, men, blacks, whites, rich, or poor may be needed. Quotas are imposed in proportion to each group's percentage of the population.

3. **Volunteer samples** use willing participants who agree voluntarily to respond to concepts and hypotheses for research purposes.

The Questionnaire

Before creating a questionnaire, whether to be mailed or emailed, a researcher must consider his or her objective in doing the study. What you seek to find out should influence the specific publics you ask, the questions you raise, and the research method you choose. After determining what you're after, consider the particular questionnaire design. Specifically, researchers should observe the following in designing their questionnaire:

1. **Keep it short.** Make a concerted attempt to limit questions. It's terrific if the questionnaire can be answered in five minutes.

2. **Use structured rather than open-ended questions.** People would rather check a box or circle a number than write an essay.

3. **Measure intensity of feelings.** Let respondents check "very satisfied," "satisfied," "dissatisfied," or "very dissatisfied" rather than "yes" or "no." One popular approach is the semantic differential technique shown in Figure 8-5.

4. **Don't use fancy words or words that have more than one meaning.** If you must use big words, make the context clear.

5. **Don't ask loaded questions.** "Is management doing all it can to communicate with you?" is a terrible question. The answer is always no.

6. **Don't ask double-barreled questions.** "Would you like management meetings once a month, or are bimonthly meetings enough?" is another terrible question.

7. **Pretest.** Send your questionnaire to a few colleagues and listen to their suggestions.

8. **Attach a letter explaining how important the respondents' answers are, and let recipients know that they will remain anonymous.** Respondents will feel better if they think the study is significant and their identities are protected. Also, specify how and where the data will be used.

9. **When mailing, hand-stamp the envelopes, preferably with unique commemorative stamps.** Metering an envelope indicates assembly-line research, and researchers have found that the more expensive the postage, the higher the response rate. People like to feel special.

FIGURE 8-5
Measuring intensity, rewarding respondents.
One common device to measure intensity of feelings is the semantic differential technique, which gives respondents a scale of choices from the worst to the best. Respondents will comply more gladly if a "crisp new bill" is included—and even more gladly to two "crisp new bills."
(Courtesy of Bauman Research & Consulting LLC)

Bauman
Research & Consulting, LLC

Dear Susan,

A few months ago you contacted XYZ company about your health condition. We'd like some feedback on how we did – and how you're doing.

Please take 5 minutes to tell us about your experiences and help us do better.

This survey is being conducted for XYZ company by an independent research firm, Bauman Research & Consulting. Your responses are completely confidential and will <u>not</u> be used for any marketing or selling purposes.

As a token of our appreciation for your participation, we have enclosed $5.

If you have any questions about this survey, please contact Sandra Bauman at sandra@baumanresearch.com or 201-444-6894.

Q1.   In general, how would you describe your own health?

EXCELLENT	VERY GOOD	GOOD	FAIR	POOR
$\square_1$	$\square_2$	$\square_3$	$\square_4$	$\square_5$

Q2.   What is your current general level of activity?

Not at all   Extremely
Active   Active

1   2   3   4   5   6   7   8   9   10

Q3.   Which joint is causing you pain? [Choose one.]

HIP	KNEE	SHOULDER	ELBOW	OTHER
$\square_1$	$\square_2$	$\square_3$	$\square_4$	$\square_5$

Q4.   How effective was XYZ company at communicating information in each of these areas?

	EXTREMELY EFFECTIVE	VERY EFFECTIVE	SOMEWHAT EFFECTIVE	NOT TOO EFFECTIVE	NOT AT ALL EFFECTIVE
a. Information about possible prescription treatment options for your joint pain	$\square_1$	$\square_2$	$\square_3$	$\square_4$	$\square_5$
b. Information about possible physical therapy options for your joint pain	$\square_1$	$\square_2$	$\square_3$	$\square_4$	$\square_5$
c. Information about possible surgical options for your joint pain	$\square_1$	$\square_2$	$\square_3$	$\square_4$	$\square_5$

➔ CONTINUED

44 Abbington Terrace, Glen Rock, NJ 07452 • Phone: 201.444.6894 • Fax: 201.701.0271 • www.baumanresearch.com

10. **Follow up your first mailing.** Send a reminder postcard three days after the original questionnaire. Then wait a few weeks and send a second questionnaire, just in case recipients have lost the first.

11. **Send out more questionnaires than you think necessary.** The major weakness of most mail surveys is the immeasurable error introduced by nonresponders. You're shooting for a 50% response rate; anything less tends to be suspect.

12. **Enclose a reward.** (One reason to mail and not email.) There's nothing like a token gift of merchandise or, better yet, money to make a recipient feel guilty for not returning a questionnaire.

Interviews

Interviews can provide a more personal, firsthand feel for public opinion. Interview panels can range from focus groups of randomly selected average people to Delphi panels of so-called opinion leaders. Interviews can be conducted in a number of ways, including face-to-face, telephone, mail, and through the Internet.

Focus Groups This approach is used with increasing frequency in public relations today. A traditional focus group consists of a 90- to 120-minute discussion among 8 to 10 individuals who have been selected based upon having predetermined common characteristics, such as buying behavior, age, income, family composition, and so on.[6]

Telephone Interviews In contrast to personal interviews, telephone interviews suffer from a high refusal rate. Many people just don't want to be bothered. Such interviews, it used to be said, introduced an upper-income bias because lower-income earners may lack telephones. However, the increasing use of unlisted numbers by upper-income people and the proliferation of "caller ID" to screen unwanted calls may severely mitigate this bias.

Email Interviews This is the least expensive approach, but it often suffers from a low response rate. Frequently, people who return email or even snail mail questionnaires are those with strong biases either in favor of or (more commonly) in opposition to the subject at hand.

Drop-Off Interviews This approach combines face-to-face and mail interview techniques. An interviewer personally drops off a questionnaire at a household, usually after conducting a face-to-face interview. Because the interviewer has already established some rapport with the interviewee, the rate of return with this technique is considerably higher than it is for straight mail interviews.

Intercept Interviews This approach is popular in consumer surveys, where researchers "intercept" respondents on the street, in shopping malls, or in retail outlets. Trained interviewers typically deliver a short (5- to 20-minute) questionnaire concerning attitudes, perceptions, preferences, and behavior.

Delphi Panels The Delphi technique is a qualitative research tool that uses opinion leaders—local influential persons as well as national experts—often to help tailor the design of a general public research survey. Designed by the Rand Corporation in the 1950s, the Delphi technique is a consensus-building approach that relies on repeated waves of questionnaires sent to the same select panel of experts.

Internet Interviews Web-based surveying is becoming more widely used. In its ubiquitous availability, the Web offers significant advantages over more traditional survey techniques. However, Internet interviews also introduce problems, among them that significant numbers of people either don't have access to or choose not to use the

Internet. Several studies have found Internet surveys have significantly lower response rates than comparable mailed surveys.[7]

Results Analysis

After selecting the sample, drawing up the questionnaire, and interviewing the respondents, the researcher must analyze the findings. Often a great deal of analysis is required to produce meaningful recommendations.

The objective of every sample is to come up with results that are valid and reliable. A margin of error explains how far off the prediction may be. A sample may be large enough to represent fairly the larger universe; yet, depending on the margin of sampling error, the results of the research may not be statistically significant. That is, the differences or distinctions detected by the survey may not be sizable enough to offset the margin of error. Thus, the margin of error must always be determined.

Popular political polls, in particular, are fraught with problems. They cannot predict outcomes scientifically. Rather, they provide a snapshot, freezing attitudes at a certain point in time—like a balance sheet for a corporation. Obviously, people's attitudes change with the passage of time, and pollsters, despite what they claim, can't categorically predict the outcome of an election. This was especially true in the 2012 Republican primary contests among eventual nominee Mitt Romney and a host of challengers, where polls taken more than three days prior to the primary weren't particularly accurate.[8] The most notorious example of polls gone awry was the political poll sponsored by *Literary Digest* in 1936, which used a telephone polling technique to predict that Alf Landon would be the nation's next president. Landon thereupon suffered one of the worst drubbings in American electoral history at the hands of Franklin Roosevelt. It was probably of little solace to the *Literary Digest* that most of its telephone respondents, many of whom were Republicans wealthy enough to afford phones, did vote for Landon.

The point is that in analyzing results, problems of validity, reliability, and levels of statistical significance associated with margins of error must be considered before concrete recommendations are volunteered.

PR Ethics Mini-Case

Sleep-Deprived Research

One publicity tactic in the arsenal of public relations professionals is the use of research studies to promote clients. Using research as publicity is a more analytical, less promotional device to burnish an organization's reputation.

As long as such studies pass empirical muster with researchers, they're fine. But when the process and measurement is questionable, the sponsoring organization suffers by association.

In February 2012, *The New York Times* published an article titled "America's 10 Most Sleep-Deprived Jobs." The piece was based on a survey supplied, coincidentally enough, by Sleepy's, the mattress chain (Figure 8-6). According to Sleepy's, it hired researchers to analyze data from the National Health Interview Survey, which interviewed 27,157 adults. Sleepy's then determined which occupations, on average, produce workers who sleep the

least. The most sleep-deprived occupations were the following:

Most Sleep-Deprived

1. 6 hr 57 min Home Health Aides
2. 7 hr Lawyer
3. 7 hr 1 min Police Officers
4. 7 hr 2 min Physicians, Paramedics
5. 7 hr 3 min Social Workers
6. 7 hr 3 min Computer Programmers
7. 7 hr 3 min Economists
8. 7 hr 5 min Financial Analysts
9. 7 hr 7 min Plant Operators
10. 7 hr 8 min Secretaries

The publicity was terrific for Sleepy's. But what about research methods? Interviewees were asked about the average number of hours of sleep they received. But could their estimates of sleep have been flawed? In other words, how accurate were the data?

The time difference between the amount of sleep stated by the #1 sleep-deprived home health aides and that of #10 secretaries was 11 minutes—not particularly meaningful. Moreover, the statistical significance of the different times couldn't be evaluated because it wasn't clear how many people were questioned in each job category.

At the other end of the Sleepy's list were those who got the "most sleep." At the top spots on this list were "Forest, Logging Workers" at 7 hours and 20 minutes and "Hairstylists" at 7 hours and 16 minutes—not a particularly large difference from the bottom 10. And ranked at #8, #9, and #10 on the most sleep list were engineers, aircraft pilots, and teachers. The average amount of sleep these people received was 7 hours and 12 minutes, a whopping four minutes longer than secretaries, at #10 on the list of most sleep-deprived.

The bottom line: Sleepy's caught the normally-vigilant *New York Times* napping.*

Questions

1. Were you Sleepy's, would you have distributed this research to the media?

2. Were you *The New York Times*, would you have run an article based on the research?

FIGURE 8-6   Sleepy's "sleepy" research.
Sleepy's research on sleep-deprived jobs found lawyers number two on the list. How do we know he's a lawyer? The shoes, the briefcase, and the thumb! *(Photo: J. KYLE KEENER KRT/Newscom)*

*For further information, see Catherine Rampell, "America's 10 Most Sleep-Deprived Jobs," *The New York Times*, February 22, 2012; and "Worst Research Study of the Year: America's 10 Most Sleep-Deprived Jobs," *Skeptical Scalpel*, March 5, 2012.

Communications Audits

Communications audits are an increasingly important method of research in public relations work. Such audits are used frequently by corporations, schools, hospitals, and other organizations to determine whether a communications group and the products it produces are realizing objectives and also how the institution is perceived by its core constituents. Communications audits help public relations professionals understand more clearly the relationships between management actions and objectives on the one hand and communications methods to promote those objectives on the other.

Communications audits are typically used to analyze the standing of a company with its employees or community neighbors; to assess the readership of routine communication vehicles, such as annual reports and news releases; or to examine an organization's performance as a corporate citizen. Communications audits often provide benchmarks against which future public relations programs can be applied and measured. The data uncovered are frequently used by management to make informed decisions about future communications needs and goals.

A communications audit is not an end in itself. Rather it must be part of a process of measurement and performance improvement.[9] In that context, an extensive audit should be conducted every couple of years to keep an organization's communications fresh and relevant and consistent with 21st-century methods and techniques.

Unobtrusive Methods

Of the various unobtrusive methods of data collection available to public relations researchers, probably the most widely used is simple fact-finding. Facts are the bricks and mortar of public relations work; no action can be taken unless the facts are known, and the fact-finding process is continuous.

Another unobtrusive method is simple content analysis, the primary purpose of which is to describe a message or set of messages. For example, an organization with news releases that are used frequently by local newspapers can't be certain, without research, whether the image conveyed by its releases is what the organization seeks. By analyzing the news coverage, the firm can get a much clearer idea of the effectiveness of its communications.

Copy testing, in which public targets are exposed to public relations campaign messages to be used in brochures, memos, online, and so on, in advance of their publication, is another viable method that ensures campaign messages are understandable and effective.

Finally, case study research that analyzes how other organizations handled similar challenges is a constructive, unobtrusive research method.

Clearly, there is nothing particularly mysterious or difficult about unobtrusive methods of research. Such methods are relatively simple to apply—and also inexpensive—yet they are essential for arriving at appropriate refinements for an ongoing public relations program.

Evaluation

No matter what type of public relations research is used, results of the research and the research project itself should always be analyzed for meaning and action. Evaluation is designed to determine what happened and why by measuring results against established objectives. As public relations researcher James Grunig has said, "The main reason to measure objectives is not so much to reward or punish individual communications managers for success or failure, as it is to learn from the research whether a program should be continued as is, revised, or dropped in favor of another approach."[10]

The key word in organizations today is *accountability,* which means taking responsibility for achieving the performance promised. With resources limited and competition fierce, managers at every level demand accountability for every activity on which they spend money. That's what evaluation is all about. Public relations professionals are obligated today to assess what they've done to determine whether the expense was worth it.

Outcome evaluation measures whether targets actually *received* the messages directed to them, *paid attention* to them, *understood* the messages, *retained* those messages, and even *acted* on them.

In many respects, a measurement of public relations outcomes is the most important barometer in assessing success or failure of a program.

Measuring Public Relations Outcomes

What kinds of tools are used to measure public relations outcomes? Here are four of the most common.

Awareness and Comprehension Measurement This measurement probes whether targets received the messages directed at them, paid attention to them, and understood them. Measuring awareness and comprehension levels requires "benchmarking," or determining preliminary knowledge about a target's understanding so that the furthering of that knowledge can be tracked.

Recall and Retention Measurement This is a commonly used technique in advertising in which sponsors want to know if their commercials have lasting impact. Such measurement analysis may be equally important in public relations. It is one thing for a target to have seen and understood a message but quite another for someone to remember what was said.

Attitude and Preference Measurement Even more important than how much someone retained from a message is a measure of how the message moved an individual's attitudes, opinions, and preferences. This involves the areas of opinion research and attitude research. The former is easier because it can be realized simply by asking a few preference questions. The latter, however, is derived from more complex variables, such as predispositions, feelings, and motivational tendencies regarding the issue in question.

Behavior Measurements This is the ultimate test of effectiveness. Did the message get people to vote for our candidate, buy our product, or agree with our ideas?

Measuring behavior in public relations is difficult, especially in "proving" that a certain program "caused" the desired outcome to occur. In other words, how do we know that it was our input in particular that caused people to contribute more to our charity, or legislators to vote for our issue, or an editor to report favorably on our organization?[11]

Regardless of the evaluative technique, by evaluating after the fact, researchers can learn how to improve future efforts. Were the right target audiences surveyed? Were the correct research assumptions applied to those audiences? Were questions from research tools left unanswered?

In the fiercely competitive, resource-dear 21st century, the practice of public relations will increasingly be called on to justify its activities and evaluate the results of its programs with formal research.

Research and the Web

Research techniques in evaluating the effectiveness of programs and products and messages on the Web are constantly being perfected.

What can today's Web analytics measure in terms of consumer-generated media (CGR, as it's known in the trade)? Lots of things. Among them:

- Unique visitors
- Returning visitors
- Costs per click through
- Total time spent on a site
- Downloads
- Costs per contact
- Links from other sites
- Google page rank
- Content popularity
- Sales

Search Engine Optimization

The most ubiquitous term in public relations relative to evaluating Websites or Webpages is Search Engine Optimization or SEO. This is the process of improving the visibility of a Website or a Webpage in a search engine's—primarily Google's—algorithmic search results. The higher ranked a site appears in the search results list, the more visitors it will receive from the search engine's users. SEO may target different kinds of search, including image search, local search, video search, academic search, industry-specific search, etc. Public relations professionals focus on SEO.

Beyond SEO, the two most frequent research terms relative to Websites are *hits* and *eyeballs*. The former refers to the number of times a Website is visited by an individual. The latter refers to the orbital lobes affixed to that hit. Obviously, these are but the most rudimentary of measurement tools in that they don't assess the visitors' interest in the product or service or information conveyed, the duration of their stay at the site, or whether they were driven to act on the information—that is, buy the product, subscribe to the service, or vote for the candidate. Indeed, the first 5,000 hits to a new Website may mean nothing more than the firm's employees checking out the latest communications tool.

One of the most popular measurement vehicles to assess Websites is Google Analytics, a free service that generates detailed statistics about site visitors. Google Analytics can track visitors from all referrers, including search engines, display advertising, pay-per-click networks, email marketing, and PDF documents.

Web Research Considerations

The value of Web-oriented research is indisputable. In preparing for such Internet evaluation—just as in preparing for any public relations research—an organization should take several factors into consideration:

1. **Establish objectives.** Again, implicit in any meaningful measurement is the setting of objectives. Why are we on the Web? What is our site designed to do? What are we attempting to communicate?

2. **Determine criteria.** Define success with tangible data—for example, percentage of people likely to purchase from the site and positive interactive publication mentions that the site will receive.

3. **Determine benchmarks.** Project the hits the site will receive. Base this on competitive data to see how this site stacks up against the competition or other forms of communication.

4. **Select the right measurement tool.** Numerous software analytical packages exist to track site traffic and provide other measurements of Internet public relations success, among them:

   - Web traffic: Clicktrax, Web trends, WebSide Story
   - Awareness/preference: SurveyMonkey, Zoomerang
   - Marketplace/Blog engagement: Type pad, Technorati
   - Messages: Dashboards, Vizu
   - Social media: Klout

5. **Compare results to objectives.** Success of online marketing and communications cannot be concluded in a vacuum. Numbers of visitors, hits, and eyeballs must be correlated with original objectives.

6. **Draw actionable conclusions.** Research indicates you've received 100,000 visitors to the site. So what? Interpret the significance of the numbers and do something with the data to make progress.[12]

Finally, in terms of researching the Web, there is the aspect of monitoring what is being said about the organization. With the proliferation of rogue sites, anti-business blogs, and chain letter email campaigns, monitoring the Web has become a frontline public relations responsibility. Web 2.0 has been called the "great equalizer," which means that all individuals can have their say—mean, nasty, belligerent—and organizations must constantly keep track of what is being said about them by consumer-generated media.

Last Word

Research is a means of both defining problems and evaluating solutions. Even though intuitive judgment remains a coveted and important public relations asset, management must see measurable results.

Nonetheless, informed managements recognize that public relations may never reach a point at which its results can be fully quantified. Management confidence is still a prerequisite for active and unencumbered programs. Indeed, the best measurement of public relations value is a strong and unequivocal endorsement from management that it supports the public relations effort. However, such confidence can only be enhanced as practitioners become more adept in using research.

Whether it's as basic as researching through the "thud factor," that is, dumping a pile of publicity on a client's desk to assessing the AVE (advertising value equivalent of publicity)—to the most sophisticated SEO optimization techniques to measure outputs and evaluate outcomes—research must be part of any 21st-century public relations enterprise.[13]

Frankly, practitioners don't have a choice. With efficiency driving today's bottom line and with communications about organizations percolating at a 24/7 clip around the world through a variety of media, organizations must always know where they stand. It is the job of public relations to keep track of, record, and research changing attitudes and opinions about the organizations for which they work.

According to Stuart Z. Goldstein, well-respected communications director of the Depository Trust & Clearing Corporation, strategic public relations research is best achieved through two obligatory databases that form the core of strategy development:

1. An integrated relational database that allows a practitioner to leverage internal information across all public relations disciplines
2. A diagnostic database that tracks and helps analyze opinion data on a wide range of issues across key segments of an organization's primary constituencies[14]

The need for greater analytical backup for public relations activities will make it increasingly incumbent on public relations people to reinforce the value of what they do and what they stand for through constantly measuring their contribution to their organization's goals.[15]

Discussion Starters

1. Why is research important in public relations work?
2. What are the differences between primary and secondary research?
3. What are the four elements of a survey?
4. What is the difference between random and stratified sampling?
5. What are the keys to designing an effective questionnaire?
6. What kinds of tools are used to measure public relations outcomes?
7. Why is evaluation important in public relations research?
8. What is Search Engine Optimization?
9. What kinds of questions are pertinent in evaluating a Website?
10. What are the characteristics that can be measured in Web-based research?

Pick of the Literature

Primer of Public Relations Research, 2nd Edition

Don W. Stacks, New York: The Guilford Press, 2011

Don Stacks has, for decades, been the quintessential public relations researcher. He literally "wrote the book" on public relations research. And this is it.

Stacks reviews the importance of research and why most public relations practitioners fear it. The essence of modern-day public relations research, says the author, is delivering evidence that the organization's bottom line has been enhanced by public relations activities. Amen.

The book reviews all matter of public relations research, including an important section on the ethics of research, as well as case studies of qualitative and quantitative research and research reporting methods. An essential text.

Case Study | Researching a Position for Alan Louis General

The administrator at Alan Louis General Hospital confronted a problem that he hoped research could help solve. Alan Louis General, although a good hospital, was smaller and less well-known than most other hospitals in Corpus Christi, Texas. In its area alone, it competed with 10 other medical facilities. Alan Louis needed a "position" that it could call unique to attract patients to fill its beds.

For a long time, the Alan Louis administrator, Sven Rapcorn, had believed in the principle that truth will win out. Build a better mousetrap, and the world will beat a path to your door. Erect a better hospital, and your beds will always be 98% filled. Unfortunately, Rapcorn learned, the real world seldom recognizes truth at first blush.

In the real world, more often than not, perception will triumph. Because people act on perceptions, those perceptions become reality. Successful positioning, Rapcorn learned, is based on recognizing and dealing with people's perceptions. And so, Rapcorn set out with research to build on existing perceptions about Alan Louis General.

He decided to conduct a communications audit to help form a differentiable "position" for Alan Louis General.

Interview Process

As a first step, Rapcorn talked to his own doctors and trustees to gather data about their perceptions not only of Alan Louis General but also of other hospitals in the community. He did this to get a clear and informed picture of where competing hospitals ranked in the minds of knowledgeable people.

For example, the University Health Center had something for everybody—exotic care, specialized care, and basic bread-and-butter care. CC General was a huge, well-respected hospital whose reputation was so good that only a major tragedy could shake its standing in the community. Mercy Hospital was known for its trauma center. And so on.

As for Alan Louis itself, doctors and trustees said that it was a great place to work, that excellent care was provided, and that the nursing staff was particularly friendly and good. The one problem, everyone agreed, was that "nobody knows about us."

Attribute Testing

The second step in Rapcorn's research project was to test attributes important in health care. He did this to learn what factors community members felt were most important in assessing hospital care.

Respondents were asked to rank eight factors in order of importance and to tell Rapcorn and his staff how each of the surveyed hospitals rated on those factors. The research instrument used a semantic differential scale of 1 to 10, with 1 the worst and 10 the best possible score. Questionnaires were sent to two groups: 1,000 area residents and 500 former Alan Louis patients.

Results Tabulation

The third step in the research was to tabulate the results in order to determine community priorities.

Among area residents who responded, the eight attributes were ranked accordingly:

1. Surgical care—9.23
2. Medical equipment—9.20
3. Cardiac care—9.16
4. Emergency services—8.96
5. Range of medical services—8.63
6. Friendly nurses—8.62
7. Moderate costs—8.59
8. Location—7.94

After the attributes were ranked, the hospitals in the survey were ranked for each attribute. On advanced surgical care, the most important feature to area residents, Laredo General ranked first, with University Health Center a close second. Alan Louis was far down on the list. The same was true of virtually every other attribute. Indeed, on nursing care, an area in which its staff thought Alan Louis excelled, the hospital came in last in the minds of area residents. Rapcorn was not surprised. The largest hospitals in town scored well on most attributes; Alan Louis trailed the pack.

However, the ranking of hospital scores according to former Alan Louis patients revealed an entirely different story. On surgical care, for example, although Laredo General still ranked first, Alan Louis came in a close second. Its scores improved similarly on all other attributes. In fact, in nursing care, where Alan Louis came in last on the survey of area residents, among former patients its score was higher than that of any other hospital. It also ranked first in terms of convenient location and second in terms of costs, range of services, and emergency care.

Conclusions and Recommendations

The fourth step in Rapcorn's research project was to draw some conclusions to determine what the data had revealed.

He reached three conclusions:

1. CC General was still number one in terms of area hospitals.
2. Alan Louis ranked at or near the top on most attributes, according to those who actually experienced care there.

3. Former Alan Louis patients rated the hospital significantly better than did the general public.

In other words, thought Rapcorn, most of those who try Alan Louis like it. The great need was to convince more people to try the hospital.

Rapcorn was confident that the data he had gathered from the research project were all he needed to come up with a winning idea.

He then set out to propose his recommendations.

Questions

1. What kind of communications program would you launch to accomplish Rapcorn's objectives?
2. What would be the cornerstone—the theme—of your communications program?
3. What would be the specific elements of your program?
4. In launching the program, what specific steps would you follow—both inside and outside the hospital—to build support?
5. How could you use the Internet to conduct more research about area hospitals and residents' perceptions of the care at these hospitals? How could you use the Internet to research the effectiveness of the communications program you implement?

From the Top

An Interview with Sandra Bauman

Dr. Sandra L. Bauman is founder and principal of Bauman Research & Consulting, LLC, a woman-owned enterprise. During her two decades in research, Dr. Bauman has designed and managed hundreds of studies for corporate and non-profit clients in the areas of corporate image and brand positioning, employee communications and commitment, strategic marketing, publicity and public affairs, and customer satisfaction and loyalty. She is expert in quantitative methodologies, including telephone, Internet and mail surveys, and her analysis skills include multivariate techniques such as segmentation and conjoint analysis. She is also adept at qualitative research; she is a trained and experienced focus group moderator and facilitator for brainstorming, ideation, and strategic planning sessions with executives.

How important is research in public relations?
Research is a means of discovery and exploration, which becomes an important tool in strategic public relations planning. There are different ways research can help in public relations: it can be used to formulate strategy, better define your target or competitors, test reactions to messages and understand the current "environment" impacting your issue or client. Research can also be used effectively for "ink"—publicity—when publicly released data from a survey serves as a "source" that is newsworthy or interesting.

What is the state of research among most public relations professionals?
I think there is a deep appreciation for research in the public relations community. Some large agencies have entire departments that support their research needs. Others use outside research companies or consultants for support. Just peruse the program of any PR conference, articles in PR journals or on the websites of PRSA or the Institute for Public Relations and you'll see how much research is a part of the profession.

Is it possible to measure public relations success?
This has been a topic of debate in the PR profession for a long time, and one that is constantly being studied, tested and refined. The short answer is yes, of course, but it can be challenging because of the complexity of environment in which PR is operating (often with factors that you can't control for, measure or even identify). First you need to set your objectives and what will determine success. Both need to be measurable. Then, there are generally three types of evaluation: outputs, outtakes and outcomes. Outputs are the easiest to measure and they occur in the short-term— how much press coverage was achieved, how many whitepapers were downloaded, number of tweets, blog posts, etc. Outtakes are more challenging and are longer-term— they involve the "reach" of the program. In order to determine who you reached and how they are affected (perceptions, attitudes, messages, awareness), you need to benchmark the "before" and measure the "after" to determine

change. Finally, there are Outcomes, which are the hardest to measure and really at the heart of the ROI debate: did your program work—by increasing sales, gaining market share, etc.

How do you respond to those who say public relations is based purely on intuition?

No profession can be based purely on intuition. Sometimes research confirms assumptions, hypotheses or conventional wisdom. That's an important role for research—now that intuition has further "proof." But it also can debunk some assumptions or help us discover new areas or relationships that we hadn't considered before.

What kinds of research are valuable for public relations professionals?

There are three types of research that are most valuable for PR professionals.

Secondary research, or desk research, involves collecting and synthesizing all available existing research and intelligence that relates to your topic. This is a critical first step—even if done more informally—before undertaking any primary research. See what's already out there, what's known and not known.

Qualitative research methods (e.g., focus groups, in-depth interviews, ethnographies) are used for discovery and exploration, to get at the "whys" of human decision making, perceptions and behaviors. Individuals are recruited to participate based on predetermined criteria; they are not a representative sample. Therefore results are directional, not statistical. We often use these methods to explore a problem area in-depth or to get reaction to proposed messages or ideas.

Quantitative research (e.g., surveys) is used when you need numeric measures to "quantify" things—behaviors, attitudes, awareness, usage, opinions, etc. Quality surveys use larger samples and statistical techniques that allow us to generalize from the findings to population at large. One caveat I will say here is that quantitative research can look "easy" but often is complex. If your study is for public release, you need to be extra careful to use a rigorous methodology in order to get attention from national media outlets that have strict "vetting" standards.

How important is reading the daily newspaper as part of public relations "research"?

The answer is obvious. That's basically informal "desk" research. Keep an eye out for how news outlets use research in their stories and you will hone your skills at being an excellent "consumer" of research. Not only will you likely inform the work you do, but you'll probably get ideas for original research to use for your clients.

What are the most important Internet research tools?

The Internet has opened up another medium for conducting research, giving us the ability to expand our geographies, find hard-to-reach populations and reduce costs. We can now do focus groups online, for example, using webcams and collaborative software. There are a number of "do-it-yourself" survey options online, many of which have free versions.

Public Relations Library

Botan, Carl H., and Vincent Hazleton. *Public Relations Theory II*. Mahwah, NJ: Lawrence Erlbaum Associates, 2009. Strong focus on academic public relations research and theory.

Kennedy, Dan. *No B.S.: Marketing to the Affluent*. Irvine, CA: Entrepreneur Media, 2008. Interesting research on the affluent in America, what makes them tick, what intrigues them, and what they buy.

Paine, Katie. *Measuring Public Relationships: The Data-Driven Communicator's Guide to Success*. Berlin, NH: K.D. Paine & Partners, 2007. One of the foremost researchers in public relations expounds on what it takes.

Pavlik, John V. *Public Relations: What Research Tells Us*. Newbury Park, CA: Sage Publications, 1987. Old, but the classic in the field.

Robbins, Donijo. *Understanding Research Methods*. Boca Raton, FL: CRC Press, 2009. Good research primer written for the public policy and nonprofit manager.

Sriramesh, Krishnamurthy, and Dejan Vercic (Eds.). *The Global Public Relations Handbook*. New York: Routledge, 2009. Good study of international public relations with strong research base.

Thomas, Alan, and Giles Mohan. *Research Skills for Policy and Development*. Thousand Oaks, CA: Sage Publications, Inc., 2007. Discussion of the research questions and approaches appropriate for policy investigation.

Van Ruler, Betteke, Ana Takalac Vercic, and Dejan Vercic. *Public Relations Metrics Research and Evaluation*. New York: Routledge, 2008. Extensive review of public relations research from the 1980s to the present.

Watson, Tom, and Paul Noble. *Evaluating Public Relations* (2nd ed.). London, England: Kogan Page Ltd., 2007. A respected treatise on public relations measurement and research, complete with online environment commentary and case studies.

www.odwyerpr.com. *Jack O'Dwyer's Newsletter* offers online logos, agency statements, and complete listings of 550 PR firms. The best choice on the Web for accessing any part of the Website, including news from the newsletter and other publications, hyperlinks to articles on PR, job listings, and more than 1,000 PR services in 58 categories.

Chapter **9**

Media

Chapter Objectives

1. To discuss the bedrock importance of media relations as the most fundamental skill in public relations work.
2. To explore media communication in all its forms—print, electronic, Internet.
3. To discuss the value of publicity as more powerful and credible than advertising.
4. To examine the proper way of dealing with journalists vis-à-vis organizational publicity.

FIGURE 9-1 **The end of the world.**
The final edition of *News of the World*, Rupert Murdoch's British tabloid, on Sunday, July 10, 2011. *(Photo: ZUMA/Newscom)*

Oy, the newspaper business!

It used to be that most citizens of the world wouldn't start their day without consulting the local paper. Boy, how times have changed. Today, with tablets, cell phones, and mobile devices of every size and shape, the news is delivered in different ways to different people. And the newspaper business has taken it on the chin.

With circulation falling and mobile news delivery rising, it doesn't help matters that distrust in the media has reached a record high.[1] And it *really* didn't help matters in the summer of 2011 when none other than global media baron Rupert Murdoch and his British tabloid, *News of the World*, were accused of hacking into the telephones of well-known and lesser-known individuals.

Not only that, but the scandal dragged in Murdoch's protégé and former *News of the World* editor Rebekah Brooks, who resigned and was arrested; caused the resignation of Britain's top law enforcement official; and even forced Murdoch's friend Prime Minister David Cameron to cut short an overseas trip and return to London to address a special session of Parliament about the hacking crisis. Ultimately, Rupert Murdoch took the unprecedented step of closing down *News of the World* after 168 years of publication, thus depriving Britons of their daily dose of scandalous news and topless beauties[2] (Figure 9-1). Twas a dark day in London town.

For public relations people, the trend toward news on the Internet, often through mobile handheld devices, greatly influenced the time-honored public relations responsibility of dealing with the media. News on the Internet was more pervasive, more intrusive, more accessible to the masses, and certainly more likely to cause problems for public relations professionals. For example:

- In 2007, in the midst of researching a story on Microsoft, *Wired* magazine reporter Fred Vogelstein received an email from Microsoft's public relations firm, Waggener Edstrom Worldwide, with a 13-page, 5,500-word internal memo attachment, meant to prepare company executives for specific media interviews—including an upcoming one with Fred Vogelstein. One sentence read, "Fred's stories tend to be a bit sensational, though he would consider them to be balanced and fair." Some public relations person at Waggener Edstrom evidently pushed the wrong button. Oops![3]

- In 2008, after Target Corp. launched a provocative woman's clothing ad to which some observers took offense, the ShapingYouth.org blog contacted the company for an explanation. What it got was the following response: "Thank you for contacting Target; unfortunately we are unable to respond to your inquiry because Target doesn't participate with nontraditional media outlets. This practice is in place to allow us to focus on publications that reach our core guest." The ensuing uproar in the blogosphere caused Target immediately to revise its policy relative to Web-based media.[4]

- That same year, when a guest Fox News talking-head psychologist described the popular *Mass Effect* as a video game that shows women only as "objects of desire, as these, you know, hot bodies," the network suffered an avalanche of criticism on global message boards, blogs, and chat rooms, all claiming the Fox commentator didn't have a clue what she was talking about. As it turned out, they were right. So overwhelming was the cyber attack that within hours of the broadcast, the embarrassed psychologist admitted she had never actually seen the game, had relied on an associate's view, and acknowledged she had been wrong.[5]

- In 2011, public relations firm Redner Group lost its largest client, another video game manufacturer, when e-zine Wired.com published threatening tweets from Redner, after its client's new action game, affectionately called *Duke Nukem Forever,* was panned. The Redner tweet said, in part, "We're reviewing who gets games next time and who doesn't—based on today's venom." Redner publicly apologized, after the client departed.[6]

The point is that in the 21st century, thanks largely to the consumer-generated media of the Internet, it's no longer your mama's media.

Where once the media were dominated by a handful of powerful, truth-seeking reporters and editors at a handful of newspapers and three national TV networks, today the media are fragmented, omnipresent, busy 24 hours a day/seven days a week, and populated by a breed of reporter—in print, on the air, and, now more than ever, online—who is aggressive, opinionated, sharp-elbowed, and more than willing to throw himself or herself personally into the story being covered, occasionally without any journalistic training whatsoever.

Not your mama's media, indeed.

This latter point presents a particular difference with the reporting style of the past century. Today, more often than not, with competition from thousands of daily and online newspapers, talk radio stations, cable TV channels, and bloggers as far as the eye can see, even journalistically trained reporters have few qualms about using anonymous sources, losing their historic anonymity, and becoming part of the story. In the old days, print reporters wouldn't risk their "objectivity" to voice their opinions on television. Today, they and their news organizations covet such attention.

And this poses a particular challenge to those who practice public relations.

As we have noted, modern public relations practice got its start as an adjunct to journalism, with former reporters, such as Ivy Lee, hired to refine the image of well-to-do clients. In the old days (before 2000), most of the professionals who entered the practice of public relations were former journalists.

Today, with public relations professionals emanating from many different fields of study and directly from college, the field is no longer dominated by former journalists. Nonetheless, the importance of the media to the practice of public relations cannot be denied.

Put simply, if you're in public relations, you *must* know how to deal with the press.

Therein lays the problem, because in the 21st century, the "press" has changed, often for the worst. As President Bush's first press secretary, Ari Fleischer, said:

We've reached a point where the press, in pursuit of its devil's advocate role, would do well to ask itself, are they "informing" the public or are they being so negative about the institutions they cover, that they're not covering all the news, but only the "bad news"?[7]

This "devil's advocate" role is the key to why many people don't like the press. As the circulation of daily newspapers continues to decline, polls suggest that Americans are growing increasingly disenchanted with the media. Going into the 2012 campaign, a Pew Research Center poll found a record high 67% of Americans saw "a great deal" or "fair amount" of "political bias" in the news media. At the end of the 2008 presidential campaign, Pew found the public "overwhelmingly"—by a 70% to 9% margin—believed that most journalists wanted to see Barack Obama, not John McCain, emerge victorious on Election Day. Bolstering this finding was research done by *Slate* magazine, which found that over the first three presidential elections of the 21st century, its reporters voted Democrat 76%, 87%, and 96% progressively. *Slate*'s findings mirrored scientific polls of so-called media elites (although conservative Fox News reporters would probably not agree!).[8]

The irrefutable fact is that most reporters in the U.S. mainstream media—or "state-run" media if you believe Rush Limbaugh—have a liberal bias. And most Americans, according to polls, acknowledge that reality when reading, listening to, or viewing the news. The real point is that in assessing and dealing with the media, public relations professionals, in particular, should base their own opinions on "objective" facts as much as possible. Stated another way, everyone is biased one way or another. As long as we accept that and try to deal from a more objective view in arriving at opinions and conclusions, our counsel will be valued.

Freedom of the press is a hallmark of American democracy. It is a right guaranteed by the First Amendment to the U.S. Constitution. Written in 1789, the 45 words contained in the First Amendment protect the freedom of speech, press, religion, and assembly.

Over the years, in pursuing that freedom, the media have regularly challenged authority with pointed, nasty, even hostile questions. Their proper role in a democracy, as embodied in the First Amendment, is to independently ferret out the truth. Often this means "breaking eggs" in the process. Whether it means hounding a public figure, invading the privacy of a private figure, or just plain being obnoxious, that is what journalists have become known to do.

What this means to public relations professionals is that dealing with the media—particularly in light of Internet journalism, where 70% accuracy is considered "acceptable"—has never been more challenging.

This is the business of the public relations professional, who serves as the client's first line of defense and explanation with respect to the media. It is the public relations practitioner who meets the reporter head on. In the 21st century, media relations is not a job for the squeamish.

Objectivity in the Media

Whether the mass media have lost relative influence to the Internet and its various vehicles, securing positive publicity through the media still lies at the heart of public relations practice.

Why attract publicity?

The answer, as we will see, is that publicity is regarded as more *credible* than advertising. To attract positive publicity requires establishing a good working relationship with the media. This is easier said than done. In the 21st century, faced with intense competition from on-air and online journalists, reporters are by and large more aggressive.

They are also decidedly less "objective."

The presumed goal of a journalist is objectivity—fairness with the intention of remaining neutral in reporting a story. But total objectivity is impossible. All of us have biases and preconceived notions about many things. Likewise, in reporting, pure objectivity is unattainable; it would require complete neutrality and near-total detachment in reporting a story. Reporting, then, despite what some journalists might suggest, is subjective. Nevertheless, scholars of journalism believe that reporters and editors should strive for maximum objectivity (Figure 9-2).

By virtue of their role, the media view officials, particularly business and government spokespersons, with a degree of skepticism. Reporters shouldn't be expected to accept on faith the party line. By the same token, once a business or government official effectively substantiates the official view and demonstrates its merit, the media should be willing to report this accurately without editorial distortion.

FIGURE 9-2
Code of objectivity.
"The Journalist's Creed" was written after World War I by Dr. Walter Williams, dean of the School of Journalism at the University of Missouri. *(Courtesy of Luce Press Clippings)*

THE JOURNALIST'S Creed

I believe IN THE PROFESSION OF JOURNALISM.

I BELIEVE THAT THE PUBLIC JOURNAL IS A PUBLIC TRUST; THAT ALL CONNECTED WITH IT ARE, TO THE FULL MEASURE OF THEIR RESPONSIBILITY, TRUSTEES FOR THE PUBLIC; THAT ACCEPTANCE OF A LESSER SERVICE THAN THE PUBLIC SERVICE IS BETRAYAL OF THIS TRUST.

I BELIEVE THAT CLEAR THINKING AND CLEAR STATEMENT, ACCURACY, AND FAIRNESS ARE FUNDAMENTAL TO GOOD JOURNALISM.

I BELIEVE THAT A JOURNALIST SHOULD WRITE ONLY WHAT HE HOLDS IN HIS HEART TO BE TRUE.

I BELIEVE THAT SUPPRESSION OF THE NEWS, FOR ANY CONSIDERATION OTHER THAN THE WELFARE OF SOCIETY, IS INDEFENSIBLE.

I BELIEVE THAT NO ONE SHOULD WRITE AS A JOURNALIST WHAT HE WOULD NOT SAY AS A GENTLEMAN; THAT BRIBERY BY ONE'S OWN POCKETBOOK IS AS MUCH TO BE AVOIDED AS BRIBERY BY THE POCKETBOOK OF ANOTHER; THAT INDIVIDUAL RESPONSIBILITY MAY NOT BE ESCAPED BY PLEADING ANOTHER'S INSTRUCTIONS OR ANOTHER'S DIVIDENDS.

I BELIEVE THAT ADVERTISING, NEWS AND EDITORIAL COLUMNS SHOULD ALIKE SERVE THE BEST INTERESTS OF READERS; THAT A SINGLE STANDARD OF HELPFUL TRUTH AND CLEANNESS SHOULD PREVAIL FOR ALL; THAT THE SUPREME TEST OF GOOD JOURNALISM IS THE MEASURE OF ITS PUBLIC SERVICE.

I BELIEVE THAT THE JOURNALISM WHICH SUCCEEDS BEST—AND BEST DESERVES SUCCESS—FEARS GOD AND HONORS MAN; IS STOUTLY INDEPENDENT, UNMOVED BY PRIDE OF OPINION OR GREED OF POWER, CONSTRUCTIVE, TOLERANT BUT NEVER CARELESS, SELF-CONTROLLED, PATIENT, ALWAYS RESPECTFUL OF ITS READERS BUT ALWAYS UNAFRAID, IS QUICKLY INDIGNANT AT INJUSTICE; IS UNSWAYED BY THE APPEAL OF PRIVILEGE OR THE CLAMOR OF THE MOB; SEEKS TO GIVE EVERY MAN A CHANCE, AND, AS FAR AS LAW AND HONEST WAGE AND RECOGNITION OF HUMAN BROTHERHOOD CAN MAKE IT SO, AN EQUAL CHANCE; IS PROFOUNDLY PATRIOTIC WHILE SINCERELY PROMOTING INTERNATIONAL GOOD WILL AND CEMENTING WORLD-COMRADESHIP; IS A JOURNALISM OF HUMANITY, OF AND FOR TODAY'S WORLD.

Walter Williams

DEAN SCHOOL OF JOURNALISM, UNIVERSITY OF MISSOURI, 1908-1935

Stated another way, the relationship between the media and the establishment—that is, public relations people—should be one of *friendly adversaries* rather than of bitter enemies. Unfortunately, this is not always the case. According to one *Washington Post* columnist, the fault may lie with the American public:

> *We are only incidentally bringing truth to the world—although don't get me wrong, from time to time we manage to do just that. But most journalists most of the time are just trying to give the public what it wants—and much of the time, the public wants trash.*[9]

That is not to say that the vast majority of journalists don't try to be fair. They do. Despite the preconceived biases that all of us have, most reporters want to get the facts from all sides. An increasing number of journalists acknowledge and respect the public relations practitioner's role in the process. (Some don't, but there are rotten apples in any profession!) If reporters are dealt with fairly, most will reciprocate in kind.

However, some executives fail to understand the essential difference between the media and their own organizations. That is:

1. The reporter wants the "story," whether bad or good.
2. Organizations, on the other hand, want things to be presented in the best light.

Because of this difference, some executives consider journalists to be the enemy, dead set on revealing all the bad news they can about their organization. These people fear and distrust the media. As a consequence, the practice of public relations—intermediary between the executive and the journalist—gets knocked as a profession of "stonewallers" intent on keeping journalists out.[10] That is an unfair and, hopefully in most cases, undeserved generalization.

Print: Hanging In

Recent years have not been kind to the print medium, particularly newspapers.

As the recession deepened, once-powerful newspapers—hit by rising costs and declining readership, not to mention challenge from Apple iPads and comparable tablets—struggled to survive. After a century of daily publishing, the *Rocky Mountain News* in Denver closed. Another mainstay, the *Philadelphia Inquirer*, declared bankruptcy. In 2009, in Seattle, the daily *Post-Intelligencer* became exclusively a Web-based newspaper. In 2012, the historic New Orleans *Times-Picayune*, which reported relentlessly on Hurricane Katrina, fired 200 people and moved to a three-days-per-week publication schedule.[11]

Despite such sour newspaper news, by the summer of 2012, print circulation seemed to be stabilizing, while newspaper reading on the Internet climbed exponentially. The most significant increase in circulation came from the venerable *The New York Times*—arguably, the world's finest newspaper—where daily circulation increased an astounding 73% over the prior year—most of it due to the introduction of paid digital subscription. The *Times'* Sunday edition, a voluminous mass of news and review, climbed to a more than two million circulation. Indeed, newspapers throughout the United States showed a slight increase in daily circulation from 2011[12] (Table 9-1).

Despite the growth of the Internet and electronic media, print still stands as an important medium among public relations professionals.

Why?

The answer probably lies in the fact that many departments at newspapers and magazines use news releases and other publicity vehicles compared to the limited opportunities for such original use on network and cable TV, which frequently schedule stories that have first attracted print coverage. In addition, online databases, blogs, and other Web-based media regularly use organization-originated material destined for print usage, so the Internet—while originating an increasing amount of original copy—still often serves as a residual target for print publicity.

Thomas Jefferson once famously said, "Were it left to me to decide whether we should have a government without newspapers or newspapers without a government, I should not hesitate a moment to prefer the latter."

TABLE 9-1   Top 100 U.S. newspapers. This list provided by Burrelles/Luce and compiled by the Audit Bureau of Circulations shows newspaper circulation through March 31, 2012. *(Courtesy of Burrelles/Luce)*

U.S. Daily Newspapers

Rank	Newspaper	Daily	Sunday	Rank	Newspaper	Daily	Sunday
1	The Wall Street Journal	2,118,315 ▲	N/A	50	The Tampa Tribune	144,510 ▲	262,369
2	USA Today	1,817,446 ▲	N/A	51	The Cincinnati Enquirer	144,165 ▲	278,607 ▼
3	The New York Times	1,586,757 ▲	2,003,247 ▲	52	The Virginian-Plot	142,476 ▼	176,705 ▲
4	Los Angeles Times	616,575 ▲	952,761 ▲	53	San Antonio Express-News	139,099 ▲	353,572 ▲
5	Daily News (New York, NY)	579,636 ▼	660,918 ▼	54	The Columbus (OH) Dispatch	136,023 ▲	264,802 ▼
6	San Jose Mercury News	575,786 ▲	690,258 ▲	55	Omaha World-Herald	135,223 ▼	168,403 ▼
7	New York Post	555,327 ▲	434,392 ▲	56	The Times-Picayune (New Orleans, LA)	133,557 ▼	154,353 ▼
8	The Washington Post	507,615 ▲	719,301 ▼	57	The Detroit News	133,508 –	N/A
9	Chicago Sun-Times	422,335 ▲	434,861 ▲	58	The Hartford Courant	132,006 ▼	191,044 ▼
10	Chicago Tribune	414,590 ▼	779,440 ▼	59	The Press-Enterprise (Riverside, CA)	131,872 ▲	156,545 ▲
11	The Dallas Morning News	405,349 ▼	702,848 ▲	60	The Oklahoman (Oklahoma City, OK)	130,177 ▼	187,240 ▼
12	The Denver Post	401,120 ▲	595,363 ▲	61	News & Observer (Raleigh, NC)	129,698 ▲	196,219 ▲
13	Newsday (Long Island, NY)	397,973 ▼	495,416 ▲	62	Austin American-Statesman	125,305 ▲	183,717 ▼
14	Houston Chronicle	384,007 ▲	916,934 ▲	63	The Commercial Appeal (Memphis, TN)	118,978 ▲	155,864 ▲
15	The Philadelphia Inquiter	325,291 ▼	517,310 ▲	64	The Tennessean (Nashville, TN)	118,589 ▼	216,434 ▼
16	The Arizona Republic (Phoenix, AZ)	321,600 ▲	538,579 ▲	65	Grand Rapids Press	114,571 ▲	149,667 ▼
17	Star Tribune (Minneapolis-St. Paul, MN)	300,330 ▲	544,186 ▲	66	Democrat and Chronicle (Rochester, NY)	114,502 ▼	167,862 ▼
18	St. Petersburg Times	299,497 ▲	432,202 ▲	67	The Providence (RI) Journal	114,013 –	122,377 –
19	The Plain Dealer (Cleveland, OH)	286,405 ▲	440,968 ▲	68	The Salt Lake Tribune	110,546 ▲	140,628 ▲
20	The Orange County (CA) Register	280,812 ▲	385,283 ▼	69	The Palm Beach Post	110,373 ▲	139,221 ▲
21	The Star-Ledger (Newark, NJ)	278,940 ▲	413,472 ▲	70	Richmond Times-Dispatch	108,559 ▼	162,769 ▼
22	The Oregonian (Portland, OR)	247,833 ▲	306,712 ▲	71	Boston Herald	108,548 ▼	81,925 ▼
23	The Seattle Times	236,929 ▼	346,589 ▲	72	The Fresno Bee	107,501 ▲	154,873 ▲
24	Detroit Free Press	232,696 ▼	668,332 ▲	73	The Birmingham News	103,729 ▲	173,187 ▼
25	The San Diego Union-Tribune	230,742 ▲	364,454 ▼	74	The Des Moines Register	101,915 ▲	211,762 ▼
26	San Francisco Chronicle	229,176 ▲	296,874 ▲	75	The Morning Call (Allentown, PA)	100,196 ▲	125,549 ▲
27	The Boston Globe	225,482 ▲	365,512 ▲	76	Daily Herald (Arlington Heights, IL)	99,670 ▲	106,326 ▼
28	Las Vegas Review-Journal	220,619 ▲	205,931 ▲	77	The Florida Times-Union (Jacksonville, FL)	98,580 ▼	157,559 ▼
29	Honolulu Star-Advertiser	209,915 ▲	164,316 ▲	78	Asbury Park Press	98,032 ▼	150,646 ▼
30	Pioneer Press (St. Paul, MN)	205,171 ▲	270,811 ▲	79	Tulsa World	97,725 ▲	140,242 ▲
31	Kansas City Star	200,365 ▲	310,487 ▲	80	Arizona Daily Star (Tucson, AZ)	96,682 ▲	154,715 ▲
32	The Sacramento Bee	196,667 ▼	271,610 ▲	81	La Opinion	95,148 ▼	38,304 ▼
33	Star-Telegram (Fort Worth, TX)	195,455 ▲	228,269 ▼	82	The Blade (Toledo, OH)	94,215 ▼	127,953 ▼
34	Pittsburgh Post-Gazette	188,545 ▲	318,962 ▲	83	Daily News (Los Angeles, CA)	94,016 ▲	97,606 ▲
35	Pittsburgh Tribune-Review	188,405 ▲	202,230 ▲	84	Dayton Daily News	93,425 ▲	154,896 ▲
36	St. Louis Post-Dispatch	187,992 ▼	333,529 ▲	85	Lexington (KY) Herald Leader	89,735 ▲	115,737 ▼
37	Milwaukee-Wisconsin Journal Sentinel	185,710 ▼	328,475 ▲	86	The Akron Beacon Journal	88,040 ▲	122,598 ▼
38	The Baltimore Sun	179,574 ▲	332,305 ▲	87	The Post and Courier (Charleston, SC)	87,817 ▲	95,291 ▲
39	Arkansas Democrat-Gazette (Little Rock, AR)	179,258 ▲	267,730 ▲	88	Northwest Indiana Times	85,692 ▼	93,019 ▲
40	The Atlanta Journal-Constitution	174,251 ▲	402,602 ▼	89	Albuquerque Journal	84,826 ▼	109,516 ▼
41	Orlando Sentinel	173,576 ▲	288,328 ▲	90	Deseret News (Salt Lake City, UT)	83,719 –	160,617 –
42	Sun-Sentinel (Ft. Lauderdale, FL)	165,974 ▲	245,869 ▲	91	The News Journal (New Castle County, DE)	83,210 ▲	122,200 ▼
43	The Indianapolis Star	164,640 ▼	304,112 ▼	92	Wisconsin State Journal (Madison, WI)	83,083 ▼	116,329 ▼
44	The Miami Herald	160,988 ▲	212,541 ▲	93	Press-Telegram (Los Angeles County, CA)	82,556 ▲	68,020 ▼
45	Investors Business Daily (Los Angeles, CA)	156,269 ▲	N/A	94	Press-Register (Mobile, Al)	82,088 ▲	103,373 ▲
46	The Record (Hackensack, NJ)	155,236 ▲	178,446 ▲				
47	The Courier-Journal (Louisville, KY)	154,033 ▲	254,685 ▼				
48	The Buffalo News	147,085 ▼	233,069 ▼				
49	Charlotte Observer	146,511 ▲	216,862 ▲				

TABLE 9-1 (*Continued*)

Rank	Newspaper	Daily	Sunday	Rank	Newspaper	Daily	Sunday
95	Knoxville News Sentinel	81,391 ▼	115,586 ▼	98	The Roanoke Times (Roanoke, VA)	78,663 ▼	92,084 ▲
96	Sarasota Herald-Tribune	79,845 –	105,470 –	99	The Post-Standard (Syracuse, NY)	78,616 ▼	137,489 ▼
97	Intelligencer Journal-Lancaster (PA) New Era	78,819 ▲	N/A	100	The News Tribune (Tacoma, WA)	78,453 ▼	105,207 ▲

Source: Audit Bureau of Circulations FAS-FAX Report for six-month period ending 03/31/12
▲ an increase in circulation for the period 9/30/11-03/31/12
▼ a decrease in circulation for the period 9/30/11-03/31/12
– did not appear on list of Top U.S. Daily Newspapers 09/30/11

While it is true that newspaper circulation in recent years has tumbled, and young readers, in particular, have turned to the Internet, the nation's largest newspapers are still powerful. Daily newspaper circulation, which stood at 62 million in 1990, fell to 43 million in 2010, a 10% decline. Sunday circulation fell by about the same percentage, although in recent years, Sunday circulation has increased. However, there is no question that the growth of alternative sources of information has hurt newspaper readership. Over the past 20 years, the number of daily American newspapers has decreased from 1,611 in 1990 to 1,387 in 2009.[13] In 2012, shortly after the *Times-Picayune* in New Orleans announced it would cut back its print schedule to three days a week, its sister publications the *Birmingham News*, the *Press-Register of Mobile,* and the *Huntsville Times* followed suit. Four days later, three Canadian newspapers, the *Calgary Herald*, the *Edmonton Journal*, and the *Ottawa Citizen*, announced they would all eliminate their Sunday editions.[14]

Despite their circulation problems, newspapers still dominate the nation's news schedule. Stated another way, what appears on the front page of the nation's leading dailies sets the news agenda for the nation. Specifically, electronic news directors and bloggers regularly check the national dailies to determine the news of the day. Moreover, newspaper readership on the Web has increased significantly, even while print circulation has declined. Newspaper Website audiences increased by 7% from 2010 to 2011. Ten percent of the nation's 1,350 daily newspapers have implemented some form of paid digital content, and this trend is expected to increase in the years ahead. *The Wall Street Journal* has charged for its online site for more than a decade and leads newspapers with 449,000 digital subscribers. In addition, newspapers and wire services are licensing content, making secondary users pay for use. And newspapers are investing in news and sales on tablets, smartphones, and social media as these vehicles become more dominant.[15] The conclusion, then, stated simply, is that even in the wired 21st century, print media newspapers still control a significant portion of the nation's news diet.

Like their newspaper brethren, U.S. magazines have also moved inexorably toward digital. In 2011, as a sign of things to come, venerable Time, Inc., the nation's largest magazine publisher, hired an expert in digital advertising to run its magazine operation. Magazines, as opposed to print newspapers, have held their own in the 21st century. There are just under 21,000 consumer and business magazines published in the United States—including 1,100 medical magazines, 978 ethnic magazines, 939 regional magazines, 829 travel magazines, 784 religious magazines, 613 business magazines, 569 college alumni magazines, and hundreds of titles for health and fitness, music, lifestyle, women and sports—not to mention titles such as *Bacon Busters* for hog hunters, *Bark* for dog lifestyle fans, and *Crappie* for enthusiasts of a particular freshwater fish[16] (Table 9-2).

TABLE 9-2 **Top 25 U.S. magazines.** This list provided by Burrelles/Luce and compiled by the Audit Bureau of Circulations shows magazine circulation, dominated by senior citizens, women, gamers, and Oprah lovers. *(Courtesy of Burrelles/Luce)*

U.S. Consumer Magazines

Rank	Magazine	Total Paid & Verified Circulation
1	AARP The Magazine	22,407,421 ▲
2	AARP Bulletin	22,171,632 ▼
3	Better Homes and Gardens	7,617,844 ▼
4	Game Informer	7,514,460 ▲
5	Reader's Digest	5,560,046 ▼
6	National Geographic	4,480,788 ▲
7	Good Housekeeping	4,341,426 ▲
8	Woman's Day	3,886,853 ▲
9	Family Circle	3,872,671 ▲
10	People	3,569,811 ▲
11	Time	3,298,390 ▼
12	Ladies' Home Journal	3,232,354 ▼
13	Taste of Home	3,230,514 ▼
14	Sports Illustrated	3,178,760 ▼
15	Cosmopolitan	3,040,013 ▲
16	Prevention	2,874,117 ▼
17	Southern Living	2,865,845 ▲
18	Maxim	2,507,318 ▲
19	AAA Living	2,471,160 ▼
20	O, The Oprah Magazine	2,380,782 ▼
21	Glamour	2,353,863 ▲
22	American Legion Magazine	2,303,613 ▼
23	Parenting	2,231,783 –
24	Redbook	2,224,418 –
25	Smithsonian	2,113,637 –

Source: ABC figures for six-month period ending 12/31/11
▲ an increase in circulation for the period 06/30/11-12/31/11
▼ a decrease in circulation for the period 06/30/11-12/31/11
– did not appear on list of U.S. Consumer Magazines 06/30/11

For the public relations professional, then, with so many print outlets—newspapers, magazines, and online publications—the area of public relations publicity remains broad and deep.

Electronic Media: Cable Ups and Downs

The first decade of the 21st century saw a dramatic increase in the number of Americans turning to cable television—CNN, MSNBC, Fox, CNBC, and even the Comedy Channel—for their daily news.

But through 2010, with challenges from Netflix, Hulu, and other on-demand viewing services, the number of daily cable watchers dropped precipitously. Audiences began returning to cable news in 2011 after a steep decline in ratings during 2010, but it depended on the channel. In aggregate, the three major cable news channels—CNN, Fox News Channel, and MSNBC—were nearly flat in terms of 2011 viewership. Median viewership in prime time was up 1% to 3.3 million. Cable television audiences fluctuated with the news, spiking when breaking news, such as the death of Osama bin Laden in 2011, dominated.[17]

Despite its fits and starts, cable TV had a dramatic impact on the nation's news consumption habits.

- ■ The impact of 24/7 cable news meant that Americans were barraged with a continuous loop of unrelated events that seemed to all run together in perpetual images, from the Kardashians and the Lohans to terrorism and missing children to insider trading scandals and pending murder verdicts. While broadcast news tried to retain at least some vestige of "impartial" journalism, cable news made no such attempt. Fox News, with lead hosts Bill O'Reilly and Sean Hannity, was clearly conservative, while MSNBC, with anchors Chris Matthews and Rachel Maddow, was unabashedly liberal. In such an environment, it was difficult to discern the truly newsworthy from the inconsequential and the hopelessly biased.

- ■ Specialized cable networks, offering everything from sports and food and fashion to weather and history, beam nonstop across the land. In the financial area, for example, CNBC, Fox Business Channel, Bloomberg Television, PBS Nightly Business Report, and other similar efforts have become enormously popular barometers of the nation's stock market appetite. The most outrageous cable phenomenon was the popularity—particularly with younger viewers—of "fake news," served up nightly by the likes of Jon Stewart and Stephen Colbert (Figure 9-3). Stewart's *The Daily Show* drew nearly two million viewers a night, and Stewart showed up fourth on a national poll of "most admired journalists"—even though he wasn't (a "journalist," that is!).[18]

- ■ Meanwhile, talk radio has become an enormous political and social force. Each week, mostly conservative talk show hosts lead call-in discussions of the issues of the day. The undisputed dean of this ilk, Rush Limbaugh—*El Rushbo*— reaches a gargantuan 15 million listeners (known as "ditto heads" because they *always* agree with the host!). In 2008, Limbaugh signed a new eight-year contract that pays $40 million annually—more than the three TV network anchors combined.[19] Following Limbaugh in the national rankings were two equally "right-minded" conservatives, Sean Hannity and Dr. Michael Savage. One liberal was able to penetrate the top 10 list in 2012, Ed Schultz, a 30-year veteran who also had his own MSNBC program.[20] Schultz was the exception. Most liberal radio just didn't work. In 2004, frustrated liberals attempted to counteract *El Rushbo* and his conservative armada with a radio network of their own, Air America, which promptly went bankrupt.

What makes the electronic media's news dominance so disconcerting—some would say scary—is that the average 30-minute television newscast would fill, in terms of words, only one-half of one page of the average daily newspaper! That means that if you're getting most of your news from television, you're *missing* most of the news.

Despite the evolving strength of the Internet as a communications medium, the electronic media undoubtedly will remain a force in the new millennium. Given the extent to which the electronic media dominate society, public relations people must become more resourceful in understanding how to deal with television and radio.

FIGURE 9-3
"Truthiness" seeker!
Fake newsman
Stephen Colbert
arrives triumphantly at
his "Rally to Restore
Sanity" on the National
Mall in 2010. *(Photo:*
TRIPPLAAR KRISTOFFER/
SIPA/Newscom)

The Internet Factor

Further complicating the relationship between journalists and executives is the Internet. To some, the Internet has ushered in a new age of journalistic reporting: immediate, freewheeling, unbridled. Indeed, when the young people of the Middle East erupted into the Arab Spring at the end of 2010, it was Twitter and Facebook that broadcast the news from Tunisia to Libya to Egypt to Syria. To others, however, the Internet is responsible for the collapse of journalistic standards and the ascendancy of rumor mongering.

As noted, while many bemoan "the end of newspapers as we know them," the fact is that newspaper Websites have grown in popularity. And smart publishers are incorporating print and online more seamlessly. Indeed when the *Washington Post* chose a new editor in 2008, it picked an outsider charged with "converting heavy Web traffic to its site into enough dollars to outweigh the loss of print advertising and circulation revenue."[21] In 2011, *The New York Times* dumped its long-time CEO, Janet Robinson, largely because the "Great Gray Lady" (the *Times*, not Robinson!) sought a more digitally oriented chief executive.[22] The point is that while print staffs and editions shrink, the online wing of many newspapers continues to expand.

TABLE 9-3 **Top 50 U.S. online newspapers.** This list provided by Burrelles/Luce indicates the popularity of online sites of the leading U.S. newspapers, most especially *The New York Times* and *The Wall Street Journal*. *(Courtesy of Burrelles/Luce)*

U.S. Daily Newspapers

Popularity	Website	Address	Popularity	Website	Address
1 *	The New York Times	nytimes.com	27 ▼	Sun-Sentinel (Ft. Lauderdale, Fl)	sun-sentinel.com
2 *	The Wall Street Journal	online.wsj.com			
3 *	The Washington Post	washingtonpost.com	28 ▲	The Baltimore Sun	baltimoresun.com
4 *	USA Today	usatoday.com	29 ▼	The Examiner (Washington, D.C.)	washingtonexaminer.com
5 *	Los Angeles Times	latimes.com			
6 *	San Francisco Chronicle	sfgate.com	30 ▼	Orlando Sentinel	orlandosentinel.com
7 *	New York Post	nypost.com	31 ▲	The Dallas Morning News	dallasnews.com
8 *	Chicago Tribune	chicagotribune.com	32 ▼	Newsday (Long Island, NY)	newsday.com
9 *	Christian Science Monitor	csmonitor.com	33 ▲	Milwaukee-Journal Sentinel	jsonline.com
10 *	Houston Chronicle	chron.com	34 *	Deseret News (Salt Lake City, UT)	deseretnews.com
11 ▲	Washington Times	washingtontimes.com			
12 ▲	The Star-Ledger (Newark, NJ)	nj.com	35 ▲	Times Union (Albany, NY)	timesunion.com
13 ▼	Chicago Sun-Times	suntimes.com	36 ▼	The Detroit News	detnews.com
14 ▼	The Atlanta Journal-Constitution	ajc.com	37 ▲	The Palm Beach Post	palmbeachpost.com
			38 ▲	Kansas City Star	kansascity.com
15 ▼	The Arizona Republic	azcentral.com	39 ▼	The Salt Lake Tribune	sltrib.com
16 ▼	The Philadelphia Inquirer	philly.com	40 ▼	Tampa Bay Times	tampabay.com
17 ▲	Boston Herald	bostonherald.com	41 ▼	The Indianapolis Star	indystar.com
18 ▲	San Jose Mercury News	mercurynews.com	42 –	The Oklahoman Online	newsok.com
19 ▼	The Denver Post	denverpost.com	43 ▼	The Seattle Times	nwsource.com
20 *	The Miami Herald	miamiherald.com	44 *	Las Vegas Review Journal	lvrj.com
21 ▲	The Seattle Post-Intelligencer	seattlepi.com	45 ▲	News & Observer (Raleigh, NC)	newsobserver.com
22 ▲	Star Tribune (Minneapolis-St. Paul, MN)	startribune.com	46 ▲	Austin American-Statesman	statesman.com
			47 *	Las Vegas Sun	lasvegassun.com
23 *	The Sacramento Bee	sacbee.com	48 –	San Antonio Express-News	mysanantonio.com
24 ▼	Detroit Free Press	freep.com	49 *	The Record (Hackensack, NJ)	NorthJersey.com
25 ▼	St. Louis Post Dispatch	stltoday.com	50 –	Buffalo News	buffalonews.com
26 ▼	Orange County Register	ocregister.com			

Source: Alexa Top Sites by News Category accessed 05/24/12
▲ an increase for 05/24/12 compared 02/27/12
▼ a decrease for the 05/24/12 compared 02/27/12
* stayed the same for 05/24/12 compared 02/27/12
– did not appear on list of Alexa Top Sites by News Category on 02/27/12

So the irony is that while the Internet may be mortally wounding the daily newspaper as we know it, it is also allowing some papers to increase their readership by quantum leaps (Table 9-3).

As to the indigenous news-oriented inhabitants of the Web, "new-age news sources" abound, from the right wing Drudge Report and NewsMax to the left wing Huffington Post and Salon, offering agreeable fodder for believers and increased targets for public relations practitioners. *The Huffington Post*, founded in 2005 by the conservative-turned-liberal gadfly Arianna Huffington, was purchased in 2011 by AOL for a whopping $315 million (Figure 9-4). (That's some gadfly!) *The Huffington Post*, with 28 million unique Website visitors per month, has been ranked as the most popular political news Website, with the conservative Drudge Report second with half the amount of estimated unique monthly users, compared to its liberal rival.[23]

Beyond the HuffPost and Drudge, millions get their daily news dose from such online sites as NBCNews.com, CNN.com, AOL.com, Yahoo!News.com, Politico.com, and a host of others.

FIGURE 9-4
Birds of a feather.
Arianna Huffington,
Huffington Post
diva-in-chief, greets
like-minded liberal
actor/activist Sean
Penn at 2010 HuffPo
Game Changers party.
*(Photo: Everett Collection/
Newscom)*

Finally, there are the blogs—all 181 million of them and counting.

Blogs come in all shapes, sizes, and pedigrees. Many are of passing interest, many more are worthless, and several—a precious few, really—have become important sources of news and commentary. Measuring agency Technorati ranks blogs by their links to Websites. The higher the number of links, the greater the ranking by Technorati. Leading blogs (Table 9-4) are all over the lot, from news sites to political sites, from gossip sites to Boing Boing.

The majority of bloggers are women, and half of bloggers are aged 18–34. About one in three bloggers are moms, and more than half are parents with children under 18 years old. Seventy percent of bloggers have gone to college.[24]

The point is that Internet reporters and bloggers from every political bias and ulterior motive remain busy 24 hours a day, seven days a week, churning out continuous stories—some true, others not—about companies, government agencies, nonprofits, and prominent individuals.

The challenge for public relations professionals in dealing with print, electronic, or online commentators is to foster a closer relationship between their organizations and those who present the news. The key, once again, is fairness, with each side accepting—and respecting—the other's role and responsibility.

TABLE 9-4   **Most popular blogs.** This list, provide by Burelles/Luce and composed by Technorati, shows the most popular English language blogs through May 24, 2012. *(Courtesy of Burrelles/Luce)*

English-Language Blogs

Rank	Blog	Blog Address	Technorati Authority Figures on 05/24/12
1	The Huffington Post	huffingtonpost.com	936 ▼
2	BuzzFeed	buzzfeed.com	866 ▲
3	The Daily Beast	thedailybeast.com	865 ▲
4	Mashable	mashable.com	864 ▼
5	TMZ	tmz.com	860 ▲
6	The Verge	theverge.com	859 ▲
7	Gizmodo	gizmodo.com	859 ▲
8	Engadget	engadget.com	848 ▲
9	Think Progress	thinkprogress.org	835 ▼
10	TechCrunch	techcrunch.com	835 ▼
11	Boing Boing	boingboing.net	832 ▲
12	Gawker	gawker.com	831 ▲
13	The Next Web	thenextweb.com	831 ▲
14	Ars Technica	arstechnica.com	825 ▲
15	Business Insider	businessinsider.com	824 ▲
16	GigaOm	gigaom.com	816 ▲
17	Kotaku	kotaku.com	813 –
18	The Blaze	theblaze.com	811 –
19	Hot Air	hotair.com	808 ▼
20	Jezebel	jezebel.com	808 ▼
21	LA Now	latimesblogs.latimes.com/lanow	808 ▼
22	VentureBeat	venturebeat.com	805 ▼
23	Deadspin	deadspin.com	803 /
24	Mediaite	mediaite.com	802 –
25	CNN Political Ticker	politicalticker.blogs.cnn.com	801 ▼

Source: Technorati Authority for the Top 100 Blogs on 05/24/12
▲ an increase in authority for 05/24/12 compared to 02/27/12
▼ a decrease in authority for 05/24/12 compared to 02/27/12
/ no change in authority for 05/24/12 compared to 02/27/12
– did not appear on list of Top English-Language Blogs 02/27/12

Dealing with the Media

It falls on public relations professionals to orchestrate the relationship between their organizations and the media, whether print, electronic, or Internet-based. To be sure, the media can't ordinarily be manipulated (and they *hate* it if you try!). They can, however, be engaged in an honest and interactive way to convey the organization's point of view in a manner that may merit being reported. First, an organization must establish a formal media relations policy (Figure 9-6). Second, an organization must establish a philosophy for dealing with the media, keeping in mind the following dozen principles:

1. **A reporter is a reporter.**   A reporter is never "off duty." Anything you say to a journalist is fair game to be reported. Remember that, and never let down your guard, no matter how friendly you are.

2. **You are the organization.**   In the old days, reporters disdained talking to public relations representatives, who they derisively labeled "flacks" (as in "catching flak," or bad news). Public relations people, therefore, were rarely quoted and remained anonymous. Today the opposite is true. The public relations person represents the policy of an organization. He or she is quoted by name and interviewed on camera, so every word out of the public relations professional's mouth must be carefully weighed in advance.

PR Ethics Mini-Case

MSNBC Cries "Wawa" with Made-Up Romney Gaffe

Some people trust reporters as far as they can throw them. And sometimes, those people are right.

Such was the case in the heated presidential election of 2012, when Republican challenger Mitt Romney squared off against President Barack Obama. MSNBC, whose advertising slogan was "Lean Forward" but whose direction was most decidedly "left," seized on an apparent Romney gaffe after ordering a hoagie sandwich in a Pennsylvania Wawa convenience store (Figure 9-5).

Romney, reported MSNBC's Andrea Mitchell, said he was "amazed" at the touch screen technology. Labeling the apparent naiveté Romney's "super market scanner moment," Mitchell compared the situation to George H.W. Bush's supposed astonishment over a scanner during his 1992 reelection campaign. The clear intent was that Romney, born with a silver spoon and oblivious about the trials and tribulations of the common man, was clearly out of touch. Left wing blogs, predictably, also seized on the incident.

But wait a minute.

Viewing the entire unedited exchange at Wawa, it was clear that Romney was well aware of touch screen technology but was making a larger point about government waste and the more efficient methods of private sector industry. Taken in context, the Romney comments made sense. But MSNBC's decision to snip the "surprise" moment out of context made Romney seem clueless.

The Romney camp immediately objected, MSNBC immediately headed for the hills, and Wawa basked as its name trended on Twitter nationwide and sparked hundreds of media articles, thus proving that one man's and network's publicity downfall can be another organization's publicity gain.

Questions

1. How would you assess MSNBC's handling of the Romney Wawa moment?

2. How would you have handled the incident were you Andrea Mitchell?*

FIGURE 9-5   Wawa scan, MSNBC scam.
Republican presidential candidate Mitt Romney shakes hands with a Wawa gas station employee at a 2012 campaign stop. *(Photo: EMMANUEL DUNAND/AFP/Getty Images/Newscom)*

*For further information, see Michael Sebastian, "MSNBC Manufacturers Romney Gaffe, Creates PR Windfall for Convenience Store," Ragan PR Daily, June 18, 2012.

3. **There is no standard-issue reporter.** The sad fact is that many business managers want nothing to do with the press. They believe them to be villains. But that isn't necessarily true. As noted, most are simply trying to do their jobs, like anyone else, so each should be treated as an individual, until, cynics might say, "proven guilty."

4. **Treat journalists professionally.** As long as they understand that your job is different than theirs and treat you with deference, you should do likewise. A journalist's job is to get a story, whether good or bad. A public relations person's job is to present the organization in the best light. That difference understood, the relationship should be a professional one. Some journalists

FIGURE 9-6 Media relations policy. Every organization should have a formal policy, such as this one from the city of Ogden, Utah, for dealing with the media. *(Courtesy of Ogden* Standard-Examiner*)*

NORTH OGDEN CITY MEDIA RELATIONS POLICY

I. GOAL:

North Ogden City seeks to establish "transparency in government" by working cooperatively with the media to disseminate information of public interest and concern in an accurate, complete and timely manner.

II. POLICY:

(1) To achieve the City's goal, the City Manager is designated as the City Public Information Officer or "CITY PIO" for North Ogden City and shall be responsible for the implementation of this policy. When the CITY PIO is unavailable, he or she shall designate one of the authorized City spokespersons as the "Acting CITY PIO."

(2) The press should be treated like a customer of the City and all City employees or officials who engage with the press shall do so in a courteous, polite and professional manner. Any media inquiries received by City staff will be referred immediately to their Department Head who, in turn, will immediately forward the contact to the CITY PIO for response.

(3) Inquiries from the news media are given a high priority by North Ogden City and should be responded to as quickly and efficiently as possible. Every effort should be made to meet media deadlines and to ensure that all information released is accurate and complete.

(4) When contacted by the CITY PIO for information to respond to a media inquiry, all department heads shall immediately provide the CITY PIO the most accurate and complete information available for the response.

(5) If the CITY PIO determines that the City's goal can best be achieved by having someone with more background or expertise speak for the City on a particular topic, he or she may designate one of the authorized spokespersons to assist with or give the City's response.

(6) To assure that the City's elected officials have accurate, complete and timely information to fulfill their responsibilities to represent the public in City affairs, they shall be immediately informed by telephone or email of the substance of every media inquiry and of the City's official response. They shall be notified of all official City press releases and other proactive media contacts prior to release of information to the media.

(7) The CITY PIO shall keep a log of all media contacts indicating the date and time of the contact, the substance of the inquiry, the substance of the City's response, the identity of the person making the response for the City and the date and time of the response.

(8) Verbal requests from the media to any City elected official or employee that are not public safety, crisis or emergency inquiries shall be sent in writing to the CITY PIO and elected officials. Responses to the media shall be sent in writing and copied to the CITY PIO and elected officials. Copies may also be sent to other City spokespersons as needed.

III. CITY SPOKESPERSONS:

Authorized City spokespersons that the CITY PIO, in his or her judgment, may designate for a particular response are:

*The Mayor and City Council members

*The Deputy City Manager

*The City Attorney

*All Department Heads

*The Police Chief

IV. RECORDS REQUESTS:

(1) Media requests for records will be handled in accordance with this policy, to the extent it is consistent with the Government Records Access and Management Act or "GRAMA" as contained in Utah Code Ann. ¬ß 63G-2-101 et. Seq.

(2) The CITY PIO will be notified of all media records requests.

(3) He or she will then forward the request to the City Recorder who is the official custodian of all City records.

(4) The Recorder will be responsible to see that media records requests are handled in an accurate, complete and timely manner.

(5) The Recorder will immediately notify all elected officials by telephone or email of each media records request received by the City.

(6) The Police Department shall continue to respond to media requests for records concerning investigations according to police department policy.

(7) Media records requests shall be made in writing on a form prepared by the City for that purpose; the form shall include:

a. an accurate and complete description of the record(s) requested;

b. the name of the person and organization making the request;

c. the date and time of the request;

d. the telephone number and mailing address of the requestor;

e. the name of the City employee assigned by the Recorder to respond to the request; and,

f. the date and time of the response.

(8) A copy of all records disclosed to the media in response to the request shall be attached to the completed form and archived by the Recorder in chronological order.

(9) The records produced in response to media requests shall be readily available for viewing at City Hall upon request by any elected official.

V. PRIVILEGED AND PRIVATE INFORMATION:

(1) The vast majority of the records and affairs of North Ogden City are public information which citizens, including the press, have the right to know. All public information should be provided to the press upon request without unnecessary delay.

(2) Some matters, however, like ongoing investigations, information regarding litigation or the threat of litigation, personnel issues, real estate transactions, medical and mental health matters, private data regarding citizens, documents in draft form, to name a few, are governed by privileges and laws intended to advance important public policy goals.

(3) When a media request for an interview or for records appears to involve a subject matter that may be privileged or private, the CITY PIO, Police PIO or Recorder should consult with the City Attorney. The City Attorney will review the request without delay and promptly provide counsel to the CITY PIO or Recorder.

(Continued)

VI. PERSONAL POINTS OF VIEW:

(1) It is recognized that all employees have the right to express their personal points of view regarding matters of general public concern.

(2) However, personal points of view may conflict with the City's official policy.

(3) Therefore, City employees who write letters to the editor may not use official City stationary. If an employee chooses to identify himself or herself as a City employee in a letter or email to the editor, he or she must state that the views set forth in the letter do not represent the views of the City but are the employee's personal opinions.

(4) A similar disclaimer must be given if an employee addresses a public meeting, participates in a radio talk show, or is interviewed for a radio or television, unless the employee has been designated by the CITY PIO as a spokesperson for the City.

VII. CITY-INITIATED INFORMATION:

(1) Proactive media contact on behalf of the City is processed through the CITY PIO—this includes press releases, media advisories and personal contacts with reporters and editors for coverage.

(2) Departments seeking publicity for events or activities, or needing to collaborate with the media to communicate important information to the public, will coordinate with the CITY PIO.

(3) Departments (except law enforcement on matters pertaining to investigations) may not unilaterally initiate media contacts.

(4) When the CITY PIO approves a proactive media contact, he or she shall notify elected officials of the substance of the contact by telephone or email prior to the information being released.

VIII. PUBLIC SAFETY ISSUES:

(1) Because the Police Department operates 24/7 and its work generates a high volume of media calls, it shall designate an officer or officers as Police Public Information Officers or "Police PIO's" and follow specific guidelines when releasing information.

(2) When the CITY PIO is notified by a City staff member of a media call regarding a police investigation or general criminal activity, the CITY PIO will immediately forward the contact to the Police PIO for the appropriate response.

(3) All information released to the media by the Police PIO should be provided immediately to the CITY PIO who will forward the information without delay by telephone or email to elected officials.

(4) Media inquiries concerning matters of police personnel, general police policies and procedures or in any way reflecting upon the competency or integrity of police personnel or police administration will be routed to and handled directly by the CITY PIO as provided in this policy.

IX. CRISIS OR EMERGENCY ISSUES:

During a crisis or major emergency (i.e. flooding, earthquake, etc.), the procedure for communicating with the media is highlighted in the City's Emergency Plan. The plan designates the CITY PIO as the main point of contact for the media. The CITY PIO is assisted by alternates, including the Police PIO, who prepare and disseminate emergency public information.

complain that "PR people are paid to twist reality into pretzels and convince you that they are fine croissants."[25] So seek to earn reporter trust.

5. **Don't sweat the skepticism.**   Journalists aren't paid to ask nice questions. They are paid to be skeptical. "Bad news" is *news*, while "good news" isn't usually *news*. Some interviewees resent this. Smart interviewees realize it comes with the territory.

6. **Don't try to "buy" a journalist.**   Never try to threaten or coerce a journalist with advertising. The line between news and advertising should be a clear one. No self-respecting journalist will tolerate someone trying to "bribe" him or her for a positive story.

7. **Become a trusted source.**   Journalists can't be "bought," but they can be persuaded by your becoming a source of information for them. A reporter's job is to report on what's going on. By definition, a public relations person knows more about the company and the industry than does a reporter. So become a source and a positive relationship will follow.

8. **Talk when not "selling."**   Becoming a source means sharing information with journalists, even when it has nothing to do with your company. Reporters need leads and story ideas. If you supply them, once again a positive relationship will follow.

9. **Don't expect "news" agreement.**   A reporter's view of "news" and an organization's view of "news" will differ. If so, the journalist wins. (It's the reporter's paper/Website/TV station, after all!) Don't complain if a story doesn't make it into publication. Sometimes there is no logical reason, so never promise an executive that a story will "definitely make the paper."

10. **Don't cop a 'tude.**   Don't have an attitude with reporters. They need the information that you possess. If you're coy or standoffish or reluctant to share, they will pay you back. Although reporters vary in look and type, they all share one trait: They remember.

11. **Never lie.**   This is the cardinal rule. As one *The Wall Street Journal* reporter put it, "Never lie to a reporter or that reporter will never trust you again."[26]

12. **Read the paper.**   The number one criticism of public relations people by journalists is that they often don't have any idea what the journalist writes, comments, or blogs about. This is infuriating, especially when a journalist is approached on a story pitch. Lesson: Read the paper!

Although some may deny it, reporters are human beings, so there is no guarantee that even if these principles are followed, all reporters will be fair or objective. Most of the time, however, following these dozen rules of the road will lead to a better relationship between the journalist and the public relations professional.

Attracting Publicity

Publicity, through news releases—mostly via email—and other methods, is eminently more powerful than advertising. Publicity is most often gained by dealing directly with the media, either by initiating the communication or by reacting to inquiries.

Although most people—especially CEOs!—confuse the two, *publicity* differs dramatically from *advertising*.

First and most important, advertising costs money—lots of it. A full-page, one-time, nonrecurring ad in the national edition of *The Wall Street Journal,* for example, costs upwards of $180,000—for one ad! A full page in *The New York Times* is just slightly lower.[27]

On the other hand, the benefits of paid advertising include the following communications areas that can be "guaranteed":

- ■ **Content:** What is said and how it is portrayed and illustrated
- ■ **Size:** How large a space is devoted to the organization
- ■ **Location:** Where in the paper the ad will appear
- ■ **Reach:** The audience exposed to the ad—that is, the number of papers in which the ad appears
- ■ **Frequency:** How many times the ad is run

Frequency is extremely important. Today, with 500 cable and broadcast television channels, thousands of newspapers and magazines, and millions more Internet sites, people often skip over or surf by the ads or commercials. The only way to get through is to repeat the ad over and over again. In that manner, the largest advertisers—McDonald's, Microsoft, Coca-Cola, and so on—blast their way into public consciousness.

Publicity, on the other hand, offers no such guarantees or controls. Typically, publicity is subject to review by news editors who may decide to use all of a story, some of it, or none of it. Many news releases, in fact, never see the light of print.

When the story will run, who will see it, and how often it will be used are all subject to the whims of a news editor. However, even though attracting publicity is by no means a sure thing, it does offer two overriding benefits that enhance its appeal far beyond that of advertising:

- ■ First, although not free, publicity costs only the time and effort expended by public relations personnel and management in conceiving, creating, and attempting to place the publicity effort in the media. Therefore, relatively speaking, its cost is minimal compared to advertising; the rough rule of thumb is 10% of equivalent advertising expenditures.

- ■ Second and more important, publicity, which appears in news rather than in advertising columns, carries the implicit *third-party* endorsement of the news source that reports it. In other words, publicity is perceived not as the sponsoring organization's self-serving view but as the view of the objective, unbiased, neutral, impartial news source. For years, for example, when surveys asked people to name their most trusted American, respondents invariably answered not the president or first lady but rather Walter Cronkite, the late former news anchor at CBS. NBC's Tom Brokaw and the late Tim Russert became equally trusted over the years. (Today, of course, it's more likely to be fake newsmen Jon Stewart or Stephen Colbert!)

So even in a cynical society, news reporters and news organizations still enjoy credibility. When an organization's publicity is reported by such a source, it instantly becomes more credible, believable, and, therefore, valuable *news.*

That, in essence, is why publicity is more powerful than advertising.

Value of Publicity

For any organization, then, publicity makes great sense in the following areas:

- **Announcing a new product or service.** Because publicity can be regarded as news, it should be used before advertising commences. A new product or service is news only once. Once advertising appears, the product is no longer news. Therefore, one inflexible rule—that most organizations, unfortunately, don't follow—is that publicity should always precede advertising.

- **Reenergizing an old product.** When a product has been around for a while, it's difficult to make people pay attention to advertising. Therefore, publicity techniques—staged events, sponsorships, and so on—may pay off to rejuvenate a mature product (Figure 9-7).

- **Explaining a complicated product.** Often, there isn't enough room in an advertisement to explain a complex product or service. Insurance companies, banks, and mutual funds, which offer products that demand thoughtful explanation, may find advertising space too limiting. Publicity, on the other hand, allows enough room to tell the story.

- **Little or no budget.** To make an impact, advertising requires frequency—the constant repetition of ads so that readers eventually see them and acknowledge the product. In the case of Samuel Adams Lager Beer, for example, the company lacked an advertising budget to promote its unique brew, so it used public relations techniques to spread the word about this different-tasting beer. Over time, primarily through publicity about its victories at beer-tasting competitions, Samuel Adams grew in popularity. It took Sam Adams'

FIGURE 9-7
Papa Spidey.
When Papa John's pizza needed a publicity boost, it teamed with the world's most famous arachnid. *(Courtesy of Odwyerpr.com)*

founder Jim Koch 12 years to be able to afford its first TV commercial.[28] Today, its advertising budget is in the hundreds of millions, but the company's faith in publicity endures.

- **Enhancing the organization's reputation.** Advertising is, at its base, self-serving. When a company gives to charity or does a good deed in the community, taking out an ad is the wrong way to communicate its efforts. It is much better for the recipient organization to commend its benefactor in the daily news columns.

- **Crisis response.** In a crisis, publicity techniques are the fastest and most credible means of response. Indeed, in the 21st century, it has become a cliché for celebrities to "apologize" for transgressions by seeking out a high-profile TV interviewer for instant publicity.

These are just a few of the advantages of publicity over advertising. A smart organization, therefore, will always consider publicity a vital component in its overall marketing plan.

Pitching Publicity

The activity of trying to place positive publicity in a periodical, on a news site, or in the electronic media—of converting publicity to news—is called *pitching*. Traditionally, public relations people "pitched" journalists through mail. Today, as more editors become more conversant in digital and social media, pitch methods are evolving. Specifically, media outlets are looking for more than text—for example, photos and videos. However, even in the second decade of the 21st century, it's important to recognize that 80% of reporters still want pitches through email; only 2% prefer social media.[29]

The following hints may help achieve placement of a written release:

1. **Be time sensitive.** The Internet means every news organization wants your news now. Even with the flexibility of the computer, newspapers have different deadlines for different sections of the paper. News events should be scheduled, whenever possible, to accommodate deadlines.

2. **Generally write first, then call.** Reporters are barraged with deadlines. They are busiest close to deadline time, which is late afternoon for morning newspapers and early afternoon for local television news. Thus, it's preferable to email news releases first, rather than try to explain them over the telephone. Follow-up calls to reporters to "make sure you got our release" also should be avoided. If reporters are unclear on a certain point, they'll call to check.

3. **Direct the release to a specific person or editor.** Newspapers are divided into departments, and bloggers have specialties: business, sports, style, entertainment, and so on. Assignment editors are generally in charge of television news. The release directed to a specific person, editor, or blogger has a greater chance of being read.

4. **Determine how the reporter wants to be contacted.** Call or write, email or tweet? Treat the reporter as the client. How he or she prefers to get the news should guide how you deliver it.

5. **Don't badger.** Journalists are generally fiercely independent about the copy they use. Even a major advertiser will usually fail to get a piece of puffery published. Badgering an editor about a certain story is bad form, as is complaining excessively about the treatment given a certain story.

6. **Use exclusives, but be careful.** News desks receive hundreds of emails daily; most, for better or worse, are considered spam. That's the reality. But reporters get credited for getting "scoops" and citing "trends." So public relations people might promise exclusive stories to particular publications. The exclusive promises one publication or other news source a scoop over its competitors. Although the chances of securing a story are heightened by the promise of an exclusive, the risk of alienating the other papers exists. Thus, the exclusive should be used sparingly.

7. **When you call, do your own calling.** Reporters and editors generally don't have assistants. Most resent being kept waiting by a secretary calling for the boss. Public relations professionals should make their own initial and follow-up calls. Letting a secretary handle a journalist can alienate a good news contact. Above all, be pleasant and courteous.

8. **Don't send clips of other stories about your client.** Rather than interesting a journalist in your story, this will just suggest that others have been there already and make the story potential less attractive.

9. **Develop a relationship.** Relationships are the name of the game. The better you know a reporter, the more understanding and accommodating to your organization he or she will be.

10. **Never lie.** This is *the* cardinal rule.

Although cynics continue to predict "the end of reading as we know it," newspapers and magazines continue to endure. Magazines, particularly special interest magazines, are proliferating. Indeed, despite early reports to the contrary, iPads and tablets aren't at all replacing magazines.[30] In fact, "controlled circulation" magazines that "pick you" now number more than 300 in the United States.[31]

Dealing with the media is among the most essential technical skills of the public relations professional. Anyone who practices public relations must know how to deal with the press. Period.

Online Publicity

With online outlets increasing in numbers and use, it is important to consider how to secure online publicity. While those who predicted that the Internet would change public relations thinking forever are wrong, it's still a "relationship business"—seeking Internet outlets for publicity is an important complement to publicity in more traditional media.

For one thing, journalists are increasingly moving toward social media, at least as a communications mechanism. According to recent studies, 75% of reporters use Facebook as a tool to assist in reporting; 69% use Twitter; 69% use mobile technology to search for stories; and 95% agree that social media has increased in journalistic import.[32]

Therefore, knowledge of social media, Web hosting and Web casting, and blogs and chat rooms and discussion groups and investor "threads" and search engine

Outside the Lines

Confessions of a Media Maven

Dealing with the media for fun and profit, even for an experienced public relations hand, is a constant learning experience. It is also risky business. Consider the real-life case of an up-and-coming, daring, but wet-behind-the-ears public relations trainee.

In the 1980s, many of the nation's largest banks were a bit jittery about negative publicity on their loans to lesser developed countries. One of the most vociferous bank bashers was Patrick J. Buchanan, a syndicated columnist who later became President Reagan's communications director and still later ran for president (Figure 9-8).

After one particularly venomous syndicated attack on the banks, the young and impetuous bank public affairs director wrote directly to Buchanan's editor asking whether he couldn't "muzzle at least for a little while" his wild-eyed columnist. The letter's language, in retrospect, was a tad harsh.

Some weeks later, in a six-column article that ran throughout the nation, Buchanan wrote in part:

> Another sign that the banks are awaking to the reality of the nightmare is a screed that lately arrived at this writer's syndicate from one Fraser P. Seitel, director of public affairs of the Chase Manhattan Bank.
>
> Terming this writer's comments "wrong," "stupid," "inflammatory," and "the nonsensical ravings of a lunatic," Seitel nevertheless suggested that the syndicate "tone down" future writings, "at least 'til the frenetic financial markets get over the current hysteria."*

Buchanan went on to describe the fallacy in bankers' arguments and ended by suggesting that banks begin immediately to cut unnecessary frills—such as "directors of public affairs!"

Moral: Never get into a shouting match with somebody who buys ink by the barrel.

Secondary moral: Just because you write a textbook doesn't mean you know everything!

*Patrick J. Buchanan, "The Banks Must Face Up to Losses on Third World Loans," *New York Post* (July 12, 1984): 35.

FIGURE 9-8   Talk to the hand.
Syndicated columnist, TV commentator, and presidential contender Patrick Buchanan wasn't amused when challenged by one bright-eyed media relations novice. *(Photo: SCOTT NELSON/AFP/Newscom)*

optimization are critical for modern public relations people. At the top of this list of Internet public relations tools is knowledge of online publicity.

- ■ Paid wires, such as PR Newswire, Business Wire (purchased in 2006 by investor Warren Buffet's Berkshire Hathaway), MarketWire, and Internet Wire, disseminate full-text news releases to media, investors, and online databases. These are wires that guarantee use of your material (you pay them!). Newsrooms regularly check the paid wires for information of interest.

- ■ All these paid wires offer services to enhance Web use, including search engine optimization and social media "tags" to encourage online sharing and a *long tail*, that is, a longer life for the release on the Internet.

- ■ Staging events is another way to draw reporters and other publics online. Popular events include movie sneak previews, concerts broadcast online, candidate debates, roundtable forums, Website grand openings, conventions, and trade shows.

- ■ As the Internet has become a more commonplace communications vehicle, the bar for Web events has been raised. A new Website is no longer cause for attention. Nor is an online news conference. So a Web event today, to attract publicity, must be really "big."[33]

Although establishing a relationship with online reporters may not be as easy as with print journalists because of the physical remoteness, the same principle still holds: The closer you are to reporters, the more fairly they will treat you.

Handling Media Interviews

A primary task of public relations people—perhaps the most essential task in the eyes of those for whom public relations people work—is to coordinate interviews for their executives with the media. Most executives are neither familiar with nor comfortable in such interview situations. For one thing, reporters ask a lot of searching questions, some of which may seem impertinent. Executives aren't used to being put on the spot. Instinctively, they may resent it, and thus the counseling of executives for interviews has become an important and strategic task of the in-house practitioner as well as a lucrative profession for media consultants.

The first question before engaging in a media interview is: What purpose will this serve the organization? If the answer is "none," then don't do it! Believe me, it ain't worth it! Before any interview, organizational goals and objectives must be considered, homework on the interviewer and outlet must be done, and statistics and figures and anecdotes to spice into the interview must be compiled.[34]

In conducting interviews with the media, the cardinal rule to remember is that such interviews are not "intellectual conversations." Neither the interviewee nor the interviewer seek a lasting friendship. Rather, the interviewer wants only a good story, and the interviewee wants only to convey his or her key messages. Period.

Accordingly, the following 11 dos and don'ts are important in media interviews:

1. **Prepare.**   An interviewee must be thoroughly briefed—either verbally or in writing—before the interview. Know the interviewer's point of view, interests, and likely questions. Preparation is key.

2. **Know your lines.** In other words, know what you will say *before* you begin the interview. This is the most important thing to remember in any interview.

Again, an interview isn't a conversation. Nor is it the place for original thought. Walk into the interview knowing the three or four points that must make it on the air or in print. Hammer away at those points, so the interviewer uses them.

3. **Relax.** Remember that the interviewer is a person, too, and is just trying to do a good job. Building rapport will help the interview. Even though a media interview isn't a "conversation," it should seem like one (Figure 9-9).

4. **Speak in personal terms.** People distrust large organizations. References to "the company" and "we believe" sound ominous. Use "I" as much as possible. Personalize. Speak as an individual, as a member of the public, rather than as a mouthpiece for an impersonal bureaucracy.

5. **Welcome the naive question.** If the question sounds simple, it should be answered anyway. It may be helpful to those who don't possess much knowledge of the organization or industry.

6. **Answer questions briefly and directly.** Don't ramble. Be brief, concise, and to the point—especially on television. An interviewee shouldn't get into subject areas about which he or she knows nothing. This situation can be dangerous and counterproductive when words are transcribed in print.

7. **Don't bluff.** If a reporter asks a question that you can't answer, admit it. If there are others in the organization more knowledgeable about a particular issue, the interviewee or the practitioner should point that out and get the answer from them. But play it straight. Bluffing will be obvious to the reporter and any readers/listeners/viewers.

FIGURE 9-9
Oshkosh, Wisconsin, you're on the air.
A media interview ought to be perceived as a "friendly chat" between acquaintances, rather than an inquisition.
(Courtesy of Fraser P. Seitel)

LOS ANGELES

NEW YORK

LARRY KING LIVE
CONDIT BREAKING SILENCE

CNN

8. **State facts and back up generalities.** Facts and examples always bolster an interview. An interviewee should come armed with specific data that support general statements. Again, the practitioner should furnish all the specifics.

9. **There is no such thing as "off the record."** A person who doesn't want to see something in print shouldn't say it. It's that simple. Print reporters, in particular, may get confused as to what was "off the record" during the interview. Although most journalists will honor an off-the-record statement, some may not. It's not generally worthwhile to take the risk. Occasionally, reporters will agree not to attribute a statement to the interviewee but to use it as background. Mostly, though, interviewees should be willing to have whatever they say in the interview appear in print.

10. **Don't say, "No comment."** "No comment" sounds evasive and suggests to people you're hiding something or worse. If you can't answer a question for confidential or proprietary reasons, explain why. "No comment" too often sounds "guilty."

11. **Tell the truth.** It sounds like a broken record, but telling the truth is the key criterion. Journalists are generally perceptive; they can detect a fraud. So don't be evasive, don't cover up, and, most of all, don't lie. Be positive but be truthful. Occasionally, an interviewee must decline to answer specific questions but should candidly explain why. This approach always wins in the long run. Remember, in an interview, your integrity is always on the line. Once you lose your credibility, you've lost everything.[35]

Outside the Lines
Two-Minute Media Relations Drill

How well would you do if you were asked to go toe-to-toe with a reporter? Take this yes-or-no quiz and find out. Answers follow:

Questions

1. When addressing a print reporter or electronic medium moderator, should you use his or her first name?
2. Should you ever challenge a reporter in a verbal duel?
3. Are reporters correct in thinking that they can ask embarrassing questions of anyone in public office?
4. Should you answer a hypothetical question?
5. Should you ever say "No comment"?
6. When a reporter calls on the telephone, should you assume that the conversation is being taped?
7. Do audiences remember most of the content of a television interview 30 minutes after it is broadcast?
8. Should you ever admit you had professional training to handle the media?
9. If you don't know the correct answer to a reporter's question, should you try to answer it anyway?

Bonus Question

What did Henry Kissinger say at the start of his press briefings as secretary of state?

Answers

1. **Yes.** In most cases, using first names is the best strategy. It makes the discussion much more conversational and less formal than using Mr. or Ms.
2. "Never say never," but the answer most often is **No.** You can and should challenge a faulty premise. But most people should try to gain goodwill in an interview. This is rarely achieved by getting into an acrimonious debate.
3. **Yes.** Journalists are suspicious of any claim by a public person that he or she is telling not only the truth but also the whole truth. Anyone in public office must be prepared to respond to such questions.
4. **No.** Avoid hypothetical questions. Rarely can you win by dealing with them.
5. **No.** It is tantamount to taking the Fifth Amendment against self-incrimination. You appear to be hiding something.

6. **Yes.** Many state laws no longer require the "beep" that signals a taped call. Always assume that everything you say is being recorded and will be used.
7. **No.** Studies have found that audiences remember less and less as time wears on. Indeed, on television (even though self-absorbed TV hosts would never admit it) it's often more important to "look good."
8. **Yes.** By all means. You should point out that good communication with the public is a hallmark of your organization and that you're proud it has such a high priority.
9. **No.** Don't be afraid to say, "I don't know." Offer to find the answer and get back to the interviewer. Don't dig yourself into a hole you can't get out of.

Bonus answer: "Does anyone have any questions . . . for my answers?"

Last Word

When journalists were asked at the beginning of the 21st century how much respect they had for public relations people, less than half answered in the affirmative. That's the bad news. The better news is that the scores accorded public relations professionals ranked higher in the eyes of these scribes than did the scores of lawyers, salespeople, celebrities, or politicians.[36] So there's always hope. On the other hand, it must be acknowledged that a good portion of journalists still seem to regard public relations people with suspicion and maybe even (though they won't admit it) envy.

As is true of any other specialty, in public relations work the key to productive media relations is professionalism. Because management relies principally on public relations professionals for expertise in handling the media effectively, practitioners must not only know their own organization and management but also be conversant in and respectful of the role and practice of journalists. That means knowing their deadlines, understanding their pressures, and returning their calls.

Indeed, public relations professionals must understand what a reporter goes through each day—intractable deadlines, spotty information, frequently uncooperative sources, and increasingly in a world marked by terrorism, mortal danger.

All that has been discussed in this chapter must be practiced: transmitting only newsworthy information to journalists; knowing how to reach reporters most expeditiously; understanding that journalists have become more pressured, by the Internet and cable, to produce material that is "immediate" and "entertaining" and therefore potentially controversial; and recognizing that a reporter has a job to do and should be treated with respect.

At the same time, all public relations practitioners should understand that their role in the newsgathering process has become more respected by journalists. As a former business/finance editor of *The New York Times* once said:

> *PR has gotten more professional. PR people can be a critical element for us. It makes a difference how efficiently they handle things, how complete the information is that they have at hand. We value that and understand all the work that goes into it.*[37]

Indeed, the best public relations–journalist relationship today—the only successful one over the long term—must still be based on mutual understanding, trust, and respect.

Discussion Starters

1. What is meant by the "devil's advocate" role of the media?
2. What is the current state of the newspaper industry?
3. What is the importance of objectivity to a reporter?
4. What are some of the key principles in dealing with the press?
5. What is the difference between advertising and publicity?
6. What is the value of publicity?
7. What are some of the keys in pitching publicity?
8. What are the several dos and don'ts of interviews?
9. What are several methods of online publicity?
10. What's the most important thing to remember in any interview?

Pick of the Literature

When the Headline Is You

Jeff Ansell with Jeffrey Leeson, San Francisco, CA: Jossey-Bass, 2010

This book, compiled by two experienced journalists for the International Association of Business Communicators, presents a different take on handling the media.

Brutally honest—for example, "The reporter's quest is for conflict, not solutions"—this book is rich in anecdotes and hypothetical cases, where the authors offer solutions. Of particular interest to public relations professionals, the book opens the kimono on news gathering and how "news" is selected. (Hint: It's often not particularly done with any empirical or merit basis in mind!)

Most public relations dilemmas are touched on here—what constitutes news, what to do in times of bad news, how to construct compelling messages. The authors also dispel pervasive myths such as "good news is no news." The most compelling part of the book, though, is the unique "take" of these two former reporters. Well worth reading.

Case Study They're Heeere!

Suppose you gave a party and *60 Minutes* showed up at the door. Would you let them in? Would you evict them? Would you commit hara-kiri?

Those were the choices that confronted the Chase Bank at the American Bankers Association convention, when *60 Minutes* came to Honolulu to "get the bankers."

The banking industry was taking its lumps. Profits were lagging. Loans to foreign governments weren't being repaid. Financings to bankrupt corporations were being questioned. And it was getting difficult for poor people to open bank accounts.

Understandably, few bankers at the Honolulu convention cared to share their thoughts on camera with *60 Minutes*. Some headed for cover when the cameras approached. Others barred the unwanted visitors from their receptions. In at least one case, a *60 Minutes* cameraman was physically removed from the hall. By the convention's third day, the *60 Minutes* team was decrying its treatment at the hands of the bankers as the "most vicious" it had ever been accorded.

By the third night, correspondent Morley Safer (Figure 9-10) and his *60 Minutes* crew were steaming and itching for a confrontation.

That's when *60 Minutes* showed up at our party.

For 10 years, with your intrepid author as its public affairs director, Chase had sponsored a private convention reception for the media. It combined an informal cocktail party, where journalists and bankers could chat and munch hors d'oeuvres, with a more formal, 30-minute press conference with the bank's president. The press conference was on the record, no-holds-barred, and frequently generated news coverage by the wire services, newspapers, and magazines that regularly sent representatives. No television cameras were permitted.

But when we arrived at Honolulu's scenic Pacific Club, there to greet us—unannounced and uninvited—were Morley and the men from *60 Minutes*, ready to do battle.

The ball was in our court. We faced five questions that demanded immediate answers.

FIGURE 9-10
Striking fear.
For half a century, this lovable band of journalistic warriors, and their successors, have terrorized even the most steely-eyed CEO or tyrannical dictator. *(Photo: BOB STRONG/AFP/Getty Images/Newscom)*

■ **First, should we let them in?** What they wanted, said Safer, was to interview our president about "critical banking issues." He said they had been "hassled" all week and were "entitled" to attend our media reception. But we hadn't invited them. And they hadn't had the courtesy to let us know they were coming. It was true that they were members of the working press. It was also true that our reception was intended to generate news. So we had a dilemma.

■ **Second, should we let them film the press conference?** Chase's annual convention press conference had never before been filmed. Television cameras are bulky, noisy, and intrusive. They threatened to sabotage the normally convivial atmosphere of our party. Equally disconcerting would be the glaring camera lights that would have to be set up. The *60 Minutes* crew countered that their coverage was worthless without film. Theirs, after all, was a medium of pictures, and without pictures, there could be no story. As appetizing as this proposition sounded to us, we were worried that if we refused their cameras, what they might film instead would be us blocking the door at an otherwise open news conference. So we had another problem.

■ **Third, should we let them film the cocktail party?** Like labor leader Samuel Gompers, television people are interested in only one thing: "More!" In the case of our reception, we weren't eager to have CBS film the cocktails and hors d'oeuvres part of our party. We were certain the journalists on hand would agree with us. After all, who wants to see themselves getting sloshed on national television when they're supposed to be working?

■ **Fourth, should we let them film a separate interview with our president?** Because few top people at the convention were willing to speak to CBS, *60 Minutes* was eager to question our president in as extensive and uninterrupted a format as possible. Safer wanted a separate interview before the formal press conference started. So we also had to deal with the question of whether to expose our president to a lengthy, one-on-one, side-room interview with the most powerful—and potentially negative—television news program in the land.

■ **Fifth, should we change our format?** The annual media reception/press conference had always been an informal affair. Our executives joked with the journalists, shared self-deprecating asides, and generally relaxed. Thus, in light of the possible presence of *60 Minutes*, we wondered if we should alter this laid-back approach and adopt a more on-guard stance.

We had 10 minutes to make our decisions. We also had splitting headaches.

Questions

1. Would you let *60 Minutes* in?
2. Would you let them film the press conference?
3. Would you let them film the cocktail party?
4. Would you let them film a separate interview with the president?
5. Would you change the format of the party?
6. How does the American Bankers Association (ABA) deal with the media today? Visit its online press room (www.aba.com /press+room/default.html). What resources can members of the press access on this site? How does ABA make it easy for reporters to make contact?

From the Top

An Interview with Al Neuharth

Al Neuharth was born a poor country boy in South Dakota in 1924. He became a self-made multimillionaire who built the nation's largest newspaper company, Gannett Co. Inc., and started the nation's most widely read newspaper, *USA Today*. Since his "retirement" from Gannett in 1989 at age 65, he has been an active author, speaker, columnist, and world traveler. He "retired a second time" on June 1, 1997, as chairperson of one of the nation's largest private charitable foundations, The Freedom Forum, which he founded in 1991 as the successor to the Gannett Foundation, established in 1935 by Frank E. Gannett. This interview was conducted in September 2007, on the occasion of *USA Today's* 25th anniversary.

How did you know *USA Today* would work?
We didn't. It was a gamble. But we did an awful lot of research. We hired the pollster Lou Harris, who extensively analyzed whether a national newspaper could make it. One of Lou's conclusions was that "The TV generation won't fight its way through dull, gray newspapers." So we shortened stories, added color, and made an exciting product.

What do you read each day?
I read *The New York Times* and *The Wall Street Journal* every day. I travel a great deal. One of the benefits I received in retiring from Gannett is that the company agreed to provide me with the *Times, Journal, USA Today,* and a local newspaper, wherever I am.

So you don't agree with Ted Turner that newspapers are dying?

No way. Critics who predict the death of newspapers are nuts. Circulation falloffs are not nearly as excessive as critics suggest. People said newspapers were dying when television first appeared. Whenever a new medium enters the picture, critics predict the demise of newspapers. The challenge for publishers is to blend newspapers with the most popular features of the Net.

By the way, I asked Ted once if he really believed what he said, and he told me, "You know me. I mix a lot of bull@#@$@ in to get people's attention!"

Do you think newspapers can compete with the Internet?

I have great confidence that executives at *USA Today*, the *Journal*, and the *Times* will find the key to successfully marrying the Internet and print. We did it at *USA Today* with the challenge of television. Look at the *Times*, under Arthur Sulzberger, its publisher, who is doing a great job. He took a risk by adding color and other things. People criticized him for changing the look of the "great gray lady." Arthur told me, "I know it's risky. But it's more risky if we didn't do it." That's the kind of attitude that will return people—even young people—to print.

What has been the role of cable television on journalism?

Cable news is largely opinion. But the good thing is that what cable forced editors and reporters to do was focus on what the public was following. If the public wants O. J. and Britney Spears, then newspaper editors can't ignore that.

But are O. J. and Britney really "news"?

According to whom? I have always felt that newspapers and the media in general must keep in mind what readers want. If the public is interested in a topic, you can't ignore it. Once upon a time, newspapers editors and reporters were convinced that they knew more than their readers. Big mistake. We've learned over the past 25 years to factor in reader judgments.

How do you feel about reporters appearing on TV and giving their opinions?

It's absolutely appropriate. For too long, publishers forbade their editors from appearing on television, because it would "compromise the integrity" of the publication. Nonsense. What it does is increase the audience for the paper.

How does this impact the "quality" of journalism?

Who defines "quality"? Readers ought to have a voice in what we're giving them. An editor's job is to diversify and debate but not to dictate. When I was CEO of Gannett, we changed the makeup of the board of directors, because we realized that a bunch of middle-aged white males couldn't possibly make appropriate decisions for a diversified audience.

How do you feel about public relations?

The job of a public relations person is to pedal propaganda. The good ones don't lie. They make it clear when they are providing facts and when they are providing something else. Our job in the media business is to make damn sure PR people aren't lying.

What's the future of the news business?

The future is bright. In the U.S., there's a great appetite for "hard news," particularly at night. That's why the "evening news" has survived. In the morning, the desire is more for "entertainment." Outside the U.S., there are few news vacuums left in the world thanks to the Net and the satellite. In places like China, Africa, India, and the like, people want more news. I see this everywhere I travel, and I travel a lot. Well, we're in the news business. So I'm optimistic.

Public Relations Library

Bland, Michael, Alison Theaker, and David Wragg. *Effective Media Relations: How to Get Results*, 3rd ed. London, UK: Kogan Page Limited, 2005. A perspective on dealing with the media from the other side of the pond.

Carney, William Wray. *In the News: The Process of Media Relations in Canada*. Alberta, Ontario: University of Alberta Press, 2008. The view of the media north of the border.

D'Vari, Marisa. *Building Buzz: How to Reach and Impress Your Target Audience*. Franklin Lakes, NJ: Career Press, 2006. A primer, from soup to nuts, on securing publicity, including news release and interview tips, media training, and branding advice.

Gianconitieri, Donna. *The Complete Guide to Getting Better Press Coverage*. Bloomington, IN: iUniverse, 2008. Former news reporter's take on dealing with the media.

Hayes, Richard, and Daniel Grossman. *A Scientist's Guide to Talking with the Media*. Cambridge, MA: Union of Concerned Scientists, 2006. Worthwhile perspective for those who must deal with technical language and experts.

Henderson, David. *Media Relations: From a Journalist's Perspective*. Lincoln, NE: iUniverse, 2005. David Henderson was an award-winning network news correspondent for CBS News, so he knows whereof he speaks. And just to make sure, Henderson interviewed 60 other journalists for insight on how public relations people can better work with the media.

Henderson, David. *Making News: A Straight Shooting Guide to Media Relations*. Lincoln, NE: iUniverse, 2006. Mr. Henderson's second work is aimed at gaining credibility and achieving media coverage.

Holstein, William. *Manage the Media: Don't Let the Media Manage You*. Cambridge, MA: Harvard University Press, 2008. Among other things, the author says that CEOs should hire a communications "consigliore" to advise them on offensive media relations. The worst thing, he cautions, is falling into the "airline syndrome," responding to media only when the organization is faced with a plane crash or similar catastrophic occurrence.

Howard, Carole M., and Wilma K. Mathews. *On Deadline: Managing Media Relations*, 4th ed. Long Grove, IL: Waveland Press, 2006. Outstanding dos and don'ts from two outstanding public relations professionals.

Johnston, Jane. *Media Relations*. Crow's Nest, Australia: Allen & Unwin, 2007. A primer from Down Under, not altogether different from dealing with the media in the United States.

Lewis, Benjamin, *Perfecting the Pitch: Creating Publicity through Media Rapport*. No. Potomac, MD: Larstan Publishing, 2008. A solid primer on how even a sole practitioner can solicit coverage by the media.

Macfarquhar, Neil. *The Media Relations Department of Hisbollah Wishes You a Happy Birthday*. New York: Public Affairs, 2009. Reporter's memoir of how times have changed in the Middle East, where many today are publicity-conscious first.

O'Dwyer, Jack (Ed.). *O'Dwyer's Directory of PR Firms*. New York: J. R. O'Dwyer, annually. This directory lists thousands of public relations firms. In addition to providing information on executives, accounts, types of agencies, and branch office locations, the guide provides a geographical index to firms and cross-indexes more than 8,000 clients.

Persinos, John. *Confessions of an Ink-Stained Wretch*. No. Potomac, MD: Larstan Publishing, 2006. This former journalist/editor/press secretary explains how marketing can mesh with media to attract publicity.

Trump, Donald, and Robert Slater. *No Such Thing as Over-Exposure*. Upper Saddle River, NJ: Pearson Prentice Hall, 2005. And there isn't, particularly if you're a self-inflated megalomaniac who can afford to hire a competent business writer willing to sacrifice his pride to extol the virtues of a somewhat questionable man of wealth and privilege. (Not that there's anyting wrong with that.)

Walker, T. J. *Media Training: A to Z*. New York: Media Training Worldwide, 2008. Media trainer Walker knows his stuff. Good advice.

Chapter 10

Social Media

Chapter Objectives

1. To discuss the phenomenon of social media and its lasting impact on the practice of public relations.
2. To explore the general parameters of public relations and the Internet.
3. To discuss the four primary social media vehicles of Facebook, Twitter, LinkedIn, and YouTube and how public relations professionals use them.
4. To examine the pros and cons of dealing with bloggers and the new journalists who populate the Internet.

FIGURE 10-1 Tough Tosh.
Raunchy comedian Daniel Tosh had reason to grimace in 2012, when an attempted joke about rape landed him in social media hot water. *(Photo: MZ1 WENN Photos/Newscom)*

In the 21st century, the face of public relations is changing, largely due to the phenomenon of social media. And that ain't always such a good thing. Just ask comedian Daniel Tosh (Figure 10-1).

By 2012, thanks to the Internet, the edgy Tosh had become a sensation. Fueled by social media, the comedian had landed his own Comedy Central *Tosh.0* show and was in demand around the country. Until the rape joke.

In July, Tosh directed a "gang rape joke" at a particular woman audience member in Los Angeles, and she stormed out of the show. An account of the Tosh "joke" and the woman's exit wound up on the Tumblr Cookies for Breakfast blog. It was then reblogged, tweeted and retweeted, until the Tosh commentary became fodder for larger Websites, from Salon to Huffington Post to Jezebel, the Gawker media female-centric blog that lambasted the comedian for thinking that rape could possibly be funny.[1]

Finally, the shaken comedian responded via Twitter that, "All the out of context misquotes aside, I'd like to sincerely apologize." Tosh's apology, wrote the Atlantic Wire, was "almost as weak as the joke itself."[2]

In the space of one short week, the same social media that had propelled Daniel Tosh to stardom had risen up and, well, bitten the raunchy comic square in the Tosh!

By the second decade of the 21st century, social media's dominance as a communication medium—for good and evil—couldn't be disputed.

- After his election in 2009, President Barack Obama created the first official White House blog, the creation of Macon Phillips, the nation's first White House Director of New Media.[3]

- That same year, when a downed plane attempted an emergency landing in New York City's Hudson River, the first reports of the floating airliner came from a nearby ferry passenger, who posted this message on Twitter: "There's a plane in the Hudson. I'm on the ferry going to pick up the people. Crazy." Within 30 minutes, the word had spread far and wide, and the original "tweeter" was interviewed live on MSNBC and CNN and would subsequently become a media star.

- Late on the night of May 2, 2011, the White House informed the nation, via Twitter, of a major presidential announcement. Within minutes, a former Defense Department official tweeted that he had been "told by a reputable person they have killed Osama Bin Laden." President Obama later confirmed the news for the nation.[4]

- A year later, the nation marveled as the social media giant, Facebook, went public and was valued at $104 billion after one hectic trading day. By the time the dust had settled, Facebook's hoodie-wearing, 28-year-old founder, Mark Zuckerberg, was worth a cool $19 billion.[5]

Such was the power of social media as a persuasive vehicle in the 21st century.

As companies tighten their spending in the face of worldwide financial challenges, inexpensive social media is clearly the new marketing and public relations frontier. As with any other phenomenon, social media offers enormous opportunities and also large pitfalls to be avoided.

While it is irrefutable that the Internet and social media have changed communication forever with newfound immediacy and pervasiveness, it isn't the case that the Internet has replaced human relationships as the essence of societal communications. Nor have the new techniques replaced human relationships as the essence of the practice of public relations.

The Internet and social media comprise important tools in the public relations arsenal. But it is important to remember, they are but "tools" nonetheless. In this chapter, we will explore how public relations professionals might harness these new technologies to more effectively communicate their messages.

Brief History of the Internet

What is the Internet? We all use it, but few of us know from whence it derived.

The Internet, technically, is a cooperatively run, globally distributed collection of computer networks that exchange information via a common set of rules. The Internet began, as President Obama noted during his 2012 campaign, as the ARPANET during the Cold War in 1969, developed by the Department of Defense and consultants who were interested in creating a communications network that could survive a nuclear attack.[6] It survived—even though there was, thankfully, no nuclear attack!—as a convenient way to communicate.

The World Wide Web, the most exciting and revolutionary part of the Internet, was developed in 1989 by physicist Tim Berners-Lee to enlarge the Internet for multiple uses. The Web is a collection of millions of computers on the Internet that contain information in a single format: HTML, or Hypertext Markup Language. By combining multimedia—sound, graphics, video, animation, and more—the Web has become the most powerful tool in cyberspace.

Without question, the Internet and the World Wide Web have transformed the way we work, the way we buy things, the way we entertain ourselves, the way business is conducted, and, most important to public relations professionals, the way we communicate with each other. The Internet phenomenon, pure and simple, has been a revolution.

By 2012, the number of worldwide Internet users had doubled in five years to 2.27 billion, with Asia dominating growth. Indeed, the growth numbers from 2007 to 2012 were staggering:

- **Africa** rose from **34 million to 140 million**, a 317% increase.
- **Asia** rose from **418 million to over 1 billion**, a 143% increase.
- **Europe** rose from **322 million to 501 million**, a 56% increase.
- **The Middle East** rose from **20 million to 77 million**, a 294% increase.
- **North America** rose from **233 million to 273 million**, a 17% increase.
- **Latin America** (South America and Central America) rose from **110 million to 236 million**, a 114% increase.
- **Oceania** (including Australia) rose from **19 million to 24 million**, a 27% increase.[7]

Perhaps even more important, the so-called digital divide between haves and have-nots was closing rapidly. In the United States, while the sharpest growth in Internet access and use was among young people, blacks and other minority members were rapidly merging onto the digital information highway. One survey of people 18 and older indicated that 74% of whites go online, 61% of African Americans do, and 80% of English-speaking Hispanic Americans do as well.[8]

In terms of commerce, the first incarnation of the Internet in the 1990s carried great—and as it turned out, unattainable—promise, with the rise and fall of such phenomena as sock puppets, push technology, and B2B (business-to-business). Most of these "great high-tech concepts" crashed and burned along with the stock market in the initial years of the 21st century.

Today, not only the giant survivors of those early days—Apple, eBay, and Amazon, among them—but also many other Internet-oriented ventures have gotten their second wind and are thriving.[9]

The new Internet explosion has taken new forms: tablets, mobile apps, blogs, podcasts, wikis, RSS feeds, and social networks from Facebook to YouTube, from LinkedIn to Pinterest. Meanwhile, Internet pioneers such as MySpace and Yahoo! have suffered in the face of fierce competition.

The pace of Internet change is so rapid and the addition of new communications vehicles so voluminous, in fact, that this summary of Web-based communications tools and tactics may be obsolete by the time you finish reading! Nonetheless, press on.

Public Relations and the Internet

The Internet has transformed the way that people communicate and make contact with each other. And the practice of public relations has responded accordingly.

Public relations departments now have interactive specialists and groups responsible for communicating via social media and the Internet. Likewise, public relations agencies boast online departments that help clients access the Internet. Although the expansive number of Internet-oriented agencies that flourished in the late 1990s has declined, a good number of firms still specialize in Internet-related communications.

Journalists, meanwhile—still the primary customers for most in public relations—have also embraced the Internet as their primary source for research and reporting. Most reporters today are online and prefer email as their primary source of public relations correspondence.[10] Nonetheless, personal contact with a journalist (i.e., building a relationship) is still the best way to ensure that your message will be heard.

Use of the Internet by public relations practitioners inevitably will grow as the century proceeds, for four reasons in particular.

- **The demand to be educated rather than sold.** Today's consumers are smarter, better educated, and more media savvy. They know when they are being hustled by self-promoters and con artists. Communications programs therefore must be grounded in education-based information rather than blatant self-promotion. The Internet is perhaps the world's greatest potential repository of such information.

- **The quest for conversation.** The Internet has enabled anyone to become a publisher, broadcasting views and opinions far and wide. In so doing, the Internet has empowered users by leveling the playing field between them and the organizations trying to reach them. The net result is that Internet dialogue is just that—a conversation—between supplier and consumer. And the more conversational and communications-savvy the organization, the more likely it will be to persuade prospects to buy its products, support its issues, and believe its ideas.

- **The need for real-time performance.** The wired world is moving quickly. Everything happens instantaneously and in real time. When insurgents in Syria blow up government leaders, the bombing is beamed immediately on the Internet around the world. Public relations professionals can use this ability to their advantage to structure their information to respond instantly to emerging issues and market changes.

- **The need for customization.** There used to be three primary television networks. Today there are hundreds of television channels. Today's consumers expect more focused, targeted, one-on-one communications relationships. Increasingly, organizations must broadcast their thoughts to ever-narrower population segments. The Internet offers such narrowcasting to reporters, shareholders, analysts, opinion leaders, consumers, and myriad other publics.

For individual public relations practitioners, then, familiarity with the Internet, mastery of it, and knowledge of its effective use have become frontline requisites of the practice. Consequently, it is important that practitioners are familiar with the primary areas of cyberspace communications.

Websites

Today, virtually all organizations, from the largest corporation to the smallest nonprofit, have a Website (Figure 10-2). Perhaps the most familiar, broadly used, and oldest social media tool, Websites provide organizations, individuals, and governmental agencies the ability to offer information to the public in an organized, consolidated manner.

Most of the time today, it is the Website that serves as an organization's "first face" to the public. Websites serve multiple functions, are commonly interactive, and afford viewers the ability to browse for information and in many cases conduct business, create profiles, manage their accounts, and a plethora of other convenient options. Websites permit an organization to speak in *its own voice*—unfettered and unadulterated by the media or other intermediaries.

Website development is very much the province of public relations professionals. Public relations professionals need to be cognizant of the methods in which audiences prefer to receive information on Websites. They need to make Websites as navigable as possible, providing the necessary tools to facilitate ease of delivery of content. "Static," non–user friendly Websites are more of a detriment than a tool. Websites also must be "media friendly"; journalists should be able to navigate the Website with ease. This means having a clearly identifiable "Media" icon and organized subsections, including a page for news and video clips, reports, and publications.

A Website gives an individual or institution the flexibility and freedom of getting news out without having it filtered by an intermediary. There are literally millions of Websites, all of them open for visitors.

Developing a Winning Website

In many ways, the organization's Website is its most important interface with the public. Today, journalists and others turn to the Website first for an introduction to the organization.

The aim of any Website is to provide information that visitors are looking for. The more you achieve that objective, the more "sticky" your site becomes. Stickiness is often measured by the amount of time visitors spend at a site and how many pages they

FIGURE 10-2
First face.
More often than not in these days of Internet dominance, a Website is the initial introduction to an organization. *(Courtesy of King Pelican Coffee)*

view. For example, if visitors spend 10 minutes at the Website and view five or more pages, you've achieved stickiness.[11]

How should you create a winning Website? By first asking and answering several strategic questions.

1. **What is our goal?** To extend the business? Sell more products? Make more money? Win support for our position? Turn around public opinion? Introduce our company? Without the answers to these fundamental questions, the what and how of a Website are inconsequential.

2. **What content will we include?** The reason some Websites are tedious and boring—and they are!—is because little forethought has gone into determining the content of a site. Simply cramming chronological news releases onto a Website won't advance an organization's standing with its publics.

3. **How often will we edit?** Often the answer to this question is "Not often enough." Stale news and the lack of updating are common Website problems. Sites must regularly be updated.

4. **How will we enhance design?** Like it or not, the style of the site is most important. If an organization's homepage isn't attractive, it won't get many hits. Good design makes complicated things understandable, and this is essential in a Website.

5. **How interactive will it be?** Traditional communication is unidirectional, one way. You read or view it, and that's where the process stops. The great attraction of the Web, on the other hand, is that it can be bidirectional.

6. **How will we track use?** As in any other communications project, the use of a Website must be measured. The most basic form of cyberspace measurement is the rough yardstick of hits to the site. But like measuring press clippings, this doesn't tell you whether your information is being appreciated, acted on, or even read. Measuring site performance, therefore, should be a multifaceted exercise that includes such analysis as volume during specific times of day, kind of access, specific locations on the site to which visitors are clicking first, and the sequencing through the site that visitors are following.

7. **Who will be responsible?** Managing a Website, if it is done correctly, must be someone's full-time job. Companies may subordinate the responsibility to someone; it is much better to treat the Website as a first line of communication to the public, which requires full-time attention.

Website developers are most concerned about SEO—search engine optimization—the tweaking of keywords, copy, and design so that a site comes up toward the top of Internet search results, primarily on Google. SEO has become an art form in itself, with Internet-oriented agencies promoting themselves as SEO specialists. The key is to identify, promote, and repeat searchable keywords and phrases that will propel a site up the search list.

Email

Research suggests that more than 90% of adult Internet users surveyed said they "regularly use email." But if you question how fast the Internet is moving, consider that in a survey of 935 teenagers, only 14% reported sending emails to their friends each day, making it the *least* popular form of social communication among teenagers. Much more highly rated were text messaging (36%), instant messaging (29%), and social network site messaging (23%).[12]

Despite teenager reluctance to stick with email, the total number of email accounts is expected to increase from 3.3 billion accounts in 2012 to more than 4.3 billion accounts by year-end 2016. Nearly half of worldwide email users are in the Asia Pacific region, with China and India pacing the growth.[13]

Email has become a pervasive internal communications vehicle. In companies, schools, media institutions, and homes, email, delivered online and immediately, has replaced traditional print and fax technology as a rapid-delivery information vehicle. Corporate email accounts, in particular, are expected to grow 13% over the next four years. Indeed, most of the world's daily email traffic emanates in the corporate world, averaging 89 billion daily emails sent and received.[14]

Although many managers are reluctant to confront employees face to face, email tends to produce more honest and immediate feedback than traditionally had been the case. Because email is quick and almost effortless, a manager can deliver praise or concern without leaving the office. Thus, email has, by and large, improved organizational communications. That is not to say that face-to-face communication isn't always best. It is. But the ease and effectiveness of email make it a viable alternative.

Email Newsletters

Email has also supplanted the traditional employee print newsletter (Figure 10-3).

Online newsletters are both more immediate and more interactive than print counterparts. Employees can "feed back" to what they've read or heard instantaneously. The organization, in turn, can apprise itself quickly of relevant employee attitudes and opinions. Such online vehicles also lend an element of timeliness that print magazines and newspapers often have a hard time offering.

Email newsletters for external use—to customers, investors, or the media—are equally popular and valuable. These differ from their print brethren in several important areas:

1. **No more than one page.**   People won't read lengthy newsletters on the computer, so writers must write short newsletters.

2. **Job relevant information.**   Employees want to know what's going on at the organization and how they fit in. So email newsletters must be strong on relevant content, short on fluff.

3. **Link content.**   Copy should be peppered with links to other material, such as teasers to full-length articles and product offers.

4. **Regular dissemination.**   It is also important to send email newsletters at regular intervals so that recipients expect them.

Instant Messaging

Instant messaging—or "IM"—is an online, nonlinear, real-time form of communication that allows two or more users to exchange information quickly via text and to send small pictures any place in the world.

IM is more closely related to conversation. Today's technology allows IM users to send text or photos to email accounts in case other users are online but busy or away from their PCs or offline. Additionally, users are able to save online conversations that can be stored or sent by email. IM is especially popular among Generation Next, which includes Americans between the ages of 18 and 25, not to mention Generation Next Next, even younger than them.

Straight Talk NCH

Healthcare System

A weekly update from management on the issues that matter most

February 12, 2009

Dear Friends and Colleagues:

There's a reason we have *two* ears and only *one* mouth – because communication is mostly *listening*!
So this week, let's "listen" to two of the many responses to last week's *Straight Talk* on **communications.**

Joe DeBellis, Director of Transportation, and a mentor to many, wrote:

> The news media communicate as much doom and gloom as possible. I find myself turning off the TV with disgust. I suggest, we "the team at NCH" spread the "good news," such as how many new employees we recently hired; how we have not cut anyone's hours and in some instances, due to need, some are getting more hours than they have in past years. Our medical benefits have been improved over the last couple of years, while some companies are doing away with them completely. We got a modest pay increase while some companies are asking employees to take pay cuts or work a shorter week. I think you get my drift. We need to remind everyone that we are in an industry that has its share of problems for sure, but we are way better off than most. That's my story and I'm sticking to it!

Bev Adams, an ever-enthusiastic and long-time NCH colleague, shared this:

> After reading your newsletter, I decided to take you up on communicating about our new and wonderful team of patient reps. We started this "Revenue Cycle" department last year. We had to apply for the position of Patient Representative and were all pretty scared of what was going to be expected.
> However, our supervisor, Sandy Nelson, kept us all upbeat and made us feel like we would become great collectors. (I personally thought she was crazy!) But she <u>has</u> made us into collectors.
> In October, when we just were getting our feet wet, we did about $40,000-$45,000 worth of collections. November was about $50,000-$55,000. Then everything seemed to start clicking. At the end of December, we collected $262,075. We were just so proud of that and our higher-ups were too. We just received our January collection total and it was $264,940 -- all from 10 reps (including Sandy). Anyways, I just wanted to let you know that this amount of money is above-and- beyond anything that is collected from the Business Office. And I thought you should know who we are: Downtown Naples – **Deborah Swilley, Linda Albanese, Dorothy Bailey, Jamie Miller, Lucille Bubnis, Bev Adams;** North Naples – **Pamela Hunt, Rosemarie Reilly, Jessica Burnside;** Supervisor **Sandy Nelson.**
>
> You're right Dr. Weiss, communication is important!

Amen, Bev. And thank you to everyone who took the time to write. Open communication helps reinforce the feelings of confidence and success we should all have as we work together to serve the community with quality care. So keep those emails coming. And we'll keep *listening*!

Respectfully,

Allen S. Weiss, M.D., President and CEO
P.S.: Feel free to share *Straight Talk* and ask anyone to email me at allen.weiss@nchmd.org to be added.

Texting

Another related messaging vehicle is text messaging or texting, the common term for sending short—160 characters or fewer—messages from cell phones, using the Short Message Service (SMS).

The most common application of the service is person-to-person messaging, but text messages are also often used to interact with automated systems, such as ordering products and services for mobile phones. There are some services available on the Internet that allow users to send text messages free of direct charge to the sender.

Text messaging started slowly but today is the most widely used mobile data service, with 35% of all cell phone users now texting.

In 2007, when a shooter killed 33 people on the Virginia Tech campus, the university was criticized for not notifying students more quickly. But later that year, when an ice storm swept over the University of Texas at Austin, administrators sent an urgent "alert" to its 67,000 students, faculty, and staff to "stay home tomorrow." Thanks to a state-of-the-art emergency communications system, students instantaneously received the alert as a text message on their cell phones and via email on their PCs. The next day, the campus was empty.[15] Indeed, texting has become a go-to crisis management mechanism, particularly on college campuses. Typical is Tufts University in Boston, where the campus was alerted by the text message Tufts Emergency Alert System in 2010 to a broken water pipe that affected millions.[16]

The point? Texting works.

Blogs

By the second decade of the 21st century, bloggers had come of age. In 2010, the Associated Press, the world's foremost network of editors and reporters, announced that henceforth, bloggers would be recognized as bona fide news sources.[17] The AP, like so many others in the news business, recognized that bloggers, who span the gamut from political to social, from entertainment to sports, deserve recognition.

A blog, technically, is an online diary, a personal chronological log of thoughts published on a Webpage, sometimes referred to as Web blog.

Once used only by fringe media, blogs have now been embraced by professional communicators as well as mainstream print and broadcast media. Blogs are used to encourage as well as enhance dialogue among publics on subjects from politics to current events, from ethical issues to hobbies and sports. Blog sharing allows individuals to locate, share, and subscribe to blogs of interest.[18]

The blogosphere is immense. With more than 156 million blogs in operation by the end of 2011, Technorati, the search engine that searches blogs, catalogued 1.5 million blog postings per day—or 17 posts per second. According to Technorati:

- The backbone of the blogosphere—60% of bloggers—are "hobbyists" who say they "blog for fun."
- Corporate blogs make up 8% of the blogosphere. These are primarily individuals paid by companies to share expertise and attract new clients. Most use their number of unique visitors to measure success.
- The leading subject blogging areas are, in order: living (health/religion/arts/food, etc.), entertainment, technology, business, and politics.[19]

Most blogs are primarily textual, although some focus on art (art blogs), photographs (photoblogs), videos (video blogs or "vlogs"), music (MP3 blogs), and audio (podcasts). Micro blogging is another type of blogging, featuring very short posts.

One reason for the proliferation of blogs is that audience preferences are shifting—many can see through a company's traditional "ad speak" and have begun to turn elsewhere for information and opinion. This phenomenon is important for public relations professionals in that it reflects the need for respected, third-party "endorsers" of products and services.

A blog gains respect thorough the support of what are called "sneezers"—or early adopters within a social group. These early adopters embrace a new trend and then spread, that is, "sneeze," the viral word by way of their own blogs.[20] An example is the advent of Gmail, Google's free email product. Instead of making Gmail available to the public, Google offered 1,000 invitation-only accounts to influential users, many of whom were high-profile bloggers in the search engine marketing industry. Google understood that these influential and respected third-party bloggers would "sneeze" Gmail to their audiences. Faster than you could say "Gesundheit," the bloggers blogged, and Gmail was "sneezed" around the globe.

The most popular blogs on the Internet are now "required reading" for journalists. Among them are politico.com, a running rundown of the latest political news and gossip; TMZ.com, a leading post for celebrity news and the latest salacious show-biz gossip; and Huffingtonpost.com, a liberal-leaning news site, purchased by AOL and begun by liberal commentator Arianna Huffington. There are blogs for every taste, including for public relations practitioners (Figure 10-4).

The vast majority of blogs on the Internet attract little following and are hardly worth the attention of public relations practitioners. And just as they do with reporters, public relations people must target bloggers they wish to reach, create relationships with them before pitching them on a particular story, personalize the appeal toward the blog targeted and have something unique to sell.[21]

The real point with blogging, as noted by one veteran blogger, was that rather than focusing on the tool itself, organizations need to zero in on "the principles behind social media that make it work, like participating in a larger community and not controlling the conversation."[22]

CEO Blogs

One phenomenon that has had intermittent success is CEO blogs, in which chief executives share their thoughts on a variety of subjects with their, well, "subjects."

CEO blogs have gotten mixed reviews. On the one hand, CEOs at companies such as Zappos, Marriott International, and Pitney Bowes have received credit for blogging

FIGURE 10-4
Premier public relations blog.
The Flack, at www .theflack.blogspot. com/, the brainchild of public relations impresario Peter Himler, provides a running commentary on all matters of pertinence to the field.
(Courtesy of The Flack)

PR Ethics Mini-Case

Blogger Backlash Crushes ConAgra Conclave

In the fall of 2011, ConAgra Foods had a great idea.

The company, which produces a full line of microwave-able delicacies, would invite food bloggers and mommy bloggers to exclusive New York City restaurant Sotto Terra, run by celebrity chef George Duran. Ostensible purpose of the free dinner, according to the Ketchum public relations invitation, was to sample Mr. Duran's "delicious four-course meal and one-of-a-kind sangria" and learn about food trends from a food industry analyst.

What Ketchum didn't reveal was that the real purpose of the festivities was to serve the guests Three Meat and Four Cheese Lasagna and Razzleberry Pie by Marie Callender's, a ConAgra frozen line. A hidden camera would record guest reactions to the company's products. Mr. Duran agreed to the ruse, because he served as a ConAgra spokesperson, most particularly for the company's Hebrew National hot dogs (Figure 10-5).

When the assembled bloggers found out about the ConAgra switcheroo, they responded in the blogosphere with great force and furious anger. To wit:

- "Our entire meal was a SHAM!" wrote Suzanne Chan, founder of the Mom Confessionals blog. "We were unwitting participants to a bait-and-switch for Marie Callender's."

- "They were serving us a frozen meal, loaded with sodium," thundered Cindy Zhou, founder of the Chubby Chinese Girl blog. "I'm NOT their target con-sumer, and they were totally off by thinking I would buy or promote their highly processed frozen foods after tricking me to taste it."

- "We discussed with the group the sad state of chemical-filled foods," wrote Lou Binder, coauthor of the FoodMayhem.com blog, "yet you still fed me the exact thing I said I did not want to eat."

As negative comments on blogs, Twitter, and Facebook grew, ConAgra canceled future similar events and vowed not to use the hidden-camera footage for promotional purposes.

FIGURE 10-5   Wassup dog?
That's what irate bloggers wanted to know when celebrity chef and ConAgra Hebrew National hot dog spokesperson George Duran hosted a stealth ConAgra product dinner at his West Village restaurant. *(Photo: Dan Barba Stock Connection USA/Newscom)*

Said the director of the Public Relations Society of America's Board of Ethics and Professional Standards, "Ketchum has an excellent reputation for high ethical stan-dards, but the social media realm is new territory for public relations practitioners, and I view this as a valuable learning opportunity."

Ya think?*

Questions

1. Had you been Ketchum, what would you have advised client ConAgra relative to its idea?

2. How would you have structured the invitation to bloggers?

*For further information, see Andrew Adam Newman, "Bloggers Don't Follow the Script, to ConAgra's Chagrin," *The New York Times*, September 6, 2011.

---

consistently in good and bad times. On the other hand, in many cases, "blogs read like tired, warmed-over press releases . . . with companies yakking away about their compa-nies and products, seemingly oblivious to whether their audience is listening or not."[23]

When this happens, what might have been "positive public relations" turns nega-tive in a hurry. To avoid such nonproductive communications, well-intentioned CEO bloggers should heed the advice of perhaps the most well-known and effective CEO blogger, Jonathan Schwartz of Sun, whose "Jonathan's Blog" was widely followed in and outside of the company, prior to Sun's purchase by Oracle in 2009. Said Mr. Schwartz:

> *We all have choices in how we communicate—I use this format because it works for me, allows me to talk to a diversity of constituents (the open source community is vastly larger than the investment community—even numerically, a stock market chat room would be a relatively inefficient forum to engage the market), and a blog is more affordable than the daily global town halls it supplants.*[24]

On the other hand, there are the random incidents when CEOs go rogue and use blogs to try to torpedo the competition. Such was the celebrated case in 2007 when Whole Foods CEO John Mackey anonymously initiated a blogging campaign impugning the financial condition of competitor Wild Oats. Eventually, Whole Foods bought Wild Oats. The Securities and Exchange Commission investigated Mackey's clandestine campaign and made Whole Foods sell 13 Wild Oats stores.

On the other, other hand, in 2009, when the Marriott Hotel in Mumbai was struck by homicide bombers, Marriott International CEO Bill Marriott immediately blogged, expressing his and the company's sorrow at the tragic events. In true reportorial form, the 76-year-old CEO's "Marriott on the Move" blog began:

> **This Senseless Tragedy . . .**
> *By: Bill Marriott*
> *Posted: September 20, 2008*
>
> *I am very sad to report a terrible tragedy at our Marriott hotel in Islamabad, Pakistan. At approximately 7:00 p.m. local time, a large truck pulled up to the security checkpoint of the heavily guarded hotel and exploded. The huge blast engulfed the front of the hotel and ruptured a gas line, which caused a large fire to break out.*[25]

The CEO's comments were picked up worldwide, demonstrating how the CEO blog could serve as well as any public relations vehicle in disseminating news.

Social Networks

The theoretical concept of social networking stemmed from an article in a telecommunications journal by David Isenberg, a former employee of AT&T Labs Research. He described the Internet as a "stupid network"—a new type of data network that relied on "dumb transport in the middle, and intelligent user-controlled endpoints" and where information was provided "by the needs of the data, not the design assumptions of the network."[26] Isenberg contrasted his "stupid network" with the outmoded "intelligent network," which relied on a technological hierarchy dictated by others.

Thus was born the "dumb transport" of social networking sites, such as MySpace and later Facebook, that allow communities of participants, who share common interests, opinions, and activities, to interact with others to manage messaging, email, video, file sharing, blogging, discussion groups, and all other manner of Internet discussion.

The growth of social networks, also called "social software," "social computing," or "Web 2.0"—from the emergence of Netscape in the 1990s to the inception of MySpace in 2004 and the phenomenon of Facebook shortly thereafter, as a nexus for young people around the world, to sites that attract a variety of age groups and interests—introduces expanding opportunities for public relations practice.

Indeed, in the second decade of the 21st century, every company, politician, non-profit organization, university, hospital, not to mention one billion citizens of the world have their own Facebook page.

The short history of social networking has been characterized by upstarts capturing tech lightning for brief stretches—see MySpace, Second Life, Bebo, Friendster, Orkut, Spotify, Quora, perhaps Pinterest?, etc.—only to sputter and fade. Thus far in the development of social networking, four sites, in particular, have stood the test of time—Facebook, Twitter, LinkedIn, and YouTube. Public relations professionals must be conversant with and proficient in using each.

Facebook

As noted, social networking sites essentially began with young people reaching out to one another. The usage and growth of sites has increased in the 21st century. So, too, has the use of social networking sites by public relations practitioners.

The biggest social networking service, with one billion members around the world, one-quarter of everyone on the Internet and growing by 5% every month, is the phenomenon of Facebook.

Founded in 2004 by Harvard sophomore Mark Zuckerberg, who was once as poor as you are, the cultural phenomenon began as a glorified, well, "Facebook," a name-and-photo directory that colleges distribute to incoming first-year students. Members answer as many questions about themselves as they feel comfortable sharing, from name and relationship status to favorite music and photos. They then search for "friends," past and present, and link up.

Facebook is ideal for sharing news, photos, and videos not only for old friends but also for groups that support various causes or interests or for sending messages or for playing games. Facebook also is prone to exposing personal information and makes money by letting advertisers place ads on the pages of targeted members, for example, divorced, 41-year-old females formerly of Stepford. Facebook went public in 2012, making its iconic founder and his colleagues instant billionaires. Zuckerberg himself was the subject of a not-so-flattering blockbuster movie, *The Social Network*, in 2010. Facebook has thoroughly eclipsed its nearest competitor and former rival, MySpace, which has become a pop music–focused site for teenagers and preteenagers. The average Facebook user spends 20 minutes on the site per visit. Fifty-three percent of users are female, 43% male.

In terms of public relations, Facebook serves multiple community-building purposes, among them the following:

■ **Attract attention.** Organizations may use their Facebook page to clarify who they are and what they stand for.

■ **Two-way communication.** The real sine qua non of Facebook, the medium can be used to "get together" virally with followers, fans, customers, and friends to help build third-party credibility.

■ **Conversation monitor.** Facebook allows one to see who's talking about us, what they are saying, and upon what basis they are making their arguments. This monitoring function, in particular, is a "must" for any organization.

■ **Interactive activities.** Many organizations sponsor opinion polls, games, contests, and other interactive platforms on their Facebook page.

■ **Internal communication.** Facebook can build morale, create employee groups, and create a sense of "community" among the staff.

■ **Halo effect.** Facebook is also excellent for promoting charitable activities or encouraging fundraising campaigns or calling a group to action to lobby for a cause.

■ **Network with the media.** Facebook may be used best when one has an existing relationship with a journalist. If so, Facebook can be an excellent medium for brainstorming story angles or in showcasing one's expertise and experience as a potential interview source.

■ **Crisis management.** Increasingly, organizations use Facebook to issue statements and post updates in times of crisis. Journalists have become accustomed to checking Facebook pages to monitor crisis management approaches.

■ **Link. Link. Link.** Finally, Facebook facilitates linking Websites, videos, content pages, hosted material, and any other sites that may be relevant to communicating an organization's view.

While it may be difficult for Facebook to continue to expand its reach—especially now that it's a more scrutinized "public company"—it is clearly here to stay as a potentially potent marketing and public relations mechanism and a powerful tool for building brand affinity.

Twitter

By the second decade of the 21st century, Twitter had graduated from the social-networking "flavor-of-the-month" to a "keeper."

Twitter is the micro blogging service that allows you to "tweet"—type short messages (140 characters maximum) to alert friends and followers "what you're doing now." Like a multi-person text message service, Twitter allows you to send and receive messages to and from tens or hundreds or even thousands of cell phones. Twitter can be used from its own Website or, more effectively, from a Twitter-reading app for a computer or phone, such as TweetDeck, Twitterific, and Twitter (the official Twitter app for the iPhone, formerly called, ugh, "Tweetie").[27]

Twitter is frequently used to follow celebrities and athletes, and, indeed, the Ashton Kutchers and Lindsay Lohans and Nicki Minajes and Shaquille O'Neals of the world pay public relations people either to tweet for them or, at least, advise them what to write (Figure 10-6). Corporations also pay celebrities to tweet about their products. Snoop Dogg, with 6.3 million followers, took in $8,000 per product plug tweet (ppt), and Paula Abdul, with 2.2 million followers, took in $5,000 per ppt.[28] Further, as Twitter has become more mainstream, it has increasingly become a source for breaking news. In 2012, Twitter broke the news about singer Whitney Houston's death 27 minutes before mainstream media reported the story. Using search.twitter.com is useful to see what others are saying about you.

In terms of public relations, Twitter can prove a powerful tool used thusly:

■ **Finding your "Tweeple."** Following conversations about your issues, product, candidate, etc. on Twitter can be enormously valuable in determining what people think is important and in building a supporter base. The Twitter search function can be used to tap into conversations on particular subjects.

■ **Finding the "Tweetfluentials."** Closely related is identifying tweeters who might be influential in speaking about your brand.

FIGURE 10-6   Shaq Tweeter-in-Chief.
The power behind the throne, responsible for her client Shaquille O'Neal's affinity to Twitter, was
Kathleen Hessert, whose firm, Sports Media Challenge, led a tweeting revolution among athletes.
(Courtesy of Sports Media Challenge)

■ **As a news source.**   As noted, Twitter increasingly has been used to break
news. Twitter, like Facebook, can be used to pitch stories. More regularly,
Twitter serves as a kind of circulatory system of the news cycle, yielding a
constant stream of commentary and information for public relations people to
observe.

■ **Providing valuable content.**   Twitter information should be less "denomi-
national" than other media. Specifically, Twitterites value insider tips and
insights and information not available elsewhere. So dull and dry corporate or
product information will backfire on Twitter.

■ **Building a community.**   That means tweeting daily to show followers you're
serious and engaged.[29]

■ **Crisis management.**   Also like Facebook, Twitter can be used to issue statements and post updates in times of crisis.

Twitter has imitators, among them Google Buzz, FriendFeed, and Facebook updates.
Twitter also has its detractors, who suggest that it is little more than a passing fad for
"people with nothing to say . . . writing for people with nothing to do." However, the
consensus seems to be that Twitter, like Facebook, is one social networking vehicle
that is here to stay.

Outside the Lines

Twouble with Twitter

The first thing to remember about Twitter—or, for that matter, anything else you type or tweet or distribute on the Internet—is that once you thumb that "send" button, it's all over.

Consider the following lost souls who learned this the hard way.

■ First, there was the Ketchum public relations vice president visiting his FedEx client in Memphis, who tweeted, "I would die if I had to live here." The tweet found its way to the client, and Ketchum had to play "catch up" to keep the account.

■ Next, there was designer Kenneth Cole, who tweeted the following after the 2011 political revolution in Egypt:

To Mr. Cole's credit, when the Twittersphere erupted in protest, he quickly apologized for mixing the quest for freedom with stupidity.

■ Then there was the Greek Olympic hurdler Voula Papachristou, who was expelled from the 2012 London Summer Games after tweeting a racist remark. She, too, sent an immediate apology tweet.

■ Even Lady Gaga, the Twitter queen with 25 million followers (Figure 10-7), had to cry "mea culpa" in 2012 when she used the hashtags #PopSingersDontEat and #IwasBornThisWay to reference her rigorous touring schedule. Gaga was criticized for insensitivity in light of her early bout with bulimia and quickly tweeted an apology.

So even the queen has to be circumspect before she tweets.

FIGURE 10-7 **It's good to be the queen.**
Twitter queen Lady Gaga had to double back in 2012 when her tweets on losing weight were misinterpreted. *(Photo: Everett Collection/Newscom)*

LinkedIn

LinkedIn is Facebook for the professional set.

The guiding concept behind LinkedIn is establishing a "who you know" network of current and former business colleagues. Begun in 2003, LinkedIn membership has grown to 200 million in more than 200 countries. Unlike Facebook, whose Initial Public Offering (IPO) in 2012 was marred by mishap, LinkedIn's public debut in 2011 saw its stock pop 90% over the IPO price. LinkedIn's revenue comes from three fairly even sources—advertising, premium subscriptions, and corporate recruiting.[30]

LinkedIn is popular with public relations professionals connected to like-minded professionals to discover new business or employment opportunities and to develop a network of contacts. LinkedIn is particularly helpful in finding a new job because you're not limited to asking immediate colleagues for referrals (Figure 10-8). LinkedIn allows you to ask colleagues of colleagues, which greatly expands one's network. Another popular LinkedIn feature called "Answers" encourages business-oriented questions of people who might know—from résumé writing tips to business software advice.[31]

In terms of public relations, LinkedIn services include the following:

- **Notes.**   Notify others of events, job openings, and vendor recommendations.
- **Groups.**   LinkedIn accesses more than 150,000 groups, including business forums, alumni groups, fan clubs, conferences, etc.
- **Answer Forum.**   Provides advice proffered by professionals, advised to "treat the discussion as you would a business lunch."
- **Polls.**   LinkedIn enables the creation of polls.
- **Card Munch.**   Mobile app that scans business cards and converts them into contacts.
- **Job Openings.**   LinkedIn has become a viable source for employment searches, as a complement to or replacement for paid search agencies.

YouTube

YouTube, hatched in 2005 as a video-sharing Website by three former PayPal employees, is already the stuff of media legend, what with its cute cats, dancing Matt, and the Mentos Diet Coke experiment. It is also the source of fantastic wealth for its founders, who sold the enterprise in 2006 to Google for $1.65 billion.

Robin Hood

Activist/ Chief Fundraiser at Nottingham

Nottingham, United Kingdom | Fund-Raising

Current	• **Activist at Nottingham** • **Mortal enemy at Sheriff of Nottingham** • **Environmentalist at Sherwood Forest**
Connections	**7 connections**

FIGURE 10-8   **Job opening.**
Had LinkedIn been around at the time, perhaps the heroic outlaw wouldn't have been forced to "rob from the rich and give to the poor."
(Ragan PR Daily)

Although YouTube has primarily served as the outlet for "15 minutes of fame" for millions of individuals around the world, organizations have increased their use of the channel for marketing purposes. One benefit is that marketers can target specific user groups for such topics as medical issues, self-help subjects, even public relations guidance. YouTube users have notoriously short attention spans, so marketing messages must be kept simple and short, and marketers have found that the more videos made available, the more YouTube traffic is generated for a particular organization's offerings.[32]

In terms of public relations, a primary use of YouTube has been as a quick response to crisis. The most famous example was Domino's use of the channel when two moronic employees posted a disgusting video, impugning the company's pizza, in 2006. Domino's CEO responded quickly—on YouTube—promising swift action against the now-former employees and reassuring the public about the goodness of the product. In more recent years, organizations from Netflix to JetBlue to RIM have all taken to YouTube to issue mea culpas for some wrong or another. In 2012, the nation was outraged when lunkheads at the U.S. General Services Administration (GSA) were seen on YouTube rapping about taxpayer naiveté at a lavish, $1 million, all-expenses-paid (by us!) junket in Las Vegas.[33] GSA officials quickly responded, via YouTube, to try to quell the uproar.

Contenders: Up-and-Coming Networking Sites

Internet aficionados and Silicon Valley venture capitalists constantly search for "the next big thing" in terms of social networks. Among those in contention as we write (meaning they'll be obsolete by next Thursday!):

Pinterest Pinterest is a social network that allows its users to share what's important to them, as long as this includes a picture somewhere on the Webpage.

The picture is displayed or "pinned" on a virtual bulletin board in Pinterest. Pinterest users can have "pinboards" that are a collection of "pins" that revolve around a common theme. Users can share their tastes and interests with others and discover like-minded people.

In 2012, Pinterest qualified as the most "addictive" new networking site, with advocates—"pinheads"— using the site as a canvas to create one's "ideal self" into one visual reflection.[34]

In terms of public relations, Pinterest advocates cite the following uses:

- **Visual stories.** Tell the story of the organization or candidate or issue or product visually, to enhance customer interest.
- **Industry stories.** Pin interesting developments in the industry and invite the community to a social media board and to Media Pinterest happenings.
- **Videos.** Tie sponsored YouTube videos to the Pinterest site.
- **Employee participation.** Ask employees to become involved by creating their own Pinterest boards.
- **Sharing.** Articles, stories, and blog posts can all be shared through Pinterest.[35]

In 2012, Pinterest took off with 10 million users out of the gate. Whether the site passes the ultimate social networking test of "staying power" remains to be seen.

Instagram   Instagram, begun in 2010, is a photo-sharing application that can be downloaded for iPhones, iPads, and Android devices. You can upload a photo from your phone or take one while using the program and then apply a filter to it to make it look weathered, faded, vintage, or enhanced in some way.

In terms of public relations, Instagram is a venue to help bolster brands. Starbucks is perhaps the most recognized brand that uses Instagram as a social channel with more than 500,000 followers; posts tend to be product-heavy but also reveal an opportunity to show a bit of personality by featuring baristas and some behind-the-scenes action as well. Another user, Vans clothing, posts photos of people using the products in their natural environment: skateboarding events, surfing, BMX events.[36]

One area where Instagram's success is irrefutable was in making its founders rich. In 2012, Mark Zuckerberg's Facebook bought the company and its 13 employees for a cool $1 billion!

Foursquare   Foursquare is an app for iPhone, Palm, BlackBerry (if it's still around when you read this!), or Android phones. It lists restaurants, bars, and shops near where you're located.

By "checking in"—tapping in the name of the venue where you are located—you broadcast your location to friends. In terms of public relations, businesses can offer free products and other incentives as you walk by. Foursquare needs more than its twenty million members—mostly bar-hopping 20 somethings—and registered businesses to qualify as a hot site.

Yelp   Yelp encompasses a huge database of restaurants, shops, hotels, doctors, museums, and attractions, with store hours, directions, and phone numbers, covering an increasing number of U.S. cities.

The key lies in "customer reviews," which can be enormously helpful—or damning—to an establishment. As more people turn to Yelp and like sites such as Open Table and Urbanspoon, it becomes increasingly important for a business to be represented.

Photo/Video-Sharing Apps   Photo/Video-sharing apps, beyond Pinterest and Instagram and YouTube, also abound, with each vying to become the next big thing.

Photo sharing sites allow users to upload, edit, print, and send their digital photos to others. Leading sites include Zoomr, Picasa, and Flickr, free sites that allow users to organize, edit, and share photos, as well as create public relations materials, such as DVD slide shows, business cards, and other printed matter.

Video sharing sites allow users to upload, view, and share video clips. Sites such as Google Video, Revver, Viddy, Klip, Shufflr, and numerous others are vying for recognition.

Second Life   Second Life is worth a mention, if only as a cautionary tale. Launched in 2003 with much pizzazz and promise, Second Life is a three-dimensional world created entirely by its members or "residents." Not exactly a game, Second Life gives members a place to congregate, chat, explore, and even fly around. And to its public relations application, companies from IBM to Reebok all initially flocked to Second Life to spread their messages.

Over time, concurrent users declined from a peak of 88,000 to 54,000 in 2010, the year that Second Life owner Linden Lab cut its workforce by 30%.

Public Relations and Social Networking

As to the use of social networking sites by public relations practitioners, public relations firms, from traditional to upstarts, have all embraced social media with a vengeance as the next frontier of communication work. One of the largest, Edelman Public Relations, headed by social media advocate and the industry's leading social media voice Richard Edelman (see From the Top in this chapter), has a division of Digital Integration, which actively markets the Internet and social media to clients.

As to measurement, the public relations industry is developing standards to track outcomes of social media use. Social media analytics target several priority areas to track, among them:

- Content sourcing and methods, so that evaluations can be standardized.

- Reach and impressions, similar to advertising analysis, which is more difficult to come by in terms of social media.

- Engagement, which might include business outcomes such as sales or less "engaging" outcomes such as blog posts, video comments, retweets, etc.

- Influence and relevance, which must be rated by more subjective human research rather than computer algorithms.

- Opinion and advocacy, also a more "qualitative" measure, analyzing feedback.

- Impact and value, including measuring financial results as well as nonfinancial factors such as "reputation impact."[37]

Again, social media measurement is just in its infancy. But just like any other public relations activity, some analytical analysis is obligatory to capture a true picture of value and contribution.

Web-Based Communication Vehicles

Any discussion of communications vehicles available on the Internet is, by definition, obsolete as soon as it hits the page. Nonetheless, public relations practitioners should be knowledgeable of the full range of Web-based communications vehicles, most certainly including the following:

- **Intranets** are a pervasive internal communications phenomenon. Generally defined, an intranet is an internal vehicle that integrates communication with workflow, process management, infrastructure, and all other aspects of completing a job. Intranets allow communicators, management, and employees to exchange information quickly and effectively, much more quickly and effectively than any similar vehicle.

- **Extranets,** on the other hand, allow a company to use the Internet to communicate information to finely segmented external groups, such as the media, investors, vendors, key customers, left-handed female reality TV stars, security-cleared video archiving soccer players, blonde East Side yoga-going supermodels, whatever. In segmenting the information in such a focused fashion—and protecting its dissemination through a complex series of firewalls—the targeted audience is assured that the data will remain confidential.

- **Wikis,** which derive from the Hawaiian word for "quick," are collaborative Websites that combine the work of many authors. Similar to a blog in structure and logic, a wiki differs from a blog in that it allows anyone to edit, delete, or modify content that has been placed on the Website, including the work of previous authors. The most prominent wiki derivative is Wikipedia, the free encyclopedia on the Web, to which anyone can contribute material, either pro or con—and often undocumented and suspect. (So don't necessarily believe it!)

■ **Podcasting**, which gained its name and fame after Apple's iPod burst onto the scene in 2001, refers to the act of making audio programs available for download to any MP3 player (although Apple still controls about 80% of the market). Listeners already have an enormous selection of podcasts from which to choose; the "pod revolution" will be limited only by the supply of and demand for content.

■ **RSS**, which literally stands for *really simple syndication,* is an easy way to distribute content on the Internet, similar to a newsgroup. RSS feeds are widely used by the blog community, for example, to share headlines or full text. Major news organizations, including Reuters, CNN, PR Newswire, and the BBC, use RSS feeds to allow other sites to incorporate their "syndicated" news services.

■ **QR Codes and LBS**, or quick response codes and location-based services, have become an essential component of the overall communication marketing experience as cell phones have overwhelmed society. QR codes, most often embedded in magazines, can be scanned by smartphones to demonstrate product uses or take advantage of special offers. Most such uses are designed to drive consumers online and visit a Website. LBS often targets consumers within close proximity to retailers selling the items identified. Both QR codes and LBS may hold potential application for public relations use.[38]

These are but a sample of the Web-based communications vehicles available to public relations professionals. The important thing for public relations people is to stay aware of the changing nature of Internet communications vehicles. The Internet menu changes at lightning speed, and it's the responsibility of the communications professional to change right along with it.

The Dark Side of Online Communications

Google the name of the world's largest retailer, and you'll discover not only the Walmart Stores Inc. homepage but also links to message boards, blogs, wikis, and online communities attacking, shellacking, and vivisecting Walmart (Figure 10-9). Welcome to the world of Internet sabotage, where no organization is immune from online attack.

As a consequence, monitoring the Internet is another frontline public relations responsibility. The World Wide Web is riddled with unhappy consumers spilling their guts, disgruntled stockholders badmouthing management in chat rooms, and rogue Websites condemning this or that organization.

The Internet is free, wide open, international, and anonymous—the perfect place to start a movement and ruin an organization's reputation. And so it is imperative that public relations people monitor the Internet in consideration of the following.

■ **Blogs** are hotbeds for discontented shareholders, unscrupulous stock manipulators, and disgruntled consumers. Any local or service provider message board that solicits public input about an organization is ripe for messaging contrary to the official position.[39] Finance boards on Yahoo! and others, for example, are the source of continuing commentary about public companies from anonymous commentators, all using mysterious pseudonyms, including Whole Foods CEO John Mackey who was caught anonymously bad-mouthing a competitor.

■ **Rogue Websites** must also be monitored by the organizations they attack. Rogue Websites seek to confront an organization by presenting negative, often-unfounded information.

A corporation's knee-jerk reaction—to call in the lawyers—hasn't resulted in great victory in battling the rogues. In perhaps the most celebrated case, Kmart sued www.kmartsucks.com, a Website hosted by a disgruntled employee. The copyright infringement suit did succeed in forcing the site to change its name—to www.martsucks.com—but the considerable national media attention the suit received helped put the rogue Website on the map. Eventually, the embattled Kmart launched its own "good news only" site, called Kmartforever.com, to combat the bashers.[40]

■ **Urban legends** are yet another requisite for online monitoring. There is a growing body of corporate horror stories from bogus Internet rumors that have taken on legendary proportions. Most are spread by email at lightning speed across the country and the world. For example:

■ Upscale retailer Neiman Marcus was accused by an anonymous emailer of charging a $200 fee for its special cookie recipe. "Outrageous," cried the thousands who received the email. It's also completely untrue. Neiman Marcus doesn't have a cookie recipe.

■ Mrs. Fields also outraged the populace when an email dispatch reported that she had sent a batch of her famous cookies to O. J. Simpson after he won his infamous 1990s murder trial. This is also totally false.

■ In perhaps the most pervasive and pernicious urban legend of all, retailer Tommy Hilfiger was, according to the official-sounding email, evicted from *The Oprah Winfrey Show* by the lady herself when the clothes manufacturer admitted his garments weren't made for "African Americans, Hispanics, and Asians" (Figure 10-10). The reality was that Tommy Hilfiger never met Oprah Winfrey, was never on her show, and certainly didn't

Subject: Tommy Hilfiger

MESSAGE:

I'm sure many of you watched the recent taping of the *Oprah Winfrey Show* where her guest was Tommy Hilfiger. On the show she asked him if the statements about race he was accused of saying were true. Statements like if he'd known African-Americans, Hispanics and Asians would buy his clothes he would not have made them so nice. He wished these people would *not* buy his clothes, as they are made for upper class white people. His answer to Oprah was a simple "yes". Where after she immediately asked him to leave her show.

FIGURE 10-10   **Stuff of legends.**
Urban legends like this email, discussing a bogus appearance by Tommy Hilfiger on *The Oprah Winfrey Show*, have become increasingly frequent as more people, some with questionable motives, access the Internet.

design his clothing solely for white people. In the end, the false Internet legend proved so virulent that Oprah invited Hilfiger on her show to "clear the air" once and for all.

What should a proper public relations response be to such online efforts to derail the organization? Typical responses range from doing nothing to throwing money at an aggrieved party to engaging the aggrieved party to releasing the lawyers. The smartest organizations adopt "inoculation strategies" that establish clear communication channels on the Web, through which customers and employees can relay concerns to management, sometimes privately, before frustrations mount. Firms such as IBM and McDonald's (see Case Study in this chapter) host secure, unedited sites where employees can openly and anonymously discuss corporate policies and strategies. Procter & Gamble sponsors an online forum where customers can express their thoughts.[41] Such preemptive public relations make solid business sense.

The real lesson: Public relations professionals must constantly monitor—and beware—the Web.

Last Word

As strange as it sounds, the Internet, as a popular communications medium, has been around barely for two plus decades. In that short time, it has evolved into an indispensable communication tool for organizations and a favored weapon for angry customers, disaffected employees, and consumer activists bent on attacking those same organizations. As a consequence, mastering and monitoring the Internet have become a front-burner priority for public relations professionals.

In the 21st century, such new techniques as blogging for promotional product buzz, setting up "blog carnivals" to inform a community about a particular topic, creating search-friendly Websites and search-optimal keywords, podcasting, videocasting, orchestrating word-of-mouth marketing campaigns, and using all aspects of social media are all part of the public relations practitioner's online tool kit.

As the number of the world's citizens using the Internet expands exponentially, it is urgent that public relations professionals understand the new technology and its capabilities and increase their competence in employing and monitoring it. Those who can blend the traditional skills of writing and media and communications knowledge with the online skills of the Internet—particularly the generation that has grown up with social media as its preferred communication default mechanism—will find a rewarding calling in the practice of public relations in the 21st century.[42]

Discussion Starters

1. What is the status of the Internet and World Wide Web in public relations today?
2. How has social media affected journalism? Commerce? Internal communications?
3. How has email changed the way people and organizations communicate?
4. How has social media changed the way journalists look at email?
5. How have blogs influenced public relations practice?
6. What is the significance of Facebook relative to public relations practice?
7. What is the significance of Twitter relative to public relations practice?
8. How have companies used YouTube in crisis?
9. How should organizations protect themselves from online attack?
10. What is the difference between an intranet and an extranet?

Pick of the Literature

Social Media and Public Relations

Deidre Breakenridge, Upper Saddle River, NJ: Pearson Education, 2012

There is no more knowledgeable public relations counselor on uses of social media and the Internet than Deidre Breakenridge. The New Jersey consultant has written a number of books on public relations uses of the new media. This is the best.

Early in the book, author Breakenridge confronts public relations practitioners with the exhortation that "Social media requires you to shift your mindset to unite communications and collaborative technology." She then goes on to introduce and explain eight new practices that social media introduces to public relations professionals: (1) policy maker, (2) internal collaborator, (3) technology tester, (4) communications organizer, (5) pre-crisis doctor, (6) relationship analyzer, (7) reputation task force member, and (8) metrics master.

She examines each of these elements in creative detail, diagramming their relationship to the overall business entity and their navigation in terms of social media. This is original thinking at its finest.

Case Study | Ronald McDonald's Brush with Antisocial Media

In the 21st century, the face of public relations is changing, largely due to the phenomenon of social media. And that ain't always such a good thing. Just ask the world's largest fast food chain, McDonald's.

McDonald's, with its franchise known throughout the world, is one of the globe's most well-known and progressive companies (Figure 10-11). And that includes its use of social media.

McDonald's has a director of social media who has instituted a robust, multiplatform program. Rick Won acknowledges that with respect to the Internet and social media, "You don't control things. You can only hope to steer things in certain directions." Indeed, Mr. Won has led the fast food franchiser with substantive offerings in terms of video campaigns, hashtags, and blogger outreach programs.

FIGURE 10-11   Ronald in happier times.
Ronald McDonald joins Olympic gold medalists Carl Lewis and Jackie-Joyner Kersee to celebrate
"Go Active Day" in Athens, Greece. *(Courtesy of O'Dwyerpr.com)*

The latter has been particularly successful, with McDonald's working with bloggers to boost its brand impact. As Mr. Won put it, "We want to be transparent in our relationships, and we want our bloggers to be authentic in their opinions."

As a consequence, McDonald's never insists that its affiliated bloggers write a word about its products. When they do, sometimes the write-up isn't flattering. Mr. Won says that's good. "We don't want them to hold back if they have an opinion that isn't totally positive."

Such an enlightened social media approach has won McDonald's viral credibility.

But there have been missteps, two in particular that McDonald's learned from but just as likely wished had never happened. Both are a reminder of how treacherous the social media terrain occasionally turns out to be.

Twitterverse Turns Racist

One weekend in June 2011, a sign, ostensibly placed in a McDonald's window, made its way around the Twitterverse, with the hashtag #seriouslymcdonalds.

The sign said, "Due in part to a recent string of robberies, African-American customers are now required to pay an additional fee of $1.50 a transaction."

Horror of horrors: Mickey D's had been disgracefully scammed.

Immediately, McDonald's responded on its Twitter page that the "pic is a senseless & ignorant hoax McD's values ALL our customers. Diversity runs deep in our culture on both sides of the counter."

The company didn't stop there, reiterating the next day on Twitter, "That Seriously McDonalds picture is a hoax."

McDonald's followers quickly chimed in that the toll-free number listed on the bottom of the phony picture belonged to competitor KFC.

Nonetheless, the hoax made the Twitter rounds on a super-sized scale.

Discomforting "Mc Nuggets"

A year later, the company tried again on Twitter by setting up a 24-hour campaign hashtag, #MeetTheFarmers, to attempt to drive people toward commercials highlighting some of the real-life farmers and ranchers who supply McDonald's with its ingredients.

The commercials were the height of "authenticity," with the farmers and ranchers dispensing nuggets of wisdom about their harvests and herds. And McDonald's thought a Twitter campaign including those nuggets would move it up the trends lists on the Twitter homepage and help the brand.

The campaign proceeded smoothly enough until social media director Won moved the conversation to another hashtag, #McDStories, to continue the conversation among their customers.

That's where the well-intentioned campaign hit the Mcrails. Social media director Won monitored in horror as a barrage of negative comments (see next page) came in fast and furious—from poor working conditions at McDonald's stores to contaminated food.

> **Tonia Leung** @ToniaLeung ← Reply ↻ Retweet ★ Favorite
> Lost my appetite RT @digitalSicilian @NikasTweets McDonald's
> hashtag campaign goes horribly wrong: read.bi/wGKKfZ #McDst
> ← In reply to Salvatore Filippone
>
> ---
>
> **Eric Miller Jr.** @EricMillerJr
> Reading all these #McDStories is helping to keep me on my diet
>
> ---
>
> **Esam Sultan** @esamsultan
> I remember in Kent with @fabrebash4 years ago he nearly choked
> bones in his nuggets. They gave him £2 refund so all was good
> #McDStories
>
> ---
>
> **Kamille Elahi** @KamilleElahi
> #McDstories saw a woman wiping a table with a dirty cloth. table
> still full of smudges of leftover burgers ew!

Oops! Within minutes, the company's social media success had crumbled to social media disaster.

A little more than an hour after the tidal wave of #McDStories negativity began, Mr. Won killed the Twitter campaign, pulling the hashtag off the Twitter homepage.

McDonald's and Mr. Won, shaken from the social media blitzkrieg, had learned some valuable lessons. It's fine to be creative with hashtags, Mr. Won said, but it's better not to create tags that people assume mean something they don't. If anything, the social media director concluded, "the lesson of #McDStories is that we can be an easy target for people who are uninformed."

Or out to get you! (Figure 10-12)

FIGURE 10-12 **Lost in space.**
Twitterspace, that is. Ronald McDonald and his colleagues were left up in the air in 2012, when a seemingly harmless Twitter campaign went horribly off the rails. *(Photo: imagostock/Newscom)*

Questions

1. What do you think of McDonald's social media strategy in general?

2. How would you characterize McDonald's handling of the racist tweet?

3. What would you have done differently relative to the #McDStories controversy?

For further information, see Brett Johnson, "McDonald's Feeling the Heat After Racist Sign Hoax," Ragan PR Daily, June 13, 2011; Keith O'Brien, "How McDonald's Came Back Bigger Than Ever," *The New York Times*, May 4, 2012; and Matt Wilson, "McDonald's Exec: 'You Don't Control' Social Media," Ragan PR Daily, May 21, 2012.

From the Top

An Interview with Richard Edelman

Richard Edelman is president and CEO of Edelman, the world's largest public relations firm with 3,500 employees in 66 offices worldwide. Mr. Edelman is also the public relations executive most associated with the Internet and new technology. Under his leadership, Edelman has distinguished itself not only in traditional public relations areas but as a pioneer in the new media. A graduate of Harvard College and the Harvard Business School, Mr. Edelman is one of the only public relations executives to write his own blog.

How has the Internet changed the public relations business?

The Web has changed the PR business by giving us access to budgets that we never saw before . . . by allowing us to make each of our clients its own media company . . . by broadening our array of addressable media to include bloggers . . . to force us to have relationships with a whole new set of influencers who may not be at top magazines but are frequently posting content.

How proficient in terms of the Net should a public relations professional be today?

The PR person who does not read important blogs (for example, in DC you should read *Drudge Report,* Politico) is missing the game. You also must be posting comments to blogs that matter. You need to be reading the mainstream media's blogs (for example, Andrew Ross Sorkin's blog at *NY Times—Deal Book*).

What are the primary online communications methods that you recommend to your clients?

Primary online methods are listening to the conversation by reading or viewing video blogs, making comments as appropriate, making relationships with key bloggers. For example, I had lunch the old-fashioned way with Laurel Touby of Mediabistro, who was Tweeting during our lunch about our conversation.

Why do you blog?

I blog because I enjoy writing, because I like to walk the talk about social media, because too few executives in PR agencies are willing to take a stand on issues.

Do you recommend that other CEOs blog internally?

I do recommend that other CEOs blog. I would rather have them make their blog posts accessible to the general public. But internal only is a good first step.

Do you recommend that clients get involved in online forums that are critical of them?

I believe that companies must participate in the horizontal axis of communications. You need to correct misinformation and to be part of the conversation. At least point people to alternative interpretations of the data on the company site or another site.

Who do you consider the leadership companies in terms of online communications?

Best companies are Walmart, GE, and GM. They offer access to mid-level staffers. Note, for example, the blog for Walmart which has buyers posting from around the world as they find new garments or electronics; also the GE research blog on future innovations.

What lies on the horizon for public relations use of the Web?

PR will have to improve the quality of its content. All of it must be ready for prime time—not as much selling mode as it will have to be conversational and factual. Also, it must include more visual content as words are no longer sufficient. We will be the means by which business can open up to conversation.

Public Relations Library

Barger, Christopher. *Social Media Strategist*. New York: McGraw-Hill, 2012. Sophisticated look at using social media strategically to accomplish public relations goals.

Bragman, Howard. *Where's My Fifteen Minutes?* New York: Penguin, 2008. Ricki Lake's public relations counselor offers behind-the-scenes secrets to optimize publicity, including using the Internet.

Breakenridge, Deirdre. *PR 2.0: New Media, New Tools, New Audiences*. Upper Saddle River, NJ: Pearson Education, 2008. This is a terrific explanation, in layperson's language, of everything one needs to know about practicing public relations on the Internet.

Evans, Liana. *Social Media Marketing*. Indianapolis, IN: Que Publishing, 2010. Solid explanation of dealing with Facebook and Twitter.

Falls, Jason, and Erik Deckers. *No Bull*&** Social Media*. Upper Saddle River, NJ: Pearson Education, 2012. My very own publisher, proving that it, too, can publish a book with a curse word in the title.

Gardner, Susannah. *Buzz Marketing with Blogs for Dummies*. Hoboken, NJ: John Wiley & Sons, 2005. This book tells you everything you need to know about blogging and bloggers.

Gehrt, Jennifer, and Colleen Moffitt. *Strategic Public Relations*. Bloomington, IN: Xlibris Corporation, 2009. General strategies including Internet discussion.

Green, Andy. *Creativity in Public Relations*, 3rd ed. London, England: Kogan Page, 2008. This updated version includes creativity via the Internet.

Handley, Ann, and C. C. Chapman. *Content Rules*. Hoboken, NJ: John Wiley & Sons, 2012. Focus on perfecting blogs, podcasts, webinars, and other Internet fare.

Kabani, Shana Hyder. *Social Media Marketing*. Dallas, TX: BenBella Books, 2010. Straightforward presentation on online marketing.

Kelleher, Thomas. *Public Relations Online*. Thousand Oaks, CA: Sage Publications, 2007. This book offers a good explanation of relationship-based interactive public relations.

Kerpen, Dave. *Likeable Social Media*. New York: McGraw-Hill, 2011. Tongue-in-cheek approach to explaining the pros and cons of avenues of social media.

King, Janice M. *Copywriting that Sells High-Tech*. Sammamish, WA: WriteSpark Press, 2006. This book is for public relations writers who deal primarily with high-tech companies and products.

Lawson, Russell. *The PR Buzz Factor*. London, England: Kogan Page, 2006. One way to create "buzz" is through a creative online presence and Website, says this counselor.

Levine, John R., Margaret Levine Young, and Carol Baroudi. *The Internet for Dummies*. Hoboken, NJ: John Wiley & Sons, 2005. For anyone feeling left behind, this is your introduction to the Internet.

Lynn, Jaqueline, Ed. *Start Your Own Public Relations Business*. New York: Entrepreneur Media, 2009. This provides a route—largely Internet-related—through which a practitioner might start his or her own public relations organization.

Martin, Gail Z. *30 Days to Social Media Success*. Pompton Plains, NJ: The Career Press, 2010. A book dedicated to getting you to rethink, restart, and reenergize your social marketing—in 30 days.

Phillips, David, and Philip Young. *Online Public Relations*. Philadelphia, PA: Kogan Page, 2011. Fine soup-to-nuts tour, including definitions and strategies, of using the Internet and social media.

Safko, Lon. *The Social Media Bible*, 3rd ed. Hoboken, NJ: John Wiley & Sons, 2012. Bible? Well, it is pretty comprehensive in discussing everything from podcasts and video sharing to social networking and micro blogging.

Scott, David Meerman. *The New Rules of Marketing and PR*, 3rd ed. Hoboken, NJ: John Wiley & Sons, 2011. Marketing-oriented text emphasizes raising online visibility to enhance sales volume.

Singh, Shiv. *Social Media Marketing for Dummies*. Hoboken, NJ: Wiley Publishing, 2010. Social media primer.

Solis, Brian, and Deirdre Breakenridge. *How Social Media Is Reinventing the Aging Business of PR*. Upper Saddle River, NJ: Pearson Education, 2009. Not sure if public relations is exactly "aging" (although your author clearly is!). But social media has, clearly, arrived, and this book is a good introduction to it.

Sponder, Marshall. *Social Media Analytics*. New York: McGraw-Hill, 2012. Searching for the Return on Investment with social media.

Sweeney, Susan, Andy MacLellan, and Ed Dorey. *3G Marketing on the Internet*. Gulf Breeze, FL: Maximum Press, 2006. It's third-generation time for the Internet, and this book provides business strategies for using the Internet today.

Chapter 11

Employee
Relations

Chapter Objectives

1. To discuss an often-overlooked but core critical constituency for organizational management, the internal public.

2. To explore the philosophy of dealing with employees in an era of layoffs and meager job growth.

3. To discuss the various tactics—print, online, and broadcast—of communicating with the internal public.

4. To examine the ways that social media have complicated and made more challenging the function of communicating with employees.

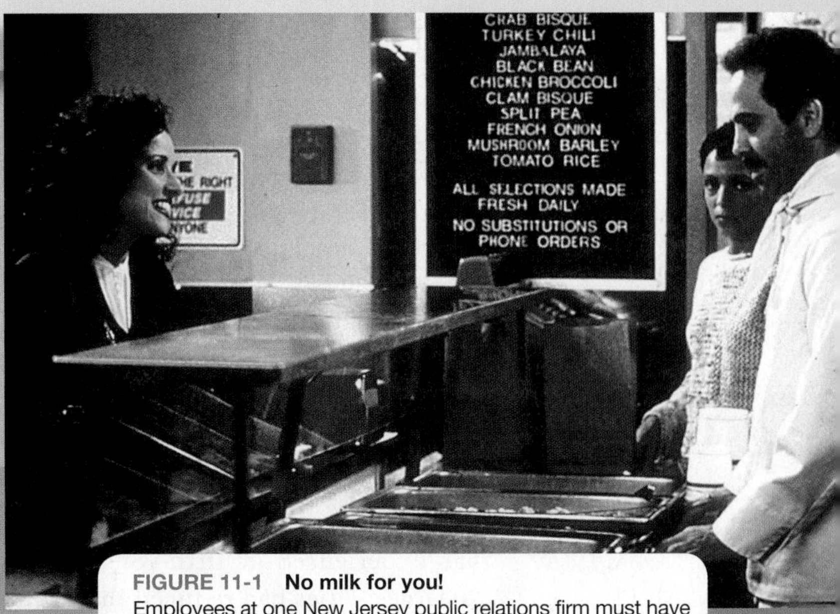

FIGURE 11-1   No milk for you!
Employees at one New Jersey public relations firm must have felt like the cast of *Seinfeld* in 2011 when their CEO lashed out about their milk consumption. *(Photo: Zuma/Newscom)*

In September of 2011, the president of a multi-million dollar public relations firm in New Jersey had had enough. The "milk situation" had to end (Figure 11-1). And so, he took matters into his own iPad.[1]

> **From: Keith Zakheim**
> **Date: September 27, 2011 8:20:21 AM EDT**
> **To: Beckerman Staff**
> **Subject: I don't know what else to do…**
>
> *I have repeatedly requested until I am blue in the face that the person that finishes the milk must replace the milk. It's not complicated and is a simple sign of respect for fellow employees.*

Thus began an impassioned email from the chagrined CEO of the Beckerman Antenna Group, who had *"stumbled in at 7:15 a.m. after enduring a typically painful Redskins loss and in dire need of a shot of caffeine."*

What he found was enough to make any Redskins sufferer cry, only three drops of milk left for the coffee; or as Mr. Zakheim put it, *"Literally 3 drops, an amount that would maybe fill the tummy of a prematurely born mouse."*

He went on to conclude that the perpetrator of this egregious offense had to be, *"incredibly lazy, obnoxiously selfish or woefully devoid of intelligence—3 traits that are consistent with the profile of FORMER Beckerman employees."*

The chief further pointed out that he paid for the milk and wouldn't tolerate future abuse of the milk privilege. *"You will be fired for not replacing the milk, and have fun explaining that one to your next employer. This is not an empty threat so PLEASE don't test me."*

And presumably, no one did.

Not surprisingly, as the U.S. and world economies continued to sputter into the second decade of the 21st century and more people either got fired or worried that unemployment might lie around the corner, the relationship between workers and bosses grew increasingly more brittle.

Layoffs across every sector of the economy were the rule. By 2012, California had experienced its fifth consecutive year of budget cuts and layoffs; the state's 20 largest cities had reduced their fulltime workforce by 10,000 people.[2] The banking industry, rocked by mismanagement and scandal, was particularly hard hit, as Bank of America fired 2,000 and Deutsche Bank 1,900 in 2012, and analysts predicted as many as 50,000 more layoffs were in the works[3] at companies from Starbucks and Yahoo! to General Motors and BMW to IBM and Blackberry. In the first six months of 2012, the U.S. Labor Department reported that nearly 770,000 people lost their jobs.[4]

No wonder only one in five workers reported giving "full discretionary effort on the job." At the same time, according to an Edelman study, companies with "highly engaged employees" outperformed the total stock market and enjoyed total shareholder returns 19% higher than the average; those with low engagement levels saw total shareholder returns 44% lower than average.[5]

So what's an organization to do, especially to reassure these younger participants in the workforce?

According to the Edelman study, rethinking employee engagement to drive better results isn't easy. Management, Edelman says, must be willing to answer several questions in attempting to lift employee morale, commitment, and engagement.

1. Is your leadership rolling out a new strategy or initiative that will require more engagement than ever from your employees?
2. Do you need to activate or reengage your employees as advocates or ambassadors?
3. How well is the urgency for change understood and acted on within your organization?
4. Should leadership communication be a critical component of delivering on your company's strategy or organizational performance goals?
5. Are you searching for novel ways to renew or reinvent the employee experience? Are leaders looking for better ways of engaging their teams?

6. Does your employee engagement research provide sufficient insights for leaders to build trust, cultivate two-way dialogue, and engage employees on critical priorities?

7. Do your current drivers of employee engagement support the business you need to become?

8. If employee engagement remains at its current level or decreases within your company, is there a downside risk?[6]

Beyond auditing an organization to begin to improve employee morale and engagement, there is the aspect of learning from "best practices." According to *Fortune* magazine, the nation's best company to work for is Google.[7] Why? Well, for one thing, Google makes meals available free to employees all day, every day. Free food is important (When Marissa Mayer left Google in 2012 to take over the CEO job at Yahoo!, the first thing she did was make the cafeteria food free!), but so is candor. The fact is that management communications to and with employees must be candid, clear, and credible. If these requisites aren't attained, then even free food may be for naught. Employees—arguably, the most savvy public with whom management must deal—just won't buy the same old, same old.

That's why organizing effective, believable, and persuasive internal communications—particularly in the midst of economic uncertainty and organizational change—is such a challenging and critical public relations responsibility in the 21st century.

Critical Internal Communications

In the 21st century, employee relations matters—a lot. Approximately 60% of corporate CEOs, according to one well-regarded survey, reported spending more of their time communicating with employees.[8]

The reason is obvious when one considers the fortunes of employees in recent years and the growing importance of internal communications.

■ First, the wave of downsizings and layoffs that dominated business and industry both in the United States and worldwide after the overleveraging in the first decade of the 21st century led to worldwide recession, and downturn in the second decade has taken its toll on employee loyalty. Although employees once implicitly trusted their organizations and superiors, today they are more hardened to the realities of a job market dominated by technological change that reduces human labor. Today, when companies lay off workers, they are often rewarded by the stock market for becoming more productive and efficient. This phenomenon has caused employees to understand that in today's business climate, every employee is expendable and there is no such thing as "lifetime employment." Consequently, companies must work harder at honestly communicating with their workers.

■ The wide gulf between the pay of senior officers and common workers is another reason organizations must be sensitive to employee communications. Income inequality between top management and common workers has exploded in recent years. This was one of the causes of the Occupy Wall Street movement (see PR Mini Case, Chapter 4) that swept the nation and the world in 2011. In that year, CEOs earned 209 times more than workers, compared to just 26.5 times more in 1978. Meanwhile, worker productivity increased by 93% between 1978 and 2011.[9] The highest paid CEO in the United States was Apple CEO Tim Cook, whose total compensation of $379 million was more than 11,000 times as much as the average worker's salary of $34,053.[10] Under Cook, Apple's stock sputtered in 2013.

■ The move toward globalization, including the merger of geographically dispersed organizations, was another reason for increased focus on internal communications. Technology has hastened the integration of business and markets around the world. Customers on far-away continents are today but a mouse-click away. Alliances, affiliations, and mergers among far-flung companies have proliferated. Organizations have become much more cognizant of the importance of communicating the opportunities and benefits that will enhance support and loyalty among worldwide staffs.

■ Finally, as the Edelman research suggested, companies that communicate effectively with their workers financially outperform those that don't. Another study found that companies with the most effective internal communications programs returned 57% more to their shareholders than companies with the least effective programs.[11]

These phenomena suggest that the value of "intellectual capital" has increased in importance. In the new information economy, business managers have realized that their most important assets are their employees. Employee communications, then, has become a key way to nurture and sustain that intellectual capital.

This was not always the case. For years, employee communications was considered less important than the more glamorous and presumably more "critical" functions of media, government, and investor relations.

Today, with fewer employees expected to do more work, staff members are calling for empowerment—for more of a voice in decision making. Just about every researcher who keeps tabs on employee opinion finds evidence of a "trust gap" that exists between management and workers. To narrow that gap demands that more effective employee communications play a pivotal role.

Dealing with the Employee Public

Just as there is no such thing as the "general public," there is also no single "employee public."

The employee public is made up of numerous subgroups: senior managers, first-line supervisors, staff and line employees, union laborers, per diem employees, contract workers, and others. Each group has different interests and concerns. A smart organization will try to differentiate messages and communications to reach these segments.

Indeed, in a general sense, today's staff is younger, increasingly female, more diverse, ambitious and career oriented, less complacent, and less loyal to the company than in the past. Today's more hard-nosed employee demands candor in communications. Internal communications, like external messages, must be targeted to reach specific subgroups of the employee public.

Grounding in effective employee communications requires management to ask three hard questions about the way it conveys knowledge to the staff.

- Is management able to communicate effectively with employees?
- Is communication trusted, and does it relay appropriate information to employees?
- Has management communicated its commitment to its employees and to fostering a rewarding work environment?

In many instances, the biggest problem is that employees don't know where they stand in the eyes of management. This is particularly true in a period of high unemployment. In addition, they often don't understand how compensation programs work or what they need to do to move ahead. This lack of understanding leads to discontent, frustration, miscommunication, problems, and eventually to the feeling that the grass is greener elsewhere.[12]

Clearly, organizing effective, believable, and persuasive internal communications in the midst of organizational change is a core critical public relations responsibility in the 21st century.

Trusted Communications in Uncertain Times

According to the coauthors of the *100 Best Companies to Work For in America*, who later became editors of the Fortune magazine exercise of the same name, six criteria, in particular, have stood the test of time:

1. **Willingness to express dissent.** Employees want to be able to "feed back" to management their opinions and even dissent. They want access to management. They want critical letters to appear in internal publications. They want management to pay attention.

2. **Visibility and proximity of upper management.** Enlightened companies try to level rank distinctions, eliminating such status reminders as executive cafeterias and executive gymnasiums. They act against hierarchical separation. Smart CEOs practice MBWA—"management by walking around."

3. **Priority of internal to external communication.** The worst thing to happen to any organization is for employees to learn critical information about the company on a renegade blog or the 10 o'clock news. Smart organizations always release pertinent information to employees first and consider internal communication primary. (That's why Barack Obama in the summer of 2008 "announced" his choice for vice president "first" to supporters via text message.)

4. **Attention to clarity.**   How many employees regularly read benefits booklets? The answer should be "many" because of the importance of benefit programs to the entire staff, but most employees never do so. Good companies write such booklets with an emphasis on clarity as opposed to legalities—to be readable for a general audience rather than for human resources specialists.

5. **Friendly tone.**   The best companies "give a sense of family" in all that they communicate. One high-tech company makes everyone wear a name tag with his or her first name in big block letters. When management creates a culture more "fiend" than "friend," employees—especially in a day of Twitter and Facebook—occasionally rebel with a vengeance (see PR Ethics Mini Case in this chapter).

6. **Sense of humor.**   People are worried principally about keeping their jobs. Corporate life for many is grim, which "puts people in strait-jackets, so they can't wait to get out at the end of the day."[13] So employees seem to enjoy themselves more at companies such as Southwest Airlines, where legendary founder Herb Kelleher used to say, "If you create an environment where people truly participate, you don't need control" (Figure 11-2).[14]

What internal communications comes down to—just like external communications—is, in a word, *credibility*. The task for management is to convince employees that it not only desires to communicate with them but also wishes to do so in a truthful, frank, and direct manner. That is the overriding challenge that confronts today's internal communicator.

FIGURE 11-2
Alien company.
Southwest Airlines is one company that prides itself on its sense of humor. Here the company, in conjunction with Sue Bohle Public Relations and Infogames Entertainment, decked out these passengers in out-of-this-world masks on the way to the E3 Entertainment Trade Show. *(Courtesy of the Bohle Company)*

PR Ethics Mini-Case

I Hate You, I'm Leaving, Where's My Check?

TODAY is my last day at Goldman Sachs. After almost 12 years at the firm—first as a summer intern while at Stanford, then in New York for 10 years, and now in London—I believe I have worked here long enough to understand the trajectory of its culture, its people and its identity. And I can honestly say that the environment now is as toxic and destructive as I have ever seen it.

To put the problem in the simplest terms, the interests of the client continue to be sidelined in the way the firm operates and thinks about making money. Goldman Sachs is one of the world's largest and most important investment banks and it is too integral to global finance to continue to act this way. The firm has veered so far from the place I joined right out of college that I can no longer in good conscience say that I identify with what it stands for.

Thus began the most poisonous pen letter in the history of the venerable investment bank of Goldman Sachs. The letter, which appeared on the Op Ed page of *The New York Times* in the spring of 2012, was written by Greg Smith, Goldman Sachs executive director and head of the firm's United States equity derivatives business in Europe, the Middle East, and Africa.

Mr. Smith chose the day of his departure from Goldman to lower the boom on his corporate benefactor of 12 years and share the news with the one million daily subscribers of the *Times*. Never mind that Goldman paid him $500,000–$750,000 a year for his unappreciated efforts, or that the firm subsidized his trips around the world. Mr. Smith simply couldn't abide a culture that had turned to thinking about "making money." So he trashed it, in *The New York Times*.

It was only the latest bad employee news for Goldman, arguably the world's most powerful investment bank. In the summer of 2010, bank CEO Lloyd Blankfein was hauled before the Senate Homeland Security and Governmental Affairs subcommittee and its fire-breathing, publicity-seeking Chair Carl Levin of Michigan (Figure 11-3).

Levin, preening as ever before the cameras, waved an internal Goldman email at Blankfein and then pointed out—by quoting verbatim—that the memo, from the head of the Goldman securities business, referred to one investment deal as "one sh*# deal."

"One sh*# deal!" Levin thundered. "Should Goldman Sachs be trying to sell a sh*&*# deal?"

In light of Levin's peacock performance at Goldman's expense before the national audience, the New York–based company wasn't about to suffer similar ignominy. A memo went out to all 34,000 traders, investment bankers, and other employees, notifying them that henceforth in emails they must refrain from profanity and be "professional, appropriate and courteous at all times."

FIGURE 11-3   Levin storm.
Grandstanding Senator Carl Levin ominously waves a Goldman Sachs, epithet-laden email, describing a company investment, at a 2010 congressional hearing designed to take the company and its CEO to the woodshed. *(Photo: Zuma/Newscom)*

CEO Blankfein and President Gary Cohn also jointly wrote another memo to the staff responding to Smith's op-ed, in which they expressed shock and disappointment at, not to mention the tardiness of, their former employee's complaints. But they also said they would also work to improve the internal climate. Shortly thereafter, Goldman canned its longtime, close-mouthed public relations director and replaced him with a high-profile, well-liked former U.S. Treasury spokesperson.

As to the aggrieved whistleblower who initiated the brouhaha, Smith chose not to continue the debate publicly, maybe because he was busy writing a book about his experiences at Goldman, for which Grand Central Publishing agreed to pay him a $1.5 million advance.*

Questions

1. How would you characterize the ethics of Smith's decision to go public with his gripes as a Goldman employee?

2. What do you think of the company's response to the controversy?

3. What advice would you give Goldman Sachs in its future public relations dealings?

*For further information, see Julie Bosman, "Former Goldman Executive Is Said to Complete Book Deal," *The New York Times*, March 30, 2012; Cassell Bryan-Low and Aaron Lucchetti, "George Carlin Never Would've Cut It at the New Goldman Sachs," *The Wall Street Journal*, July 29, 2010; "Goldman Sachs Response to Greg Smith's Op-Ed," Bloomberg Businessweek, March 14, 2012; and Greg Smith, "Why I Am Leaving Goldman Sachs," *The New York Times*, March 14, 2012.

Credibility: The Key

The employee public is a savvy one. Employees can't be conned because they live with the organization every day. They generally know what's going on and whether management is being honest with them. That's why management must be truthful.

Employees want managers to level with them. They want facts, not wishful thinking. The days when management could say "Trust us, this is for your own good" are over. Employees like hearing the truth, especially in person. Indeed, survey after survey suggests that face-to-face communication—preferably between a supervisor and subordinate—is the hands-down most effective method of employee communications.

Employees also want to know, candidly, how they're doing. Research indicates that trust in organizations would increase if management (1) communicated earlier and more frequently, (2) demonstrated trust in employees by sharing bad news as well as good, and (3) involved employees in the process by asking for their ideas and opinions. Effective employee communication means that an organization's leaders have taken the time to clearly and succinctly articulate the vision of the business, show how employees can contribute to it, and demonstrate how it can be "lived" in the daily jobs.[15]

Today, smart companies realize that well-informed employees are the organization's best goodwill ambassadors. Managements have become more candid in their communications with the staff. Gone are the days when all the news coming from management is all good. In today's environment, being candid means treating people with dignity, addressing their concerns, and giving them the opportunity to understand and share in the realities of the marketplace (Figure 11-4).

FIGURE 11-4
Market debut.
Palo Alto Networks President and CEO Mark D. McLaughlin, along with members of his leadership team, celebrate the company's first day on The New York Stock Exchange by ringing the opening bell.
(Courtesy NYSE Euronext)

S-H-O-C the Troops

Enhancing credibility, being candid, and winning trust must be the primary employee communications objectives in the new century. Earning employee trust may result in more committed and productive employees. But scraping away the scar tissue of distrust that exists in many organizations requires a strategic approach.

The question is: How does management build trust when employee morale is so brittle?

Part of the answer lies in an approach to management communication built around the acronym S-H-O-C. That is, management should consider a four-step communications approach—built on communications that are **strategic**, **honest**, **open**, and **consistent**—to begin to rebuild employee trust.

- **First, all communications must be strategic.**   What strategic communication essentially boils down to is this: Most employees want you to answer only two basic questions for them:
  1. Where is this organization going?
  2. What is my role in helping us get there?

  That's it. Once you level with the staff as to the organization's direction and goals and their role in the process, even the most ardent bellyachers will grudgingly acknowledge your attempt to "keep them in the loop" (Figure 11-5).

- **Second, all communications must be honest.**   The sad fact is that while most executives may pay lip service to candor and honesty, in the end, too many turn out like the managements at Bear Stearns, Washington Mutual, Lehman Brothers, Countrywide Financial, and all the other 21st-century companies caught dissembling, obfuscating, pulling their punches, and eventually fading into oblivion.

  They seem to fear, as Jack Nicholson raged in *A Few Good Men*, that the staff "can't handle the truth."

  Such trepidation is foolish. For one thing, the staff already may discount anything management tells them. For another, you can't hope to build credibility through prevaricating or sugarcoating.

- **Third, all communications must be open.**   This is another way of saying that there must be feedback. The best communications are two-way communications. That means that no matter how large the organization, employee views must be solicited, listened to, and most important, acted on.

  That latter aspect is most important. Often, managers stage elaborate forums and feedback sessions, listen to employee gripes and suggestions, and yet do nothing. The key must be *action*.

- **Fourth, all communications must be consistent.**   Once you've begun to communicate, you must keep it up. Maintain a regular, on-time, and predictable program of internal newsletters, employee forums, leadership meetings, and reward celebrations.

  On-again, off-again communications or programs that start with bold promises only to peter out question management's commitment to keeping the staff informed.

  This obviously is wrong. Communications, if they are to work, must be steadily, sometimes painfully, consistent.[16]

Straight Talk NCH

Healthcare
System

A weekly update from management on the issues that matter most

March 15, 2012

Dear Friends and Colleagues,

"Be Aware for Safe Care."

That's the theme we have shared with colleagues throughout the system, as NCH strives to be a *"no guilt culture,"* where patient safety is a daily way of life for every one of us. To help us achieve that goal, NCH is a proud partner of the National Patient Safety Foundation. Our Patient Safety Awareness Task Force, led by Associate Chief Nursing Officer **Laurie Zone-Smith**, PhD, RN, NE-BC and Risk Manager **Barb Bixby**, RN was excited to participate very recently in Patient Safety Awareness Week.

Among last week's activities, we sponsored our very own Starbucks-like *"Safe Care Café,"* where we reviewed our ongoing hand washing initiative with an educational glow germ demonstration. The display revealed effectiveness in hand washing through applying a non-toxic invisible material to hands to simulate contact with germs, followed by normal hand washing, to see how much of the invisible material is left when hands are placed under a special glow light. I'm pleased that more than 95% of us have completed a hospital-wide hand washing initiative. (http://www.glogerm.com/using.html)

Attaining a *"no guilt culture"* means knowing whenever and wherever we can improve. Nearly half of national healthcare workers feel their mistakes and unfortunate events are held against them, according to a recent *American Medical News* report. In our own confidential patient survey last year, 97% of the 544 respondents rated NCH "very good" or "excellent." With "5" representing a possible perfect score for patient safety, we recorded a 3.96. We are repeating this confidential inquiry this year and are hopeful for improvement. I will let you know the results.

Meanwhile, we are actively focusing on areas for self-improvement in patient safety. Our profession has been criticized in the past for not being proactive, transparent or self-correcting. We are doing much to counteract that impression. For example, the Florida Hospital Association, where I am privileged to participate on the Quality Committee, reported that more than 25% of Florida's 400 hospitals have participated in a collaborative effort to decrease readmissions. That resulted in 11% fewer readmissions statewide, saving $25 million. Additionally, 67 Florida hospitals are participating in the nation's largest surgical quality effort to decrease surgical site infections, prevent urinary tract infections post-op, and improve both colectomy (bowel resection) outcomes and surgical outcomes in the elderly (http://www.fha.org/patientsafety/safteytoolkit.html). Another state program, of which NCH was an initial member, targets the prevention of blood stream infections. Proudly, NCH has not had a central line infection for many months in the following units—North Naples ICU for 10 months, Progressive Care and Surgical ICU 15 months, Downtown ICU 22 months and Cardiovascular Unit 25 months, a significant achievement.

All in all, NCH continues to devote considerable resources to improving healthcare for ourselves, our community and our country by sharing best practices in all quality areas. One of our most important objectives is to make NCH safer for our patients. Achieving this mandate is not only lifesaving for patients, but also helps all of us feel better about what we do every day, and burnishes our reputation as a nationally-ranked healthcare provider. All of this underscores the recognition of Southwest Florida as a medical tourist attraction, helping our economy recover. So being *"aware for safe care"* helps us all.

Respectfully,

Allen

Allen S. Weiss, M.D., President and CEO
P.S. Feel free to share *Straight Talk* and ask anyone to email me at allen.weiss@nchmd.org to be added.

FIGURE 11-5 In the loop.

Employees at NCH Healthcare System in Naples, Florida, know what's going on around them, as long as they read the weekly email update from their CEO.
(Courtesy NCH Healthcare)

Employee Communications Tactics

Once objectives are set, a variety of techniques can be adopted to reach the staff. The initial tool again is research. Before any communications program can be implemented, communicators must have a good sense of staff attitudes.

Internal Communications Audits

Both a strategy and a tactic, the internal communications audit is the most beneficial form of research on which to lay the groundwork for effective employee communications. Ideally, this starts with old-fashioned, personal, in-depth interviews with both top management and communicators. It is important to find out from top management what it "wants" from the communications team. It is also important to find out what communicators "think" management wants. Often the discontinuities are startling. The four critical audit questions to probe are:

1. How do internal communications support the mission of the organization?
2. Do internal communications have management's support?
3. Do internal communications justify the expense?
4. How responsive to employee needs and concerns are internal communications?[17]

Online Communications

The age of online communications has ushered in a whole new set of employee communications vehicles—from instant messaging to email to voicemail to tailored organizational intranets to employee and CEO blogs. Such vehicles are more immediate than earlier print versions. They reach employees at their desks and are more likely to be read, listened to, and acted on. Indeed, employees without computer access are increasingly losing their "voice" and ability to be heard, especially the ability to submit ideas for improvement or to access a company intranet remotely.

Online communications also have the capability of reaching virtual employees at their desks in their homes, on their handheld devices, in their cars, or wherever they remotely may be.

As print publications become steadily fewer, tailored online newsletters have begun to replace them. In many cases, organizations are using print vehicles to push readers to new intranet portals.[18]

Among growing online, internal communications vehicles are the following:

■ *Blogs* provide an easy way for employees to post opinions and views of the company on the Internet.

■ *Podcasts*, in which audio or video monologue, interview or on-location content is broadcast online to employees. At Hewlett-Packard, for example, division presidents are podcasting discussions of new products and organizational developments with rank-and-file employees. The HP podcasts have proven immensely popular.[19]

■ *Wikis,* a dynamic Website to which any user can add pages, modify content, and comment on existing content, may be better suited than a blog for a smaller group, and their ability to provide instant interactive capabilities is unmatched.[20]

In addition to these online tactics, social media, primarily through Facebook and Twitter, have caused companies to adopt specific social media policies and strategies, which we will discuss in a moment.

The Intranet

Today, in many organizations, the intranet has overtaken and even emulsified print communications. Intranet investments remain strong as companies continue to convert sites to portal technology and add streaming video capability. At IBM, for example, where just about everyone is computer savvy, the company has eliminated every other internal communications medium but the corporate intranet to reach IBM's 300,000 employees.[21]

At British American Tobacco, 25,000 intranet users can create their own Facebook-like profiles and networks by linking with other members. Members of the company's *Connect* network can link up with others in the 40-country company through a variety of social media derivatives.[22]

Unfortunately, having an intranet site doesn't mean employees will necessarily go there for information. Sites high in visual appeal but low in usefulness will likely be ignored. To prevent that, intranet creators should keep in mind several important considerations, learned early on in the intranet experience:

1. **Consider the culture.** If the organization is generally collaborative and collegial, it will have no trouble getting people to contribute information and materials to the intranet. But, if the organization is not one that ordinarily shares, a larger central staff may be necessary to ensure that the intranet works.

2. **Set clear objectives and then let it evolve.** Just as in setting up a corporate Website, intranets must be designed with clear goals in mind: to streamline business processes, to communicate management messages, and so on.

3. **Treat it as a journalistic enterprise.** Company news gets read by company workers. Employees must know what's going on in the company and complain bitterly if they are not given advance notice of important developments.

4. **Market, market, market.** The intranet needs to be "sold" within the company. Publicize new features or changes in content. Weekly emails can be used to highlight noteworthy additions and updates.

5. **Link to outside lives.** Some CEOs may not recognize it, but employees have lives outside the corporation. An intranet site that recognizes that simple fact can become quite popular.

6. **Senior management must commit.** Just like anything else in an organization, if the top executive is neither interested nor supportive, the idea will fail. Therefore, the perceived value of an organization's intranet will increase dramatically if management actively supports and uses it.[23]

Print Publications

The advent of online internal communications has been hard on print publications. It's happening all over corporate America.

Print defenders argue that print still must play a role, particularly in helping create a "climate" that bears the stamp of management (Figure 11-6). After British Petroleum suffered the disastrous spill in the Gulf of Mexico in 2010 (see Case Study, Chapter 1),

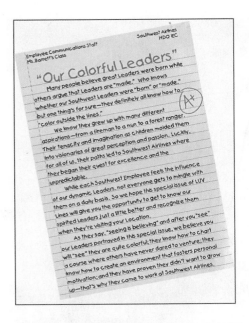

FIGURE 11-6
Prince of print.
Southwest Airlines is a one-of-a-kind company, thanks principally to its founder and former CEO Herb Kelleher. For five decades, Kelleher helped build a climate of creativity, productivity, and fun at Southwest by sponsoring some of the most far-out internal print publications ever seen on this planet (and perhaps any other!).
(Reprinted courtesy of Southwest Airlines)

the company used its internal publication, "Planet BP," to update employees on the efforts to clean up the gulf and help damaged communities.[24]

Writing and editing employee newsletters are traditional entry-level public relations responsibilities (your author was one who started as internal newsletter editor). In many firms, the mandate is to integrate print and online publications, with each vehicle realizing a different communication objective (Figure 11-7).

One organization devoted originally to internal communications, the International Association of Business Communicators (IABC), founded in 1970, has come to rival the older Public Relations Society of America. With more than 15,000 members throughout the United States and in 80 countries, the IABC helps set journalistic standards for internal communicators of both print and online publications.

FIGURE 11-7
Edgy photo.
Publicity photos for internal and external uses don't have to be mundane. So when the CN Tower in Toronto, declared one of the modern Seven Wonders of the World by the American Society of Civil Engineers, created a publicity photo, it captured the world's highest full circle hands-free walk, 168 stories above the ground.
(Courtesy CN Tower)

Bulletin Boards

Bulletin boards—not necessarily *electronic* ones but the decidedly low-tech kind—may be among the most ancient of employee communications vehicles, but they have made a comeback in recent years.

For years, bulletin boards were considered second-string information channels, generally relegated to the display of federally required information and policy data for such activities as fire drills and emergency procedures. Most employees rarely consulted them. But the bulletin board has experienced a renaissance and is now being used to improve productivity, cut waste, and reduce accidents on the job. Best of all, employees are taking notice.

How come?

For one thing, yesterday's bulletin board has become today's news center. It has been repackaged into a more lively visual and graphically arresting medium. Using enlarged news pictures and texts, motivational messages, and other company announcements— all illustrated with flair—the bulletin board has become an important source of employee communications (Figure 11-8).

Suggestion Boxes and Town Hall Meetings

Two other traditional staples of employee communication are the suggestion box and the town hall meeting.

In the old days, suggestion boxes were mounted on each floor, and employees, often anonymously, deposited their thoughts on how to improve the company and its processes and products. Often rewards were awarded for the most productive or profitable suggestions.

ETHICS
QUESTIONS OR CONCERNS

Setting the Standard

For help...

STEP 1

Contact your supervisor. If necessary, take it up the chain of command at your location.

STEP 2

Contact your Company Ethics Officer in person, by phone, or by mail.

LMASC Ethics Director:	Tom Salvaggio
Location:	B-2, 2nd Floor, Col. 28
Phone:	Helpline Coordinator, (770) 494-3999
Mailing Address:	LMASC Ethics Office
	P O Box 1771
	Marietta, GA 30061

STEP 3

If the first two steps do not resolve the matter, contact the Corporate Office of Ethics and Business Conduct for confidential assistance:

Helpline:	800 LM ETHIC (800 563-8442)
Fax:	(818) 876-2082
Or Write:	Corporate Office of Ethics and Business Conduct
	Lockheed Martin Corporation
	P O Box 34143
	Bethesda, MD 20827-0143

STEP 4

Contact the Department of Defense Hotline to report fraud, waste and abuse, and/or security violations.

Hotline:	800 424-9098
Or Write:	Defense Hotline
	The Pentagon
	Washington, DC 20301-1900

IDENTITIES OF WRITERS AND CALLERS ARE FULLY PROTECTED.

LOCKHEED MARTIN

FIGURE 11-8
Comeback kid. Among important announcements included on organizational bulletin boards are updates on key corporate issues such as ethical questions and concerns.

Today, the only necessity in implementing a successful suggestion box program is to ensure that there is "feedback"—that is, that management takes action to deal with valid suggestions and then communicates what it did to respond.

Town hall meetings are large gatherings of employees with top management, where no subject is off limits and management–staff dialogue is the goal. That was the conclusion of one study of 200 employees, some of whom labeled these vehicles "charades, phony, management games, and a joke."[25]

Town hall meetings must encourage unfettered two-way communication. That is, when managers tell town hall meeting goers they will "look into" something or "get action" on something, they need to do it. If not, they impair their own credibility.

Internal Video

As important as YouTube and broadcast and cable television are as communication media in society today, video has had an up-and-down history as an internal communications medium. On the one hand, internal television, including streaming video, can be demonstrably effective. A 10-minute Web video of an executive announcing a new corporate policy imparts hundreds of times more information than a podcast of that same message, which in turn contains hundreds of times more information than a printed text of the same message.

On the downside, internal video is a medium that must be approached with caution. Unless video is of broadcast quality, few will tolerate it—especially an audience of employees weaned on television. So there are always risks in producing an internal video.

The keys to any internal video production are first to examine internal needs; next to plan thoughtfully before using the medium; and finally to keep it short and keep it exciting.[26] Broadcast quality is a tough standard to meet. If an organization can't afford high-quality video, it shouldn't get involved.

Face-to-Face Communications

The best communications vehicle to reach employees is neither online nor social, but rather face-to-face, preferably from a supervisor. Supervisors, in fact, are the preferred source for the vast majority of employees, making them the top choice by far. The reason is obvious. You report to your supervisor, who awards your raise, promotes you, and is your primary source of corporate information.

Some departments formalize the meeting process by mixing management and staff in a variety of formats, from gripe sessions to marketing or planning meetings. Many organizations embrace the concept of skip-level meetings in which top-level managers meet periodically with employees at levels several notches below them in the organizational hierarchy. As with any other form of communication, the value of meetings lies in their substance, their regularity, and the candor managers bring to face-to-face sessions.[27]

Outside the Lines

Takes Juan to Know Juan

In 2010, National Public Radio (NPR) unceremoniously dumped longtime news analyst Juan Williams for saying, on Fox News, that he got nervous upon seeing people in "Muslim garb" on an airplane.

NPR CEO Vivian Schiller's decision to dump the popular analyst was met with outrage from employees. So Schiller sent an internal memo to ease concern. In the follow-up,

she spelled out the reasons for showing Mr. Williams the door. Among them:

■ The role of an NPR journalist is distinctly different from that of a new commentator. She said news analysts, like Williams, may not take personal public positions on controversial issues, because it undermines their credibility as analysts.

■ She said NPR brass had many conversations and issued warnings over the years, but that Mr. Williams continued to violate this principal.

■ Mr. Williams' comments on Fox news, in addition to others he made in the past, violated NPR's code of ethics. She pointed out that in appearing on TV or other media, NPR journalists should not express views they would not air in their role as an NPR journalist. Further, she said they should not participate in shows that encourage *"punditry and speculation rather than fact-based analysis."*

■ She said Mr. Williams' comments on Fox violated NPR standards and offended many in doing so.

■ When making media appearances outside their role at NPR, journalists are still expected to adhere to NPR standards. She concluded that the decision was a tough one.

Schiller's candid note to the staff, exposing Williams' past infractions, didn't do much to endear the executive's

decision to the staff. Within months, it was Schiller, herself, who was shown the door by NPR's board of directors (Figure 11-9).*

FIGURE 11-9   NPR...No President Remaining.
After National Public Radio President Vivian Schiller fired correspondent Juan Williams in 2011, the president, herself, was the next to go in the fallout from the firing.
(Photo: LUCAS JACKSON/REUTERS/Newscom)

*For further information, see Mark Memmott, "NPR CEO Vivian Schiller Resigns after Board Decides She Should Go," NPR, March 9, 2011.

Internal Social Media

The popularity of social media among employees has caused problems for employers. About half of U.S. employers block their employees from using social media sites at work.

Typical was the experience of Procter & Gamble, which blocked 129,000 employees from accessing video-streaming site Netflix and music site Pandora. Why? Employees were watching so many movies and downloading so many songs, it was "hobbling the company's digital backbone to the point of slowing down Internet service."[28]

An increasing number of companies have social media policies. The best are based in common sense.

■ Best Buy's policy is underpinned by an approach that dictates: "Be smart. Be respectful. Be human." Because Best Buy's 170,000 employees are mostly young people, the company allows employees to use social media, including sponsoring a "Watercooler" online forum that allows employees to voice concerns, uncensored by management. Employees also participate in great numbers in the company's "Twelpforce" Twitter account, which is also open to customers.[29]

■ FedEx "moderates," that is, reviews, all comments posted to its internal blog. Blog comments are screened for relevance to the topic and compliance with the company's "Rules of Engagement." Email addresses are mandatory for posted comments.

- Wells Fargo, too, moderates all comments on its internal community blogs, ensuring that submissions subscribe to guidelines relative to such things as personal attacks, offensive language, confidential information, or spam designed to sell products.

- Walmart reminds any of its 2.2 million associates around the world that if they want to use any of the company's Twitter sites—among them, "walmartmeeting," "samsclubrobert," and "walmartgames"—they must identify themselves on a "landing page" where identities are captured.

Just like any other communications vehicle, for social media to be effective within an organization environment, it (1) must have a business purpose, (2) be entertaining as well as informative, and (3) be composed of riveting content.

The Grapevine

In far too many organizations, it's neither print nor social media that dominate communication but rather the company grapevine. The rumor mill can be treacherous. As one employee publication described the grapevine:

Once they pick up steam, rumors can be devastating. Because employees tend to distort future events to conform to a rumor, an organization must work to correct rumors as soon as possible.

Identifying the source of a rumor is often difficult, if not impossible, and it's usually not worth the time. However, dispelling the rumor quickly and frankly is another story. Often a bad-news rumor—about layoffs, closings, and so on—can be dealt with most effectively through forthright communication. Generally, an organization makes a difficult decision after a thorough review of many alternatives. The final decision is often a compromise, reflecting the needs of the firm and its various publics, including, importantly, the workforce.

In presenting a final decision to employees, management often overlooks the value of explaining how it reached its decision.

A company grapevine can be as much a communications vehicle as internal publications or employee meetings. It may even be more valuable because it is believed, and everyone seems to tap into it.

Last Word

The best defense against damaging social media discussion and grapevine rumors is a strong and candid internal communication system. Employee communication, for years the most neglected communications opportunity in corporate America, is today much more appreciated for its strategic importance. Organizations that build massive marketing plans to sell products have begun today to apply that same knowledge and energy to communicating with their own employees.

A continuing employee relations challenge for public relations communicators is to work hand in hand with human resources officials. In the 1950s, personnel departments began to change their name to "human resources" to more accurately reflect the personal focus of their responsibilities. Over the past half century, human resources functions have concentrated on such areas as organization, staffing, benefits, and recruitment rather than communications.

The responsibility for communicating to employees has largely fallen on the public relations function, which must coordinate its initiatives with human resources priorities to create a culture of professionalism, accountability, and candor.

In the 21st century, organizations have no choice but to build rapport with and morale among employees. The shattering of morale and distrust of top management prevalent in the early years of the century will take time to repair. Building back internal credibility is a long-term process that depends on several factors—among them, listening to employees, developing information exchanges to educate employees about changing technologies, empowering them with new skills and knowledge through strategic business information they require, and adapting to the new culture of job "mobility" that is replacing job "stability."

Most of all in this new century, effective employee communications requires openness and honesty on the part of senior management. Public relations professionals must seize this initiative to foster the open climate that employees want and the two-way communications that organizations need.

Discussion Starters

1. What societal factors have caused internal communications to become more important today than in the past?
2. What is the general mood of the employee public today?
3. What are the key elements to effective employee relations?
4. What are some important employee communications strategies today?
5. What are the key questions of an employee communications audit?
6. What is the status of internal print communications?
7. What are the key considerations in communicating through an intranet?
8. How should an organization respond to and use social media with employees?
9. What are the primary considerations in adopting internal social media?
10. What is the best way to combat the grapevine?

Pick of the Literature

Inside the Organization: Perspectives on Employee Communications

Jack LeMenager, Winchester, MA: Fells Publishing, 2011

Communications counselor LeMenager was driven to write this book in the wake of the raft of downsizings in the newspaper industry and others in the second decade of the 21st century.

The book's overriding theme is to treat employees as "human beings," especially in terms of trusting them and letting them know what's going on around the organization at which they spend most of their daily lives. It is a modern-day, common sense approach to internal communication, emphasizing such pertinent 21st-century issues as "communicating after layoffs," "keeping connected after a merger," and "the value of saying 'thank you.'"

LeMenager also offers advice on the more prosaic areas of employee communication, including counseling management, winning converts in meetings, and creating effective communication plans.

Case Study

Consultant Drops F-Bomb, Chrysler Drops Consultant

Beware the perils of social media—especially if you're an employee.

That's the mantra that everyone who works for anyone else today must keep in mind, as the temptations of the thumb, launching that Facebook response or tweet, perpetually loom.

Case in point: The sad saga of an employee of New Media Strategies (NMS), ironically a social media advisory firm, who accidentally dropped the dreaded f-bomb in a tweet from client Chrysler's Twitter account. The employee was exasperated with the navigating habits of Detroit drivers, so he tweeted, "I find it ironic that Detroit is known as the motor city and yet no one here knows how to f-ing drive!"

Why the employee was tweeting at the wheel was unknown. But what was known was that the consulting firm employee thought he was tweeting from a private Twitter account. He wasn't. Rather, the New Media staffer was logged into the @ChryslerAutos account.

As the world was soon to learn.

Ghost Tweeting

How, you might ask, did the consulting firm employee have access to the Chrysler Twitter account? The answer is that Chrysler, like many organizations and celebrities, hires others to write tweets throughout the day. This so-called ghost tweeting appears to come directly from the sender but, like other public relations vehicles such as speeches and testimony, is actually anonymously authored by public relations professionals.

After the expletive went out, it was quickly deleted. But with social media, once you press "send," you're stuck. The original expletive tweet was retweeted by several Chrysler followers and spread to blogs. Chrysler was duly embarrassed about the remarks about its headquarters city.

Said a Chrysler spokesperson, "Even if it had gone out under their private account, we would have had issues with it as indirectly referenced a Chrysler ad and violated the company's policy about texting while driving."

The fact that NMS chose to fire the employee for the tweeting lapse was scant consolation to the Chrysler client. The day after the tweet went out, Chrysler relieved NMS of its consulting duties, with Chrysler tersely announcing that "NMS's contract will not be renewed for the balance of 2011."

The CEO of NMS issued a statement that the agency "regrets this unfortunate incident. It certainly doesn't accurately reflect the overall high-quality work we have produced for Chrysler. We respect their decision and will work with them to ensure an effective transition of this business going forward."

But evidently the NMS CEO himself had incurred the wrath of his Chrysler clients for talking about the company's two-minute Super Bowl ad, headlined "Imported from Detroit" and starring Detroit native Eminem, the Friday before the game on a national TV news program; Chrysler had earlier sworn staff and agencies to secrecy about Eminem's use until kickoff (Figure 11-10).

FIGURE 11-10 **Will the real Slim Tweety please shut up!** Chrysler spokesperson and outspoken Detroit native Eminem was positively deferential compared to the company's tweet-happy former social media agency. *(Photo: Detroit Free Press/MCT/Newscom)*

For its part, Chrysler was unsympathetic to its former agency's apology.

One Chrysler staffer, in the wake of the flare-up, wrote on the automaker's blog, "The tweet denigrated drivers in Detroit and used the fully spelled-out F-word. It was obviously meant to be posted on the person's personal Twitter account and not the Chrysler Brand account where it appeared. So why were we so sensitive? That commercial featuring the Chrysler 200, Eminem, and the City of Detroit wasn't just an act of salesmanship. The company is committed to promoting Detroit and its hard-working people."

Public Relations v. Marketing

Underscoring the Chrysler f-bomb incident was the battle shaping up between the public relations and marketing departments as to who should be in charge of corporate social media.

In many companies, the two departments fight over social media turf and budget, just as public relations used to fight with human resources over the internal communication function. At Chrysler, social media interface was complicated, with the marketing department in charge of social media accounts that were "consumer facing," and the communication (public relations) department in charge of separate Twitter, Facebook, YouTube, and Flickr accounts that were meant to be "media facing."

The mixed responsibility of the social media function added to Chrysler's dilemma in responding in a coordinated manner to the errant tweet.

At other car companies, Jaguar and Land Rover, for example, a small internal communication group is responsible for social media postings. Social media, according to Jaguar-Land Rover's communication director, just makes sense.

"Communications is better trained and oriented to deal with the real-time and back-and-forth nature of social media," she explained.

Despite internal finger-pointing, it likely would have made little difference had social media been the province of public relations or marketing. The vulgar tweet went public with a slip of a consultant's thumb.

In that one instantaneous action, the consultant lost his job and his agency lost a client—a cautionary tale for any employee.*

*For further information, see "Chrysler Splits with New Media Strategies Over F-Bomb Tweet," *Advertising Age*, March 10, 2011; Stuart Elliott, "When the Marketing Reach of Social Media Backfires," *The New York Times*, March 15, 2011; and David Kiley, "What Lurks Behind Chrysler's F-Bomb? Social-Media Turf War," *Advertising Age*, March 14, 2011, pp. 1–20.

Questions

1. How do you feel Chrysler handled the tweet controversy?

2. What new internal client rules would you enforce were you the CEO of NMS?

3. Should social media report to marketing or public relations? Why?

4. What are the larger lessons here for any public relations professional?

From the Top

An Interview with Craig Rothenberg

Craig Rothenberg is vice president, Corporate Communication, with responsibility for organizational communication at Johnson & Johnson. Mr. Rothenberg is a driving force behind the Academy for Communication Excellence and Leadership, a first-of-its-kind program designed to further the professional and career development for communication professionals across the company. Mr. Rothenberg is on the faculty at the New York University School of Continuing and Professional Studies Master's Degree Program in Public Relations.

How would you assess the level of trust between management and employees?

Employees' trust in management is critical. Managers need to be credible and believable, so building trust is a critical task for communicators. Communication is one of the best levers for building trust in an organization. Communicating at a regular cadence and with the information that employees need to do their jobs efficiently and effectively is invaluable (and costs little!). You also build trust by listening—really listening—to employees. When companies do that, they foster a culture of trust, and that almost always correlates to the alignment of your workforce and better business outcomes.

What do employees want to know from management?
First, they want to know what's happening across the business. Updates—good and bad—to let employees know how the business is tracking and what's expected of them, and a regular cadence or rhythm are critical.

Second, employees want to have reasons to believe in the future, and know that there are clear plans and strategies in place to get the company to that future.

Third, employees want to know that the company's fundamental mission and purpose is unchanged from what it was when they first joined.

Are print publications still effective in dealing with employees?
In some cases they still are. While we have generally moved away from print publications, for some segments of our workforce, print is still the best way to reach them. That's mostly true for employees who work in a manufacturing or operations environment, where people do not have ready access to computers, and we need to rely on printed collateral and newsletters to share information.

Not surprisingly, much of our communications today is driven out to our employees electronically, and also through the many portals that connect our employees around the world.

How has the Internet affected employee communications?
Like everything else in business *and in life*, technology—not just the Internet—plays a major role in employee communications. With respect to the Internet specifically, we

recognize that employees have access to more information today than ever before. So we need to respect and appreciate that, and know that when we want employees to hear from us, we need to be early, nimble and frequent in our communications to them, especially when it comes to company information. That means utilizing multiple channels to get employees timely information, and also the perspectives of our leaders and management so they hear first (or at least very early) from the Company.

What can management do to improve the climate of trust within an organization?

Simply put, communication is key. When employees feel they have the information they need to fully operate, they are more trusting, more willing to exercise discretionary effort, and more likely to fight for the company.

A big part of communication is listening—arguably the biggest part. Establishing both formal and informal mechanisms to foster listening and enhanced communication may be the single most important thing leaders can do to build a climate of trust. And by the way, with that climate of trust, come better business outcomes, greater employee satisfaction and retention, an improved Company reputation/profile, and so much more.

What communications advice would you give any CEO?

Treat communication as the leadership and management function that it is. The best leaders I have worked with view the function of Communication, and the act of communicating, as "one of the most important things I do—every day." A CEO who treats the Communication function and transactions that way, invariably has a more aligned and engaged workforce.

What can students do to prepare for internal communications work?

Beyond all else—and I say this to my students and also the teams and individuals I have led through my years here—learn the business you are in. Learn it and be as knowledgeable about it as you can be, from the R&D side, to the supply chain . . . learn how products reach customers . . . learn how customers think about your Company's products and services . . . learn how they view and interact with the company . . . understand as much as you can, and include in that a deep understanding of the external environment . . . the competitive landscape.

Relating to and communicating with your workforce may be the most important thing you and the executive team do.

Public Relations Library

Davis, Allison (Ed.). 21 *Strategies for Improving Employee Communications.* Glen Rock, NJ: Davis & Company, Inc., 2005. Introduction to internal communication planning, measuring, acting.

Drake, Susan M., Michelle J. Gullman, and Sara M. Roberts. *Light Their Fire.* Chicago, IL: Dearborn Trade Publishing, 2005. Internal marketing to encourage employees to get with the program.

Duncan, Wendy. *Lead Employees to Success.* Parker, CO: Books to Believe In, 2010. An explanation of what constitutes an internal "leader."

Falcone, Paul. *101 Tough Conversations to Have With Employees.* New York: Amacom, 2009. The rules of engagement in dealing with employees.

Guffey, Mary Ellen, and Dana Loewy. *Essentials of Business Communications,* 9th ed. Mason, OH: South-Western, 2013. Comprehensive text on business communication.

Holtz, Shel. *Corporate Conversations: A Guide to Crafting Effective and Appropriate Internal Communications.* New York: Amacom, 2004. One of the most learned Internet experts presents a guidebook to managing all aspects of internal communications.

Leat, Mike. *Exploring Employee Relations,* 2nd ed. Burlington, MA: Butterworth-Heinemann, 2007. Used in colleges, this text is an excellent introduction to the art of dealing with employees.

MacDonald, Lynda. *Managing Email and Internet Use,* 2nd ed. London, England: Reed Elsevier, 2004. Solid review of the boundaries and legalities of internal email and Internet usage.

Quirke, Bill. *Making the Connections,* 2nd ed. Hampshire, England: Gower Publishing Limited, 2008. Outstanding analysis of how businesses can use internal communications to enhance everything from productivity to differentiation.

Ragan PR Daily and Ragan Report. Chicago: Ragan Communications. Daily online report and weekly newsletter, written in an irreverent tone, that captures the best and worst in internal communications.

Runion, Meryl. *Perfect Phrases for Managers and Supervisors,* 2nd ed. New York: McGraw-Hill, 2010. Among them: "synergize, dynamize, personalize."

Vengel, Alan. *20 Minutes to a Top Performer.* New York: McGraw-Hill, 2010. A primer on how to motivate, develop, and engage employees.

Xenitelis, Marcia. *Repositioning Employee Communications.* Camberwell, Australia: Communication at Work, 2009. The internal view from Down Under.

Chapter **12**

Government
Relations

Chapter Objectives

1. To discuss the prevalence of government at all levels of daily life and the impact that public relations plays in communicating the platforms and programs of legislators.

2. To review the unusual distinction that the practice of "public relations" has played in government history.

3. To discuss the use of public relations by the president and in government departments, agencies, and at the state and local levels.

4. To examine the role, responsibilities, and tactics of those who "lobby" the government to influence legislation.

FIGURE 12-1 "I hereby resign."
Traveling Press Secretary Rick Gorka was relieved of his duties by candidate Mitt Romney in the summer of 2012, after suggesting that discourteous members of the traveling press corps smooch an element of his anatomy.
(Photo: ERIK S. LESSER/EPA/Newscom)

In America, politics is a contact sport.

In the summer of 2012 in the midst of the presidential campaign, Republican Mitt Romney went overseas to meet U.S. allies. At his first stop in London, Romney, former head of the Olympics, told an interviewer that the British were rightfully concerned about security preparations for the summer games. The American press corps traveling with the candidate excoriated him for embarrassing his hosts. At the next stop in Israel, Romney complimented his hosts on their successful "culture." The rival Palestinians objected, and once again the U.S. press condemned Romney for his gaffes on foreign soil.

While Romney announced that, as was custom, he wouldn't criticize a sitting president while he was on foreign soil, President Obama's henchman extended no such courtesy to the challenger. Obama's perpetually glum-faced Press Secretary Jay Carney, a former journalist who replaced Obama's close friend and advisor Robert Gibbs, pointedly observed, "I think one thing news reports remind us of is that when American presidents, American senators and congressmen and would-be leaders—what they say is placed under a magnifying glass. It carries great impact."[1]

By the time the Romney party reached last stop Poland, nerves were so frayed that when a *New York Times* reporter yelled out a question to Romney about the trip's gaffes, Romney traveling press secretary Rick Gorka told her to kiss his posterior (in more descriptive terms). The video of Gorka's outburst went viral, and the traveling press secretary was relieved of his campaign duties[2] (Figure 12-1).

Such is the "contact sport" nature of politics.

Politics, especially the American kind, is also dominated by social media. In the 2008 presidential campaign, Barack Obama became the first candidate to use social media as a communication focal point—especially to reach younger voters. In August, after he had won his party's nomination, Senator Obama decided on a novel way to name his vice presidential pick—text messaging supporters at 3 o'clock in the morning:

> *Barack has chosen Senator Joe Biden to be our VP nominee. Watch the first Obama-Biden rally live at 3pm ET on www.BarackObama.com. Spread the word!*[3]

By 2012, 98% of Congress was using at least one social media platform, with 72% using the big three platforms of Twitter, YouTube, and Facebook. Both 2012 presidential candidates had digital media directors and were active social media users. The Obama camp, however, with close to 18 million Twitter followers and 27 million Facebook followers dwarfed the Romney efforts.[4] Obama won.

The practice of public relations, whether social media–based or not, is a huge factor in politics and government around the world. By 2012, the faith in governments across the globe—what with financial meltdowns, bank bailouts, near collapse of the European Union, censorship in China, nuclear disasters in Japan, and Arab revolutions in the Middle East—stood at an all-time low. According to the Edelman Trust Barometer, trust in global government showed the biggest decline in the survey's 11-year history.[5]

In light of the universal mistrust of government agencies and officials, the importance of honest and open communication can't be understated. This is the role of public relations in government work; although as we will see, in the United States, at least, the term "public relations" is rarely used in government.

Don't Call It "Public Relations"

It is ironic that the practice of "public relations"—so defined—has been barred from the federal government since 1913. Congress at the time was worried that those who inhabited the corridors of power might be tempted to use the privileges granted and the attention paid to them by the American people for the advancement of their own agendas or, heaven forbid, the promotion of themselves.

One wonders, therefore, how the legislators of that day would think of their 21st-century publicity-seeking successors.

Every day, the Washington, D.C., seat of the federal government is a public relations free-for-all, with 435 congressmen and congresswomen, 100 senators, 15 cabinet secretaries, and thousands of federal employees supporting them, all jockeying to make the morning newspapers and evening talk shows. One U.S. senator, Democrat Charles Schumer of New York, is legendary for holding press conferences every Sunday—some (most?) of dubious value—simply because Sunday is a notoriously slow news day. Schumer's push for personal publicity knew no bounds. On the state and local levels, where the situation is just slightly less blatant, politicians similarly jockey for attention in the media.

Legislators in the 21st century, it seems, have come a far distance from the days of President Dwight D. Eisenhower, a former general, who once famously remarked, "If the Army is good, the story will be good, and the public relations will be good. If the Army is bad, the story will be bad, and the public relations will be bad."[6]

Today, by contrast—good, bad, or indifferent; story or no story—politicians crave publicity; apparently, according to most Americans, in lieu of seeking meaningful policy change. Indeed, by the start of 2013, with the American government hopelessly mired in dysfunction, upwards of 80% of Americans "disapproved" of Congress and an abysmal 14% "approved."[7]

In many ways, the importance of constant government communications became more profound after the terrorist attacks on America on September 11, 2001.

The war on terrorism depended on candid, frank, and informative communications with the American people and the world. Said President Bush's first press secretary, Ari Fleischer, "The American people are appreciative of the forthrightness of the government. I think the government has an obligation to be forthright."[8]

"Why do they hate us?" the president asked rhetorically about the Muslim attackers and their sympathizers in his historic speech before Congress the week after the terrorist attacks.[9] To combat such hate and to reassure the American people about the goodness of the war effort, the government's public relations initiatives took center stage, particularly in the initial stages of the conflict. Ironically, it was Bush—not a particularly adept communicator—who put in place lasting public relations measures. Among those initiatives were the following:

- The White House created a permanent Office of Global Communications to coordinate the administration's foreign policy message and supervise America's image abroad.[10]

- Bush mounted the "bully pulpit" of the American presidency often in the first days of the war to win public support. In a riveting speech before Congress and the nation, Bush vowed: "I will not yield. I will not rest. I will not relent in waging this struggle. We will not tire. We will not falter, and we will not fail."[11]

- The position of Undersecretary for Public Diplomacy and Public Affairs was created in the State Department, immediately after the 2001 attacks, to work to convince the Muslim world of the true values and ethics of America. In 2005, to spearhead this effort, President Bush named his longtime, close public relations advisor, Karen Hughes, to be Undersecretary of State for Public Diplomacy and Public Affairs. Hughes was largely ineffective in the job.

Ironically, while George W. Bush and his administration used public relations to build support for the early stages of the war, they dissipated most of the nation's goodwill, so that at the end of Bush's presidency, with the nation facing ferocious economic crisis, the clout of the "bully pulpit" had withered. In his last months as president, Bush's popularity had sunk precipitously.

Enter a challenger gifted in oratory and steeped in the promise of "hope and change." Barack Obama's march to the White House in 2008 was built largely on his superior communication skills and the promises he offered. Obama used the media more than any previous president, even agreeing from time to time to be interviewed by the "enemy," staunchly conservative network Fox News. Unable to resurrect a damaged economy, Obama's communication prowess seemed to dissipate as the nation's economic fortunes languished. Nonetheless, Obama prevailed again in 2012.

It is indisputable that the practice of public relations is broadly represented throughout government—not only at the presidential level but in each government branch, in all government agencies, on the state and local levels, and also in lobbying the government to maintain or change legislation. All of these functions are part of the multiple levels of public relations communication in and around government.

Public Relations in Government

The growth of public relations work both with and in the government has exploded in recent years. Although it is difficult to say exactly how many public relations professionals are employed at the federal level, it's safe to assume that thousands of public relations–related jobs exist in the federal government and countless others in government at the state and local levels. Thus, the field of government relations is a fertile one for public relations graduates.

Since the 1970s, more than 20 new federal regulatory agencies have sprung up—including the Office of Homeland Security, the Environmental Protection Agency, the Consumer Product Safety Commission, the Department of Energy, the Department of Education, and the Drug Enforcement Administration. Moreover, according to the Government Accounting Office (GAO), more than 120 government agencies and programs now regulate business. As society is shaken by new problems, the government response is to create a new bureaucracy. Such was the case when the near-total collapse of the financial system in 2007–2008 gave rise to the Dodd-Frank Bill and another new agency, the Consumer Financial Protection Bureau.

The nation's defense establishment offers some 27,000 jobs for recruiting, advertising, and public relations—although, again, none are labeled "public relations" in Department of Defense (DOD) military and civilian positions. Indeed, with military service now purely voluntary and an increasingly difficult war on terrorism nearly a decade old, the nation's defense machine must rely on its public information, education, and recruiting efforts to maintain a sufficient military force. One 2009 audit found that the DOD budget to win "hearts and minds" increased by 63% in one year alone to $4.7 billion.[12]

As noted, the public relations function has traditionally been something of a "poor relation" in the government. In 1913, Congress enacted the Gillette Amendment, which almost barred the practice of public relations in government. The amendment stemmed from efforts by President Theodore Roosevelt to win public support for his programs through the use of a network of publicity experts. The law was a specific response to a Civil Service Commission help wanted advertisement for a "publicity man" for the Bureau of Public Roads. Congress, worried about the potential of this unlimited presidential persuasive power, passed an amendment stating: "Appropriated funds may not be used to pay a publicity expert unless specifically appropriated for that purpose."

Several years later, still leery of the president's power to influence legislation through communication, Congress passed the gag law, which prohibited "using any part of an appropriation for services, messages, or publications designed to influence any member of Congress in his attitude toward legislation or appropriations." Even today, no government worker may be employed in the "practice of public relations." Public affairs, yes. But public relations, no. As a result, the government is flooded with "public affairs experts," "information officers," "press secretaries," and "communications specialists."

Government Practitioners

Most practitioners in government communicate the activities of the various agencies, commissions, and bureaus to the public. As consumer activist and never-ending presidential candidate Ralph Nader has said, "In this nation, where the ultimate power is said to rest with the people, it is clear that a free and prompt flow of information from government to the people is essential."

It wasn't always as essential to form informational links between government officials and the public. In 1888, when there were 39 states in the Union and 330 members in the House of Representatives, the entire official Washington press corps consisted of 127 reporters. Today, as cutbacks have occurred in the ranks of mainstream media reporters, there has been a surge in niche media representatives, among the more than 2,000 full-time journalists covering the capital. In addition the contingent of foreign reporters covering Washington has grown to nearly 10 times the size it was a generation ago, with 1,500 foreign journalists based in the nation's capital.[13]

The closest thing to an audit of government public relations functions came in 1986 when former Senator William Proxmire, a notorious gadfly, asked the GAO to tell him "how much federal executive agencies spend on public relations."

At the time, the GAO reported that the 13 cabinet departments and 18 independent agencies spent about $337 million for public affairs activities during fiscal 1985, with almost 5,600 full-time employees assigned to public affairs duties. In addition, about $100 million was spent for congressional affairs activities, with almost 2,000 full-time employees assigned.

Now fast-forward to 2005, where a similar GAO report revealed that the Bush administration paid $1.6 billion—that's $1.6 *billion*—on advertising and public relations contracts over a two-and-a-half-year period, with $88 million spent in 2004 alone. The DOD spent $1.1 billion of that for recruitment campaigns and public relations efforts. A total of 54 public relations firms were contracted as part of this effort.[14]

And then, of course, there are the monumentally expensive campaigns for national office, in which virtually all spending is for public relations and advertising. By the summer of 2012, the Obama campaign had spent a record $400 million on its reelection efforts—and the campaign still had four months to go.[15]

Two Prominent Departments

Even before the war on terrorism, the most potent public relations voices in the federal government, exclusive of the president, were, first, the U.S. Department of State, and second, the U.S. Department of Defense. After the terrorist attacks of September 11, 2001, the communications importance of both increased, but their relative positions were reversed.

The State Department The State Department, like other government agencies, has an extensive public affairs staff, responsible for press briefings; maintaining secretary of state homepage content; operating foreign press centers in Washington, New York, and Los Angeles; as well as managing public diplomacy operations abroad.

In October 1999, as part of the Foreign Affairs Reform and Restructuring Act of 1998, the State Department inherited the United States Information Agency (USIA), from 1953 the most far-reaching of the federal government's public relations arms, devoted to "public diplomacy." USIA had been an independent foreign affairs agency within the executive branch created in 1953 by President Dwight Eisenhower. Its job was to explain and support American foreign policy and promote U.S. national interests through a wide range of overseas information programs and educational and cultural activities.

The State Department consolidated USIA's 6,352 employees, of whom 904 are foreign service personnel and 2,521 are locally hired foreign service nationals overseas. There are 2,927 civil service employees based in the United States, of whom 1,822 work in international broadcasting and 1,105 are engaged in USIA's educational and informational programs.

The director of the USIA had reported directly to the president and received policy guidance from the secretary of state. Under the 1999 integration plan, an undersecretary for public diplomacy and public affairs within the State Department was chosen to head the operation. The USIA's annual appropriation has exceeded $1 billion since the late 1980s.

In the 21st century, with America's motives for the war on terrorism challenged around the world, the former USIA's mission—"to support the national interest by conveying an understanding abroad of what the United States stands for"—has been modified to include new challenges:

- Build the intellectual and institutional foundations of democracy in societies around the globe.
- Support the war on drugs in producer and consumer countries.
- Develop worldwide information programs to address environmental challenges.
- Bring the truth to any society that fails to exercise free and open communication.

In its nearly half a century, the USIA was a high-level public relations operation and not without controversy. Under the direction of such well-known media personalities as Edward R. Murrow, Carl Rowan, Frank Shakespeare, and Charles Z. Wick, the agency prospered. In 2002, the Voice of America (VOA), the State Department's leading voice overseas, named veteran *Time* magazine correspondent David Jackson as director. Jackson lasted until 2006, when his relations with the BBG apparently grew frosty over charges that the board sought to "politicize" the VOA.[16] Jackson was succeeded by Dan Austin, a 36-year veteran of Dow Jones & Company. Current director of VOA is former ABC correspondent David Ensor.

The communication initiatives of the successor to USIA to spread the "gospel of America" are far-reaching. Among them are the following:

1. **Radio.**   VOA, which first went on the air in 1942, broadcasts more than 1,000 hours of programming weekly in 45 languages, including English, to an international audience of more than 100 million listeners. In 2006, the U.S. Congress appropriated $166 million for VOA. In addition to VOA, the USIA in 1985 began Radio Marti, in honor of José Marti, father of Cuban independence. Radio Marti's purpose was to broadcast 24 hours a day to Cuba in Spanish and "tell the truth to the Cuban people" about ruler Fidel Castro and communism. With Raul Castro having succeeded his brother in 2008 and Cuba–U.S. relations thawing a bit, it remains to be seen whether Radio Marti's mandate will change. In 2002, a new Arabic service, called the Middle East Radio Network or Radio Sawa, was instituted, with an initial budget of $22 million. Radio Sawa offered mostly Western and Middle Eastern popular songs with periodic brief news bulletins. In 2010, VOA added radio broadcasts in Sudan to coincide with growing U.S. interests in Southern Sudan.

2. **Film and television.**   VOA annually produces and acquires an extensive number of films and videocassettes for distribution in 125 countries. VOA produces more than 30 hours of television per week in 24 languages, from Albanian to Urdu. TV Marti in Cuba, for example, telecasts four-and-a-half hours daily.

3. **Internet.**   VOA uses a distributed network, including more than 14,000 servers in 65 countries, to deliver Internet content. News is also available via email subscription service in English and an increasing number of broadcast languages. Electronic journals were created to communicate with audiences overseas on economic issues, political security and values, democracy and human rights, terrorism, the environment, and transnational information flow.[17]

4. **Education.**   The agency is also active overseas in sponsoring educational programs through 111 bi-national centers where English is taught and in 11 language centers. Classes draw about 350,000 students annually.

The Defense Department   The importance of Department of Defense (DOD) communications has been intensified in wartime. The DOD's public affairs network is massive—3,727 communicators in the Army, 1,250 in the Navy, 1,200 in the Air Force, 450 in the Marines, and 200 at headquarters. The DOD public affairs department is headed by an assistant secretary of defense for public affairs, one of six direct reports to the deputy secretary of defense (Figure 12-2).

With the DOD consisting of more than three million active duty forces, reserves, and civilian employees, information is the strategic center of gravity. Communications must be organized, secure, and rapid to fulfill the department's mission.

Although each service has its own public affairs organization and mission, DOD's American Forces Information Service (AFIS) promotes cooperation among the various branches. AFIS is responsible for maintaining the Armed Forces Radio and Television Service, *Stars and Stripes* newspaper, communications training at the Defense Information School, and a variety of other functions (Figure 12-3).

Public relations efforts of the DOD in the 21st century have run the gamut from drawing universal praise to generating opprobrium. When the United States invaded Iraq in 2003, the department was lauded for "embedding" reporters with the troops in the field in order for Americans to get firsthand information about the battle.

By 2005, with the war now decidedly unpopular with the public and with much of the criticism focusing on the Guantanamo Bay detention center, a group of retired military officers took to the airwaves to defend the Bush administration. The soldiers, most of them generals, appeared frequently on talk shows as "analysts" on the war and its aftermath, frequently agreeing with the DOD. The only problem was, as *The New York Times* revealed three years later, most of the retired officers had ties to military contractors and were largely directed by the Pentagon. Said one retired Green Beret and former Fox News analyst about the "guidance" he received from DOD, "It was them saying, 'We need to stick our hands up your back and move your mouth for you.'" Clearly, the Pentagon's public relations initiative did little to endear the department with the media.[18]

By 2012, with unmanned drone attacks being criticized for killing civilians in Pakistan and Afghanistan, the industry that supplied drones to the DOD launched a full-scale public relations effort to deal with the fallout (see PR Ethics Mini-Case in this chapter).

Other Government Agencies   Beyond the State and Defense departments, other government departments also have stepped up their public relations efforts. The

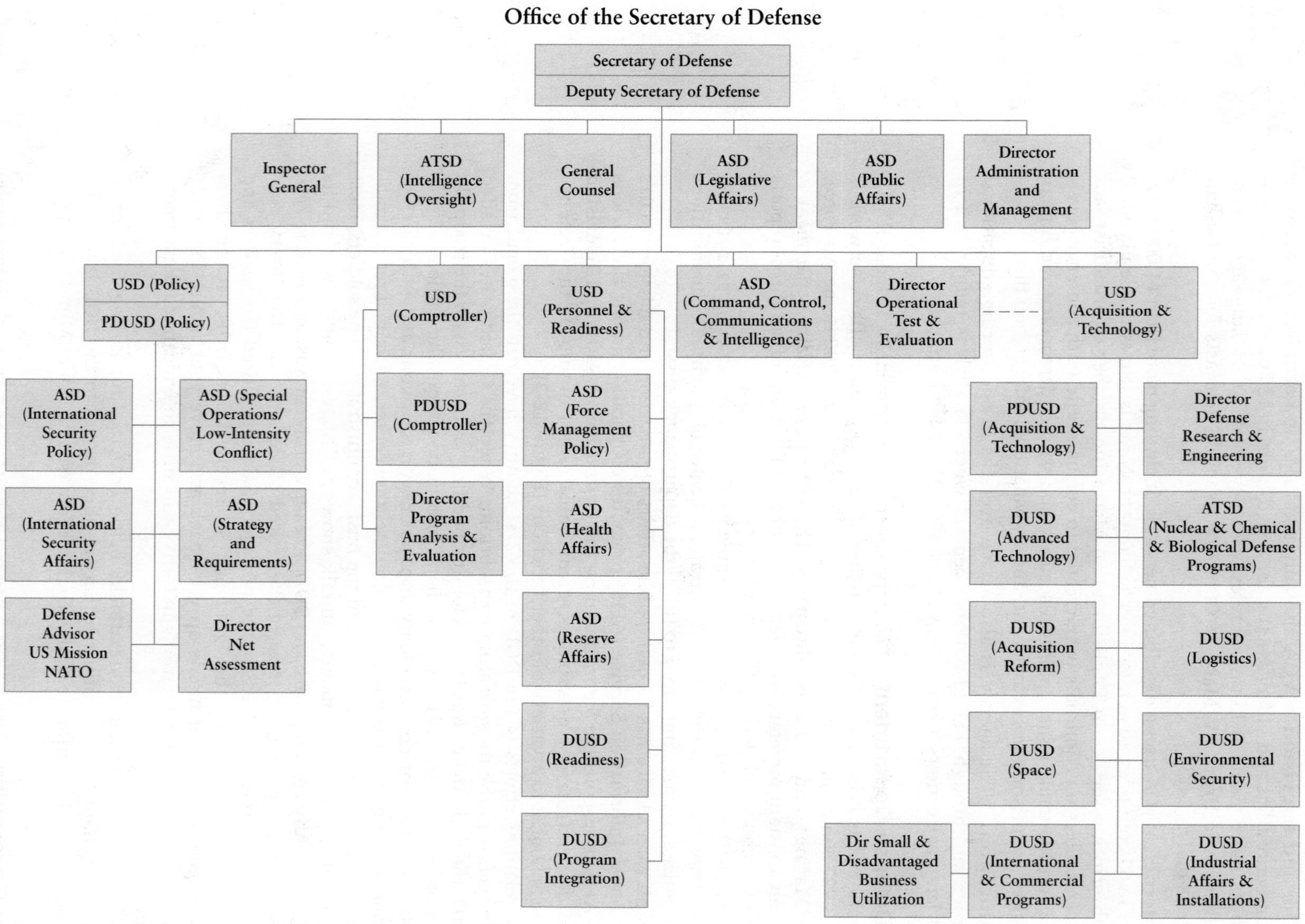

Office of the Secretary of Defense

FIGURE 12-2 DOD public relations organization.
The Assistant Secretary of Defense for Public Affairs was one of six who reported to the Defense Secretary's chief deputy. *(Courtesy of Department of Defense)*

FIGURE 12-3 **AFIS.** The primary mission of the American Forces Information Service is to integrate the vast communications resources of the various military branches under one communications umbrella. *(Courtesy of Department of Defense)*

Department of Health and Human Services has a public affairs staff of 700 people. The Agriculture, State, and Treasury departments each have communications staffs in excess of 400 people, and each spends more than $20 million per year in public relations–related activities. One of the most controversial public relations operations was housed in the U.S. Department of Homeland Security, created in 2003 to combine

PR Ethics Mini-Case

Drowning Out the Drone Attacks

Among the most significant weapons advances of the 21st century was the unmanned aviation vehicle, widely known as the missile-firing drone. Some drones were used to kill enemies; others used for remote surveillance.

By 2012, after drone attacks aimed at Al Qaeda fighters instead killed scores of civilians in the mountains of Pakistan, the drone industry found itself under mounting hostility not only from the poor people of Pakistan (Figure 12-4), but from the left and right in America as well. The opposition was fueled by reports of drone "scares," in particular when an unidentified flying object nearly collided with a plane over Denver and rumors circulated of a surveillance drone flying near the NATO summit in Illinois in the summer of 2012.

Some conservatives, concerned about privacy, called for a "ban on drones" and "shooting down drones." Liberals,

meanwhile, were equally aghast at the loss of innocent life due to drone attacks in overseas warzones.

Enter the Association of Unmanned Vehicle Systems International (AUVSI), the industry's trade group in Washington. The association president, Michael Toscano, a former manager of the Pentagon's robotics program, declared, "We're going to do a much better job of educating people about unmanned aviation, the good and the bad." One irritant to the AUVSI was the use of the term, "drones," itself. Said the president, "People who don't know what they're talking about say these are spy planes or killer drones. They're not." He said "remotely piloted vehicles" is the more accurate name.

Toscano set out on an aggressive media relations blitz to remind the public of the value of unmanned vehicles in war. "If you want to say we shouldn't be involved in these wars, that's fine. But if our military has already been committed to do this and we are putting men and women in harm's way, I want to do it with the least amount of risk to them."

As to the deaths of civilians in Pakistan, Toscano was equally candid. "Car crashes kill 35,000 people a year. But we don't talk about banning cars. We need to be honest about the costs and the benefits."

The other aspect of drones was that the technology responsible for them could also be used for humanitarian purposes, such as fighting forest fires or finding missing persons. In any event, drone industry executives seemed united in confronting their public relations problem.

Said Toscano, "This is like motherhood and apple pie for them. They concur we need to act. We can't stick our heads in the sand."*

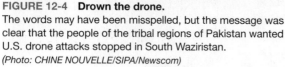

FIGURE 12-4   Drown the drone.
The words may have been misspelled, but the message was clear that the people of the tribal regions of Pakistan wanted U.S. drone attacks stopped in South Waziristan.
(Photo: CHINE NOUVELLE/SIPA/Newscom)

Questions

1. What do you think of the industry's public relations approach and messages in response to its critics?
2. Were you organizing the drone industry's public relations approach, what elements would you add?

*For further information, see "Jefferson Morley, 'Drones' New Weapon: P.R.," Salon.com, May 22, 2012.

the two dozen or so agencies that dealt with protecting the nation's homeland. Even the U.S. Central Intelligence Agency has three spokespersons. Out of how many CIA public relations people, you ask? Sorry, that's classified.

The President

Despite early congressional efforts to limit the persuasive power of the nation's chief executive, the president today wields unprecedented public relations clout. The president travels with his own media entourage, controls the "bully pulpit," and with it, a large part of the nation's agenda. Almost anything the president does or says makes news.

The broadcast networks, daily newspapers, and national magazines follow his every move. His press secretary provides the White House press corps (a group of national reporters assigned to cover the president) with a constant flow of announcements supplemented by daily press briefings. Unlike many organizational press releases that seldom make it into print, many White House releases achieve national exposure.

Prior to President Obama, Ronald Reagan and Bill Clinton were perhaps the most masterful, modern presidential communicators. Reagan gained experience in the movies and on television, and even his most ardent critics agreed that he possessed a compelling stage presence. As America's president, he was truly the "Great Communicator." Mr. Reagan and his communications advisors followed seven principles in helping to "manage the news":

1. Plan ahead.
2. Stay on the offensive.
3. Control the flow of information.
4. Limit reporters' access to the president.
5. Talk about the issues you want to talk about.
6. Speak in one voice.
7. Repeat the same message many times.

George H. W. Bush was not as masterful as his predecessor in communicating with the American public. Indeed, Bush met his communications match in 1992 when Bill Clinton beat him soundly in the presidential race.

The press had a love–hate relationship with President Clinton. On the one hand, Clinton's easygoing, "just folks" demeanor, combined with an unquestioned intelligence and grasp of the issues, was praised by the media. On the other hand, the president's legendary "slickness," accentuated by his false statements and downright lying to the American people during the Monica Lewinsky affair, caused many journalists to treat him warily.[19]

President Clinton's accessibility to the media—except during the saga with the White House intern—and his common sense approach to dealing with media were greatly responsible for his popularity, despite a series of embarrassing scandals afflicting his administration during both terms of his presidency. (Of course, a booming economy helped, too!)

George W. Bush, like his father, wasn't particularly comfortable with the press and public speaking. After the terrorist attacks of September 11, 2001, Bush delivered a historic speech before Congress, addressed workers at the World Trade Center site through a bullhorn, and conducted frequent press conferences in Washington and at his ranch in Crawford, Texas. The terrorist challenge of Bush's first term had awakened his communications instincts (Figure 12-5).

In his second term, however, particularly due to his premature announcement of "Mission Accomplished" in Iraq and disastrous handling of Hurricane Katrina in New Orleans, Bush's relationship with the media soured significantly. As his presidency limped to a close in 2008, Bush's public attempts to reassure Americans about the resilience of the falling economy were largely ignored, and his "approval rating" sunk to an unprecedented level of 27%, with 72% "disapproving."[20]

In his first months in office in 2009, President Barack Obama proved himself an adept communicator with a natural, easygoing, and believable style. Faced with

FIGURE 12-5
Hail to the public relations chief.
As a wartime president, George W. Bush, here with first-term Press Secretary Ari Fleischer, met the media challenge immediately after 9/11 with strength and confidence.
(Courtesy of the White House Photo Office)

mounting economic crises, Obama immediately became the most telegenic president in U.S. history, with daily televised press conferences and announcements characterizing his early presidential tenure. As the rigors of the presidency wore on and the nation's economy staggered along, Obama drew criticism, ironically, for "over-communicating" particularly on television, where some accused it of being, "All Obama All the Time."[21] In 2012, even though much of his early communications luster had worn off, Barack Obama proved worthy enough to stave off the Mitt Romney challenge and was reelected.

The President's Press Secretary

The press secretary to the President of the United States is the most visible public relations position in the world.

Some have called the job of presidential press secretary the second-most-difficult position in any administration. The press secretary is the chief public relations spokesperson for the administration. Like practitioners in private industry, the press secretary must communicate the policies and practices of the management (the president) to the public. Often it is an impossible job.

In 1974, Jerald ter Horst, President Ford's press secretary, quit after disagreeing with Ford's pardon of former President Richard Nixon. Said ter Horst, "A spokesman should feel in his heart and mind that the chief's decision is the right one so that he can speak with a persuasiveness that stems from conviction."[22]

A contrasting view of the press secretary's role was expressed by ter Horst's replacement in the job, former NBC reporter Ron Nessen, who said, "A press secretary does not always have to agree with the president. His first loyalty is to the public, and he should not knowingly lie or mislead the press."[23] A third view of the proper role of the press secretary was offered by a former public relations professional and Nixon speechwriter who became a *New York Times* political columnist, William Safire:

> *A good press secretary speaks up for the press to the president and speaks out for the president to the press. He makes his home in the pitted no-man's land of an adversary relationship and is primarily an advocate, interpreter, and amplifier. He must be more the president's man than the press's. But he can be his own man as well.*[24]

In recent years, the position of press secretary to the president has taken on increased responsibility and has attained a higher public profile. Jimmy Carter's press secretary, the late Jody Powell, for example, was among Carter's closest confidants and frequently advised the president on policy matters. He went on to found his own Washington public relations agency. James Brady, the next press secretary, who was permanently paralyzed in 1981 by a bullet aimed at President Reagan, later joined his wife, Sarah, to lobby hard for what would become known as the Brady Bill, establishing new procedures for licensing handguns.

Over time, the position of press secretary has been awarded more to career political public relations people than to career journalists. Larry Speakes, who followed Brady, was a former Hill and Knowlton executive and was universally hailed by the media for his professionalism. During Reagan's second term, Speakes apparently was purposely kept in the dark by Reagan's military advisors planning an invasion of the island of Grenada. The upset press secretary later apologized to reporters for misleading them on the Grenada invasion.

The next press secretary was a low-key, trusted, and respected lifetime government public relations professional, Marlin Fitzwater. His successor was another career political public relations professional, Dee Dee Myers, who was respected by the media and brought a refreshing perspective to her role as President Clinton's press secretary. She went on to become a cable talk show host and magazine editor.

The trend toward retaining experienced communications people continued in the second Clinton White House, with the president hiring political public relations veteran Mike McCurry. When McCurry left in 1998 to help form a new Washington public affairs agency, he was replaced by another public relations veteran, Joe Lockhart.

President George W. Bush appointed another government communications veteran, Ari Fleischer, as his press secretary. Upon taking over, Fleischer looked at the challenge optimistically, "I may be crazy, but I like working with reporters."[25] In his second term, Bush appointed his longtime Texas press aide Scott McClellan as press secretary.

McClellan, a member of a prominent Texas political family, had his hands full as White House reporters grew increasingly testy when Bush's second term ran into problems.[26] McClellan wilted under the pressure. His ineffectual performance as press secretary made him an easy target for the press and only added to Bush's public relations problems in his second term. In April 2006, McClellan was dumped and replaced by Fox News host Tony Snow. One year later, the bitter McClellan wrote a blistering, tell-all book about President Bush and the administration he had served.

Snow was everything his predecessor was not—smart, quick, self-assured. Snow regained the upper hand at the briefing podium, bringing a renewed sense of vitality and respect—both absent during the tenure of the hapless McClellan—back to the office of presidential press secretary. Snow was an iron-fisted charmer, standing up for his president but always delivering his message with confidence, flair, and humor. Some, like former White House operative David Gergen, objected to Snow's outspoken support of Bush and his policies. Tut-tutted Gergen, "If he is seen as wearing two hats, reporters as well as the public will inevitably wonder: Is he speaking to us now as the traditional press secretary, or is he speaking to us as a political partisan."[27] That Snow was a lightning rod for controversy only added to the credibility he brought to his job. And when Snow resigned from the White House to fight a battle with cancer, he received universal praise from friend and foe alike. Tony Snow died at the age of 53 in July 2008.

For his first choice as White House Press Secretary, President Barack Obama chose Robert Gibbs (see From the Top in this chapter), a career political public relations strategist who gained the new president's trust over four years as a wise and trusted advisor

(Figure 12-6). Gibbs, in the tradition of the best press secretaries, was an alter ego to Obama. Because of his closeness, Gibbs could speak with impunity and absolute confidence in the name of the president.

When Gibbs left the administration to help run Obama's reelection campaign, he was replaced by Jay Carney, a former *Time* magazine journalist and communications director for Vice President Joe Biden. Unlike Gibbs, Carney had no particular relationship with President Obama, and it showed. Carney was hesitant, uncertain, painfully deliberative in his responses, always giving the impression of "walking on eggshells" each time he responded to a reporter's question. Carney's shaky tenure as press secretary underscored the importance of a strong relationship between principal and spokesperson; which the unsteady Carney apparently didn't enjoy.

Over the years, the number of reporters hounding the presidential press secretary—dubbed by some "the imperial press corps"—has grown from fewer than 300 reporters during President Kennedy's term to around 3,000. During the Obama administration, the position of director of new media was created. With the White House having 1.7 million followers on Twitter, 500,000 fans on Facebook, and 70,000 email subscribers, the traditional power of the press corps following the president began to erode.[28]

Dealing with the media on an international stage is no easy task, and the role of press secretary is never simple nor totally satisfactory. As former press secretary McCurry, who began the practice of televising the daily White House press secretary press briefing, put it, "Having a single person standing at a podium and answering questions and trying to explain a complicated world is not a very efficient way to drive home the idea that government can make a difference."[29] Perhaps President Lyndon Johnson, the first chief executive to be labeled an "imperial president" by the Washington press corps, said it best when asked by a television reporter what force or influence he thought had done the most to shape the nature of Washington policy. "You bastards," Johnson snapped.[30]

Lobbying the Government

The business community, foundations, and philanthropic organizations have a common problem: dealing with government, particularly the mammoth federal bureaucracy. Because government has become so pervasive in organizational and personal life, the number of corporations and trade associations with government relations units has grown steadily in recent years.

The occupation of lobbyist has shown steady growth. The number of registered lobbyists in Washington, many of them situated along legendary K Street, totals 11,268, responsible for spending at an annual level of more than $3 billion—more than $8 million a day—to influence legislators and legislation.[31] Who spends the most to lobby the federal government? At the top of the lobbying chart was Exxon Mobil, which spent nearly $82 million over three years; next were Verizon Communications, General Electric, AT&T, and Altria.[32] Trade associations, led by the U.S. Chamber of Commerce, the American Medical Association, American Hospital Association, Pharmaceutical Manufacturers of America, and the American Association of Retired Persons, also spend millions annually to influence legislation.

Beyond federal government lobbying, state government and local lobbying is only slightly less active. In 2009, local, state, and territorial governments spent more than $83.5 million of taxpayer money lobbying federal lawmakers and public officials. And who leads the parade in local lobbying? Believe it or not, Puerto Rico—since 1998 the top overall spender on lobbying, beating all other states, cities, territories, and municipalities. The reason seems to be that Puerto Rico, a U.S. territory with only four million people, has one non-voting delegate in Congress. So the Island needs to spend money to ensure its voice is heard.[33]

To the uninitiated, Washington (or almost any state capital) can seem an incomprehensible maze. Consequently, organizations with an interest in government relations usually employ a professional representative, who may or may not be a registered lobbyist, whose responsibility, among other things, is to influence legislation. Lobbyists are required to comply with the federal Lobbying Act of 1946, which imposed certain reporting requirements on individuals or organizations that spend a significant amount of time or money attempting to influence members of Congress on legislation.

In 1995, the Lobbying Disclosure Act took effect, reforming the earlier law. The new act broadened the activities that constitute lobbying and mandated government registration of lobbyists. Under the new law, a lobbyist is an individual who is paid by a third party to make more than one "lobbying contact," defined as an oral or written communication to a vast range of specific individuals in the executive and legislative branches of the federal government.

Lobbyists, at times, have been labeled everything from influence peddlers to fixers to downright crooks. In 2005, with the admissions of convicted super-lobbyist Jack Abramoff—and his equally convicted public relations consigliore, Michael Scanlon—about luring members of Congress on golf outings and in the process ripping off Native American tribe clients for millions of dollars, the practice of lobbying reached a new low. President Obama made a point of going after lobbyists in his campaigns and State of the Union messages. But his Democrat colleagues, typical of Washington's tradition of not wanting to bite the hand that feeds it, failed to pass legislation in 2010 that would have required greater disclosure of donors to outside spending groups, an issue the president emphasized that year.[34]

Despite the slings and arrows and Congressional reluctance to do anything about the influence of lobbyists, the fact is that today's lobbyist is likely to be a person who is well informed in his or her field and who furnishes Congress with facts and information necessary to make an intelligent decision on a particular issue. This task—the lobbyist's primary function—is rooted in nothing less than the First Amendment right of all citizens to petition government.

What Do Lobbyists Do?

For sure, lobbying has become big business.

But what exactly do lobbyists do?

The essence of a lobbyist's job is to inform and persuade. The specific activities performed by individual lobbyists vary with the nature of the industry or group represented. Most take part in these activities:

1. **Fact-finding.** The government is an incredible storehouse of facts, statistics, economic data, opinions, and decisions that generally are available for the asking.

2. **Interpretation of government actions.** A key function of the lobbyist is to interpret for management the significance of government events and the potential implications of pending legislation. Often a lobbyist predicts what can be expected to happen legislatively and recommends actions to deal with the expected outcome.

3. **Interpretation of company actions.** Through almost daily contact with congressional members and staff assistants, a lobbyist conveys how a specific group feels about legislation. The lobbyist must be completely versed in the business of the client and the attitude of the organization toward governmental actions.

4. **Advocacy of a position.** Beyond the presentation of facts, a lobbyist advocates positions on behalf of clients, both pro and con. Hitting a congressional representative early with a stand on pending legislation can often mean getting a fair hearing for the client's position.

5. **Publicity springboard.** More news comes out of Washington than from any other city in the world. It is the base for thousands of social media, press, television, radio, and magazine correspondents. This multiplicity of media makes it the ideal springboard for launching organizational publicity. The same holds true, to a lesser degree, in state capitals.

6. **Support of company sales.** The government is one of the nation's largest purchasers of products. Lobbyists often serve as conduits through which sales are made. A lobbyist who is friendly with government personnel can serve as a valuable link for leads to company business.[35]

Emergence of E-Lobbying As it has in every other area of society and public relations work, the Internet has influenced the practice of lobbying as well. In terms of political campaigning and grassroots lobbying, as noted, the two-term Presidency of Barack Obama cemented the role of the Web in political campaigning. Obama became the first "digital presidential candidate." He raised millions in campaign contributions via the Internet. He announced his vice presidential running mate via instant messaging. He created a blog, "Fight the Smears," to extinguish scurrilous rumors. He had more than 1.5 million "friends" on MySpace and Facebook and 45,000 followers on Twitter. His facility with the Web allowed the Obama campaign to get its word out in lightning, unprecedented speed to vast numbers of voters.[36] The 2012 Obama campaign replicated the social media penetration.

The Obama campaigns were the greatest indication that social media and the Internet had changed politics and lobbying forever. One Democratic Website, in particular,

MoveOn.org, financed by the billionaire George Soros, was credited as "one of the most influential . . . organizations in U.S. politics."[37] Founded in 1998 by Clinton sympathizers opposed to impeachment and eager for the Congress to "move on," the site has become a rallying point for liberal issues. A host of conservative sites, including The Drudge Report, News Max, and Real Clear Politics, fuel the fervor on the other side of the aisle.

Political Action Committees

The rise of political action committees (PACs) has been among the most controversial political developments in recent years—second only to the rise in 2012 of the "super" political action committee (super PAC).

A political action committee is the name commonly given to a private group, regardless of size, organized to elect political candidates. In the mid-1970s, there were about 600 PACs. By 2009, there were more than 4,600 PACs, which are formed by companies, unions, or other groups to raise and spend money to help presidential and congressional candidates. The largest PACs were Emily's List, the Service Employees International Union, American Federation of Teachers, American Medical Association, National Rifle Association, Teamsters Union, and the like—all donating millions of dollars to get candidates elected.[38]

Each PAC can give a maximum of $5,000 to a federal candidate in a primary election and another $5,000 for the general election. The top 50 PACs contribute in excess of $60 million annually. An organization with many individual PACs can have a tremendous monetary influence on an election. And during an election, PACs are constantly seeking campaign contributions. Every day, in fact, political PACs reach out along these lines:

> *Rosemary—*
>
> *I'm here to tell you, really quickly, about why tonight's fundraising deadline matters.*
>
> *The past couple of months, our president has been vastly outraised by Republicans. Democrats in races across the country are up against the same thing, with outside groups pouring millions in to drag us down.*
>
> *If we don't stop this trend, and start closing the gap, 2012 could go down as the year that powerful special interests learned that elections can have a price tag.*
>
> *I'm not willing to accept that—and I hope you aren't either.*
>
> **I promise this will be the last email you get from me for a while.**
>
> *Will you help close that fundraising gap?*
>
> *https://my.democrats.org/July-Deadline*
>
> *Thanks,*
>
> *Debbie*
>
> *Debbie Wasserman Schultz*
>
> *Chair*
>
> *Democratic National Committee*
>
> *P.S.—We've got less than 100 days left until Election day. Thank you for everything you've done, and everything you do these next 98 days to* **help Democrats win.** *You won't regret it.*

PAID FOR BY OBAMA VICTORY FUND *2012*, *A JOINT FUNDRAISING COMMITTEE AUTHORIZED BY OBAMA FOR AMERICA, THE DEMOCRATIC NATIONAL COMMITTEE, AND THE STATE DEMOCRATIC PARTIES IN THE FOLLOWING STATES: CO, FL, IA, NV, NH, NC, OH, PA, VA, AND WI.*

Contributions or gifts to Obama Victory Fund 2012 are not tax deductible.

Democratic National Committee, 430 S. Capitol St. SE, Washington DC 20003

Source: Democratic National Committee

The increased influence of such groups on candidates is one reason why Senators John McCain and Russ Feingold led the Congress in 2002 to pass new strictures on campaign financing and particularly advertising for or against a candidate just prior to an election. But then in 2010, in the landmark case *Citizens United v. Federal Election Commission*, the U.S. Supreme Court held that the First Amendment to the U.S. Constitution prohibited the government from restricting independent political expenditures by corporations and unions.

And so the gate was lifted for the introduction of super PACs, groups able to accept unlimited political donations to use in favor of or against a particular candidate. In the 2012 campaign, the market was flooded with ads sponsored by the likes of former George W. Bush advisor Karl Rove's "Crossroads GPS," conservative billionaire brothers David and Charles Koch's "Americans for Prosperity," and billionaire casino owner Sheldon Adelson. All Republicans, these contributors helped Mitt Romney raise an unprecedented $140 million through July 2012.[39] Romney still lost the election.

While some pointed to super PACs as merely exercising free speech, critics argued that the tremendous amount of money being spent—mostly by Republicans—on negative advertising would unfairly influence elections and steer "political favors" to megadonors. And so, inevitably, in 2012 was born the first "anti-super PAC super PAC." Jonathan Soros, son of billionaire Democrat George, started a new super PAC aimed at lessening the impact of other super PACs. The younger Soros set out to use $5–$8 million for negative ads aimed at politicians who oppose campaign finance reform.[40]

Good luck. With the approval ratings of politicians at an all-time low, largely because of their never-ending quest for money, the likelihood that money and politics would be inextricably linked for the foreseeable future looked to be strong.

Dealing with Local Government

In 1980, Ronald Reagan rode to power on a platform of New Federalism, calling for a shift of political debate and public policy decisions from national to state and local levels. Presidents Clinton and Bush picked up the same initiative when they assumed power. But by the time the second decade of the 21st century rolled around, after financial system collapse, auto industry implosion, terrorism not only overseas but in Colorado, Wisconsin, and around the corner, and persistent economic problems, sentiment shifted back to a more fortified national government role and increased regulation. Indeed, this battle between federal vs. local government power largely framed the narrative of the 2012 presidential election.

Although the federal government's role in wielding power and employing public relations professionals is significant, state and local governments also are extremely important. Indeed, one viable route for entry-level public relations practitioners is through the local offices of city, county, regional, and state government officials.

Local agencies deal directly—much more so than their counterparts in Washington—with individuals. State, county, and local officials must make themselves available for local media interviews, community forums and debates, and even door-to-door campaigning. In recent years, local and state officials have found that direct

Outside the Lines

Congress of the Absurd

So you're one of those cynics who believes the U.S. Congress is the nation's biggest laughing stock. How dare you! On the other hand . . .

In the winter of 2010, with the Congress again putting off a decision to extend the Bush tax cuts lest voters accuse members of increasing taxes, they decided to change the subject. Specifically, a hearing was called to discuss the issue of the nation's migrant farm workers. To underscore the issue, Democrats invited comedian Stephen Colbert to testify before the Subcommittee on Immigration, Citizenship, Refugee, Border Security, and International Law, in character as a buffoonish right-wing anchorman (Figure 12-7).

Whaaaaa?

The stunt backfired immediately, with Republicans leaping to be heard.

"They've got time to bring a comedian to Washington, D.C., but they don't have time to eliminate the uncertainty by extending all of the current tax rates," thundered House Leader John Boehner. "All Democrats showed the American people with this stunt is how out of touch they are," the Republican National Committee wrote in introducing a quickie video entitled, "The Colbert Congress."

For his part, comedian Colbert must have felt emboldened. Two years later, he applied for and was granted permission to start a super PAC, "Americans for a Better Tomorrow, Tomorrow," and raised $794,000 to commit mayhem in the 2012 campaign for the White House.

The last laugh, cynics concluded, was on the taxpayers.*

FIGURE 12-7 Feelin' truthie.
Comedian Stephen Colbert greets a fan as he prepares to "testify" before Congress in 2010.
(Photo: TRIPPLAAR KRISTOFFER/SIPA/Newscom)

*For further information, see Russell Goldman, "Stephen Colbert Raises More Than PAC Backing Ron Paul," ABC News, April 25, 2012; and Byron York, "Unable to Govern, Dems Turn to Stephen Colbert," *The Examiner*, September 27, 2010.

contact with constituents—often through call-in radio programs—is invaluable not only in projecting an image but also in keeping in touch with the voters.

The public information function at state and local levels—to keep constituents apprised of legislative and regulatory changes, various government procedures, and notices—is a front-line public relations responsibility on the local level.

Last Word

The pervasive growth of government at all levels of society may not be welcome news for many people. But with the nation and the world confronting unprecedented economic challenges in the second decade of the 21st century, an increased government role is inevitable.

Government's growth has stimulated the need for increased public relations support and counsel. On the one hand, the importance of communicating directly with individual voters has become paramount for politicians. On the other hand, individuals disgusted with the system where "money talks" need communication mechanisms to fight back. Such was the case in 2011 when Starbucks CEO Howard Schultz launched an effort to convince his fellow CEOs to forego giving political donations to any candidate until Washington "delivers a fiscally, disciplined long term debt and deficit plan to the American people."[41] Valiant idea, but again, good luck!

The fact is we're stuck with this massive federal government bureaucracy, organized through individual agencies that seek to communicate with the public. The best news is that this means a vast repository of public relations jobs. Indeed, the most powerful government position in the Free World—that of President of the United States—has come to rely on public relations counsel to help maintain a positive public opinion of the office and the incumbent's handling of it.

On state and local levels, public relations expertise also has become a valued commodity. Local officials, too, attempt to describe their programs in the most effective manner. In profit-making and non-profit organizations alike, the need to communicate with various layers of government also is imperative.

Like it or not, the growth of government in our society appears unstoppable, particularly now that the United States is faced with continued economic challenges and engaged in a long-term war on terror. One direct outgrowth is that need for public relations support in government relations will clearly continue to grow in the 21st century.

Discussion Starters

1. Why is the public relations function regarded as something of a stepchild in government?
2. What is the current status of the Voice of America, and what are its responsibilities?
3. What is meant by the term *embedded reporter*?
4. Why was Ronald Reagan called the Great Communicator?
5. Contrast the performances of Scott McClellan and Tony Snow as White House press secretaries.
6. What are the objectives of government relations officers?
7. What are the primary functions of lobbyists?
8. What impact has the Internet had on lobbying?
9. What are the pros and cons of PACs?
10. What is the significance of the *Citizens United* Supreme Court case?

Pick of the Literature

All the Presidents' Spokesmen
Woody Klein, Westport, CT: Praeger Publishers, 2008

A former *Washington Post* reporter reviews the ups and downs of press secretaries through the ages. With forewords by former press secretaries Marlin Fitzwater and Dee Dee Myers, Klein discusses the special responsibilities that press secretaries share. The book begins with Franklin Roosevelt and his press secretary, Stephen Early. It then tracks through history through the presidency of George W. Bush, describing in some detail every press secretary to occupy the White House briefing room podium.

Klein focuses on seminal events, from Pearl Harbor and Vietnam to Richard Nixon's pardon and Hurricane Katrina. He extensively examines "spin" and how beauty—or more specifically, "truth"—lies in the eye of the administration and the spokesperson representing it.

Case Study | Anthony Weiner Texts His "Anthony"

There are many reasons why Americans don't trust, don't like, and don't want to put up with the arrogance that resonates among members of Congress. One, in particular, was a Democrat with a long face and huge ego, who hailed from the borough of Queens, New York.

Anthony Weiner, the congressman from Queens, was an up-and-coming Democrat star. A protégé of New York Senator Chuck Schumer, himself the most self-servingly successful publicity-seeker this side of Donald Trump, Weiner distinguished himself in 11 years in Congress as one of Washington's most savvy purveyors of public relations.

The combative and charismatic congressman was a familiar face on cable TV, even including the dreaded Fox News, where Weiner was a lone liberal willing to mix it up with antagonistic conservative hosts. Weiner was one of the only Democrats with nerve enough to battle with Foxcasters Don Imus or Megyn Kelly. And he gave as good as he got.

Weiner was also ambitious. Not content with the life of a low-clout, albeit highly recognized, congressman, Weiner had his sights set on replacing Michael Bloomberg as mayor of New York City in 2013.

Suicidal Sexting

But Congressman Weiner's talent led to unbridled arrogance, which, coupled with his failure to face reality and the unforgiving pervasiveness of the Internet, resulted in a fall from grace that was unprecedented in its velocity.

One day at the end of May 2011, Representative Weiner issued a strange announcement via Twitter. Weiner tweeted that his Twitter account had been hacked and a sexually suggestive photo sent in his name to a young woman in the Northwest. The photo, of someone's crotch, was removed from Congressman Weiner's Twitter account immediately. Nonetheless, reporters were intrigued.

But when they tried to follow up, the normally effusive congressman was uncharacteristically circumspect and more characteristically combative. He insisted his account had been hacked and attempted to deflect the conversation to "issues of much greater importance to our nation." When reporters pressed, he punched back, labeling one CNN journalist a "jackass" for refusing to desist in pressing the sexting issue.

Typical of Weiner's response to the controversy he couldn't quite get rid of was his tête-a-tête with ABC's Jonathan Karl.

> **Karl:** *"Is it inappropriate for a member of Congress to be following young women on a Twitter account?"*
>
> **Weiner** (snarling): *"That's outrageous. Ya know, that's really outrageous. The implication is outrageous. Your question had a pretty charged supposition, 'Do you think there's anything wrong with following young women on Twitter?' Do you really think that's a fair question?"*

Rep. Weiner evidently failed to understand that to a reporter in the 21st century, no issue is of "greater importance" than sex. He suggested to reporters that he had hired an Internet securities attorney to look further into the case. Nonetheless, the congressman made no calls to authorities; nor did he report the alleged account tampering, as was required by Congressional rules.

Despite his repeated attempts to change the subject, not only couldn't Weiner shake the controversy, his curious attempts at deflection served only to attract more journalistic interest.

Smile, You're on Stranded Camera

Within days of his staunch denials, Anthony Weiner started backtracking from his original story. His comments were less certain and more cagey, as if there might have been more to the story.

Within a week of the first revelation, the "more" of the story was announced by combative conservative blogger Andrew Breitbart, who claimed to have additional photos of women sent from the congressman's Twitter account; these photos were saucier than the original. Not only that, Breitbart had names of the women to whom the snapshots were sent. And he named them.

The truth, said Breitbart, was that Anthony Weiner, himself, had sent the suggestive photo—in fact, *a lot* of suggestive photos—for several years to a healthy list of female Twitter pals. It didn't help matters that the congressman had recently married a well-liked official in the Hillary Clinton State Department.

The next afternoon, Anthony Weiner staged a hastily called 4 p.m. press conference to set the record straight. The surreal press conference was one for the ages.

It began with Andrew Breitbart—yes, *that* "Andrew Breitbart"—taking the stage prior to the congressman arriving. Breitbart answered questions from the media about his role in the scandal. Weiner's aides evidently rushed to tell the congressman that his press conference was being hijacked by his accuser. Once Weiner arrived, he and Breitbart uncomfortably shared the stage for a stretch.

When Representative Weiner finally got a chance to make a statement, he broke down in tears, confessing that he had sent explicit photos and messages to at least six women and blatantly lied about it to anyone who asked. He apologized over and over to his wife and the women he had tweeted and took full responsibility for making "terrible mistakes" (Figure 12-8).

And, oh yes, he steadfastly refused to resign.

Rather, said Weiner, he would seek help for whatever it was that afflicted him, get cured, cooperate with any ethics investigation his colleagues thought appropriate, but then return to the House to complete the important business for which his constituents had sent him to Washington.

Not So Fast, Tweetie

Maybe Anthony Weiner saw no problem in returning to congressional action. But others had other ideas.

In the days following the press conference, news outlets and Websites began to report on other racy and explicit messages and photos from Weiner's online accounts to other women. The BigGovernment.com Website that published the first crotch shot

FIGURE 12-8 Don't cry for me, Anthony Weiner.
The final press conference. *(Photo: John Angelillo/UPI/Newscom)*

came up with another photo from another woman of a man's shirt-less torso. (Guess who?) RadarOnline.com reported that a Nevada woman claimed to have 200 explicit messages from Weiner via a Facebook account. Other sites leaked photos they claimed to be Anthony Weiner's genitalia.

Finally, three weeks after the emergence of the telltale tweets, Anthony Weiner called yet another press conference at a senior center in his Queens district. The press conference—interrupted yet again by a Howard Stern confederate screaming "pervert"—lasted all of four minutes.

Rep. Weiner made the following statement:

> *I am here today to again apologize for the personal mistakes I have made and the embarrassment I have caused. I am announcing my resignation from Congress, so my colleagues can get back to work, my neighbors can choose a new representative and most important so that my wife and I can continue to heal from the damage I have caused.*

And with that, mercifully, Anthony Weiner was gone.*

Questions

1. Had you been Anthony Weiner's public relations advisor, what would you have counseled him prior to going public about the tweets?

2. What general advice relative to social media communicating would you offer anyone in the public eye?

3. Do you think Anthony Weiner can make a political comeback? If he came to you with that question, what would you advise him?

*For further information, see Andrea Canning, "Rep. Anthony Weiner's Sexting Scandal: Why Did He Do It?" ABCNews.com, June 6, 2011; Raymond Hernandez, "Weiner Resigns in Chaotic Scene," *The New York Times*, June 16, 2011; and "Rep. Weiner Admits to Sending Lewd Twitter Photo, Acknowledges Other Explicit Conversations," FoxNews.com, June 7, 2011.

From the Top

An Interview with Robert Gibbs

Robert Gibbs served as senior advisor to President Barack Obama during the 2012 reelection campaign. Earlier, he was named the nation's 28th White House Press Secretary in January 2009. An experienced political public relations counselor, Mr. Gibbs was communications director for Senator Obama, for whom he had worked since 2004, and for Senator Obama's 2008 presidential campaign. Prior to that, Mr. Gibbs served as press secretary of Senator John Kerry's 2004 presidential campaign. He also served as communications director for the Democratic Senatorial Campaign Committee and for four individual Senate campaigns, including those of Mr. Obama in 2004 and Fritz Hollings in 1998. Mr. Gibbs was also press secretary for Congressman Bob Etheridge. (This interview was conducted after Mr. Gibbs' first 100 days as press secretary in the White House.)

How would you describe your job?
This is the most fun I've ever had in a job in my life. It is the best job that you could have.

What do you consider your primary mission as press secretary?
I am the primary representative for the President with the White House press corps. I help them get access to the information and facts they need to cover what the President does each day.

What is a typical day for the White House Press Secretary?

I try to be on the job about 6 o'clock in the morning, and sometimes I get home to read to my son at 8:30. But most nights, I'm not able to do that. And so far, we've worked every day of every weekend. The President, of course, lives above the "company store," which has its advantages!

How much access do you have to the President?

I see him every day in several meetings in the Oval Office. Most important, if I need anything at any point during the day, I can walk in and ask him a question. A press secretary has to have the ability to do that, or it's very tough to do your job.

How does President Obama feel about the press?

He understands very much the role they play in a representative democracy. He understands that that democracy is as strong as the people who cover the President and help the public understand what government is doing and holding it accountable.

How would you characterize the White House press corps?

They do a remarkable job under difficult circumstances. It's a grueling pace in terms of time and what you give up in terms of your personal life.

Is the press "fair" in its coverage of the President?

Absolutely. They ask the right questions. They're tough, but they're fair.

What should be the proper relationship between the press secretary and the press?

I think it's important to have good relationships. We can disagree, but we can do it in a way that is respectful and personable. I've been told this by my predecessors—that the Press Secretary occupies a unique position in the physical structure of the White House. Your office is equidistant from the Oval Office and the Briefing Room. So your role is one of spokesperson to and advocate for the President, but you are also the representative of the press inside the White House, in order for them to get the facts, information, and access they need. So there's a dual role you must play to serve both of the people you are tasked to work for.

Do you consider yourself a "counselor" to the President?

The role that I play in parts of my day would typically be reserved for more of a behind-the-scenes advisor. While that does take some of my day away from dealing with reporters, I believe it helps the press get a better sense for who the President is and the reasons for his decisions. It allows me to speak more authoritatively for his viewpoint.

How does being the President's press secretary differ from other public relations jobs?

This job has evolved into one where you play the traditional role of working with reporters but with the added responsibility of hosting your own cable TV show. I literally spend half of my day getting ready for the one hour that I spend in front of the press corps on camera. This requires a great deal of preparation and study.

How does someone become the President's Press Secretary?

You have to get good work experience in government, in press, and public relations. Also, because of the daily on-camera responsibilities, you have to be someone who is intellectually curious and can understand the rigors of the job. You have to also be *"lucky"* because you have to pick the right guy or woman. I wouldn't disavow anybody of the luck that's involved.

Public Relations Library

Bacevitch, Andrew J. *The Limits of Power*. New York: Henry Holt and Company, 2008. A university international relations professor analyzes what's behind America's international relations problems.

Beck, Glenn. *An Inconvenient Book: Real Solutions to the World's Biggest Problems*. New York: Simon & Schuster, 2007. The conservative commentator takes 'em all on—from poverty and marriage to liberalism and radical Islam.

Chemerinsky, Erwin. *Enhancing Government: Federalism for the 21st Century*. Stanford, CA: Stanford University Press, 2008. A political science professor explores the evolution of government in U.S. society.

Clarke, Torie. *Lipstick on a Pig*. New York: Free Press, 2006. The former Department of Defense communication director and originator of the effort to "embed" reporters in warzones offers a worthwhile memoir of her time running perhaps the largest government public relations operation.

Dunn, Geoffrey. *The Lies of Sarah Palin*. New York: St. Martin's Press, 2011. A less-than-friendly portrait of the woman who might have been second-in-command.

Fleischer, Ari. *Taking Heat: The President, the Press and My Years in the White House*. New York: HarperCollins, 2005. Firsthand account from President Bush's first press secretary, who answered the media mob during wartime.

Lee, Mordecai, Grant Neeley, and Kendra Stewart. *The Practice of Government Public Relations*. Boca Raton, FL: CRC Press, 2012. Dissection of various government relations functions by guest chapter writers.

Levin, Linda Lottridge. *The Making of FDR*. Amherst, NY: Prometheus Books, 2008. The story of Stephen T. Early, FDR's and America's first modern-day press secretary.

McClellan, Scott. *What Happened*. New York: Perseus Books Group, 2009. Hatchet job from a disappointed and disappointing George W. Bush spokesman.

Morris, Dick, and Eileen McGann. *Fleeced*. New York: HarperCollins, 2008. A reborn, former Bill Clinton advisor rants about what's wrong with liberals.

Murray, Ian. *Stealing You Blind*. Washington, DC: Regenery Publishing, 2011. Red meat for conservatives, where the "rich" are composed primarily of Democrats.

Nessen, Ron. *Making the News*. Middletown, CT: Wesleyan University Press, 2011. Memoir from a press secretary to President Richard Nixon.

Phillips, Kevin. *Bad Money*. New York: Penguin Group. 2008. A sobering look at American foreign policy from a former White House strategist.

Smith, Kevin R. (Ed.). *State and Local Government 2007–2008 Edition*. Washington, DC: CQ Press, 2008. Practitioners discuss various aspects of government on the state and municipal levels.

Smith, Sally Bedell. *For Love of Politics*. New York: Random House, 2007. The unadulterated story of America's favorite political couple, Bill and Hillary Clinton.

Woodward, Bob. *The War Within: A Secret White House History 2006–2008*. New York: Simon & Schuster, 2008. The *Washington Post* reporter convinced Bush administration people to speak with him about this inside story. They learned to regret it.

Woodward, Bob. *Obama's Wars*. New York: Simon & Schuster, 2010. The same reporter also convinced the Obama administration people to speak with him. They, too, learned to regret it.

Chapter 13

Community Relations

Chapter Objectives

1. To discuss the importance of dealing with "communities," both geographic and ethnic.
2. To review the tradition of corporate social responsibility that has uniquely characterized U.S. institutions.
3. To discuss the multicultural publics that populate society, including Hispanics, blacks, Asians, and groups beyond nationalities, such as seniors and gays.
4. To examine the role of public relations in orchestrating the activities of nonprofit organizations.

FIGURE 13-1 Seeing pink.
Susan G. Komen Race for the Cure participants show their disapproval of Komen's threat to stop funding Planned Parenthood. *(Photo: Jeff Malet Photography/Newscom)*

In the 21st century, most organizations—companies, hospitals, schools, sports teams, etc.—understand they have an obligation to their communities, including supporting nonprofits. But in times of economic downturn and scarce corporate resources, charitable groups have found it much harder to raise the funds they require to do their good works.

As society gets more polarized, with interest groups for every imaginable subset—from liberals to conservatives, gays to straights, senior citizens to Generation Xers—demanding their voice be heard, dealing "correctly" with all these constituencies has caused many nonprofits to tread carefully, lest they turn out like Susan G. Komen for the Cure.

Susan G. Komen for the Cure was founded in 1980 by Nancy G. Brinker, whose sister died of breast cancer. The charity took Ms. Brinker's sister's name and dedicated itself to eradicating that awful disease. In 30 years, the Komen charity raised over a billion dollars—through Races for the Cure and the proliferation of trademark pink T-shirts—toward research screening and awareness of breast cancer.

Nancy Brinker's public relations fundraising ability was heroic, spawning Kites for a Cure, Par for the Cure, Surfing for a Cure, Cupcakes for a Cure, and even a dog-sledding event called Mush for the Cure. Susan G. Komen for the Cure had become one of the nation's most laudable, beloved, and successful charities—until it all came crashing down in 2012.

In February, Komen quietly announced its long-standing contributions to Planned Parenthood's breast screenings would stop due to "newly-adopted criteria barring grants to organizations that are under investigation by local, state or federal authorities." The new policy was advocated by a relatively new Komen hire, Vice President for Public Policy Karen Handel. Handel, an unsuccessful conservative Tea Party candidate for governor of Georgia, had campaigned on an anti–Planned Parenthood agenda.

Komen supporters were outraged, contributions and support plummeted, and ultimately, CEO Brinker reversed the decision, and Vice President Handel resigned[1] (Figure 13-1). In August, founder Brinker herself stepped down as Susan G. Komen CEO, the final casualty from the Planned Parenthood uprising.

In the second decade of the 21st century, not even a nonprofit devoted to an issue as unsullied as women's health care was free from controversy.

Multicultural Diversity

Today's society is increasingly multicultural. America has always been a melting pot, attracting freedom-seeking immigrants from countries throughout the world. Never has this been more true than today, as America's face continues to change. In 2012, America hit a demographic milestone, with new census figures showing for the first time more than half the children born in the United States were minorities. That percentage just barely eked over the halfway mark, with minorities making up 50.4% of U.S. births, compared to 37% of births in 1990.[2]

While minorities seemed to have slowed down growth rates in the second decade of the 21st century, their march to majority status in the United States appeared inexorable. Consider the following:

- By 2010, 48 million Hispanics represented about 16% of the U.S. population, and 14 million Asians represented almost 5% of the U.S. population. Both groups were growing at a rate of about 3% a year, well ahead of blacks, who numbered 40 million or about 12% of the population, and were growing at a 1% per year rate. At the same time, the U.S. white population, representing about 243 million people or 65% of the country, remained flat.[3] Put another way, over the first 10 years of the 21st century, minority populations grew eight times faster than the majority white, non-Hispanic population in the United States.[4]

- Multiracial Americans, the fastest growing U.S. demographic group, are also adding to minority gains. About 5.3 million Americans recognize themselves as "multiracial," up 3% per year. American Indians/Alaska Natives also comprise about 3 million people.

- While whites are getting older, minorities generally are getting younger. Latest census numbers indicate that the median age for Hispanics and Asians edged lower—to 27 and 35, respectively. The median age for blacks was unchanged at 31, while whites rose slightly to 41, due mostly to an aging boomer population.

- The largest numbers of immigrants flock to six U.S. states—California, New York, Texas, Florida, Illinois, and New Jersey.[5]

- The minority population's buying power has been increasing as its numbers have grown. Today, Hispanic buying power alone in the top 20 U.S. markets approximates $850 billion out of total U.S. consumer spending of $10 trillion. In 2009, Procter & Gamble spent nearly $160 million and DirecTV $133 million on ads in Hispanic media.[6]

■ The Asian population is the fastest-growing racial or ethnic group in the United States. Asians are more highly concentrated than Hispanics. One-third of all U.S. Asians live in California and another 10% live in New York State. Texas, New Jersey, Illinois, and Hawaii each have more than half a million Asian residents. The importance of this for public relations professionals is that Asian median household income is the highest of any racial category, 26% above the media income for white, non-Hispanic households. Indeed, the Asian population is the only race or ethnic market segment that is both rapidly growing and affluent.[7]

Such is the multicultural diversity enjoyed today by America and the world. The implications for organizations are profound. For example, women now receive about 60% of university degrees and, for the first time in American history, represent a majority of the workforce.[8]

As the arbiters of communications in their organizations, public relations people must be sensitive to society's new multicultural realities.

CSR—Corporate Social Responsibility

In the old days—1980s—corporations prided themselves on their "social responsibility." Their premise was that with the great opportunities they were afforded, companies needed to "give back" to society through participation in and contributions to not-for-profit organizations committed to confront society's most pressing problems—from poverty to education to cultural and health enrichment (Figure 13-2).

FIGURE 13-2
Mighty community relations.
Catan Communications created the Mighty Milk Nutritional Drink campaign, devising the "Be Mighty, Get Active" essay contest to raise awareness among children to learn about living a healthier lifestyle. Winners got to meet the one and only former pro basketball giant Shaquille O'Neal.
(Courtesy of O'Dwyer Company)

Then came the go-go 1990s and the "bubble years" of the early 2000s, when Internet stocks zoomed to dizzying heights, and corporate social responsibility took a backseat to making money—as much money as possible. When the stock market bubble burst, and economic doldrums morphed into worldwide recession and then near-systemic Armageddon in the second decade of the 21st century, companies cut back again on charitable support and charities struggled to support their constituents.

The concept of "corporate social responsibility"—of "giving back" to one's community and the larger society through voluntarism and financial support—is very much an American phenomenon, slow to catch on around the world.

In light of the increasing diversity of U.S. society, both profit and nonprofit organizations are also becoming more diverse and learning to deal and communicate with those who differ in work background, education, age, gender, race, ethnic origin, physical abilities, religious beliefs, sexual orientation, and other perceived differences.

In 2012 alone, 13 companies donated more than $100 million in cash, with Walmart at $342 million and Goldman Sachs with $337 million leading the way. Meanwhile, donations of products are growing faster than donations of cash, with Pfizer and Oracle leading the way with cash and product donations, $3 billion and $2.3 billion, respectively.[9] Most companies today donate a percentage of their profits to nonprofit organizations—schools, hospitals, social welfare institutions, and others. Charitable giving in the United States was estimated to be more than $306 billion in 2007, the first time in history such giving exceeded $300 billion.[10] That's good. On the other hand, in the face of the global economy's economic downturn in 2012, giving by America's corporations decreased slightly from the year earlier, to slightly under $300 billion.

Corporate giving in the second decade of the 21st century also has shown three decided trends:

■ **Corporate giving is becoming more focused.**   Companies are choosing to make larger gifts to fewer causes. Only 4% gave to a wide variety of charities in 2012, with 31% giving at least half their charitable dollars to a single program area.

■ **Matching gifts are a high priority.**   Companies with a workplace giving campaign rose to 59% in 2012, and those with a "dollars for doers" program encouraging volunteerism rose to 63%. Matching gifts are a great way for employees to maximize the value of their personal giving.

■ **International giving is on the rise.**   This is partly driven by overseas profits, which are difficult to bring home without incurring big tax liabilities. But overseas giving also rose as a result of company-sponsored volunteerism, where employees are given time off to take part in local causes around the world. Indeed, employers are increasingly willing to let workers engage in causes that are important to them anywhere in the world. Companies, increasingly, are embracing the "giving back" mindset and establishing the strategies and programs to back it up.[11]

Increasingly, corporate leaders—long absent from the public dialogue on community issues—have begun again to take an active stance in confronting societal challenges, such as protecting the environment. General Electric CEO Jeffrey Immelt, for example, led his company's effort to reduce its greenhouse gas emission by 1% over time, really a 40% reduction when factoring in GE's presumed growth. Ford Motor Company executives also have worked to shift the company's energy use to renewable sources, which account for 3% of Ford's energy use.[12] Tiger Management founder and legendary Wall Street investor and hedge fund legend Julian Robertson has also devoted significant foundation money to curbing greenhouse gasses.

FIGURE 13-3
From this . . .
*(Courtesy of Alex's
Lemonade Stand
Foundation)*

Again, corporate contributions like these depend on profits. In the case of car companies and financial companies, the economic crisis brought about by the U.S. financial meltdown and recession effectively derailed CSR initiatives. Indeed, in 2010, financial firms accounted for $2.11 billion of corporate donations, but after the financial industry's near collapse, contributions dipped considerably.[13]

Another element of CSR "giving back to the community" is voluntarism. As noted, a new generation—Gen X—of employees has entered the business world, aware of and concerned about their own and their firm's contribution to society.[14] At the Walt Disney Company, for example, Disney VoluntEARS spent more than 800,000 hours in volunteer services over a two-year span. At Volvo, hundreds of car dealers join forces to raise funds for pediatric cancer research at local hospitals (Figure 13-3, Figure 13-4).

Companies have also more recently attempted to gain increased recognition for their eleemosynary efforts. With corporations and CEOs back to being held in low esteem, some firms haven't been content to hide their charitable light under a bushel. In 2011, JP Morgan Chase financed and sponsored the "American Giving Awards," an NBC broadcast hosted by Bob Costas profiling recipients of Chase donations, bookended by Chase commercials, including regular announcements that the two-hour TV extravaganza was "presented by Chase."[15]

Most companies today understand that in the 21st century an organization must be a *citizen* of the community in every respect and accept its role as an agent for social change in the community.

Community Relations Expectations

For an organization to coexist peacefully in its community, three skills in particular are required: (1) determining what the community knows and thinks about the organization, (2) informing the community of the organization's point of view, and (3) negotiating

or mediating between the organization and the community and its constituents should there be a significant discrepancy.

Basically, every organization wants to foster positive reactions in its community. This becomes increasingly difficult in the face of protests from and disagreements with community activists. Community relations, therefore—to analyze the community, help understand its makeup and expectations, and communicate the organization's story in an understandable and uninterrupted way—are critical.

What the Community Expects

Communities expect from resident organizations such tangible commodities as wages, employment, and taxes. But communities have come to expect intangible contributions, too:

- **Appearance.** The community hopes that the firm will contribute positively to life in the area. It expects facilities to be attractive, with care spent on the grounds and structures. Increasingly, community neighbors object to plants that belch smoke and pollute water and air.

- **Participation.** As a citizen of the community, an organization is expected to participate responsibly in community affairs, such as civic functions, park and recreational activities, education, welfare, and support of religious institutions.

- **Stability.** A business that fluctuates sharply in volume of business, number of employees, and taxes paid can adversely affect the community through its impact on municipal services, school loads, public facilities, and tax revenues. Communities prefer stable organizations that will grow with the area.

■ **Pride.** Any organization that can help put the community on the map simply by being there is usually a valuable addition. Communities want firms that are proud to be residents. For instance, to most Americans, Battle Creek, Michigan, means cereal; Armonk, New York, means IBM; and Hershey, Pennsylvania, *still* means chocolate. Organizations that help build the town generally become revered symbols of pride.

What the Organization Expects

Organizations, in turn, expect to be provided with adequate municipal services, fair taxation, good living conditions for employees, a good labor supply, and a reasonable degree of support for the business and its products. When some of these requirements are missing, organizations may move to communities where such benefits are more readily available.

New York City at the turn of the century, for example, experienced a substantial exodus of corporations to neighboring Connecticut and New Jersey and the Sun Belt states of the Southeast and Southwest, because of high taxes and decidedly anti-business politicians. New York's state and city legislators responded to the challenge by working more closely with business residents, and business-oriented billionaire Mayor Michael Bloomberg led a successful effort to bring business back to New York. In the second decade of the 21st century, as the economy suffered, states such as Texas made a concerted push to attract business. The combination of improved infrastructure, low cost of living, and pro-business policies relative to taxation, innovation, and technology made Texas the most "business friendly state in the nation."[16]

Community Relations Objectives

Research into community relations indicates that winning community support for an organization is no easy matter. Studies indicate difficulty in achieving rapport with community neighbors, who expect support from the company but object to any dominance on its part in community affairs.

Organizations profit by a written community relations policy that clearly defines the philosophy of management as it views its obligation to the community.

Typical community relations objectives may include the following:

1. To tell the community about the operations of the firm: its products, number of employees, size of the payroll, tax payments, employee benefits, growth, and support of community projects.

2. To correct misunderstandings, reply to criticism, and remove any disaffection that may exist among community neighbors.

3. To gain the favorable opinion of the community, particularly during strikes and periods of labor unrest, by stating the company's position on the issues involved.

4. To inform employees and their families about company activities and developments so that they can tell their friends and neighbors about the company and favorably influence opinions of the organization.

5. To inform people in local government about the firm's contributions to community welfare and to obtain support for legislation that will favorably affect the business climate of the community.

6. To find out what residents think about the organization, why they like or dislike its policies and practices, and how much they know of its policy, operations, and problems.

7. To establish a personal relationship between management and community leaders by inviting leaders to visit the plant and offices, meet management, and see employees at work.

8. To operate a profitable business to provide jobs and to pay competitive wages that increase the community's purchasing power and strengthen its economy.

9. To cooperate with other local businesses in advancing economic and social welfare through joint community relations programs.

Community Relations on the Web

At the heart of the Internet is a sense of community.

From this concept of community has emerged an effort to use the Internet for social good, to expand educational and commercial opportunities for minority communities as well as provide a philanthropic forum. For example:

- The world famous Mayo Clinic in Minnesota stands at the health care forefront in using social media to educate the public about staying healthy in general and its works in particular. Mayo sponsors a YouTube channel, a Twitter account, and more than 53,000 Facebook connections. In 2011, Mayo went one step further by creating the world's first medical provider group online community. A goal of the community was to connect former Mayo patients with others facing similar health concerns.[17]

- Black Entertainment Television created BET.com to bring "connectivity, content, and commerce" to African Americans, a community relatively underrepresented in cyberspace. Internet access in African American homes is 60% less than in Caucasian households. So, armed with $35 million, the largest online investment ever aimed at African Americans, BET.com hoped to help African Americans become more computer savvy. Although some black-oriented sites, like other so-called vertical Websites, among them the NetNoir.com pop culture portal and the urban youth-oriented Volume.com portal, have suffered cutbacks in recent years, established media companies have used the Web to attract minority followers. Early in the century, Time Warner paid $10 million for Africana.com in an effort to attract more African American users to AOL.[18] And in 2008, the *Washington Post* launched *The Root*, an online magazine focused on black culture and society.[19]

- Less successful have been socially responsible Websites wholly devoted to raising e-commerce funds for charity. One of the most ambitious, GreaterGood.com, closed in 2001, unable to sustain itself.[20] In less prosperous economic times, a more viable model seemed to be one where for-profit and nonprofit organizations alike devoted part of online purchases toward charitable causes. In addition, a number of sites offering "socially responsible shopping" and allying themselves with causes ranging from helping wounded vets to greening the planet have continued to pop up.

Although the Web may be characterized by some as anonymous, acrimonious, and heartless, efforts such as these underscore the Internet's immense potential in furthering human relations and progress—across common communities and for the larger society.

Serving Diverse Communities

What were once referred to as minorities are rapidly becoming the majority. Today, 40 million Americans, or 13% of the population, are foreign born—the highest level since 1920, despite the nation's various adversaries around the world.[21] The U.S. Census Bureau reports that more than two-thirds of current U.S. and future population growth is and will be the result of immigration.

According to the 2010 Census Bureau census, Hispanics have overtaken African Americans as the America's largest minority group, reaching 50.5 million in 2010, compared to about 39 million blacks and 18 million Asians.[22]

Women, African Americans, Hispanics, Asians, gays, seniors, persons with disabilities, and a variety of other groups have become not only important members of the labor force but also important sources of discretionary income.

Public relations professionals must be sensitive to the demands of all for equal pay, promotional opportunities, equal rights in the workplace, and so on. Communicating effectively in light of the multicultural diversity of society has become an important public relations challenge.

Women

In the 21st century, women became the majority of the workforce in the United States, making up 51% of U.S. professional workers.

According to the Bureau of Labor Statistics, women hold 51% of managerial and professional jobs—up from 26% in 1980. Women are 54% of all accountants and hold about half of all banking and insurance jobs. Women are about one-third of the physicians and 45% of the associates in law firms—and both percentages are rising fast. And, in the European Union, women have filled six million of the eight million new jobs since 2000.

Women today head large corporations from Avon to Hewlett Packard to Pepsi Cola, represent about 20% of U.S. representatives and senators, hold the highest positions in the American government from Secretary of State to Secretary of Homeland Security, and have been major party candidates for every government job exclusive of the President of the United States. And that will occur soon enough.

The point is that in the 21st century, women have made great strides in leveling the playing field between their roles and compensation schedules and those of their male counterparts. The days of "mommy tracks" and "mommy wars," glass ceilings and pink-collar ghettos are rapidly falling by the wayside.

So, too, in public relations, women have steadily climbed into middle- and upper-management positions, both at corporations and public relations agencies. Indeed, with the Public Relations Student Society of American now reporting 90% women, the field is among the strongest for opportunities for women.[23] One blemish, however, remains in the area of equal pay. According to a Public Relations Society of America (PRSA) study conducted through January 2011, women made 78 cents on the dollar compared to men. While an improvement over prior decades, researchers concluded that "gender discrimination as related to pay" still exists in public relations.[24]

Hispanics

There is little question that companies need to reach Hispanics. Currently 50 million strong, Hispanics are the fastest growing minority in the nation. From 2000 to 2010, more than half of the nation's population growth was due to Hispanics. The Census

Bureau predicts that by 2050, they will comprise one-third of the population, nearly 100 million people.

The U.S. Hispanic population already ranks as the fifth largest in the world, behind Mexico, Spain, Colombia, and Argentina. In the United States, 77% of Hispanics reside mainly in six states—California, Texas, Florida, Arizona, New Jersey, and Illinois. Each has more than a million Hispanic residents and collectively, 31% of their population is Hispanic. As a group, those states house 30 million Hispanics, according to the 2010 Census.[25]

New York City has the largest Latin population with 2.3 million residents. Los Angeles rates second with 1.8 million. Mexicans, numbering 32 million, are by far the biggest national group within the United States, accounting for 63% nationwide and constituting the majority of Latinos in 40 of the 50 states.

Next come the nearly five million from Puerto Rico, who are U.S. citizens by birth, followed by the nearly two million people of Cuban origin. Three other Hispanic national groups reached or surpassed the 1 million mark between 2000 and 2010: Salvadorans, Dominicans, and Guatemalans.

Accordingly, Latinos comprise a potent political and economic force. In the 2012 presidential election, Hispanics were perhaps the most coveted voting group; San Antonio Mayor Julian Castro keynoted the Democrat National Convention, and New Mexico Governor Susana Martinez, the first female Hispanic governor in the United States, spoke at the Republican National Convention. The Hispanic vote went convincingly to Democrats.

Latinos are voracious media consumers, relying heavily on television and radio to stay informed. Two large Spanish-programming networks, Univision and Telemundo, dominate the airwaves, with Univision drawing 83% of the country's adult, prime-time, Spanish-language viewing audience. CNN also offers a daily program in Spanish for its Latin American viewers.

Magazines also are a great source of entertainment to the Latino community, with more than 200 Hispanic publications hitting the market in the last 10 years, including *Latin CEO* for top executives to *Latina* magazine for teenage girls to *Healthy Kids en Español* for parents to the general-interest *Latina* and *People en Español*.[26]

Thirty years ago, there were 67 Spanish-language radio stations in the United States; today that number has increased fivefold. By 2008, African Americans and Spanish-dominant Hispanics had the highest radio listening levels of all demographic groups, propelling urban and Spanish-language stations to the top in major U.S. markets, including New York, Chicago, and San Francisco.[27]

In terms of the importance of the Latin community to marketers and organizations of all types, Hispanic buying power is worth $1 trillion now and is expected to grow another 50% to $1.5 trillion in the next five years. Moreover, Hispanic households earning more than $50,000 are projected to grow at a faster rate than the total number of households.[28]

African Americans

The black population has stabilized its growth at 39 million in recent years. New York has the largest black population, followed by Florida, Texas, Georgia, and California. For the bulk of the past century, most blacks lived in the south. By 2010, the south had 22 of 39 million blacks, for 56%, still a sizeable majority. New York City, with three million black people, leads the nation, followed by Atlanta, Chicago, and Washington, D.C.[29] The latter, a traditional hub of black culture and politics, traditionally had a more than 50% black population (Figure 13-5). In addition, foreign-born blacks have increased materially in numbers. In Miami, the West

FIGURE 13-5
Hizzoner.
Washington, D.C., Mayor Vincent C. Gray, here announcing VeriFone's selection as vendor for the city's Taxicab Smart Meter System, presided over a city historically more than half black residents.
(Photo: Lateef Mangum, Audiovisual Producer/ Photographer, Executive Office of the Mayor)

Indian population makes up nearly 50% of the black population. In New York, nearly a third of the black population is foreign-born.

The socioeconomic status of blacks has improved in recent years primarily due to large increases in women's incomes. While black median family income has improved, black men have recently experienced a decline in income. Median family income of blacks ages 30 to 39 was only 58% that of white families in the same age group ($35,000 for blacks compared to $60,000 for whites).[30]

Black disposable income has increased markedly in recent years, now nearly $1 billion yearly. Black buying power is expected to continue its trajectory— from $316 billion in 1990 to $600 billion in 2000, to $947 billion in 2010, to $1,038 billion in 2012 and a projected $1,307 billion in 2017.[31]

Despite their continuing evolution in the white-dominated workplace, the nation's 41 million blacks can still be reached effectively through special media:

- Black Entertainment Television is a popular network that has done well.
- Local African American radio stations have prospered.
- Pioneering Internet sites, such as TheRoot.com, BlackFamilies.com, Blackvoices.com, NetNoir.com, and the Black World Today (www.tbwt.com), have created a culture of acceptance and desirability for Web access among African Americans.
- Publications such as *Black Enterprise* and *Essence* are national vehicles. *Ebony,* the largest African American–oriented publication in the world and publishing since 1945, has a circulation of 1.6 million.[32]

One area of frustration in improving the livelihood of African Americans is the practice of public relations. The field has failed to attract sufficient numbers of African American practitioners to its ranks. In recent years, the Public Relations Society of America has increased outreach efforts to attract and retain African Americans. In 2008, the PRSA launched a three-year "State of Multicultural Public Relations" initiative to assess the gains and needs in increasing the diversity of public relations practitioners.

Attracting African Americans to the field remains a great challenge to public relations leaders in the new century.

Asians/Muslims

The U.S. Asian population totals nearly 18 million and grew faster than any other major race group between 2000 and 2010, increasing by 43%, about 5% of the U.S. population. By 2010, Asians had surpassed Hispanics as the primary immigrants to the United

States, as 430,000 Asians—or 36% of all new immigrants, legal and illegal—moved to the United States in 2010, compared with 370,000 Hispanics, or 31% of all new arrivals.

Asians in the United States, according to studies, are distinguished by their emphasis on traditional family mores, such as having a successful marriage and being a good parent. Asians also place greater importance on career and material success, values reflected in child-rearing styles. About 62% of Asians in the United States believed that most American parents do not put enough pressure on their children to do well in school.[33]

Finally, there is perhaps the most misunderstood and put-upon public in this post-9/11 world: Muslims. Since the attacks on America in 2001, life has become more difficult for many of the estimated 2.6 million Muslims living in the United States. In terms of U.S. media, Arabic television stations such as Al Jazeera or PTV, the state-run Pakistan Television, are accessible and frequently employ American journalists. In 2004, Bridges TV, an English-language network with programming aimed at American Muslims, made its debut. The primary purpose of Bridges TV, said its founder, was to "build bridges of understanding between American Muslims and mainstream America."[34]

Gays, Seniors, and Others

In the 21st century, a diverse assortment of special communities has gravitated into the mainstream of American commerce. One such group is the gay market. To some, homosexuality may remain a target of opprobrium, but in the 21st century, the gay market, estimated at 15 million Americans, comprises a target of opportunity estimated at $690 billion.

An increasing number of marketers, including IBM, United Airlines, and Anheuser-Busch, run advertisements with gay themes. Accordingly, a vibrant gay media market—from magazines *The Advocate* and *Out* to Internet portal GayWired .com to premium gay cable TV network Here—has emerged.[35]

Attitudes toward gay people, too, are changing. The number of Americans who think gays should have access to equal rights in employment and public accommodations rose from 56% in 1977 to 83% in 2000.[36] And gay marriage has become a front burner issue around the country. President Obama, in the midst of his 2012 reelection campaign, announced that he supported gay marriage. However, Americans remained divided—sometimes vocally so—on the concept during the 2012 presidential election (see Ethics Mini-Case in this chapter).[37]

Senior citizens also have become an important community for public relations professionals and the organizations they represent. The baby boomer generation has begun to steam into their Social Security years. Together, the over-50 crowd controls more than 50% of America's discretionary income. The American Association of Retired Persons, founded in 1958 for women and men over 50, has a membership of more than 35 million, about half of whom, despite the group's name, still work for a living.

Nonprofit Public Relations

Among the most important champions of multiculturalism in any community are not-for-profit or just plain *nonprofit* organizations. Nonprofit organizations serve the social, educational, religious, and cultural needs of the community around them. So important is the role of public relations in nonprofit organizations that this sector is a primary source of employment for public relations graduates.

PR Ethics Mini-Case

Playing "Chicken" with Gay Marriage

Freedom of speech is a bedrock principal in the American Constitution, but in the summer of 2012, one corporate CEO learned that he could only take the concept so far.

In an interview with a Baptist publication and appearance on a devotional radio program, Dan Cathy, CEO and president of the family-owned fast food chain Chick-fil-A, railed against same-sex marriage as "violating God's plan."

"We are very much supportive of the family—the biblical definition of the family unit," he told the Biblical Recorder. On the radio, he observed: "I think we are inviting God's judgment on our nation when we shake our fist at him and say we know better than you as to what constitutes a marriage."

The CEO's unburdening, publicized as it was after President Obama said he "supported" gay marriage, ignited a firestorm of controversy, with gays vowing to boycott the chain and conservatives vowing to support it. Former Arkansas Governor Mike Huckabee, now a radio and TV personality, called for Bible-loving conservatives to show up at the restaurants in a "Chick-fil-A Appreciation Day." The day produced lines around the block at many locations and contributed to the largest revenue day in Chick-fil-A history. Opponents answered with a "Chick-fil-A Kiss In," in which members of the same sex puckered up for the cameras (Figure 13-6).

Adding to the furor, liberal politicians from Boston to Chicago railed against the insensitivity of the chain's CEO and dug in to rid their localities of Chick-fil-A. Chicago Mayor Rahm Emanuel, whose city was faced with an out-of-control murder wave, was more than willing to deflect attention to anything—especially an easy target like the fast food chain. The mayor speculated self-righteously on the possibility of such a franchise invading his fair city, "Chick-fil-A values are not Chicago values. They disrespect our fellow neighbors and residents. This would be a bad investment, since it would be empty."

The uproar reached its peak when an out-of-sorts and outraged (not to mention, slightly cuckoo) medical supply firm financial manager drove through a Tucson Chick-fil-A and filmed himself, unmercifully berating the poor server at the drive-in window. The seeker of truth then posted his video on YouTube, where it became an overnight sensation, getting him fired in the process. The man subsequently apologized, the server was rewarded for keeping her cool, and the Chick-fil-A gay marriage controversy eventually subsided.

And there was one sad postscript. Shortly after the controversy erupted onto the national stage, the 60-year-old Director of Public Relations for the Chick-fil-A company, a veteran of 29 years with the Atlanta-based firm, dropped dead of a heart attack.*

Questions

1. Was the CEO wise in making his anti-gay marriage views known, exposing his company to such controversy?

2. Had you been advising Mr. Cathy, what would you have counseled him?

FIGURE 13-6
Lip lickin' good.
Supporters of same-sex marriage staged a "Chick-fil-A Kiss-In" in 2012 to rebut the views of CEO Dan Cathy, who publicly opposed gay marriage.
(Photo: GSA/ZOJ WENN Photos/Newscom)

* For further information, see "Adam Smith, Chick-fil-A Drive-Through Bully Hassles Fast Food Employee and Gets Fired," Huffington Post, August 2, 2012; Michael Hiltzik, "Chick-fil-A Gets a Lesson on Corporate Outspokenness," *Los Angeles Times*, July 31, 2012; Michael Sebastian, "Chick-fil-A's PR Crisis," Ragan PR Daily, July 25, 2012; and Michael Winter, "Chick-fil-A Spokesman Dies Amid Furor Over Same Sex Marriage," *USA Today*, July 28, 2012.

FIGURE 13-7 Follow the sun. One hundred students created Quantum, a car powered solely by the sun, which uses the same amount of energy to power a hair-dryer and reaches speeds of more than 105 miles per hour.
(Handout photo via Avery Dennison)

The nonprofit sector is characterized by a panoply of institutions: hospitals, schools, trade associations, labor unions, chambers of commerce, social welfare agencies, religious institutions, cultural organizations, and the like. Unlike corporations, nonprofits also seek to broaden volunteer participation in their efforts, often through the use of controversial communications tactics to raise public awareness through *media advocacy*. Media advocacy, simply defined, is public relations without resources. Protests, marches, demonstrations, media photo opportunities, stealth Internet campaigns, and the like are all fair game in media advocacy (Figure 13-7).

Master of Many Trades

Also unlike corporations, nonprofits generally don't have much money for key activities—especially in times of economic downturn. That's why public relations professionals in nonprofits must be masters of many functions; key among them are positioning the organization, developing a marketing or promotional plan, orchestrating media relations, and supporting fundraising.

Positioning the Organization   With thousands of competitors vying for support dollars, a nonprofit must stand out from the rest. This positioning initiative, to differentiate itself, depends largely on the public relations function.

No organization, particularly a resource-challenged nonprofit, can afford to be all things to all people. The best nonprofits, like the best corporations, stand for something. And they are unafraid to "break a few eggs" in order to achieve a clear and differentiable identity (Figure 13-8).

Developing a Marketing/Promotional Plan   Often in nonprofits, the public relations director serves as the marketing director, advertising director, and promotion

FIGURE 13-8   Grin and bear it.
A "polar bear" sliced into the world's largest "Baked Alaska" during an "Earth Day" demonstration against drilling in the Arctic National Wildlife Region.
(Courtesy of O'Dwyer Company)

director. The job, simply, is marketing the organization to raise its profile, respect, and levels of support. This requires planning in terms of audiences, messages, and vehicles to deliver those messages to those audiences. Crucial in framing these messages is to recognize the *cause-related* quotient—that is, what the organization stands for—around which the marketing campaign is based.

Media Relations   Because most nonprofits lack sufficient resources for advertising or formal marketing, the use of "free" media is a critical public relations function. As the late National Public Radio broadcaster Daniel Schorr once put it, "If you don't exist in the media, for all practical purposes you don't exist." Nonprofits desperately need media advocates who champion their cause and mission.

Supporting Fundraising   Nonprofits depend on donors for support. Fundraising, therefore, is a key nonprofit challenge that must engage the attention of the organization's key executives. Public relations professionals must be intimately involved in fundraising communications and appeals so that messages can be targeted and consistent with the organization's general position.

A successful fundraising campaign should include the following basic steps:

1. **Identify campaign plans and objectives.** Broad financial targets should be set. A goal should be announced. Specific sectors of the community from which funds might be extracted should be targeted in advance.

2. **Organize fact-finding.** Relevant trends that might affect giving should be noted. Relations with various elements of the community should be defined. The national and local economies should be considered, as should current attitudes toward charitable contributions.

3. **Recruit leaders.** The best fundraising campaigns are those with strong leadership. A hallmark of local United Way campaigns, for example, is the recruitment of strong business leaders to spearhead contribution efforts.

4. **Plan and implement strong communications activities.** The best fundraising campaigns are also the most visible. Publicity and promotion must be stressed. Special events should be organized, particularly featuring national and local celebrities to support the drive.

Outside the Lines

13 Rules for Radicals

Want to know how to organize a winning protest on campus with no money?

No problem.

Here are the time-honored suggestions of labor leader Saul Alinsky, from his 1971 classic *Rules for Radicals* (see Pick of the Literature in this chapter). They are just as relevant now as they were nearly four decades ago. *(Just don't tell anybody where you learned 'em!)*

1. Power is not only what you have but what the enemy thinks you have.
2. Never go outside the experience of your people.
3. Whenever possible, go outside the experience of the enemy.
4. Make the enemy live up to its own book of rules.
5. Ridicule is a person's most potent weapon.
6. A good tactic is one that your people enjoy.
7. A tactic that drags on too long becomes a drag.
8. Keep the pressure on.
9. The threat is usually more terrifying than the thing itself.
10. The major premise for tactics is the development of operations that will maintain a constant pressure on the opposition.
11. If you push a negative hard and deep enough, it will break through to its counter side.
12. The price of a successful attack is a constructive alternative.
13. Pick the target, freeze it, personalize it, and polarize it.

---

5. **Periodically review and evaluate.** Review the fundraising program as it progresses. Make midcourse corrections when activities succeed or fail beyond expectations. Evaluate program achievements against program targets. Revise strategies constantly as the goal becomes nearer.[38]

Because many public relations graduates enter the nonprofit realm, knowledge of fundraising strategies and techniques is especially important. Beginning practitioners, once hired in the public relations office of a college, hospital, religious group, charitable organization, or other nonprofit organization, are soon confronted with questions about how public relations can help raise money for the organization.

Last Word

The increasing cultural diversity of society in the 21st century has spawned a wave of "political correctness," particularly in the United States. Predictably, many have questioned whether sensitivity to women, people of color, the physically challenged, gays, seniors, and other groups has gone too far. One thing, however, is certain. The makeup of society—of consumers, employees, political constituents, and so on—has been altered inexorably. The number of discrete communities with which organizations must be concerned will continue to increase.

Intelligent organizations in our society must be responsive to the needs and desires of their communities. Positive community relations must begin with a clear understanding of community concerns, an open door for community leaders, an open and honest flow of information from the organization, and an ongoing sense of continuous involvement and interaction with community publics.

The public relations profession, responsible as it is for managing the communications of an organization, must take the lead in dealing with diversity. Since 2004, when the Public Relations Society of America initiated Advancing Diversity, a national initiative uniting various elements to promote multiculturalism in both the public relations industry and the business community, the PRSA has worked on promoting diversity in the profession.[39] The society's Public Relations Student Society of America has chapters at 13 historically black colleges, and 27 schools have been accredited by the Hispanic Association of Colleges and Universities. Still, 87% of PRSA membership has remained Caucasian, with only a 6% increase in minority membership since 2005. So there is a ways to go for the profession.

Community relations itself is only as effective as the support it receives from top management. Once that support is clear, it becomes the responsibility of the public relations professional to ensure that the relationship between the organization and all of its multicultural communities is one of mutual trust, understanding, and support.

Discussion Starters

1. How is the atmosphere for community relations different today than it was even at the turn of the century?
2. What is meant by the term *multicultural diversity*?
3. In general terms, what does a community expect from a resident organization?
4. What are typical community relations objectives for an organization?
5. What was the philosophy of corporate responsibility espoused by economist Milton Friedman?
6. What is meant by the term *media advocacy*?
7. Why do companies need to reach the Hispanic community?
8. What are the primary responsibilities of a non-profit public relations professional?
9. What is meant by the term *corporate social responsibility*?
10. What are the basic steps of a fundraising campaign?

Pick of the Literature

Rules for Radicals: A Practical Primer for Realistic Radicals

Saul D. Alinsky, New York: Vintage Books, 1989

Sure it's ancient, but so am I, and besides . . . Alinsky's *Rules for Radicals*, originally published in 1971, is still the classic handbook for those bent on organizing communities, rattling the status quo, and effecting social and political change as well as for those who wish to learn from a legendary master.

Alinsky, a veteran community activist who fought on behalf of the poor from New York to California, provides strategies for building coalitions and for using communication, conflict, and confrontation advantageously.

In "Of Means and Ends," Alinsky lists his 13 tactics of engagement (see Outside the Lines in this chapter) and 11 rules of ethics that define the uses of radical power.

Alinsky supports his principles with numerous examples, the most colorful of which occurred when he wanted to draw attention to a particular cause in Rochester, New York. Alinsky and his group attended a Rochester Symphony Orchestra performance—after a meal of nothing but beans. The results were predictable—and very funny.

Alinsky died in 1972, but his lessons endure in this off-beat guide to seizing power. Whether your goal is to fluster the establishment or defend it, *Rules for Radicals* is the organizer's bible.

Case Study   The Silence of the Lions

The Nittany Lions of Penn State University were synonymous with two things: a winning football program and a legendary and revered coach.

Joseph Vincent "Joe" Paterno was Penn State's beloved "JoePa," the head coach for 46 years. During that period, the man who originally planned to be a lawyer coached five undefeated teams, won two national championships, went to 37 post-season bowl games, and was inducted into the College Football Hall of Fame as a coach.

Joe Paterno and his football program *were* Penn State University. No one on the campus they called "Happy Valley"—including the university president—outranked the coach. And no institution on campus had more clout than the vaunted Nittany Lions football program.

Until it all came crumbling down.

Going the Second Mile

For most of his tenure, Paterno's right-hand man was defensive coach Jerry Sandusky. Sandusky, a giant of a man, was just slightly less revered on campus as JoePa.

Sandusky was a highly respected defensive strategist. He coached a number of future National Football League stars and was named the nation's Assistant Coach of the Year twice. Sandusky also authored several books related to his football coaching experiences.

Sandusky was beloved in State College, Pennsylvania, not only for his leadership on the football field but also for founding The Second Mile, a nonprofit for at-risk children in Pennsylvania.

Second Mile provided services for more than 100,000 children through camp programs, anti-bullying kits, friend fitness programs, and mentoring. It was active in almost all 501 school districts and 67 counties in the state.

Second Mile was doing the Lord's work. And the face of Second Mile was Jerry Sandusky.

Then, inexplicably, at the end of the 1999 season, Jerry Sandusky resigned. In his final game at the Alamo Bowl, Sandusky's defense shut out Texas A&M, 24-0, and his players carried the defensive coach off the field on their shoulders; high praise for an assistant.

Unease in Happy Valley

On April 1, 2011, the *Harrisburg Patriot-News* ran a story that Jerry Sandusky was under investigation by a grand jury for inappropriate conduct with a teenager who was part of a football program that Sandusky helped coach. The paper said the investigation had been ongoing for 18 months. ESPN picked up the story, but it died shortly thereafter.

Second Mile defended its founder and the organization, pointing out that the program had a spotless record in behalf of the safety and well-being of the children in its care. The organization talked of its background checks, child line checks, and similar safeguard processes.

For its part, Penn State and its well-respected President Graham Spanier, who had helped improve the school's academic standing to rival its reputation on the gridiron, were decidedly low-key about the Sandusky investigation.

The story stayed controlled for six months and then exploded on the national stage. *The New York Times'* November 5 front-page headline said it all:

Former Coach at Penn State Is Charged With Abuse

The story explained how a grand jury investigation had revealed that over a 15-year period, the now 67-year-old Sandusky had sexually abused eight boys in his care. Sandusky was arrested and released on $100,000 bail, charged with 40 counts of sexual abuse (Figure 13-9). Gary Schultz, Penn State's senior vice president for finance, and Tim Curley, the school's athletic director, were also charged with perjury and failure to report to authorities what they knew of the allegations, as required by state law.

President Spanier, who acknowledged that he had been made aware of the 2002 incident, issued a statement expressing "complete confidence" in how Schultz and Curley handled the situation.

One who wasn't charged but whom Penn State watchers wondered about was the school's 85-year-old head football coach.

Paterno, according to the grand jury, learned of one allegation of abuse in 2002 and immediately reported it to Curley. While the coach wasn't implicated by the grand jury, it remained unclear whether Paterno ever followed up after his initial report.

FIGURE 13-9   Evil.
Jerry Sandusky after conviction for sexual abuse.
(Photo: Zuma/Newscom)

Death of a Legend

In the months that followed, the awful truth about Sandusky quickly emerged.

For years, according to individuals who came forward, Sandusky would use Second Mile to gain access to hundreds of boys, many of whom were vulnerable due to their economic and social situations.

According to the grand jury report—most of which became public—Sandusky would use the Penn State football facilities to abuse the boys, none of whom were believed to be older than 13 when they first met the coach. The gruesome report detailed how Sandusky brought one boy to the Alamo Bowl and then threatened to send him home when the boy resisted the coach's sexual advances. Another boy attended as many as 15 football games as Sandusky's guest and was abused in the Penn State shower room by the coach.

When, in 2002, a former player and then assistant coach witnessed Sandusky sexually assaulting a boy in the locker room shower, he reportedly alerted Paterno, who told Curley.

After the horror of the grand jury report, events quickly escalated.

While students converged on the campus home of Coach Paterno to show their support, Paterno himself tried to take control of the rapidly deteriorating situation by securing a better contract and announcing that he would serve one more year as coach and then resign.

It was too late.

On November 9, four days after the grand jury report went public, the Penn State Board of Trustees announced that Spanier had resigned and that Joe Paterno—the most hallowed name in college football coaching history, a statue of whom stood triumphantly outside Penn State's Beaver Stadium—had been fired.

Ultimately, Jerry Sandusky was found guilty on 45 of 48 charges and will spend the rest of his life in jail. In January 2012, two months after he had been fired, Joe Paterno died of complications from lung cancer.

On July 22, 2012, in the final blow to his reputation, Joe Paterno's seven foot, 900-pound statue outside Beaver Stadium was removed by forklift, because, said Penn State's new president, the statue had become "a source of division and an obstacle to healing in our university and beyond" (Figure 13-10).*

Questions

1. What would you have advised Second Mile to do when apprised of the charges against its founder?

2. What would you have counseled President Spanier to do when apprised of the charges against Sandusky?

3. What would you have counseled Coach Paterno to do when apprised of charges against his assistant?

4. Do you agree with Penn State's decisions after the grand jury revelations?

5. Was the school fair in its treatment of Joe Paterno?

FIGURE 13-10 Over.
The statue of Joe Paterno, which once stood triumphantly in front of Beaver Stadium, stands no more.
(Photo: PAT LITTLE/Reuters/Newscom)

*For further information, see Jo Becker, "Paterno Won Sweeter Deal Even as Scandal Played Out," *The New York Times*, July 14, 2012; Maureen Dowd, "Paterno Knocked Off His Pedestal," *The New York Times*, July 21, 2012; Shannon Doyne, "Jury Finds Jerry Sandusky Guilty," *The New York Times*, June 25, 2012; Don Van Natta Jr., "Joe Paterno Statue Taken Down," ESPN.com, July 23, 2012; and Mark Viera, "Former Coach at Penn State Is Charged With Abuse," *The New York Times*, November 5, 2011.

From the Top

An Interview with Mike Paul

Mike Paul, the "Reputation Doctor," is a veteran of strategic public relations, corporate communications, and reputation management. He is president and senior counselor of MGP and Associates PR (MGP). MGP was founded by Paul in 1994 and is a leading boutique public relations and reputation management firm based in New York, providing senior counseling services to top corporate, government, nonprofit, sports, and entertainment clients. In 2012, Trust Across America named Mr. Paul one of the "Top 100 Thought Leaders in Trustworthy Behavior."

How important is an organization's or individual's reputation?
Reputations of all types are so important, I made it our firm's tag line: "Because Your Reputation Is Everything!"™ A reputation is the greatest asset we have, for both a public company and an individual. It must be built, maintained, and repaired to thrive for a lifetime. Sadly, many corporations, organizations, and individuals talk the talk of the importance of reputation, but don't walk the walk.

How can reputation be managed?
The big "bricks" of managing an excellent reputation include truth, humility, transparency, accountability, consistency. Honesty and humility are the most important tools in a reputation management tool belt. Like any disease, a reputation in crisis is a disease that can be cured or can grow out of control and cause severe damage in other areas. Admitting

mistakes, lies, and deceit is the first step in reputation management.

What is the state of community relations among organizations today?
Community relations among U.S. organizations are becoming much better, but there is still much work to be done and further commitment and accountability from senior management is necessary to achieve excellence. For example, many community organizations are not teaming up with similar organizations in their arena to achieve community goals. Many are islands among themselves and believe partnering with other community organizations is not part of their mission. One goal of any community relations campaign should be to mirror the population in which you serve.

What is the state of social responsibility among corporations?
Corporate social responsibility has become a key communications and business tool for most corporations today. However, corporations must realize social responsibility has both a community responsibility and a business obligation. For example, a successful social responsibility campaign—local, national, or global—cannot be just a pet project of a CEO or senior management. It must include social and community responsibility interests important to many key audiences, including employees, investors, customers, and the communities in which the corporation operates.

How important is it for an organization to focus on dealing with minorities?
Minorities have become the majority in many communities across the United States and around the world. As a result, minority is not an accurate word to use any more for communities or people of color. People, employees, or executives of color are now the appropriate terms to use because of the huge demographic shift in the world. As a result, corporate America and other organizations have begun to truly embrace diversity, but there is much more work to be done. However, the executive ranks are still void of many people of color, and sadly, racism is still alive in many corporations, organizations, and communities in the United States and around the world.

What is the state of African Americans in the public relations business?
Two words: in crisis. There are still few African Americans in public relations overall and even fewer executives of color in leadership positions. Most work for community organizations and in government. There has still not been an African American CEO within any of the top 10 global PR firms and very few top global corporate communications executives. Until the CEOs of PR firms and corporate America embrace

the problem with the same intensity from both the bottom and the top levels, diversity in PR will continue to be in crisis. Accountability and transparency are both necessary to develop lasting change.

What advice would you give young minority members interested in a public relations career?

First, for young people of color, there are not many executives of color in our business. As a result, seeking a career in our business is a tougher road. The numbers don't lie. Second, seek employment at a top global PR firm to best learn the business and work in as many different divisions as possible. The training programs at these firms are superior to others, and the type of clients you will work with are top notch and best for building skills and an excellent resume. Third, seek out an excellent mentor, and the mentor does not have to be an executive of color. For example, I have the best mentor in our business, Harold Burson of Burson-Marsteller. He gave me excellent advice years ago when I was at B-M, and he still gives me excellent advice today. Many young professionals of color make the mistake of only seeking executives of color. This is a big mistake.

Public Relations Library

Banks, James A., and Cherry Banks. *Multicultural Education: Characteristics and Goals*. Hoboken, NJ: John Wiley & Sons, 2005. A compilation of leading academic scholars and researchers about multiculturalism.

Benn, Suzanne, and Dianne Bolton. *Key Concepts in Corporate Social Responsibility*. Thousand Oaks, CA: Sage Publications, 2011. Strong discussion on sustainability and environmental programs.

Burke, Edmund. *Managing a Company in an Activist World*. Westport, CT: Praeger Publishing, 2005. Outstanding explanation of corporate outreach to enhance community citizenship.

Derickson, Rossella, and Krista Henley. *Awakening Social Responsibility*. Silicon Valley, CA: Derickson and Henley, 2007. This text calls for individuals to lead their companies down the path of sustainable development, business ethics, philanthropy, and giving.

Dresser, Norine. *Multicultural Manners: Essential Rules of Etiquette for the 21st Century*. Hoboken, NJ: John Wiley & Sons, 2005. The do's and don'ts of dealing in business with people of different backgrounds.

Fineglass, Art. *The Public Relations Handbook for Nonprofits*. San Francisco: Jossey-Bass, 2005. All a nonprofit organization needs to organize and implement an effective public relations program.

Harrison, E. Bruce. *Corporate Greening 2.0: Create and Communicate Your Company's Climate Change and Sustainability Strategies*. Exeter, NH: Publishing Works, 2008. The most knowledgeable person in public relations about climate change analyzes the positions on the environment of 40 companies and business groups.

Haywood, Roger. *Corporate Reputation: The Brand and the Bottom Line*. 3rd ed. London, England: Kogan Page, Ltd., 2005. Storehouse of case studies on institutions that have successfully managed their reputations.

Kotler, Philip, and Nancy Lee. *Corporate Social Responsibility: Doing the Most Good for Your Company and Your Cause*. Hoboken, NJ: John Wiley & Sons, 2005. Real-world advice from noted marketing professor Kotler and a respected colleague.

Levine, Bertram. *Resolving Racial Conflict*. Columbia, MO: University of Missouri Press, 2005. The former community relations director of the U.S. Justice Department traces the history of the civil rights movement in America.

McElhaney, Kellie A. *Just Good Business*. San Francisco, CA: Berret-Koehler Publishers, 2008. Step-by-step approach in implementing CSR.

Tench, Ralph, and Liz Yeomans. *Exploring Public Relations*. Essex, England: Pearson Education, 2006. A general public relations text, written by British authors, with a strong section on community and society, as well as corporate social responsibility.

Visser, Wayne, Dirk Matten, Manfred Pohl, and Nick Tolhurst. *The A to Z of Corporate Social Responsibility*. Chichester, England: John Wiley & Sons, 2007. Literally soup to nuts in organizing for corporate social responsibility.

Vogel, David. *The Market for Virtue: The Potential and Limits of Corporate Social Responsibility*. Washington, DC: The Brookings Institution, 2005. A candid look at the constant business battle of "doing what's right" versus "doing what makes the most money."

Werther, William B., Jr., and David Chandler. *Strategic Corporate Responsibility*, 2nd ed. Thousand Oaks, CA: Sage Publications, 2011. Good primer on the various elements of corporate social responsibility.

Chapter 14

International Consumer Relations

Chapter Objectives

1. To examine the important public of "consumers," both in the United States and around the world.

2. To explain the nuances of consumer relations; dealing persuasively with customers and prospects to build an agreeable consumer experience.

3. To discuss the growth of the "consumer movement" in America and around the world.

4. To explore the building of worldwide brands through positive public relations activities, conducted on a consistent basis throughout geographic markets.

FIGURE 14-1 **Out from the weed(s).**
General Mills had no problem pushing the envelope in bringing back 1970s pothead heroes Cheech and Chong to star on YouTube about Fiber One brownies.
(Photo: FRED PROUSER/REUTERS/Newscom)

Just like everything else in the 21st century, social media have changed, inexorably, the way companies deal with consumers—even conservative, traditional, and solidly entrenched companies.

Like General Mills, for example.

In 2011, General Mills, the keeper of Cheerios and Betty Crocker and the Jolly Green Giant, literally "went to pot" using social media. The $12 billion, family-friendly, Midwestern company decided in 2011 to market its Fiber One brand of brownies by bonding with the two biggest burnouts in movie making history, Cheech and Chong.

Specifically, the company chose the now nearly septuagenarian potheads—most famous for their immortal film, *Cheech and Chong: Up In Smoke*—to star in a YouTube video, entitled *Magic Brownie Adventure,* to tout the "magic ingredient" in Fiber One brownies (Figure 14-1). The ingredient, of course, turned out to be "fiber," not marijuana. "Because now that you are getting older, you need a new kind of magic from your brownie," intones an announcer. The over-the-edge video proved a viral sensation for General Mills and Fiber One.[1]

Social media and the Internet have, indeed, changed people's buying habits. In 2012, U.S. online shoppers were expected to spend upwards of $224 billion—on books, apparel, computers, you name it—up 15% from the year earlier.[2]

Thanks largely to e-commerce, the world has continued to evolve into a society of consumers, with increased consumption propelling economies in good times and declining consumption perplexing economies in bad times.

Dealing with consumers around the world—often in conjunction with product and marketing professionals—is another front-line responsibility of public relations. At the core of international consumer relations lies an attitude of delivering dependable products in a manner that is service-oriented and ethical. As in all areas of public relations, the aim is to offer products and brands that are stellar not only in quality but also in reputation.

Worldwide Consumer Class

Notwithstanding the economic malaise that gripped the globe in the second decade of the 21st century, nearly two billion people worldwide now belong to the "consumer class"—the group of people characterized by diets of highly processed food, the desire for bigger houses and more and bigger cars, higher levels of debt, and lifestyles devoted to the accumulation of nonessential goods. Rising consumption has helped meet basic needs and create jobs around the world. Today, nearly half of global consumers reside in developing countries, including 240 million in China and 120 million in India—markets that, even with recession, still command the highest potential for expansion.

Nowhere was the worldwide consumer class more on display than at the 2012 Summer Olympics in London, where companies from McDonald's and Coca-Cola in the United States to Taiwan's Acer electronics company and France's Atos technology company joined six other global corporations to pay nearly $1 billion for the privilege of sponsoring the games. Nonetheless, the problems that multinational companies suffer in a society of "Occupy" movements were also vividly on display in London.

McDonald's, the world's largest restaurant chain and perhaps the lead Olympic sponsor among lead sponsors, was vilified for selling unhealthy foods, even by the Olympic executives who just signed the company up for an eight-year sponsorship extension. McDonald's also constructed the world's largest McDonald's restaurant inside the Stratford, London, Olympic Park (Figure 14-2). When the British Green Party pointed out that 25% of the British population was obese and then publicly denounced the company for "promoting obesity," International Olympic Committee Chair Jacques Rogge knuckled under and agreed with the critics. "We've said to them: 'Listen, there is an issue in terms of the growing trend on obesity, what are you going to do about that?'" the IOC chair said.[3]

Globalization and the spread of social media and the Internet have introduced fresh pressures on companies such as McDonald's to walk a fine line between behaving "responsibly" and promoting their products. More often than not, meeting this challenge means differentiating one's product from all the rest. Often it is public relations techniques and societal sensitivities that help distinguish a company and its products from the competition.

- In the prior Summer Olympics in Beijing, 2008, the General Electric (GE) Company launched its "EcoMagination" campaign on the Olympic grounds to showcase the company's environmentally friendly products from wind turbines to LED lighting to eco-friendly nanofiltration and recycling water systems. Three years earlier, GE CEO Jeff Immelt announced the global company would bet its future on environmentally hospitable products.[4]

- The Walt Disney company, addressing the concerns of parents over child nutrition, decided to curtail the use of its name and popular characters such as Buzz

FIGURE 14-2
Biiiiig Mac.
The world's largest
McDonald's inside
The Olympic Park,
Stratford, London,
in 2012. *(Photo: Sue
Andrews/Photoshot/
Newscom)*

Lightyear and Lightning McQueen with food items that didn't meet acceptable nutritional standards. The new guidelines affected Disney licensing agreements with a variety of snacks and foods that were too rich in sugar, calories, and fat.[5]

- The Mattel Company battled ferociously to protect the reputation of its toys. A lead paint scandal emanating from China, where many of the company's toys were made, caused Mattel to revamp safety measures at Chinese manufacturing plants and caused the firm's CEO to film an online video apology to parents.[6]

- Meanwhile, Burger King, the world's second largest hamburger chain behind McDonald's, announced it would begin buying eggs and pork only from suppliers that did not confine their animals in cages and crates. The decision was hailed by animal rights activists as a "historic advance."[7]

Such were the socially responsible public relations initiatives companies used to enhance consumer relations.

In an era overwrought with advertising "noise"—tens of thousands of blaring messages beamed in the direction of a single consumer—public relations solutions can help cut through the clutter and distinguish one company from the next, enhancing the sale of a firm's products. This chapter examines how public relations helps attract, win, and keep consumers.

Consumer Relations Objectives

Building sales is the primary consumer relations objective. A satisfied customer may return; an unhappy customer may not. Here are some typical goals:

- **Keeping old customers.** Most sales are made to established customers. Consumer relations efforts should be made to keep these customers happy.

FIGURE 14-3
The butler is out and about.
BlazePR used traditional and social media to introduce the upscale consumers of Los Angeles to BrunchButler, a 24/7 luxury brunch delivery and catering service from Switzerland, in 2012. *(Courtesy BlazePR)*

- **Attracting new customers.**   Every business must work constantly to develop new customers. In many industries, the prices and quality of competing products are similar. In choosing among brands, customers may base decisions on how they have been treated.

- **Marketing new items or services.**   Customer relations techniques can influence the sale of new products. When GE's research revealed that consumers want personalized service and more information on new products, it established the GE Answer Center, a national toll-free, 24-hour service that informs consumers about new GE products and services. Building such company and product loyalty lies at the heart of a solid consumer relations effort (Figure 14-3).

- **Expediting complaint handling.**   Few companies are free of complaints. Customers protest when appliances don't work, errors are made in billing, or deliveries aren't made on time. Many large firms have established response procedures, often outsourcing call centers to places like Lakeland, Florida; Johnson City, Tennessee; or Bangalore, India.

- **Reducing costs.**   For three decades, the Sym's clothing company used to advertise that "An educated customer is our best customer." Indeed, to most companies, an educated consumer is the best consumer.

Consumer-Generated Media

For decades, publicity to consumers about products and services revolved around the mass media. While the traditional media are still important avenues through which to promote organizational offerings, the new lead voice in town is social media. It has given consumers a voice, a publishing platform, and a forum where their collective voices on products and services can be heard, shared, and researched.

Consumer-generated media (CGM) encompass the millions of consumer-generated comments, opinions, and personal experiences posted in publicly available online sources on a wide range of issues, topics, products, and brands. CGM is also referred to as "online consumer word-of-mouth," originated from a variety of sources:

- blogs
- message boards and forums
- public discussions (Usenet newsgroups)
- discussions and forums on large email portals (Yahoo!, AOL, MSN)
- online opinion/review sites and services
- online feedback/complaint sites

Consumers seem to place trust in their fellow consumers. For any marketer trying to be heard or to break through the clutter, understanding and managing CGM may be critical. Then, too, CGM is increasingly easy and inexpensive to create. Online discussion forums, membership groups, boards, blogs, and Usenet newsgroups are all easy to access.[8]

Handling Consumer Complaints

Research indicates that only a handful of dissatisfied customers—4%—will ever complain. But that means that there are many others with the same complaint who never say anything. And the vast majority of dissatisfied customers won't repurchase from the offending company.

In the old days, a frequent response to complaint letters was to dust off the so-called *bedbug letter*—a term that stemmed from occasional letters to the railroads complaining about bedbugs in the sleeper cars. To save time, railroad consumer relations personnel simply dispatched a prewritten bedbug letter in response. Today, with the volume of mail, email, and faxes at a mountainous level, 21st-century versions of the bedbug letter still appear from time to time. Really good companies, however, understand the benefit of applying the "personal touch" to rectify consumer problems (Figure 14-4).

FIGURE 14-4
Personal touch.
There's a reason Four Seasons hotel chain is always ranked at the top of customer service lists; it takes pains to deal properly with clients.
(Courtesy Fraser Seitel)

Dear Mr. Seitel,

I'm writing to apologize for the email sent to you on April 13th, 2012, which incorrectly identified you as "Mr. Mamela".

The error occurred during the programming of the salutation and resulted in the email being addressed to a Four Seasons employee (the recipient for purposes of testing), instead of you, the intended recipient. This technical oversight is not representative of the standard we have set for ourselves in creating customized experiences and communications for our guests. We have put measures in place to ensure that it does not happen again.

At Four Seasons, we take guest privacy very seriously. Please rest assured that your personal data has not been compromised in any way and your Four Seasons guest profile remains secure.

I apologize for any inconvenience or concern this may have caused you.

Sincerely,

Susan Helstab
Executive Vice President, Marketing
Four Seasons Hotels and Resorts

Today, the risk of consumer complaints going viral is always present. Airlines seem to suffer more than others. In 2010, when a young couple missed their Alaska Airlines flight after arriving one minute late because of a baby diaper emergency, they were forced to pay thousands of dollars in rebooking fees. The couple took their disapprobation out in a blog, and Alaska Airlines was vilified coast to coast.[9]

To respond quickly to complaints, companies established ombudsperson offices. The term *ombudsman* originally described a government official—in Sweden and New Zealand, for example—appointed to investigate complaints about abuses committed by public officials. Today, more often than not, the ombudsperson function is outsourced to a central (often overseas) location that customers can call to seek redress of grievances.

Typically, call center personnel monitor the difficulties customers are having with products. Often they can anticipate product or performance deficiencies. Corporate complaint handlers are in business to inspire customer confidence and to influence an organization's behavior toward improved service.

The companies that express such understanding and courtesy will be the ones that keep the business.

PR Ethics Mini-Case
Kenneth Cole's Egyptian "Twagedy"

There's a way to conduct online international relations. And there's a way not to.

American shoe designer Kenneth Cole found out the hard way in 2011 that "humor" doesn't translate well beyond international boundaries. As the world focused on Arab Spring uprisings across the Middle East and North Africa, Cole seized the opportunity to tweet about his new fall collection:

> **KC** @KennethCole
> Kenneth Cole
>
> Millions are in uproar in #Cairo. Rumor is they heard our new spring collection is now available online at http://bit.ly/KCairo -KC
>
> 2 hours ago via Twitter for BlackBerry® ☆ Favorite ↄ Retweet ↵ Reply

First, not funny. Second, offensive. Third, displayed around the world. (Other than that, it was great!) The criticisms of the Cole tweet were instantaneous.

TechCrunch's Michael Arrington tweeted:

> **Michael Arrington**
> WTF is wrong with you, @KennethCole?
> http://twitter.com/#!/KennethCole/status/33177584262971393 less than a minute ago via web

Others added to the anti-Cole chorus:

> **Jennifer Lizak**
> @KennethCole Totally poor taste. People are dying in the streets and you want to advertise your fashions? #boycottKennethCole.

In predictable Internet fashion, a parody @kennethcolepr account was quickly created, and the #KennethColeTweets hashtag took off. A sample:

> **KennethColePR**
> "People from New Orleans are flooding into Kenneth Cole stores!"
> #KennethColeTweets less than a minute ago

To his credit, within two hours of his initial tweet, Mr. Cole tweeted an apology and posted a longer mea culpa to his blog, saying: "I apologize to everyone who was offended by my insensitive tweet about the situation in Egypt. I've dedicated my life to raising awareness about serious social issues and in hindsight my attempt at humor regarding a nation liberating themselves against oppression was poorly timed and absolutely inappropriate."

Ya think?*

Questions

1. What would you have advised that Kenneth Cole tweet about the Arab Spring?

2. In light of this contretemps, what policy would you recommend Mr. Cole follow in future tweets?

*For further information, see Rupal Parekh, "The Seven Stages in the Life Cycle of a Social-Media Sin," *Advertising Age*, February 7, 2011, 6; and Mary Phillips-Sandy, "Kenneth Cole's Egypt Tweet Offends Just About Everyone on Twitter," *The Huffington Post*, February 3, 2011.

The Consumer Movement

Although consumerism is considered to be a late 20th-century concept, legislation to protect consumers first emerged in the United States in 1872, when Congress enacted the Criminal Fraud Statute to protect consumers against corporate abuses. In 1887, Congress established the Interstate Commerce Commission to curb freewheeling railroad tycoons.

However, the first real consumer movement came right after the turn of the century when journalistic muckrakers encouraged legislation to protect the consumer. Upton Sinclair's novel *The Jungle* revealed scandalous conditions in the meatpacking industry and helped usher in federal meat inspection standards as Congress passed the Food and Drug Act and the Trade Commission Act. In the second wave of the movement, from 1927 to 1938, consumers were safeguarded from the abuses of manufacturers, advertisers, and retailers of well-known brands of commercial products. During this time, Congress passed the Food, Drug, and Cosmetic Act.

Later, the movement was boosted by the activities of a lone consumer crusader, Ralph Nader, who brought the world's most powerful auto company, General Motors, to its knees. Nader's thin 1965 book, *Unsafe at Any Speed,* pointed out how the GM Corvair was literally a "death trap." After trying to stop Nader at every turn—including assigning private detectives to trail his every move—GM relented and stopped production of the Corvair. Consumerism had won its most significant battle.

By the early 1960s, the movement had become stronger and more unified. President John F. Kennedy, in fact, proposed that consumers have their own bill of rights, containing four basic principles:

1. **The right to safety:**   to be protected against the marketing of goods hazardous to health or life.

2. **The right to be informed:**   to be protected against fraudulent, deceitful, or grossly misleading information, advertising, labeling, or other practices and to be given the facts needed to make an informed choice.

3. **The right to choose:**   to be assured access, whenever possible, to a variety of products and services at competitive prices.

4. **The right to be heard:**   to be assured that consumer interests will receive full and sympathetic consideration in the formulation of government policy.

Subsequent U.S. presidents have continued to emphasize consumer rights and protection. Labeling, packaging, product safety, and a variety of other issues continue to concern government overseers of consumer interests. Indeed, the federal consumer-protection bureaucracy extends through multiple agencies, which protect everything from trade and product performance to stock holder rights and financial disclosure. The most recent such agency was the Consumer Financial Protection Bureau, created in the wake of Wall Street scandals in 2011 "to promote fairness and transparency for mortgages, credit cards and other consumer financial products and services."

Operating Around the Globe

The actions of individuals and organizations in one part of the world are felt instantly and irrevocably by people around the globe. As a consequence, multinational corporations, in particular, must be sensitive to how their actions might affect people of different cultures in different geographies.

2011 Ranking of the Top 20 Brands						
Rank	Previous Rank	Brand	Region/ Country	Sector	Brand Value ($m)	Change in Brand Value
1	1	Coca-Cola	United States	Beverages	71,861	2%
2	2	IBM	United States	Business Services	69,905	8%
3	3	Microsoft	United States	Computer Software	59,087	-3%
4	4	Google	United States	Internet Services	55,317	27%
5	5	General Electric	United States	Diversified	42,808	0%
6	6	McDonald's	United States	Restaurants	35,593	6%
7	7	Intel	United States	Electronics	35,217	10%
8	17	Apple	United States	Electronics	33,492	58%
9	9	Disney	United States	Media	29,018	1%
10	10	HP	United States	Electronics	28,479	6%
11	11	Toyota	Japan	Automotive	27,764	6%
12	12	Mercedes	Germany	Automotive	27,445	9%
13	14	Cisco	United States	Business Services	25,309	9%
14	8	Nokia	Finland	Electronics	25,071	-15%
15	15	BMW	Germany	Automotive	24,554	10%
16	13	Gillette	United States	FMCG	23,997	3%
17	19	Samsung	South Korea	Electronics	23,430	20%
18	16	Louis Vuitton	France	Luxury	23,172	6%
19	20	Honda	Japan	Automotive	19,431	5%
20	22	Oracle	United States	Business Services	17,262	16%

FIGURE 14-5
Global brand leaders.
And the Top 10 winners are . . . all from the good-old US of A.
(Courtesy of Interbrand)

Companies, in fact, have become the most prominent standard bearers of their countries. American companies, with the 10 most powerful brands in the world (Figure 14-5), are the most prominent of the prominent.

Consider the challenges multinational companies face.

■ In 2012, both McDonald's and Coca-Cola, two core sponsors of the London Summer Olympics, drew criticism from local politicians and nongovernmental organizations for offering products that promote obesity. That same year, McDonald's, Burger King, and KFC were subject to a new law in Chile, barring them from offering toys with children's meals. Like the Brits, Chilean officials worried about their increasingly chubby children.[10]

■ That same year, the European Union, concerned about antitrust violations of American companies, reopened an investigation into whether Microsoft had kept the antitrust commitments it made in 2009 and warned that penalties for noncompliance would be "severe."[11] Earlier, a similar investigation had been launched against Google. And in 2009, the EU fined Intel a whopping $1.45 billion in antitrust fines. Intel appealed.

■ And also in 2012, the mighty Apple company found itself embroiled in a scandal involving working conditions at the Chinese plants manufacturing its iPads and iPhones. One iPad factory in Foxconn, near the booming southern city of Shenzhen, experienced a spate of 13 suicides or attempted suicides. Amid increased criticism, Apple called in assessors from the same organization that was set up to stamp out sweatshops in China's clothing industry a decade earlier.[12]

All foreign companies operating internationally must constantly reinforce the notion that they are responsible and concerned residents of local communities. Most resort to the public relations philosophy of leading with proper action and then communicating it. KFC, for example, has 158 franchises in Indonesia, most of which are locally owned and operated. McDonald's has a poster in the window of the Jakarta McDonald's that reads:

> *In the name of Allah, the merciful and the gracious, McDonald's Indonesia is owned by an indigenous Muslim Indonesian.*

Smart multinationals also support local causes and incorporate international audiences and celebrities in their philanthropic efforts. Stated another way, the most well-known companies and best brands in the world observe a mantra of "thinking global, acting local" to win lasting friendship and support in other countries.

Consumer Internet Activists

In the 21st century, with the Internet as stimulus, organic consumer movements—directed at individual companies, industries, or even multinational agencies such as the World Trade Organization—have spread like wildfire around the globe. As one harassed executive put it, "In the old days, if you had an unlisted number, it was hard to find you. Now you do a Google search and find out the most intimate details."[13]

Such was the case in 2011 when the Occupy Wall Street movement rallied its troops with ongoing social media contact about rallies and protests, not to mention marches to the Manhattan homes of several Wall Street big shots, including JP Morgan CEO Jamie Dimon, News Corp. CEO Rupert Murdoch, and several hedge fund billionaires, all addresses compliments of Internet search.

Likewise, although private testing organizations that evaluate products and inform consumers about potential dangers have proliferated, the most significant activity to keep companies honest has occurred on the Internet.

Perhaps the best-known testing group, Consumers Union, was formed in 1936 to test products across a wide spectrum of industries. It publishes the results in a monthly magazine, *Consumer Reports*, which reaches about 3.5 million readers. Often an evaluation in *Consumer Reports*, either pro or con, greatly affects how customers view particular products. Occasionally *Consumer Reports* flubs its reviews, such as the famous case in 2007 when the magazine embarrassingly backed off its negative report on infant car seats, when manufacturers complained that test crashes were conducted at speeds higher than the publication claimed.[14]

The Consumer Federation of America was formed in 1968 to unify lobbying efforts for pro-consumer legislation. Today the federation consists of 200 national, state, and local consumer groups, labor unions, electric cooperatives, and other organizations with consumer interests.

With 513 million Chinese, 240 million Americans, 121 million Indians, 101 million Japanese, and millions of others around the world accessing the Internet annually, online consumer activism has become much more prominent.[15] Internet activism uses Internet communications technologies to enable faster communications and coordination by citizen movements.

The most striking example of Internet activism stemmed not from consumers but from political activists throughout the Middle East from Tunisia to Egypt to Syria, who raged against established dictatorships to bring them down.

Although companies often find such activists' criticism annoying, the emergence of the consumer watchdog movement has generally been a positive development for consumers. Ralph Nader, still going strong into the 21st century, and others have forced organizations to consider, even more than usual, the downside of the products and services they offer. Smart companies have come to take seriously the pronouncements of consumer activists.

Outside the Lines
Think Multilingual—or Else

Steve Rivkin is America's foremost "nameologist," having written extensively on what organizations and products must consider before they choose a name (Figure 14-6). When it comes to organizations dealing overseas, the nameologist warns, you'd better think multilingual—or else.

Or else what? Or else this:

- A food company named its giant burrito a *Burrada*. Big mistake. The colloquial meaning of that word in Spanish is "big mistake."

- Estée Lauder was set to export its Country Mist makeup when German managers pointed out that *mist* is German slang for, uh, well, to put it gently, "manure." (The name became Country Moist in Germany.)

- Colgate introduced a toothpaste in France called Cue, the name of a notorious French porno magazine.

- The name Coca-Cola in China was first rendered as *ke-kou-ke-la*. Unfortunately, Coke did not discover until after thousands of signs had been printed that the phrase means "bite the wax tadpole." Coke then researched 40,000 Chinese characters and found a close phonetic equivalent, *ko-kou-ko-le*, which loosely translates as "happiness in the mouth." Much better.

- A leading brand of car de-icer in Finland will never make it to America. The brand's name: *Super Piss*.

FIGURE 14-6 Namemeister extraordinaire.
Steve Rivkin. *(Courtesy of Rivkin & Associates, Inc.)*

- Ditto for Japan's leading brand of coffee creamer. Its name: *Creap*.

Outside the Lines

Straighten Out Your English—or Else

On the other hand, it might be equally beneficial for our friends in foreign lands to make sure of their own English.

Consider these actual signs posted in various establishments around the world.

- In a Copenhagen airline ticket office: "We take your bags and send them in all directions."
- In a Norwegian cocktail lounge: "Ladies are requested not to have children in the bar."
- At a Budapest zoo: "Please do not feed the animals. If you have any suitable food, give it to the guard on duty."
- In a doctor's office in Italy: "Specialist in women and other diseases."

- In a Paris hotel elevator: "Please leave your values at the front desk."
- From the brochure of a Tokyo car rental firm: "When passenger of foot heave in sight, tootle the horn. Trumpet him melodiously at first, but if he still obstacles your passage then tootle him with vigor."
- In an advertisement by a Hong Kong dentist: "Teeth extracted by the latest Methodists."
- In an Acapulco hotel: "The manager has personally passed all the water served here."
- In a Bucharest hotel lobby: "The lift is being fixed for the next day. During that time we regret that you will be unbearable."

Business Gets the Message

Obviously, few organizations can afford to shirk their responsibilities to consumers. Consumer relations divisions have sprung up, either as separate entities or as part of public relations departments.

In many companies, consumer relations began strictly as a way to handle complaints, an area to which all unanswerable queries were sent. Such units have frequently provided an alert to management. More recently, companies have broadened the consumer relations function to encompass such activities as developing guidelines to evaluate services and products for management, developing consumer programs that meet consumer needs and increase sales, developing field-training programs, evaluating service approaches, and evaluating company effectiveness in demonstrating concern for customers.

The investment in consumer service apparently pays off. Marketers of consumer products say that most customer criticism can be mollified with a prompt, personalized reply. Throw in a couple of free samples and consumers feel even better. In any case, consumers are impressed when a company takes the time to drop them a line for whatever reason.

On the other hand, failing to answer a question, satisfy a complaint, or solve a problem can result in a blitz of bad word-of-mouth advertising.

In adopting a more activist consumerist philosophy, firms have found that consumer relations need not take a defensive posture. Consumer relations professionals must themselves be activists to make certain that consumers understand the benefits and realities of using their products.

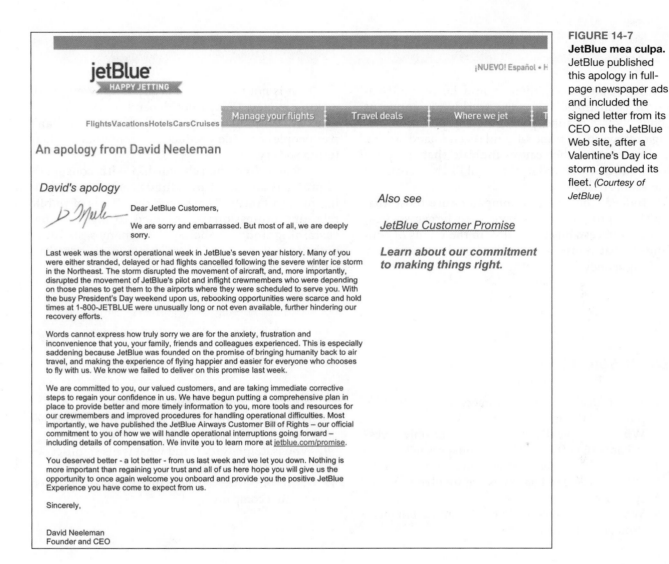

FIGURE 14-7
JetBlue mea culpa. JetBlue published this apology in full-page newspaper ads and included the signed letter from its CEO on the JetBlue Web site, after a Valentine's Day ice storm grounded its fleet. *(Courtesy of JetBlue)*

The consumer philosophy of Jet Blue Airways, embodied in the company's "Customer Bill of Rights," is typical of the more enlightened attitude of most companies today.[16]

JetBlue issued its Customer Bill of Rights in 2007, a week after a disastrous Valentine's Day ice storm stranded thousands of customers and saddled the formerly beloved airline with oppressive national opprobrium. Said embattled CEO David Neeleman (who was replaced shortly thereafter), *"We had a weakness in our system. We were completely overwhelmed. I don't blame our customers for being upset with this. This was a big wakeup call for JetBlue."* (Figure 14-7)

No question that in the second decade of the 21st century, business understood that with heightened competition, scarcer resources and more immediate and public ways to complain, the consumer most certainly was "king."

Last Word

Without consumers, there would be no multinational companies. Increased worldwide concerns about climate change, packaging and pollution, rising outrage about trans fats and second hand smoke, and numerous other causes indicate that the push for product safety and quality will likely increase in the years ahead.

Indeed, the smartest companies are those that tie their products and services to larger societal causes, thus establishing a link in the minds of consumers that represents "loftier" goals than merely making money.

That is not to say there is anything wrong with making money. Companies depend on their profits to exist. Without profitability, corporations can't pay people, provide products, or contribute to bettering society.

Safeguarding the relationship with consumers of products and services is fundamental to continuing to earn profits. That's why the efforts of public relations professionals, assigned to maintaining, sustaining and enhancing a company's standing with its customers, is a core communications challenge in the 21st century.

Discussion Starters

1. Why is dealing with consumers so important for public relations?
2. What are typical consumer relations objectives?
3. What is the office of the ombudsperson?
4. What is consumer-generated marketing?
5. What key federal agencies are involved in consumerism?
6. What is the purpose of the Consumer Financial Protection Bureau?
7. What is a consumer bill of rights?
8. What is the impact of the Internet on a company's consumer relations?
9. Who is Ralph Nader, and what is his significance to consumerism?
10. What constitutes a quality international consumer-oriented company?

Pick of the Literature

Business As Usual

Brian Solis, Hoboken, NJ: John Wiley & Sons, Inc., 2012

A young, Silicon Valley-based, new media expert dissects the new ways that business reaches consumers.

His premise is that new communication networks—through social media, the mobile Web, gamification and other Web-based technology—have created an ever-expanding "egosystem," such that each individual believes he or she deserves 24-hour customer service.

The author attempts to decipher the significance of all this socializing and egotism and draw lessons for business so that organizations might understand how to respond to this new breed of consumer.

Case Study   Linsanity

For one brief shining moment in the early months of 2012, there arose a basketball phenomenon that spread beyond sports to embrace the entire world.

Jeremy Lin, an obscure, unheralded, 22-year-old Asian American, evangelical Christian, backup point guard—a Harvard graduate, no less—came off the bench for the New York Knicks and lit up the New York sky with hard court exploits that left mouths agape throughout the globe.

Linsanity was born.

And the public relations ramifications were breathtaking.

Intervention from On High

Jeremy Lin began as a high school phenom in Palo Alto, California, attracting attention as a tall—6'3"—Asian American basketballer who led his team to a state championship. He was offered no college scholarships but went on to star on an over-achieving Harvard team and set many Ivy League records.

Nonetheless, Lin wasn't good enough to be drafted by a single National Basketball Association (NBA) team. But he persevered and tried out anyway, gaining a spot with the Golden State Warriors.

Lin barely played in that rookie year and was subsequently cut by the Warriors in year two. He found a temporary position with the Houston Rockets, but that team, too, felt obliged to cut the young Ivy Leaguer before the season. So Lin toiled for a time in the NBA's Development League, where the Knicks—the league's perennial underachievers—picked him up, looked at him in pre-season, and then sent him back down.

One day in January 2012, after toiling admirably for the Erie BayHawks in the D-League, Lin got a call that would change his life forever. The Knicks recalled him as a fourth-string backup. But again, Lin played only 55 minutes in 23 games, mostly at what the players called "garbage time," when the game was out of reach.

Once again, Lin so much feared being cut that he asked a chaplain at a pregame prayer session to pray for him.

Evidently, the chaplain did.

With the Knicks suffering injuries and poor play, the Knicks coach, in "desperation," inserted his fourth-string point guard into the lineup.

The results were instantaneous and miraculous.

Lin lit up the court with baskets from all over and dazzling passing. The Knicks, losers of 11 of 13 prior games without Lin in the lineup, went on a winning streak with the young point guard at the helm.

And Jeremy Lin never looked back.

From Nowhere to Everywhere

Lin's play for the Knicks that winter was "off the charts."

He regularly scored 20 points a game against the best and highest paid players on the planet. His play was electric, with alley-oop passes, daring drives, and crushing falls to the floor after making circus shots.

On February 14, with less than a second remaining in a game with Toronto, Lin launched a three-point shot that won the game.

FIGURE 14-8   Lincredible.
The cover of China Times Publishing Company's 2012 release on the life and times of the world's fastest rising superstar, Jeremy Lin. *(Photo: Newscom)*

Lin became the first NBA player to score at least 20 points and have seven assists in each of his first five starts. Lin scored 89, 109, and 136 points in his first three, four, and five career starts, respectively, all three the most by any player since the merger between the American Basketball Association and the NBA in 1976–77.

The New York media ate it up with new headlines every day.

- "Linsane"
- "Lincredible"
- "Linsational"
- "Linvincible"
- "Lintoxicating"

The puns were, well, "Lin-itless."

Within three weeks of his first game as a starter, at least seven e-books were being published on Lin, and the Global Language Monitor declared that "Linsanity" had met its criteria to be considered a bona fide English-language word.

International media also flocked to New York to see the Asian savior. Indeed, with the retirement of 7'4" Yao Ming from China,

Jeremy Lin seemed poised to inherit Yao's mantle as the most popular athlete in China (Figure 14-8). In rapid order:

■ Lin's name was the most searched athlete on the Internet in China, eclipsing basketball's Kobe Bryant and soccer star Ronaldo.

■ While Lin's U.S. twitter account attracted 6 million followers (not too shabby), his Chinese twitter account attracted 26 million followers!

■ In 2011, China's *Vivid Magazine* named Lin one of its top eight influential Chinese Americans.

■ Lin's Chinese name, "linshuhao," was put up for auction in China for 260,000 yuan, or $41,080 (again, not too shabby).

■ Lin signed a two-year marketing partnership contract with Volvo to serve as advertising spokesperson in China and other Chinese-speaking Asian areas.

In addition, Lin and his marketing/public relations team quickly moved to trademark the word "Linsanity" for use on T-shirts, hoodies, mugs, energy drinks, duffel bags, fruit juices, nightshirts, scarves, socks, underwear, sandals, visors, bandannas, footwear, and action figures, all listed on Lin's trademark application. The trademark would provide him with legal protection against others who wanted to stamp, sew, or print the "Linsanity" name on their merchandise.

With continued prominence on the court, the international marketing and public relations opportunities for Jeremy Lin would be astounding.

The Next Challenge

As in most fairy tales, Jeremy Lin's magic season ended abruptly as an injury caused him to miss the last months of the Knicks' season.

In the off-season of 2012, Lin was the subject of a bidding war between the Houston Rockets—Yao Ming's team in a city with a huge Asian American population— and the Knicks. Eventually, the Rockets, who had once before cut Lin because they saw no future for him, signed the player to a three-year contract, the Houston general manager admitting that the first time around, he "made a mistake."

The price of Lin's new contract?

Twenty-five million dollars.

Not bad for a young man who, a year earlier, didn't know where his next paycheck was coming from.

The moral: Everybody loves a Linner.*

Questions

1. Was Jeremy Lin smart to take advantage of marketing/public relations deals and trademark immediately after his breakout month with the Knicks?

2. How would you market Lin in Houston?

3. What public relations contingency plans would you make for Jeremy Lin, were you the Houston Rockets?

*For further information, see Howard Beck, "Growing Doubts on Lin's Return to Knicks," *The New York Times*, July 15, 2012; Richard Sandomir, "Knicks' Lin Is Guarding a Word that Defined a Craze," *The New York Times*, June 23, 2012; Nate Taylor, "Lin Follows Yao in More Ways Than One," *The New York Times*, July 24, 2012; and Dave Zirin, "Jeremy Lin Inspires a Nation," *The Nation*, February 29, 2012.

From the Top

An Interview with Kathy Bloomgarden

Dr. Kathy Bloomgarden is CEO of Ruder Finn, one of the world's leading independent public relations agencies, serving more than 250 corporations and nonprofit organizations. With more than 25 years of experience in communications for multinational companies, Dr. Bloomgarden has developed particular skills in global communications consulting. She is a member of the Council on Foreign Relations and the Atlantic Council and author of *Trust: The Secret Weapon of Effective Business Leaders*.

What is the key to doing public relations work in international markets?

It is absolutely critical to distinguish between global PR—using channels and thought leadership that have the flexibility to be relevant to people worldwide—and execution of PR in local markets around the world—tailoring approaches to specific audiences. While some campaigns can be broad enough to have a universal impact, it is often necessary to adjust strategies for each country or region. For example, since countries have varying levels of Internet usage, the channels used to reach target audiences must be adjusted by market.

In particular, it is crucial to understand that different markets often have vastly different needs and cultural nuances. Today, the simplicity of disseminating messages instantly and globally through the Internet can easily camouflage the importance of language and culture needed to engage local audiences.

What is the largest difference between public relations work in the United States and overseas?

Some international markets, like those in Western Europe, are actually quite similar to the United States, especially with respect to the position of journalists, the ways people consume media, and levels of government involvement. For example, in both the United States and France, Germany, Italy, Spain and the UK, consumers are likely to access media through their phones. However, the approach to PR content and messaging to the media in the United States is often more technical and in-depth than in other markets, like the UK, where journalists tend to prefer succinct messaging and colloquial language.

On the other hand, PR in emerging markets is distinct from the United States and can vary drastically between countries. For example, while Internet penetration is still spotty in India, China has the largest population of Internet users in the world. This allows PR campaigns to reach large audiences through these channels. Cultural differences also affect PR messaging and approach. In the West, for instance, differing opinions are usually valued, while in China, a higher premium is placed on consensuses. Taking this cultural dissimilarity into account can help PR practitioners ensure that they target the right influencers.

What is the most advanced international location for public relations?

If you think of PR in terms of traditional media relations, London is among the most advanced international locations because its media culture is probably the most established in the region and absolutely ingrained in popular culture. Germany is similar in rank and is important due to its economic role in Europe and geographic position at the heart of the continent. There is a high concentration of international journalists based in these locations—some international publications, such as *Al Hayat* and *Al-Arab*, have their global headquarters in London despite the fact that their distributions are concentrated in the Middle East.

Beijing is also very developed in certain PR specialty areas, such as Corporate Social Responsibility, the environment, mobile technology, and luxury.

What is the most common mistake that American firms make in international public relations?

Many American agencies use a one-size-fits-all approach, failing to take into account the scale and diversity of their target audiences, and, with budget constraints in mind, stick to regional planning without adequate local budgets for adaptation and execution. The "Europe-in-a-box" approach, for example, in which agencies run a continent-wide campaign from one location with a limited budget, almost never works. Pitching media in France and Spain from an office in London is not the same as securing coverage in Illinois and Ohio from a desk in New York!

What is the state of public relations in Europe?

It's very difficult to generalize when it comes to Europe. The continent has some very mature and developed PR markets such as the UK, Germany, and France, which are on a par with the United States, and the Nordic countries, which are similar, but have a more limited media environment. However, other countries, such as Poland and the Czech Republic, have a less developed PR industry, but are moving quickly and showing signs of progress.

What is the state of public relations in Latin America?

With increased focus on Brazil and other emerging economies in Latin America, there is a growing demand for public relations services in this region. This market is particularly dynamic due to the demographic differences and similarities across the region. For example, PR can benefit from the fact that, with the notable exception of Brazil, the vast majority of people in this region speak Spanish, but must also consider that drastic income and wealth disparity impacts how audiences can be reached. Age demographics, such as the fact that half of Mexico's population is under the age of 27, also influence the content and channels that are effective in particular areas.

What is the state of public relations in Asia generally?

Public relations in Asia varies tremendously by market, primarily due to differences in economic development and the extent of government involvement in the media. In countries that have a robust economy and low government control, like the Philippines, the practice of PR is more similar to developed markets like the United States and Western Europe. On the other hand, in countries where the government has more influence over the media, like Singapore, China, and Indonesia, public relations operates differently, as local contexts must be taken into account.

In particular, differing demographics play a large role in PR across the region. India, for example, is a relatively young market age-wise and the population speaks more than 22 languages.

What is the state of public relations in China?

China is a very dynamic and fast-growing market for public relations. We've seen the market dramatically evolve, from 15 years ago, when the government led all media, and 10 years ago, when business and commercial publications began to take over, to today, when social plays a critical role in influencing young audiences. Third party influencers are also a growing factor, as NGOs increase their presence.

Public relations in China has flourished, developing at an annual growth of around 30% over the past 10 years, according to the China International Public Relations Association.

With the boom of the PR industry there are also a lot of issues to deal with today in China. For instance, PR needs to be more clearly defined for the public if we don't want it to be known as buying ads or paying media. The PR industry needs to tackle these ethics issues and educate clients and the public about what behaving responsibly means for the industry.

Public Relations Library

Bloom, Robert H., and Dave Conti. *The Inside Advantage: The Strategy that Unlocks the Hidden Growth in Your Business.* New York: McGraw-Hill, 2007. The premise here is that in order to grow your consumer base, a firm must tap its "inner strength" by looking internally for that which differentiates you.

Burley, Ron. *Unscrewed.* Berkeley, CA: Ten Speed Press, 2006. A consumer's guide to getting what you pay for.

Carland, Maria Pinto, and Candace Faber. *Careers in International Affairs,* 8th ed. Washington, DC: Georgetown University Press, 2008. Fine primer on what it takes to serve in international relations and how to secure employment.

Cone, Steve. *Powerlines: Words that Sell Brands, Grip Fans & Sometimes Change History.* New York: Bloomberg Press, 2008. These are the lines that moved marketing, according to the author, from "Only You Can Prevent Forest Fires" to "Virginia is for Lovers."

Eisenberg, Bryan, and Jeffrey Eisenberg. *Waiting for Your Cat to Bark?* Nashville, TN: Thomas Nelson Publishers, 2006. The Eisenberg brothers are best-selling authors who have made their living examining the communication gap between marketers and the buying public, and what marketers can do to redress the problem. They begin by declaring "mass marketing" deader than Saddam Hussein.

Epstein, Charlotte. *The Power of Words in International Relations.* Boston, MA: Massachusetts Institute of Technology, 2008. This is a fascinating analysis of how the whaling industry evolved from an attitude of widespread acceptance to one of worldwide opprobrium.

Jackson, Robert, and George Sorenson. *Introduction to International Relations: Theories and Approaches.* New York: Oxford University Press, 2007. An excellent introductory text to international relations.

Johnson, Lisa, and Cheri Hanson. *Mind Your X's & Y's: Satisfying the 10 Cravings of a New Generation of Consumers.* New York: Free Press, 2006. There are 62 million Americans aged 27–41 and 74 million aged just below. This book tells how to reach these Gen X and Yers, who grew up on the Internet.

Martin, Dick. *Rebuilding Brand America.* New York: Amacom, 2007. Dick Martin is a longtime public relations professional and a smart fellah. His prescription to build back the American brand makes great good sense.

McPhail, Thomas L. *Global Communication: Theories, Stakeholders and Trends,* 2nd ed. Malden, MA: Blackwell Publishing, 2006. In addition to tracking the elements that impact global communication, the author also provides a primer on the latest global theories of communication, from electronic colonialism theory to world-system theory.

Ries, Laura, and Al Ries. *The Fall of Advertising and the Rise of PR.* New York: Harper Business, 2002. Legendary positioning guru and his talented daughter declare that their former business has had it. Long live public relations!

Schiffman, Stephan. *E-Mail Selling Techniques: That Really Work.* Avon, MA: Adams Media, 2007. This book is all about creating targeted emails to reach potential customers and earn coveted face time with them.

Spizman, Robyn, and Rick Frishman. *Where's Your WOW? 16 Ways to Make Your Competitors Wish They Were You.* New York: McGraw-Hill, 2008. All about growing creatively by seeking and winning new business.

Stevens, Howard, and Theodore Kinni. *Achieving Sales Excellence: The 7 Customer Rules for Becoming the New Sales Professional.* Avon, MA: Platinum Press, 2007. The result of 14 years of research into how people can become better salesmen. (And all of us in public relations are—"salespeople.")

Wilkinson, Paul. *International Relations.* New York: Oxford University Press, 2007. Learned treatise on government entities and the challenges they face.

Chapter **15**

Public Relations
Writing

Chapter Objectives

1. To discuss the reasons that the public relations professional must be the best writer in the organization.
2. To explore the fundamentals of writing, from drafting to style to ensuring worthwhile content.
3. To discuss, in detail, the rationale for and elements of the news release, the most practical and ubiquitous of public relations writing vehicles.
4. To examine the requisites of writing for the Internet and social media.

Report Card

Agency	Basic Act Requirements	Supporting Activities
Department of Agriculture (USDA)	A	B
Department of Defense (DOD)	B	D
Department of Homeland Security (DHS)	D	D
Department of Justice (DOJ)	C	D
Department of Labor (DOL)	B	F
Department of Transportation (DOT)	C	F
Environmental Protection Agency (EPA)	C	F
Health and Human Services Department (HHS)	C	B
National Archives and Records Administration (NARA)	B	C
Small Business Administration (SBA)	C	C
Social Security Administration (SSA)	C	C
Veterans Affairs Department (VA)	F	F

A — Excellent B — Good C — Satisfactory D — Needs Improvement F — Fail

Name: _Annetta L. Cheek_   Date: _7.19.12_
Chair, Center for Plain Language

FIGURE 15-1 Plain-speaking bureaucrats (not yet). The Center for Plain Language graded 12 federal agencies on (1) how well they followed the new federal law and (2) how well they supported the "spirit" of the law. *(Courtesy of Center for Plain Language)*

Have you ever wondered after reading a correspondence from the Internal Revenue Service or the motor vehicle bureau—that you didn't understand—whether there might be something wrong with you?

Well, rest easy. You're fine. *Nobody* understands what the government is writing.

Latest proof came in a "report card" issued by the nonprofit Center for Plain Language in 2012. The organization "graded" 12 federal agencies (alas, neither the motor vehicle bureau nor the IRS were included) on how well they met the requirements of the 2010 Plain Writing Act, a law mandating government bureaus to cut the "bureaucratese" in dealing with the public. The Center awarded two grades based on how well the agencies met the letter and spirit of the law (Figure 15-1).

The "good news" is that if you're a farmer or defense contractor, you're in good shape; the Department of Agriculture received an A, and the Department of Defense received a B. The "bad news" is that if you're a veteran, fuggedaboutit! The Veterans Affairs Department received a big, fat F.

Center Chairperson Annetta L. Cheek concluded that the government was paying more attention to including more plain language in its communication to the public but, "We still have a long way to go."[1]

Even in the age of social media and the Internet, writing remains the key to public relations: Public relations practitioners are professional communicators. And communications means writing.

All of us know how to write and speak—even government bureaucrats! But public relations professionals should write and speak *better* than their colleagues. Communication—that is, effective writing and speaking—is the essence of the practice of public relations.

There is no substitute for clear and precise language in informing, motivating, and persuading. The ability to write and speak with clarity is a valuable and coveted skill in any organization. Stated another way, the pen (or keyboard, if you will) is, indeed, mightier than the sword.

The ability to write easily, coherently, and quickly distinguishes the public relations professional from others in an organization. It's not that the skills of counseling and marketing and judgment aren't just as important; some experts argue that these skills are often *more* important than knowing how to write. Perhaps. But not knowing how to write—how to express ideas on paper—may reduce the opportunities to ascend the public relations success ladder.

Stated bluntly, beginning public relations professionals are expected to have mastery over the written word. So this chapter will explore the fundamentals of writing: (1) discussing public relations writing in general and the staple of that writing, news releases, in particular; (2) reviewing writing for reading; and (3) discussing writing for listening.

Writing for the Eye and the Ear

The sad fact is that public relations people, by and large, are horrible writers. This is the unfortunate conclusion of public relations teachers, supervisors, and executive recruiters assigned to find jobs for public relations applicants.[2] That is unacceptable in a field in which the fundamental skill must be the ability to write.

What does it take to be a public relations writer?

For one thing, it takes a good knowledge of the basics. Although practitioners probably write for a wider range of purposes and use a greater number of communications methods than do other writers, the principles remain the same whether writing for the Internet, an annual report or a case history, an employee newsletter, or a public speech.

Writing for a reader differs dramatically from writing for a listener. A reader has certain luxuries a listener does not have. For example, a reader can scan material, study printed words, dart ahead, and then review certain passages for better understanding. A reader can check up on a writer; if the facts are wrong, for instance, a reader can find out pretty easily. With the emergence of online reading, the requirements and scrutiny have increased. Online readers are fickle and impatient. Unless your copy corrals them, they move on. To be effective then, especially in the second decade of the 21st century, writing for the eye must be able to withstand the most rigorous standards.

The stakes are even higher with writing for listening. A listener gets only one opportunity to hear and comprehend a message. If the message is missed the first time, there's usually no second chance. This situation poses a special challenge for the writer—to grab the listener quickly. A listener who tunes out early in a speech or a broadcast is difficult to draw back into the listening fold.

Public relations practitioners—and public relations students—should understand the differences between writing for the eye and the ear. Although it's unlikely that any beginning public relations professional would start by writing speeches, it's important to understand what constitutes a speech and how it's prepared and then be ready for the assignment when opportunity strikes. Because writing lies at the heart of the public relations equation, the more beginners know about writing, the better they will do.

Again, your *primary* skill as a public relations professional is "writing."

Any practitioner who doesn't know the basics of writing and doesn't know how to write—even in the age of social media—is vulnerable and expendable.

Fundamentals of Writing

Few people are born writers. Like any other discipline, writing takes patience and hard work. The more you write, the better you should become, provided you have mastered the basics. Writing fundamentals do not change significantly from one form to another.

What are the basics? Here is a foolproof, four-part formula for writers, from the novice to the novelist:

1. **The idea must precede the expression.**   Think before writing. Few people can observe an event, immediately grasp its meaning, and sit down to compose several pages of sharp, incisive prose. Writing requires ideas, and ideas require thought.

   Sometimes ideas come quickly. Other times, they don't come at all. But each new writing situation doesn't require a new idea. The trick in coming up with clever ideas lies more in *borrowing* old ones than in creating new ones. What's that, you say? Is your dear old author encouraging "theft"? You bet! The old cliché "Don't reinvent the wheel" is absolutely true when it comes to good writing. So never underestimate the importance of maintaining good files.

2. **Don't be afraid of the draft.**   After deciding on an idea and establishing the purpose of a communication, the writer should prepare a rough draft. Drafting is a necessary and foolproof method for avoiding a mediocre, half-baked product. Writing, no matter how good, can usually be improved with a second look. The draft helps you organize ideas and plot their development before you commit them to a written test. Sadly, few public relations writers go through the drafting process. (That's why public relations people, by and large, are horrible writers!) Writing clarity is often enhanced if you know where you will stop before you start.

3. **Simplify, clarify.**   In writing, the simpler, the better. Today, with more and more consumers reading from computer screens, simplicity is imperative. The more people who understand what you're trying to say, the better your chances for stimulating action. Shop talk, jargon, and "in" words should be avoided. Standard English is all that's required to get an idea across. In practically every case, what makes sense is the simple rather than the complex, the familiar rather than the unconventional, and the concrete rather than the abstract. Clarity is another essential in writing.

4. **Finally, writing must be aimed at a particular audience.**   The writer must have the target group in mind and tailor the message to reach that audience. To win the minds and hearts of a specific audience, one must be willing to sacrifice the understanding of certain others. Writers, like companies, can't expect to be all things to all people.

Outside the Lines

The Greatest Public Relations Writer of All Time

You're too young to remember Sir Winston Churchill. (Actually, so am I!)

But the former Prime Minister of Great Britain, who led the Brits to victory in World War II, was history's greatest public relations writer, an inspiration to any poor schnook who ever pecked at a keyboard. Churchill, also one of history's greatest speakers, began as a back bencher in Parliament, who lacked confidence because of a stutter.

But Churchill worked hard at his writing and, through it, developed into one of history's most charismatic figures, with memorable passages that will live forever (Figure 15-2).

How did he do it? Here's the writing formula Churchill followed.*

1. **He got straight to the point.**
   Churchill delivered bad news, in particular, in a no-nonsense, straightforward way, for example, "The news from France is very bad."

   So get to your point.

2. **He wrote the truth.**
   Jack Nicholson famously intoned in the movie *A Few Good Men* that "You can't handle the truth."

   Well, Churchill could and did, all the time.

   "The whole fury and might of the enemy must very soon be turned on us," he told the British people about the Nazis. It was true, and they needed to hear it.

3. **He painted pictures.**
   Writing teachers in the 21st century talk about "telling stories" and "painting pictures." Churchill did this beautifully a full century earlier.

   When he talked of the evil Hitler, Churchill told his countrymen and women, "If we can stand up to him, all Europe may be freed and the life of the world may move forward into broad, sunlit uplands.

   "But if we fail, then the whole world, including the United States, including all that we have known and cared for, will sink into the abyss of a new dark age made more sinister and perhaps more protracted, by the lights of perverted science."

   Nuff said.

4. **He used simple words.**
   "Let us therefore brace ourselves to our duties, and so bear ourselves, that if the British Empire and its Commonwealth last for a thousand years, men will still say. 'This was their finest hour.'"

FIGURE 15-2 **Sir Winston: History's greatest public relations writer.**

(Photo: akg-images/Newscom)

Simple, straightforward, perhaps the most famous written passage in military history.

5. **He worked his verbs.**
   In writing, verbs are always the key. Churchill understood that and wouldn't be caught using an "is" or "am" or "achieve." Rather, the Churchill verb lexicon stressed words of action:

   - Grieve
   - Fall
   - Rise
   - Defend
   - Fight

   Not a dead, corporate verb among 'em.

*Based on Clare Lynch, "5 Writing Tips from Winston Churchill," Ragan's PR Daily, May 15, 2012.

Flesch Readability Formula

Through a variety of writings, the late Rudolf Flesch staged a one-man battle against pomposity and murkiness in writing. According to Flesch, anyone can become a writer. He suggested that people who write the way they talk will be able to write better. In other words, if people were less inclined to obfuscate their writing with 25-cent words and more inclined to substitute simple words, then not only would communicators communicate better but receivers would also receive more clearly.

There are countless examples of how Flesch's simple dictum works.

- Few would remember William Shakespeare if he had written sentences such as "Should I act upon the urgings that I feel or remain passive and thus cease to exist?" Shakespeare's writing has stood the test of centuries because of sentences such as "To be or not to be?"

- A scientist, prone to scientific jargon, might be tempted to write, "The biota exhibited a 100 percent mortality response." But how much easier and infinitely more understandable to write, "All the fish died."

- One of President Franklin D. Roosevelt's speechwriters once wrote, "We are endeavoring to construct a more inclusive society." FDR changed it to "We're going to make a country in which no one is left out."

- Even the most famous book of all, the Bible, opens with a simple sentence that could have been written by a 12-year-old: "In the beginning, God created the heaven and the earth." Simple but brilliant!

Outside the Lines
Churchill's Worst Nightmare

Worried about fitting in a corporate environment? Concerned that the suits speak and write a different language than do you—more convoluted, hyperextended, and obtuse?

Relax. You can rely on the following "Jargon Master Matrix," developed by a former bank communicator, a chart consisting of three columns of jargon words that can be mixed and matched for any occasion.

Just select any three words from the three columns, such as *value-based process model* or *overarching support centralization*, and you will fit right in. (Just don't tell Sir Winston!)

1. overarching	visionary	objectives
2. strategic	support	alternatives
3. special	customer-oriented	expectations
4. specific	stretch	excellence
5. core	planning	assessment
6. long-term	marketing	update
7. quality	service	model
8. technology-based	process	product
9. formal	fundamental	centralization
10. exceptional	sales	incentive
11. value-based	budget	initiatives
12. executive	operating	feedback
13. immediate	discretionary	infrastructure
14. interactive	tracking	proposition

Flesch gave seven suggestions for making writing more readable.

1. Use contractions such as *it's* and *doesn't*.
2. Leave out the word *that* whenever possible.
3. Use pronouns such as *I, we, they,* and *you*.
4. When referring back to a noun, repeat the noun or use a pronoun. Don't create eloquent substitutions.
5. Use brief, clear sentences.
6. Cover only one item per paragraph.
7. Use language the reader understands.

The Beauty of the Inverted Pyramid

Journalistic writing style is the Flesch approach in action.

Reporters learn that words are precious and are not to be wasted. In their stories every word counts. If readers lose interest early, they're not likely to be around at the end of the story. That's where the inverted pyramid comes in. Newspaper story form is the opposite of that for a novel or short story. The climax of a novel comes at the end; but the climax of a newspaper story comes at the beginning.

Generally, the first tier, or lead, of the story is the first one or two paragraphs, which include the most important facts. From there, paragraphs are written in descending order of importance, with progressively less important facts presented as the article continues—thus, the term *inverted pyramid*.

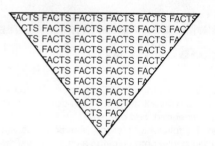

The lead is the most critical element, usually answering the questions concerning who, what, why, when, where, and occasionally how. For example, the following lead effectively answers most of the initial questions a reader might have about the subject of the news story.

Columbia Pictures announced today it had signed Mila Kunis and Ryan Gosling to a three-film deal for $60 million each.

That sentence tells it all; it answers the critical questions and highlights the pertinent facts. It gets to the point quickly without a lot of extra words. In just about 20 words, it captures and communicates the essence of what the reader needs to know.

This is the style of straightforward writing that forms the basis for the most fundamental, practical, ubiquitous, and easiest of all public relations tools: the news release.

The News Release

A valuable but much-maligned device, the news release is the granddaddy of public relations writing vehicles. The first recorded news release was issued by Ivy Lee in October of 1906, as a "Statement from the Road," offering an explanation from client Pennsylvania Railroad about that month's crash that killed 50 people. The release was published verbatim by *The New York Times*. (That may have been the last release the *Times* ever published verbatim!)

Most public relations professionals swear by news releases. Some editors and reporters swear *at* them. Some, in fact, have predicted that with social media and Internet communicating, the "end of news releases" is nigh. Nah. Releases, done correctly, are the easiest, most straightforward, most understandable, and ubiquitous communication vehicles. Indeed, PR Newswire, a paid wire service used by public relations people, distributes hundreds of news releases—virtually all by email—every day to more than 5,000 Websites and online databases.

A news release may be written as the document of record to state an organization's official position—for example, in a court case or in announcing a price or rate increase. More frequently, however, releases have one overriding purpose: to influence a publication to write favorably about the material discussed. Each day, in fact, professionals email releases to editors in the hope of stimulating favorable stories about their organizations.

Most news releases are not used verbatim, although there are occasional exceptions (Figures 15-3 and 15-4). Rather, they may stimulate editors to consider covering a story.

NEWS RELEASE

**CONSUMERS PREFER "HOSPITALS" OVER "MEDICAL CENTERS,"
ACCORDING TO NEW SURVEY**

June 21, 2011 – Do consumers prefer a "Hospital" over a "Medical Center," or vice versa? According to a new survey of 1,027 American adults, the clear answer is: "Hospital."

On four separate measures, consumers showed strong preferences for a "Hospital" over a "Medical Center." Survey highlights:

	HOSPITAL	MEDICAL CENTER
Which would have a wider range of services?	61%	31%
Which would provide better care?	32	52
Which would be on the cutting edge of medicine?	53	37
Which would have physicians who are experts?	46	34

These consumer perceptions come from a survey conducted this month by Rivkin & Associates LLC and Bauman Research & Consulting LLC, both based in Glen Rock, NJ.

"The conventional wisdom for years has been that the word 'Hospital' was tired and old-fashioned," said Steve Rivkin, founder of Rivkin & Associates, a marketing and communications consultancy. "As a result, hundreds of hospitals have dropped the word and renamed themselves Medical Centers."

"Our data indicates this conventional wisdom is wrong," said Sandra Bauman, PhD, founder of Bauman Research & Consulting. "This national study shows that consumers favor a 'hospital' across the board on the four attributes we measured."

Survey results were consistent across respondents' gender, age, income, race, region, household income, size of household and educational levels, according to Dr. Bauman.

"We've encountered many internal reasons for using the term 'medical center,'" said Rivkin. "As hospitals expanded, added facilities and services, and partnered with physicians, they came to see themselves as 'centers' of healthcare for their communities. And for some, the term 'medical center' also has an academic pedigree, conveying prestige to physicians and other practitioners."

FIGURE 15-3 Ready for prime time news release. So...
This release concerns a captivating topic and is well-written and newsworthy.
(Courtesy Rivkin & Associates)

FIGURE 15-4
....Prime time.
Sometimes (not always), news releases serve their purpose perfectly.
(Courtesy Rivkin & Associates)

L-2 THE RECORD   **LOCAL**

HEALTH CARE NEWS

⬆ Submit news items to **northjersey.com/calendar**

Most favor hospitals over medical centers, poll shows

By BARBARA WILLIAMS
STAFF WRITER

Americans believe they will receive better services in a "hospital" than in a "medical center," according to a phone survey conducted by two local consulting firms.

More than 1,000 people were asked four questions about whether they believed they would have better outcomes in a hospital or medical center during the survey conducted by Rivkin & Associates LLC and Bauman Research & Consulting LLC, both based in Glen Rock.

When asked "which would have a wider range of services," 61 percent said a hospital and 31 percent chose a medical center. Six percent said there would be no difference, and 2 percent didn't know or refused to answer.

Fifty-two percent said a hospital provides "patients with better quality medical care" while 32 per-

> "The conventional wisdom for years has been that the word 'hospital' was tired and old-fashioned."
>
> STEVE RIVKIN,
> RIVKIN & ASSOCIATES

cent said a medical center. Twelve percent thought the care would be the same; 4 percent weren't sure.

Asked "which would be on the cutting edge of medicine, using the most up-to-date technologies and procedures," 53 percent chose a hospital while 37 percent picked a medical center. Just 8 percent thought there would be no difference.

Forty-six percent said they thought a hospital would have "physicians who are experts in their fields" compared with 34 per-

cent who thought a medical center would have more expertise, and 19 percent who thought there would be no difference.

"The conventional wisdom for years has been that the word 'hospital' was tired and old-fashioned," Steve Rivkin, founder of Rivkin & Associates, said in a statement. "As a result, hundreds of hospitals have dropped the word and renamed themselves medical centers."

But "our data indicates this conventional wisdom is wrong," Sandra Bauman, founder of Bauman Research, said in a statement. "This national study shows that consumers favor a "hospital" across the board on the four attributes we measured."

The survey was conducted in June using random-digit dialing to 1,027 people nationwide who were at least 18 years old.

E-mail: williamsb@northjersey.com

In other words, the release becomes the point of departure for a newspaper, magazine, radio, or television story. Professor Linda Morton of the University of Oklahoma's Herbert School of Journalism suggested five newsworthy topics for news releases:

- *Impact:* a major announcement that affects an organization, its community, or even society.
- *Oddity:* an unusual occurrence or milestone, such as the one-millionth customer being signed on.
- *Conflict:* a significant dispute or controversy, such as a labor disagreement or rejection of a popular proposal.
- *Known principal:* the greater the title of the individual making the announcement—president versus vice president—the greater the chance of the release being used.

- *Proximity:*   how localized the release is or how timely it is, relative to the news of the day.[3]

Beyond these characteristics, *human interest* stories, which touch on an emotional experience, are regularly considered newsworthy.

With this as a backdrop, it is not surprising that research indicates that in terms of the popular press, most news releases never see the light of print. Early studies, in fact, even before the exponential growth of releases, indicated that less than 10% of all news releases were published.[4] Nonetheless, each day's *The Wall Street Journal, The New York Times, USA Today,* CNN, Fox News, MSNBC, CNBC, Associated Press wire, Yahoo News, Google News, and other daily media around the nation and world are filled with stories generated from news releases issued by public relations professionals.

So the fact is that the news release—despite the harsh reviews of some—remains the single most important public relations vehicle.

News Release News Value

The key challenge for public relations writers is to ensure that their news releases reflect news. What is *news*? That's an age-old question in journalism. Traditionally, journalists said, when "dog bites man, it's not news, but when man bites dog, that's news." The best way to learn what constitutes news value is to scrutinize the daily press and broadcast news reports and see what they call news. In a general sense, news releases ought to include the following elements:

- Have a well-defined reason for sending the release.
- Focus on one central subject in each release.
- Make certain the subject is newsworthy in the context of the organization, industry, and community.
- Include facts about the product, service, or issue being discussed.
- Provide the facts "factually"—with no puff, no bluff, no hyperbole.

Outside the Lines

Write the Release

Writing in news release style is easy. It is less a matter of formal writing than it is of selecting, organizing, and arranging facts in descending sequence.

Here are 10 facts:

Fact 1: Supreme Court Chief Justice John Roberts will speak in Madison, Wisconsin, tomorrow.

Fact 2: He will be keynote speaker at the annual convention of the American Bar Association.

Fact 3: He will speak at 8 p.m. at the Kohl Center.

Fact 4: His speech will be a major one.

Fact 5: His topic will be capital punishment.

Fact 6: He will also address university law classes while in Madison.

Fact 7: He will meet with the university's chancellor while in Madison.

Fact 8: He became the 17th Chief Justice, replacing the late William Rehnquist in 2005.

Fact 9: He is a former practicing attorney.

Fact 10: He has, in the past, steadfastly avoided addressing the subject of capital punishment.

Organize these facts into an American Bar Association news release for tomorrow morning's Wisconsin State Journal newspaper. One right answer appears soon in this chapter. Just don't peek.

- Rid the release of unnecessary jargon.
- Include appropriate quotes from principals but avoid inflated superlatives that do little more than boost management egos.
- Include product specifications, shipping dates, availability, price, and all pertinent information for telling the story.
- Include a brief description of the company (also called a "boilerplate") at the end of the release—what it is, and what it does.
- Write clearly, concisely, forcefully.

News Release Content

When a release is newsworthy and of potential interest to an editor, it must be written clearly and concisely in proper newspaper style. It must get to the facts early and answer the six key questions. From there it must follow the inverted pyramid structure to its conclusion. For example, consider the following lead for the John Roberts news release posed in this chapter's "Outside the Lines."

MADISON, WISCONSIN—Supreme Court Chief Justice John Roberts will deliver a major address on capital punishment at 8 p.m. tomorrow in the Kohl Field House before the annual convention of the American Bar Association.

This lead answers all the pertinent questions:

1. Who? Chief Justice John Roberts
2. What? a major address on capital punishment
3. Where? Kohl Field House
4. When? tomorrow at 8 p.m.
5. Why? American Bar Association is holding a convention

In this case, *how* is less important. Whether or not the reader chooses to delve further into the release, the gist of the story has been successfully communicated in the lead.

To be newsworthy, news releases must be objective. All comments and editorial remarks must be attributed to organization officials. The news release can't be used as the private soapbox of the release writer. Rather, it must appear as a fair and accurate representation of the news that the organization wishes to be conveyed.

And news releases—even email or tweet releases—must also be written in a certain professional style, or there can be real trouble (see PR Ethics Mini-Case in this chapter).

News Release Essentials

Beyond the necessity of being newsworthy, news releases must include several time-honored essentials that will help get them considered for inclusion in print.

- **Rationale.**   There must be a well-defined reason for sending the release. Releases should answer the two critical questions: *What's new?* and *So what?* Stated another way, the subject matter of the release must be relevant to the readers or viewers of the target media. Lack of relevance should be enough to scuttle the release.
- **Focus.**   Each release should speak about only one central subject. Lack of focus—that is, discussing many different things—is a guaranteed non-starter for a journalist.

PR Ethics Mini-Case
Bad Taste Tweet Release

Never forget that any time you put keyboard to word, you are taking your life into your hands.

Just ask James Taranto, experienced columnist for *The Wall Street Journal* and a member of the editorial board, who writes well and writes quickly. Sometimes too quickly.

In the summer of 2012, after the nation was stunned when a deranged shooter killed innocent people at a Colorado movie theater midnight show, Taranto tweeted:

> **James Taranto**
> @jamestaranto
>
> I hope the girls whose boyfriends died to save them were worthy of the sacrifice.
>
> 24 Jul 12

The journalist's intent was to underscore the heroism of several boyfriends and brothers in the crowd, who selflessly shielded loved ones from the murderous rampage. The immediate response on Twitter ranged from calling the journalist "disgusting" to referring to him as something not suitable for a family textbook.

Taranto was quick to apologize, with a mea culpa column in the *Journal*. His purpose, he wrote, was to point out the ultimate sacrifice these men made to prove the depth of their devotion.

"We intended this to be thought-provoking," he wrote, acknowledging that, instead, "the vast majority found it offensive and insulting."

Taranto's mea culpa column was far longer than a tweet or a news release, and it conveyed more accurately what he wanted to say. The point is that in confronting difficult subjects, a tweet or a news release may not suffice.

As the columnist admitted, "This column has often argued that a failure of public communication is the fault of the public communicator, and that's certainly true in this case."

Question

1. How would you have advised James Taranto to word his tweet about the Colorado massacre?

For further information, see Michael Sebastian, "WSJ Editor Offers Mea Culpa for Tweet about Colorado Shooting," *Ragan's PR Daily*, July 26, 2012.

- **No puffery.** Releases, to paraphrase Fox News commentator Bill O'Reilly, should be "puffery-free zones." Even mediocre reporters can sniff out hyperbole and puffiness, which may make them suspicious of the entire product. At all costs, avoid the buzzwords and taboo terms listed in the next Outside the Lines box.

- **Nourishing quotes.** Include quotes, but make them count. "We think this is the best product of its type" doesn't add much. But "This product will add 20% to our annual revenue growth" advances the story by providing important projections that will help put the announcement in corporate context.

- **Company description.** Many reporters may not be familiar with a particular organization and what it does. Therefore, a succinct organizational description, commonly called *boilerplate*, is eminently appropriate to conclude a release. The best boilerplate should contain market position, scope of business activity, geographic coverage, aspiration, size, and even company personality.[5]

- **Spelling, grammar, punctuation.** Ask journalists to describe the *quality* of the public relations releases they receive, and they'll invariably roll their eyes. If the most rudimentary writing principles of spelling, grammar, and punctuation aren't observed, how important can the release be? And how important can the reporter recipient be if the public relations writer doesn't even take the time to proofread?

Outside the Lines
News Release Taboo Terms

Back in the old days of 1978, the late comedian George Carlin found himself in deep turbulence for uttering seven "dirty words" that the Supreme Court found to be "patently offensive" to radio listeners. (Because this is a "family textbook," we will leave the seven words to your imagination or your next visit to the *Howard Stern Show* on satellite radio.)

In the second decade of the 21st century, there is nothing more patently offensive to a reporter than a news release that contains the following 25 most overused buzzwords in public relations news releases—in the following order—as compiled by social media specialist Adam Sherk:

1	leader	5	solution
2	leading	6	largest
3	best	7	innovative
4	unique	8	innovator

9	award winning	18	state of the art
10	exclusive	19	flexible
11	extensive	20	cutting edge
12	leading provider	21	biggest
13	innovation	22	world class
14	real-time	23	next generation
15	fastest	24	revolutionary
16	easy to use	25	best practices
17	dynamic		

In writing a news release, then, forget these terms. Use some originality. Be more creative. Don't succumb to cheap and easy—and, as it turns out, journalistically suicidal—superlatives.*

*For further information, see Adam Sherk, "The Most Overused Buzzwords and Marketing Speak in Press Releases," www.adamsherk.com/public-relations/most-overused-press-release-buzzwords/, June 29, 2010.

- **Clarity, conciseness, commitment.** The best releases from the best organizations are straightforward, understated, and confident. Just like any other communications vehicle, a public relations news release can reveal much about the company that produces it.[6]

News Release Style

The style of writing, particularly news release writing, is almost as critical as content. Alas, many in the public relations profession overlook the importance of proper writing style. Sloppy style can break the back of any release and ruin its chances for publication. Style must also be flexible and evolve as language changes.

Most public relations operations follow the style practiced by major newspapers and magazines rather than that of book publishers. This news style is detailed in various guides published by such authorities as the *Associated Press* and *The New York Times*.

Because the press must constantly update its style to conform to changing societal concepts, news release style is subjective and ever changing. However, a particular firm's style must be consistent from one release to the next. The following are examples of typical style rules:

- **Capitalization.** Most leading publications use capital letters sparingly; so should you. Editors call this a down style because only the most important words begin with capital letters.

- **Abbreviations.** Abbreviations present a many-faceted problem. For example, months, when used with dates, should be abbreviated, such as Dec. 11, 2009. But when the day of the month is not used, the month should be spelled out, such as December 2009. Days of the week, on the other hand, should never be abbreviated. In addition, first mention of organizations and agencies should be spelled out, with the abbreviation in parentheses after the name, such as Securities and Exchange Commission (SEC).

- **Numbers.**   There are many guidelines for the spelling out of numbers, but a general rule is to spell out numbers zero through nine and use figures for 10 and up. Yet numerals are perfectly acceptable for such things as election returns, speeds and distances, percentages, temperatures, heights, ages, ratios, and sports scores.

- **Spelling.**   Many words, from *advisor* to *zucchini,* are commonly misspelled. The best way to avoid misspellings is to have a dictionary always within reach. When two spellings are given in a dictionary, the first spelling is always preferred.

These are just a few of the stylistic stumbling blocks that writers must consider. In writing a news release, style should never be taken lightly, not even for the Internet. The style, as much as any other part of the release, lets an editor know the kind of organization that issued the release and the competence of the professional who wrote it.

Social Media Releases

The Internet has revolutionized news releases and news release writing. Before the Internet, public companies would issue news releases only when they had newsworthy announcements to make. Today, companies regularly issue releases merely to be included on online databases—Google News, Yahoo News, MSN News, AOL News, etc.

Social media releases (SMRs) are designed to reach nontraditional journalists, such as bloggers and podcasters. Technically, to qualify for an SMR, a release only needs a photo. Often, SMRs might use other technological tools—video, audio, links, etc.—to mash up their own multimedia news stories (Figure 15-5).

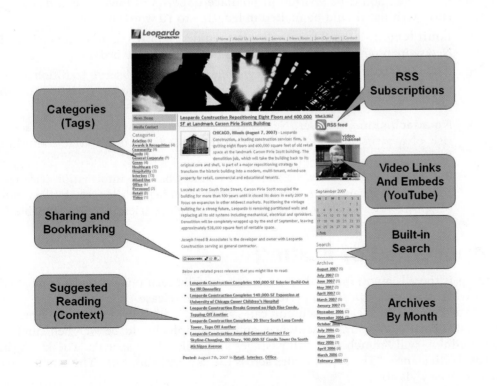

FIGURE 15-5
The SMR.
The blog-based corporate newsroom of Leopardo Companies, Inc., enlists all manner of social networking vehicles in its social media releases.
(Courtesy of Leopardo Companies, Inc.)

Like any other release, SMRs should contain contact information, boilerplate, and quotes. Unlike traditional releases, SMRs can embed head shots and logos; include video, audio, and photos; as well as link to additional material that might be relevant.

In addition, SMRs include tags to social bookmarking services, such as Delicious and Technorati. SMR writers should include as many tags as they can to ensure that the SMR is easily found; indeed, it's the tags that help distinguish the SMR as "social."[7]

Beyond disseminating a news release throughout the Web, social media news releases are best used at an organization's Website to stimulate "conversation."

Writing Releases for the Internet

As noted, the vast majority of journalists today prefer to receive news releases via email.[8]

In terms of news release writing for the Internet, brevity and succinctness are paramount. Reading from a computer screen is more difficult and tedious than extracting from paper. Therefore, Internet news release writing must conform to the following requisites:

- **One reporter per "To" line.** Nobody—least of all, reporters—likes to be lumped in with everybody else. That's why journalists despise press conferences. They want to be considered "special." So don't group journalists together on the "To" line of an email release.

- **Limit subject line headers.** Most reporters are cursed with a daily email inbox that runneth over. Therefore, enticing them with a provocative subject line is a necessity if you want your release to be considered. You should limit subject headers to four to six words, no more.

- **Hammer home the headline.** Email release headlines are as important as print headlines to attract immediate interest and subsequent coverage. Email headlines should be written in boldface upper- and lowercase and, as in all email writing, should be limited in length—to 10 words or less.

- **Limit length.** Email news releases should be shorter than print versions; PR Newswire reports that the average print release is 500 words.

- **Observe 5W format.** Email news releases should observe traditional news release style, leading with the 5W format, to answer the key questions of who, what, why, when, where, and even how.

- **No attachments.** Never. Never. Never. Journalists wish neither to face the risk of a virus nor take the time to download. So don't attach anything. Rather . . .

- **Remember readability.** Email releases must balance information with readability. That means short paragraphs, varied paragraph length, bullets, numbers, lists—devices that make the release more eye-friendly and scannable.[9]

Importance of Editing

Editing is the all-important final touch for the public relations writer. You must edit your work. One error can sink a perfectly worthwhile release.

In a news release, a careful self-edit can save the deadliest prose. An editor must be judicious. Each word, phrase, sentence, and paragraph should be weighed carefully. Good editing will "punch up" dull passages and make them sparkle. The key again: verbs. For instance, "The satellite flies across the sky" is dead, but "The satellite roars across the sky" is alive.

Outside the Lines
Twitterspeak

The Internet and social media, particularly Twitter, have a writing style all their own. In chat rooms, a correctly spelled word may be a sign of the inarticulate. Consider, for example, this conversation:

Wuzup?
n2m
well g/g c ya

The translation by anyone who spends 8 to 10 hours a day texting or tweeting: Not too much is up with the respondent, and so the writer has got to go and will see his friend later.

Indeed, in terms of email vocabulary, the following shortened vernacular can be adjudged as "chat ready":

- please   pls
- feel free   flfre

- by the way   btw
- be right back   brb
- best friend forever   bff
- in my humble opinion   IMHO
- laughing out loud   lol
- rolling on the floor laughing rotfl
- you are   u r
- information   info
- document   doc
- conversation   convo
- later   latr

Latr.

In the same context, good editing will get rid of passive verbs. Invariably, this will produce shorter sentences. For example, "George Washington chopped down the cherry tree" is shorter and better than "The cherry tree was chopped down by George Washington."

A good editor must also be gutsy enough to use bold strokes—to chop, slice, and cut through verbiage, bad grammar, misspellings, incorrect punctuation, poorly constructed sentences, misused words, mixed metaphors, non sequiturs, clichés, redundancies, circumlocutions, and jargon. Redundant sentences such as "She is the widow of the late Marco Picardo." and "The present incumbent is running for reelection." are intolerable to a good editor.

Editing should also concentrate on organizing copy. One release paragraph should flow naturally into the next. Transitions in writing are most important. Sometimes it takes only a single word to unite two adjoining paragraphs.

Writing, like fine wine, should flow smoothly and stand up under the toughest scrutiny. Careful editing is a must.

Last Word

Writing is the essence of public relations practice. The public relations professional, if not the best writer in his or her organization, must at least be one of the best.

That means mastering the traditional fundamentals of sound writing and staying aware of changing, 21st-century techniques in writing. Specifically, "in an era where buttoned-up corporate culture is giving way to hoodie-clad executives and job titles like 'chief happiness officer,'" public relations people must be sensitive to stylistic writing changes brought about by blogs, tweets, to say nothing of haiku.[10]

It's up to the public relations professional to decide which of these new wrinkles is either lasting or worth considering. Indeed, writing remains the communications skill that sets public relations professionals apart from others.

Or should.

The most frequent complaint of employers is that "public relations people can't write." That's why any public relations student who "can write" is often ahead of the competition.

Some writers are born. But most are not.

Writing can be learned by understanding the fundamentals of what makes interesting writing; by practicing different written forms; and by working constantly to improve, edit, and refine the written product. When an executive needs something written well, one organizational resource should pop immediately into his or her mind: public relations.

Discussion Starters

1. What is the foremost technical skill of public relations professionals?
2. What are several of the writing fundamentals one must consider?
3. What is the essence of the Flesch method of writing?
4. What is the purpose of a news release?
5. What is the inverted pyramid, and why does it work?
6. What is the essential written communications vehicle used by public relations professionals?
7. What are style considerations of news releases?
8. What is an SMR and what distinguishes it?
9. What are the keys in writing releases for the Internet?
10. Why shouldn't public relations writers include attachments on email releases?

Pick of the Literature

The Public Relations Writer's Handbook 2nd ed.

Merry Aronson, Don Spetner, and Carol Ames, San Francisco, CA: Jossey-Boss, 2007

The second edition of the *Public Relations Writer's Handbook* offers a simple, step-by-step approach to creating a wide range of writing, from basic news releases, pitch letters, biographies, and media alerts, to more complex and sophisticated speeches, media campaign proposals, crisis responses, and in-house publications. The authors provide a rich blend of academic, corporate, and executive search experience to provide practical tips, particularly in writing in the digital age.

Case Study   The Raina, Inc. News Release

Background: The Raina carborundum plant in Blackrock, Iowa, has been under pressure in recent months to remedy its pollution problem. Raina's plant is the largest in Blackrock, and even though the company has spent $5.3 million on improving its pollution-control equipment, black smoke still spews from the plant's smokestacks, and waste products are still allowed to filter into neighboring streams. Lately, the pressure on Raina has been intense.

- On April 7, J. K. Krafchik, a private citizen, called to complain about the "noxious smoke" fouling the environment.
- On April 8, Janet Greenberg of the Blackrock Garden Club called to protest the "smoke problem" that was destroying the zinnias and other flowers in the area.

- On April 9, Clarence "Smoky" Salmon, president of the Blackrock Rod and Gun Club, called to report that 700 people had signed a petition against the Raina plant's pollution of Zeus Creek.
- On April 10, WERS Radio editorialized that "the time has come to force area plants to act on solving pollution problems."
- On April 11, the Blackrock City Council announced plans to enact an air and water pollution ordinance for the city. The council invited as its first witness before the public hearing Leslie Sludge, manager of the Raina carborundum plant.

News Release Data

1. Leslie Sludge, manager of Raina's carborundum plant in Blackrock, appeared at the Blackrock City Council hearing on April 11.

2. Sludge said Raina had already spent $5.3 million on a program to clean up pollution at its Blackrock plant.

3. Raina received 500 complaint calls in the past three months protesting its pollution conditions.

4. Sludge said Raina was "concerned about environmental problems, but profits are still what keeps our company running."

5. Sludge announced that the company had decided to commit another $2 million for pollution-abatement facilities over the next three months.

6. Raina is the oldest plant in Blackrock and was built in 1900.

7. Raina's Blackrock plant employs 10,000 people, the largest single employer in Blackrock.

8. Raina originally planned to delay its pollution-abatement program but speeded it up because of public pressure in recent months.

9. Sludge said that the new pollution-abatement program would begin in October and that the company projected "real progress in terms of clean water and clean air" as early as two years from today.

10. Five years ago, Raina received a Presidential Award from the Environmental Protection Agency for its "concern for pollution abatement."

11. An internal Raina study indicated that Blackrock was the "most pollutant laden" of all Raina's plants nationwide.

12. Sludge formerly served as manager of Raina's Fetid Reservoir plant in Fetid Reservoir, New Hampshire. In two years as manager of Fetid Reservoir, Sludge was able to convert it from one of the most pollutant-laden plants in the system to the cleanest, as judged by the Environmental Protection Agency.

13. Sludge has been manager of Blackrock for two months.

14. Raina's new program will cost the company $2 million.

15. Raina will hire 100 extra workers especially for the pollution-abatement program.

16. Sludge, 35, is married to the former Polly Yurathane of Wheeling, West Virginia.

17. Sludge is author of the book *Fly Fishing Made Easy.*

18. The bulk of the money budgeted for the new pollution-abatement program will be spent on two globe refractors, which purify waste destined to be deposited in surrounding waterways, and four hyperventilation systems, which remove noxious particles dispersed into the air from smokestacks.

19. Sludge said, "Raina, Inc., has decided to move ahead with this program at this time because of its long-standing responsibility for keeping the Blackrock environment clean and in response to growing community concern over achieving the objective."

20. Former Blackrock plant manager Fowler Aire was fired by the company in July for his "flagrant disregard for the environment."

21. Aire also was found to be diverting Raina funds from company projects to his own pockets. In all, Aire took close to $10,000, for which the company was not reimbursed. At least part of the money was to be used for pollution control.

22. Aire, whose whereabouts are presently not known, is the brother of J. Derry Aire, Raina's vice president for finance.

23. Raina's Blackrock plant has also recently installed ramps and other special apparatus to assist employees with disabilities. Presently, 100 workers with disabilities are employed in the Raina Blackrock plant.

24. Raina's Blackrock plant started as a converted garage, manufacturing plate glass. Only 13 people worked in the plant at that time.

25. Today the Blackrock plant employs 10,000 people, covers 14 acres of land, and is the largest supplier of plate glass and commercial panes in the country.

26. The Blackrock plant was slated to be the subject of a critical report from the Private Environmental Stabilization Taskforce (PEST), a private environmental group. PEST's report, "The Foulers," was to discuss "the 10 largest manufacturing polluters in the nation."

27. Raina management has been aware of the PEST report for several months.

Questions

1. If you were assigned to draft a news release to accompany Sludge to the Blackrock City Council meeting on April 11, which items would you use in your lead (i.e., who, what, why, where, when, how)?

2. Which items would you avoid using in the news release?

3. If a reporter from the *Blackrock Bugle* called and wanted to know what happened to former Blackrock manager Fowler Aire, what would you tell the reporter?

4. How could Raina use the Internet to research public opinion of the pollution problem? How could the company use the Internet to communicate its position in advance of the Blackrock City Council meeting?

From the Top

An Interview with Chuck Suits

Charles R. Suits has taught public relations and mass media law as an adjunct professor at Florida Atlantic University for the past 12 years. Entering military duty in 1967, he served in the Republic of Vietnam as a detachment commander of an American Forces Radio and Television station serving the largest audience in that country. He was awarded the Bronze Star medal for his combat service in Vietnam. He was special assistant to Secretary Caspar Weinberger at the Department of Defense, and was responsible for media activities and public events involving strategic defense initiatives. Later, he served as a Presidential Communications Officer for President Ronald W. Reagan. He left the U.S. Army as a lieutenant colonel and served in public relations positions in industry and government.

How important is public relations writing?

Writing clearly and concisely with a focus on purpose is paramount for today's public relations practitioner. Sometimes, especially in financial relations writing, we may revert to terms of art. Similarly, in announcing compliance with (or defiance of) governmental regulatory actions, avoid the "alphabet soup" and explain in plain English what management plans to do and what outcome might be expected. Lo these long years, my steadfast companion is still *The Elements of Style.*

What's the caliber of public relations writers?

After 20 years of teaching English composition, public relations and advertising as an adjunct professor at the university level (which wasn't my day job), I was fortunate to have good students who applied themselves. I was also fortunate in early life, while working at four daily metropolitan newspapers, that my deadline only came once a day. Today, thanks to the Internet and media websites, daily newspaper reporters must scramble just like a wire service reporter.

Fast is the enemy of good. Sometimes we see poorly edited and vetted stories online. The good reporter will correct previous errors in a subsequent update. As for public relations practitioners, they should allow ample time for coordinating an announcement or news release. I tell my students, you have only one opportunity to commit news; get it right the first time.

Are public relations writers "born," or can they be taught?

Growing up, I had a natural curiosity that put me in good stead as a reporter starting with my high school and college newspapers. The five Ws and the H seemed hard-wired into my gray matter. Also, I was born into a family of writers. My mother worked in the public relations departments of four corporations in St. Louis and my step-father wrote for *The Associated Press*. In addition to those genes, I was fortunate to attend the world's first school of journalism at the University of Missouri where I received my master's degree. For me, "born" or taught is not an either/or choice, it's both.

What's the secret to effective public relations writing?

In my public relations course, I teach the inverted pyramid style of writing and how it developed as a telegraphic style replacing the interpretive narrative style of the past. For comparison of writing styles then and contemporary, I cite some stories from the first (and only) edition of our country's first newspaper, *Publick Occurrences both Foreign and Domestick*, from September 25, 1690. If I'm writing hard news, then the inverted pyramid is my bread and butter. Conversely, if I'm pursuing a soft-news feature story, I'll want a creative, catchy and intriguing lead.

How important is speech writing in a public relations career?

Speech writing is one challenge that I find more difficult if I'm writing as a surrogate or ghostwriter. The more you know about the persona of your principal, the better you will be in crafting the message to match the message-bearer. As an Army officer working in public affairs, a general once asked me to draft a speech and his final comment was, *"Make me sound like Patton."* His intended audience, however, was a women's club and not airborne troops in a marshaling area.

If I am the intended presenter, I will undertake my own audience analysis, consider the topic, time and location before I even start the first draft. As a public relations practitioner, speaking well should be second-nature to writing well.

How important is writing in a public relations career?
In my career, writing quickly and well is my supreme consideration. Seldom, however, do I have all the information at hand to accomplish my purpose.

In addition to one's writing skill, your knowledge of your company's history, products and services, executives, vision and financials is vital. In short, you have to know where to go to get the answers quickly. My public relations experience has always been with large organizations. Combined with the key to good communication is good coordination: ensure the company president, the CEO or the county administrator sees and approves your news release *before* they read about it in tomorrow's paper.

The *Rubaiyat* says, "The moving finger writes; and, having writ, moves on . . ." Meanwhile, you're left with indelible words on paper that may displease management and not ". . . all your piety nor wit shall lure it back to cancel half a line."

Public Relations Library

Altman, Rick. *The Most PowerPoint Presentations Suck*. Pleasanton, CA: Harvest Books, 2007. This book, from a computer expert, is worth the time for anyone who complements presentations with PowerPoint. And that's everyone!

Bartlett, David. *Making Your Point*. New York: St. Martin's Press, 2008. This comprehensive book covers every area of how to communicate more effectively in today's society.

Bivins, Thomas. *Public Relations Writing*, 7th ed. Lincolnwood, IL: NTC/Contemporary Publishing Group. 2010. A popular text, updated to include all aspects of public relations writing, including writing for digital media.

Foster, John. *Effective Writing Skills for Public Relations*, 4th ed. Philadelphia, PA: Kogan Page, 2008. Another solid writing text from a former journalist and public relations professional.

Newsom, Doug, and Jim Haynes. *Public Relations Writing*, 9th ed. Boston, MA: Wadsworth, 2011. Outstanding, long-lasting, and comprehensive writing manual.

Pacelli, Lonnie. *The Truth about Getting Your Point Across . . . and Nothing but the Truth*. Saddle River, NJ: Prentice Hall, 2006. This is a guide to communicating in all settings—at meetings, presentations, interviews, and more.

Scott, David Meerman. *The New Rules of Marketing and PR*. Hoboken, NJ: John Wiley & Sons, 2007. This book primarily discusses the Internet and how such vehicles as news releases and blogs should be used.

Shapiro, Roger A. *Write Right*. Bloomington, IN: AuthorHouse, 2005. This paperback guide offers 26 tips that get down to the nitty-gritty, such as avoiding prepositions and being bold. Good primer.

Smith, Ronald D. *Becoming a Public Relations Writer*, 4th ed. New York: Routledge, 2012. Important section on "ethical writing"; good primer.

Strunk, W., and E. B. White. *Elements of Style*. New York: Allyn & Bacon, 1999. A classic that *must* be in any public relations writer's library.

Treadwell, Donald, and Jill B. Treadwell. *Student Workbook for Public Relations Writing*. Thousand Oaks, CA: Sage Publishing, 2005. This presents an interesting approach to work for one hypothetical client, preparing all matter of public relations writing vehicles.

Walker, T.J. *Presentation Training A–Z*. New York, NY: Media Training Worldwide, 2005. The author traces what one needs to do to ensure the audience understands you, remembers what you said, and is motivated to tell others.

Weinbroer, Diana Roberts, Elaine Hughes, and Jay Silverman. *Rules of Thumb for Business Writers*, 2nd ed. New York: McGraw-Hill, 2005. The answers to every writing or grammar question that a business writer might have.

Weissman, Jerry. *Presenting to Win: The Art of Telling Your Story*. Upper Saddle River, NJ: Prentice-Hall, Inc., 2006. An experienced speech trainer shares his secrets.

Wilcox, Dennis L. *Public Relations Writing and Media Techniques*, 6th ed. Boston, MA: Allyn & Bacon, 2009. Comprehensive review of writing skills and media relations principals.

Chapter 16

Integrated Marketing
Communications

Chapter Objectives

1. To discuss the synthesis of advertising, marketing, and public relations to yield an integrated marketing approach in promoting products, services, and brands.

2. To explore the distinctions among advertising, marketing, and public relations.

3. To discuss, in detail, the two marketing differentiators of public relations—publicity and third-party endorsement.

4. To examine the various tactics and techniques that distinguish integrated marketing, from the traditional—public relations advertising, trade shows, cause-related marketing, etc.—to the 21st-century innovations—social media marketing, brand integration, buzz marketing, etc.

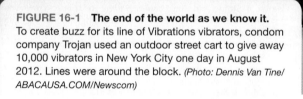

FIGURE 16-1   The end of the world as we know it. To create buzz for its line of Vibrations vibrators, condom company Trojan used an outdoor street cart to give away 10,000 vibrators in New York City one day in August 2012. Lines were around the block. *(Photo: Dennis Van Tine/ ABACAUSA.COM/Newscom)*

In these days of 24/7 media, social media networks, and uber-competition among products and services in every sector, it sure ain't "your mother's marketing" environment.

- In 2000, a Russian rocket emblazoned with a giant Pizza Hut logo carried advertising into outer space.

- In 2001, novelist Fay Weldon wrote a book commissioned by the jewelry company Bulgari; in exchange for payment, she agreed to mention Bulgari jewelry in the novel at least a dozen times.

- In the 2008 season finale of *CSI: NY*, information about a shooting was shared on what was referred to as a "TelePresence screen." The unlikely—and unmentioned—supporting player in the episode was Cisco Systems, manufacturer of the TelePresence videoconferencing system, who paid for the prominent inclusion.[1]

- In 2012, *U.S. News & World Report* magazine offered the hospitals it ranked in its "Top 100 Hospitals" a complete merchandising package to promote the distinction, including sample news releases, promotional badges for use in electronic media, print media and broadcast media, reprints, Best Hospitals 2012–13 lapel pins, and advertising on USNews.com.

■ Also in 2012, New York Life Insurance signed a deal with 10 Major League Baseball teams that triggers a promotional plug every time a player slides safely into home plate. When the umpire calls the runner safe, a corporate logo appears on the TV screen, and the play-by-play announcer is contracted to say, "Safe at home. Safe and secure, New York Life."[2]

What's going on here?

Welcome to the global market society where, according to one expert, "everything is up for sale. . . . where market values govern every sphere of life."[3] Perhaps that's an overstatement. But it is true that the various discrete disciplines that have always added up to "marketing" are, today, integrated more than ever before.

Integrated marketing is the intersection of public relations and publicity, advertising, sales promotion, and marketing to promote organizations, products, and services. Creating marketing-oriented tweets and Facebook messages, YouTube videos, Internet publicity, using celebrities as spokespersons, inserting product placements in movies, sponsoring concerts, creating street theater, and a host of other publicity-seeking techniques are all examples of *integrated marketing communications* (Figure 16-1).

All are important to sell products and ideas.

While traditional advertising and marketing can build brand awareness, public relations establishes credibility and tells the brand story more comprehensively. Database marketing touches consumers one-on-one. Sales promotion motivates them to action.

The integration of these marketing techniques helps build a cohesive presence for a brand.

Some have suggested that advertising is dying and that public relations is taking over. That may be a bit overzealous.[4] Advertising isn't quite dead yet—especially with Procter & Gamble spending $11 billion a year in ads, Unilever spending $5 billion, and formerly bankrupt General Motors spending $4 billion.[5] Neither is marketing. But it is true that public relations and publicity integrated with these other disciplines are very much the rule in many organizations today.

Therefore, the need for integration . . . for *communications cross-training*—to learn the different skills of marketing, advertising, sales promotion, and public relations—becomes a requirement for all communicators.

Public Relations vs. Marketing vs. Advertising

What is the difference between marketing, advertising, and public relations?

Marketing, literally defined, is the selling of a service or product through pricing, distribution, and promotion. Marketing ranges from concepts such as free samples in the hands of consumers to buzz campaigns.

Advertising, literally defined, is a subset of marketing that involves paying to place your message in more traditional media formats, from newspapers and magazines to radio and television to the Internet and outdoors.

Public relations, liberally defined, is the marketing of an organization and the use of unbiased, objective, third-party endorsement to relay information about that organization's products and practices.[6]

With so many media outlets bombarding consumers daily, most organizations realize that public relations can play an expanded role in marketing.

In the past, marketers treated public relations as an ancillary part of the marketing mix—almost an afterthought. They were concerned primarily with making sure that their products met the needs and desires of customers and were priced competitively, distributed widely, and promoted heavily through advertising and merchandising. Gradually, however, these traditional notions among marketers began to change.

The increased number of advertisements in newspapers and on the airwaves caused clutter and placed a significant burden on advertisers who were trying to make the public aware of their products. In the 1980s, the trend toward shorter television advertising spots contributed to three times as many products being advertised on television as there were in the 1970s. In the 1990s, the spread of cable television added yet another multi-channeled outlet for product advertising. In the 2000s, the proliferation of cable TV and Internet advertising intensified the noise and clutter.

Against this backdrop, the potential of public relations as an added ingredient in the marketing mix has become an imperative. Indeed, marketing guru Philip Kotler was among the first to suggest two decades ago that to the traditional four Ps of marketing—product, price, place, and promotion—a fifth P, *public relations*, should be added.[7]

In the second decade of the 21st century, Kotler's suggestion has increasingly become reality.

Product Publicity

To many, product publicity is the essence of the value of integrating public relations and marketing. In light of how difficult it now is to raise advertising awareness above the noise of so many competitive messages, marketers are turning increasingly to product publicity as an important adjunct to advertising. Although the public is generally unaware of it, a great deal of what it knows and believes about a wide variety of products comes through press coverage.

In certain circumstances, product publicity can be the most effective element in the marketing mix. For example:

- **Introducing a revolutionary new product.** Product publicity can start introductory sales at a much higher level of demand by creating more awareness of the product.

- **Eliminating distribution problems with retail outlets.** Often the way to get shelf space is to have consumers demand the product. Product publicity can be extremely effective in creating consumer demand.

- **Small budgets and strong competition.** Advertising is expensive. Product publicity is cheap. Often publicity is the best way to tell the story. That's why Samuel Adams Boston Lager beer became a household name—and a huge franchise—almost solely through publicity opportunities.

- **Explaining a complicated product.** The use and benefits of many products—particularly financial services—are difficult to explain to mass

FIGURE 16-2
The king.
Maybe not of "burgers" but certainly of corporate icons. Ronald McDonald, here with former Olympic gold medalists Carl Lewis and Jackie-Joyner Kersee to celebrate "Go Active Day" in Athens, Greece. *(Courtesy of O'Dwyerpr.com)*

audiences in a brief ad. Product publicity, through extended news columns, can be invaluable.

■ **Tying the product to a unique representative.** Try as it might, the advertising industry can't escape the staying power of unique mascots who become tied inextricably to products. Consider the following:

- Morris the Cat was one answer to consumer disinterest in cat food for the 9 Lives Cat Food Company in 1968 and still appears today, well into middle age.
- The Jolly Green Giant has "ho ho ho'ed" so long at General Mills that he now has his own Green Giant Food Company and Website.
- Burger King's "King" is back with a vengeance in the new century, cavorting on football fields and in other venues for a whole new generation.[8]
- The real "king" is McDonald's standard bearer, Ronald McDonald, who first appeared in 1963 and has since starred on national television, at Academy Awards ceremonies, and around the world. No other iconic figure in history has become more synonymous with any company (Figure 16-2).

Third-Party Endorsement

Perhaps more than anything else, the lure of third-party endorsement is the primary reason smart organizations value product publicity as much as they do advertising. Third-party endorsement, as noted, refers to the tacit support given a product by an "objective" third-party observer—a blog, newspaper, magazine, or broadcaster—who mentions the product as news.

Advertising often is perceived as self-serving. People know that the advertiser not only created the message but also paid for it. Publicity, on the other hand, which often appears in news columns, carries no such stigma. Editors, after all, are considered objective, impartial, indifferent, neutral. Therefore, publicity appears to be news

FIGURE 16-3   **It's my third-party, and I'll sign if I want to.** Actress and former Girl Scout Elizabeth Banks supplies third-party endorsement to Nestle, signing a poster and talking about Nestle Crunch Girl Scout Candy Bars. *(Courtesy of O'Dwyerpr.com)*

and is more trustworthy than advertising that is paid for by a clearly nonobjective sponsor.

Editors, sensitive to the proliferating raft of product placements in the media, have become sensitive to mentioning product names in print. Some, in fact, have a policy of deleting brand or company identifications in news columns. Bloggers, new to the media world, often have no such reluctance. Indeed, Brooklyn Blogfest 2010 was sponsored by Absolut Vodka. Absolut also offered gifts, including a bottle of the new vodka and a small digital video camera, to bloggers in exchange for coverage. Nine accepted the vodka and eight got cameras.[9] (Meanwhile, Walter Cronkite was rolling over in his grave!)

In recent years, one practice that has drawn journalistic scorn is that of organizations—particularly corporations—using well-known spokespersons to promote products without identifying that they are being paid for the endorsement. Journalists argue that such presentations are patently unethical paid endorsements designed to appear objective.[10] CNN, for one, imposed a strict policy on paid spokespersons after suffering an embarrassing incident with actress Kathleen Turner, who promoted drug company products without disclosing her financial relationship with the company.[11] Nonprofits seem to suffer decidedly less anguish when they use celebrities to promote their activities (Figure 16-3).

Building a Brand

The watchword in business today is branding—creating a differentiable identity or position for a company or product.

In more traditional times, it took years for brands such as Pepsi, Coke, McDonald's, Hertz, FedEx, and Walmart to establish themselves. Today, with the advent of the World Wide Web, thriving Internet companies such as Apple, Google, Amazon, and eBay have become household words in a historical nanosecond. Using integrated marketing communications to establish a unique brand requires adherence to the following principles.

- **Be early.**   We remember the "first" in a category because of the *law of primacy*, which posits that people are more likely to remember you if you were the first in their minds in a particular category.

- **Be memorable.**   Equally important is to fight through the clutter by creating a memorable brand. With hundreds of participants in categories from bottled water to bathing suits, a brand needs to stand out by distinguishing itself in some way—through uniqueness or advertising slogan or social responsibility or whatever. Creating brand awareness requires boldness.

- **Be aggressive.**   A successful brand also requires a constant drumbeat of publicity to keep the company's name before the public. Potential customers need to become familiar with the brand. Potential investors need to become confident that the brand is an active one. So take it to the customers aggressively (Figure 16-4). The new competitive economy leaves little room for demure integrated marketing communications.

- **Use heritage.**   Baby boomers are old. Gen Xers are getting older. And *heritage* is very much in vogue. This means citing the traditions and history of a product or organization as part of building the brand. As consumers live longer, an increasing number of citizens long for "the good old days."

- **Create a personality.**   The best organizations are those that create "personalities" for themselves. Who is number one in rental cars? Hertz. What company stands for overnight delivery? FedEx. What's the East Coast university that boasts the best and the brightest? Harvard. Or at least that's what most people think. The organization's personality should be reflected in all communications materials the organization produces.

FIGURE 16-4   Street cred.
Friendly Ice Cream Corporation took to the streets with free samples in an effort to reinforce brand recognition. *(Courtesy of O'Dwyerpr.com)*

Outside the Lines
World's #1 Sports Brand

What sports franchise is the number-one integrated marketer in the world?

If you answered mighty Manchester United, the British soccer (or football, if you prefer) powerhouse, you were almost right. ManU has the second most powerful sports brand in the world. Spanish football franchises Real Madrid and Barcelona also are not far behind, ranking in the Top 10. As to U.S. football franchises, the Dallas Cowboys, New England Patriots, Washington Redskins, and New York Giants pace the field.

But the clear overall winner in terms of integrated marketing is the mighty New York Yankees, whose brand name is worth $328 million—with a total worth of close to $3 billion—according to *Forbes*.

The Yankees, who opened a new stadium in 2010 and are perennial favorites to win the World Series, were molded largely by the late George Steinbrenner, a colorful and flamboyant owner who purchased the very best players and dominated the newspaper back pages. Steinbrenner also instilled into his executives and players the importance of integrated marketing.

- Steinbrenner and the Yankees founded the Silver Shield Foundation to support the families and children of slain New York Police Department officers.
- A pretend Steinbrenner (played by comedian Larry David) was a regular fixture on the most popular situation comedy TV show of all time, *Seinfeld.*
- Steinbrenner funded the West Tampa Boys and Girls Clubs, in the city where the Yankees conduct spring training.
- Yankee players are constant presences in the New York community, working with charities from the New York Blood Center to the Make-A-Wish Foundation to Mayor Bloomberg's efforts to combat truancy and chronic absenteeism in schools.
- Yankee players are trained assiduously, more than any other team, in dealing with the media. As General Manager Brian Cashman put it, "We want to be the guardrail at the top of the cliff, rather than the ambulance at the bottom."

FIGURE 16-5   Jeter in training.
Extensive integrated marketing activities have made the New York Yankees name the most hallowed in all of sports.
(Photo by Raina Seitel, courtesy of Fraser Seitel)

No question, the focus on integrated marketing has helped make the New York Yankees the most revered name in sports (Figure 16-5).

For further information, see Steve McIntyre, "What the New York Yankees Can Teach You about Branding," Change Conversations, August 9, 2010; Peter J. Schwartz, "The Most Valuable Sports Team Brands," *Forbes*, May 18, 2010; and Paul White, "Yankees 'Proactive' in Training Players about News Media," *USA Today*, April 12, 2012.

As more and more companies each year attempt to bust through the advertising and marketing clutter by resorting to such marketing devices as social media, banner ads, proprietary Websites, free classified advertising, e-zines and email marketing, the challenge to create a differentiable brand becomes that much more difficult.

Public Relations Advertising

Traditionally, organizations used advertising to sell products. In 1936, a company named Warner & Swasey initiated an ad campaign that stressed the power of America as a nation and the importance of American business in the nation's future. Warner & Swasey continued its ads after World War II and thus was born a unique type of advertising—the marketing of an image rather than a product. This technique became known variously as institutional advertising, image advertising, public service advertising, issues advertising, and ultimately public relations—or nonproduct—advertising.

In the 1980s, image advertising became *issues advertising*, which advocated positions from the sponsor's viewpoint. Often these concerned matters of some controversy. The practice was spearheaded by the outspoken Mobil Corporation—now ExxonMobil. ExxonMobil's practice of placing an issues ad on the op-ed page of *The New York Times* and other leading newspapers each Thursday began in the 1960s and today has morphed into ExxonMobil instituting its own blog. Nonprofits, too, are often outspoken—and controversial—in the cause of such issues advertising (Figure 16-6).

Traditional public relations advertising—as opposed to image or issue positioning—is still widely used. Such advertising can be appropriate for a number of activities:

FIGURE 16-6   Advertising with attitude.
Never one to back away from controversy, Los Angeles Lakers basketballer Metta World Peace, aka Ron Artest, starred in this controversial ad for the People for the Ethical Treatment of Animals. *(Courtesy of PETA)*

1. **Mergers and diversifications.**   When one company merges with advertising provides a quick and effective way to convey this message.

2. **Personnel changes.**   A firm's greatest asset is its employees. Presenting staff members in advertising not only impresses a reader with the firm's pride in its workers but also helps build confidence among employees themselves.

3. **Organizational resources.**   The scope of a company's services also says something positive about the organization.

4. **Manufacturing and service capabilities.**   The ability to deliver quality goods on time is something customers cherish. A firm that can deliver should advertise this capability.

5. **Growth history.**   A growing firm, one that has developed steadily over time and has taken advantage of its environment, is the kind of company with which people want to deal. Growth history, therefore, is a worthwhile subject for nonproduct advertising.

6. **Financial strength and stability.**   A picture of economic strength and stability—particularly in times of financial crisis—is one that all companies like to project. Advertisements that highlight the company's financial position earn confidence and attract customers and investors.

Traditional Integrated Marketing

Among the more traditional public relations activities used to market products are article reprints, trade show participation, use of spokespersons, cause-related marketing, and in-kind promotions.

Article Reprints

Once an organization has received product publicity in a newspaper or magazine, whether in print or online, it should market the publicity further to achieve maximum sales punch. Marketing can be done through article reprints aimed at that part of a target audience—wholesalers, retailers, or consumers—that might not have seen the original article. Reprints, included on a Website and direct mailed, also help reinforce the reactions of those who read the original article.

Trade Show Participation

Trade show participation enables an organization to display its products before important target audiences. The decision to participate should be considered with the following factors in mind:

1. **Analyze the show carefully.** Make sure the audience is one that can't be reached effectively through other promotional materials, such as article reprints or local publicity. Also, be sure the audience is essential to the sale of the product.

2. **Select a common theme.** Integrate public relations, publicity, advertising, and sales promotion. Unify all organizational elements for the trade show to avoid any hint of interdepartmental rivalries.

3. **Emphasize what's new.** Talk about the new model that's being displayed. Discuss the additional features, new uses, or recent performance data of the products displayed. Trade show exhibitions should reveal innovation, breakthrough, and newness.

4. **Consider local promotional efforts.** While in town during a trade show, an organization can enhance both the recognition of its product and the traffic at its booth by doing local promotions.

5. **Evaluate the worth.** Always evaluate whether the whole exercise was worth it. This involves counting, qualifying, and following up on leads generated as well as looking at other intangibles to see if marketing objectives were met.[12]

Spokespersons

In our celebrity-dominated culture, the use of spokespersons to promote products has increased. As noted, spokespersons shouldn't disguise the fact that they are advocates for a particular product.

Spokespersons must be articulate, fast on their feet, and thoroughly knowledgeable about the subject. When these criteria are met, the use of spokespersons as an integrated marketing tool can be most effective. As the music business has been hit by a barrage of negative factors, from recession to free downloads, rockers, in particular, have joined the ranks of spokespersons. The rock band Kiss was among the most prolific merchandisers, selling products ranging from condoms to musical toothbrushes to baby booties to the ever-fashionable "Kiss Kasket," a limited-edition coffin.[13]

In recent years, the use of spokespersons to promote products has become so crazed that in 2003, Coca-Cola signed high school basketball phenom LeBron James to a six-year, $12 million contract to promote Sprite. James hadn't even stepped foot onto an NBA court. At the time Coke signed him, the Ohio high schooler already had signed a shoe deal with Nike for a cool $100 million. And it all paid off for the sponsors, as King James has become one of the world's premier players and pitchmen.[14]

Cause-Related Marketing

Public relations sponsorships tied to philanthropy are another effective integrated marketing device. Again, in an economy where advertising is omnipresent and differentiation is at a premium, companies turn to sponsorship of the arts, education, music, festivals, anniversaries, sports, and charitable causes for promotional and public relations purposes[15] (Figure 16-7).

Cause-related marketing will continue to grow in the 21st century. Middle-aged baby boomers, in particular, are more concerned about issues that affect their lives, such as protecting the environment and aiding the less fortunate. This, coupled with the need of corporations to reassure the citizenry that are "not evil," should drive the creation of events and decision making by corporate sponsors.

FIGURE 16-7 Yes we can.
Cause-related marketing was very much on the mind of real estate executive and philanthropist Connie Milstein when her Connie's Bakery, dedicated to job training for low-income New Yorkers, baked and then gave away 20,000 brownies in Washington to celebrate the inauguration of President Barack Obama. *(Courtesy of Connie's Bakery)*

In-Kind Promotions

When a service, product, or other consideration in exchange for publicity exposure is offered, it is called an *in-kind promotion*. Examples of in-kind promotions include the following:

1. Providing services or products as prizes offered by a newspaper or charity in exchange for being listed as a cosponsor in promotional materials.

2. Providing services or products to a local business in exchange for having fliers inserted in shopping bags or as statement stuffers.

3. Providing services or products to doctors' offices, auto repair shops, or other businesses in exchange for having brochures prominently displayed.

4. Providing posters of the product or service at well-trafficked locations.

The point of in-kind promotions is to leverage the name and use of products and services, so that more potential buyers are exposed to the organization.

21st-Century Integrated Marketing

Beyond advertising, marketing, and public relations techniques, integrated marketing, too, must keep pace with the ever-changing world of promotional innovations to help sell products and services. Among them are television brand integration, infomercials, word-of-mouth marketing, television and movie product placement, and more.

Online/Social Media Marketing

The fastest growing category of advertising in the 21st century is online. And the most rapidly emerging integrated marketing technique is using social media and the Web to create "buzz" for a product.

Traditional marketers from Coca-Cola to Kraft Foods to Procter & Gamble have all shifted significant marketing dollars to online marketing. In 2008, Pepsi-Cola went one step further by introducing a line of no-calorie carbonated beverages, with a campaign that bypassed altogether mainstream media such as television and print. Even more unique, the beverages weren't aimed at social media–savvy younger consumers but rather at a demographic target of men and women aged 35 to 49.

Pepsi's fruit-flavored, caffeine-free Tava line received a spirited send-off with its own Website, banner ads, promotions, and offbeat buzz-building stunts such as sampling events at popular shops and the delivery of free samples to the employees of prominent companies such as Google and MTV.[16] With social media accounting for one out of every four minutes spent online in the United States, marketers must become proficient in reaching customers through Facebook and Twitter and YouTube and all the rest. Social media advertising, increasingly on mobile devices, is one of the fastest-growing advertising segments, exceeding $2.5 billion annually. In 2010, media-buying firm Universal McCann launched its Rally service to help marketers develop social media campaigns, track online chatter about their brands, and measure how those campaigns perform.[17] Similar services were launched by other advertising and public relations agencies.

Television Brand Integration

The latest phenomenon in television is to integrate products into the fabric of what is being presented on the screen. When one of ABC's *Desperate Housewives* found herself hard up for cash, she donned an evening gown and extolled the virtues of a Buick Lacrosse at a car show. One of the stars of Warner Brothers' *What I Like About You* raved about Fruity Pebbles and competed to win a role in an Herbal Essences commercial.

Such product emphases were not just coincidence.

As technology and clutter blunt the effectiveness and reach of traditional 30-second commercials, more advertisers are paying to integrate their products directly into the action of a show or film. In 2012, in fact, an entire episode of the hit NBC sitcom *30 Rock* was devoted to a look back in time to what the announcer called "The Kraft Product Placement Comedy Hour, sponsored by Kraft Singles. It's the cheese that won World War II." The bit made sense because not only was Kraft an early NBC sponsor, but the corporation also entered into a "branded integration" contract that combined real-life commercials with fake on-the-air ones.[18]

The process of brand integration owed its start to CBS's *Survivor*, which financed itself largely through product tie-ins with advertisers whose products were mentioned in the course of the show. This was a far cry from serendipitous—that is, unpaid—product mentions, such as Junior Mints and Pez on *Seinfeld*.[19]

Product Placements

Once removed from brand integration are product placements—in novels, TV programs, movies, video games, and even cartoons. These have proliferated at a rapid—and to some, alarming—rate. As one watchdog put it, product placements are "a huge, out-of-control issue."[20]

- Advertisers from Dunkin' Donuts to Intel to Honda have all signed up with the publishers of game consoles to embed their messages in video games.[21]

- Comedy Central introduced its adult cartoon show, *Shorties Watchin' Shorties*, which prominently featured Domino's Pizza, Red Bull energy drink, and Vans sneakers.[22]

PR Ethics Mini-Case

Shilling the Morning Joe

Brand integration and product placement are realities of 21st-century television, particularly in dramatic programs and situation comedies.

But as MSNBC's *Morning Joe* found out in the spring of 2011, TV news-oriented programs must walk a finer line when it comes to shilling for a product.

Morning Joe was a popular news talk program that starred former Republican Congressman Joe Scarborough and former ABC correspondent Mika Brzezinski (Figure 16-8). The program was famously "brewed by Starbucks," as the anchors sipped coffee from Starbucks' cups and various video billboards reminded viewers each morning.

This stemmed from a reportedly $10 million deal that the coffee maker made with the program two years earlier to become a "name sponsor," so that Starbucks, according to executives, could reach "affluent, sophisticated consumers."

Nothing wrong with that—especially since at the time of the unusual deal, MSNBC's president vowed that his news anchors would never shy away from asking hard questions of Starbucks if the matter demanded.

But there may, however, have been something wrong when Ms. Brzezinski sat down one morning in March 2011 to interview Starbucks CEO Howard Schultz on the subject of the coffee chain's 40th anniversary. Nothing was mentioned about the program's sponsorship agreement with Mr. Schultz's company. This, in itself, was odd since MSNBC had earlier suspended Scarborough for making donations to political operatives without disclosing the conflict on the air.

The interview with Mr. Schultz was clearly of the "decaf" variety, largely softball questions and lots of panning to bags of Starbucks java sitting on the news desk. Ms. Brzezinski did ask about low-calorie options for teenagers, but in the main, the interview served as a seven-minute infomercial for Starbucks.

MSNBC defended its decision not to mention the Starbucks sponsorship during the interview. "We've been

FIGURE 16-8 **Morning java.**
MSNBC's Mika Brzezinski and Joe Scarborough sans Starbucks. *(Photo: Cindy Barrymore/ABACAUSA.COM/Newscom)*

upfront about our relationship with Starbucks," a spokesperson said. "Our regular viewers are well aware that *Morning Joe* is 'Brewed by Starbucks.'"

Perhaps. But somewhere, Walter Cronkite is spinning in his grave (again!).*

Questions

1. Do you agree with MSNBC's decision not to mention the Starbucks's sponsorship in its segment with Howard Schultz?

2. Were you public relations advisor to MSNBC, what would you have counseled the network do with respect to the Schultz interview?

3. Were you a Starbucks's advisor, what would you have counseled CEO Schultz to do during the interview?

*For further information, see Brian Steinberg, "Tuning In: MSNBC's Java Sponsorship Gets Overcaffeinated," *Advertising Age*, March 8, 2011.

■ General Motors (GM), seeking new ways to market cars in its comeback, made its Camaro and Traverse brands central parts in the NBC series, *My Own Worst Enemy*. Unfortunately for GM, the show was canceled after only four episodes.[23]

■ Also in 2008, TiVo, the Silicon Valley company that invented skipping over annoying commercials, reversed course completely. Teaming up with Amazon.com, TiVo introduced on-screen links to product ads for CDs, DVDs, and books that guests promote on talk shows such as *Imus in the Morning* and *The Daily Show*.[24]

And according to one study, the proliferation of product placements in all forms of media—or *ad creep*, if you prefer—is just going to continue to grow around the world. Summarized the study's organizer, "There's a new media order emerging, fueled by a fear of ad-skipping technology, doubts about traditional advertising's effectiveness, and, in some countries, a search for new revenue streams as government subsidies decline."[25]

Stated another way, product placements are here to stay.

Infomercials

Infomercials were greeted with universal catcalls in the 1980s when they were introduced as program-length commercials, shamelessly hawking products.

Nonetheless, infomercials remain strong for one reason: They work. Americans spend more than $8.5 billion a year on infomercial products from baldness cures to fitness equipment to potato peelers and sauna belts.[26]

Indeed, former boxing champion George Foreman's immortal infomercial about his Lean Mean Fat-Reducing Grilling Machine reportedly earned him in excess of $137 million! Between $1 billion and $2 billion worth of merchandise is sold each year—from dicing and slicing kitchen utensils to exercise paraphernalia to psychic hot lines—despite condemnation and even lawsuits. Celebrities from Chuck Norris to Suzanne Somers to Donald Trump are staples among the growing parade of shameless infomercial hawkers.

Buzz Marketing

Also known as word-of-mouth, *buzz marketing* is another alternative to traditional advertising that enlists "influencers" or "trend setters" to spread the word about a particular product.

The practice began with teenagers, who appeared to be popular. Today, marketers have graduated to reaching out for "evangelists" who are already diehard fans of a particular product and persuading them to "spread the gospel." Its proponents hail word-of-mouth as the most honest and ethical of advertising media. "People don't want to hurt their friends and family and colleagues with bad information," is the way one believer put it.[27]

Social marketing, too, has quickly graduated to a leading mechanism for buzz. One service, Klout, is a sophisticated ranking system that analyzes one's activity on social networks and assigns a score to that individual based on his or her ability to influence others. Like Google, Klout uses a complex algorithm to determine how many times followers click on Twitter feeds, for example. Among marketers working with Klout include Starbucks, CoverGirl, Dannon Yogurt, Virgin America, and Fox—all interested in spreading product buzz.[28]

You Name It

What other 21st-century integrated marketing venues exist? How fertile is your imagination? Consider the following:

- **Song placements.**   Marketers now compete to get brands mentioned in best-selling records. Thanks primarily to hip-hop luminaries such as Jay-Z and Ludacris, brands such as Nike, Mercedes-Benz, Hennessy, Louis Vuitton, and Lamborghini all benefit from the "street cred" embodied in popular music. In 2005 alone, Nike was mentioned in 63 hip-hop songs.[29]

- **Sports teams.**   It used to be that stadiums were named for the highest bidder. Today, the team itself takes on the name of the sponsor who pays for it. Venues such as the St. Louis Cardinals' Busch Stadium and the Washington Redskins' FedEx Field have given way to teams such as the New York Red Bulls, the Major League Soccer franchise named after the sports energy drink, which paid more than $100 million for the integrated marketing privilege. But when the New York Giants tried to sell stadium naming rights to a German insurance company linked to the Nazis, the franchise was forced to reverse field and shelve the $25-million-a-year bonanza.[30] The venue is now called MetLife Stadium, a much safer choice.

- **Online game shows.**   What national advertiser hasn't sponsored a game show? But what JetBlue did in 2012 was waaaay different. JetBlue designed its own online game show to be the centerpiece of a $2 million campaign to build awareness of its JetBlue vacation package travel service. The show was to take place on the JetBlue Website for one week, complete with its own slick host and fabulous prizes for contestant volunteers.[31]

- **Whaaaa?**   No space is too odd to integrate marketing messages. US Airways sells ads on airsickness bags. School districts sell ads on the outside of school buses. Hands down, the most bizarre 21st-century integrated marketing technique was the use of a person's body for marketing purposes. In 2008, a father looking for money to buy a new car sold rights to a permanent tattoo on his neck to Web-hosting company Globat. And if that wasn't enough, the same company purchased a temporary tattoo ad on the pregnant belly of a St. Louis woman—to promote its product (not the woman's baby).
    Ridiculous? Perhaps. But if we're writing about it here—it worked!

Last Word

The key marketing question in the 21st century is, *How do we generate buzz?* How do we distinguish ourselves and get our voice heard in the midst of hundreds of thousands of competing voices?

To marketing expert Al Ries, who cut his teeth in the advertising industry, the answer was obvious.

"In the past, it may have been true that a beefy advertising budget was the key ingredient in the brand-building process. . . . Today brands are born, not made. A new brand must be capable of generating favorable publicity in the media or it won't have a chance in the marketplace."[32]

In other words, said Ries, it is public relations and its attendant communications forms—not advertising alone—that differentiate an organization, product, or issue.

Perhaps more precisely stated, what is needed now is an integrated approach to communications, combining the best of marketing, advertising, sales promotion, and public relations with all forms of media from online to print to broadcast to face-to-face.

The clear marketing need for organizations and those who serve them is to build lasting client relationships. A successful communications professional must be knowledgeable about all aspects of the communications mix. Integrated marketing communications, then, becomes paramount in preparing public relations professionals for the challenges of the second decade of the 21st century.

Discussion Starters

1. What is meant by *integrated marketing communications*?
2. Describe the differences among advertising, marketing, and public relations.
3. What is meant by *third-party endorsement*?
4. In what situations is product publicity most effective?
5. Describe the pros and cons of using a well-known individual as a spokesperson.
6. What is *cause-related marketing*?
7. How can integrated marketing help build a brand?
8. What are the purposes of public relations advertising?
9. What is the significance of Warner & Swasey and Mobil Oil in terms of public relations advertising?
10. What are several 21st-century techniques of integrated marketing communications?

Pick of the Literature

Strategic Integrated Marketing Communications

Larry Percy, Oxford, UK: Elsevier, 2008

This is a straight-talk, no-nonsense excursion through the various communication venues of integrated marketing communications.

The author begins by tracing the history of integrated marketing communications, stretching back to 1989 when the American Association of Advertising Agencies formed a task force to study the concept.

The book talks about managing for IMC, including a discussion of the "barriers" that afflict silo-oriented departments, most interested in protecting their own turf. It then spends quality time on discussing positioning and branding and how a product or service can differentiate itself from the competition. The author spends ample time on reputation, how it's built and perpetuated, and the various techniques of "promotion," including and in addition to formal advertising.

Case Study | Resurrecting Brand Vick

On July 1, 2011, Michael Vick, starting quarterback for the Philadelphia Eagles, signed an endorsement deal with Nike, the world's largest sporting-goods company, for a multiyear contract. Star athletes sign endorsement deals all the time; nothing unusual about that.

But Nike's resigning of Michael Vick, after a four-year absence, was perhaps the most significant story of integrated marketing redemption in the history of sports.

Five years earlier, Michael Vick was a convict, convicted of unspeakable crimes against animals. He was friendless and bankrupt, and few gave him much chance of ever again playing professional football, much less being signed for endorsement contracts by image-conscious corporations.

How he did it is a testimony to the power of public relations.

Fickle Fingers of Fate

As the 2006 National Football League season began, Michael Vick stood as an integrated marketing whirlwind.

The top pick in the NFL's 2001 draft, the southpaw quarterback, who ran faster and threw farther than most anyone else, had become a three-time all-pro for the Atlanta Falcons. Vick's endorsement income from contracts from Nike, EA Sports, Coca-Cola, and other top corporations had earned him 33rd place on Forbes' list of *Top 100 Celebrities in 2005*. One magazine reported him as "one of the top 10 richest athletes in the United States."

Michael Vick was on top of the sports celebrity world—until it all came crashing down.

In April, Vick settled a lawsuit by a woman who claimed the player knowingly gave her herpes.

In November, after a particularly disappointing game where his receivers dropped a boatload of passes, Vick was booed by the hometown Atlanta fans (Figure 16-9). As he walked off the field after the 31-13 loss to the New Orleans Saints, Vick held up both hands and flashed two well-publicized fingers at the fans—a "double-barreled salute," as one reporter labeled it.

Vick issued a statement through the team Sunday night, saying, "First and foremost, I would like to apologize for my inappropriate actions with fans today. I was frustrated and upset at how the game was going for my team, and that frustration came out the wrong way. That's not what I'm about. That's not what the Atlanta Falcons are about. I simply lost my cool in the heat of the moment. I apologize and look forward to putting this incident behind me."

Vick paid a $10,000 team fine and donated another $10,000 to charity.

The issue was defused. But it was a sign of trouble to come.

In January 2007, Vick reluctantly surrendered a water bottle to security at Miami International Airport. The bottle smelled like marijuana and contained a substance in a hidden compartment. The police report characterized the substance as a residue that is "closely associated with marijuana."

Ten days later, Vick was exonerated, as no marijuana was found in the bottle.

FIGURE 16-9   Hard landing.
Michael Vick had a tough game against the New Orleans Saints in 2006 and later took out his displeasure on the unsympathetic Atlanta fans. *(Photo: Johnny Crawford/AJC/Newscom)*

Going to the Dogs

In April 2007, Michael Vick's reputation crumbled.

A report circulated that an elaborate, illegal dogfighting complex, owned by the Atlanta Falcons quarterback, was discovered in Surry County, Virginia. State and federal authorities were investigating.

In subsequent months, as details emerged about his "Bad Newz Kennels," Vick was considered a pariah by many, both animal lovers and non-animal lovers alike.

Reports from the complex were chilling.

Federal officials reportedly found equipment associated with dogfighting, blood stains on the walls of a room, and a blood-stained carpet stashed on the property. They reportedly removed more than 60 dogs.

In July, Vick and three associates were indicted on charges of conducting illegal dogfighting. The indictment alleged that Vick and his associates bought the property in 2001, expressly as the main staging area for housing and training pit bulls involved in dogfighting. They built "a fence to shield the rear portion of the compound from public view and multiple sheds used at various times to house training equipment, injured dogs, and organized fights."

Vick himself, according to the indictment, was highly involved in the operation, attended fights, and paid off bets when his dogs lost.

Vick was also cited for being involved with "the execution of dogs that didn't perform well." The indictment reported that Vick and his colleagues "executed approximately eight dogs that did not perform well in 'testing' sessions by various methods, including hanging, drowning, and/or slamming at least one dog's body to the ground."

Although Vick was only accused—and not found guilty—of these frightening charges, his sponsors didn't hesitate. AirTran dropped him as a spokesperson for its airline. Nike, which at first said it would "stand by" the standard bearer of its planned new Vick shoe, quickly reversed its stand and canceled the shoe and its multimillion dollar contract with Vick. Other sponsors quickly followed suit.

Next Stop: The Slammer

At first, Vick seemed like he might fight the charges.

He immediately issued a statement apologizing to the people of Atlanta and Falcons' owner Arthur Blank, "who I love sincerely, I've put him though a lot. And you know it hurts me to put him through these situations."

Vick refused to acknowledge his guilt, saying, "There are a lot of things that needed to be worked out."

By August 2007, Michael Vick had gotten religion—literally. He formally accepted a plea agreement from the federal government and held a press conference, at which he said he sought God's help to cure him. "Dogfighting is a terrible thing. I reject it," he said at the press conference (Figure 16-10).

Vick vowed to "redeem" himself and willingly serve his time in jail. His prison sentence was 23 months in Leavenworth, Kansas (where he played for the prison football team), with release in the summer of 2009.

Meanwhile, in 2008, Vick filed for personal reorganization bankruptcy protection, listing assets of $16 million and liabilities of $20 million. In 2009, Vick sued his former financial advisor for $2 million, claiming she used his money for her personal and business expenses.

FIGURE 16-10 Doing time.
Michael Vick accepted his punishment in the fall of 2008, vowing to make a comeback after his time in the slammer.
(Courtesy of Fox News)

Still a young man, not yet 30, Michael Vick hoped to return to football. As his attorney told the bankruptcy court in 2008, "He has every reason to believe that upon his release, he will be reinstated into the NFL, resume his career, and be able to earn a substantial living."

Sure enough, in 2009, after two years in prison, the NFL allowed Michael Vick to resume his career with the Philadelphia Eagles.

IM Redemption

After his reentry into society, Michael Vick became a spokesperson for the Humane Society and gave speeches on the depravity of the dogfighting activities with which he formerly was associated.

On the field, Vick regained his old magic and was named the National Football League's Comeback Player of the Year in 2010.

By 2011, Nike, which four years earlier had labeled Vick's crimes "inhumane and abhorrent" and cut him from its roster, had had a change of heart.

"Michael has acknowledged his past mistakes. We do not condone those actions, but we support the positive changes he has made to better himself off the field," the company said in a statement, announcing Vick's re-signing. Vick's Nike contract contained a commitment to work with camps and youth programs, Nike said.

Vick's agent said his client was "ecstatic" that he was back in the Nike fold—the first time a company had brought back a celebrity it had previously dropped.

Michael Vick had come full circle.

Questions

1. What do you think of Michael Vick's decision to accept jail time and hold a press conference?

2. If you were advising Vick, how would you suggest he comport himself now that he is back in the NFL? What should he do, in a public relations sense, when he is freed?

3. If you were advising the National Football League, how would you suggest it handle Vick's reinstatement?

4. If you were advising corporate sponsors, what would you suggest they do relative to Michael Vick, now that he is back in the NFL?

5. What do you think of Nike's decision to reinstate him as an endorser?

For further information, see Larry O'Dell, "Michael Vick Sues Former Financial Adviser," Associated Press (January 27, 2009); Mark Maske, "Falcons' Vick Indicted in Dog Fighting Case," *Washington Post* (July 18, 2007); Michael S. Schmidt, "Vick Pleas Guilty in Dog-Fighting Case," *The New York Times* (August 27, 2007); "Michael Vick's Water Bottle Raises Suspicion at Miami Airport," *USA Today* (January 19, 2007); "Nike Re-Signs Michael Vick to Endorsement Deal," *Bloomberg News*, July 1, 2011; and Mary Elizabeth Williams, "Why Is Michael Vick Shilling for Nike?" Salon.com, July 5, 2011.

From the Top

An Interview with Tadd Schwartz

Tadd Schwartz is the founder and president of Schwartz Media Strategies, a public relations, marketing, and digital media firm based in Miami, Florida. Schwartz Media Strategies has national practices in real estate; financial and legal services; hospitality and lifestyle; destination marketing; consumer affairs; and cultural arts. Offering services ranging from media relations, crisis management and targeted marketing, to Hispanic communications and social media, the firm helps clients reach their core audiences with the goal of generating new business and building increased brand value.

How helpful can public relations be for a marketer?
Public relations amplifies the value of a marketing campaign, lending an element of third party credibility to advertising, direct marketing, collateral material development, and even events. Prospective clients or customers who have read about your business or product in the news are much more likely to accept your marketing proposition when it comes time to reach out to them directly.

How can public relations help build a brand?

Every brand has a story, and public relations is a vehicle for broadcasting that story, whether it's through traditional media or social media. Publicity gives your brand a sense of depth and substance that can't be bought. It has to be earned.

Is public relations more important than advertising in selling products?

Depends who you ask, but no matter your school of thought, a well-balanced communications campaign is one that combines several mediums—PR, marketing, social media, and advertising in many cases. Public relations provides the credibility that comes when someone else is talking about your business or product. The challenge is that you don't control the message, which is why a strategic media relations counselor is so valuable when it comes to managing the message. Advertising allows you to convey your points in a predictable manner, but it lacks the journalistic integrity that comes with earned editorial coverage.

How important is social media in public relations work?

It's everything. In today's 24/7 world where information can be shared with the click of a mouse, or the tap of an app, a savvy PR campaign doesn't solely focus on traditional media or social media. It emphasizes and gives equal weight to all media, period. And in many cases, journalists are relying on social media for news tips and expert source identification. Media, whether it's social engagement or publicity and marketing driven, is all encompassing and really includes any forum in which you are communicating publicly.

What social media devices are most important?

It depends on the client, and we tailor our campaigns accordingly. A hotel or consumer product launch will rely heavily on photo and video-centric social media platforms such as Pinterest or Instagram; a real estate client with a clearly-identified target customer base is a good fit for Facebook; a business-to-business company may be a better fit for LinkedIn. There's no catch-all strategy for any one client. A successful campaign will align the social media tactics with the client's underlying business goals. The one common denominator is that all social media platforms have the potential to drive brand awareness if implemented strategically.

How important is a knowledge of mobile devices for public relations professionals?

PR professionals must use social media every day to communicate with their followers, to raise awareness and start meaningful conversations. Twitter, Facebook, YouTube and others, have quickly become important tools in a PR person's communications toolkit.

Food for thought: Every year, fewer people read print or use computers, and are communicating and consuming their news via mobile devices. According to Microsoft Tag, by 2014, mobile Internet should take over desktop Internet usage! One half of all local searches are performed on mobile devices, and 91 percent of mobile Internet access is to socialize. This gives PR professionals many other avenues to connect and inform the public.

Public Relations Library

Belch, George, and Michael Belch. *Advertising and Promotion: An Integrated Marketing and Communications Perspective.* New York: McGraw-Hill, 2008. A view of integrated marketing from the advertising side of the house.

Cone, Steve. *Steal These Ideas.* New York: Bloomberg Press, 2005. An experienced brand manager offers his version of the marketing concepts that are most compelling and memorable.

D'Vari, Marissa. *Building Buzz.* Franklin Lakes, NJ: Career Press, 2005. Concepts such as visualization and getting your name in the media are reviewed.

Gospe, Mike. *Marketing Campaign Development.* Silicon Valley, CA: Happy About, 2008. How a guerilla marketer might use integrated marketing.

Hanlon, Patrick. *Primal Branding.* New York: Free Press, 2006. The author says there is a "primal code" that makes a product successful, all based on creating a "belief system" for your brand.

Kabani, Shama Hyder. *The Zen of Social Media Marketing.* Dallas, TX: Ben Bella Books, 2012. A non-stress introduction to social media marketing, if you've got the "zen."

Percy, Larry. *Strategic Integrated Marketing Communications.* Oxford, England: Butterworth-Heinemann, 2008. Chapter and verse discussion of the roots and implementation of integrated marketing communications.

Rein, Irving, and Philip Kotler. *High Visibility.* New York: McGraw-Hill, 2006. What do Oprah Winfrey, Donald Trump, and Bill Gates have in common? High visibility, which the authors claim is necessary to succeed today.

Rostica, Christopher, with Bill Yenne. *The Authentic Brand: How Today's Top Entrepreneurs Connect with Customers.* Paramus, NJ: Noble Press, 2007. Case studies from the viewpoint of CEOs, whose companies stood apart from the competition.

Schaefer, Mark W. *Return on Influence.* New York: McGraw-Hill, 2012. Excellent explanation and discussion about Klout scores and how they're derived and used.

Shiffman, Denise. *The Age of Engage: Reinventing Marketing for Today's Connective, Collaborative and Hyperinteractive Culture.* Ladera Ranch, CA: Hunt Street Press, 2008. This book charts a way to market on the Web and has a very long title.

Shimp, Terence A. *Advertising, Promotion and Other Aspects of Integrated Marketing Communications.* Mason, OH: South-Western Cengage Learning, 2008. Good discussion here of introducing new brands.

Chapter **17**

Crisis Management

Chapter Objectives

1. To discuss the importance in counseling on the actions and managing the communication of an organization in crisis.
2. To explore the role of public relations in managing issues and risks and communicating in a crisis.
3. To discuss, in detail, the aspects of crisis planning, message mapping, and implementing crisis communication.
4. To examine how media relations differs in time of crisis than in normal everyday operations.

FIGURE 17-1 **Face of evil.**
The outrage around the world was palpable in 2012, when a crazed killer murdered innocent people in a Colorado movie theater premiere of Warner Brothers' *The Dark Knight Rises*. (*Photo: RICHARD B. LEVINE/ Photoshot/Newscom*)

"A lie," Mark Twain once said, "can travel half-way around the world while the truth is still putting on its shoes."

In the age of social media and the Internet, so can a crisis.

No individual or organization—no matter how public, how large, or how newsworthy—is immune from crisis. Public relations professionals must be ready to confront crisis at any moment—whether said crisis has been festering for years or occurs in an instant. Consider the following international thunderbolts that struck in 2012.

In July, Warner Brothers planned the premiere of its biggest movie of the season, *The Dark Knight Rises*, the dark and violent culmination of its Batman films, in which a masked super villain inflicts violence on the residents of Gotham City.

Appropriately, midnight shows were planned in major U.S. cities as well as around the world.

Typically, the Friday midnight premiere in Denver suburb Aurora was sold out when the unthinkable happened. A masked, costumed, red-headed intruder armed with a trove of weapons and ammunition opened fire on hapless moviegoers. By the time police subdued the deranged gunman, he had killed 12 and wounded 58 others (Figure 17-1).

The mass shooting tragedy forced Warner Brothers immediately to reevaluate its marketing and public relations plans for the movie, expected to gross more than $1 billion worldwide.

The studio moved quickly to defer the movie's major premieres in Paris, Mexico City, and Tokyo. It canceled all advertising, valued at $3–5 million for its opening weekend. It asked networks to pull all spots planned to review the movie. And the movies stars, Christian Bale and Anne Hathaway, were flown to Colorado to comfort and support the victims. The studio also suspended trailers for another Warner release, *Gangster Squad*, which depicted four men shooting up a movie theater.[1]

Warner Brothers' quick crisis management drew positive reviews, although the tragedy that befell its movie would cast a reputational pall on the film forever.

A month later in August, a crisis of a far different complexion led the morning news, this one years in the making.

Lance Armstrong, seven-time winner of cycling's highest prize, the Tour de France, and long suspected of "doping" to summon extra strength, suddenly announced he would immediately drop his defense against anti-doping charges (Figure 17-2).

The announcement, after Armstrong, who miraculously battled cancer and had for years vociferously denied that he had ever taken any illegal substances, stunned the cycling community and the world. Tour de France authorities, who had challenged his claims of innocence, immediately announced that Armstrong would be stripped of his titles. A few months later, in January 2013, Armstrong admitted to Oprah Winfrey that his life was a lie; that he had, in fact, doped throughout his cycling career.

His sponsors, at first, seemed to appreciate Armstrong's crisis management. Said longtime sponsor Nike, "Lance has stated his innocence and has been unwavering on this position."[2] But Nike changed its tune and dropped Armstrong in late 2012, just before his Oprah revelation, when the suggestion of his doping became incontrovertible.

In the second decade of the 21st century, thanks to the digital speed of the Internet and the pervasiveness of social media and viral communications, organizations and individuals are always one step away from crisis.

FIGURE 17-2 **Dope.** Cyclist Lance Armstrong holds up seven fingers to signal how many Tour de France titles he had won, before they were all stripped (the titles, not the fingers), after Armstrong announced in 2012 he would drop his fight against anti-doping charges. *(Photo: OLIVIER HOSLET/ EPA/Newscom)*

Crisis Pervades Society

Crisis has become so pervasive, so crippling, that insurance companies, such as AIG and Chubb, now offer crisis management insurance to pay for corporations turning to crisis management agencies for help in defending damaged brands from such issues as food contaminations, environmental disasters, executive scandals, or even government bailouts (which AIG, by the way, received as a result of the U.S. financial meltdown!).[3]

Indeed, in recent years, the practice of public relations has become most well known for assisting those who find themselves in such crises and, as a consequence, has benefitted handsomely.

Crisis, which public relations counselor James Lukaszewski once described as "unplanned visibility," can strike anyone at any time.[4] Indeed, in the new century, among the most well-regarded and highest-paid professionals in public relations are those who have achieved this status through their efforts in attempting to "manage" crises.

In a world of instantaneous Internet communications, round-the-clock social media, cable news commentary, talk radio, tabloid news journalism, and exploding communications challenges, the number and depth of crises affecting business, government, labor, nonprofits, and even private individuals have expanded exponentially.

No sector of society is immune from crisis.

- In *government,* scandals—from the tax finagling of New York Congressman Charley Rangel to the impeachment of former Illinois Governor Rod Blagojevich to the sexual shenanigans of a host of Democrats and Republicans—have recurrently dominated the news.

- In business, the outrageous ineptitude of the financial industry leading to the subprime lending crisis of 2008 and the subsequent financial meltdown, complemented by the outrageous pay packages awarded failed CEOs, caused sweeping changes in government regulation of business during the Obama administration.

- In *education,* a scandal at Duke University in 2006, involving bogus accusations of rape and racism among the college's lacrosse players, and the awful Penn State University child sex scandal of 2011 (see Case Study, Chapter 13) rocked both respected universities.[5]

- In the *health care* sector, the CEO of giant HealthSouth, Richard Scrushy, was indicted in a government corruption case in 2006 after being ousted from the company he allegedly bilked for a personal fortune.[6]

- In the area of *religion,* the Catholic Church, under Pope Benedict XVI and his successor in 2013, was still recovering, two decades later, from the shame of the pedophile priest scandals at the beginning of the decade.

- In the world of *charitable institutions,* in January 2009 universities and foundations across the nation discovered their investment portfolios savaged by the actions of one rogue investor, Bernard Madoff, a former chair of the NASDAQ Stock Exchange. Madoff's actions caused a crisis of biblical proportions for charities, which suffered the brunt of the $60 billion he had reportedly bilked investors.[7]

- In *journalism,* a story created out of whole cloth by *Newsweek* in 2005, alleging that guards at the U.S. detention center at Guantanamo Bay flushed a copy of the Koran down a toilet, triggered Muslim world outrage and left as many as

17 dead and scores injured in Afghanistan.[8] Meanwhile, plagiarism scandals at the offices of *The New York Times*, *New Yorker*, CNN, *Washington Post*, *Boston Globe*, and elsewhere tarnished the reputation of reporters and editors.

■ Nor was scandal absent in the *public relations* industry. The Burson-Marstellar Facebook–Google scandal of 2011 (see PR Ethics Mini-Case, Chapter 2) was just the latest controversy that affected the field. Scandals in 2005 involving Ketchum Public Relations in a pay-for-play broadcaster scheme and Fleishman-Hillard in padding bills brought crisis to the crisis counselors themselves.

The list of such issues—and of the crises they often evoke—is unending. In the second decade of the 21st century, society is flooded with front-burner issues that affect individuals and organizations. From war to peace, poverty to abortion, discrimination to downsizing, environmentalism to energy conservation, the domain of "issues management" has become increasingly important for public relations professionals.

Issues Management

In guarding against crisis, public relations professionals must constantly be aware of the primary issues that impact their organizations. The term *issues management* was coined in 1976 by the late public relations counselor W. Howard Chase, who defined it this way:

Issues management is the capacity to understand, mobilize, coordinate, and direct all strategic and policy planning functions, and all public affairs/public relations skills, toward achievement of one objective: meaningful participation in creation of public policy that affects personal and institutional destiny.[9]

In specific terms, issues management encompasses the following elements:

■ **Anticipate emerging issues.**   Normally, the issues management process is about precrisis planning. It deals with an issue that will hit the organization a year later, thus distinguishing the practice from the normal crisis planning aspects of public relations.

■ **Identify issues selectively.**   An organization can influence only a few issues at a time. Therefore, a good issues management process will select several—perhaps 5 to 10—specific priority issues with which to deal.

■ **Deal with opportunities and vulnerabilities.**   Most issues, anticipated well in advance, offer both opportunities and vulnerabilities for organizations. For example, in assessing higher oil prices, an insurance company might anticipate that fewer people will be driving and therefore there will be fewer accident claims. This would mark an opportunity. On the other hand, higher gas prices might mean that more people are strapped to pay their premiums. This would be a vulnerability that a sharp company should anticipate well in advance.

■ **Plan from the outside in.**   The external environment—not internal strategies—dictates the selection of priority issues. This is especially true in a day where social media and the Internet set the conversation. This approach differs from the normal strategic planning approach, which, to a large degree, is driven by internal strengths and objectives. Issues management is driven by external factors.

■ **Bottom-line orientation.** Although many people tend to look at issues management as anticipating crises, its real purpose should be to defend the organization in light of external factors as well as to enhance the firm's business by seizing imminent opportunities.

Risk Communication and Message Mapping

Risk communication is an outgrowth of issues management. Risk communication began as a process of taking scientific data related to health and environmental hazards and presenting them to a lay audience in a manner that is both understandable and meaningful.

Models of risk communication have been developed based on the position that *perception is reality*—a concept that has been part of public relations for years. Indeed, the disciplines of risk communication and public relations have much in common. Risk communication is based on behavioral scientific research, which shows how behavior changes when a person processes messages during high-stress situations. When stressed, the ability to hear, understand, and remember diminishes. Research indicates that in times of high stress, people can miss up to 80% of message content. Of the 20% they do hear, most messages are negative. In crisis, you must adjust for these effects to communicate effectively.

To confront this reality, risk communicators have developed a message-mapping process, based on seven steps.

1. Identify stakeholders.
2. Determine specific concerns for each stakeholder group.
3. Analyze specific concerns to fit underlying general concerns.
4. Conduct structured brainstorming with input from message-mapping teams.
5. Assemble supporting facts and proof for each key message.
6. Ask outside experts to systematically test messages.
7. Plan delivery of resulting messages and supporting materials.[10]

Message maps generally adhere to the following standard requirements:

■ Three key messages
■ Seven to 12 words per message
■ Three supporting facts for each key message

Like any other area of public relations, risk communication depends basically on an organization's actions. In the long run, deeds, not words, are what count in communicating risk.

Signs of a Crisis

The most significant test for any individual or organization comes when it is hit by a major accident or disaster—that is, a *crisis.*

What is a crisis? According to the *Harvard Business Review*, "A crisis is a situation that has reached a critical phase for which dramatic and extraordinary intervention is necessary to avoid or repair major damage."[11] Others define a crisis more simply, as "anything the CEO says it is!"

A corporate "problem" is generally a more short-term issue that affects one element or department of the organization and can be limited. A "crisis," on the other hand, is a longer-term issue that impacts the entire organization, affects many parts of that organization, and runs the risk of damaging the organization's reputation.

How an individual or organization handles itself in the midst of a crisis may influence how it is perceived for years to come. Poor handling of events with the magnitude of past crises such as Exxon's *Valdez* oil spill, Netflix's 2011 pricing debacle, President Bush's handling of Hurricane Katrina, President Obama's handling of the BP oil spill (see Case Study, Chapter 1), Denny's racial bias accusations, Wall Street's banking crisis, or Major League Baseball's steroids scandal can cripple a reputation and cause it enormous monetary loss (Figure 17-3). On the other hand, thinking logically and responding thoughtfully and quickly in a crisis, such as how Johnson & Johnson (see Case Study, Chapter 2) reacted to its Tylenol tablet poisoning episodes, can cement a positive reputation and establish enormous goodwill for an organization.

It is essential, therefore, that such emergencies be managed intelligently and forthrightly with the news media, employees, and the community at large.

As any organization unfortunate enough to experience a crisis recognizes, when the crisis strikes, seven instant warning signs invariably appear:

1. **Surprise.**   When a crisis breaks out, it's usually unexpected. Often it's a natural disaster—a tornado or hurricane, for example. Sometimes, it's a human-made disaster—robbery, embezzlement, or large loss. Frequently, a public relations professional first learns of such an event when the media calls and demands to know what immediate action will be taken.

FIGURE 17-3
Throwing away a pot of dough.
Oakland Athletics pitcher Bartolo Colon forfeited $750,000 from his contract and the chance to make an additional $850,000 in playoff money when he was suspended for violating baseball's drug policy in the final months of the 2012 season. *(Photo: JOSE CARLOS FAJARDO/MCT/ Newscom)*

2. **Insufficient information.**   Many things happen at once. Rumors fly. Blogs come alive with wild stories. Wire services want to know why the company's stock is falling. It's difficult to get a grip on everything that's happening.

3. **Escalating events.**   The crisis expands. The stock exchange wants to know what's going on. Will the organization issue a statement? Are the rumors true? While rumors run rampant, truthful information is difficult to obtain. You want to respond in an orderly manner, but events are unfolding too quickly.

4. **Loss of control.**   The unfortunate natural outgrowth of escalating events is that too many things are happening simultaneously. Erroneous stories hit the Internet, the wires, and the airwaves.

5. **Increased outside scrutiny.**   Bloggers, the media, stockbrokers, talk-show hosts, and the public in general feed on rumors. "Helpful" politicians and observers of all stripes comment to cable television on what's going on. Talk radio is abuzz with innuendo. The media want responses. Investors demand answers. Customers must know what's going on.

6. **Siege mentality.**   The organization understandably feels surrounded. Lawyers counsel, "Anything we say will be held against us." The easiest thing to do is to say nothing. So, "No comment" is urged by the attorneys. But does that make sense?

7. **Panic.**   With the walls caving in and with leaks too numerous to plug, a sense of panic pervades. In such an environment, it is difficult to convince management to take immediate action and to communicate what's going on.[12]

Planning in a Crisis

The first rule of crises is that they never appear on your schedule. But that doesn't mean you shouldn't plan as much as you can for the inevitable.

Thus, heightened preparedness is always in order, with five planning issues paramount.

- **First, for each potentially impacted audience, define the risk.**   "The poison in the pill will make you sick." "The plant shutdown will keep you out of work." "The recall will cost the stockholders $100 million." The risk must be understood—or at least contemplated—before framing crisis communications.

- **Second, for each risk defined, describe the actions that mitigate the risk.**   "Don't take the pill." "We are recalling the product." "We are studying the possibility of closing the plant." If you do a credible job in defining the risk, the public will more closely believe in your solutions. In 2006, for example, when bird flu pandemic threatened the world, the parent of Kentucky Fried Chicken readied a consumer education and advertising program to reassure consumers that eating cooked chicken is perfectly safe.[13]

- **Third, identify the cause of the risk.**   If the public believes you know what went wrong, it is more likely to accept that you will quickly remedy the problem. That's why people get back on airplanes after crashes.

- **Fourth, demonstrate responsible management action.**   Most essential to the planning phase is to move toward fixing the problem—in other words, take proper action. Cosmetics are never the solution. Much more important is acting to correct the issue that got you in the soup in the first place.

PR Ethics Mini-Case

Kobe's Nimble Public Relations Once Again Saves the Day

Kobe Bryant suffered a near-celebrity death experience when charged with sexual assault in Colorado in 2003.

Bryant, in an unprecedented move, got in front of the charges by calling his own press conference, his wife by his side, and acknowledged that he had sexual relations with another woman, but that there was no "assault" involved. The aggressive public relations set the public agenda for the debate and rescued the NBA superstar from disaster. The case was settled out of court.

Eight years later, Bryant was back in the news, in the middle of another public relations predicament. And once again, quick thinking in terms of strategic communication saved the day.

After receiving a technical foul in a game in 2011, Bryant lashed out at the referee with a curse and a homophobic slur (Figure 17-4). Since virtually every sports contest today from Little League on up is recorded, Bryant's nasty remark was heard by one and all and repeated in sports shows throughout the day. Gay and lesbian groups, in particular, took great umbrage at the remarks and demanded that Bryant be disciplined.

Having learned from the Colorado incident that the best defense is a good offense, Bryant immediately went on radio the next day in Los Angeles to clear the air. "The concern that I have is for those who follow what I say, don't take what I said as a message of hate or a license to degrade or embarrass or tease. That's something I don't want to see happen. It's o.k. to be who you are." Bryant concluded by reassuring listeners that what he said was wrong and not what it was perceived to be.

Bryant then personally worked with the Gay and Lesbian Alliance Against Defamation to, as he put it, "bring awareness and turn this into a positive. It's not o.k. to insult or disrespect and we must do whatever we can to prevent violence or hate crimes."

Ultimately, the NBA fined Bryant $100,000 for his remarks, which Bryant appealed.

In the end, the fine was a small price to pay if the rapid public relations efforts Bryant took helped retain Kobe's fans and sponsors and extinguish the crisis. Which, in fact, they did.*

FIGURE 17-4 Say what?
Kobe Bryant can't believe ref's technical foul call. What Bryant said next got him in deep trouble, to be rescued only by quick-thinking public relations. *(Photo: LUCY NICHOLSON/REUTERS/Newscom)*

Questions

1. How do you think Kobe Bryant handled the gay slur controversy?

2. Were you a Bryant sponsor, would you take action against him?

3. Were you a Bryant advisor, how would you have counseled him to handle the NBA fine?

*For further information, see "How to Handle a PR Crisis: Kobe's Homophobic Slur, the Lakers and the NBA," *Psychology Today*, April 18, 2011.

■ **Fifth, create a consistent message.**   Agree on an official spokesperson who can disseminate one voice for the organization. Most of all, be honest, and never, ever cover up or lie. That just exacerbates the crisis.[14]

Letting people know that the organization has a plan and is implementing it helps convince them that you are in control. Defining the issues means both having a clear sense internally of what the focus of action should be and communicating that action into the marketplace to reach key constituents.

Communicating in a Crisis

The key communications principle in dealing with a crisis is not to clam up when disaster strikes. A lawyer, correctly, is focused on defense in a court of law and advises clients to say nothing.

Public relations advice, on the other hand, is concerned about a different court—the court of public opinion—and therefore takes a different tack.

Keep in mind that every crisis is different. And just like anything else in public relations, there is no one answer to solve every crisis. Sometimes, an organization shouldn't say something—especially if it doesn't know the facts or the answer will just lead to more trouble.[15]

However, in a general sense, in saying nothing, an organization is perceived as already having made a decision. Indeed, research sponsored by public relations agency Porter Novelli suggests that when most people—upwards of 65%—hear the words "no comment," they perceive the no-commenter as guilty. Silence angers the media and

Outside the Lines

When "No Comment" and "Comment" Are Equally Catastrophic

Normally, public relations crisis counselors advise avoiding "no comment" at all costs. White House press secretaries, working for administrations generally disdainful of the media's prying eyes, constantly have to parry reporters' questions with the dreaded phrase.

President George W. Bush's press secretary Scott McClellan, for example, had to invoke the phrase repeatedly in the summer of 2005 when White House senior advisor Karl Rove was alleged to have identified Valerie Plame, the wife of an administration critic, as an undercover CIA officer.

McClellan's denials recalled the days of President Clinton's Press Secretary Mike McCurry, who had to invoke a similar Kabuki-dancing strategy when his boss got mixed up with a White House intern and went public to adamantly deny the liaison (Figure 17-5). McCurry, who later intimated he had his doubts about his boss's honesty, refused, personally, to deny the allegations—because he wasn't privy to the facts—and salvaged his own reputation.

On the other hand, sometimes a comment is even worse than "no comment." This turned out to be the case in early 2006, when 12 miners were caught in a West Virginia mine explosion. After 41 hours underground, the miners, according to a statement by the mine's owner, were "found alive." The media communicated the news, and the nation rejoiced.

A day later, the earlier report was found to be mistaken—wishful thinking based on misunderstood communications.

FIGURE 17-5 "I did not have sex with that woman." Well.........never mind. *(Photo: CHUCK KENNEDY KRT/Newscom)*

The CEO of the mine company apologized immediately and profusely, but the damage perpetrated by the false report had been done.

compounds the problem. On the other hand, inexperienced spokespersons, speculating nervously or using emotionally charged language, are even worse.

Most public relations professionals consider the cardinal rule for communications during a crisis to be *Tell it all and tell it fast!*

As a general rule, when information gets out quickly, rumors are stopped and nerves are calmed. There is nothing complicated about the goals of crisis management. They are (1) terminate the crisis quickly, (2) limit the damage, and (3) restore credibility. If this requires taking quick, remedial action, then that's what should be done.

Engaging the Media

Handling the media is the most critical element in crisis. Normally, treating the press as friendly adversaries makes great sense. But when crisis strikes, media attention quickly turns to "feeding frenzy." So dealing with the media in crisis demands certain "battlefield rules," among them:

- **Set up media headquarters.**   In a crisis, the media will seek out the organizational soft spots where the firm is most vulnerable to being penetrated. To try to prevent this, organizations in crisis must immediately establish a media headquarters through which all authorized communication must flow.

- **Establish media rules.**   In a crisis, the media are sneaky. Their goal is to unearth any salient or salacious element that will advance the story line of the crisis. It is imperative, therefore, that the organization in the crucible set firm rules—which parts of the operation are off limits, which executives won't be available, and so on—for the media to follow.

- **Media live for the "box score."**   Crisis specifics make news—the grislier, the better. Stated another way, crisis is about numbers. And an organization in crisis must be ready to provide enough numbers to keep the media at bay.

- **Don't speculate.**   If you don't know the numbers or the reasons or the extent of the damage, don't pretend you do. Speculation is suicidal in crisis.

- **Feed the beast.**   The media in crisis are insatiable. Blogs, cable news, and wire services all must be fed 24/7. In the 21st century, with faux journalists blogging and tweeting round the clock, the media never sleep. "Nature abhors a vacuum," goes the old saying.

    So a smart organization in crisis will strive to keep the media occupied— even distracted—with new information that advances the story.

- **Speed triumphs.**   In crisis, the media mantra is speed first, accuracy second. This sad but true fact holds major implications for public relations people, who must monitor what is being wrongly reported so that it can be nipped quickly before others run with the same misinformation.

As to what is said to the media, the following 10 general principles apply:

1. Speak first and often.
2. Don't speculate.
3. Go off the record at your own peril.
4. Stay with the facts.
5. Be open and concerned, not defensive.

6. Make your point and repeat it.
7. Don't wage war with the media; when you do, you lose (Figure 17-6).
8. Establish yourself as the most authoritative source.
9. Stay calm and be truthful and cooperative.
10. Never lie.[16]

Social Media Crisis Management

In the Internet Age, some believe social media set the tone for most crises. Not true—at least not yet.

Traditional media still dictate the vast majority of crises. So the rule of thumb is to communicate well with mainstream media and monitor social media 24/7.[17]

One social media strategy increasingly popular for corporations is the development of a so-called dark Website, a pre-developed site that doesn't become "live" until crisis strikes. A dark Website is equipped with documents perceived to be necessary in a crisis. When the crisis hits, the dark Website is activated, and other documents, graphics, videos, etc., are added, as needed. Once again, the point of a dark Website—just as any other communication vehicle—is to serve as a source of information for the outside world, so that the organization becomes the go-to contact for explanations and updates about the crisis.[18]

Last Word

In 2012, angry MSNBC anchor Rachel Maddow labeled crisis communication specialists "disgusting," "mercenary," "open sewer," and "the most morally repellant, indefensible thing out of American corporate culture." Tsk. Tsk. (Maybe the liberal lady was just having a bad day.)[19]

The fact is that in the second decade of the 21st century, although prevention remains the best insurance for any organization, crisis management has become one of the most revered skills in the practice of public relations. Organizations of every variety are faced, sooner or later, with a crisis. The issues that confront society—from energy and the environment, to health care and nutrition, to corporate accountability and minority rights—will not soon abate.

Social media and the Internet, with blogs and tweets and Facebook friends banging about at all times, has added a new dimension of complexity to communicating in crisis. Nonetheless, research indicates that in time of crisis, consumers still turn to traditional media. Half of those polled turn to network television in times of crisis, followed by 42% radio; 37% newspapers; 33% cable networks; and 25% the Internet.[20]

All of this suggests that experienced and knowledgeable crisis managers who can skillfully navigate and effectively communicate, turning crisis into opportunity, will be valuable resources for organizations in the 21st century.

In the final analysis, communicating in a crisis depends on a rigorous analysis of the risks versus the benefits of going public. Communicating effectively also depends on the judgment and experience of the public relations professional. Every call is a close one, and there is no guarantee that the organization will benefit, no matter what course is chosen. One thing is clear: Helping to navigate the organization through the shoals of a crisis is the ultimate test of a public relations professional. And crisis managers are very much in demand.

In the years ahead, as the world continues to present new and more complex challenges, crisis management promises to be a *growth* area in the *growth* profession that is the practice of public relations.

Discussion Starters

1. What is meant by the term *issues management*?
2. How can an organization influence the development of an issue in society?
3. What is meant by "message mapping"?
4. What is meant by the term *risk communications*?
5. What are the usual stages that an organization experiences in a crisis?
6. What are the principles in planning for crisis?
7. What are important rules in dealing with the media in crisis?
8. What is the cardinal rule for communicating in a crisis?
9. What are the keys to successful crisis communication?
10. What is a dark Website?

Pick of the Literature

Crisis Management in the New Strategy Landscape

William "Rick" Crandall, John A. Parnell, and John E. Spillan, Thousand Oaks, CA: Sage Publications, 2010

This book presents a solid framework in crisis management, from planning to execution.

The emphasis here is on strategy, including the context of crisis and the elements that must be considered in preparing for a crisis and extricating the organization. Case studies are liberally mentioned, including weather-related disasters, Royal Caribbean hijacking, Perrier water contamination, and others.

The back part of the book deals with implementation, in terms of the action that crisis managers must take in dealing with customers, media, social media, etc. Finally, the extensive discussion on ethics in a crisis is a welcome addition to a comprehensive text.

Case Study   Carnival's Crisis Cruise

By 2012, Miami-based Carnival Cruise Lines was the behemoth of the cruise industry.

Dubbed "Carnivore Cruise Lines," Carnival, under high-profile CEO Micky Arison, had gobbled up competing lines around the world to build the globe's largest fleet of cruise ships—incorporating 11 global cruise ship brands. Arison's management style was to decentralize operations and allow local operators the flexibility to run their own fleets.

Carnival was a pioneer in the concept of shorter, less-expensive cruises. Its fleet—known as "The Fun Ships"—were renowned for Las Vegas–style decor and entertainment.

Carnival's Italian line was the *Costa Concordia*, the name *Concordia* intending to denote "continuing harmony, unity, and peace among European nations."

And so it was until the evening of January 13, 2012, when *Costa Concordia* and its parent ran into a major crisis.

Between a Rock and Disaster

A "major crisis" was not the only thing the *Costa Concordia* ran into on that fateful night.

The ship, under the command of Captain Francesco Schettino and in calm seas, stuck a rock in the Tyrrhenian Sea, just off the eastern shore of scenic Giglio Island. The impact tore a 160-foot gash on the port side, and the ship began taking on fearsome quantities of water. The ship listed back toward the island, running aground just 1,600 feet away, lying on her starboard side in shallow water with most of her starboard side underwater.

Despite its closeness to shore, an order to abandon ship, inexplicably, wasn't issued until more than an hour after the initial impact. Although international maritime law requires all passengers to be evacuated within 30 minutes of an order to abandon ship, the evacuation of *Costa Concordia* took more than six hours. Also inexplicably, not all passengers were evacuated. In fact, 300 passengers were left on board and had to be evacuated by helicopters or motorboats in the area.

Of the 3,229 passengers and 1,023 crew known to have been aboard, 32 people perished; 30 bodies were found and two more passengers were missing and presumed dead.

It was a tragedy of the highest order. And the crisis reverberated around the world, when pictures of the dying *Costa Concordia* carcass were broadcast on stations everywhere (Figure 17-7).

The Captain and the Dancer

In the days following the ship's crash, attention centered on the captain, who reportedly had deviated from the ship's computer-programmed route to treat people on the nearby island to a "near shore salute," in which the ship got close (as it turned out, too "close") to the island.

Captain Schettino was also accused by some of spending most of the night just prior to the crash in the ship's bar, wrapped around the arm of a young, attractive blonde woman—one of the ship's dancers, as it turned out—laughing, drinking, and in high spirits. One witness, quoted in the Italian media, claimed he had seen the Captain drain "at least a whole decanter of wine." Even worse, when the ship hit the rock, the captain reportedly abandoned ship even before most of the passengers.

FIGURE 17-7
Tragedy at sea.
The hulk of the *Costa Concordia* lies adrift off the coast of Italy.
(Photo: MASSIMO PERCOSSI/EPA/ Newscom)

FIGURE 17-8
Captain Coward.
The hottest selling outfit at the 2012 carnival ceremonies in Milan was the Schettino costume, patterned after the dress whites worn by the floundering skipper of the *Costa Concordia. (Photo: Gio Francesco Lombardi/ ZUMA Press/Newscom)*

Not surprisingly, Schettino, dubbed "Captain Coward" in the press, was arrested on preliminary charges of multiple manslaughter in connection with causing a shipwreck, failing to assist 300 passengers, and failing to be the last to leave the wreck. He was subsequently also charged with failing to describe to maritime authorities the scope of the disaster and with abandoning incapacitated passengers.

As a consequence of the bumbling captain's notoriety, the "Schettino captain's costume" was the biggest seller at that season's Milan carnival (Figure 17-8).

The Silence of the CEO

Perhaps most surprising was the absence in any sort of damage control of Carnival CEO Micky Arison.

Arison, who also owned the star-studded Miami Heat basketball team and was a regular courtside spectator, stayed strangely distant from the crisis enveloping his company, in spite of the fact that the company's bookings and stock sank and it was royally pilloried on social media. Nonetheless, Carnival and Arison stayed relatively aloof.

Carnival's first response on Facebook came shortly after the crash.

"Our thoughts are with the guests and crew of the Costa Concordia. We are keeping them in our hearts in the wake of this very sad event."

Then, six days after the accident, the company's Facebook update read:

"Out of respect for all those affected by the recent events surrounding our sister line, Costa cruises, we are going to take a bit of a break from posting on our social channels."

Arison, himself, corroborated that same sentiment, when he tweeted: "I won't be as active on Twitter for next while. Helping our @costacruises team manage this crisis is my priority right now. Thnx - @Mickey Arison"

Facebook and Twitter followers weren't impressed with the company's minimalist response. Typical was this post:

—Sorry, Carnival, you don't have a heart. Only bags of money. And stop calling Costa a "sister" line – it is a SUBSIDIARY of CARNIVAL. Carnival owns all of its TEN LINES! Even if Micky Arison stays away from the scene of his latest crime the world is watching and everyone will know who is behind this tragedy. The company is at fault. I wish Arison would stop trying to hide in order to avoid losing money on his other CARNIVAL owned cruise ships.

In the weeks that followed, media attacks on Carnival and its subsidiary continued. *Costa Concordia* offered to pay 11,000 euros ($14,500) in compensation to each of the more than 3,000 passengers and also—in clearly the most tone deaf public relations move in maritime history—offered "discounts" of 30% off on future cruises.

Meanwhile, three weeks after the crash, Carnival Cruise Lines returned to its regular social media commentary. And a few weeks after that, CEO Arison was back entertaining at Miami Heat games (Figure 17-9). And six months after his company suffered one of history's most tragic sea crashes, Arison's Heat won the NBA championship.

FIGURE 17-9   Back to courtside. One month after the deadly crash of one of his ships, Micky Arison, CEO of Carnival Cruise Lines and owner of the Miami Heat, was back at the game entertaining a friend. *(Photo: David Santiago/ MCT/Newscom)*

Questions

1. What do you think of Carnival Cruise Line's response to its crisis?

2. What role would you have advised of Carnival's CEO?

3. How do you feel about the "settlement" offer and the discount that *Costa Concordia* offered?

4. In retrospect, what public relations changes, if any, would you advise Carnival in the event of a similar tragedy in the future (such as the one that hit it in the winter of 2013)?

For further information, see Frances Demilio, "Francesco Schettino, Costa Concordia Captain, Makes Shocking Revelations on Crash," *News of the World*, July 10, 2012; Gini Dietrich, "Carnival Cruise Lines Commits Big Social Media Mistake," *Ragan PR Daily*, February 17, 2012; Steven Erlanger, "Oversight of Cruise Lines at Issue after Disaster," *The New York Times*, January 16, 2012; Marissa McNaughton, "Crisis Communications: Will Carnival Maintain Social Media Silence about the Costa Allegra, Too?" *Realtime Report*, February 27, 2012; and Michael Sebastian, "PR Blunder? Owner of Wrecked Cruise Liner Offering Survivors 30 Percent Off," *Ragan PR Daily*, January 23, 2012.

From the Top

An Interview with John Stauber

John Stauber is every public relations person's worst crisis. Mr. Stauber, who stepped down in 2009 after 16 years as executive director of the Center for Media and Democracy and the publisher of PRWatch.org, has made it his life's work to scrutinize the public relations business. Together with Sheldon Rampton, he authored several books about PR crisis: *Toxic Sludge Is Good for You!*, *Mad Cow U.S.A.*, and *Trust Us, We're Experts!* Mr. Stauber is as "outspoken" a critic of the public relations industry as there is (as you will detect from his answers to the following questions). But despite that, he's a real good guy. So read on—if you've got the guts.

How would you describe the practice of public relations?
In a single word, and quoting the father of "spin" Edward Bernays, public relations is propaganda. PR is a multibillion dollar business conducted by professionals trained in communications and politics and employed primarily by

businesses and governments to strategically manage public perceptions, opinions, information, and policy.

How is public relations looked at by journalists?
Most media professionals seem to flatter and fool themselves that they are immune to PR manipulations, while using public relations professionals to further their journalistic goals.

How much influence does public relations exert on the media?
PR professionals have tremendous influence with the media although media professionals generally fail to admit or recognize this fact. Of course, it is in the interest of PR professionals to also downplay their influence with the media to preserve the public myths of vetted journalism and courageous, independent news reporting. Academic studies attempting to measure how much of the news results from PR have typically found that 40 percent or more of what is read, seen, and heard in mainstream media is the result of, or heavily influenced by, public relations. For example, most Americans get most of their news from television, yet every year thousands of Video News Releases (VNRs) are aired by TV news producers as if they were their own independent reporting, constituting the largest ongoing plagiarism scandal in U.S. history.

What is the proper relationship between a reporter and public relations professional?
From the standpoint of the reporter, the relationship must be viewed as adversarial, although of course the PR professional

generally strives to position him or herself as a helpful facilitator or gatekeeper for the reporter.

Were you a reporter, how would you approach your dealings with public relations professionals?
I *am* a reporter and I view my relationship with any PR professional as adversarial.

Do you think public relations professionals serve any purpose?
PR professionals make life much easier for lazy and compliant journalists, and they generally strive to protect their clients in government and business from scrutiny, criticism, and reform.

If you could "fix" the practice of public relations, what steps would you take?
Propaganda will always exist within a democracy, but it's a nemesis. I strive to fix and strengthen news reporting by educating and informing journalists, researchers, citizens, and policy-makers about the realities of PR and propaganda. PR works best when it is an invisible manipulator of public perceptions; my job is to spray paint that Invisible Man with a bright safety orange. Democracies function best without hidden persuaders.

Public Relations Library

Anthonissen, Peter. *Crisis Communication*. London, England: Kogan Page, 2008. This book was written by members of the IPREX group of 64 worldwide, independent public relations agencies and offers a novel take on crisis communications in the 21st century; the Internet, they say, has changed everything.

Barton, Laurance. *Crisis Leadership Now*. New York: McGraw-Hill, 2008. This book is written from the perspective of averting corporate disasters, from threats to sabotage to scandal.

Boin, Arjen, Paul t'Hart, Eric Stern, and Bengt Sundelius. *The Politics of Crisis Management*. Cambridge, England: Cambridge University Press, 2006. This is a treatise on major government crises, including 9/11 and the anthrax scare in the United States.

Coombs, W. Timothy. *Ongoing Crisis Communication*, 2nd ed. Thousand Oaks, CA: Sage Publications, 2007. This is a well-researched explanation, complemented by real-life case studies.

Devlin, Eric S. *Crisis Management Planning and Execution*. Boca Raton, FL: Auerbach Publications, 2007. This is a good compilation of case studies, emphasizing the planning aspects that go into crisis management.

Dezenhall, Eric, and John Weber. *Damage Control*. New York: Penguin Group, 2008. The authors contend that "everything you learned about crisis communication is wrong." (Not quite.) But they have a new chapter on Wikileaks.

Fearn-Banks, Kathleen. *Crisis Communications*, 4th ed. New York: Routledge, 2011. Solid primer on full spectrum of crises and how to handle them.

George, Bill. *Seven Lessons for Leading in Crisis*. San Francisco, CA: Jossey-Bass, 2009. If only it were this easy.

Gilpin, Dawn R., and Priscilla J. Murphy. *Crisis Management in a Complex World*. New York: Oxford University Press, 2008. This book does a good job of tracing the roots and progression of crises, including the long, sad saga of Enron.

Glaesser, Dirk. *Crisis Management in the Tourism Industry*. Burlington, MA: Butterworth-Heinemann, 2003. With people falling overboard and other crises popping up in the tourism industry, this book is particularly timely.

Henry, Rene. *Communicating in Crisis*. Seattle, WA: Gollywobbler Productions, 2008. Leaning on his 40 years of experience in industry, sports, education, and government, the author warns, "Lawyers make little money preventing crisis and a lot resolving them."

Jordan-Meier, Jane. *The Four Stages of Highly Effective Crisis Management*. Boca Raton, FL: CRC Press, 2011. Focus here is on managing the media in a digital age.

Levick, Richard, and Larry Smith. *Stop the Presses*, 2nd ed. Ann Arbor, MI: Watershed Press, 2008. The authors contend that one important change in 21st-century crisis communication is the "sea change in Internet communications that now ties the world's most powerful corporations to the humblest public interest groups in an unholy dance of 'gotcha' and 'gotcha back.'"

Lewis, Gerald. *Organizational Crisis Management*. Boca Raton, FL: Auerbach Publications, 2006. This book focuses on crises involving personnel, premises, and the like, all affecting reputation.

Martin, Dick. *Tough Calls*. New York: AMACOM, 2005. A former communications director of AT&T presents a riveting account of what led to that great firm's destruction as an independent company.

McCusker, Gerry. *Tailspin*. Sterling, VA: Kogan Page, 2005. This book covers some of the biggest public relations disasters in recent years, from 9/11 to Martha Stewart.

O'Dwyer, Jack (Ed.). *Jack O'Dwyer's Newsletter* (271 Madison Ave., New York, NY 10016). The industry bible.

Powell, Conrad. *Sandy Hook Slaughter*. New York: First World Publishing, 2012. A quickly-done e-book that details the horrendous shooting of elementary school children in Connecticut and how authorities reacted to the crisis.

Rampton, Sheldon, and John Stauber. *The Best War Ever*. New York: Penguin Press, 2006. Two industry critics offer a thorough trashing of the War on Terror, the Bush administration, and the entire public relations industry. (Look out below!)

Regester, Michael, and Judy Larkin. *Risk Issues and Crisis Management*, 3rd ed. London, UK: Michael Regester and Judy Larkin, 2005. Interesting dissertation on issues management and managing risk.

Smith, Denis, and Dominic Elliot. *Key Readings in Crisis Management*. New York: Routledge, 2006. A series of essays on major international crises and how they were handled.

Stein, Matthew. *When Disaster Strikes*. White River Junction, VT: Chelsea Green Publishing Company, 2011. Written from the point of view of what to do when disaster strikes you or your family; not exactly traditional crisis management but, hey, 377 pages ain't easy to fill!

Ulmer, Robert Ray, Timothy L. Sellnow, and Matthew Wayne Seeger. *Effective Crisis Communication*. Thousand Oaks, CA: Sage Publications, 2011. This provides a good explanation of steps in crisis management, illustrated by famous cases.

Zdziarski, Eugene L., Norbert W. Dunkel, and J. Michael Rollo. *Campus Crisis Management*. San Francisco, CA: Jossey-Bass, 2007. This provides background on university crises, beginning with the University of Texas tower shootings in 1966 to the present.

Chapter 18

Launching
a Career

Chapter Objectives

1. To discuss how a public relations student or novice finds a position in the practice of public relations.

2. To explore the role of public relations in time of economic uncertainty, charting how the field has improved its position even in times of stress.

3. To discuss, in detail, the aspects of organizing the search, job letters, résumés, interviewing, and follow-up.

4. To examine how an individual can map his or her course for long-term public relations success.

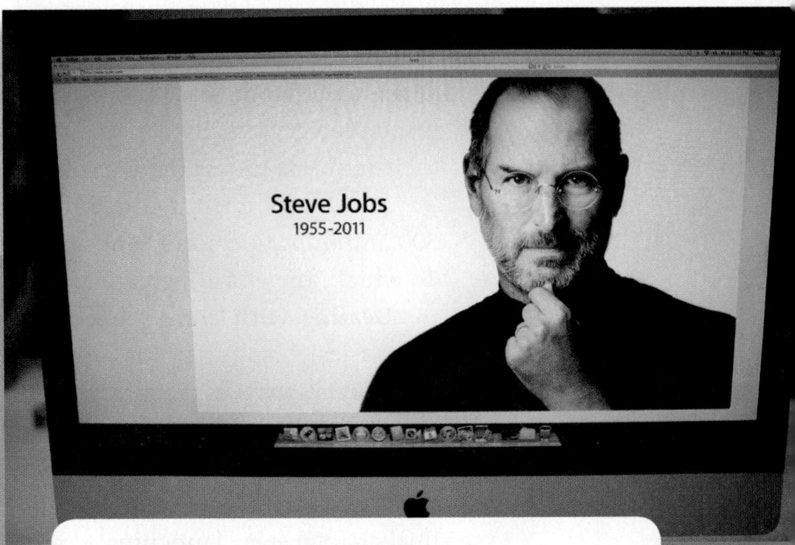

FIGURE 18-1 **Student unfriendly.**
Apple CEO Steve Jobs, who died in 2011, created products that were inarguably "consumer friendly," but he didn't always treat struggling students with the same considerate regard. *(Photo: EMMANUEL DUNAND/AFP/Getty Images/Newscom)*

In the old days, you got a job in public relations by "networking."

In the new days, you get a job in public relations by "networking" in social media.

At least that's how young David Murray found communications work in 2009.

 First, he reached out to followers on his Twitter account that he was officially "looking for work." He immediately received several prime leads.

 Second, he augmented these by entering keywords in Twitter Search, like "Hiring Social Media," "Online Community Manager," and "Blogging Jobs."

 Third, he pulled RSS feeds of his keyword conversations into Google Reader and checked his incoming mail every morning.

 Fourth, he followed up on promising leads by introducing himself via Twitter, inquiring about job leads, some of which hadn't been officially posted. Several executives were receptive to his social media entreaties.

And before he knew it, voilà, he had landed a Web-based communications post at a Website design firm.[1]

As positive as Mr. Murray's experience in reaching out to corporate bigwigs for assistance, there are others who are less fortunate, such as Long Island University senior Chelsea Kate Issacs, who in 2010 had a most unpleasant exchange with a well-known CEO (Figure 18-1).

Ms. Issacs emailed none other than living (at the time) legend Steve Jobs, founder and

CEO of Apple, and asked why the Apple public relations department refused to give her a quotation for a school project on the use of iPads in academic settings.[2]

Wonder of wonders, Mr. Jobs himself, the iconic Apple impresario emailed back—bluntly: "Our goals do not include helping you get a good grade. Sorry."

Ms. Issacs was shocked by the dismissive tone and emailed again, wondering again whether it was Apple's job to be responsive to the public. Mr. Jobs again responded cryptically: "Nope. We have over 300 million users and we can't respond to their requests unless they involve a problem of some kind. Sorry."

Ms. Issacs tried again, informing the CEO that she was, in fact, "one of the 300 million Apple users" and asked if she might, simply, receive the quote she sought. To which, the world's greatest innovator responded: "Please leave us alone."

Dealing with cranky executives—and sometimes even worse, their protective secretaries!—isn't easy for public relations students. Finding a job in the practice of public relations—especially in times of economic downturn—is probably the most formidable task that an entry-level communicator faces. Once inside an organization, competence rises to the top. So if you're competent, you've got it made. But how do you get "through the door" in the first place? The challenge—the one we'll focus on in this final chapter—is "launching a career."

Public Relations in Economic Downturn

Traditionally, public relations jobs were the first to fall when economic times got rough. Not so much anymore.

Smart organizations today understand the critical importance of communications that are honest, candid, and transparent. Moreover, the advent of social media and the Internet have made the traditional corporate "vow of silence," especially in the face of continuous criticism, a dangerous proposition. CEOs, who by nature are tight-lipped, need only consider the carcasses of once-great companies laid to waste by arrogant leaders, who, in recent years, refused to level with the public about the state of their corporations (Figure 18-2).

As a consequence, the impact on the public relations industry of the economic downturn that afflicted the United States and the world in the second decade of the 21st century was rather muted. A study of nearly 200 organizations by the University of Southern California indicated that public relations and communications functions of U.S. companies suffered only moderate decreases as the recession wore on. Instead of cutting staffs, as had been done in previous downturns, most companies opted to freeze or reduce staff compensation, rather than cutting headcount.[3]

The understanding and mastery of social media proved a primary reason in the renewed popularity and staying power of public relations positions in economic downturn. As one Toronto marketing CEO, whose firm purchased three public relations agencies, told *The New York Times*: "Marketers want to find firms that can deliver performance, and public relations agencies are excelling in understanding the changing dynamics of the marketplace, as what happens with a campaign in social media and earned media has become as important as its presence in paid media and owned media."[4]

FIGURE 18-2
Everybody's crazy 'bout a sharp-dressed man.
The media couldn't get enough of flamboyant and quotable Countrywide Financial Founder and CEO Angelo Mozilo, until he and his company crumbled in 2008.
(Photo: CD1 WENN Photos/Newscom)

While the practice of public relations isn't immune from cuts in bad times, it is no longer "the first to go." Most important, organizations today understand that especially in bad times, candid communication isn't an option; it's a necessity.

Getting a Jump

Public relations jobs used to be available for anybody who wanted them. Since nobody understood exactly what public relations was, standards weren't high. (How d'ya think I got a job?) But today, with standards raised, competition fierce, and the labor market contracted, the search for a public relations position must begin in school.

The reality today is that when a potential employer considers a candidate, he or she is also thinking, as Pulitzer Prize–winner Tom Friedman has put it, "Can this person add value every hour, every day—more than a worker in India, a robot or a computer? Can he or she help my company adapt by not only doing the job today but also reinventing the job for tomorrow? And can he or she adapt with all the change, so my company can adapt and export more into the fastest-growing global markets? In today's hyperconnected world, more and more companies cannot and will not hire people who don't fulfill those criteria."[5]

For public relations students, this translates into using the college years to get a jump on the competition by doing the following:

1. **Improve your communication skills.**   Communication is what you do in public relations. So make sure you do it better than others.

2. **Start networking.**   Don't wait until you're submitting your résumés before you begin networking. Start doing it now. Make friends and keep them. Attend business gatherings and get around.

3. **Focus . . .**   on what you do—and like—best. Which part of public relations do you like the most—corporate, agency, nonprofit, political, what?

4. **Look at companies you like.**   Keep a running roster of the public relations firms or companies to which you'd like to apply. Follow them on LinkedIn for news on the company and to learn who is leaving and moving up the ladder.

5. **Intern, intern, intern.**   Use college to try employment during the off months. Sure, you may not get paid and may be given tedious assignments that others don't want. But it's worth it—a great way to get your foot in the door, both literally and figuratively.

To paraphrase the old saw, an education is a terrible thing to waste—so get started in the field before you graduate.[6]

Organizing the Job Search

Organizing a job search, in good times or bad, requires just that—"organization."

Just as in any assignment, public relations job seekers should follow a predetermined path to get them through the door to meet a person with a potential job offer. Again, it's getting *through* the door that's the problem.

As public relations practice has become more enticing to communications students, lawyers, journalists, and others, positions in the field have become more competitive.

So what's an entry-level, fresh-eyed graduate to do as he or she commences the post-commencement job search?

According to experienced public relations executive and teacher Martin Arnold, the following ought to be considered:

- **First, consider what interests you, and start early.**
  Determine where, if you had your druthers, you would like to work. In sports? Fashion? Government? Big business? With a grassroots nonprofit? Where?

- **Second, get a name.**
  Avoid writing blind to potential employers.
  To avoid the "dead letter response," network with colleagues to see if an associate might suggest a name at a target organization. Failing that, consult directories to discover the names of public relations professionals on staff. Failing that, call the organization directly and secure the name of the public relations director.

- **Third, dispatch a personal letter.**
  Write directly to the contact, requesting an interview. Explain in the note who you are, your rationale for choosing this organization as a target, and why you're interested in speaking with the addressee.
  But don't make the interview contingent on job openings at the company in question. Even if no job is currently available—and most of the time that's the case—you still want to get through the door.

- **Fourth, call.**
  The sad truth is that few job applicants ever do.
  While it's true that some potential employers—the nasty ones—refuse to be "bothered" by job seekers, most potential public relations employers are nicer than that. Some, in fact—the enlightened ones—will even allow you 30 minutes to come in and discuss opportunities.

- **Fifth, prepare an elevator speech.**
  Be prepared with a 30-second talk on who you are, what you are doing, and what you are trying to achieve. Memorize it and use it whenever you can. Most people will help if they know what you want.[7]

Organizing the Résumé

Just like everything else in the second decade of the 21st century, résumés have become big business, with their own set of consultants to help you master the process. As to what to do—and not to do—here are some "dos" from résumé consultant extraordinaire Paulette Barrett:

1. What's your intro? Who are you? What do you want? Why should anyone care?

2. What three impressions do you want to create immediately?

3. What can you say about your achievements that will make someone say, "Tell me more."

4. Be able to cover a time sequence, most recent, backward. Don't leave any gaps.

5. How did you add value in each slot? Solve a problem? Lead colleagues? Sell more?

6. Have an anecdote about each post.

7. List your professional awards, educational achievements, and community service.

8. Aim for a 2-page résumé with no less than 12 pt. type.[8]

As to the "don'ts," here are some of the more egregious from career expert Dawn Rasmussen:

1. **Goofy or inappropriate email address.**   Grow up. Don't use your hotlix23@ aol.com account on your résumé. Names like that suggest that you aren't taking your job search seriously, and quite possibly lead to a "delete."

2. **Including an objective statement.**   Employers don't care what *you* want; they care what you are going to do for *them*.

3. **Forgetting skill sets.**   Knock, knock. Who's there? Keywords. Keywords who? Keywords are key to getting your résumé noticed. Okay, that's a lousy joke, but it's not any worse than a résumé without keyword skill sets included. (The Website onetonline.org offers the mother lode of keywords. Pass it on.)

4. **Placing awards and top achievements at the end of the document.** Please, insert a "Notable Achievements" section right after the top third of the résumé where you've included your keywords. Remember, the cream rises to the top.

5. **Lumping multiple jobs at one employer into one position.**   This is a deal-breaker. Some people have had a wonderful career at one employer, holding multiple positions as they worked their way to the top. However, this does *not* entitle them to lump the entirety of their time at that employer under that one position. It's a *big* no-no.

6. **Stretching your employment dates.**   If you started on 11/2007 and left in 2/2008, that does not mean you can put "2007–2008" on your résumé. That's called lying.

7. **Upgrading your job title.**   The title listed on the résumé should match what is on file in the personnel office—or you're creating a terrible first impression.

8. **Not keeping up to date.**   If the last class you took to boost your on-the-job knowledge was in 1999, then you need to get cracking. Employers are hiring subject matter experts, and your job—until you retire (I know, tall order)—is to constantly think about the professional development classes, workshops, conferences, etc., that will enhance your job knowledge. Because there is no such thing as job security anymore—even in public relations.[9]

Outside the Lines
Online Public Relations Job References

The Internet offers an expanding list of reference sites that access "public relations openings." Among them:

- **Bulldog Reporter PR Job Mart**
  Bulldog's PR Job Mart is an active, updated source for agency and corporate jobs at various levels. As with other free public relations sites, Bulldog's non-agency roster is flooded with hospitals, academic institutions, and nonprofits looking for public relations help. Bulldog also provides email updates of job openings each week to its subscriber list. (http://bulldogreporter.com/ME2/dirmod.asp)

- **Indeed.com**
  The job search engine Indeed.com is an excellent resource for finding public relations job listings fast. Indeed.com is free and enables you to search millions of job listings from thousands of Websites, job boards, newspapers, blogs, company career pages, and associations to find job listings that match or are similar to your search query. Indeed.com has the look and feel of Google and the other top search engines. It's user friendly, uncluttered, and simple and easy to navigate. (www.Indeed.com/)

- **International Association of Business Communicators (IABC)**
  The IABC's site lists 240 or so primarily internal communications openings at corporations and nonprofits. With its significant presence in Canada, IABC boasts the added advantage of listing Canadian job openings. (http://jobs.iabc.com/home/index.cfm?site_id=65)

- **Media Bistro**
  This site lists all manner of media jobs, from online and newspaper editors to broadcast journalists. It also includes a healthy sampling of public relations posts. (www.mediabistro.com/joblistings/)

- **Monster**
  Every day, approximately 20–50 "new" public relations positions are listed. Many are of the promotional/marketing cold call variety, but others are at legitimate public relations firms. Monster.com is a good source for "public relations" positions that often don't appear elsewhere. (http://jobsearch.monster.com/Browse.aspx)

- **O'Dwyer**
  Among its 70 or so availabilities, the inestimable Odwyerpr.com site generally lists higher level openings at firms, nonprofits, and companies. In addition to the high-level posts, O'Dwyer also lists a number of "intern" availabilities. (http://jobs.odwyerpr.com/home/index.cfm?site_id=258)

- **PR News Online**
  PR News offers another excellent online source for corporate, nonprofit, and agency public relations positions. As with other sites, PR News offers a service for job seekers to post résumés for employers to peruse. (www.prnewsonline.com/resources/pr_jobs.html)

- **PRSA Job Center**
  The Public Relations Society of America (PRSA) site lists 1,700 job openings, many from agency members from around the nation. In addition, individual PRSA chapters, such as Cleveland and Houston, keep their own local job openings updated on a regular basis. (www.prsa.org/jobcenter/)

- **PR Talent**
  This service, begun by several public relations professionals, says that it "operates much like an entertainment talent agency, except that we identify and represent top full-time and freelance public relations and communications talent." (www.prtalent.com/jobSearch.aspx)

- **Public Affairs Council**
  The Public Affairs Council in Washington lists primarily lobbying, government relations, and government agency job openings, not only in the nation's capital but throughout the nation. (http://pac.org/jobs)

- **Ragan Communications Career Center**
  Ragan.com's 250 or so offerings span the gamut from internal to external positions, including public relations posts at government agencies, such as the U.S. Coast Guard and the IRS. (www.ragan.com/jobadvice/)

- **The Fry Group**
  The Fry Group is a public relations executive search firm that lists some of its job searches on the Internet, where interested talent may inquire. Other search firms offer similar job quests in progress. (www.frygroup.com/listings.php)

Many of the job opening postings on these sites are redundant from one site to the next. Some are recurring month-to-month adverts designed to troll the waters to see what turns up. Still others are little more than low-level sales come-ons, looking for warm bodies.

Whatever.

All these site are worth a look from prospective public relations job seekers.

Remember, it only takes one.

Organizing the Job Interview

Once an applicant is fortunate enough to land an interview, he or she must understand that 9 times out of 10, it is their responsibility to control the meeting agenda.

This meeting is your chance—often your *only* chance—to find out the information you need about other firms and other individuals to keep your search progressing.

So walk in with a game plan and the "script" that will keep the interview going.

- **First, take charge.**   To take your best shot, you have to—in a nice and subtle way—take charge of the interview.

    So lead. Don't wait to be asked. Raise questions about the organization and the interviewer.

    Demonstrate your interest in the organization and a job by taking charge of the interview.

- **Second, lead with your knowledge and strength.**   Suggest through your questions and answers that you've done your homework on the organization. Show the interviewer that you've gone the extra mile by researching the firm and becoming knowledgeable about it.

- **Third, beware the "gotcha" questions.**   Every interviewer asks standard questions. They seem innocuous enough, but cuidado: They're tricky. Here are a few:

    - **Do you have any questions?**   This is a great opportunity to turn around the interview. The best way to answer this standard question is to stir up a conversation by asking the interviewer more about how he or she started at the company, and even what he or she loves most about the job.

    - **What is your biggest weakness?**   This is dangerous. The standard "weakness" question is usually answered with a strength by the majority of job applicants. But careful, hiring managers are tired of hearing every single candidate that walks through the door stating that being a "perfectionist" is their biggest weakness.

    - **Tell me about yourself.**   Your answer to this interview question is where your "elevator pitch" can work like a charm. Be prepared for it.

    - **What do you know about our company?**   The best strategy you can have in tackling this question is to research the most recent news about the employer and turn this interview question around by starting a conversation about the direction the business is moving in. On the other hand, the biggest mistake an applicant can make in answering this common interview question is to not know anything about the company at all.[10]

- **Fourth, indicate what you'll add to the mix.**   Take the opportunity to allude to what that college training has afforded you, particularly in enhancing the expertise and scope of the department you'd love to join.

    For example, all those social media tools that you took for granted in school—Facebook, Twitter, Tumblr, Pinterest, blogs, and all the rest—may reveal potential new avenues for an interviewer. Your facility with such social media may, therefore, suggest attractive possibilities to the interviewer.

    Also, smile. As Professor Martin Arnold observes, "First and foremost people want to work with people they like."[11]

- **Fifth, get more names.**   This is your most important task at the interview.

    Use the interviewer to provide more names—advice, leads, contacts, colleagues at competitors with whom you might speak, etc. Don't walk out the door unless you have been given two or three other people you can call to continue the job search.

■ **Sixth, follow up.**   Ensure that the interviewer won't mind if you "keep in touch," as situations with you and at the organization change. Once you've made the contact, you don't want to lose it.

The reassuring point to keep always in mind is that as frustrating and maddening and ego-deflating as the job-seeking process sometimes seems to be, all it takes is one "You're hired" to start you on a lifelong career.

Ensuring Public Relations Success

For years, practitioners of the practice of public relations have searched for the "holy grail" to advise them on getting ahead.

While many have speculated on achieving senior management success in public relations, a comprehensive study of 97 highest-level public relations leaders isolated the seven factors that can help pave the way to the top of the practice.

Recruiter William C. Heyman (see From the Top in this chapter) and University of Alabama Professor Bruce Berger produced a study that pinpointed what it takes to pursue a successful career in public relations. They discovered seven keys—some expected, others counterintuitive—to a successful public relations career.

1. **Diversity of experience.**   While the executives polled averaged 23 years of experience, most indicated that it was "the accumulation of experiences over time" that forged the "tipping point" in their success. Study recipients clearly felt that focusing on one specialty throughout a career was counterproductive.

2. **Performance.**   Successful public relations executives must deliver one tangible commodity—results. Survey respondents agreed that the power of performance—solving problems, meeting goals, providing counsel, and producing results—was an absolute requirement for success in public relations.

3. **Communications skills.**   Public relations practitioners are, at base, professional communicators. Therefore, highly honed technical communications skills, according to the study—from writing and design to the production of sophisticated communication materials—are imperative for public relations success.

4. **Relationship building.**   Common wisdom suggests that in public relations, "it's not what you know but who you know that counts." To a great degree, according to the study, common wisdom is correct.

    Nearly half of the executives, in fact, said the most valuable source of influence they possessed was relationships with senior executives, peers, and subordinates. Indeed, the findings hint that relationships may provide more power to professionals than their titles or formal positions in their organization.

5. **Proactivity and passion.**   The executives said that public relations people must be go-getters, self-starters, risk-takers, opportunity-seekers with boundless energy, great curiosity, and passionate in their commitment to the practice.

6. **Teamliness.**   Most respondents agreed that achievement depended on three levels—the individual, organizational, and group or work unit, in that order.

7. **Intangibles.**   Chemistry. Likeability. Personality. Presence. Cultural fit.

Nearly 90% of the executives polled cited positive personal character traits as the single most desired characteristic among job candidates.

One disturbing aspect of their study, said the researchers, was that nearly half of those interviewed said the most significant limitation on public relations practice and influence was the "inaccurate or incomplete perceptions of the function's role and value," particularly among organizational executives.

One way to upgrade that perception is for those who practice public relations—particularly young practitioners—to take seriously the list of successful attributes revealed in the Heyman-Berger study.[12]

Outside the Lines
Don't You Dare . . .

After all this, anyone guilty of repeating the following 20 faux pas in their cover letters or résumés for employment (culled from the files of career expert Andrew Kucheriavy) deserve what they get:

20. "I have a known track record and excellent experience with accurancy and fixing erors"

19. "Strong Work Ethic, Attention to Detail, Team Player, Attention to Detail"

18. "My experience include filing, billing, printing and coping"

17. "Demonstrated ability in multi-tasting."

16. "My work ethics are impeachable."

15. "I have nervous of steel."

14. "I consistently tanked as top sales producer for new accounts."

13. "I am a perfectionist and rarely if if ever forget details."

12. "Dear Sir or Madman,"

11. "I can type without looking at the keyboard."

10. "Instrumental in ruining entire operation for a Midwest chain store."

9. "I am anxious to use my exiting skills"

8. "Speak English and Spinach"

7. "I am a Notary Republic"

6. "I attended collage courses for minor public relations"

5. "Following is a grief overview of my skills."

4. "I'm attacking my resume for you to review."

3. "I am experienced in all faucets of accounting."

2. "Hope to hear from you, shorty."

And the most embarrassing one to finish off our list:

1. "Directed $25 million anal shipping and receiving operations." **

**Andrew Kucheriavy, "Top 20 of the Most Hilarious Mistakes on Resumes and Cover Letters," www.resumark.com/blog/author/andrew/, March 19, 2010.

Outside the Lines
The Old Man and the Chair

Finally, lest you still doubt the power and value of public relations, consider how the penultimate moment of the 2012 Republican Convention was capsized by poor public relations planning.

That was the moment when octogenarian actor Clint Eastwood—the original *Dirty Harry*—who hadn't rehearsed, didn't have a script, and, most important, hadn't been vetted by Mitt Romney public relations advisors, took the stage and, in the most bizarre 12 minutes of campaign history, kidnapped the convention (Figure 18-3).

Eastwood, using an empty chair to symbolize President Obama, conducted a rambling, slightly off-color, and largely off-message conversation with the absent president that brought angst and dismay to the otherwise buttoned-up Mitt Romney team.

FIGURE 18-3   Talk to the chair.
Clint Eastwood in a 2012 convention moment that will live
in infamy. *(Photo: Ron Sachs/CNP/AdMedia/Newscom)*

It was excruciating and "a reminder," as *The New York Times* wrote, "of how carefully staged events can be upset by an unpredictable turn."*

In other words, to be effective, everyone must follow sound principles of public relations. In other words, they need people like you.

*For further information, see Michael Barbaro and Michael D. Shear, "Before Talk with Chair, Clearance from the Top," *The New York Times*, pp. A1–15.

Last Word

Public relations dialogue still revolves around finding that elusive "seat at the management table," that is, convincing management that the public relations function is as imperative as legal or human resources or finance. To be sure, the practice has come a long way since patriarchs such as Edward Bernays and Ivy Lee first practiced the art form in the early 20th century.

Indeed, notwithstanding the tremendous strides the field has made in recent years, the practice is still often challenged by those who don't fully understand or appreciate it. The burden, then, is on the public relations practitioners of the 21st century.

Employers will increasingly seek experienced and competent public relations professionals to help them communicate. How can entry-level professionals accommodate this Catch-22 need for "experience"? According to experienced counselor and LIM College public relations professor Barry Zusman, at least three specific courses should be considered:

■ **Hone writing skills.**   Says Professor Zusman, "While the current generation gets it as far as technology and digital media are concerned, we don't yet live in a world ruled by 140 Twitter characters." Well-written content is still king.

■ **Seize internships.**   These are among the best ways to learn about the field with real-life experience. Although many internships are unpaid, they're still often worth it, since firms hire based on internship experience.

■ **Join a professional communications organization.**   And become involved in professional committees. Says Zusman, "Listen and learn everything you can from the organization's members, who have been in the field and can serve as mentors."[13]

To the Zusman Principles, others suggest five additional keys to moving ahead in public relations.

1. **Use technology to your advantage.**   You can often teach employers how to use social media for public relations value, so don't be shy.

2. **Pay attention to details.**   Treat everything like a "big deal," using every opportunity to demonstrate your worth.

3. **Read, read, read.** The key to good writing, say veterans, is "good reading," so pick up newspapers, magazines, and books, and then *read* them.

4. **Be a student.** Just because you've graduated into the workplace doesn't mean you should stop *learning*. Learn constantly.

5. **Find a mentor.** Often, the old adage is right: It's not what you know but who you know that counts. So find someone or *someones* who can advise and help you as you proceed through the public relations profession.[14]

As it heads into the second decade of the 21st century, the practice of public relations has never been stronger or more valuable to the individuals and organizations that depend on it. The field still has its share of debates—the value of a public relations degree vs. a degree in liberal arts, the role and

knowledge of digital media vs. traditional media, the goodness of a public relations education vs. on-the-job training, the relative pay of women vs. men, whether marketing should be subordinated to public relations, etc. Indeed, as the CEO of Ketchum public relations put it, "The fact there's debate over whether marketing and public relations should remain separate is evident of PR's growing importance."[15]

One point, however, is incontestable: The practice of public relations has never been as accepted or respected as it is today. That's why jobs in the field are coveted, and competition is great. But for an individual of dedication and competence, who writes well and communicates clearly and who understands that integrity and reputation are critical for success—the practice of public relations will continue to offer bountiful opportunities for generations to come.

Discussion Starters

1. How is the practice of public relations doing in the midst of economic downturn?
2. What steps can a college student take to get a jump on public relations employment?
3. Is it worth sending a form letter to a potential public relations employer?
4. Why is it important to have a "name" at an organization before applying?
5. What are the elements that make a winning job letter?
6. What are the principles in creating an effective résumé?
7. How can an applicant "control the agenda" of a job interview?
8. Should an interviewee follow-up the interview with further communication?
9. What additional steps should an up-and-coming professional follow to ensure success?
10. How important is writing in a public relations career?

Pick of the Literature

Ready to Launch: The PR Couture Guide to Breaking into Fashion PR
Crosby Noricks, New York: Crosby Noricks, 2011

Sure, this is self-published, but it's good.

A great many public relations students today, infused by Fashion Week and VH1, wish to enter the wild world of fashion public relations. This is a great introduction to that ethereal world.

The book begins by distinguishing among marketing, advertising, and public relations, emphasizing that it is media relations and publicity that largely defines the latter (true, especially in the fashion world).

The book takes the novice through interviewing, pitching, social media networking, and what to expect from a career in fashion public relations. Written by an agency executive knowledgeable in the subject matter, this book provides a true-to-life explanation about what public relations—at least as it relates to fashion—is all about.

From the Top

Ultimate Word to the Wise (Student):
An Interview with Bill Heyman

Bill Heyman, founder, president, and CEO of Heyman Associates, has been the dean of public relations recruiters for more than two decades. He manages senior-level searches for blue-chip and emerging companies, leading public relations firms, nonprofit organizations, and government agencies. He is a board member of the Lagrant Foundation, which awards scholarships to minority students planning public relations careers. He is also an inaugural member of the advisory board for the Plank Center for Public Relations Studies in the College of Communication and Information Sciences at the University of Alabama. For additional information about Heyman Associates, visit www.heymanassociates.com.

What is the employment outlook for public relations graduates today?

Public relations has become an essential business tool, not something that could be eliminated. On the whole, companies want to do a better job telling their stories. But, job seekers need to be realistic: The employment market is tied to the performance of capital markets. Those seeking jobs must recognize that salaries and perks will not match those of only a few years ago, when "new economy" companies ruled, and that more will be expected from them for lower initial salaries. It also is likely to take longer for most to earn their stripes—[that is, job seekers can expect to] rise more slowly within an organization, because organizations are smaller and leaner.

Where are the most attractive public relations employment skill areas?

The most employment opportunities today are in media relations, internal communications, issues management, financial public relations, branding and image development, and social responsibility. Each one of these specialties tends to target an audience that was underserved prior to corporations' rebuilding their images. Companies are no longer taking any audience for granted. Transparency is critical.

What are the most attractive industries for public relations employment?

The health care industry consistently looks at communications as an important way to deliver its message. Pharmaceutical and biotechnology companies lead the public relations job market. Almost on a level field is the financial services industry. Also, an increased number of the largest corporations are in the process of remaking their images, especially those whose reputations have been challenged. With communications, they can demonstrate they are broad thinkers, technologically advanced, and contemporary.

What's the best preparation for public relations employment?

Become a strong writer. There is no greater need than having a strong writing ability. Key areas of employment today are in media relations and speechwriting, and both require strong writing skills.

Students must take as many writing classes as possible and intern (for pay or not) in places where they can get real-world experience (local newspapers, public relations agencies, companies, or philanthropic organizations).

And, because they must be increasingly well-rounded in their knowledge, they need to take a wide range of liberal arts classes (especially ethics) and meld that with exploring cultural experiences in the community (opera, theater, museums, etc.) and read, read, read newspapers, magazines, corporate Websites, and books.

The most successful practitioners will be those that the CEO will want as a seatmate flying across the country or at a dinner table with the organization's most important client.

What is the ideal starting point for public relations beginners?

Often, an agency is the best training ground because of the diverse experiences. The broader the experience, the better it is. Corporate jobs, especially entry-level, tend to be more narrowly focused. Starting at a news organization enables people to learn up close what a reporter goes through and needs every day. Another area where people can consider working in the early stages of their career is a political campaign.

What are the public relations prospects in the nonprofit sector?

Public relations is becoming a valued commodity in the nonprofit sector, especially after 9/11. These jobs tend to have lower salaries, but the experience can be similar to that of a public relations agency and therefore a good training ground. Also, corporate foundations are doing more to articulate their specific business message and are looking for strong public relations executives.

What are the essential characteristics that public relations employers look for in potential employees?

There are five nontechnical characteristics that are most important: one, integrity; two, self-confidence; three, likeability (including respect for others); four, energy (including noticeable enthusiasm); and five, intellect (including business knowledge and judgment).

Added to that are two technical characteristics: the ability to write and to present well. These seven criteria transcend communications posts and organizations.

What's the best way to find a public relations job?

There is no greater way to find a position than to develop a network from the earliest stages of your career.

■ Contacting people, joining professional organizations, and being involved in volunteer work are all critical ways to meet other people.

■ Conducting research and learning more about the companies you want to work for is key, as is finding a specific contact within each company.

■ Learning about the alumni association at your college or university and who might be working within the field can help you start your career.

■ During internships, reach out to anyone you meet.

■ Always follow up with people, writing courteous notes asking for help. Two key characteristics in finding a job are to be courteous and tenacious. Always let people know how appreciative you are of any time they spend with you.

Public Relations Library

Aronson, Merry, Don Spetner, and Carol Ames. *The Public Relations Writer's Handbook*. San Francisco, CA: Jossey-Bass, 2007. This presents a good explanation of how the digital age has altered the requirements in the public relations field.

Breakenridge, Deirdre. "Social Media and Public Relations." Upper Saddle River, NJ: Pearson Education, 2012. The queen of social media public relations holds forth on a comprehensive explanation of what social media means to the practice of public relations.

Careers in Advertising and Public Relations. San Francisco, CA: WebFeet, 2005. This guide offers an analysis of whether an advertising or public relations firm is right for a writer.

Croft, A. C. *Managing a Public Relations Firm for Fun and Profit*. Binghamton, NY: Haworth Press, 2006. Once you've entered the field, prospered in it, and now are ready to become your own CEO, read this book to find out how to do it.

Field, Shelly. *Career Opportunities in Advertising and Public Relations Rev. Ed*. New York: Checkmark Books, 2005. This presents a full roster of jobs in the communications industry and what each requires.

Fitzpatrick, Kathy, and Carolyn Bronstein. *Ethics in Public Relations*. Thousand Oaks, CA: Sage Publishing, 2006. This offers a fresh approach on why public relations people should be "responsible advocates" for the views they represent.

Freitag, Alan R., and Ashli Quesinberry Stokes. *Global Public Relations*. New York: Routledge, 2009. This presents the cross-border cultural impact of different societies on public relations practice.

Green, Andy. *Creativity in Public Relations*, 3rd ed. London, England: Kogan Page, 2007. The author emphasizes "creative thinking" as the road to inspired public relations.

Hall, Phil. *The New PR*. N. Potomac, MD: Larsten Publishing, 2007. Emphasis here is on how "experiential marketing strategies" will change the face of public relations.

Harris, Thomas L., and Patricia T. Whelan. *The Marketer's Guide to Public Relations in the 21st Century*. Mason, OH: Texere, 2006. The emphasis here is on marketing public relations.

Henderson, David. *Making News*. Lincoln, NE: iUniverse Star, 2006. This is an experienced look at how to effectively practice media relations.

Kelleher, Tom. *Public Relations Online*. Thousand Oaks, CA: Sage Publications, 2007. This is a fine explanation of the new technologies in public relations and how to use them.

Morris, Trevor, and Simon Goldworthy. *PR: A Persuasive Industry?* New York: Palgrave MacMillan, 2008. The authors describe public relations as more gray than black and white, in terms of ethics; as "amoral," neither a tool for good nor bad but rather dependent on the specific ethic or motives of its professionals. They deride journalists who deride public relations, because without the field, "there would be little news."

Weiner, Mark. *Unleashing the Power of PR*. San Francisco, CA: Jossey-Bass, 2006. A measurement expert reminds practitioners that public relations measurement has become essential.

Yaverbaum, Eric. *Public Relations for Dummies*, 2nd ed. Hoboken, NJ: Wiley Publishing, 2006. A seasoned public relations professional talks about how "word of mouth" can move mountains.

Zappala, Joseph M., and Ann R. Carden. *Public Relations Worktext*. Mahwah, NJ: Lawrence Erlbaum, 2008. This is an excellent writing resource for the public relations professional.

Appendix A

PRSA Member Code of Ethics 2000

Approved by the PRSA Assembly October, 2000

Letter from the PRSA Board of Directors

It is with enormous professional pleasure and personal pride that we, the Public Relations Society of America Board of Directors, put before you a new Public Relations Member Code of Ethics for our Society. It is the result of two years of concentrated effort led by the Board of Ethics and Professional Standards. Comments of literally hundreds and hundreds of members were considered. There were focus groups at our 1999 national meeting in Anaheim, California. We sought and received intensive advice and counsel from the Ethics Resource Center, our outside consultants on the project. Additional recommendations were received from your Board of Directors, PRSA staff, outside reviewers, as well as District and Section officers. Extensive research involving analysis of numerous codes of conduct, ethics statements, and standards and practices approaches was also carried out.

In fact, this Member Code of Ethics has been developed to serve as a foundation for discussion of an emerging global Code of Ethics and Conduct for the practice of Public Relations.

This approach is dramatically different from that which we have relied upon in the past. You'll find it different in three powerfully important ways:
1. Emphasis on enforcement of the Code has been eliminated. But, the PRSA Board of Directors retains the right to bar from membership or expel from the Society any individual who has been or is sanctioned by a government agency or convicted in a court of law of an action that is in violation of this Code.
2. The new focus is on universal values that inspire ethical behavior and performance.
3. Desired behavior is clearly illustrated by providing language, experience, and examples to help the individual practitioner better achieve important ethical and principled business objectives. This approach should help everyone better understand what the expected standards of conduct truly are.

Perhaps most important of all, the mission of the Board of Ethics and Professional Standards has now been substantially altered to focus primarily on education and training, on collaboration with similar efforts in other major professional societies, and to serve an advisory role to the Board on ethical matters of major importance.

The foundation of our value to our companies, clients, and those we serve is their ability to rely on our ethical and morally acceptable behavior. Please review this new Member Code of Ethics in this context:

- Its Values are designed to inspire and motivate each of us every day to the highest levels of ethical practice.
- Its Code Provisions are designed to help each of us clearly understand the limits and specific performance required to be an ethical practitioner.
- Its Commitment mechanism is designed to ensure that every Society member understands fully the obligations of membership and the expectation of ethical behavior that are an integral part of membership in the PRSA.

This approach is stronger than anything we have ever had because:

- It will have a daily impact on the practice of Public Relations.
- There are far fewer gray areas and issues that require interpretation.
- It will grow stronger and be more successful than what we have had in the past through education, through training, and through analysis of behaviors.

The strength of the Code will grow because of the addition of precedent and the ethical experiences of other major professional organizations around the world.

Our new Code elevates our ethics, our values, and our commitment to the level they belong, at the very top of our daily practice of Public Relations.

PRSA Board of Directors

A Message from the PRSA Board of Ethics and Professional Standards

Our Primary Obligation

The primary obligation of membership in the Public Relations Society of America is the ethical practice of Public Relations.

The PRSA Member Code of Ethics is the way each member of our Society can daily reaffirm a commitment to ethical professional activities and decisions.
- The Code sets forth the principles and standards that guide our decisions and actions.
- The Code solidly connects our values and our ideals to the work each of us does every day.
- The Code is about what we should do, and why we should do it.

The Code is also meant to be a living, growing body of knowledge, precedent, and experience. It should stimulate our thinking and encourage us to seek guidance and clarification when we have questions about principles, practices, and standards of conduct.

Every member's involvement in preserving and enhancing ethical standards is essential to building and maintaining the respect and credibility of our profession. Using our values, principles, standards of conduct, and commitment as a foundation, and continuing to work together on ethical issues, we ensure that the Public Relations Society of America fulfills its obligation to build and maintain the framework for public dialogue that deserves the public's trust and support.

The Members of the 2000 Board of Ethics and Professional Standards

Robert D. Frause, APR,
Fellow PRSA
Chairman BEPS
Seattle, Washington

Kathy R. Fitzpatrick,
APR
Gainesville, Florida

Linda Welter Cohen,
APR
Tucson, Arizona

James R. Frankowiak,
APR
Tampa, Florida

James E. Lukaszewski,
APR, Fellow PRSA
White Plains, New York

Roger D. Buehrer, APR
Fellow PRSA
Las Vegas, Nevada

Jeffrey P. Julin, APR
Denver, Colorado

David M. Bicofsky,
APR, Fellow PRSA
Teaneck, New Jersey

James W. Wyckoff, APR
New York, New York

Preamble

Public Relations Society of America Member Code of Ethics 2000

- Professional Values
- Principles of Conduct
- Commitment and Compliance

This Code applies to PRSA members. The Code is designed to be a useful guide for PRSA members as they carry out their ethical responsibilities. This document is designed to anticipate and accommodate, by precedent, ethical challenges that may arise. The scenarios outlined in the Code provision are actual examples of misconduct. More will be added as experience with the Code occurs.

The Public Relations Society of America (PRSA) is committed to ethical practices. The level of public trust PRSA members seek, as we serve the public good, means we have taken on a special obligation to operate ethically.

The value of member reputation depends upon the ethical conduct of everyone affiliated with the Public Relations Society of America. Each of us sets an example for each other—as well as other professionals—by our pursuit of excellence with powerful standards of performance, professionalism, and ethical conduct.

Emphasis on enforcement of the Code has been eliminated. But, the PRSA Board of Directors retains the right to bar from membership or expel from the Society any individual who has been or is sanctioned by a government agency or convicted in a court of law of an action that is in violation of this Code.

Ethical practice is the most important obligation of a PRSA member. We view the Member Code of Ethics as a model for other professions, organizations, and professionals.

PRSA Member Statement of Professional Values

This statement presents the core values of PRSA members and, more broadly, of the public relations profession. These values provide the foundation for the Member Code of Ethics and set the industry standard for the professional practice of public relations. These values are the fundamental beliefs that guide our behaviors and decision-making process. We believe our professional values are vital to the integrity of the profession as a whole.

Advocacy
- We serve the public interest by acting as responsible advocates for those we represent.
- We provide a voice in the marketplace of ideas, facts, and viewpoints to aid informed public debate.

Honesty
- We adhere to the highest standards of accuracy and truth in advancing the interests of those we represent and in communicating with the public.

Expertise
- We acquire and responsibly use specialized knowledge and experience.
- We advance the profession through continued professional development, research, and education.
- We build mutual understanding, credibility, and relationships among a wide array of institutions and audiences.

Independence
- We provide objective counsel to those we represent.
- We are accountable for our actions.

Loyalty
- We are faithful to those we represent, while honoring our obligation to serve the public interest.

Fairness
- We deal fairly with clients, employers, competitors, peers, vendors, the media, and the general public.
- We respect all opinions and support the right of free expression.

PRSA Code Provisions

Free Flow of Information

Core Principle
Protecting and advancing the free flow of accurate and truthful information is essential to serving the public interest and contributing to informed decision making in a democratic society.

Intent
- To maintain the integrity of relationships with the media, government officials, and the public.
- To aid informed decision making.

Guidelines
A member shall:
- Preserve the integrity of the process of communication.
- Be honest and accurate in all communications.
- Act promptly to correct erroneous communications for which the practitioner is responsible.
- Preserve the free flow of unprejudiced information when giving or receiving gifts by ensuring that gifts are nominal, legal, and infrequent.

Examples of Improper Conduct Under this Provision
- A member representing a ski manufacturer gives a pair of expensive racing skis to a sports magazine columnist, to influence the columnist to write favorable articles about the product.
- A member entertains a government official beyond legal limits and/or in violation of government reporting requirements.

Competition

Core Principle
Promoting healthy and fair competition among professionals preserves an ethical climate while fostering a robust business environment.

Intent
- To promote respect and fair competition among public relations professionals.
- To serve the public interest by providing the widest choice of practitioner options.

Guidelines
A member shall:
- Follow ethical hiring practices designed to respect free and open competition without deliberately undermining a competitor.
- Preserve intellectual property rights in the marketplace.

Examples of Improper Conduct Under This Provision
- A member employed by a "client organization" shares helpful information with a counseling firm that is competing with others for the organization's business.
- A member spreads malicious and unfounded rumors about a competitor in order to alienate the competitor's clients and employees in a ploy to recruit people and business.

Disclosure of Information

Core Principle
Open communication fosters informed decision making in a democratic society.

Intent
- To build trust with the public by revealing all information needed for responsible decision making.

Guidelines
A member shall:
- Be honest and accurate in all communications.
- Act promptly to correct erroneous communications for which the member is responsible.
- Investigate the truthfulness and accuracy of information released on behalf of those represented.
- Reveal the sponsors for causes and interests represented.
- Disclose financial interest (such as stock ownership) in a client's organization.
- Avoid deceptive practices.

Examples of Improper Conduct Under this Provision
- Front groups: A member implements "grass roots" campaigns or letter-writing campaigns to legislators on behalf of undisclosed interest groups.
- Lying by omission: A practitioner for a corporation knowingly fails to release financial information, giving a misleading impression of the corporation's performance.
- A member discovers inaccurate information disseminated via a Web site or media kit and does not correct the information.
- A member deceives the public by employing people to pose as volunteers to speak at public hearings and participate in "grass roots" campaigns.

Safeguarding Confidences

Core Principle
Client trust requires appropriate protection of confidential and private information.

Intent
- To protect the privacy rights of clients, organizations, and individuals by safeguarding confidential information.

Guidelines

A member shall:

- Safeguard the confidences and privacy rights of present, former, and prospective clients and employees.
- Protect privileged, confidential, or insider information gained from a client or organization.
- Immediately advise an appropriate authority if a member discovers that confidential information is being divulged by an employee of a client company or organization.

Examples of Improper Conduct Under This Provision

- A member changes jobs, takes confidential information, and uses that information in the new position to the detriment of the former employer.
- A member intentionally leaks proprietary information to the detriment of some other party.

Conflicts of Interest

Core Principle

Avoiding real, potential, or perceived conflicts of interest builds the trust of clients, employers, and the publics.

Intent

- To earn trust and mutual respect with clients or employers.
- To build trust with the public by avoiding or ending situations that put one's personal or professional interests in conflict with society's interests.

Guidelines

A member shall:

- Act in the best interests of the client or employer, even subordinating the member's personal interests.
- Avoid actions and circumstances that may appear to compromise good business judgment or create a conflict between personal and professional interests.
- Disclose promptly any existing or potential conflict of interest to affected clients or organizations.
- Encourage clients and customers to determine if a conflict exists after notifying all affected parties.

Examples of Improper Conduct Under This Provision

- The member fails to disclose that he or she has a strong financial interest in a client's chief competitor.
- The member represents a "competitor company" or a "conflicting interest" without informing a prospective client.

Enhancing the Profession

Core Principle

Public relations professionals work constantly to strengthen the public's trust in the profession.

Intent
- To build respect and credibility with the public for the profession of public relations.
- To improve, adapt, and expand professional practices.

Guidelines
A member shall:
- Acknowledge that there is an obligation to protect and enhance the profession.
- Keep informed and educated about practices in the profession to ensure ethical conduct.
- Actively pursue personal professional development.
- Decline representation of clients or organizations that urge or require actions contrary to this Code.
- Accurately define what public relations activities can accomplish.
- Counsel subordinates in proper ethical decision making.
- Require that subordinates adhere to the ethical requirements of the Code.
- Report ethical violations, whether committed by PRSA members or not, to the appropriate authority.

Examples of Improper Conduct Under This Provision
- A PRSA member declares publicly that a product the client sells is safe, without disclosing evidence to the contrary.
- A member initially assigns some questionable client work to a non-member practitioner to avoid the ethical obligation of PRSA membership.

Resources

Rules and Guidelines
The following PRSA documents, available in The Blue Book, provide detailed rules and guidelines to help guide your professional behavior:
- PRSA Bylaws
- PRSA Administrative Rules
- Member Code of Ethics

If, after reviewing them, you still have a question or issue, contact PRSA headquarters as noted below.

Questions

The PRSA is here to help. Whether you have a serious concern or simply need clarification, contact Judy Voss at judy.voss@prsa.org.

PRSA Member Code of Ethics Pledge

I pledge:

To conduct myself professionally, with truth, accuracy, fairness, and responsibility to the public; to improve my individual competence and advance the knowledge and proficiency of the profession through continuing research and education; and to adhere to the articles of the Member Code of Ethics 2000 for the practice of public relations as adopted by the governing Assembly of the Public Relations Society of America.

I understand and accept that there is a consequence for misconduct, up to and including membership revocation.

And, I understand that those who have been or are sanctioned by a government agency or convicted in a court of law of an action that is in violation of this Code may be barred from membership or expelled from the Society.

_____

Signature

_____

Date

Public Relations Society of America
33 Irving Place
New York, NY 10003
www.prsa.org

Appendix B

PRIA Code of Ethics

The Public Relations Institute of Australia is a professional body serving the interests of its members. In doing so, the Institute is mindful of the responsibility which public relations professionals owe to the community as well as to their clients and employers. The Institute requires members to adhere to the highest standards of ethical practice and professional competence. All members are duty-bound to act responsibly and to be accountable for their actions.

The following Code of Ethics binds all members of the Public Relations Institute of Australia.

1. Members shall deal fairly and honestly with their employers, clients and prospective clients, with their fellow workers including superiors and subordinates, with public officials, the communications media, the general public and with fellow members of PRIA.
2. Members shall avoid conduct or practices likely to bring discredit upon themselves, the Institute, their employers or clients.
3. Members shall not knowingly disseminate false or misleading information and shall take care to avoid doing so inadvertently.
4. Members shall safeguard the confidences of both present and former employers and clients, including confidential information about employers' or clients' business affairs, technical methods or processes, except upon the order of a court of competent jurisdiction.
5. No member shall represent conflicting interests nor, without the consent of the parties concerned, represent competing interests.
6. Members shall refrain from proposing or agreeing that their consultancy fees or other remuneration be contingent entirely on the achievement of specified results.
7. Members shall inform their employers or clients if circumstances arise in which their judgment or the disinterested character of their services may be questioned by reason of personal relationships or business or financial interests.
8. Members practising as consultants shall seek payment only for services specifically commissioned.
9. Members shall be prepared to identify the source of funding of any public communication they initiate or for which they act as a conduit.
10. Members shall, in advertising and marketing their skills and services and in soliciting professional assignments, avoid false, misleading or exaggerated claims and shall refrain from comment or action that may injure the professional reputation, practice or services of a fellow member.
11. Members shall inform the Board of the Institute and/or the relevant State/Territory Council(s) of the Institute of evidence purporting to show that a member has been guilty of, or could be charged with, conduct constituting a breach of this Code.
12. No member shall intentionally injure the professional reputation or practice of another member.
13. Members shall help to improve the general body of knowledge of the profession by exchanging information and experience with fellow members.

14. Members shall act in accord with the aims of the institute, its regulations and policies.
15. Members shall not misrepresent their status through misuse of title, grading, or the designation FPRIA, MPRIA or APRIA.

Adopted by the Board of the Institute on November 5, 2001, this Code of Ethics supersedes all previous versions.

End Notes

Chapter 1

1. Stuart Elliott, "Public Relations Defined, After an Energetic Public Discussion," *The New York Times* (March 1, 2012).
2. Ibid.
3. Peter Baker, "Recovered Bin Laden Letters Show a Divided Al Qaeda," *The New York Times* (May 3, 2012).
4. U.S. Bureau of Labor Statistics, U.S. Department of Labor, Occupational Outlook Handbook 2012–13 Edition, Public Relations Managers and Specialists, www.bls.gov/ooh/Management/Public-relations-managers-and-specialists.htm, March 29, 2012.
5. Kirk Hallahan, "Challenges Confronting PR Education," Public Relations Society of America website, www.prsa.org, November 2005.
6. O'Dwyer's, 2011 Worldwide Fees of Top Independent PR Firms with Major U.S. Operations, www.odwyerpr.com/pr_firm_rankings/independents.htm, May 2012.
7. "Company Expands Its Management Committee to Include Communicator," *Ragan Report* (September 19, 2005): 2.
8. "The Design for Undergraduate Public Relations Education," a study cosponsored by the public relations division of the Association for Education and Journalism and Mass Communication, the Public Relations Society of America, and the educators' section of PRSA, 1987, 1.
9. Cited in Glen M. Broom, *Cutlip and Center's Effective Public Relations*, 10th ed. (Upper Saddle River, NJ: Prentice Hall, 2008).
10. Edward L. Bernays, *Crystallizing Public Opinion* (New York: Liveright, 1961).
11. Rex F. Harlow, "Building a Public Relations Definition," *Public Relations Review 2*, no. 4 (Winter 1976): 36.
12. John E. Marston, *The Nature of Public Relations* (New York: McGraw-Hill, 1963): 161.
13. "Denny Griswold, PRN Founder and Industry Luminary, Dies at 92," *Public Relations News* (March 12, 2001): 1.
14. Dr. Melvin L. Sharpe, professor and coordinator of the Public Relations Sequence, Department of Journalism, Ball State University, Muncie, IN 47306.
15. John Dewey, *The Public and Its Problems* (Chicago: Swallow Press, 1927).
16. Linda P. Morton, "Segmenting Publics by Lifestyles," *Public Relations Quarterly* (Fall 1999): 46–47.
17. Dr. Melvin L. Sharpe, op. cit.
18. Timothy L. O'Brien, "Spinning Frenzy: P.R.'s Bad Press," *The New York Times* (February 13, 2005): B1.
19. Derrick Jensen, "The War on Truth: The Secret Battle for the American Mind," interview with John Stauber, www.mediachannel.org (June 7, 2000).
20. Fraser P. Seitel and John Doorley, *Rethinking Reputation* (New York: Palgrave Macmillan, 2012): 187–189.
21. "White House Official I. Lewis Libby Indicted on Obstruction of Justice, False Statement and Perjury Charges Relating to Leak of Classified Information Revealing CIA Officer's Identity," news release of Office of Special Counsel (October 28, 2005), www.usdoj.gov/usao/iln/osc.
22. Seitel and Doorley, op. cit., 149–151.
23. "Heyman Associates Study Finds Critical Patterns for Public Relations Success," news release of Heyman Associates (June 28, 2004), www.heymanassociates.com.
24. Fraser P. Seitel, "Relax Mr. Stauber, Public Relations Ain't That Dangerous," www.mediachannel.org (June 7, 2000).
25. Abraham Lincoln, Lincoln–Douglas Debates, Ottawa, IL, August 21, 1858.

Chapter 2

1. Natasha Singer and Reed Abelson, "After Recalls of Drugs, a Congressional Spotlight on J&J's Chief," *The New York Times* (September 28, 2010).
2. World Internet Users December 2007, Internet World Stats: Usage and Population Statistics, www.internetworldstats.com, Miniwatts Marketing Group, 2008.
3. Scott M. Cutlip, Allen H. Center, and Glen M. Broom, *Effective Public Relations,* 8th ed. (Upper Saddle River, NJ: Prentice Hall, 2000): 102.
4. Fraser P. Seitel, "The Company You Keep," www.odwyerpr.com (July 22, 2002).
5. Donadio, Rachel, "Vatican Tells Bishops to Set Clear Strategy Against Abuse," *The New York Times* (May 16, 2011), A1,8.
6. Harold Burson, speech at Utica College of Syracuse University, Utica, NY (March 5, 1987).
7. Ray Eldon Hiebert, *Courtier to the Crowd: The Story of Ivy L. Lee and the Development of Public Relations* (Ames: Iowa State University Press, 1966).
8. John E. Harr and Peter J. Johnson, *The Rockefeller Century: Three Generations of America's Greatest Family* (New York: Simon & Schuster, 1988): 130.
9. Interview with David Rockefeller, New York, NY, November 30, 2005.
10. Cited in Alvin Moscow, *The Rockefeller Inheritance* (Garden City, NY: Doubleday, 1977): 23.
11. Interview with Stuart Ewen, "Spin Cycles: A Century of Spin," CBC Radio (January 19, 2007).
12. Interview with Fraser Seitel, "Spin Cycles: A Century of Spin," CBC Radio (January 19, 2007).
13. Edward L. Bernays, "Bernays: 62 Years in Public Relations," *Public Relations Quarterly* (Fall 1981): 8.
14. Interview with Stuart Ewen, op. cit.
15. "Burson Hailed as PR's No. 1 Influential Figure," *PR Week* (October 18, 1999): 1.
16. Cited in Noel L. Griese, "The Employee Communications Philosophy of Arthur W. Page," *Public Relations Quarterly* (Winter 1977): 8–12.
17. Noel L. Griese, *Arthur W. Page: Publisher, Public Relations Pioneer, Patriot* (Tucker, GA: Anvil Publishers, 2001).
18. Fraser P. Seitel, "An Afternoon with Peter Drucker," *The Public Relations Strategist* (Fall 1998): 10.
19. "Internet Users in the Americas December 31, 2011," World Stats—Web Site Directory, Miniwatts Marketing Group, 2012.
20. Cara Pring, "100 Social Media, Mobile and Internet Statistics for 2012 (March)," http://thesocialskinny.com/100-social-media-mobile-and-internet-statistics-for-2012.
21. John L. Paluszek, "Public Relations Students: Today Good, Tomorrow Better," *The Public Relations Strategist* (Winter 2000): 27.
22. "'Churnalism' Study Claims News Mainly PR and Wire Copy," www.pressgazette.co.uk/story.asp?storycode=40123, February 1, 2008.
23. Bureau of Labor Statistics, U.S. Department of Labor, *Occupational Outlook Handbook, 2012–13 Edition*, Public Relations Specialists, www.bls.gov/oco/ocos086.htm., March 29, 2012.
24. Jack O'Dwyer (Ed.), *O'Dwyer's Directory of Corporate Communications* (New York: J. R. O'Dwyer Co., 2005).
25. Jack O'Dwyer (Ed.), *O'Dwyer's Directory of Public Relations Firms* (New York: J. R. O'Dwyer Co., 2011).

Chapter 3

1. Wikipedia, Aboutwikipedia.org.
2. Noam Cohen, "After False Claim, Wikipedia to Check Degrees," *The New York Times* (March 12, 2007).
3. Interview with Raymond Siposs, Director, Carnet Media, San Diego, CA (May 24, 2012).
4. Patrick Jackson, "The Unforgiving Era," *Currents* (October 1998).

5. Thomas H. Bivins, *Public Relations Writing,* 7th ed. (New York: McGraw-Hill, 2010): 31–32.

6. Serge Moscovici, "Silent Majorities and Loud Minorities," *Communication Yearbook* 14 (1991): 298–308.

7. J. Delia, B. O'Keefe, and D. O'Keefe, "The Constructivist Approach to Communication," *Human Communication Theory* (New York: Harper and Row, 1982): 147–191. Also see E. Griffin, *A First Look at Communication Theory,* 4th ed. (New York: McGraw-Hill, 2000): 110–120; J. T. Wood, *Communication Theories in Action: An Introduction* (Belmont, CA: Wadsworth, 1997): 182–184.

8. W. B. Pearce and V. Cronen, *Communication, Action and Meaning: The Creation of Social Realities* (New York: Praeger, 1980). Also see G. Philipsen, "The Coordinated Management of Meaning: Theory of Pearce, Cronen, and Associates,"*Watershed Research Traditions in Human Communication Theory,* Donald Cust and Branislave Kovocic, Eds. (Albany, NY: State University of New York Press, 1995): 13–43.

9. James E. Grunig and Todd Hunt, *Managing Public Relations* (New York: Holt, Rinehart and Winston, 1984): 21–27. See also Anne Lane, "Working at the Interface: The Descriptive Relevance of Grunig and Hunt's Theories to Public Relations Practices in South East Queensland Schools," http://praxis.massey.ac.nz/working_interface.html, 2003.

10. "DealBook Online," *The New York Times,* May 25, 2012, B4.

11. "McDonald's Launches Face-Saving Petition," *Bulldog Reporter's Daily Dog* (May 25, 2007).

12. Richard Lederer, "The Way We Word," *AARP Magazine* (March/April 2005): 86–93.

13. Justin Elliott, "GOP Message Man 'Frightened to Death' of Occupy," Salon.com, December 1, 2011.

14. M. E. McCombs, D. L. Shaw, and D. L. Weaver, *Communication and Democracy: Exploring the Intellectual Frontiers in Agenda-Setting Theory* (Mahwah, NJ: Lawrence Erlbaum, 1997).

Chapter 4

1. Rene Lynch, "Trayvon Martin's Parents Oppose How 'Stand Your Ground' Law Used," *Los Angeles Times,* June 12, 2012.

2. Salvador Rizzo, "Johnson & Johnson Becomes First N.J. Company to Part Ways with ALEC," *Newark Star-Ledger,* June 12, 2012.

3. Colleen Jenkins, "John Edwards' Reputation Tarnished After Trial, Scandal with Rielle Hunter," Reuters, June 1, 2012.

4. Michael S. Schmidt and William Neuman, "U.S. Expands Inquiry of Suspected Misconduct by Agents in Colombia," *The New York Times,* April 19, 2012.

5. Sheryl Gay Stolberg and Michael S. Schmidt, "Agency Trip to Las Vegas Is the Talk of Washington," *The New York Times,* April 3, 2012.

6. Cited in Edward L. Bernays, *Crystallizing Public Opinion* (New York: Liveright, 1961): 61.

7. Cited in Harwood L. Childs, *Public Opinion: Nature, Formation, and Role* (Princeton, NJ: Van Nostrand, 1965): 15.

8. James E. Grunig and Todd Hunt, *Managing Public Relations* (New York: Holt, Rinehart & Winston, 1984): 130.

9. Leon A. Festinger, *A Theory of Cognitive Dissonance* (New York: Harper & Row, 1957): 163.

10. Richard M. Perloff, *The Dynamics of Persuasion: Communication and Attitudes in the 21st Century,* 2nd ed. (Mahwah, NJ: Lawrence Erlbaum Associates, 2003). Ample discussion of social judgment theory, pioneered by Muzafer and Carolyn Sherif in 1967.

11. Abraham Maslow, *Motivation and Personality* (New York: Harper & Row, 1954).

12. R. E. Petty and J. T. Cacioppo, *The Elaboration Likelihood Model of Persuasion* (New York: Academic Press, 1986).

13. T. C. Brock and S. Shavitt, *Persuasion: Psychological Insights and Perspectives* (Chicago: Allyn & Bacon, 1999).

14. Saul D. Alinsky, *Rules for Radicals* (New York: Vintage Books, 1971): 81.

15. Robert L. Dilenschneider, *Power and Influence* (New York: Prentice Hall, 1990): 5.

16. Hadley Cantril, *Gauging Public Opinion* (Princeton, NJ: Princeton University Press, 1972): 226–230.

17. D. T. Max, "The 2,988 Words That Changed a Presidency: An Etymology," *The New York Times* on the Web (October 7, 2001).

18. Saad Abedine, "U.S. Death Toll in Iraq Reaches 2000," *CNN.com* (October 26, 2005).

19. Richard Benedetto, "Business News Alters Perceptions of Bush," *USA Today* (July 10, 2002): 6A.

20. Tom Vanden Brook, "U.S. Formally Declares End of Iraq War," *USA Today* (December 15, 2011).

21. Clifford Kraus, "Rockefeller Family Members Press for Change at Exxon," *International Herald Tribune* (May 26, 2008).

22. "Doorley Is Selling CEOs on the Value of Reputation," *PR Week* (November 18, 2002).

23. John Naisbitt and Patricia Aburdene, *Megatrends 2000* (New York: Morrow, 1990).

24. Philip Lesly, "How the Future Will Shape Public Relations—and Vice Versa," *Public Relations Quarterly* (Winter 1981–82): 7.

Chapter 5

1. "The Heat Is (Back) On: CEO Turnover Rate Rises to Pre-Recession Levels, Finds Booz and Company Study," Governance and Compliance, June 7, 2012.

2. Jonathan Ratner, "RIM Plunges 9% Despite Management Shakeup," *Financial Post,* January 23, 2012.

3. "Ding Dong! Coty Says Avon Took Too Long," *The Daily Mail,* May 16, 2012.

4. Jessica Silver-Greenberg, Ben Protess and Michael J. De La Merced, "Dimon Testifying Before House, Stays on Message," *The New York Times,* June 19, 2012.

5. James E. Grunig and Todd Hunt, *Managing Public Relations* (New York: Holt, Rinehart, & Winston, 1984): 89–91.

6. "Study Results Find Communications Competence Must Be Combined with Knowledge of the Business," study sponsored by Deloitte & Touche and IABC Research Foundation, June 14, 2001.

7. "Study Results Find Communications Competence Must Be Combined with Knowledge of the Business," study sponsored by Deloitte & Touche and IABC Research Foundation, June 14, 2001.

8. Stuart Z. Goldstein, "Building Reputation through Communication," *Strategic Communication Management 8,* no. 6 (October/November 2004): 23.

9. Lester R. Potter, "How to Be a Credible Strategic Counselor to Your Organization," delivered at IABC International Conference, Chicago, June 2002.

10. Stuart Z. Goldstein, "Information Preparedness," *Strategic Communication Management 3,* no. 1 (December/January 1999).

11. Richard Virgilio, "Is The Road to ROI Paved With Pay-for-Placement PR?" *PR News,* August 10, 2005.

12. "O'Dwyer's Director of Corporate Communications 2005" (New York: J. R. O'Dwyer Company, 2005): A5.

13. Remarks by Harvey Greisman, senior vice president/group executive global communications group, MasterCard Worldwide, May 15, 2007, Tarrytown, NY.

14. Karl Greenberg, "Survey Shows Strong Agency CEO Billing Rates," *PR Week* (July 31, 2006).

15. Paul Holmes, "Global Ranking 2011: Industry Up 8 Percent to Around $8.8 Billion," *The Holmes Report,* September 5, 2011.

16. Michael Sebastian, "At 84 Years Old, Hill & Knowlton Rebrands," *Ragan PR Daily,* December 2, 2011.

17. Thomas Murray, "In Retreat from Excellence," *Ragan Report* (June 11, 2007): 1.

18. Pete Engardio and Michael Arndt, "What Price Reputation?" *Business Week* (July 9, 2007): 70.

19. Ken Wheaton, "NBA's Stern Gets It: Brand Image Is Key to Game Plan," *Advertising Age* (June 23, 2008).
20. Salary Survey 2008," *PR Week* (February 25, 2008).
21. Susanne Craig, "Goldman Hires a New P.R. Chief," *The New York Times*, March 13, 2012.
22. Fraser P. Seitel, "Reputation Management," odwyerpr.com (July 9, 2002).
23. Frances Martel, "Pope Benedict XVI Hires Fox News Correspondent to Beef Up PR Wing," *Mediaite*, June 23, 2012.
24. "Public Relations Specialist: Job Profile & Salary," *U.S. News & World Report*, copyright 2012.
25. "Salaries for PR Professionals," PRSA Job Center, www.prsa.org/jobcenter/career_resources/resource_type/tools_tactics/salary_information/salaries_pr/, adopted from "The Official PR Salary and Bonus Report—2012," Spring Associates, Inc., New York, NY.
26. "2012 Salary Guide," The Creative Group, creativegroup.com, 2012.
27. Kristin Piombino, "Typical PR Vice President Is Female, Married and Earns Six Figures," *Ragan PR Daily*, March 2, 2012.
28. "The Chief Communications Officer," Korn/Ferry's 2012 Survey of Fortune 500 Companies, Korn/Ferry International, 2012.
29. Russell Working, "Women Dominate the PR Industry: Why?" *Ragan PR Daily*, October 4, 2010.
30. Bey-Ling Sha, PR Women: New Data Show Gender-Based Salary Gap Is Widening," *Ragan PR Daily*, March 8, 2011.
31. Romy Frohlich, "The Friendliness Trap," *Communication Director*, April 2010.
32. David M. Dozier, "No Equal Pay in PR: Today's Gender Pay Gap of 14% Can Be Blamed on Discrimination," COMMPRO.Biz LLC, August 4, 2011.
33. "The Chief Communications Officer," op. cit.
34. Richard Bailey, "A Glass Ceiling in PR?" *PR Studies* weblog from Leeds Business School at Leeds Metropolitan University, http://prstudies.typepad.com (April 2, 2005).
35. "Best Jobs in America," *CNN Money*, Cable News Network, 2012.
36. "Salary Survey 2005," *PR Week* (February 21, 2005).

Chapter 6

1. Kevin Roderick, "Former LA PR Exec Dowie Must Begin Prison Term," Associated Press, January 7, 2011.
2. Carol J. Williams, "Douglas Dowie Loses Appeal of Prison Sentence in Fraud Case," *Los Angeles Times*, January 8, 2011.
3. Grant Gross, "FTC Settles Complaint about Fake Video Game Testimonials," IDG News Service, August 26, 2010.
4. Justin Elliott, "The Lobbyist and the Despot," *Salon*, December 22, 2010.
5. Alice Hines, "Stephanie Hartnett, Member of PR Team Hired by Walmart, Fired for Posing as Reporter," *The Huffington Post*, June 14, 2012.
6. Andy Newman, "Rangel's Ethics Violations," *The New York Times*, November 16, 2010.
7. Raymond Hernandez, "Weiner Resigns in Chaotic Final Scene," *The New York Times*, June 16, 2011.
8. Jim Vertuno, "Lance Armstrong Doping Charges: USADA Makes New Allegations," *The Huffington Post*, June 13, 2012.
9. Andrew McGill, "Penn State President Graham Spanier Resigns in Wake of Scandal," *The Morning Call*, November 10, 2011.
10. "Charity Fraud: Disabled Veterans National Foundation Squanders Millions on Marketing Services," *The Huffington Post*, May 8, 2012.
11. "In Public Relations, 25% Admit Lying," *The New York Times* (May 8, 2000): C20.
12. "2011 National Business Ethics Survey," Ethics Resource Center, 2011.
13. A. Larry Elliott and Richard J. Schroth, *How Companies Lie: Why Enron Is Just the Tip of the Iceberg* (New York: Crown Publishers, 2002).
14. Henry M. Paulson, Address to the National Press Club, Washington, DC (June 5, 2002).
15. CSR, "Ethics and the Board of Directors," *Ethisphere*, Q3 (2007): 8.

16. Eyder Peralta, "Congress' Approval Rating Improves Slightly," NPR, April 19, 2012.
17. "Internet 20120 in Numbers," Pingdom, January 12, 2011.
18. Scott Shane and Andrew W. Lehren, "Leaked Cables Offer Raw Look at U.S. Diplomacy," *The New York Times*, November 28, 2010.
19. Howard Kurtz, "ABC Bans Paying News Subjects," *The Daily Beast*, July 25, 2011.
20. "CNN Hits a Primetime Ratings Low," *The Huffington Post*, May 22, 2012.
21. "Honesty/Ethics in Professions," Gallup Poll, 2011 November 29–December 1.
22. Jennifer Harper, "Supreme Court Justices Rank Highest in Credibility, Index Says," *Washington Times* (July 8, 1999): 20.
23. Fraser Seitel, "Public Relations Ethics," *O'Dwyer's PR Report* (April 2007): 36.
24. Teresa M. McAleavy, "Survey: Ethics Abuses on Rise," *The Record* (October 13, 2005): B1.
25. James Patrick Thompson, "Enforcing the Code of Conduct," *NYSE Magazine* (January 2006): 23.

Chapter 7

1. Julie Jargon, Emily Steel, and Joann S. Lublin, "Taco Bell Makes Spicy Retort to Suit," *The Wall Street Journal*, January 31, 2011.
2. Gerhart L. Klein, *Public Relations Law: The Basics* (Mt. Laurel, NJ: Anne Klein & Associates, 1990): 1–2.
3. William Raspberry, "In the Plame Case, Losers All Around," washingtonpost.com (May 9, 2005).
4. Scott Shane and Eric Lichtblau, "Scientist Is Paid Millions by U.S. in Anthrax Suit," *The New York Times* (June 28, 2008): 1.
5. John Burns and Ravi Somaiya, "Wikileaks Founder on the Run, Trailed by Notoriety," *The New York Times*, December 23, 2010.
6. Dennis L. Wilcox and Glen T. Cameron, *Public Relations Strategies and Tactics*, 8th ed. (Boston: Allyn & Bacon, 2002): 265.
7. Thomas K. Grose, "$50 Million Lawsuit Against WSJ and Burrough May Make Some Authors-to-Be Think Twice," *TFJR Report* (April 1992): 3.
8. "Judge Tosses Out NY Businessman's 'Borat' Lawsuit," *Associated Press* (April 2, 2008).
9. Denise Lavoie, "Media Troubled by Libel Ruling that Excludes Truth as Defense," *The Record* (March 8, 2009): A-10.
10. Jennifer Preston, "Courtney Love Settles Twitter Defamation Case," *The New York Times*, March 4, 2011.
11. Constance L. Hays, "Aide Was Reportedly Ordered to Warn Stewart on Stock Sales," *The New York Times* (August 6, 2002): C1–2.
12. Wil Deener, "Lights, Camera, Madness: Cramer Is CNBC's Best," *Dallas Morning News* (February 4, 2006).
13. Andrew Clark, "Brunswick Executive Suspended After Husband Is Charged Over Insider Trading," *The Guardian*, December 23, 1908.
14. "Managing Tidal Wave of Corporate Disclosure," *Business Wire Newsletter* (April 2002): 2.
15. Joseph Nocera, "For All Its Costs, Sarbanes-Oxley Is Working," *The New York Times* (December 3, 2005): C1.
16. Alix M. Freedman and Suein L. Hwang, "Brown & Williamson Faces Inquiry," *The Wall Street Journal* (February 6, 1996): A1.
17. Richard L. Hasen, "Money Grubbers," Slate.com, January 21, 2010.
18. Wilcox and Cameron, op. cit, *Public Relations Strategies and Tactics*, 271.
19. Harold W. Suckenik, "PR Pros Should Know the Four Rules of 'Fair Use,'" *O'Dwyer's PR Services Report* (September 1990): 2.
20. Saul Hansell, "The Associated Press to Set Guidelines for Using Its Articles in Blogs," *The New York Times* (June 16, 2008).
21. Linda Greenhouse, "What Level of Protection for Internet Speech?" *The New York Times* (March 24, 1997): D5.
22. Steven Levy, "U.S. v. the Internet," *Newsweek* (March 31, 1997): 77.
23. Linda Greenhouse, "Decency Act Fails," *The New York Times* (June 27, 1997): 1.
24. Javier C. Hernandez, "Google Calls for Action on Web Limits," *The New York Times*, March 24, 2010.

25. Kristi Heim, "Inside China's Teeming World of Fake Goods," *Seattle Times* (February 12, 2006).

26. Jonathan Weisman, "After an Online Firestorm, Congress Shelves Anti-Piracy Bills," *The New York Times*, January 20, 2012.

27. Eric Pfanner, "Europeans Reject Treaty to Combat International Piracy," *The New York Times*, July 5, 2012.

28. Howard Beck, "Bosh's Win Over Cybersquatter Frees 800 Domain Names," *The New York Times*, October 14, 2009.

29. "In Pursuit of Cybersquatters," *CFO Magazine* (November 1999): 16.

30. David Hanners, "Travelers in a Spat over Catty E-Chat," *St. Paul Pioneer Press* (March 13, 2008).

31. Kevin Lee, "Click Fraud: What It Is, How to Fight It," *ClickZ Experts* (February 18, 2005).

32. Steven Greenhouse, "Company Accused of Firing Over Facebook Post," *The New York Times*, November 8, 2010.

33. Ibid.

34. Mary Pilon, "Maryland Bill Addresses College Athletes' Social Media Policy," *The New York Times*, February 3, 2012.

35. Greg Hazley, "PR, Legal Need to Play on Same Team," *O'Dwyer's PR Services Report* (December 2005): 1.

36. James E. Lukaszewski, "Managing Litigation Visibility: How to Avoid Lousy Trial Publicity," *Public Relations Quarterly* (Spring 1995): 18–24.

37. "Reverberations: The FTC Means Business and What PR Firms Should Do," Firm Voice, Council of Public Relations Firms, September 8, 2010.

Chapter 8

1. Mark Penn, "In Search of the Changing American Voter," *Time*, June 21, 2012.

2. Interview with Steve Rivkin, July 5, 2012. Based on "Record High 40% of Americans Identify as Independents in '11," *Gallup Politics*, January 9, 2011.

3. Katie Delahaye Paine, "Measuring Social Media, Can You Track the Wild West?" Address to Ragan Communications Conference (September 2007).

4. Jennifer Nedeff, "The Bottom Line Beckons: Quantifying Measurement in Public Relations," *Journal of Corporate Public Relations Northwestern University* (1996–1997): 34.

5. Gary Holmes, "Nielsen Media Research Reports Television's Popularity Is Still Growing," Nielsen Media Research (September 21, 2006).

6. Tom Greenbaum, "The Gold Standard: Why the Focus Group Deserves to Be the Most Respected of All Qualitative Research Tools," *Quirk's Marketing Research Review* (June 2003).

7. David J. Solomon, "Conducting Web-Based Surveys," *Practical Assessment, Research and Evaluation* (August 23, 2001).

8. Nate Silver, "A Warning on the Accuracy of Primary Polls," *The New York Times*, March 1, 2012.

9. "Guidelines and Standards for Measuring and Evaluating PR Effectiveness," The Institute for Public Relations Commission on PR Measurement and Evaluation (2003).

10. Katie Delahaye Paine, op. cit.

11. Ibid.

12. Frank Walton, "Expect More from PR Research," PR Café, CommPro.biz, September 13, 2011.

13. Clare Dowdy, "How to Measure the Value of Public Relations," *Financial Times* (June 20, 2006).

14. Fraser P. Seitel, "Strategic PR Research and Analysis," odwypr.com (January 26, 2004).

15. Jennifer Nedeff, op. cit.

Chapter 9

1. Lymari Morales, "Majority in U.S. Continue to Distrust Media, Perceive Bias," Gallup Daily, September 22, 2011.

2. Michael Rundle, "Murdoch Sorry 'For Serious Wrongdoing' in Newspaper Ad Campaign," Huffington Post, July 16, 2011.

3. Angela Macropoulos, "A Misfired Memo Shows Close Tabs on Reporter," *The New York Times* (April 2, 2007): C4.

4. Michael Sebastian, "Target Shuns Bloggers and Almost Pays the Price," *Ragan Report* (January 28, 2008): 4.

5. Seth Schiesel, "Author Faults a Game and Garners Flame Back," *The New York Times* (January 26, 2008).

6. "Redner Group Loses Biggest Client Over Tweet," *Advertising Age*, June 15, 2011.

7. Interview with Ari Fleischer, for *The Practice of Public Relations*, 9th ed. (August 7, 2002).

8. Rich Noyes, "Updated for 2012: The MRC 'Media Bias 101,'" Media Research Center, April 22, 2012.

9. David T. Z. Mindich, "The New Journalism," *The Wall Street Journal* (July 15, 1999): A18.

10. Satham Sanghera, "How Corporate PR Has Turned into the Art of Stonewalling," *Financial Times* (February 10, 2006).

11. "Times-Picayune Editor on Commitment, Accountability amid Cutbacks," PBS News Hour, June 13, 2012.

12. Tanzina Vega, "Small Gain in Newspaper Circulations, Aided by Digital Subscriptions," *The New York Times*, May 1, 2012.

13. "The State of the News Media 2012," The Pew Research Center's Project for Excellence in Journalism, 2012.

14. Christine Haughney, "Newspapers Cut Days from Publishing Week," *The New York Times*, June 3, 2012.

15. Rick Edmonds, "6 Trends for Newspapers in 2012, from a Sunday Boom to an Executive Bust," Poynter, March 9, 2012.

16. "Number of Magazines by Category 1999-2009," National Directory of Magazines, 2011, Oxbridge Communications.

17. "The State of the News Media 2012," op. cit.

18. Michiko Kakutani, "Is Jon Stewart the Most Trusted Man in Television?" *The New York Times*, August 15, 2008.

19. Zev Chafets, "Late-Period Limbaugh," *The New York Times* (July 6, 2008).

20. "2012 Heavy Hundred," *Talkers Magazine*, Talk Media, Inc., 2012.

21. Richard Perez-Pena, "Washington Post Signals Shift with a New Editor," *The New York Times* (July 8, 2008): 1.

22. Russell Adams and Christopher S. Stewart, "Digital Strategy Undid Times CEO," *The New York Times*, December 17, 2011.

23. Jeremy W. Peters and Verne G. Kopytoff, "Betting on News, AOL Is Buying the Huffington Post," *The New York Times*, February 7, 2011.

24. "Buzz in the Blogosphere: Millions More Bloggers and Blog Readers," Nielsen Wire, March 8, 2012.

25. Bruce Buschel, "The Problem with Public Relations," *The New York Times*, February 22, 2011.

26. Lee Berton, "Avoiding Media Land Mines," *Public Relations Strategist* (Summer 1997): 16.

27. Josh Feldman, "MSNBC Shells Out Big Bucks to Congratulate Rachel Maddow in Full Page NY Times Ad," Mediaite, April 1, 2012.

28. "Jim Koch on the Secret to Effective (and Cheap) Marketing," Inc., April 1, 2007.

29. Michael Sebastian, "7 Things PR Pros Should Know about Shifting Media Landscape," *Ragan PR Daily*, January 26, 2012.

30. Ibid.

31. Michael Hastings and Yepoka Yeebo, "Luxurious Reading," *Newsweek* (October 17, 2005): E24.

32. "Journalists' Use of Facebook, Twitter, Blogs and Company Websites to Assist in Reporting Surges from 2009/2010 Study," Society for New Communications Research and Middleberg Communications, May 6, 2011.

33. Steve O'Keefe, *Complete Guide to Internet Publicity* (New York: John Wiley & Sons, 2002).

34. Kaylen McNamara, "Interview Savvy: How Spokespeople Can Avoid Media Blunders," *Ragan PR Daily*, September 28, 2010.

35. Fraser P. Seitel, "Preparing the CEO for a Print Interview," odwyerpr.com (July 11, 2001).

36. Adam Leyland, "Journalists Grudging Respect for PR Execs," *PR Week* (September 20, 1999): 1.

37. "Getting into the Times: How Andrews Views PR," *Across the Board* (August 1989): 21.

Chapter 10

1. Michael Sebastian, "Comedian Daniel Tosh Tweets Sincere Apology for Rape Joke," *Ragan PR Daily*, July 11, 2012.
2. Adam Martin, "Daniel Tosh's Apology for Gang Rape Joke Almost as Weak as the Joke Itself," Atlantic Wire, July 10, 2012.
3. Eric Benderoff, "Macon Phillips: Obama's New-Media Messenger," *Chicago Tribune* (March 9, 2009).
4. Michael Calderone, "Bin Laden Killed: Media Scrambles to Cover News," The Backstory, May 2, 2011.
5. Evelyn M. Rusli and Peter Eavis, "Facebook Raises $16 Billion in IPO," *The New York Times*, May 17, 2012.
6. "Facts and Figures," www.internetindicators.com.
7. "World Internet Population Has Doubled in the Last 5 Years," Pingdom blog, April 19, 2012.
8. Michael Marriott, "Blacks Turn to Internet Highway and Digital Divide Starts to Close," *The New York Times* (March 31, 2006): A1.
9. Dan Fost, "Festival Organizers Say Internet Bouncing Back with a Vengeance," *The Record* (March 11, 2006): A7.
10. "Journalists' Use of Facebook, Twitter, Blogs and Company Websites to Assist in Reporting Surges from 2009/2010 Study," Society for New Communications Research and Middleberg Communications, May 6, 2011.
11. "Corporate Websites Still Coming Up Short," *The Holmes Report* (February 18, 2002): 1–2.
12. Rachel Leibrock, "Teens Treating E-mail as Too Old-Fashioned," *The Record* (July 8, 2008): A-7.
13. "Email Statistics Report, 2012–2016," The Radicati Group, Inc., Palo Alto, CA, April 2012.
14. Ibid.
15. Li Yuan, Corey Dad, and Paulo Prada, "Texting When There's Trouble," *The Wall Street Journal* (April 18, 2007).
16. Lisa Gualtieri, "Social Media in Crisis Management and Public Health Emergencies," Medpage Today's KevinMD.com, 2011.
17. Lauren Fisher, "AP Begins Crediting Bloggers as News Sources," TNW Social Media, September 7, 2010.
18. Fraser P. Seitel, "Blog-Communications Weapon," *O'Dwyer's PR Services Report* (November 2005): 39.
19. "State of the Blogosphere 2011," Technorati Media, November 4, 2011.
20. Seth Godin, "Unleash Your Ideavirus," *Fast Company* (December 19, 2007).
21. Lisa Barone, "5 Dos & Donts For Getting Blog Coverage," *Ragan PR Daily*, June 30, 2010.
22. Beth Snyder Bulik, "Does Your Company Need a Chief Blogger?" *Advertising Age* (April 14, 2008): 24.
23. Chris Kent, "Why Your CEO's Blog Is Fading into Oblivion," *The Ragan Report* (December 2008): 9.
24. David Murray, "Rules for Blogging at Sun: 'Don't Do Anything Stupid,'" ragan.com (May 1, 2008).
25. Bill Marriott, "This Senseless Tragedy," Marriott on The Move blog (September 20, 2008).
26. D. Isenberg, "The Rise of the Stupid Network," *Computer Telephony* (August 1997): 16–26.
27. David Pogue, "For Those Facebook Left Behind," *The New York Times*, July 7, 2010.
28. Vicki Flaugher, "Being Kim Kardashian: Are You Willing to Sell Your Social Media Audience," 101 and Beyond: Social Media How To, February 1, 2012.
29. Sally Falkow, "10 Steps for Putting Twitter to Use as a Potent PR Tool," *Ragan PR Daily*, April 8, 2010.
30. Irina Slutsky, "Why LinkedIn Is the Social Network that Will Never Die," *Advertising Age*, December 6, 2010.
31. David Pogue, op. cit.
32. Christa Toole, "Ten Tips for Those Who Still Aren't Using YouTube," *Advertising Age*, October 19, 2010.
33. Steve Tetreault, Laura Myers, and Peter Urban, "GSA Video Clip Inflames Spending Scandal," *Las Vegas Review-Journal*, April 5, 2012.
34. "The Ultimate Guide to Pinterest," *Copyright © 2012* http://eReleases.com.
35. Gin Dietrich, "16 Ways to Use Pinterest for PR," *Ragan PR Daily*, May 10, 2012.
36. Kevin Allen, "A Complete Guide to Instagram," *Ragan PR Daily*, May 21, 2012.
37. Angela Jeffrey, "PR Industry Developing Social Media Measurement Standards," *Ragan PR Daily*, July 24, 2012.
38. JoAnn De Luna, "QR Codes," www.dmnews.com, May 2012.
39. Charles Pizzo, "Shield Your Company's Reputation from the Dark Side of Cyberspace," P.R., Inc., New Orleans, LA, P.O. Box 172846, Arlington, TX 76003-2846.
40. Ibid.
41. Christopher L. Martin and Nathan Bennett, "What to Do about Online Attacks," *The Wall Street Journal* (March 10, 2008): R6.
42. Fraser P. Seitel, "Know Your Social Media," *O'Dwyer's PR Report* (November 2006): 34.

Chapter 11

1. "PR Firm President to Staff: 'You Will Be Fired For Not Replacing the Milk,'" Gawker Daily, February 28, 2011.
2. Phillip Reese, "California's Largest Cities Shed 10,000 Jobs," *The Sacramento Bee*, July 29, 2012.
3. Linette Lopez, "Deutsche Bank to Lay Off 1,900, as Meredith Whitney Predicts 50k Wall Street Layoffs," Business Insider, July 31, 2012.
4. "Mass Layoff Statistics," Bureau of Labor Statistics, August 1, 2012.
5. "Edelman Change and Employee Engagement," Edelman Company, May 22, 2012, p. 2.
6. Ibid.
7. "100 Best Companies to Work For," *Fortune*, February 6, 2012.
8. "CEOs Rely Most on Public Relations Professionals for Reputation Management," Burson-Marsteller news release (November 12, 2004).
9. Bonnie Kavoussi, "CEO Pay Grew 127 Times Faster Than Worker Pay Over Last 30 Years: Study," *The Huffington Post*, May 2, 2012.
10. Laura Clawson, "CEOs at Top Companies Earned 380 Times the Average Worker's Income in 2011," *Daily Kos Labor*, April 19, 2012.
11. "Effective Employee Communication Linked to Stronger Financial Performance," Watson Wyatt news release (November 8, 2005).
12. Paul Dorf, "Is Turnover Back in Vogue?" Ezinearticles.com (November 2005).
13. Milton Moskowitz and Robert Levering, "Beyond Perks: Lessons from Tracking the '100 Best,'" *Fortune*, January 20, 2011.
14. "Edelman Change and Employee Engagement," op cit.
15. "Management Failing to Connect with Employees at Almost Half of Companies," Right Management Consultants (October 11, 2005).
16. Fraser P. Seitel, "Rebuilding Employee Trust through S-H-O-C," odwyerpr.com (July 11, 2005).
17. Jerry Stevenson, "How to Conduct a Self-Intranet Audit," *Ragan Report* (August 19, 2002): 7.
18. Kevin J. Allen, "Overhaul Your Intranet from A to Z," ragan.com (October 24, 2007).
19. Steve Crescenzo, "How to Make Social Media Successful at Your Company," ragan.com (February 28, 2008).
20. "New Frontiers in Employee Communications: Current Practices and Future Trends," survey of Edelman Public Relations (2004).
21. "All Intranet, All the Time," *Ragan Report* (May 14, 2001): 6.
22. Jamie Pietrus, "Employee Networking: The Next Generation," ragan.com (October 2, 2008).
23. John R. Kessling, "Maintaining a Successful Intranet: The KGN Experience," *PR Tactics* (November 1999): 20.
24. Michael Sebastian, "BP Internal Pub Extols the Virtues of the Oil Disaster," *Ragan PR Daily*, June 23, 2010.
25. John Guiniven, "Suggestion Boxes and Town Hall Meetings: Fix 'Em or Forget 'Em," *PR Tactics* (February 2000): 22.

26. Michael Sebastian, "Video 101 from the *New York Times'* Tech Critic," ragan.com (January 2, 2008).
27. Robert J. Holland, "Seven Ways to Use Face-to-Face Communication," ragan.com (August 7, 2008).
28. Matt Wilson, "P&G Blocks Employee Access to Pandora, Netflix," *Ragan PR Daily*, April 6, 2012.
29. Matt Wilson, "Best Buy Engages Young Staff through Online Dialogue," *Ragan PR Daily*, December 15, 2011.
30. "Talking to the Troops," *Business Week* (July 5, 1999): 62.

Chapter 12

1. Ashley Killough, "Team Obama: Romney Trip 'Embarrassing Disaster,'" CNN, July 31, 2012.
2. Jack Mirkinson, "Rick Gorka, Romney 'Kiss My A--_Spokesman' Taking a Break from Campaign," *The Huffington Post*, August 3, 2012.
3. Adam Nagourney and Jeff Zeleny, "Obama Chooses Biden as Running Mate," *The New York Times* (August 23, 2008).
4. Jamar Hudson, "Election 2012: Sizing Up the Social Media Battle," *PR News*, July 18, 2012.
5. Kevin McCauley, O'Dwyer's PR Services Report, February 2012, 6.
6. David Murray, "PR Is Not the Problem—or the Solution," *Ragan Report* (November 24, 2003): 1.
7. Andrew Taylor and Donna Cassata, "Congress Breaks for 5 Weeks but Much Work Undone," *Associated Press*, August 4, 2012.
8. Fraser P. Seitel, *The Practice of Public Relations,* 9th ed. (Upper Saddle River, NJ: Prentice-Hall, 2004): 341.
9. Karen De Young, "Bush to Create Formal Office to Shape U.S. Image Abroad," *Washington Post* (July 30, 2002): A1.
10. Sonya Ross, "White House Opens Office to Put a Better Face on U.S. Policy and Messages Abroad," *Associated Press* (July 30, 2002).
11. Fraser P. Seitel, "Words of Speech = Weapons of War," odwyerpr.com (October 15, 2001).
12. "Pentagon Spending Billions on PR to Sway World Opinion," *Associated Press*, February 5, 2009.
13. "The New Washington Press Corps," Journalism.org, July 16, 2009.
14. "GAO: Bush Administration Paid $200M for PR," *Jack O'Dwyer's Newsletter* (February 22, 2006): 2.
15. "Obama Campaign Spending Too Much Too Soon," Upi.com, August 5, 2012.
16. Alvin Snyder, "The Changing Voice of America," USC Center on Public Diplomacy (October 27, 2006).
17. "About VOA," Voice of America, Office of Public Affairs, 330 Independence Avenue, S.W., Washington, D.C. 20237.
18. Mark Hertsgaard, "Journalists Played Dead for Reagan—Will They Roll Over Again for Bush?" *Washington Journalism Review* (January–February 1989): 31.
19. "Give Him an 'F,'" *The Scudder Media Report* (October 1998): 1, 6.
20. "President Bush Overall Job Rating," CNN/Opinion Research Corp. (October 17, 2008).
21. Roger Simon, "It's All Obama All the Time," Politico.com, April 16, 2009.
22. Robert U. Brown, "Role of Press Secretary," *Editor & Publisher* (October 19, 1974): 40.
23. William Hill, "Nessen Lists Ways He Has Improved Press Relations," *Editor & Publisher* (April 10, 1975): 40.
24. William Safire, "One of Our Own," *The New York Times* (September 19, 1974): 43.
25. Laurence McQuillan, "Ari Fleischer Warms Up for Grillings," *USA Today* (January 23, 2001): 6A.
26. Richard W. Stevenson, "Press Secretary on Trial in the Briefing Room," *The New York Times* (November 3, 2005): A25.
27. Sheryl Gay Stolberg, "Bush's Press Secretary Is Out Raising Money, and Some Eyebrows," *The New York Times* (October 16, 2006): A16.
28. Lloyd Grove, "Death of the White House Press Corps," *The Daily Beast*, April 3, 2010.
29. Remarks by Mike McCurry, "A View from the Podium," New York (May 5, 1999).

30. Michael J. Bennett, "The 'Imperial' Press Corps," *Public Relations Journal* (June 1982): 13.
31. "Lobbying Database," OpenSecrets.org, July 31, 2012.
32. Luke Johnson, "Corporations That Spent the Most on Lobbying Saw Tax Rates Decline: Report," *The Huffington Post*, April 17, 2012.
33. Summer Lollie, "State and Local Governments Aggressively Lobby the Federal Government in Hope of Federal Aid," Open Secrets Blog, July 2, 2010.
34. Dan Eggen, "The Influence Industry: Obama's Ban on Lobbyist Bundlers Has Unclear Prospects," *Washington Post*, February 1, 2012.
35. Fraser P. Seitel, "Lobbying Do's and Don'ts," *O'Dwyer's PR Services Report* (December 2005): 31.
36. Andy Sullivan, "Obama Launches Web Site to Fight Rumors," *Reuters* (June 12, 2008).
37. Robert Stacy McCain, "MoveOn.org: Don't Believe the Hype," *Ripon Forum* (Fall 2004): 16.
38. Alan Fram, "Number of Political Action Committees Hits Record," *Associated Press*, March 14, 2009.
39. Chris Cillizza and Aaron Blake, "How Super Pacs are Saving Mitt Romney," *Washington Post*, July 24, 2012.
40. Michael D. Shear, "The Super PAC That Aims to End Super PACS," *The New York Times*, July 17, 2012.
41. Charles Riley, "Starbucks CEO to DC: You've Been Cut Off," CNN Money, August 16, 2011.

Chapter 13

1. Mary Elizabeth Williams, "Komen Scandal: Goodbye, Karen Handel," Salon.com, February 7, 2012.
2. "Minorities Now Surpass Whites in U.S. Births, Census Shows," FoxNews.com, May 17, 2012.
3. Hope Yen, "U.S. Minority Population Could Be Majority By Mid-Century, Census Shows," *Associated Press*, June 10, 2010.
4. Peter Francese and Matt Carmichael, "Five Surprising Faces Marketers Should Know About 2010 Census Stats," *Advertising Age*, April 4, 2011, 8–9.
5. Robert Bernstein, "U.S. Hispanic Population Surpasses 45 Million, Now 15 Percent of Total," U.S. Census Bureau (May 1, 2008).
6. Hispanic Fact Book 2010 Edition, *Advertising Age*, July 26, 2010.
7. Francese and Carmichael, op. cit.
8. Marsha Clark, "Six Facts about Women in the Workforce," W2wlink, October 2011.
9. "Most Big Companies Expect Flat Giving, Despite 2011 Gains," *Chronicle of Philanthropy*, July 22, 2012.
10. Sharon Bond, "U.S. Charitable Giving Estimated to be $306.39 Billion in 2007," Giving USA Foundation (June 23, 2008).
11. Dan Kadlec, "Charitable Giving: How Companies Are Doing More with Less," *Time*, June 5, 2012.
12. "CEO Forum: Environmental Impact," *NYSE Magazine* (January/February 2006): 13.
13. Ben Protess and Kevin Roose, "Charities Struggle with Smaller Wall Street Donations," *The New York Times*, August 30, 2011.
14. Beckey Bright, "How More Companies Are Embracing Social Responsibility as Good Business," *The Wall Street Journal* (March 10, 2008).
15. Brian Stelter, "For Chase, A TV Show to Promote Its Charity," *The New York Times*, December 9, 2011.
16. Scott Cohn, "Texas Is America's Top State for Business 2012," CNBC.com, July 10, 2012.
17. "Mayo Clinic Launches Social Network," Minnesota Public Radio, July 8, 2011.
18. Daniel Golden, "Time Warner to Buy Henry Gates's Africana.com," *The Wall Street Journal* (September 7, 2000): B1–4.
19. Richard Perez-Pena, "Washington Post Starts an Online Magazine for Blacks," *The New York Times* (January 28, 2008).
20. John Cook, "Charity Web Site Greatergood.com Shuts Down," *Seattle Post Intelligencer* (July 21, 2001).
21. Rebecca Trounson, "13% in U.S. Foreign Born, A Level Not Seen Since 1920," *Los Angeles Times*, May 11, 2012.

22. "2010 Census Shows America's Diversity," U.S. Census Bureau News, U.S. Department of Commerce, March 24, 2011.
23. Tom Martin, "A Few Good Men," *PR Week* (July 21, 2008).
24. Bey-Ling Sha, "PR Gender Gap Research Under Fire," CommPRO.biz, May 20, 2011.
25. Jeffrey S. Passel, "How Many Hispanics in the U.S.?" Pew Hispanic Center, March 15, 2011.
26. "Hispanic Pubs Surge," *Jack O'Dwyer's Newsletter* (January 25, 2006): 3.
27. "Urban, Spanish-Language Stations Dominate Major Radio Markets," Arbitron marketingcharts.com, October 7, 2008.
28. Doris Nhan, "Buying Power of Hispanics Worth $1 Trillion, Report Says," *National Journal*, May 8, 2011.
29. "Ten Major Cities with the Largest Black Populations," MadameNoir.com, September 24, 2011.
30. Julia B. Isaacs, "Economic Mobility of Black and White Families," Brookings Institution (November 2007).
31. Jeffrey M. Humphreys, "Black Buying Power Continues to Rise," ReachingBlackConsumers.com, 2012.
32. Richard Prince, "Ebony and Jet Increase Circulations," TheRoot.com, August 14, 2011.
33. Kirk Semple, "In a Shift, Biggest Group of Migrants Is Now Asian," *The New York Times*, June 18, 2012.
34. Laurie Goodstein, "Start-Up Television Venture Is Aiming Its Programming at American Muslims," *The New York Times* (November 29, 2004): C7.
35. Claudia Eller, "Building an Empire of Gay Media," *Los Angeles Times* (June 29, 2008): C2.
36. "What's So Important about Diversity?" *Ragan Report* (August 9, 2004): 3.
37. Aaron Blake, "Obama's Gay Marriage Support Fails to Sway Americans," *Washington Post*, July 31, 2012.
38. Nicole Lewis, "Multiple Missions and a Thousand Ideas," *Chronicle of Philanthropy*, December 8, 2005: 37.
39. "Public Relations Society of America Launches National Diversity Initiative," Public Relations Society of America news release, September 14, 2004.

Chapter 14

1. E.J. Schultz, "General Mills Marketing Goes Up in Smoke With Pot-Linked Brownie Pitch," *Advertising Age*, September 26, 2011.
2. Thad Rueter, "Online Shoppers Will Boost Shopping 15% This Year," Internet Retailer, April 5, 2012.
3. "Food Fight Continues Over McDonald's Sponsorship of Olympic Games," Agence France Presse, July 16, 2012.
4. "The General Electric Green Beijing Olympics, 2008," *Ecofuss*, www.ecofuss.com (August 11, 2008).
5. Landon Thomas, Jr., "Disney Says It Will Link Marketing to Nutrition," *The New York Times* (October 17, 2006).
6. Nicholas Casey and Nicholas Zamiska, "Mattel Does Damage Control After New Recall," *The Wall Street Journal* (August 15, 2007): B1.
7. Andrew Martin, "Burger King Shifts Policy on Animals," *The New York Times* (March 28, 2007): C1.
8. "Consumer-Generated Media Exceeds Traditional Advertising for Influencing Purchasing Behavior," *PR Newswire-Intelliseek* (September 26, 2005).
9. Gus Lubin, "After Diaper Incident, Alaska Airlines Has a Major PR Debacle on Its Hand," *Business Insider*, November 8, 2010.
10. Luis Andres Henoa, "No McDonald's Happy Meal Toy? Chile Bans Toys in Children's Meals," *Christian Science Monitor* (August 2, 2012).
11. James Kanter, "EU Opens New Microsoft Inquiry," *The New York Times* (July 17, 2012).
12. Matt Warmen, "iPhone Workers Beg Apple for Better Working Conditions," *The Telegraph* (February 23, 2012).
13. Noam Cohen, "Doorstep Protest: Very Real, Very Virtual," *The New York Times* (November 26, 2007): C3.
14. Jim Fitzgerald, "Consumer Reports' Flubs Relatively Few but Notable," *Associated Press* (January 21, 2007).

15. "Top 20 Internet Countries 2012 Q1," Miniwatts Marketing Group, June 19, 2012.
16. *JetBlue Airways Customer Bill of Rights*, JetBlue Airways, Forest Hills, NY.

Chapter 15

1. Richard Simon, "Plain-Language Report Card: Agriculture Gets A; VA Gets F," *Los Angeles Times*, July 23, 2012.
2. Fraser P. Seitel, "PR Pros Are Horrible Writers," odwyerpr.com, March 5, 2001.
3. "How to Get Editors to Use Press Releases," *Jack O'Dwyer's Newsletter*, May 26, 1993: 3.
4. Linda P. Morton, "Producing Publishable Press Releases," *Public Relations Quarterly*, Winter 1992–1993: 9–11.
5. Jonathan Grieb, "Make Your Press Release Boilerplate Sizzle," *Ragan PR Daily*, September 16, 2010.
6. Fraser P. Seitel, "News Release Essentials," odwyerpr.com, July 18, 2001.
7. Amanda Laird, "Social Media Release Checklist," *Beyond the Wire*, May 10, 2010.
8. "2011 Journalist Survey," op cit.
9. Fraser P. Seitel, "E-mail News Releases," odwyerpr.com, February 23, 2004.
10. Kevin Roose and Peter Lattman, "New-Form Press Release, in Blog, Tweet and Haiku," *The New York Times*, September 8, 2011.

Chapter 16

1. Stephanie Clifford, "Product Placements Acquire a Life of Their Own on Shows," *The New York Times* (July 14, 2008).
2. Thomas L. Friedman, "This Column Is Not Sponsored by Anyone," *The New York Times*, May 12, 2012.
3. Ibid.
4. Al Ries and Laura Ries, *The Fall of Advertising and the Rise of PR* (New York: Harper Business, 2002): 251.
5. "100 Global Marketers," *Advertising Age*, December 5, 2011, 6.
6. "Getting Word Out Involves 3 Strategies," *Poughkeepsie Journal* (October 16, 2005).
7. Tom Harris, "Kotler's Total Marketing Embraces MPR," *MPR Update* (December 1992): 4.
8. Daniel Gross, "Ho Ho Ho Classic," *US Airways Magazine* (February 2006): 26.
9. J. David Goodman, "Now in Blogs, Product Placement," *The New York Times*, June 11, 2010.
10. James Bandler, "How Companies Pay TV Experts for On-Air Product Mentions," *The Wall Street Journal* (April 19, 2005): A1.
11. "CNN Clamps Down on 'Stealth' Guests," *Jack O'Dwyer's Newsletter* (September 4, 2002): 3.
12. Kathy Burnham, "Trade Shows: Make Them Worth the Investment," *Tactics* (September 1999): 11.
13. Janet Morrissey, "If It's Retail, Is It Still Rock?" *The New York Times* (October 28, 2007).
14. Chad Terhune and Brian Steinberg, "Coca-Cola Signs NBA Wunderkind," *The Wall Street Journal* (August 22, 2003): B5.
15. Jessica Sidman, "20,000 Brownies for Obama," *Washingtonian* (January 16, 2009).
16. Stuart Elliott, "For a New Brand, Pepsi Starts the Buzz Online," *The New York Times* (March 14, 2008).
17. Suzanne Vranica, "Social Media Draws a Crowd," *The Wall Street Journal*, July 18, 2010.
18. Stuart Elliott, "'30 Rock' Satire of Kraft Sponsorship Is Sponsored by Kraft," *The New York Times*, April 27, 2012.
19. Lorne Manly, "On Television, Brands Go from Props to Stars," *The New York Times* (October 2, 2005): B1.
20. Clifford, op. cit.
21. Matt Richtel, "A New Reality in Video Games: Advertisement," *The New York Times* (April 11, 2005).
22. Stuart Elliott, "Product Placement Moves to Cartoons," *The New York Times* (October 21, 2004).

23. Brian Stelter, "Low Ratings End Show and a Product Placement," *The New York Times* (November 14, 2008).

24. Brad Stone, "TiVo and Amazon Team Up," *The New York Times* (July 22, 2008).

25. Stuart Elliott, "A Column on (Your Product Here) Placement," *The New York Times* (August 16, 2006).

26. Damon Darlin, "Words to Live by in an Infomercial World: Caveat Emptor," *The New York Times*, April 8, 2006.

27. Julie Bosman, "Advertising Is Obsolete: Everyone Says So," *The New York Times* (January 23, 2006): C7.

28. David Teicher, "Need a Reservation? That Could Depend On How Big You Are on Twitter (Really)," *Advertising Age*, September 30, 2010.

29. "The Age of Nikes, Cars and Guns—Not Roses," *Barron's* (January 16, 2006): 14.

30. Clyde Haberman, "Sell the Naming Rights and You May Sell Much More," *The New York Times* (September 16, 2008).

31. Stuart Elliott, "Live and Online, a Game Show Developed for the Internet Age," *The New York Times*, June 4, 2012.

32. Al Ries and Laura Ries, op. cit.

Chapter 17

1. Cynthia Littleton, "Studio in Crisis—Management Mode in Wake of Deadly Shootings," *Variety*, July 20, 2012.

2. Richard Sandomir, "Backing, Not Backing Away From, Armstrong," *The New York Times*, August 24, 2012.

3. Erik Holm, "Got a Crisis? Tap AIG (Really)," *The Wall Street Journal*, October 12, 2011.

4. Helio Fred Garcia, *Crisis Communications 1* (New York: American Association of Advertising Agencies, 1999): 9.

5. Ed Wiley III, "Duke Lacrosse Suspended Amid Rape Charges," BET.com (March 29, 2006).

6. Philip Rawls, "Magistrate Rejects Scrushy's Arguments of Prosecutor Misconduct," *Associated Press* (March 27, 2006).

7. Vernon Silver and David Glovin, "Madoff Scandal Ensnares Patron Saint for Moralists," *Bloomberg News* (February 13, 2009).

8. Richard Lacayo, "When a Story Goes Terribly Wrong," *Time* (May 22, 2005).

9. "Issues Management Conference—A Special Report," *Corporate Public Issues 7*, no. 23 (December 1, 1982): 1–2.

10. Richard C. Hyde, "In Crisis Management, Getting the Message Right Is Critical," *The Strategist* (Summer 2007): 32–35.

11. Richard K. Long, "Seven Needless Sins of Crisis (Mis)management," *PR Tactics* (August 2001): 14.

12. Fraser P. Seitel, "Spotting a Crisis," odwyerpr.com (March 20, 2001).

13. Kate MacArthur, "KFC Preps Bird-Glue Fear Plan," *Advertising Age* (November 7, 2005): 1.

14. Todd Gutner, "Dealing with PR Crisis Takes Planning and Truth," *The Wall Street Journal* (March 25, 2008).

15. Rick Amme, "9 Popular Crisis Responses That Don't Always Work," *Ragan PR Daily*, May 7, 2012.

16. Fraser P. Seitel, "Crisis Management Lessons from the Astor Disaster," *O'Dwyer's PR Report* (December 2006): 30.

17. Rick Amme, op. cit.

18. Melissa Agnes, "Dark Websites as a Social Media Crisis Management Strategy," White Paper, www.MelissaAgnes.com, 2012.

19. Shel Holtz, "In Defense of Crisis PR: An Open Letter to Rachel Maddow," *Ragan PR Daily*, August 8, 2012.

20. "Traditional Media Still Win in Crises," *Jack O'Dwyer's Newsletter* (October 9, 2006): 8.

Chapter 18

1. David Meerman Scott, "How David Murray Found a New Job via Twitter," ragan.com (February 25, 2009).

2. "Steve Jobs in Email Pissing Match with College Journalism Student," Gawker.com, September 16, 2010.

3. Lindsey Miller, "Recession Reprieve for Communicators," ragan.com (February 27, 2009).

4. Stuart Elliott, "Growing Appreciation for P.R. on Madison Avenue," *The New York Times* (September 8, 2010).

5. Thomas L. Friedman, "The Start-Up of You," *The New York Times* (July 12, 2011).

6. Mickie Kennedy, "5 Things Students Should Do Now to Secure a PR Job Later," *Ragan PR Daily*, (July 5, 2011).

7. Fraser P. Seitel, "Finding a PR Job," odwyerpr.com (June 13, 2005).

8. Paulette Barrett, "Working with a Resume Consultant: 10 Tips to Help You through the Process," thehiringclub blog, July 22, 2011.

9. Dawn Rasmussen, "12 Dangerous Résumé Mistakes," *Ragan PR Daily*, May 15, 2012.

10. Christine Rochelle, "Standard Interview Questions That Will Make or Break You," AOL.jobs, February 26, 2010.

11. Fraser P. Seitel, "Finding a Job in Public Relations," odwyerpr.com (May 12, 2008).

12. Fraser P. Seitel, "The 7 Keys to Success in Public Relations," odwyerpr.com (July 15, 2004).

13. Interview with Barry Zusman (March 2, 2009).

14. Jessica Levco, "Veteran Communicators Share Advice with Newbies," ragan.com (March 16, 2009).

15. Michael Bush, "How Social Media Is Helping Public-Relations Sector, Not Just Survive but Thrive," *Advertising Age* (August 23, 2010).

Index

Page numbers followed by "*f*" refer to figures and "*t*" refer to tables.